W9-BJB-062

The Papers of
Henry Laurens

Frontispiece: Henry Laurens c. 1778. Engraving by John B. Neale (1818) for Joseph Delaplaine, after a portrait by Charles Willson Peale.

The Papers of
Henry Laurens

Volume Fourteen: July 7, 1778–December 9, 1778

David R. Chesnutt, Editor

C. James Taylor, Editor

Peggy J. Clark, Assistant Editor

SOUTH
CAROLINA

Published for the South Carolina Historical Society by the

UNIVERSITY OF SOUTH CAROLINA PRESS

11/1/94, 4:58 PM

COLUMBIA, S.C.

FIRST EDITION

Copyright © 1994 by the South Carolina Historical Society

Published in Columbia, S.C. by the
University of South Carolina Press, 1994

International Standard Book Number: 1-57003-030-8

Library of Congress Catalog Card Number: 67-29381

Manufactured in the United States of America

CONTENTS

Introduction

"*I again recommend to your serious Consideration the near approach of the 1ˢᵗ of November. I do not say that I shall leave Philadelphia immediately after its arrival, nor can I promise not to leave it on the 2ⁿᵈ. I have a duty to you, to your Brother, to your sisters, and some to myself which call loudly on me. My Country is like all other collective Bodies extremely easy when they can get a Man to serve them diligently and faithfully, be the consequence to himself what it may, even Ruin.*"—HL to John Laurens, September 17, 1778

INTRODUCTION TO VOLUME FOURTEEN

The fourteenth volume of *The Papers of Henry Laurens* is the third of three volumes which cover the period from November 1, 1777, to December 9, 1778, when Laurens served as president of the Continental Congress. This volume opens with HL's letter of July 7, 1778, congratulating George Washington on his success at the Battle of Monmouth. It ends with HL's resignation speech to Congress on December 9, 1778, and two sets of notes which HL prepared to explain various points in his speech. These last months of Laurens's presidency were marked by the ebb and flow of American optimism which had become almost commonplace in his tenure.

As his first letter in the volume notes, Laurens had finally been able to muster a quorum of Congress on July 7— thus reestablishing Philadelphia as the center of the American government. One of Congress's first actions on its return was to correct the engrossed copy of the Articles of Confederation and to begin the signing by states. HL and his fellow South Carolina delegates— William Henry Drayton, Thomas Heyward, Jr., Richard Hutson and John Mathews—signed the Articles on July 9. By the end of October, the Articles had been signed by all of the states except Delaware, New Jersey and Maryland. In his letters to Caesar Rodney in November, HL urged Rodney to call the Delaware assembly together to act on the Confederation. New Jersey signed later that month, but HL's presidency ended with the Confederation still lacking the signatures of the Delaware and Maryland delegates.

American optimism had been renewed in early July with the news of the arrival of the French fleet commanded by Count d'Estaing. With the fleet came both Silas Deane, one of the American commissioners to Paris, and Conrad-Alexandre Gérard, the first French minister to the United States. The arrival of d'Estaing and Gérard provoked a flurry of activity on both the military and diplomatic fronts.

Congress ordered Washington to coordinate his efforts with d'Estaing and HL's son John soon distinguished himself as the liaison between the two commanders. Rhode Island became the focus for the first Franco-American thrust against the British. By early August, Maj. Gen. John Sullivan's troops were pressing the British garrisons and expecting reinforcements from d'Estaing's troops. The arrival of a small British fleet tempted d'Estaing into pursuit. An untimely storm left both the French and British fleets in disarray and ultimately proved to be the undoing of the Rhode Island campaign. By the end of August, Sullivan felt he had no choice but to evacuate his forces which he did on the night of August 30–31. D'Estaing had repaired to Boston for supplies and refitting and would soon move his theater of operations to the West Indies. As Laurens's own letters and those of his correspondents reveal, the Rhode Island episode shook American confidence in the efficacy of the Franco-American alliance.

Gérard's arrival marked the first formal diplomatic encounter for the American congress. Uncertain of the protocol of European diplomacy, the delegates took their lead from Gérard who explained his mission and the nature of his rank and powers in private conversations with Laurens. Gérard met informally with HL on several occasions. The two discussed Gérard's mission and the question of his powers as minister plenipotentiary to America. Laurens was much taken with Gérard. In a letter to Rawlins Lowndes several days after their early discussions, he described Gérard as "A Man of politeness, Good Breeding and affability without troublesome ceremony." HL declared that he did not often form judgements about character upon such short acquaintance, but that he had "seen many marks which induce[d]" him to "believe well of this Gentleman's candour and integrity of Heart." (p. 34) Gérard's suggestion that the American ministers in Paris be elevated to equivalent status was not acted upon until Congress, on September 14, named Benjamin Franklin as the sole minister to France with the rank of minister plenipotentiary.

Even before the arrival of the French fleet, Laurens and his fellow delegates had steadfastly refused to treat with Britain's peace commissioners headed by the Earl of Carlisle. By making recognition of American independence the *sina qua non* for negotiations, the delegates left the peace commissioners with few options. Commissioner George Johnstone's thinly veiled attempts to bribe American leaders succeeded only in provoking a congressional resolution condemning his activities. The commissioners' final "Manifesto and Proclamation," an appeal to the citizenry of America for support of reconciliation, was ridiculed by HL's colleague William Henry Drayton. And when the delegates learned that the commissioners intended to distribute the document, they promptly labeled it an act of sedition and ordered the arrest of anyone distributing the document. Late in November, the commissioners acknowledged the futility of further efforts and embarked at New York for their return to London.

After the abortive Rhode Island campaign, Washington's forces were content to keep a wary surveillance of Sir Henry Clinton's forces in New York. In the midst of rumors that the British intended to shift their focus to Georgia and South Carolina came confirming reports from an unexpected source: one of Laurens's old South Carolina acquaintances. The warning in September came from Robert Williams, a prominent Loyalist and well-known Charleston lawyer, then waiting in New York for transport to Charleston under a British flag of truce. Williams's verbal message to HL was delivered by another South Carolinian, Richard Beresford, who was returning from England where he had been studying law. About the same time, at the urging of Laurens and his fellow delegates, Congress replaced Robert Howe with Benjamin Lincoln as commander of the Southern department and called on North Carolina and Virginia to assist the two southern colonies.

The shift in command for the Southern department came in the wake of South Carolina and Georgia's ill-fated expedition against the British in East Florida which had broken up in mid-July. Just as British officers often found it difficult to work with colonial troops in earlier wars, Continental officers often encountered the same problems. The state troops of Georgia and South Carolina answered to their own commanders—John Houstoun and Andrew Williamson—while the Continental forces were headed by Maj. Gen. Robert Howe. Beset by lack of adequate supplies and sickness, the expedition slowly ground to a desultory halt, exacerbated by disagreements among the commanding officers. Nor were Georgia and South Carolina better prepared four months later when British forces moved into the coastal frontier areas of Georgia—the opening gambit in Britain's southern campaign. Savannah would fall before year's end.

Although HL was much occupied by his concern for the safety of South Carolina and Georgia, he perceived a growing factionalism among his fellow delegates which was equally disturbing. At the center of this worrisome situation was Silas Deane and the question of Deane's conduct while serving as an American commissioner in Paris. Allegations that Deane had mixed public and private business had led Congress to issue a recall in November 1777. Laurens pointedly took a neutral position as Congress reviewed Deane's conduct. Deane's oral account of his mission in August was followed by an examination in September and October of William Carmichael who had assisted Deane in Paris. At that point, Congress entered a lengthy series of deliberations on the matter despite Deane's repeated requests for a hearing and a speedy resolution of the issue. The frustrated Deane finally resorted to a public defense of his conduct which was published in the *Pennsylvania Packet* of December 5. Laurens was incensed because he felt that Deane had challenged the integrity of Congress. When Congress failed to take strong measures against Deane and rejected HL's own resolution for an inquiry, Laurens resigned as president on December 9. Though HL stepped down from the chair, he would remain in Congress as one of its most active delegates until November 1779.

EDITORIAL POLICY

The increased number of documents for the period of HL's presidency has led the editors to exercise even greater selectivity than in previous periods of his life. The increased selectivity is also in part dictated by our continuing concern with rising costs and the threat of dwindling resources. A fully-indexed supplement is planned after publication of the printed volumes to achieve comprehensiveness.

Principles of Selection

Documents printed in this volume were selected on the basis of two principles—their intrinsic value and their representative quality. The first principle could be restated as simply "letting the documents speak for themselves." The materials in this volume reflect HL's role as president and the issues confronting Congress; his continuing concerns about his own affairs and the affairs of his home state of South Carolina; and his personal views of the American situation both in and out of Congress. The editors have attempted to balance his public correspondence with documents that reveal his personal concerns for his family and business interests. This selection gives the fullest documentation of those themes possible within the confines of this volume. The second principle of selection, to present a representative group, is not meant in a statistical sense. Rather, an effort has been made to achieve a selection which provides a sense of the breadth and the depth of the documents. To further this goal, many of the documents which are not printed have been employed in the annotation.

This volume is the third of the Laurens series which is fully paralleled in another modern edition. As a member of the Continental Congress, HL's letters are published in *Letters of Delegates to Congress, 1774–1789*, edited by Paul H. Smith and his colleagues at the Library of Congress. While the two projects have a cooperative history which dates from the early 1970s, the Laurens editors have long realized that the publication of the *Delegate Letters* would have a significant effect on the selection policies for the *Laurens Papers*. The Smith edition includes almost every letter written by HL while he was in Congress. To merely duplicate that effort would be of little service to scholarship and a waste of scarce resources. At the same time, to omit previously published letters completely would obviously vitiate the Laurens edition. To strike a balance, this volume includes approximately one-fourth of HL's correspondence during this period.

One factor which distinguishes the two projects is that the Smith edition includes none of the letters written to the delegates unless one delegate is writing to another delegate. On the other hand, the Laurens edition has traditionally included incoming letters in order to provide a fuller understanding of Laurens and his world—a policy continued here. Most of the letters he received as president have been preserved in the Papers of the Continental Congress. Many of the private letters he received in this period have also survived and are in the Henry W. Kendall Collection of Laurens Papers or in the Laurens Papers at the South Carolina Historical Society. Thus, the number of incoming letters which survived from this period differs markedly from earlier periods in Laurens's life—a factor which is recognized by the inclusion of a large number of incoming letters in this volume. Publication of both sides of Laurens's correspondence allows the documents to speak for themselves with minimal annotation.

HL's letters can be generally divided between those he wrote in his official capacity as president and those he wrote as a private person. Letters written to Laurens also fall into the same categories. In the selection of material for this volume, this proved to be an important distinction. The official correspondence establishes the issues which confronted the delegates on a day-to-day basis; the private correspondence provides a more candid view of those same issues as well as additional information. Most of HL's private correspondence is published in this volume. Among the more important correspondents in this group were his son John Laurens, George Washington, the Marquis de Lafayette, Baron von Steuben, William Livingston, Rawlins Lowndes, John Rutledge, John Wells, Jr., and John Lewis Gervais. The private letters are in turn balanced by selections from the official correspondence which provide a framework for the course of events with which Laurens was intimately involved.

Textual Principles

The shift to a more literal rendering of the text initiated in Volume Ten continues in this volume. The text contains no silent editorial changes. Editorial changes which affect all documents are discussed below; changes which apply to particular documents are reported in textual notes.

When multiple copies of a document are available, the editors have chosen that copy which is closest to the author as the basis for the published text in this edition. For example, a letter signed by the author carries more authority than a letterbook copy created by a clerk. Less obvious is the choice between a letterbook copy and a contemporary copy based on the recipient's copy of the original letter. In those instances where multiple texts are available, the texts have been collated and an appropriate publication text has been chosen. The basis of that decision is reported in the textual annotation.

The conversion of hand-written manuscripts into typescript or printed pages inevitably alters certain characteristics of those manuscripts. The reader of a transcribed document cannot see a hasty scrawl, the ill-formed letters of an author who is suffering from illness, or even instances when text is substituted over an erasure. Textual notes are used to alert the reader to such characteristics when editorial conventions cannot suffice. A case in point is the letterbook which HL used for his private correspondence. The emendations throughout the letterbook in HL's hand give the letterbook added authority in the absence of recipient copies of the letters. Particularly striking are those instances when he drafted a letter, had his clerk copy it, and then used the letterbook copy itself as a second draft for the final letter—either changing the text extensively as in his letter of July 31 to George Washington or deleting significant passages as in his letter of August 26 to William Maxwell.

Other variations between documents and the transcriptions thereof are created by editorial decisions to use typographical conventions which include justifying the right margin as well as the left, adopting standards for indenting paragraphs and extracts, and adopting rules for vertical spacing. The document format and the conventions used in presenting the documents in this volume are identical to those listed in Volume Ten.

The textual conventions and typographical symbols used in this volume are listed below.

[roman][1]	Text supplied from another source identified in footnote, or text set apart when editorial clarification required.
[*italic*]	Editorial insertion or conjectural reading supplied by the editors when text is damaged.
↑text↓	Interlineations above line in text.
↓text↑	Interlineations below line in text.
~~text~~	Canceled text which has been recovered.
~~*illegible*~~	Illegible canceled text.
℗	Per sign.
þ	Thorn.
˜	Raised tilde. Used for writer's flourish at the end of a word which signals the omission of characters.
ˉ	Macron. Bar over character in word indicating the omission of one or more characters.
/	Virgule. Indicates line breaks in text. Commonly used in the complimentary close and the source notes.
./.	Special symbol denoting a full stop or used as an abbreviation for et cetera. Written in manuscript either as period-slash-period or period-slash-dash.

ACKNOWLEDGEMENTS

Many persons and organizations have contributed to The *Papers of Henry Laurens*. The most important of those individuals is George C. Rogers, Jr., Distinguished Professor Emeritus and the former senior editor of the *Laurens Papers*. His personal friendship and his wise counsel are ever at our disposal and have helped us over many a rough spot. Others who have given particular help for this volume include: N. Louise Bailey, Lester Duncan, Herbert J. Hartsook, Martha J. King, Charles Lesser, Thomas A. Marcil, Gregory D. Massey, Joel Myerson, Barbara Oberg, Douglas Southard, Michael E. Stevens, Allen H. Stokes, Rita F. Wallace, Robert M. Weir, the staff of the Thomas Cooper Library interlibrary loan office, the staff at the South Carolina Archives reading room, and the staff of the Kendall Whaling Museum.

Permission to publish documents from their collections has been given by the American Antiquarian Society, the Feinstone Collection on deposit at the American Philosophical Society, the Archives of the Moravian Church, Bethlehem, Pennsylvania, the Archives Nationale, Paris, France, the Archive du ministère des affaires étrangère, Paris, France, the Boston Public Library, Columbia University Libraries, the Connecticut Historical Society, the Georgia Historical Society, Harvard University, the Historical Society of Delaware, the Henry E. Huntington Library, the Historical Society of Pennsylvania, the Illinois State Historical Library, the Kendall Whaling Museum, the Library of Congress, the Maryland Hall of Records, the Massachusetts Historical Society, the Maine Historical Society, the National Archives and Records Administration, the New Hampshire Historical Society, the New-York Historical Society, the New York Public Library, the New York State Library, the North Carolina Department of Archives and History, the Pierpont Morgan Library, the Public Record Office, London, the Rhode Island Archives, the Philip H. and A.S.W. Rosenbach Foundation, St. Mary of the Lake Seminary, Mundelein, Illinois, the South Carolina Historical Society, the Southern Historical Collection at the University of North Carolina, and the Yale University Libraries.

The preparation of this volume was made possible in part by grants from the Division of Research Programs of the National Endowment for the Humanities, the National Historical Publications and Records Commission, and the South Caroliniana Society of the University of South Carolina. Lawrence S. Rowland, of Beaufort, South Carolina, is a long-time friend and supporter of the project whose personal contributions have been especially meaningful. The editors also wish to acknowledge with appreciation the continuing support of the History Department, the College of Humanities and Social Sciences, and the administration of the University of South Carolina. And last, but certainly not least, is our appreciation for the continued support of the South Carolina Historical Society, the founding sponsor of the edition.

LIST OF ABBREVIATIONS
AND SHORT TITLES

Adams Papers (Taylor) for *The Adams Papers, Series III, General Correspondence and Other Papers of the Adams Statesmen: The Papers of John Adams*, ed. Robert J. Taylor, et al. (8 vols. to date: Cambridge, Mass., 1979–   ).

Alden, *Charles Lee* for John Richard Alden, *General Charles Lee, Traitor or Patriot?* (Baton Rouge, La., 1951).

Balch, *French in America* for Thomas Balch, *The French in America During the War of Independence of the United States 1777–1783* (2 vols.: Philadelphia, 1891, 1895. Reprint. Boston, 1972).

Bennet and Lennon, *A Quest for Glory* for Charles E. Bennet and Donald R. Lennon, *A Quest for Glory, Major General Robert Howe and the American Revolution* (Chapel Hill, N.C., 1991).

Brown, *Empire or Independence* for Weldon A. Brown, *Empire or Independence, A study in the failure of Reconciliation, 1774–1783* (Baton Rouge, La., 1941).

Carp, *To Starve the Army at Pleasure* for E. Wayne Carp, *To Starve the Army at Pleasure: Continental Army Administration and American Political Culture, 1775–1783* (Chapel Hill, N.C., 1984).

Claghorn, *Naval Officers,* for Charles E. Claghorn, *Naval Officers of the American Revolution: A Concise Biographical Dictionary* (Metuchen, N.J., 1988).

Clinton Papers (Hastings) for *The Public Papers of George Clinton, first Governor of New York, 1777–1795, 1801–1804*, ed. Hugh Hastings (10 vols.: New York and Albany, 1899–1914).

Cobbett's *Parliamentary History* for *The Parliamentary History of England from the Earliest Period to the Year 1803*, printed by T.C. Hansard (36 vols.: London, 1806–1820).

Collections of SCHS for *Collections of the South-Carolina Historical Society* (5 vols.: Charleston, S.C., 1857–1897).

DAB for *Dictionary of American Biography*.

Delegate Letters (Smith) for *Letters of Delegates to Congress, 1774–1789*, ed. Paul H. Smith (21 vols. to date: Washington, D.C., 1976–   ).

Diary of John Baker for *The Diary of John Baker*, ed. Philip C. Yorke (London, 1931).

Directory of the S.C. House for *Biographical Directory of the South Carolina House of Representatives*, ed. Walter B. Edgar, N. Louise Bailey, and Alexander Moore (5 vols. to date: Columbia, S.C., 1974–   ).

Documents of the American Revolution (Davies) for *Documents of the American Revolution 1770–1783*, ed. K.G. Davies (21 vols.: Colonial Office Series, Shannon, Ireland, 1972–   ).

Dull, *French Navy* for Jonathan R. Dull, *The French Navy and American Independence* (Princeton, N.J., 1975).

Fowler, *Rebels Under Sail* for William M. Fowler, Jr., *Rebels Under Sail* (New York, 1976).

Franklin Papers (Labaree) for *The Papers of Benjamin Franklin*, ed. Leonard W. Labaree, William B. Willcox, Barbara Oberg, et al. (29 vols. to date: New Haven, Conn., 1959–   ).

Gazette of the State of S.C. for *The Gazette of the State of South-Carolina*.

Greene Papers (Showman) for *The Papers of General Nathanael Greene*, ed. Richard K. Showman, et al. (6 vols. to date: Chapel Hill, N.C., 1976–   ).

Gruber, *Howe Brothers* for Ira D. Gruber, *The Howe Brothers & the American Revolution* (New York, 1972).

Hamilton Papers (Syrett) for *The Papers of Alexander Hamilton*, ed. Harold C. Syrett, Jacob E. Cooke, et al. (27 vols.: New York, 1961–1981).

Heitman, *Continental Officers* for Francis Bernard Heitman, *Historical Register of Officers of the Continental Army during the war of the Revolution, April, 1775, to December, 1783* (Washington, D.C., 1914).

HL Papers for *The Papers of Henry Laurens*.

HL Correspondence, 1762–1780, PHi for Henry Laurens Correspondence, 1762–1780, Collection 356, PHi.

JCC for U.S. Continental Congress, *Journals of the Continental Congress, 1774–1789*, ed. Worthington C. Ford, et al. (34 vols.: Washington, D.C.: 1904–1937).

Kendall Collection for the Henry W. Kendall Collection of Laurens Papers, Kendall Whaling Museum, Sharon, Massachusetts.

Lafayette Papers (Idzerda) for *Lafayette in the Age of the American Revolution, Selected Letters and Papers, 1776–1790*, ed. Stanley J. Idzerda, et al. (5 vols.: Ithaca, N.Y. and London, 1977–1983).

Livingston Papers (Prince) for *The Papers of William Livingston*, ed. Carl E. Prince, et al. (5 vols.: Trenton, N.J., 1979–1988).

Loyalist Transcripts for Transcripts of the Manuscript Books and Papers of the Commission of Enquiry into Losses and Services of the American Loyalists held under Acts of Parliament of 23, 25, 26, 28, and 29 of George III preserved amongst the Audit Office Records in the Public Record Office of England, 1783–1790, 59 vols. made for the New York Public Library, microfilm, ScA.

Moss, *S.C. Patriots* for Bobby Gilmer Moss, *Roster of South Carolina Patriots in the American Revolution* (Baltimore, Md., 1983).

Moultrie, *Memoirs* for William Moultrie, *Memoirs of the American Revolution* (New York, 1802. Reprint. New York, 1968).

Naval Documents (Clark) for *Naval Documents of the American Revolution*, ed. William B. Clark, et al. (9 vols. to date: Washington, D.C., 1964–   ).

Nordholt, *Dutch Republic and American Independence* for Jan Willem Schulte Nordholt, *The Dutch Republic and American Independence,* translated by Herbert H. Rowen (Chapel Hill, N.C., 1982).

OED for *Oxford English Dictionary.*

Palmer, *Biographical Sketches of Loyalists* for Gregory Palmer, *Biographical Sketches of Loyalists of the American Revolution* (Westport, Conn., 1984).

Palmer, *Von Steuben* for John McAuley Palmer, *General Von Steuben* (Port Washington, N.Y., 1966).

Pa. Archives for *Pennsylvania Archives. Selected and Arranged from Original Documents in the Office of the Secretary of the Commonwealth* (119 vols.: Philadelphia and Harrisburg, 1852–1935).

Pa. Gazette for *The Pennsylvania Gazette, and Weekly Advertiser.*

Pa. Packet for *The Pennsylvania Packet, or the General Advertiser.*

PCC for Papers of the Continental and Confederation Congresses and the Constitutional Convention, Record Group 360, DNA.

PMHB for *Pennsylvania Magazine of History & Biography.*

Revolutionary Records of Georgia (Candler) for Allen D. Candler, ed., *The Revolutionary Records of the State of Georgia....* (3 vols.: Atlanta, Ga., 1908).

Risch, *Supplying Washington's Army* for Erna Risch, *Supplying Washington's Army* (Washington, D.C., 1981).

Rogers, *Evolution of a Federalist* for George C. Rogers, Jr., *Evolution of a*

Federalist: William Loughton Smith of Charleston, 1759–1812 (Columbia, S.C., 1962).

Ryden, *Caesar Rodney* for *Letters to and from Caesar Rodney, 1756–1784*, ed. George H. Ryden (Philadelphia, 1933).

S.C. Country Journal for *South Carolina Gazette & Country Journal.*

S.C. Gazette for *South-Carolina Gazette*; after April 9, 1777, *Gazette of the State of South-Carolina.*

S.C. General Gazette for *South Carolina and American General Gazette.*

SCHM for *The South Carolina Historical Magazine.*

S.C. Statutes for *The Statutes at Large of South Carolina,* ed. Thomas Cooper and David J. McCord (10 vols.: Columbia, S.C., 1837–1841).

Searcy, *Georgia-Florida Contest* for Martha Coudray Searcy, *The Georgia-Florida Contest in the American Revolution, 1776–1778* (University, Ala., 1985).

State Records of North Carolina for *The State Records of North Carolina. Pub. under the supervision of the Trustees of the public libraries, by order of the General Assembly* (26 vols.: Goldsboro, N.C., 1886–1907).

Sullivan Papers (Hammond) for *Letters and Papers of Major-General John Sullivan Continental Army,* ed. Otis G. Hammond. (3 vols.. Concord, N.H., 1930–1939.

Tilley, *British Navy* for John A. Tilley, *The British Navy and the American Revolution* (Columbia, S.C., 1987).

Walker, *Engineers of Independence* for Paul K. Walker, *Engineers of Independence, A Documentary History of the Army Engineers in the American Revolution 1775–1783* (Washington, D.C., n.d.).

Washington Papers, DLC for the papers of George Washington, Manuscript Division, Library of Congress.

Washington Writings (Fitzpatrick) for *The Writings of George Washington from the Original Manuscript Sources 1745–1799,* ed. John C. Fitzpatrick (39 vols.: Washington, D.C., 1931–1944).

Willcox, *Portrait of a General* for William Bradford Willcox, *Portrait of a General: Sir Henry Clinton in the War of Independence* (New York, 1964).

Wright, *Continental Army* for Robert K. Wright, *The Continental Army* (Washington, D.C., 1983).

Writings of Christopher Gadsden (Walsh) for *The Writings of Christopher Gadsden, 1746–1805,* ed. Richard Walsh (Columbia, S.C., 1966).

LOCATION SYMBOLS

Archives Nationales for Archives Nationales, Paris, France.

CSmH for Henry E. Huntington Library, San Marino, California.

CtHi for Connecticut Historical Society, Hartford, Connecticut.

CtLHi for Litchfield Historical Society, Litchfield, Connecticut.

CtY for Yale University, New Haven, Connecticut.

DeHi for Historical Society of Delaware, Wilmington, Delaware.

DLC for Library of Congress.

DNA for National Archives and Records Administration.

DNDAR for National Society of the Daughters of the American Revolution, Washington, D.C.

GHi for Georgia Historical Society, Savannah, Georgia.

IHi for Illinois State Historical Library, Springfield, Illinois.

IMunS for Saint Mary of the Lake Seminary, Mundelein, Illinois.

MB for Boston Public Library, Boston, Massachusetts.

MdAA for Hall of Records Commission, Annapolis, Maryland.

MeHi for Maine Historical Society, Portland, Maine.

MH for Harvard University Library, Cambridge, Massachusetts.

MHi for Massachusetts Historical Society, Boston, Massachusetts.

MiU-C for The William L. Clements Library, University of Michigan, Ann Arbor, Michigan.

Nc-Ar for North Carolina State Department of Archives and History, Raleigh, North Carolina.

Nh-Ar for New Hampshire Department of Administration and Control, Division of Archives and Records Management, Concord, New Hampshire.

NHi for the New-York Historical Society, New York, New York.

NjP for Princeton University, Princeton, New Jersey.

NN for The New York Public Library, New York, New York.

NNC for Columbia University Library, New York, New York.

NNPM for Pierpont Morgan Library, New York, New York.

PBMCA for Archives of the Moravian Church, Bethlehem, Pennsylvania.

PHi for The Historical Society of Pennsylvania, Philadelphia, Pennsylvania.

PPAmP for The American Philosophical Society, Philadelphia, Pennsylvania.

PRO for Public Record Office, London, England.

PWacD for David Library of the American Revolution, Washington Crossing, Pennsylvania, on deposit at the American Philosophical Society.

RPB for Brown University Library, Providence, Rhode Island.

ScHi for South Carolina Historical Society, Charleston, South Carolina.

SHC (NcU) for Southern Historical Collection, University of North Carolina, Chapel Hill, North Carolina.

SCL (ScU) for South Caroliniana Library, University of South Carolina, Columbia, South Carolina.

PRINCIPAL DATES OF LAURENS'S LIFE

1724	*Feb. 24.* Born in Charleston, S. C.
1744–1747	Received business training with James Crokatt in London.
1747	*June 3.* Arrived in Charleston from London; began mercantile career.
1750	*June 25.* Married Eleanor Ball.
1754	*Oct. 28:* His son John Laurens born.
1757	*Sept.* First elected to S. C. Commons House of Assembly.
1759	*Nov. 3.* His daughter Martha Laurens born.
1761	*April 2–Nov. 14.* Engaged in Cherokee campaign.
1762	*June 5.* Purchased Mepkin plantation.
1763	*July 23.* His son Henry Laurens, Jr. , born.
1765	*Nov. 26.* His son James Laurens born.
1767–1769	Embroiled in controversy with Charleston customs officers over seizure of three of his vessels; engaged in pamphlet war with Egerton Leigh, judge of the Charleston vice-admiralty court.
1770	*April 26.* His daughter Mary Eleanor Laurens born.
	May 22. His wife Eleanor Ball Laurens died.
1771	*Sept. 9.* Sailed from New York.
	Oct. 9. Arrived at Falmouth, Eng.
1772–1774	Toured England, France, the Low Countries and Switzerland. Placed his sons in schools in Geneva and England.
1774	*Nov. 7.* Sailed from Falmouth for Charleston aboard the *Le Despenser* packet.
	Dec. 11. Landed in Charleston.
1775	*Jan. 9.* Elected to Provincial Congress.
	May 1. Elected chairman of Charleston General Committee.
	June 1. Elected president of Provincial Congress.
	June 1. His brother James, sister-in-law Mary, and daughters Mary Eleanor and Martha sailed for England.
	June 16. Elected president of Council of Safety.
	Sept. 5. His son James Laurens died.
	Oct. 17. Duel with John Faucheraud Grimké.
1776	*March 26.* S. C. Constitution adopted.
	March 26. Elected vice president of S. C.
	June 28. Battle of Fort Moultrie.
	Aug. 5. News of the Declaration of Independence reached Charleston.
1777	*Jan. 10.* Elected to Continental Congress.
	July 22. Seated as delegate for S. C. in the Continental Congress.
	Aug. 1. Appointed to committee to investigate the fall of Fort Ticonderoga.
	Aug. 9. John Laurens joined George Washington's staff.
	Sept. 19. Congress evacuated Philadelphia.
	Sept. 30. Congress reconvened in York.
	Oct. 17. General John Burgoyne surrendered at Saratoga.
	Nov. 1. Elected president of the Continental Congress.
	Nov. 28. Transmitted Articles of Confederation to states for approval.
	Dec. 12. Requested permission to resign as president of Congress because of ill health.
	Dec. 19. Washington's army went into winter quarters at Valley Forge.
1778	*Jan. 8.* Congress passed resolution calling for suspension of embarkation of Convention troops.
1778	*Jan. 21.* Reelected as delegate to Continental Congress.

Feb. 6. Treaties of alliance and commerce with France signed in Paris.
April 22. Congress rejected North's Conciliatory proposals.
May 4. Congress ratified treaties with France.
May 11. Sir Henry Clinton assumed British command.
May 15. Congress adopted half pay compromise.
June 6. Carlisle Commissioners arrived at Philadelphia.
June 18. British evacuated Philadelphia.
June 26. Congress ordered engrossing of Articles of Confederation.
June 27. Left York after Congress adjourned.
June 28. Battle of Monmouth.
June 30. Returned to Philadelphia.
July 7. Congress reconvened in Philadelphia.
July 9. French fleet commanded by Count d'Estaing and carrying Conrad-Alexandre Gérard and Silas Deane arrived in Delaware Bay.
July 9. Signed the Articles of Confederation.
July 12. Maj. Gen. Robert Howe withdrew Continental troops from American expedition against East Florida.
July 14. Conferred informally with French minister Gérard on mission and powers of minister plenipotentiary.
Aug. 6. Gérard met formally with Congress.
Aug. 11. Congress denounced peace commissioner George Johnstone for attempts to bribe American leaders.
Aug. 11. French and British fleets off Rhode Island severely damaged by storm.
Aug. 17–21. Silas Deane gave Congress an oral account of his mission to France.
Aug. 30–31. American forces evacuated Rhode Island after learning French fleet could not rejoin the expedition.
Sept. 25. Maj. Gen. Benjamin Lincoln ordered to command the Southern Department, replacing Maj. Gen. Robert Howe.
Sept. 28–Oct. 16. William Carmichael examined regarding allegations of misconduct by Silas Deane.
Oct. 3. Carlisle peace commissioners issued "manifesto and proclamation" appealing to citizenry of America.
Oct. 31. Offers to resign as president but persuaded to continue by unanimous vote of delegates.
Nov. 19. British forces from East Florida entered Georgia, marking the opening of the Southern campaign.
Nov. 27. Carlisle peace commissioners embark at New York for return to England.
Dec. 5. Silas Deane's defense of his conduct published in *Pennsylvania Packet*.
Dec. 9. Resigned as president when Congress failed to adopt his resolution on Deane's letter of December 5.

1779   *Oct. 21–Nov. 1.* Appointed to negotiate a loan and treaties of amity and commerce with Holland.
1780   *Sept. 3.* Captured by the British while on his way to Holland.
         Oct. 6. Imprisoned in the Tower of London.
1781   *Dec. 31.* Released from the Tower of London.
1782   *Aug. 27.* John Laurens killed near the Combahee River, S. C.
         Nov. 30. Signed, with other commissioners, preliminary treaty of peace between the United States and Great Britain.
1792   *Dec. 8.* Died at Mepkin

TO GEORGE WASHINGTON

Philadelphia, July 7, 1778

Dear Sir.

I have had the honor of presenting to as many Members of Congress as have been convened in this City since the adjournment from York, Your Excellency's several favors of the 28th. & 30th June & 1st Inst: & at their special Instance have caused them to be printed for the information of the Public.[1]

I arrived here on Tuesday last but hitherto have not collected a sufficient number of States to form a Congress,[2] consequently I have received no Commands. Your Excellency will therefore be pleased to accept this as the address of an Individual intended to assure you Sir of my hearty congratulations with my Country Men on the success of the American Arms under Your Excellency's immediate Command in the late Battle of Monmouth & more particularly of my own happiness in the additional Glory atcheived by Your Excellency in retrieving the honor of these States in the Moment of an alarming dilemma.[3]

It is not my design to attempt encomiums upon Your Excellency, I am as unequal to the task as the Act is unnecessary, Love & respect for Your Excellency is impressed on the Heart of every grateful American, & your Name will be revered by Posterity. Our acknowledgements are especially due to Heaven for the preservation of Your Excellency's person necessarily exposed for the Salvation of America to the most imminent danger in the late Action; that the same hand may at all times guide & Sheild Your Excellency is the fervent wish of

Dear Sir__ / Your much obliged & / faithful humble servant
Henry Laurens[4]

---

[1] HL sent Washington's letters to *Pennsylvania Packet* printer John Dunlap and requested that he "print the following Letters from his Excellency General Washington, together with the return of killed, wounded, &c. for the information of the good people of these United States." Dunlap published the letters with HL's request in a July 6 "Supplement." *Pa. Packet,* July 6, 1778.

[2] According to its journal, Congress held its first session, upon returning to Philadelphia, on that same day, July 7, 1778. *JCC,* XI, 672-673.

[3] As the American troops were retreating under Gen. Charles Lee, Washington personally countermanded the order and rallied them to an eventual face-off with the British. The episode is vividly described in John Laurens to Henry Laurens, June 30, 1778, *HL Papers*, XIII, 532-537.

[4] Washington replied with an equally effusive letter on July 11, 1778. RC, in private hands. Copy, HL Papers, ScHi.

SOURCE: ALS, Washington Papers, DLC; addressed below close "His Excellency / General Washington__"; dated "York Town / Philadelphia 7ᵗʰ July 1778". LB, HL Papers, ScHi. Copies (2), MH.

FROM GEORGE CLINTON

Poughkeepsie, N.Y., July 8, 1778

Sir.

I have to acknowledge the Receipt of your Excellency's Letters of the 10th. and 20ᵗʰ· of June last and to inform you that the Legislature of this State have, at their last Meeting, enactd Laws;

> for appointing suitable Persons to procure military Accoutrements
> for the Quota of Drafts for filling up the continental Battalions raised under the Direction of this State.
> For suspending the Law for regulating Prices.__ And
> For exempting from military Duty, Deserters from the british Army and Navy (not being Subjects of this State) and disqualifying them from acting as Substitutes in the Militia during the present War.[1]

Copies of these Acts together with such other as have before been passed in consequence of Recommendations of Congress, and have not been already forwarded, shall as soon as they are printed be transmitted to Congress.

It is with the utmost Regret, Sir, I find myself constrained again to intrude upon the deliberations of Congress, and to entreat their Attention to a Matter of the greatest Importance and which requires their immediate Interposition.

The Disorders which have long prevailed in the Northeastern Parts of this State, where the deluded Inhabitants have at-

---

[1] The New York legislature's session had ended June 30. The act appointing suitable persons (governor, lieutenant governor, or president of the Senate) to procure military accoutrements passed February 4. The act for completing the five Continental battalions raised under the direction of the state passed April 1. And, the acts suspending price regulation and disqualifying British deserters from militia duty passed June 29. *Laws of the State of New York Passed at the Sessions of the Legislature 1777-1784* (Albany, N.Y., 1886), I, 1, 8, 51, 83, 84.

tempted a separation from us, and to erect themselves into an independent State under the Style of the <u>State of Vermont</u> are fast approaching to a serious and alarming Crisis, and unless Measures are speedily adopted to prevent it, we shall very soon be involved in a civil War.[2]

As we have considered the whole Continent eventually interested in the issue of this Affair equally with ourselves, the Legislature of this State were determined to use no compulsory Means for the reestablishment of their Authority in that part of the Country 'till we were previously favored with the Sentiments and Advice of Congress, and had these unhappy People contented themselves with barely denying our Jurisdiction, matters might have remained in that Situation 'till, having expelled our external Enemy, Congress might then have entered upon the business with more leisure and deliberation; but their Proceedings have of late been such, that we shall very soon, from mere Motives of self Defence be obliged to have recourse to Arms.

The Inhabitants of several Towns within the claim of this pretended State distinguishing between the former and present Government of this, conscious that all the Grievances which they may have suffered arose from Abuses under the former, and that they had every Thing to expect from the Justice and Generosity of the latter, have been constantly and warmly attached to us, and are confirmed in this Attachment by the equitable Proposals in the Resolutions of both Houses of the 21st. of february last,[3] and relying on us for Assistance are determined at every hazard to resist this unwarrantable Usurpation.

In consequence of an Act of the pretended Legislature of Vermont a Draft of every fourth Man throughout that Territory, including these Towns, are to be made to compleat Colo. Warners

---

[2] Vermont had written its own constitution in July 1777 and by March 1778 had its own legislature, governor, lieutenant governor, treasurer, and council members. See George Clinton to HL, April 7, 1778, *HL Papers*, XIII, 86-88.

[3] One of two acts passed February 21 by the New York legislature provided "For the distribution of sundry charitable donations to certain distressed inhabitants on the frontiers of this State." *Laws of the State of New York Passed at the Sessions of the Legislature 1777-1784* (Albany, N.Y., 1886), I, 12.

Regiment[4] (tho' in Justice to this Gentleman I must observe it does not appear to have been done upon his Application) and Assessments are making in order to raise a Tax. As the well affected Towns will refuse to furnish their respective Aids (under that usurped Authority) either of Men or Money, force will probably be used to compel them; which will be opposed by force.___

The Wisdom of Congress will naturally suggest to them what the consequence will be and what a disagreable Influence a Contest of this kind ~~will~~ may have not only on the Minds of the Inhabitants of this State, but upon the Affairs of the whole Confederation; and therefore trust it will command a proportionable Degree of their Care and Attention, to prevent this unhappy Dispute from being bro't to so fatal an Issue.___

Whether the very important Matters now before Congress will admit them to enter fully upon the Business of this Controversy is with them to determine tho' I could wish it might not be deferred longer. I must however for the present intreat at least a Resolution expressly disapproving of the Conduct of these People in this Instance and a positive Order to Col[o.] Warner not to receive any of the Drafts into his Regiment.___ This appears to be necessary to prevent the immediate shedding of Blood and without it I fear all those Calamities and Misfortunes which are the natural attendants of a civil War.___[5]

---

[4] Seth Warner (1743-1784) was a militia officer who became a leader of the Green Mountain Boys. He participated in the capture of Ticonderoga, Longueuil, and the battles of Hubbardton and Bennington. On March 20, 1778, he was promoted to brigadier general of the Vermont militia, having been given the grade of colonel of one of the "Additional Continental Regiments." A bill to raise men to fill Warner's regiment was presented by the Council of Safety on March 21, 1778, and approved by the Vermont legislature on March 23, 1778. *Vermont State Papers: being a collection of records & documents, connected with the assumption and establishment of government by the people of Vermont; together with the Journal of the Council of Safety...(Middlebury, Vt., 1823)*, pp. 264-265.

[5] HL did not answer this letter; however, New York delegates William Duer and Gouverneur Morris, whom Clinton had addressed July 7 on the same problem, did respond on July 21. They could only offer a committee report with amendments that supported New York's position. But Congress took no action concerning Vermont and as late as June 1, 1779, despite attempts by the New York delegation to initiate resolutions on the matter, resolved unanimously "That the President inform the governor of the State of New York that a more early attention would have been paid to the pressing applications...relating to the disturbances...had it not been prevented by matters of the greatest importance; and that Congress will continue to pay equal attention to the rights of that State with those of other states in the union." *Delegate Letters* (Smith), X, 330-338; *JCC*, XIV, 631-633, 673-675.

I have the honor to be, with the / highest Esteem and Respect / Your Excellency's / most Obedient Servant

Geo: Clinton

SOURCE: RC, PCC (Item 78), DNA; addressed below close "His Excellency / Henry Laurens Esquire President of Congress.__"; dated "Poughkeepsie July 8th. 1778"; docketed "Letter from Gov Clinton / July 8. 1778 / Read 18 Sept.".

FROM COUNT D'ESTAING[1]

Aboard the *Languedoc*, July 8, 1778

Sir.[2]

I have the honour to inform you Excellency and by you to acquaint Congress, of the arrival of his Majesties Squadron on the Coasts of the united states of America.

Honour'd with his Majesties full Powers, to treat with Congress. I have the honour Sir to remit to your Excellency coppy of my Credential Letter on this subject,[3] the honour of presenting it myself, the desire I have of paying my Court to the Respectable Representatives of a Free Nation, my Eagerness to go and Reverence ~~in them~~ the high qualifications of Wisdom and stedfastness which C↑h↓aracterise[4] them__[5] Virtues which all Europe Admires, and France Cherishes, is a happiness which can be retarded only by the desire I have to render my self worthy of the Favour of the United States, by fulfilling the Duties which circumstances and my

---

[1] Charles-Henri, Count d'Estaing (1729-1794), who had been a lieutenant general in the French army before receiving a vice-admiralship in 1777, sailed April 13 from Toulon aboard his flagship the 90-gun *Languedoc* at the head of a fleet of twelve warships and five frigates. Balch, *French in America*, II, 117-120; Dull, *French Navy*, pp. 67, 112.

[2] D'Estaing may not have known HL's full name. The recipient's copy is addressed "Monsieur Laurens". This translation was addressed "[*blank*] Laurens". HL himself filled in the blank with "Henry".

[3] In a commission dated March 28, 1778, Louis XVI granted full power to Count d'Estaing as Vice Admiral for France. The monarch encouraged the United States to "give Faith and Credit to whatever he will communicate to you in our Name and to place confidence in his Zeal and his talents." PCC, Item 59, Vol. 2, p. 85.

[4] Interlineation by HL.

[5] HL inserted the dash over a comma.

Military station require; I hope this will be a sufficient Excuse to your Excellency and that you will render it acceptable to Congress.

I have the Honour to write to General Washinton and shall send successively to his Camp Two Officers with offers to combine my movements with his.[6] The deserved Reputation that so great a Warrior has so justly acquired, leave no doubt of his being convinced of the value of the first moments.#[7] I hope that his Authority from Congress will leave him at Liberty to make use of them, and that we may from this moment and without any delay Act in consort for the good of the common Cause. and it seems to me that Orders of Congress should ~~raise~~ ↑remove↓ every difficulty which might happen as quickly as possible, but perhaps none Exist.

M[r.] De Chouin Major of Infantry and related to M[r.] de sartine[8] is charged to present this Letter to your Excellency, he is one of the Officers which I send to General Washington.

The Diligence with which his Excellency M[r.] Gerard his Majesty's Minister Plenipotentiary will hasten to go and reside near Congress and Display the Character with which the King has invested him, will remedy all the delays which our Military Opperations might suffer by my remoteness.# I have the honour to assure your Excellency, that I shall regard it as a pleasing Duty to Execute every Engagement of M. Gerard, and whatever he may promise you, will need no other Ratification from me than the possibility of ~~the~~ execution by the Military or Sea Officer.

A Minister who has been so happy as to have had the Indelible ~~Gloury~~ Glory of Signing a treaty which unites two Powers whose Interests are so intimately connected, is fit to preserve the greatest influence on my furthermost Views__#[9] the Retinue which conducts him, that by which the King caused his Excellency M[r.] Silas Dean to be conducted back to the United States is without doubt the most brilliant Pomp that ever accompanied Ambassadors, and I

<hr>

[6] Washington apparently did not receive the July 8 letter from d'Estaing until July 14 when a copy of it arrived with another of July 13. George Washington to d'Estaing, July 17, 1778, *Washington Writings* (Fitzpatrick), XII, 185.

[7] Crosshatches here and below inserted by HL.

[8] André Michel Victor, Marquis de Choin (1744-1829), served as an aide-de-camp to d'Estaing. *Lafayette Papers* (Idzerda), II, 502. Antoine Raymond Jean Gualbert Gabriel de Sartine was the French Minister of Marine.

[9] HL inserted the dash over a comma.

dare hope it will become advantageous to the Interest of the two Nations.[10]

The finest moment of my Life will be that in which I may be able to contribute towards it, in any manner, I shall at the same time fulfill my Duty as intrusted with his Majesty's Commands, and satisfy[11] my private desire and Inclination.

I have the honour to be with Respect. / Your Excellencys / Most humble and most Obedient servant

Estaing

PS. Permit me to recommend to the Congress's favour Mess[rs.] John Nicholson, Elias Johnson and Henry Johnson.[12] M[r] Nicholson has preserved the ship the Tonnant which is the second of the squadron and M[r.] Elias Johnson has conducted himself with the greatest Zeal and Bravery on board the Frigate the Engagente in the Engagement she had in taking the Privateer[13] Rose[14] in Chesapeek Bay

SOURCE: Translation, Kendall Collection; addressed at bottom of first page "To His Excellency Henry Laurens Esq[r.] President of the Congress of the / United American States at Philadelphia"; dated below close "At Sea July 8. 1778."; docketed "The Count d'Estaing's Letter / at Sea July 8th 1778__". RC (French), PCC (Item 164), DNA. Translation, PCC (Item 164), DNA. Copy (French), PCC (Item 111), DNA. Copy (French), PCC (Item 114), DNA.

FROM PATRICK HENRY

Williamsburg, Va., July 8, 1778

Sir

Some Resolutions of Congress & proceedings of the Board of War, have been lately transmitted to me by which it appears that

---

[10] France's new Minister Plenipotentiary to the United States, Conrad-Alexandre Gérard, and American commissioner Silas Deane had accompanied d'Estaing on the *Languedoc*.

[11] "y" written over "ie".

[12] Capt. John Nicholson, of the sloop *Hornet*, had been captured in April 1777. Eleazer Johnson, of the privateer brig *Dalton*, had been captured in December 1776, and Henry Johnson of the brig *Lexington* had been taken in September 1777. The three had escaped from Mill Prison in Plymouth, England. *Franklin Papers* (Labaree), XXV, 415n, 571n.

[13] HL inserted an asterisk at this point to refer to his note "supposed to mean Lydia__" written below the postscript.

[14] The *Rose* was a 20-gun frigate in the British fleet. *Naval Documents* (Clark), IX, 259.

an Expedition against Fort Detroit is resolved on.[1] In order to effect the purposes of it 2000 of the Militia together with Amunition, provisions, Horses, Military Stores, Cloathing &c. &c. are requested to be furnished by this State. I should most chearfully exert myself in accomplishing the Desires of the Board of War & to provide without Delay whatever this Country could afford for the Expedition, agreeable to the Resolution of Congress, did not Reasons of the greatest Importance arrest me in the first Step. I entreat for the Candour and attention of Congress while I submit to their Consideration some of the Reasons which have induced me to think the Expedition to Detroit as announced to me by the Board of War, utterly impracticable at this Season of the year, & under our present Circumstances. In the first place it is impossible to procure Flour in Time. I observe it is proposed to be purchased in the County of Goochland. Neither that, or the adjacent Counties, or adjacent Country can afford the Quantity wanted. Suppose the Contrary, the transportation of it, is absolutely impossible by the Time required.

The Horses may possibly be got but I will venture to say that the immediate purchase of 5000 & upwards which are required will raise the price to four Times the Estimate, and amount I think to near half a million of pounds.

Indeed I am satisfied upon a View of the Articles wanted for this Expedition, that the preparations ought to have begun early in the Winter, & that those now making cannot be compleated before next Spring. 5000 pack saddles, tight seasoned Casks for carrying the powder, collecting the Cattle together, transporting 30,000 lbs. Lead from the Mines, fabricating 1000 horse Bells 400 felling Axes 3000 Hatchets, Kettles made of rolled Iron, procuring Tents, Knapsacks, Haversacks, complete suits of Clothes for the Regulars, the recruiting, Arming, accoutring & Disciplining them; forming Magazines of provisions & military Stores, finding the Means of transportation thro that Country. These and a vast Variety of other particulars which I do not enumerate, cannot be accomplished of a Sudden: On the contrary, from a Scarcity of Workmen & Materials,

---

[1] HL had sent Governor Henry a copy of Congress's June 11 resolution which called for troops to be raised for the purpose of repelling hostile Indians by carrying out an expedition against them including the capture of Fort Detroit if necessary. HL to Patrick Henry, June 13, 1778, PCC, Item 13; *JCC*, XI, 587-589.

from the want of Waggons, from the exhausted State of this Country, as to several Articles called for, and the distressed Situation of our people, Resources & Supplies, I think the next Spring is as soon as the march proposed can be thought of.

My perfect Reliance on the Wisdom of Congress makes me wish by no means to touch upon any matter that lays within their province to determine. And I should not say any thing now touching the general Expence of this Expedition, did not the advanced price of most Articles in this Country, joined to the nature of the proposed Service & the plan for effecting it make it my Duty to hint, that in my Opinion the amount will far exceed the Ideas of Congress; & perhaps approach to a Comparison with the Sum which the grand Army of Infantry cost the united States for the same length of Time. All I request is that Congress will be pleased to review the Estimate of Expences the nature of the Business and the Time for executing it; And if they shall be pleased to persist in the first plan, I shall think it my Duty to forward to the utmost what they direct

In the mean Time, Lieutenant Colonel Campbell[2] who brings me the Despatches on this Subject, is now here, having the Stores of the State thrown open to him, & is desired to select such Articles of Clothes as the Troops to be raised, may want & can be found in them. Orders to the Leadmines will also be sent to forward some Lead towards Fort Randolph or Pittsburgh.

The Miseries of the people of Virginia who live exposed to the Assaults of the Savages, affect me most Sensibly. And in my anxiety to see some thing doing for their protection, I hope for Excuse from Congress when I suggest, that if an Expedition is directed against the Hostile Tribes nearest our Frontiers, very good Consequences might result. Such a Step seems to be free from the Objections which are hinted against the Attack of Detroit, where a post will be difficult to maintain while the great intermediate Country is occupied by Hostile Indians, & from which it seems easy

---

[2] Maj. Richard Campbell (d. 1781) of the 13th Va. Regiment had been given a brevet lieutenant colonel's commission through the intercession of Lachlan McIntosh and George Washington in mid June. He was stationed in the western department under McIntosh after that. George Washington to HL, June 10, 1778, PCC, Item 152, Vol. 6, p. 97ff.

for the enemy to retreat with all their Stores while they are superior upon the adjacent Waters

Our Frontier people wish for offensive Measures against the Indian Towns & will enlist freely for that purpose. But I cannot help doubting whether the apparent Difficulties of succeeding against Detroit at present, will not be an Obstacle with them against engaging in the Service.

I beg to be favoured with the Decisions of Congress upon this matter quickly as possible, that necessary Measures may not be delayed, or useless purchases or Expenditures for preparations be made by the several Agents who are already engaged in their respective Departments.[3]

The Sentiments contained in this Letter come from a full Board of Council ↑as well↓ as from me.

I beg to be informed whether it is necessary to push forward the Cavalry & Infantry voted by the last Assembly here. They are to serve but a short Time & if they are not wanted, much Expence will be saved by knowing it in Time & preventing their Inlistments which will be made upon a most expensive plan & which nothing but a supposed necessity induced the Legislature to adopt.

With great Regard I have the Honor to be / Sir / Your most obedient & / very humble Servant

P. Henry

P.S. The Express has Orders to wait for an Answer to this, & indeed the State of affairs seems to require it speedily

SOURCE: RC, PCC (Item 71), DNA; addressed below close "The honble / Henry Laurens Esqr. / President of Congress"; dated "Wmsburg July 8th 1778"; docketed by HL "Govr Henry / 8th. July 1778 / Recd late PM 18th."; and in another hand "Read 20. / Referred to the board of war / who are directed to take the / same under their immediate / consideration & report there / on as soon as possible.".

---

[3] Governor Henry followed this letter with a July 10 note in which he further discouraged the expedition by underscoring the difficulty he would have furnishing beef cattle. Congress on July 25, largely in response to Henry's advice, suspended the plans for the expedition against Detroit. Patrick Henry to HL, July 10, 1778, PCC, Item 71, Vol. 1, p. 169; *JCC*, XI, 720-721.

TO RICHARD CASWELL

Philadelphia, July 9, 1778

Sir

By Captain Cottineau I had the honor of writing to Your Excellency from York the 20th Ult°.

Inclosed herein Your Excellency will receive Copy of a Letter from the Commissioners at Paris, which I had the honor of receiving and presenting to Congress yesterday.__ [1] The English fleet mentioned in that Letter is supposed were equipped for intercepting a French squadron intended for some part of North America, probably Chesapeak bay. Your Excellency is therefore requested to pursue the most effectual measures to apprize the Commander of the French squadron Le Compte d'Estaing of any English ships of War which may come into any of the Harbours or Inlets of the state of North Carolina, their force, number and station, and to accommodate the squadron or any of the ships of our Ally the King of France with proper Pilots, if required. [2]

Monsr. Gerard in the Character of Plenipotentiary from the Court of Versailles to these states, is ~~illegible~~ expected in the French fleet which consists of twelve sail of the Line, six Frigates &c

I shall add printed Papers containing much public intelligence, to which I beg leave to refer.

A private Letter from Genl. Washingtons Army of the 7th informs me "the Army was then in motion from Brunswick for

---

[1] The American commissioners sent twenty copies of this circular letter, dated Paris, May 18, 1778, "to the Governor or any Counsellor, or Senator or Member of any House of Representatives, in any of the Thirteen United States of America." Congress received its copy enclosed from William Heath June 30, 1778. Congress had the letter printed as a broadside. "Certain Intelligence having been received, that Eleven British ships of War, viz. One of 90 Guns, Nine of 74, and one of 64 Guns, are in the Road of St. Hellens, near Portsmouth, bound for North-America, and the United States being in Alliance with France, you are requested, as speedily as possible, to convey this information to the Commander of any French Fleet, or Ships of War in America, by sending them this Letter, and also to publish the Contents of it in all the Continental News-Papers." A copy of the broadside from the Archives Nationale, Marine, Paris, B4, v. 146 is used as an illustration in *Adams Papers: Diary and Autobiography of John Adams,* IV, following page 99. A note at the bottom of that copy in HL's hand reads "This Fleet I trust will be curbed by the Ships at Brest__". William Heath to HL, June 30, 1778, PCC, Item 157, p. 166ff.

[2] Congress resolved July 9, that the governors of Maryland, Virginia, North Carolina, South Carolina, and Georgia "be severally requested to take proper measures for giving the earliest intelligence to any French fleet...of a fleet of British ships of war being ready to sail for North America". And, that they assist any French "ships of war with good pilots for bringing them safely into the [*Chesapeake*] Bay, should they incline to come there." *JCC,* XI, 675-676.

North River. the Enemy had passed the Breach between Sandy
Hook and the Main, and had taken up their Bridge after them, they
were embarking with the greatest expedition, had left a number of
Waggons behind them and cut the throats of many horses, three
signal Guns had been fired from the fleet on the 5th. and the whole
were under sail the 6th in the Morning__ uncertain whither bound__
Colonel Morgan had taken about 30 Prisoners and received about
100 Deserters."[3]

English Papers of the middle of April shew the Debates in
both Houses of Parliament to have been on a motion for acknowledging American Independence, and the whole Nation in great
distraction.[4]

I have the honor to be &c

SOURCE: LB, PCC (Item 13), DNA; addressed "Governor Caswell / North
Carolina / by Johns"; dated "9th July".

TO COUNT D'ESTAING

Philadelphia, July 10, 1778

Sir

Congress received Intelligence this Morning of the arrival
on this Coast of a fleet of Men of War under Your Excellencies
command.[1]

The Packet which I have the honor of transmitting you
herewith reached my hands on the 8th Instant,[2] together with the

---

[3] John Laurens to HL, July 7, 1778, Kendall Collection.

[4] On April 9, David Hartley offered a motion in the House of Commons to end the
American war. He addressed the cost of the war which he projected through 1778 to be almost
£33 million sterling. He suggested Britain "seek the alliance and friendship of America" and
"cement the two countries...by a mutual naturalization in all rights and franchises to the
fullest extent." The following day Thomas Powys offered a motion that because of the debt
already incurred and the threat of war with France that the peace commission recognize
American independence as a means of ending the conflict. Cobbett's *Parliamentary History*,
XIX, 1068-1088.

[1] The first word of d'Estaing's arrival off the Maryland coast was delivered to Congress by
Blair McClenachan before noon on July 10. HL to George Washington, July 10, 1778.

[2] HL informed Lafayette the same day that "A large Mail arrived a few days ago in Congress
from France, I found it to contain many Packets for Monsr. Gerard." The packets sent to
d'Estaing probably arrived in this mail. Because he was uncertain where d'Estaing would be,
HL sent two packets, one directed to Henry Fisher at Lewistown, Del., and another to Richard
Wescott "at the Forks of Little Egg Harbour," N.J. HL to Lafayette, July 10, 1778, HL Papers,
ScHi; HL to Henry Fisher, July 10, 1778, PCC, Item 13; HL to Richard Wescott, July 28, 1778.

[3] See HL to George Washington, July 10, 1778, for a list of the British warships.

Inclosed intelligence of an English squadron lying near Portsmouth on the 18th of May, supposed to have been intended to annoy
your Excellencies progress towards this shore__ to the force of that
squadron your Excellency will be pleased to add the Inclosed
enumeration of the English ships of War supposed to be in the
harbour of New York, which is the most accurate we have been able
to collect.[3]

   If it shall be your Excellency's design to act offensively
against the British Marine, it may conduce to success, that the
Commander in Chief of the forces of these United States should
cooperate in the measures intended to be pursued on your part__
I beg leave therefore to inform you, Sir, that His Excellency General
Washington with the Army under his command, is at this time
between Morris town in New Jersey and the North river which forms
part of the waters which encircle New York.__

If your Excellency should be pleased to open a Communication
with General Washington, your dispatches will be quickly conveyed
to him by means of the Inclosed Warrant to be sent on shore with
Your Excellency's Packets.

   To the several Papers already said to be inclosed with this,
I add three which will lay before Your Excellency the proceedings
and determinations of Congress consecutive upon the various
attempts of the British Parliament and Administration for effecting
a Reconciliation between Great Britain and the United States of
America; as Your Excellency cannot have seen these papers on the
other side the Atlantic, a perusal of them will afford some amusement at the same time that you will learn from the contents the
firmness of the good People of this Country.[4]

   I have the Honor to assure you, Sir, if it shall be necessary
after referring to the papers last mentioned that Congress will be
ready to render you every service in their power for facilitating your
oper Excellency's operations against our common Enemy.

---

[4] The three documents rebuffing the Carlisle Commission to which HL refers here were
probably the Congressional resolution of April 22, HL's Clinton/Howe letter of June 6, and
his letter to the Carlisle Commission on June 17. *JCC* X, 374-380; *HL Papers*, XIII, 409-410,
470-471.

I have the Honor to be / With the highest Esteem and Regard / Sir / Your Excellency's / Most Obedient & / Most Humble Servt.

SOURCE: LB, PCC (Item 13), PCC; addressed "His Excellency Admiral Count d'Estaing / by Anthony Daugherty. Duplicate by Charles Freeman"; dated "10th July".

TO GEORGE WASHINGTON

Philadelphia, July 10, 1778

Sir.

I had the honor of writing to Your Excellency by Major Putnam the 8th Inst__

Congress while sitting before Noon received intelligence of the following import.

Mr. Blair MLenahan[1] said he had seen a Capt. Selby[2] or Selwin off Chincoteague who had fallen in with the French Fleet Eastward of Bermuda__ the Admiral had taken him on board & enjoined him to Pilot the ffleet to this Coast, the ffleet arrived near Chincoteague in the Evening of the 5th. Inst.__ there they found the Ship Lydia of 26 Guns from New York on a Cruise__ she was sunk by a french Frigate of 36 Guns__ On Monday Capt. Selby was sent on Shoar in order to procure Pilots he engaged six to go on board the French ffleet upon Wednesday__ the Fleet consisted of the Admiral Count d'Estaing of 90 Guns__ 2 Ships of 80__ 8 of 74__ 1 of 64.__ 4 of 36. & said to have 12000 Men__ they had taken a Ship of 18 Guns from Providence before they had made the Land.

War was to be declared against England by France & Spain on the 19th. May__ they had originally intended for Delaware but hearing that the Enemy were gone to New York they required Pilots

---

[1] Blair McClenachan (d. 1812), an Irish-born Philadelphia merchant, was active during the Revolution in fitting out privateers. He participated in politics after the war serving as chairman of the Anti-Federalist convention held at Harrisburg in 1788, as a state legislator 1790-1795, and as member of Congress 1797-1799. John H. Campbell, *History of the Friendly Sons of St. Patrick and the Hibernian Society for the Relief of Emigrants from Ireland* (Philadelphia, 1892), p. 126; *Biographical Directory of Congress*.

[2] Probably William Selby of Pitts Landing, Va., who had been enlisted to unload a schooner in Chincoteague Inlet in 1776. *Naval Documents* (Clark), V, 792.

to conduct them to Sandy Hook, they had then six Months provision on board.

Your Excellency will perceive by the inclosed Printed Paper that a Fleet had been prepared at Portsmouth in order to intercept or annoy this Fleet of which 'tis possible the Count d'Estaing may be ignorant as he sailed from Toulon the 15th April; 'tis possible also that a Check may have been put upon that by a Fleet from Brest, be that as it may, Count d'Estaing should be apprized of this important circumstance & also of the strength of the British Marine power in New York, which from the best accounts we have been able to collect is made up of the following Ships__

Boyne	70 Guns.	Centurion	50.	Roebuck	44
Eagle	64.	Experiment	50.	Phœnix	44.
St. Alban	64.	Preston.	50.	& many Frigates	
Ardent.	64.	Renown.	50.		
Sommerset	64.	Chatham	50.		
Trident	64.	Isis	50.		
Vigilant formerly	64.				

I shall endeavour to reach Count d'Estaing with the necessary advices on the Coast of New Jersey or ↑off↓ the Capes of Delaware__ Your Excellency will, if he shall have proceeded nearer Sandy Hook endeavor to meet him with a Letter where it may reach him, & you will also concert measures for improving the force under Your Excellency's immediate Command & that under the direction of Major General Gates, in the present critical conjuncture.

Your Excellency will also if you have a more exact Account of the British Fleet at New York make proper corrections upon the list above enumerated__

I have the honor to be / With the highest Esteem & / Respect Sir / Your Excellencys / Most obedient & most hum̄ / servant

Henry Laurens.
President / of Congress

It is almost unnecessary to intimate to Your Excellency the propriety of opening & keeping up a correspondence with the Admiral Count d'Estaing__

SOURCE: ALS, Washington Papers, DLC; addressed below close "His Excel-

lency / General Washington."; dated "Philadelphia / 10ᵗʰ· July 1778__";
docketed "Congress 10 July 78 / ansᵈ_ 14__ / Advising of the Arrival / of
Count D'Estaing". LB, PCC (Item 13), PCC.

TO RICHARD WESCOTT[1]

Philadelphia, July 10, 1778

Sir

The Bearer hereof will will also deliver to you a Packet
directed to His Excellency Count d'Estaing, Commander of a
French fleet of ships of War which were a few days ago at
Chincoteague, and said to be bound for Delaware or Sandy Hook.
If the fleet shall be accessible I request you in the name of Congress
to send the Packet at all expence to the Admiral, otherwise be
pleased to return it by the same hand which will deliver it to you.[2]

I have the Honor to be &c.

SOURCE: LB, PCC (Item 13), DNA; addressed "Richard Westcott at the Forks
of Little Egg Harbour / by Charles Freeman at ½ past 10 at night"; dated
"10ᵗʰ July".

FROM SILAS DEANE

Delaware Bay, July 10, 1778

Sir

I have now the pleasure of acquainting your Excellency of
my Arrival here yesterday on board the Languedoc commanded by
his Excellency Count D'Estaing, with a fleet of twelve Sail of the Line
and four Frigates. We sailed from Toulon the 10ᵗʰ of April last,
presume therefore that I have no intelligence from Europe so late
as what you must be possessed of already. Finding that the Enemy
had escaped the Admiral resolved instantly to pursue them to New
York and will sail this morning for that Port, but he has no pilot; If

---

[1] The name appeared as Westcott in HL's letterbook but was clearly signed Wescott in the reply. Richard Wescott's sloop *Betsey* had been captured and sunk by HMS *Phoenix* in April 1776 upon the vessel's return from Dominque. He received a letter of marque for the boat *Chance* in March 1778. PCC, Item 196, Vol. 2, p. 26.

[2] HL sent a similar letter to Henry Fisher at Lewistown the same day covering a duplicate packet for d'Estaing. PCC, Item 13.

therefore pilots can be sent to meet him on his arrival, it will be of the utmost service to the expedition. I shall embark this afternoon in company with his Excellency Monsr· Gerard for Philadelphia, and hope soon to have the honor of paying my respects to your Excellency and the honorable Congress in person, and to congratulate you on the late glorious events. I have sent Comm^r· Nicholson express who can inform you of our situation, permit me to recommend him as an active, Spirited Officer, to whom the Admiral has been much obliged by his services during our passage.

I have the Honor to be with the most pro / found Respect / Your Excellency's / most obedient & very hble. Ser^t·

(signed) Silas Deane

P.S His Excellency the Admiral desires, that on the arrival of the pilots at the hook where they will find his Fleet, that they would make a Signal with a white Flag, either on board their Boat, if they have one, or from the Shore, formed in a triangle. Monsr· Chouen who will wait on you with a Letter from the Admiral sets out suddenly and may want money to bear his expences on his further Journey, Monsr· Gerard desires he may be supplied on his Account, with any sum to the Amount of twenty thousand Livres.

SOURCE: Copy, PCC (Item 103), DNA; no address; dated "Delaware Bay 10th July 1778".

CIRCULAR TO SEVERAL STATES[1]

Philadelphia, July 10, 1778

Sir

Congress intent upon the present and future security of these United States has never ceased to consider a Confederacy[2] as the great principle of Union, which can alone establish the Liberty of America and exclude for ever the hopes of its Enemies.

Influenced by motives[3] so powerful, and duly weighing the difficulties which oppose the expectation of any plan being formed

---

[1] This letter, sent to New Jersey, Maryland, Delaware, and Georgia, was prepared by a committee headed by Richard Henry Lee. The draft is in Lee's hand and was amended in Congress on this date. Some of the amendments to the draft are recorded in HL's hand; the final text is identical in wording to the copy in the presidential letterbook. *JCC,* XI, 681.

[2] "Confederation" in draft.

[3] "considerations" in draft.

that can exactly meet the wishes and obtain[4] the approbation of so many States, differing essentially in various points, Congress have, after mature deliberation agreed to adopt without amendments the Confederation transmitted to the several States for their approbation. The States of New Hampshire, Massachusetts Bay, Rhode Island & Providence Plantations,[5] Connecticut, New York, Pennsylvania, Virg[a], North Carolina and South Carolina,[6] have ratified the same & it remains only for your State with those of [blank] and [blank][7] to conclude the Glorious Compact, which, by uniting the wealth, strength and Councils of the whole, may bid defiance to external violence[8] and internal dissentions,[9] whilst it secures the Public Credit both at home and abroad. Congress is willing to hope that the Patriotism and good sense of Your State will be influenced by motives so important, and they request Sir, that you will be pleased to lay this Letter before the Legislature of [blank] in order that if they judge it proper, their Delegates may be instructed to ratify the Confederation with all convenient dispatch, trusting to future deliberation to make such alterations and amendments as experience may shew to be expedient and just.[10]

I have the Honor to be &[c.]

P.S. to Georgia, (only)[11]

It cannot be doubted that Georgia so distantly situated will consider that new Delegates are to be appointed to meet in Congress under Articles of Confederation on the 1st Monday in Nov[r.] & give suitable dispatch to this important business.

SOURCE: LB, PCC (Item 13), DNA; addressed "Governor Houston, Georgia / Governor Johnson Maryland / Presiden Rodney, Delaware / & Governor Livingston, New Jersey / the Blanks will [be] filled with the Names of the States / Mutatis Mutandis__ / Gov[r] Johnson by the Virginia Express__ Gov[r] Livingston by Baldwin / Gov[r] Houston, by [blank] / President Rodney by [blank]"; dated "10th July". Draft, PCC (Item 47), DNA.

---

[4] "secure" in draft.

[5] "& Prov" in draft.

[6] "making nine [illegible]" cancelled in draft.

[7] "Delaware, Maryland, and Georgia" in draft.

[8] Other text replaced by "violence" in draft.

[9] "or domestic dissention" in draft.

[10] Draft read "request, Sir that your Delegates in Congress may be authorized to ratify the Convention with all convenient dispatch, trusting to future deliberation and to time itself [illegible] for a more perfect accomodation of opinions. I have the honor to be &[c.]".

[11] "(only)" inserted by HL.

TO GEORGE WASHINGTON

Philadelphia, July 11, 1778

Sir.

I beg leave to refer Your Excellency to the contents of a Letter which I had honor[1] of writing to you last Evening by Barry.

The present Cover will convey to Your Excellency two Acts of Congress of this date.

1. Empowering Your Excellency to call in the Aid of such Militia as shall appear to be necessary from the four Eastern States, from New York & New Jersey for carrying on operations in concert with Count d'Estaing.[2]

2. Intimating the desire of Congress that Your Excellency Co-operate with Vice Admiral Count d'Estaing in the Execution of such offensive operations as against the Enemy as shall appear to be necessary.

Congress have directed me to propose for Your Excellencys consideration an attack by Vice Admiral Count d Estaing upon the British Ships of War & Transports in the harbor of Rhode Island, by which possession of a safe Port may be gained & the retreat of the British forces on that Island be cut off, as an alternative to a hazardous or ineligible attempt upon the British Squadron within Sandy Hook.

I have the honor to be / With the highest Esteem & Respect / Sir Your Excellency's / Most obedient & most / humble servant

Henry Laurens.

President / of Congress.

Some time ago I informed Your Excellency that Congress had adopted the Stile of "North America" to these States__ this day that Resolution was reconsidered & reduced to the former mode of "America"[3]

---

[1] Letterbook reads "the honor".

[2] HL addressed a circular letter dated July 12 to the executives of New Hampshire, Connecticut, Massachusetts, and Rhode Island as well as New York and New Jersey enclosing the act empowering Washington to call out the militia of those states. PCC, Item 13.

[3] Congress on May 19, 1778, had passed a resolution to designate the country "the United States of North America." This July 11 resolution removed the word "North" returning to the form "United States of America" as styled in the Articles of Confederation. *JCC*, XI, 683.

Congress Resolved on the 9th. Inst that the Committee appointed to arrange the Army do repair without delay to Head Quarters for that purpose as Your Excellency will perceive by the Inclosed Certified Order.__4

SOURCE: ALS, Washington Papers, DLC; addressed below close "His Excellency / General Washington__"; dated "Philadelphia 11th. July 1778__"; docketed "Congress 11 July 1778 / ansd 22. / Enterprize against / Rhode Island, suggested / Power to call in / Militia. / Committee of Arrangemt / ordered to Camp". LB, PCC (Item 13), DNA.

FROM CARLISLE COMMISSION

New York, July 11, 1778

Gentlemen

We received soon after our Arrival at this place your Answer to our Letter of the 10th of June1 and are sorry to find on your part any difficulties raised which must prolong the Calamities of the present War.

You propose to us as matter of Choice one or other of two Alternatives which you state as Preliminaries necessary even to the beginning of a Negociation for Peace to this Empire.__

One is an explicit acknowledgement of the Independence of these States. We are not inclin'd to dispute with you about the meaning of Words: But so far as you mean the entire Priviledge of the People of North America to dispose of their Property and to Govern themselves without any reference to Great Britain, beyond what is necessary to preserve that Union of Force in which our mutual safety and advantage consist: We think that so far, their Independency is fully acknowledged in the Terms of our Letter of

---

4 Congress had adopted on May 27 a detailed plan for the organization of the American army and had appointed Joseph Reed and Francis Dana on June 4 to assist Washington in implementing the plan. In effect, this resolution ordered Reed and Dana to carry out their assignment. *JCC,* XI, 538–543, 570, 676.

1 The letter from the Carlisle Commission was actually dated June 9, rather than June 10, 1778. *HL Papers,* XIII, 424–427.

the 10^{th:} June.__ And we are willing to enter upon a fair discussion with you of all the Circumstances that may be necessary to ensure or even to enlarge that Independency.__

In the other Alternative you propose That His Majesty should withdraw His Fleets and His Army.__

Although we have no doubt of His Majesty's disposition to remove every Subject of uneasiness from the Colonies, Yet there are Circumstances of Precaution against our Ancient Enemies, which joined to the regard that must be paid to the safety of many who from Affection to Great Britain have exposed themselves to suffer in this Contest and to whom Great Britain owes support at every expence of Blood and Treasure, that will not allow us to begin with this Measure. How soon it may follow the first Advances to Peace on your part will depend on the favorable prospect you give of a reconciliation with your fellow Citizens of this Continent and with those in Britain. In the mean time we assure you that no Circumstance will give us more Satisfaction than to find that the Extent of our future Connection is to be determined on principles of mere Reason and the Considerations of mutual Interest on which we are willing likewise to rest the Permanency of any Arrangements we may form.

In making these Declarations we do not wait for the decision of any Military Events. Having determined our Judgement by what we believe to be the Interests of our Country we shall abide by the declarations we now make in every possible Situation of our Affairs.__

You refer to Treaties already subsisting but are pleased to withhold from us any particular Information in respect to their nature or tendency.__

If they are in any degree to affect our Deliberations we think that you cannot refuse a full Communication of the particulars in which they consist both for our Consideration and that of your own Constituents who are to Judge between us whether any Alliance you may have Contracted be a sufficient reason for continuing this unnatural War. We likewise think ourselves entitled to a full Communication of the Powers by which you conceive yourselves Authorized to make Treaties with Foreign Nations.

And we are led to ask Satisfaction on this point because we have observed in your proposed Articles of Confederation N^{os:} 6 and

9 it is Stated that you should have the Power of entering into Treaties and Alliances under certain Restrictions therein specified yet we do not find promulgated any Act or Resolution of the Assembly's of particular States conferring this Power on you.__

As we have Communicated our Powers to you and mean to proceed without reserve in this business we will not suppose that any objection can arise on your part to our Communicating to the Public so much of your Correspondence as may be necessary to explain our own proceedings.[2] At the same time we assure you that in all such Publications the Respect which we pay to the great Body of People you are supposed to represent shall be Evidenced by us in every possible mark of Consideration and Regard

We are with perfect respect / Gentlemen / Your most Obedient and / Most humble Servants

Carlisle.__

H Clinton

Wm. Eden

Geo. Johnstone.

SOURCE: Copy, Force Collection, DLC; addressed "To / His Excellency Henry Laurens / The President and other The Members / of Congress"; dated below close "New York / 11th. July 1778"; docketed "Letter from Carlisle / ᴳ H ꟻ Clinton / Wm. Eden / Geo Johnstone / New York 11 July 1778 / Read 18.__". Copy, CO 5/180, PRO. Copy, Kendall Collection.

FROM EBENEZER HAZARD [1]

Philadelphia, July 11, 1778

Sir,

Viewing Congress as the Friends of Science, as well as the Guardians of our Liberties, I flatter myself there can be no Impropriety in solliciting their Patronage and Assistance for a Collection

---

[2] Congress stole a march on the Commission by ordering this letter to be published along with Congress's resolution of July 18 explaining why this letter would not be answered. *JCC,* XI, 701–702. The letter and the resolution were published in the *Pa. Packet,* July 21, 1778. That issue also included an open letter from William Henry Drayton to the Commission which is printed in *Delegate Letters* (Smith), X, 295–302.

[1] Ebenezer Hazard (1744–1817), the father of American historical editing, surveyor of the post in the eastern department at this time, served as postmaster general from 1782 to 1789.

of American State Papers, which, from its evident Utility, I am confident they will deem not unworthy of either.

The Design of it is to furnish Materials for a good History of the United States, which may now be very well done, for so rapid has been our political Progress that we can easily recur to the first Step taken upon the Continent, and clearly point out our different Advances from Persecution to comparative Liberty, and from thence to independent Empire. In this Particular we have the Advantage of every Nation upon Earth, and Gratitude to Heaven and to our virtuous Fathers, Justice to ourselves, and a becoming Regard to Posterity strongly urge us to an Improvement of it, before Time and Accident deprive us of the Means.

The Undertaking will appear, at first View, to be too great for an unassisted Individual; and Experience has convinced me that although several Years incessant Application has produced an important Collection, yet, so numerous are the Materials, and so much dispersed, that a whole Life would be insufficient to compleat it in the Way in which I have been hitherto obliged to proceed. I now propose to visit each State for that Purpose, and must request of Congress a Certificate of their Approbation of my Design, should they approve of it, and a Recommendation to the several Governors and Presidents to grant me free Access to the Records of their respective States, and Permission to extract from them such Parts as may fall within the Limits of my Plan.__

To enable them to judge of the Nature of the Collection, I beg Leave to enclose the Titles of some of the Materials of which it is to consist, which please to lay before them,[2] and believe me to be, Sir, / Your most obedient & very hum[l.] Serv[t.]

Eben Hazard

He produced two volumes of *Historical Collections of State Papers and Other Authentic Documents, intended as Materials for an History of the United States of America* (Philadelphia, 1792, 1794) before poor sales ended the project. Fred Shelley, "Ebenezer Hazard: America's First Historical Editor," *WMQ*, XII (1955):44–73.

[2] Congress referred this letter to a committee consisting of Richard Henry Lee, William Duer, and Samuel Adams who recommended that Congress appropriate $1,000 to help defray Hazard's expenses. The committee also urged the states to cooperate with Hazard's collection of state papers: "that, for this purpose, he be admitted to an inspection of public records, and be furnished, without expence, with copies of such papers as he may judge will conduce to the valuable end he hath in view." The report was submitted and adopted by Congress on July 20. *JCC*, XI, 705–706.

SOURCE: RC, Continental Congress Miscellany, DLC; addressed on cover "The Honorable / Henry Laurens Esq$^{r.}$"; addressed below close "The Hon$^{ble.}$ Henry Laurens Esq$^{r.}$"; dated "Philadelphia July 11$^{th.}$ 1778"; docketed "Letter from Ebenezer Hazard / July 11. 1778 / Read & freferred to M^r R H Lee / M Duer / M S. Adams." Copy, with committee report and resolutions, Peter Force Papers, MiU-C. Committee Report, PCC, Item 19, Vol. 3, p. 75.

FROM RICHARD WESCOTT

Egg Harbor, N.J., July 12, 1778

Sir

I had the honor of Receiving your favour of the 10th Insant with the dispatches for his Excellency Count de Estaing and have dispatch'd the Lexington, Privateer Schooner Capt Cook[1] with them who saw the Fleet of Barnagat Inlett last ~~week~~ ↑Saturday.↓ Should any misfortune attend the Lexingtons going in Quest of His Excellency with them I have Engaged Congress will make him every Reasonable Compensation__ I doubt not he will deliver them Safe

And have the Honor to be / with the greatest Respect / Sir / Your Obed$^{t.}$ / Hble Servt

Rich$^{d.}$ Wescott

SOURCE: RC, PCC (Item 78), DNA; addressed on cover "The Honble Henry Laurens Esqr / President of Congress / in / Philadelphia"; addressed below close "Hon$^{ble.}$ Henry Laurens Esq$^{r.}$"; dated "Forks Egg-harbour July 12th / 1778"; franked "On public Service"; docketed "J Letter from R Wescot / Forks little Egg harbour / July 12. 1778 / Read 15.".

FROM JOHN LAURENS

Paramus, N.J., July 13, 1778

I have[1] barely[2] time my dearest friend and Father to say that my heart overflows with gratitude at the repeated proofs of your tender love__ and must defer answering your kind letters of the 6th

---

[1] Joseph Cook of Massachusetts took command of the schooner *Lexington*, with 16 swivel guns and 25 men, on April 10, 1778. Claghorn, *Naval Officers.*

[1] "I have" written over other text.

[2] "1" written over "a".

and 10th 'till my return from Count D'Estaing's Fleet, where the[3] General has thought proper to send me with dispatches__ I must immediately prepare for my Journey and Voyage__ I could wish that Mons[r.] Le Comte were furnished with a proper number of intelligent Coast pilots__ that as many pilot boats Schooners and other small swift sailing Vessels were employed under the conduct of judicious Se[a]mean to reconnoitre the Enemys fleet whenever it appears at Sea__ and give the french Admiral the earliest account of their Strength, &ca__ as well as keep him constantly advised afterwards of all their motions__

The movement of our Army across the North River, to make demonstration near N. York, may have a happy effect in preventing the English Admiral from making his Fleet so strong as he otherwise would__

God protect you my dear Father.

John Laurens.

SOURCE: ALS, Kendall Collection; no address; dated "Head Quarters 13th July 1778.".

FROM CONRAD-ALEXANDRE GÉRARD

Philadelphia, July 14, 1778

The Squadron which the King my Master has sent to Act in consort with the United States against the common Ennemy, having taken some Prisoners in its Passage, the keeping of which on board the Ships would be troublesome and even dangerous, The under written begs ~~that~~ ↑the↓[1] Congress ↑of the said United States↓ would be pleased to direct that those Prisoners may, be received on Shore as well as those that the Kings Squadron may hereafter take in the Course of its Operations, and that Provision may be made for their Security and Subsistence in the same manner as is practised with

---

[3] "His" altered to "the".
[1] Interlineations here and below by HL.

their own Prisoners and that they may remain at the Kings disposal and to the Orders of his Ex^cy· M the Count d'Estaing Vice Admiral of France and Commander of his Majesties Squadron.[2]

   The underwritten will take care at the times assignd and in the manner Congress will be pleased to point out, to Pay all the Expences this affair may occasion.

                                                        Gerard

SOURCE: Translation, PCC (Item 94), DNA; no address; dated below close "Philadelphia July 14. 1778"; noted "Memorandum Concerning the Prisoners". RC (French), PCC (Item 94), DNA.

FROM CONRAD-ALEXANDRE GÉRARD

                                    Philadelphia, July 14, 1778

[His Excellency M. the Count d'Estaign Vice Admiral of France, Commanding the Kings Squadron desiring to procure to all the Armements either Public or private in the United States of ↑North↓[1] America the means of making the greatest advantage of the Operations of this Squadron, in order to make Prizes on on the common Ennemy. The under written has the Honour to inform Congress, that all such Armaments shall enjoy the most extensive Protection from his most Christian Majesties Squadron, and that the Prizes they may take shall belong to them only without any division], he referrs to the Wisdom of Congress to draw from this disposition all the Advantage it is capable of admitting. [The American Vessells who will apply to his Excellency the Vice Admiral will receive the Necessary Signals] and the under written will Successively deliver ↑them↓ to Congress, in order that they may inform those who will sail from the different Ports. he reposes himself on the Prudence of

---

[2] The following day Congress responded with resolves which directed the commissary general of prisoners to accept these prisoners, provide "safe custody and subsistance," make monthly returns on expenditures, and hold them "subject to the orders of his excellency Mons. the Count d'Estaing". *JCC*, XI, 690–691.

[1] Interlineation by HL.

Congress in relation to the Measures Necessary to secure ~~the greatest~~ Success.[2]

Gerard

SOURCE: Translation, PCC (Item 94), DNA; no address; dated below close "Philadelphia July 14. 1778."; docketed "Message from the S* / Gerard relative to en / couragement given by / the Count d'Estaign to / American armed vessels / whether public or private / read 15 July 1778.__ / Entered.__". RC (French), PCC (Item 94), DNA.

FROM THE MARQUIS DE LAFAYETTE

Paramus, N.J., July 14, 1778

dear Sir

I [torn] honor'd with your favor of the 10th last, and beg you would Receiv[e] [torn] Sincere thanks for the important intelligence you are pleas'd to Communicate to me__ as the division of the army ↑I command↓ is just going to March, I will confine myself in very few lines.

I beg leave to mention a thing which seems to me of the highest importance the french admiral will no doubt want frequent intelligences, and great many accidents may happen to those which will be sent to him__ I think therefore that an immense plenty of boats schould be Ready and fitted out in every part of the Continent, that if one do'nt arrive, others may Reach him__ no time ~~no expense~~ schould be lost or expense spar'd for to convey the least news, as they may prouve of [torn] [conse]quence__ do'nt you think also, Sir, that our fleet may be in nee[d] [of so]me [p]ilots__ I have wrote[1] to the Count destaing in a letter which gāl Wa[shington] is going to send him.[2]

---

[2] Congress responded the following day by ordering that an extract of this letter "relative to the encouragement given by Count d'Estaing to American armed vessels" be published. *JCC*, XI, 691. The sections of this translation marked with brackets in the manuscript itself made up the "extract" published in the *Pa. Packet*, July 16, 1778, and in the *Boston Gazette*, Aug. 10, 1778.

[1] "w" written over other text.

[2] Lafayette's July 14 letter to d'Estaing was carried by John Laurens, who was going as Washington's messenger. Lafayette introduced John as "a young man of wit, learning, and

I beg you would make apologies to Mr Richard henry Lee for my not answering to him, and Communicate this schort letter to that gentleman or other members of Congress who may have any influence in sending intelligences to our Admiral.

with the highest Regard and most sincere affection I have the honor to be / dear Sir / Yours

the m$^{\overline{is}}$ de Lafayette

SOURCE: RC, HL Papers, ScHi; addressed on cover "private / to / The honorable henry laurens Esq. / President of Congress / At / Philadelphia"; dated "Camp Near Paramus 14th july 1778"; docketed by HL "Marquis delafayette / 14 July 1778. / Ans^d 18th".

TO JOHN LEWIS GERVAIS

Philadelphia, July 15, 1778

Dear Sir

I confirm and beg leave to refer to the preceding duplicate of a Letter which I had the honor of writing to you the 23^d June by way of Maryland.__

I could now if circumstances permitted fill two or three pages with important Intelligence and nothing would give me more pleasure than devoting an hour or two to your service or amusement, but I am limited__ I was not allowed to write a single line to any body by M$^{r.}$ Archibald Brown[1] who left me the 9th Instant, and I believe waited on the road a day in expectation of Letters from me. At present I must be brief and refer you for particulars where you can find them in papers which will be wrapped up with this, and to our friend M$^{r.}$ Lowndes, to whom I shall send other papers and write a little more copiously, you will learn also almost every thing from

the greatest patriotism. You will greatly please the general and Congress by receiving him with distinction and *that will have many good effects.*" *Lafayette Papers* (Idzerda), II (translation and annotation), 106–107, (French) 402–404.

[1] The *S.C. General Gazette* of Aug. 13, 1778, mentioned an Archibald Brown of S.C. who had recently "returned from Europe, by way of the Northern States."

the Chief Justices communications, he devotes all his leisure minutes to collecting and transmitting news, and I help him upon all
occasions with materials__ he is a perfect Miser in gathering but very
liberal in diffusing and by his means Carolina will be fully informed,
the great end will therefore be answered and I must avail myself of
the advantage of so good a Colleague__ if I have any objection to his
conduct 'tis that he will not frame public Letters to be subscribed by
all the Delegates which ought to be done, but here he is a Miser
again, why should I write, says he, for A.B.C.__[2] from one and
another you must therefore expect to collect all that is fit and
necessary to offer.__

You will have such free access to the Papers in the hands of
His Excellency as will save you the trouble of reading here, what
passes away like a shadow, news only begets appetite for more and
never satisfies. When you are told that Monsr· or Le S^r· Gerard is
arrived, you will be anxious to learn the reception he has met, and
the important concerns he is charged with.__ That Monsr· le Count
d'Estaing had passed Barnagat and had anchored off Sandy Hook,
there will be a chasm, and a painful one too on your mind until you
hear whether he has Burgoyned the British Fleet and Army at New
York or caught a Tartar.

Informing you that I have transmitted orders to General
Washington to co-operate with the French Vice Admiral, to dispose
of the Army under General Gates at North River, and to call in the
aid of the Militia from the six northern and eastern States__ the
wonder will be, whether General Pigot surrendered his Garrison at
Rhode Island, or made his escape, or maintained his ground? when
I tell you that hitherto Congress have only talked of a Table[3] but
seem to evade all Measures for covering one, either with an House
or Viands, that I am forced every day to entertain Delegates,
Strangers and sometimes Minister plenipo: you will naturally ask,
will Mount Tacitus Mepken &c. support the expence? I can assure
you their produce must be uncommonly ample if they answer in the
affirmative__ if my diurnal Account amounted at York Town to near

[2] HL had previously complained about colleague William Henry Drayton's refusal to
share the credit for the compilations Drayton sent to South Carolina. *HL Papers,* XIII, 550.
[3] Congress, in mid May, took up the issue of providing an allowance to the president but
did not act until Dec. 16, 1778. *HL Papers,* XIII, 321; *JCC,* XII, 1213–1214.

fifty Dollars, what will be the sum in Philadelphia, I hope not much more, be that as it may, I must bear it until the Celebration of All Saints__ the first time I ever wished for the arrival of a Saints day since I left school; then by the Grace of God I mean to break up.__ [4]

You will see that your friend Col⁰· Laurens has again been in the way of danger and honor, besides having his horse fall under him by a deadly shot ↑he↓ has received a slight contusion from a spent ball which he has not mentioned. I learnt it from Colonel Boudinot.[5]

When General Lee's tryal is ended, you shall be informed of certain particulars which had excited my jealousy of my old friend antecedent to the march from Valley Forge__ he has written two Pieces and caused them to be published in the Jersey Gazette relative to the Battle of Monmouth, I have not read them, but have been informed they contain no proofs of his discretion.__ [6]

I intend to draw on M⁻· Nutt for eight hundred and ten Pounds Sterling, which will produce me here at least ten thousand two hundred and sixty dollars, perhaps five hundred and forty more I am offer'd 475 Currency for 1 Sterling, and am taught to expect five for one.__ You will take this under consideration in lodging the attachment if he pays my Bill the expence of the attachment will of course be mine, & contra, the precaution will be found to have been necessary.[7]

---

[4] HL, partly with the one-year term limitation prescribed by the Articles of Confederation in mind, had at this time decided to continue as president until Nov. 1, 1778, but would later defer his resignation. The French Minister reported that HL was "determined" to resign at the end of his year in office because he believed so strongly in the "principle of indefinite rotation." Baisnée and Meng, "French Diplomacy," LVII (1946),182.

[5] Reports of John Laurens's bravery, perhaps foolhardiness, at Monmouth had been conveyed to Elias Boudinot by James McHenry and Alexander Hamilton. *HL Papers*, XIII, 536n.

[6] Charles Lee wrote two letters dated July 3 that appeared in the *New-Jersey Gazette* July 8, 1778. The first complained that the account of the battle of Monmouth which appeared in the July 1 *New-Jersey Gazette* was "a most invidious, dishonest, and false relation." Lee promised that "Before long they 'shall have a minute, just, and faithful account.'" The second letter, printed immediately below, Lee described "as a postscript to the note I have already addressed to you." He requested that his letters also be published in the Philadelphia press and offered a brief laudatory account of the actions of officers and men at Monmouth.

[7] Laurens's problems in collecting his funds from the London merchant John Nutt are reviewed in *HL Papers*, XIII, 128. The 12 to 1 ratio which HL used in converting Nutt's debt was apparently the ratio of paper dollars to sterling at this time. In his report to Vergennes on Sept. 10, 1778, Gerard gives a good overview of exchange rates as well as an assessment of America's national debt. Baisnée and Meng, "French Diplomacy," LVIII (1947), 221–225.

18th. My Letter has been kept open, and the Messenger detained in hopes of procuring one Morning or Evening for filling a page or two of news to you, but all such expectations are vain, I must therefore, again refer you, my Friend, to his Excellency as first Magistrate without attention to my respect for the Man, he is justly entitled to the first fruits of intelligence_ you will there learn all I could say in a dozen sheets.

Your friend Colonel Laurens is detached upon a very honorable Embassy by his General to Count d'Estaing, his knowledge of the French tongue in some measure qualifies him for the errand, and I trust he will not be found deficient in other necessary qualifications, making reasonable considerations for his Youth, when I learn particulars from him, you shall be informed._ 'Tis highly probable, Count d'Estaings' squadron will capture many English Vessels while lying at Sandy Hook, but I have doubts concerning their getting within; the large Men of War draw 25 to 27 feet water_ if they fail at that place, I think Rhode Island must be their next object, there they must succeed._

My best Compliments, Love and Respects to Mrs. Gervais Mr. and Mrs. Manigault &c. &c. &c._ My Dear friend,

Adieu

SOURCE: LB, HL Papers, ScHi; addressed "Colo. John L. Gervais / Charles town / Sent by Barry to the sign of the Black Horse / and there to be delivered Sharp."; dated "15th July".

TO RAWLINS LOWNDES

Philadelphia, July 15, 1778

Dear Sir

I had the Honor of addressing Your Excellency the 27th Ulto. through the hands of Governor Henry vîa Williamsburg. On that day I left York Town and arrived here the 30th_ from various impediments I could not collect a sufficient number of States to form a Congress earlier than the 7th Instant; one was the offensiveness of the air in and around the State House, which the Enemy had made an Hospital and left it in a condition disgraceful to the

Character of civility. Particularly they had opened a large square pit near the House, a receptacle for filth, into which they had also cast dead horses and the bodies of Men who by the mercy of death had escaped from their further cruelties. I cannot proceed to a new subject before I add a curse on their savage practices.[1]

Congress in consequence of this disappointment have been shuffling from Meeting House to College Hall[2] the last seven days & have not performed half the business which might and ought to have been done, in a more commodious situation.

The several Papers which Your Excellency will receive within the present cover, N[o.] 1 to N[o.] 15 will contain much Intelligence of our Public Affairs,[3] and more minutely than my time will allow me to repeat in a Letter, wherefore Sir, I beg leave to refer to these and request you will communicate to ↑M[r.]↓ Wells all that Your Excellency shall judge proper for publication, he is very good in sending me his Gazettes and other Intelligence and my duties will not always permit me to make exact and direct returns.

On sunday last the Committee appointed for the purpose received Mons[r.] Gerard at Chester,[4] and under a respectible Cavalcade conducted him to temporary Apartments at General Arnold's, where the Committee, a few other Members of Congress including myself dined with him, on Monday he dined with me, walk'd an hour in the Evening and yesterday Morning Mons[r.] Gerard breakfasted with me and explained his Mission for the information of Congress. He intimated to me his powers for appearing in the Character of Minister Plenipotentiary, or, more simply a Resident;

---

[1] Josiah Bartlett, in a letter to John Langdon on July 13, also noted that "the State House was left by the enemy in a most filthy and sordid situation." *Delegate Letters* (Smith), X, 268.

[2] College Hall, built in 1740 as a tabernacle for George Whitefield and located on Fourth Street between Market and Arch, was deeded in 1750 to the trustees of the Philadelphia Academy and later became the nucleus of the University of Pennsylvania. William L. Turner, "The Charity School, The Academy, and The College," *Transactions of the American Philosophical Society*, n.s., XLIII (1953), 179–186.

[3] The *S.C. General Gazette*, Aug. 13, 1778, printed a variety of items "received last night by an express" from Philadelphia which included the Carlisle Commission's letter of July 11 to Congress; the July 18 Congressional resolution not to respond to the Commission; an estimate of British losses at the Battle of Monmouth Courthouse; as well as information on the British and French fleets and strength of the Spanish navy. These were probably the enclosures to which HL refers here.

[4] The reception committee included former president John Hancock, Richard Henry Lee, William Henry Drayton, Daniel Roberdeau, and William Duer. *JCC*, XI, 685.

"that which he should assume awaited the determination of Congress respecting the public Character of their Minister or Ministers at the Court of Versailles, who without full powers would in many instances find themselves incapable of accomplishing essential services to these States."__[5]

He marked the distinction of Ambassador, a character in which he did not appear, and put into my hands Copy of the Kings' sign Manual appointing him Minister Plenipo: another by which he is appointed Consul General in the several United States with powers to depute and several other Papers, Copies of some of these Your Excellency will find among the numbers abovementioned__ N[o.] [*blank*] respecting Prizes which may be made by American Vessels of War is another mark of the good will of our illustrious Ally and ought to be published immediately.[6] These Papers I laid before Congress and reported all the necessary articles of ~~communication~~ conversation with Mons[r.] Gerard, a Committee of three are appointed for considering & reporting upon the subject and upon a proper mode for receiving Mons[r.] Gerard in form.[7]

The Court of France ~~coul~~ probably could not have discovered a Man in Europe so equal to the task assigned the Minister Plēnipo: as is Mons[r.] Gerard__ a Man of Politeness, Good Breeding and affability without troublesome ceremony. Of good sense and quick perceptions without shew or ostentation, and well read in the History of Man__ very seldom, Sir, do I suffer myself to pronounce an opinion of any Man upon so short and slight an acquaintance; even the present Case, although I have seen many marks which

---

[5] Congress accepted Gérard's commission as minister plenipotentiary on July 14, but took no action on Gérard's suggestion to HL that Congress expand the powers of their own commissioners in Paris. *JCC*, XI, 688. The "notorious" dissentions among the commissioners which HL mentions below may account for the lack of action at this time.

[6] The *S.C. General Gazette*, Aug. 13, 1778, published d'Estaing's offer to cooperate with American privateers. The text is almost identical to the translation of Gérard's letter to HL, July 14, 1778, which is printed above.

[7] The committee on Gérard's reception appointed July 14 included Richard Henry Lee, Samuel Adams, and Gouverneur Morris. Their report recommended the protocol for three classes of diplomats: ambassadors, ministers plenipotentiary or envoys, and residents. Discussed at length on July 16 and 17, and again on July 20, the procedures for receiving Gérard were adopted but the issue of ambassadors and residents was postponed. *JCC*, XI, 688, 696–697, 698–701, 707–708. However, Gérard was not formally received until almost two weeks later on August 6. *JCC*, XI, 753–757.

induce me to believe well of this Gentlemans' candour and integrity of Heart. I proceed in my judgment not a step beyond visibility, and keep as I hold we ought all to keep upon every Stranger in high Character, ~~all the necessary Guards,~~ all the necessary Guards awake. One article of Conversation with the Sier Gerard I ought not to omit, I think it important, and that it will please Your Excellency.__ With a view of learning what reception at home those French Gentlemen had met, who had returned some eight or nine Months ago murmuring and dissatisfied; I took occasion to intimate some concern at the disappointment which many of them had suffered, and in honor of Congress added brief Accounts of what had been granted to numbers of French Officers now in our Army, that it had been impossible to gratify the wishes of every one for grade, that in general such as had been Commissioned by Congress had performed good service, and done honor to their Nation, that some of these Gentlemen from their bravery and propriety of conduct were held in the highest esteem &c. &c. M[r.] Gerard replied, the Court had seen with pain so many French men applying for permission to resort to the American Army, very few of whom had received encouragement, the Court were sensible that crouds of Foreigners applying for Commissions would tend to embarrass Congress__ that since his arrival in Philadelphia there had been many applications made to him for recommendations, every one of which he had refused to listen to, and that I might rest satisfied Congress would never be troubled with Petitions under his auspices.__

M[r.] Silas Deane is returned to Congress in pursuance of an Order in the last Winter, the dissentions among our croud of Commissioners at Paris are become notorious and I was going to add scandalous, particulars have been imparted to me in several Letters, but I have hitherto sealed my lips, and I hope Congress will, by a judicious ~~choice~~ seperation, supercede the Call for investigation and avert the impending evil of keeping jarring minds in one employ.

M[r.] Deane has delivered me an handsome testimonial in his favor from Mons[r.] Vergennes one of the Ministers at the Court of Versailles, signed by the Kings order, and accompanied with his Majestys' Picture ↑in a Gold Box↓ ,[8] superbly surrounded by two

---

[8] Interlineation by HL.

rows of Diamonds__ Le Sier Gerard speaks of and entertains him with distinguishing respect__ Doctor Franklin has also written to me, expressing an high sense of M^r. Deanes' merits__ those who differ in opinion with the Doctor, say all these recommendations are mere etiquette and partiality.__ ⁹ I shall form no conclusion until I learn much more than has hitherto come to my knowledge. I believe they are all good Men, but I know there are in some of them vile tempers, which alloy their general goodness.

Inclosed herein your Excellency will find a Bill dated 4th June 1778 by the Marquis de la Fayette on Messrs. John Crips and Comp. for seven thousand dollars, and a Promisary note by Archibald Browne, Esqr. 7th July for £1726.5.__ Carolina Currency sums which I supplied those Gentlemen respectively as a good means of removing so much out of the public treasury here into our own, and shall with the concurrence of my Colleagues remit all that remains after ascertaining a sum necessary to be reserved for the use of the Delegates, unless Your Excellency and the Privy Council shall otherwise direct.

I had relied on my Colleague the Chief Justice for the frame of a general Address from the Delegates from our State to Your Excellency, accounting for our proceedings respecting Confederation, but am disappointed, I believe he has written fully on the subject in his private Letters to Your Excellency to his Advices therefore I beg leave at present to refer, but I shall urge the propriety and necessity for laying before the Legislature from whom we derived our authority a proper report of our conduct.

I foresee I shall be obliged to detain this Messenger a day or two, in which time articles of Intelligence will accumulate, whatever happens worthy Your Excellencys notice shall be transmitted in the Packet which shall be kept open to the last moment. I have taken the liberty to refer the late President and M^r. Gervais as well as M^r. Wells to Your Excellency for news, in my present circumstances 'tis barely possible for me to keep pace with my public duties, my own private concerns receive not the smallest attention from me.

---

⁹ The French Ministry apparently interpreted Deane's recall as a victory for an anti-alliance faction in Congress. The portrait and the testimonial were intended to show their displeasure with Congress. Coy Hilton James, *Silas Deane: Patriot or Traitor?* (Ann Arbor, Mich., 1975), p. 58.

Your Excellency's favors of the 28th May and 17th June lie before me, and I had intended to pay the respect due to them by this Messenger, but 'tis now impossible. I therefore intreat your indulgence Sir, until the next__ and that you will be assured ~~Sir~~ I Am with very great Esteem and Respect

Sir / Your Excellency's &c.

SOURCE: LB, HL Papers, ScHi; addressed "President Lowndes / South Carolina / By Barry to the Black Horse Tavern / there to be deliver'd Sharp"; dated "15th July". Copy (19th century), HL Papers, ScHi.

FROM THÉVENEAU DE FRANCY

Williamsburg, Va., July 15, 1778

Honorable Sir.

give me leave to Congratulate you upon the happy & glorious news which have Succeeded one another So rapidly Since I left york town. it is a Circumstance Very remarkable, & which must give to Such patriot as you are, the greatest pleasure to See that all the Events which were to fix & ascertain for ever the independence & freedom of America, have taken place under your presidency. what Satisfactory reward for all your generous & infatiguable Exertions in the defense of this noble Cause: how Sweet & agreable Shall be the rest which you will take now! what delicious prospect it must be for you to imagine that all the future generations Will celebrate & bless your name as long as America shall be Wise enough to Enjoy its liberty.

I have been very much pleased by the news of a french fleet arrived at new york; it is a proof that our government wishes most Earnestly to keep up the alliance, I have not the least doubt but Congress is in the Same disposition, however we Cannot but See that the most part of the nation is So Strongly prejudiced against us that every well-wisher may fear the Consequences, a good administration will I hope prevent any bad effect.

I Should hear with a very great pleasure that Some of the officers of a french fleet Specially the Vice-admiral M[r.] Le Comte d'estaing who is the particular friend of Mr de Beaumarchais was at philadelphia: it Should be then very easy to know what Sort of man he is, what influence he had in the Sending of all the munitions, goods &ca. for which I came here to ask the payment in his name. the H^ble· the Commercial Committee Should learn then, that he did deserved to have his letter answered, ~~illegible~~ they Would not have Certainly treated him as he has been & as he is even now when a Contract has been Signed between the Committee & me by which he is acknowledged to be the creditor of the 13 united States.[1] I have the honour to Send you inclosed a copy of the letter which I write to-day to the Committee on that report, it will inform you what reasons I have to Complain, & if you think it proper, I Should be glad ↑to have↓ that letter read in Congress,[2] because it is not probable that that debt having been acknowledged by ↑the↓ majority of the representative body of the nation, the Commercial Committee Should be directed to Send the Vessel of the public to different merchants in france & not a Single one to M^r· de Beaumarchais. I remember with a very great pleasure that from the first time I Spoke to your excellency you was Convinced of M^r· de Beaumarchais's right in claiming the munitions & goods Sent by the house of Roderigue Hortalez & Cie·;[3] but it has not been a So Easy matter to Convince Every gentleman of Congress: however I was in hope, after the Contract has been Signed, that in expecting the general invoice & the necessary papers to Eclairise all what Could have remained obscure, the honorable the congress Would order that Some remittance Should be made ↑in beginning of payment,↓ as

---

[1] The contract between Congress and Jean Baptiste Théveneau de Francy as the agent for Caron de Beaumarchais and Beaumarchais's firm, Roderigue Hortalez & Co., was agreed to on April 7, 1778. Under its terms, the United States was to remit payments to the firm through consignments of American produce to pay for both previous and future shipments of supplies and munitions. *JCC*, X, 315–319.

[2] This copy of De Francy's July 15, 1778, letter to the Committee of Commerce is in the HL Papers, ScHi. The letter was read in Congress July 25 and referred to the Committee of Commerce. The committee reported August 1 and a letter signed by chairman Francis Lewis, based on that report, was addressed to De Francy. *JCC*, XI, 716, 738–740; Francis Lewis to De Francy, Aug. 3, 1778, HL Papers, ScHi.

[3] Although De Francy considered HL sympathetic to Beaumarchais's claims for payment of the goods shipped by Roderigue Hortalez & Co., HL had written to James Duane on April 7, the day of the contract signing, "If you delight in contracting an enormous debt to a Crafty powerful foreign State, your absence from this Mornings service [*session*] has lost you much pleasure__". *HL Papers*, XIII, 83.

there is nothing in contest but the munitions that was repeatedly promised to me by the whole Winter last: therefore I have the honour of demanding to the Committee of Commerce or to the Honorable the Congress in the name of M^r· de Beaumarchais Some remittances, or a refusal of paying the debt owed to him. as I intend to be very particular with him when I Shall write by his large Vessel, I beg to have a[4] positive answer to that question. at the Same time I must observe to your Excellency that I Should wish most Sincerely for the honour of this Country that M^r· de Beaumarchais had no reasons of complaint. M^r· Carmichael & M^r· Deane if he is arrived, Will Say what he has done & what he is capable to do, & as his Exertions have been known almost to Every body, in france, it Shall appear Very Strange if he has any occasion to repent of what he has done.

as the cargo of his Vessel <u>Le fier Roderigue</u> was all Sold when I arrived here, it has not been in my power to get the article which you did asked me, even there was no linnen fit for making Shirts for you, there was no Cambrick at all nor Super fine Cloth. I could get those article here in town, but as they are at an Extravagant price & as it is possible you may have them cheaper in philadelphia, I Shall wait ↑for↓ your Commands before I procure any. the Burgundy Wine which Was[5] on board, has lost its colour in the passage, it was of a Very good quality, but I Should not like to recommend it as it is now, it is Said that the quality is not much altered. there ~~sh~~ is Some pretty good claret, you will be So kind as to let me Know if you want any. I have besides a Single case of malaga which you will Command.

I had promised to M^r· jame cutter[6] to get Some linnen for him, I don't find any at the price which he has fixed, I beg you will let me know if I am to buy Some at the best rate ↑to which↓ I can get it.

I have the honour to Send you inclosed Some letters for the camp & one for Captn· Landais,[7] I beg you will be pleased to forward them; as I Expect you will have received many for me Since my departure from york, you will be So obliging as to Send them to me

---

[4] "an" altered to "a".
[5] "W" written over other text.
[6] James Custer.
[7] Pierre Landais. *HL Papers*, XIII, 370n.

by my Servant whom I have Sent on purpose to get an immediate answer I intreat your Excellency to have him Sent back to me directly, as I must Wait his return for the fitting on of my vessel which Shall be ready in less than 20 days from this date.

I am with Every Sentiment of respect & the most Sincere Esteem / Honorable Sir / your most obed^t. / & Very humble Servant

De francy

P.S. will you be pleased to make my respectfull compliments to M^r. Drayton.

SOURCE: RC, HL Papers, ScHi; addressed above salutation "His Excellency Henry Laurens Esqr. / president of Congress."; dated "Williamsburgh 15th July 1778."; docketed by HL "Laz. de Francy / 15 July 1778 Rec^d. 24th. / Answered 26th.".

FROM JOHN LEWIS GERVAIS

Charles Town, July 16, 1778

Dear Sir

I write to you the 2^d. & 6th.– Instant to which I beg leave to refer. The Boat with Ruff Rice ↑arrived↓ last Week, but I am Sorry to acquaint you that Tom Peas is also dead__[1] poor Tom Peas, I am Sorry you have lost him, upon the whole he was a good Negro__ The Ruff Rice Sells at 20/. but not readily, it has been a little damaged for want of Care__

I am at a loss for a Patroon, white Men are not to be hired__ In this Situation Mr Loveday advises me to take Scaramouch, I will try him & if he behaves well & I will give him some encouragement;[2]

---

[1] Tom Peas, one of HL's slaves, had been the "patroon" in the rice boat. Gervais had had a "falling out" with Tom but after a reconciliation admitted that he did "tolerably well" overseeing the slave boatmen. *HL Papers*, XIII, 274, 539-540.

[2] Scaramouch had been in charge of one of HL's plantation boats as early as 1766. Viewed at that time as a reliable hand, he came to be regarded as a rebellious troublemaker during HL's sojourn in England and Europe (1771-1774). When HL again prepared to leave Charleston for an extended period in 1777, Scaramouch threatened to run away until HL persuaded him to stay. That Scaramouch should be placed in charge of a coastal vessel used to carry rice cargoes from HL's southern plantations was an obvious risk. *HL Papers*, V, 86; VIII, 355; XI, 386.

Whenever the Ruff Rice is sold I will send the Boat back to Wright Savannah for a Load of Clean Rice, as I find it sells again notwithstanding the embargo at £3.₩ Ct.__ For more particulars I shall refer you to another Letter I intend to write by Mr Galvan,[3] if I am able, for I am writing this on the bed tortured by a Rhumatism, or a Cramp in my left Leg & can hardly put myself in a posture to write__

It is reported to day that the Ennemy have left Philadelphia the 18 June, I wish it may be true. M^rs. Gervais presents her Compliments and I am truly

Dear Sir / Your affectionate & most / Obed^t. Servant

SOURCE: RC, Gervais Papers, in private hands; addressed on cover "Honourable Henry Laurens Esquire / President of Congress / York Town__ / P^r favour of / Mr Carson."; dated "Charles Town 16. July 1778__"; docketed by HL "John L Gervais / 16 July 1778 / Rec̄d 17 Sept^r.".

FROM JACOB READ

Charles Town, July 16, 1778

Honoured Sir

By my Brother Doctor William Read who left Carolina for Head Quarters in the Month of May last I did myself the Honour to address you, and relying on your known Philanthropy and Generosity took the Liberty to Introduce that young Gentleman to your Acquaintance and to request your Countenance and Support for

---

[3] William Galvan (d. 1782), a French adventurer who had come to South Carolina by way of Martinique in September 1776, served as a lieutenant in the 2nd S.C. Regiment. He returned to France to obtain a cargo of arms and ammunition which he delivered to South Carolina in August 1777. He traveled north at this time seeking a Continental commission. He failed to obtain a commission in part because of the impression he made on HL, but went on to serve as an aide-de-camp to General De Kalb and was a "volunteer in Gen. Gates's family" in December 1779 when he again appealed to Congress for a commission. In January 1780 he became a major in the Continental Army and served as an inspector until March 1782. *HL Papers*, XI, 460-461; John Lewis Gervais to HL, July 6, 1778, Gervais Papers, in private hands; Jacob Read to HL, July 16, 1778; HL to John Laurens, Aug. 29, 1778; William Galvan to Congress, Dec. 28, 1778, PCC, Item 78, Vol. 10, p. 191ff; *Delegate letters* (Smith), XIV, 307; Francis Galvan Bernoux Petition, March 15, 1784, PCC, Item 42, Vol. 3, p. 264ff.

him,__[1] I was sorry to hear from him that his Servant had very Carelessly mislaid my Letter; he was not without hopes of finding it among his Baggage least he shou'd not have been so lucky   I now take the Liberty of once more addressing you in his Behalf, If in any Case I cou'd altogether Pardon myself for this Intrusion it wou'd be in this Wherein I am serving my Brother and nearest friend, on the foot of my brotherly affection to him I must ground my Defence to the Charge which I am obliged to bring against myself of making too free not doubting that if Indeed I am found Guilty you will generously pardon me

Bred to Physick and Chirurgery in the Colledge of Philadelphia and in Savannah my Brother was to have finished his Education & professional Studies in Scotland London and Paris but unluckily poor fellow he[2] has not been able to do so, from the Convulsions of the times and the want of friends who cou'd advance him money in Europe, his Genius however Soars above the Grovelling Station of a Country Doctor nor can he Submit to attend Negro Houses and feel pulses of the sooty Sons of Afric, ~~and~~ his Diffidence and want of Experience or that which Viginti Annorum Lucubrationes[3] wou'd warrant (according to Custom) the[4] assuming a formal Consequence prevents his settling in a Town where he woud have to struggle with Difficulties Incident to Every beginner, he therefore at the earnest Intreaty of his friend Doctor Rush makes a Tour to the Hospital to Improve his Hand in Surgery and as every Camp or Hospital in a Country in Actual War must afford a variety of Cases in Physick he flatters himself with an Idea of great advantage from an attendance of a few months,   Those under whom he studied have been ever Lavish in his praise. I hope he will Continue to deserve every Encomium that application sobriety and a Polite Conduct will warrant

I request of you Sir to shew him that Countenance he may deserve   also to Assist him if at any time the high price of goods or other Casualties shoud make it necessary for him to ask your Assistance in the Pecuniary Line, I pledge myself that his Draft[s] on

---

[1] Jacob Read to HL, April 5, 1778, *HL Papers,* XIII, 78-79.
[2] "he" written in left margin.
[3] Working by lamplight for twenty years.
[4] "this" altered to "the".

me at any Sight you may Choose shall be Honoured or the Sum replaced on the Earliest Notice in any place in America that you may Desire, He is Intitled to a Considerable property as a Dividend of my Fathers Estate (whose death you may probably have heard of)[5] and I am ready to advance every Shilling I may earn in my profession toward the Advancement of my Brothers and Sisters[6]   their Welfare Seems to Engross at present more of my attention than any lucrative views for myself

The present Letter is forwarded by Mons.[r] Galvan late an Officer in the Second Regiment who comes to Head Quarters in quest of Employment and promotion   He is the Gentleman who first arrived here from Martinico and Who rendered this state such Essential Services in france, but on seeing him you will readily recollect these facts

Of the State of this Country he will be able to give you very Satisfactory Accounts   the progress of the Southern Expedition and Departure of the Tories Engage us at present   tho' we anxiously wish to hear from your Quarter   that the Intelligence may be agreeable I most heartily wish

Were I a Planter I might attempt to give you my Ideas of the Prospects of Crops but as I know not how to Cultivate any other than the Sterile Plant Law I shall be Excused on that Subject, from the Excessive fall of rains for a Month past however I fear the Indico Planters must suffer greatly

I pray a tender of my best Compliments to my gallant Friend Colonel John Laurens   I most heartily Congratulate you and him on the Laurels he has won

I am Sir with the most perfect Esteem / Your much obliged / most Obedient Servant

Jacob Read

SOURCE: RC, Gratz Collection, PHi; addressed below close "His Excellency / Henry Laurens Esq.[r] / president of Congress"; dated "Charles Town 16[th:] July 1778__". Copy (19th century), HL Papers, ScHi.

---

[5] James Read, a merchant of Charleston and Savannah, became a member of the Georgia Royal Council in 1756. He died in March 1778. HL occasionally did business with Read in the 1750s and 1760s. *HL Papers*, III, 136n; *SCHM*, XXV (1924), 9.

[6] In addition to his brother William, Jacob Read had two younger brothers, George and James, and two younger sisters, Elizabeth and Susannah. *SCHM*, XXV (1924), 9-10.

FROM WILLIAM LIVINGSTON

Morristown, N.J., July 17, 1778

Sir

Heartily congratulating you upon the arrival of the French Fleet, & Monsieur Gerard; I have the pleasure to acquaint you that on my receipt of the Committees Letter of the 14th instant,[1] I immediately set off, tho' greatly indisposed, to engage Capt Dennis[2] a hearty & trusty whig, & acquainted with all the best Pilots in these parts, to secure a competent Number for the purpose__ He set off upon the Business before I left his house, so that I doubt not in less than 24 hours after, the fleet was supplied with the Complement. Least however more may be wanted than may be procured by him, I have sent a List to General Washington of all those at Peeks Kill, and about King's Ferry.[3]

I am honoured with your Favour of the 12 instant inclosing an Act of Congress of the 11th. recommending it to certain of the States to exert themselves in forwarding the force which may be required from them for enabling General Washington to carry on his operations in concert with Count d'Estaing which I will make it by Business to ↑have↓ enforced as far as the Circumstances of this harrassed state will admit of

I am also to acknowledge the receipt of your Favour of the 10th. which, agreable to the request of Congress, I am to lay before the Legislature of this state (unfortunately not to meet till the second Wednesday in September) "in order that if they judge it proper, their Delegates may be instructed to ratify the Confederation with all convenient dispatch, trusting to future Deliberations to make such Alterations and Amendments as Experience may show to be expedient & just"__ Congress may depend upon my laying the Letter before the Legislature as soon as ever they shall make a house, & on my using my utmost Endeavours to expedite the ratification of the Confederacy, for which I long been exceedingly

---

[1] A committee consisting of William Duer, Jonathan Bayard Smith, and Elias Boudinot had been ordered to "take the speediest measures for furnishing Count d'Estaing with a sufficient number of skilful pilots." *JCC*, XI, 683.

[2] Patrick Dennis, a pilot. *Livingston Papers* (Prince), II, 391.

[3] Livingston listed William Dobbs, Dennis McQuire, and Isaac Symondson at Peekskill and William Sloan at Kings Ferry. William Livingston to George Washington, July 16, 1778. *Livingston Papers* (Prince), II, 392.

anxious; but I sincerely hope that this state will never ratify it, till Congress is explicit in doing us that Justice respecting the common Lands, which I think no man of common Sense, or the least acquainted with human Nature would trust to the <u>future Deliberations</u> of any Body of Men (I speak it with the highest respect for that Assembly which I verily believe to be the most illustrious upon earth) a considerable part of which must necessarily be gainers by a contrary determination.[4] I have the honor to be with the greatest Regard

Sir / your most humble & / most obedient Servt

Wil: Livingston

SOURCE: RC, PCC (Item 68), DNA; addressed on cover "To / The honourable Henry Laurens Esqr / President of Congress / In / Philadelphia__"; addressed below close "The honorable / Henry Laurens Esqr / President of Congress"; dated "Morris Town 17 July 1778"; docketed "Letter from Govr Livingston / Morristown July 17__ 1778 / read 18.".

TO JOHN HOUSTOUN

Philadelphia, July 18, 1778

Dear Sir

I had the honor of addressing you under the 10th and the same date in public Letters which this will accompany.[1] The subjects contained in those are now obsolete, nevertheless I do not think it proper to suppress them__ Georgia has at present only one Delegate in Congress who alone cannot on her part ratify a confederation. I am very unhappy from having received no further commands from Congress respecting poor little Georgia; in hopes of such I had detained the Bearer three days, but the arrival of a French squadron and a Minister Plinipotentiary has accumulated the labours of

---

[4] New Jersey and other states like Maryland and Delaware that did not have additional land claims questioned Article Nine of the Confederation which stated in part that "no State shall be deprived of territory for the benefit of the United States." The New Jersey legislature offered an amendment to the article but ratified unconditionally Nov. 26, 1778. *Articles of Confederation*, pp. 196-197, 267.

[1] The two public letters of July 10 included the circular requesting action on the Articles of Confederation and another, also sent to Rawlins Lowndes, concerning information about the English squadron that HL wished to have conveyed to d'Estaing. PCC, Item 13.

Congress insomuch that many necessary considerations for the benefit of particular States unavoidably lie dormant__ the first hour of leisure I will give M^r· Telfair all the aid in my power to bring his state on the tapis.[2]

Count d'Estaing is exceedingly chagrined at the impracticability of attacking the English ships of War, who lie in his sight within Sandy Hook__ his large ships draw too much water for the Bar and keep him without, where prizes are daily dropping into his net, and not a few very valuable. I presume he has already lessened the number of British Seamen 500__ if he proceeds to Rhode Island he will probably recover that place, capture the Garrison said to be upwards of 3,000, make prizes of some ships, and secure a good Harbour

I shall have the honor of writing to you again in[3] a few days, at present must content myself with subscribing, D^r· Sir

With great Regard and Esteem / Your Obedient Humble Servt·

P.S.
I send you a few News papers

SOURCE: LB, HL Papers, ScHi; addressed "Governor Houston / Georgia / by Barry to the Black Horse / there to be deliver'd Sharp"; dated "18th July". Copy (19th century), HL Papers, ScHi.

TO THE MARQUIS DE LAFAYETTE

Philadelphia, July 18, 1778

Sir

I have with pleasure executed an Order of Congress by signing and delivering a Brevet to the Marquis de Vienne to rank Colonel in the Army of the United States of America__ [1] My pleasure

---

[2] On July 23, John Walton joined Edward Telfair as Georgia's representatives in Congress and on July 24 they signed the ratification for their state. *JCC*, XI, 712, 714.

[3] "i" written over "o".

[1] Louis-Pierre, marquis de Vienne, arrived in America in May aboard the *Deane*. Lafayette recommended him as "the son of a much reputed general officer" and an officer with 24 years experience "in the service." Congress acted quickly and commissioned him a brevet colonel July 15. Lafayette to HL, June 23, 1778, HL Papers, ScHi; *JCC*, XI, 692-694.

as an individual would not have been less if my name had been
ordered to a full Commission, such an one I make no doubt will be
readily granted if the Marquis de Vienne shall think it more valuable
than the present, when he shall be returning to his Native Clime.
Your Excellency cannot conceive the embarrasment which ~~grant-~~
~~ing~~ is often occasioned to Congress by granting Commissions to
foreign Gentlemen to the prejudice of rank to many of our own
↑home↓ [2] born Officers, who have served the public with honor
from the very commencement of the War

The Board of War have not yet reported on the application
in favor of Mons[r.] Touzard, possibly there may be policy and good
will towards that Gentleman concealed in the delay__ [3] requests do
not so well succeed, when crouded together; be this as it may for I
know not how it be, when Gentlemen recommend an A. or B. a
Foreign[4] Gentleman of great merit to receive a Commission far
above any which he had formerly enjoyed it is natural, and Your
Excellency's Candour will admit that it is[5] also just, for other
Gentlemen to produce in contrast the merits of American Officers
in the Army who are, and must be content to wait for grade until they
shall be entitled to advancement in due course.

When it is urged that French Gentlemen have come a long
Voyage and at great expence to serve the United States, the reply
without observing that the Act was voluntary, is, that many of our
American Officers have abandoned[6] their Homes, all their domestic happiness, the education of their Children, the improvement of
their fortunes, &c. &c. and in the course of three years hard duty,
have advanced gradation to the heighth of Captain or Major and
have the mortification of being commanded by Gentlemen who
had held Lieutenancies in their Native Country, and who were
promoted here after one battle to Lieutenant Colonels, Colonels,

---

[2] Interlineation by HL.

[3] Lafayette had recommended that Louis de Tousard be promoted from captain to major.
HL Papers, XIII, 401, 450. Congress referred the matter to the Board of War on June 9, but took
no action until October when Tousard lost his arm in an action against the British. He was
then breveted a lieutenant colonel with a pension of $30 per month for life. *JCC*, XI, 580; XII,
1068.

[4] "or" written over other text.

[5] "was" altered to "is".

[6] "e" written over other text.

and in some instances, As[7] it is said, to higher ranks__ such opposition my dear Marquis, is not to be answered by an ingenuous mind.__ Your Excellency must not think me from these observations less devoted to your service upon every occasion, in which your own impartiality and wise discernment shall be pleased to command.

The Marquis de Vienne is so polite as to afford me the present opportunity of Paying my respects to your Excellency and at the same time of acknowledging the receipt of your Excellency's favor of the 15th Instant__ [8] conscious of being greatly in arrears, I am grieved that I cannot go back to several Letters which your Excellency has lately honored me with, and which require such notice as my present circumstances will not allow me to go into__ surely I shall be Blessed with one day in the course of next week which may be apply'd to a serious review of the Marquis de la Fayette's Letters, I will embrace the first leisure hour for this purpose. I know I am immensely in debt I do not want candour to acknowledge, and I trust Your Excellency will find that I am not deficient in honesty to pay, to the utmost of my abilities__ at present indulge me, Dear Sir, in confining myself to that which lies immediately before me.

I have the satisfaction to assure Your Excellency that from the first moment we were apprized of the arrival of Count d'Estaing's squadron on this coast, Congress have vigorously pursued every measure for facilitating and effectuating the Vice Admirals' operations against the Enemy. We were not unmindful of the great utility of Advice Boats__ but, alass! such are not to be built in so short a time as we can write the name, and you well know, Sir, the Enemy while they had possession of this river stretched an unsparing firebrand over all our navigation which they could reach and could not carry off, consequently they have left us very little, and none of the sorts which you allude to. I have great hopes that Count d'Estaing will find means for supplying himself with necessary Vessels for contingent services upon the Coast and within the Harbour of New York, in the mean time, Congress will in every respect contribute to his success and the mutual honor and benefit of the Alliance.

---

[7] "A" written over other text.
[8] Lafayette's letter to HL was dated July 14, 1778.

But here comes Marquis Vienne and indeed has been waiting half an hour in the Audience Room, there's for you Dear Marquis. I am not quite so squeezed up as at York Town when Miss Katy and Your Humble Servant lay within very narrow bounds and without the smallest breach of decorum__[9] Yes Sir, I have now what M[r.] Burgoyne could not obtain in America, a little Elbow room, how happy should I be to be honored with the Company of the Marquis de la Fayette at the consumption of a great Turtle tomorrow in addition to Mons[r] Girard &c. &c.__ but I flatter myself the time will soon come, when without impeachment of honor or danger to the State Your Excellency may sit quietly under the Roof of

    Your Excellency's much obliged &c.

    And longer under your own__

SOURCE: LB, HL Papers, ScHi; addressed "The Marquis de la Fayette / Head Quarters / by the Marquis de Vienne"; dated "18th July".

FROM JOHN LAURENS

Black Point, N.J., July 18, 1778

Sir

Admiral Count d'Estaing to whom I had the honor of bearing dispatches from His Excellency Gen[l.] Washington__ finding that he cannot detain his prisoners on board the fleet without considerable expence of provision and much inconvenience[1] in other respects__ has taken the resolution to land them, in confidence that Congress will order them to be provided for, at the expence of His most Christian Majesty__

    In pursuance therefore of general directions given me by the Commander in chief to give every possible assistance to the Admiral, I have ordered Lieuten[t.] de Clos[2] with a party of Continental Troops to escort such prisoners as the Admiral may choose to

---

[9] Both Lafayette and HL admired Catherine Alexander, Lord Stirling's daughter, who lodged at Thomas Hartley's York, Pa., home while HL resided there.

[1] "inc" written over other text.

[2] Lt. Francis DuClos of the 2nd N.J. Regiment.

have landed__ from hence to Philadelphia__ and deliver them there into the custody of the Town Major, until farther arrangements shall be made respecting them by Congress or the Minister of France__[3]

The Count d'Estaing desires[4] me to mention to you farther, as he has not prepared his dispatches for Congress__ that there is the most urgent necessity for his being instantly joined by the Frigate la Chimere__

I have the honor to be / with the most profound Respect / Sir / Your most obed Serv[t.]

John Laurens
Aide de Camp.

SOURCE: ALS, PCC (Item 65), DNA; addressed on cover "The honble / Henry Laurens Esq[r.] / President of Congress / Philadelphia"; addressed below close "The honorable Henry Laurens Esq[r] / President / of Congress__"; dated "Black point 18th July 1778."; franked "(On public Service)"; docketed by HL "John Laurens / 18 July 1778 / Rec̄ d 19th-" and in another hand "Read 20.__".

FROM JOHN LAURENS

Black Point, N.J., July 18, 1778

I have barely had time paper and ink to write my dear father a hurried official letter__ upon my arrival here with dispatches from the General to Admiral d'Estaing__ I found that the Fleet laboured under the greatest difficulty in procuring water__ its distance from the shore was too great to roll the Casks down to the place of embarkation__ the disaffected inhabitants either refused their waggons or granted them only at an exhorbitant price__ I have done every thing in my power to remedy this evil__ but as we cannot have too many resources__ I would propose that any fast sailing small craft in the delaware may be immediately employed in

[3] D'Estaing's plans changed and on August 4 JL informed his father, from Providence, R.I., that rather than send the prisoners to Philadelphia, the admiral "disembarrassed himself of his prisoners" in Rhode island. JL to HL, Aug. 4, 1778.
[4] Final "s" written over "d".

bringing water round__ the southerly winds which prevail on the coast at this season will give them a quick voyage__ and they will be in time if they arrive with la Chimere__

It would give me pleasure to speak to you particularly of the great qualities of the Admiral__ he has inspired me in the short acquaintance I have had with him, with uncommon respect__ he laments the insipid[1] part he is playing__ keeping the English fleet blocked up within sandy hook and taking prizes within their view every day, does not satisfy a man of his great ideas__ When six prizes were brought into him yesterday__ he desired the Major of the Fleet to give some directions about those <u>Drugs</u>___ and sighed at not being engaged in a way ↑in↓ which more honor was to be acquired__ two of the prizes that have been taken since my being here are armed one with 14 and the other with 10 Guns__ [2] One had a quantity of specie on board, the profits of prizes taken from us__ The fleet, men and officers appear to be in fine health__ and eager to distinguish themselves in a naval Combat__ as much as it is against my desire, I must break off__ and express rider must be diligent__

My dearest friend and / father I pray God to protect you__

John Laurens__

SOURCE: ALS, Kendall Collection; addressed on cover "(Private) / The honble / Henry Laurens Esqr- / President of Congress / Philadelphia"; dated by HL below close "Black Point / 18 July 1778__"; docketed by HL "John Laurens / 18 July 1778 / Rec^d 19th-".

FROM COMMISSIONERS AT PARIS

Passy, France, July 20, 1778

Sir

We have the honor to inform Congress that the Spy Captain Nyles[1] has arrived at Brest, and brought us a ratification of the

---

[1] HL did not like the way JL had written "insipid" so he interlined it below the line.
[2] Admiral d'Estaing captured several British vessels off Sandy Hook. Included in the number were the armed sloop *York* and a bomb tender, as well as the unlucky brig *Stanley*, Whitworth, that upon returning from a successful cruise, with five prizes, mistakenly anchored at night among the French vessels. *Documents of the American Revolution* (Davies), XV, 167; Tilley, *British Navy*, p. 144.
[1] The schooner *Spy*, Robert Niles.

Treaties with his most Christian Majesty, which has given much satisfaction to this Court and Nation. On the 17[th.] instant we had the honor of exchanging ratifications with his Excellency the Count de Vergennes. The Treaties ratified, signed by his Majesty, and under the great Seal of France, are[2] now in our possession, where perhaps considering the danger of Enemies at Sea, it will be safest to let them remain for the present. Copies of them we shall have the honor to transmit to Congress by this opportunity. War is not yet declared between France and England by either Nation but hostilities at Sea have been already commenced by both; and as the French fleet from Brest under the command of the Count d'Orvilliers, and the British fleet under Admiral Keppel are both at Sea, we are in hourly expectation of a rencounter between them.[3]

The Jamaica fleet, the windward Island fleet, and a small fleet from the Mediterranean have arrived at London, which has enabled them to obtain by means of a violent impress, perhaps a thousand ~~of~~ ↑or↓ fifteen hundred Seamen, which will man two or three Ships more, in the whole making Admiral Keppels fleet some what nearer to an equality with the French. In the mean time the Spanish Flota has arrived, but the Councils of that Court are kept in a secrecy so profound that we presume not to say with confidence what are her real intentions. We continue however to receive from various quarters encouraging assurances, and from the situation of the powers of Europe it seems highly probable that Spain will join France in case of war.

A war in Germany between the Emperor and King of Prussia, seems to be inevitable, and it is affirmed that the latter has marched his army into Bohemia so that we apprehend that America has at present nothing to fear from Germany.

We are doing all in our power to obtain a Loan of Money, and have a prospect of procuring some in Amsterdam, but not in such quantities as will be wanted.[4] We are constrained to request Congress to be as sparing as possible in their drafts upon us. The drafts already made; together with the great expence arising from

---

[2] "are" written over "is".

[3] The naval battle of Ushant between Augustus Keppel and d'Orvilliers was fought July 27, 1778. Tilley, *British Navy*, pp. 129-130.

[4] Loan negotiations between the American Commissioners and Amsterdam bankers during the summer and fall of 1778 proved abortive. *Franklin Papers* (Labaree), XXVI, 338n.

the frigates which have been sent here, together with the expences of the Commissioners, the maintenance of your Ministers for Vienna and Tuscany, and of[5] prisoners who have made their escape, and the amount of Cloaths and munitions of war, already sent to America, we are under great apprehensions ~~your~~ that our funds will not be sufficient to answer the drafts which we daily expect for the interest of Loan-Office Certificates, as well as those from Mr. Bingham.[6] We have the honor to enclose copy of a Letter from Mr. de Sartine, the Minister of Marine, and to request the attention of Congres to the subject of it.[7]

We are told in several Letters from the honorable Committee for foreign affairs, that we shall receive instructions and authority for giving up on our part the whole of the 11th. article of the Treaty, proposing it as a condition to the Court of France, that they on their part should give up the whole of the 12th. But unfortunately these instructions and authority were omitted to be sent with the Letters, and we have not yet received them. At the time of the exchange of ratification[ns] we mentioned this subject to the Count de Vergennes and gave him an extract of the Committee's Letter. His answer to us was that the alteration would be readily agreed to, and he ordered his Secretary not to register the ratification until it was done. We therefore request that we may be honored with the instructions and authority of Congress, to set aside the two articles, as soon as possible and while the subject is fresh in memory.[8]

The Letter to Mr. Dumas is forwarded and in answer to the Committee's enquiry, what is proper for Congress to do for that Gentleman, we beg leave to say that his extreme activity and

---

[5] "of" written in left margin.

[6] On April 16, 1778, Congress empowered William Bingham, the Continental agent at Martinique, to draw on the commissioners to a maximum of 100,000 livres. *JCC*, X, 356.

[7] Gabriel de Sartine, in his July 14 note to the commissioners, requested American assistance in sending supplies to the French islands of St. Pierre and Miquelon. PCC, Item 105, p. 106; *Franklin Papers* (Labaree), XXVII, 87, 128.

[8] Despite ratifying the Treaty of Amity and Commerce unanimously and without reservation on May 4, Congress resolved the following day to instruct the commissioners "to use their best endeavours to procure the abolition of the said 11 and 12 articles of the said treaty." The commissioners received the official instruction August 3 but the formal deletion of the articles did not take place until November. *JCC*, XI, 457, 459-460; *Franklin Papers* (Labaree), XXVII, 330-331.

diligence, in negociating our affairs, and his punctuality in his correspondence with Congress as well as with us, and his usefulness to our cause in several other ways, not at present proper to be explained, give him in our opinion a good title to two hundred pound sterling a year at Least.[9]

The other things mentioned in the Committee's Letter to us shall be attended to as soon as possible. We have received also the resolution of Congress of 9th. February, and the Letter of the Committee of the same date, empowering us to appoint one or more suitable persons ~~to~~ ↑as↓ Commercial Agents for conducting the Commercial business of the United States in France and other parts of Europe. But as this power was given us before Congress received the Treaty, and we have never received it but with the ratification of the Treaty and as by the Treaty Congress is empowered to appoint consuls in the ports of France, perhaps it may be expected from us, that we should wait for the appointments of consuls. At present Mr. John Bonfield[10] of Bourdeaux[11] and Mr. J. D. Schweighauser at Nantes,[12] both by the appointment of Mr. William Lee, are the only persons authorised as Commercial Agents. If we should find it expedient to give appointments to any other persons, before we hear from Congress, we will send information of it by the next opportunity. If Congress should think proper to appoint Consuls, we are humbly of opinion, that the choice will fall most justly as well as ~~natuarl~~ naturally on Americans, who are in our opinion better qualified for this business than any others, and the reputation of such an office, together with a moderate Commission on the business they may tran↑s↓ act, and the advantages to be derived from trade, will be a sufficient inducement to undertake it,

----

[9] Charles W.F. Dumas, who acted as Congress's agent at The Hague, received payment beginning in April 1777 and thereafter until May 1785. The commissioners at Paris had agreed to pay him 100 Louis d'or semiannually and only three days before Dumas had requested the second payment for 1778. *Adams Papers* (Taylor), VI, 73n; *Franklin Papers* (Labaree), XXVII, 117.

[10] "e" written over "l".

[11] John Bondfield, a Canadian merchant, had moved to Bourdeaux by way of Philadelphia. *Franklin Papers* (Labaree), XXIV, 403n.

[12] Jean-Daniel Schweighauser replaced Thomas Morris as the agent at Nantes.

and a sufficient reward for discharging the duties of it.[13]
    We have the honor to be &c.

(signed)   B: Franklin

A. Lee

J. Adams

SOURCE: Copy, PCC (Item 85), DNA; addressed above salutation "To the President of Congress"; dated "Passy 20 July 1778"; noted "Copy from a Vol. of the / Commissioners Letters kept by Mr Lee / Henry Remsen Junr.". Copies, PCC (Items 84, 102, 105), DNA. Extract, PCC (Item 83), DNA. LB, Adams Papers, MHi.

FROM SAMUEL A. OTIS

Boston, July 20, 1778

Sir

    I have not done myself the Honor of addressing you these few last weeks, upon a Supposition that your attention was called to the peculiarly important business of the field & cabinet, but as Genl. Washington is pushing the War at a distance from Congress, & a degree of tranquility is taking place in your quarter, I must ask a moments attention to a matter in w^h I think I have hardly been treated with delicacy__

    About the 20th of May, when the Marine board of this department had filled all their Stores, upon offering to rec^t the 13.000 Su^ts of Cloaths arrived in the Dean Frigate, they delivered them to the Cloth^g Agents, Some indeed were damaged, were opened & dried, & Congress or the C General, being informed what was done, I waited further Orders__ In the mean time a pressing order came for 10.000 Shirts & overals, which the materials for which could not be got in time any other way, or if they could it would have been a miserable waste of public money to purchase them when much lay unappropriated, tho ready paid for accordingly application was made to the Marine Board, & they delivered part of the

---

[13] Despite the fact that Article 29 of the Franco-American Treaty of Amity and Commerce provided for the appointment of consuls and other agents and that France appointed consuls for Philadelphia, Baltimore and Charleston by the end of 1778, Congress did not act until November 1780 when it appointed William Palfrey consul in France. *Adams Papers* (Taylor), VIII, 390n.

articles requested, every ell & yard being regularly apprized & receipted, & your agents holding themselves accountable for the same___ A like pressing order came in fav^r of Count Polaskis Legion, there was neither blue Cloth or money to purchase any, & applying to the marine Board they delivered sufficient Cloth for this Corps, like Rec^{ts} being given, & these with some blankets from Bilboa sent on are all the articles I recollect receiveing; But Sir was it for a too forward assiduity, or what other Cause, that the Board of War have been pleased to appoint another Agent, and ordered that agent, in case of refusal, to appoint a Substitute, or refer the matter to the Council of this State?

The agent appointed declined, alledging friendship &^{c}, as a reason, In consequence hereof, the Council who are men of like passions, chose a Committee upon the matter, the Chairman of which, Thos Cushing Esqr dictated the proper Agent, none seemed so proper to him as a near kinsman of ruined fortune, and thus the public are set upon enquiry for what crime neglect or incompetence, the former agents are laid aside___[1] We dont dispute the right of Congress to dismiss their Servants, but it is seldom done without reason, unless thro the machinations of malevolent people, When public business always begets Enemies, I have frm various Causes a double portion, I know Mr Rayn^{olds} agent for RI state is doing me all the injury in his power, as he is restricted from my representation from purchaseing out of that State; for tho' the interfearance in his department, most certainly hurts the publick, it as certainly helps his private Interest___[2]

But Sir let the Causes of rancour flow frm provocation, innate malice, or whatever cause will Congress, whose justice, whose steadiness & whose magnanimity, the world contemplate with pleasure, suffer at least faithful servants to be neglected, & disgraced unheard & unnoticed.

---

[1] The Board of War initially appointed George Williams of Salem, Mass., as their agent to collect the clothing which had recently arrived in New England. When Williams declined, he was replaced by Samuel Fletcher. Although Otis & Andrews were ordered to cease purchasing clothing for the army, Fletcher turned over large quantities of cloth to Otis & Andrews for the purpose of having uniforms made. Risch, *Supplying Washington's Army*, p. 293.

[2] Samuel Otis had complained to HL in May 1778 that John Reynolds had purchased across state lines and forced prices higher while criticizing Otis for paying high prices for clothing. Otis suggested that "he thinks the Ruin of his Neighbours reputation the best foundation to build his own upon." *HL Papers*, XIII, 363.

It was not for one expected pecuniary reward I ever received the imported goods, the allowance will be trifling for that business, because it deserves but little, but it looks like distrust and disapprobation to have a fresh hand thrust in to wrest the business from its proper department, nor does <u>that</u> induce me to covet earnestly the agency, for however idle chattering people may amuse themselves, application to private business will do much greater things, Large quantities of goods arrived & arriving will hardly make it an object for the pecuniary advantage, but a superceedence at the moment I was assured of the Confidence of Congress is dishonorary, discouraging, & unaccountable.

I regret Sir so much trouble to my friends as I am sensible my affairs have given you, but they were so connected with the public, <u>that</u>, encouraged my applications, I thank you for your attention to them, & still flatter myself with a dependance upon your patronage, to sheild me from the aspersions of the envious, & the malevolent insinuations of persons disposed to do unpro↑voked↓ injury___

The Clothier Gen[l] tho requested has never wrote a Line upon this Subject, as he seems to have no violent passion for writing I wonder less at it, and indeed the u↑n↓ settled State of things in Pensylv[a] is an apology, If however Sir you could spare me a Line it would be rec[d] with usual pleasure & ranked with the honors of

Your Most Humble Ser[t]

Sam A Otis

SOURCE: RC, Kendall Collection; addressed on cover "Hon[ble] / Henry Laurens Esq[r] / President of / Congress / Philadelphia"; addressed below close "Hon[be.] Pres[t] Laurens__"; dated "Boston July 20[th.] 1778"; docketed by HL "Sam. A. Otis / 20 July 1778 Rec[d] 3 Aug[t.]". Copy (19th century), HL Papers, ScHi.

TO JOHN NUTT

Philadelphia, July 21, 1778

Dear Sir

As I have not had the pleasure of a line from you since I left London in October 1774 I know nothing more of my Account than appears in the state which you delivered to me while I was with you, except that the Ship Heart of Oak had been sold and one fourth part of the Amount passed to my Credit ~~with you~~__ the former balance $1/4$ of the ships value together with growing Interest according to my computation will Amount upward of £850 Sterling.[1]

You cannot have forgot the motives which induced me to leave a balance in your hands for a considerable time before I left England as well as at the time of my departure__ you had repeatedly intimated to me that the use of the Money would be a convenience to you, and you know I had another friend who would have been equally glad to have had the little deposit lodged in his hands, but delicacy towards you forbad my[2] drawing it out of yours__ the same consideration for you has restrained me from securing myself and giving your honor ~~illegible~~ ↑or↓ Credit the smallest wound by means which have been often practised on both sides the water. I reflected that the use of such means being extreamly expensive in these times, would also give a deep wound to your Purse.

The time is come when I find it convenient to myself to draw for a part of the sum which I suppose stands to my Credit in your Books. I have therefore under the present date passed a Bill on you ↑payable↓ at thirty days sight to the Order of Sarah Yard[3] ↑for eight hundred & ten pounds↓ [4] to which you will give due honor, and pay the whole, if the balance due to me extends so far or so much of it as my said balance will reach, and send the remainder or the whole as you shall judge proper to determine to my friend William Manning Esquire, who I am sure will find means for shewing my Draft compleat honor, but I dare not indulge a thought so injurious to your Character as a Man of Honor and gratitude as that you will send the bills out of your own house, even admitting it shall appear I have overdrawn a few Pounds__ the time is not very far distant when a free correspondence will be opened between your kingdom and these Confederated United States. In the mean time let our whole conduct distinguish between private mutual faith and honor, and the necessary unavoidable Acts of authoriz'd public seizures and hostilities. I have been tenacious on my part in all my proceedings during this ↑little↓ War to avoid every Act which might prove

---

[1] John Nutt was a London merchant with whom HL had left a £400 sterling balance in 1774. This balance increased with the sale of the *Heart of Oak* in 1777 for £1,450. *HL Papers*, XIII, 128.

[2] "my" written over other text.

[3] Sarah Yard was landlady to several members of Congress.

[4] The bill was copied into the letterbook above the letter.

a Bar to a revival of those happy friendships in Great Britain which I had long enjoyed__ under a persuasion of your having been actuated by the same principles, I freely and respectfully subscribe,

Dear Sir / Your Most Obedient and / Most Humble Servt.

SOURCE: LB, HL Papers, ScHi; addressed "John Nutt Esquire / London"; dated "21st July".

TO DENIS COTTINEAU

Philadelphia, July 22, 1778

Sir

I was honored with your favor of the 30th Ult^o. three days ago

Congress are not disposed to grant Marine Commissions for Vessels in distant States unless descriptions more special than those you left are laid before them; in order therefore to avoid as much as possible any disappointment to you and to promote the general Interest of the Allied Powers of France and these United States I shall transmit by this conveyance to His Excellency Governor Caswell a number of Commissions, Instructions and Bonds, from whom you may obtain so many as he shall judge proper.[1]

From the conversation at York Town when you were going to Camp, I had expected you would have renewed it at your return and that some Plan for your proceeding on a voyage in joint concern would have been reduced to writing, but as you did not even touch upon the subject, I concluded you had determined your Affairs to go in some other Channel, and now a concern in the extent you mark, would not be convenient to me even if I were as much disposed as I was at York, because I had the very day before your Letter reached me agreed to draw for a considerable part of the Money I had lodged in England, besides, I cannot venture to risque the good opinion of my friends by an attempt to persuade them into an Association where so large a sum as £6000 Sterling is

---

[1] HL sent Richard Caswell "six Marine Commissions Instructions, & Bonds" and explained that Captain Cottineau had "applied to me in York Town for a Commission for his own Ship & for one or two which he said he intended to equip & to form a little squadron." HL left the decision to Caswell who was "capable of judging of the propriety of Capt. Cottineau's pretensions." HL to Richard Caswell, July 23, 1778, Nc-Ar.

required on their part, without having a Plan of particulars for their consideration, hence Sir, you will after one moments reflection perceive how impossible it is for me to return a more direct answer__ and will govern your future determinations accordingly.[2]

We have received no certain account of a Declaration of War, but beyond all dispute hostilities are mutual between France and England, and captures made upon every occasion__ already the Count d'Estaing has taken a great number of British ships, and some he has destroyed, among them it is said five armed Vessels, and I know he is exceedingly chagrined, because he cannot get into Sandy Hook with his large ships. His intention was to have tried the powers of the English squadron under the command of Lord Howe at New York__ failing in this place the Admiral is gone to Rhode Island, where he may play a smaller Game than he had aspired to__ but will render much service to the common cause.

You perceive Sir, from this intelligence, which is the best I can give, that you are at liberty to enrich yourself from the spoils of the Enemy__ an Enemy who a very little time ago panted for our destruction and had avowed their designs to accomplish it.__

Accept my wishes for your prosperity, and believe me to be with great Regard

Sir / Your Obedient Servant

SOURCE: LB, HL Papers, ScHi; addressed "Captain Cottineau / North Carolina / by Governor Henrys' Messenger"; dated "22nd July 1778".

FROM WILLIAM LIVINGSTON

Morristown, N.J., July 22, 1778

Dear Sir

I find that the greatest Multiplicity of Business does not prevent you from remembering your Friends, or of obliging with Intelligence one who will ever be as proud of that distinction, as he

---

[2] The friends HL mentioned may have been Lachlan McIntosh and Joseph Clay. In January 1777, HL had rejected their invitation to join them in a privateering venture, but promised he would "enter into any connection...which we three, shall determine to be feasible & for the benefit of our Country or the honest improvement of our fortunes". *HL Papers*, XI, 287.

is sorry that he has it not in his Power to return you an equivalent.

I am greatly obliged to you for your Favours of the 17th & 18th Instant accompaned with the Instruments for Privateers, & the second overtures of the British Commissioners, who, if of the romish communion, would certainly be ranked among the order of Mendicants.

As the English will never be undeceived till they are ruined, it seems those poor devils are now made to believe that the Congress does not speak the Sentiments of the People at large; but that an harangue to the Mobility will do mighty matters, & raise a great Mob in favour of Despotism. I suppose the Gentlemen have read the Story of Jack Straw & Watt Tyler,[1] & now for a popular[2] Sermon out of Rivington's Pulpit upon the advantages of the old & the tyranny of the new Government,[3] which will have about as much effect, and make as many converts, as would a Sermon upon holyness delivered by Beelzebub, What a piece of Impudence to demand from Congress, at the same time that they affect to acknowledge our Independence, their authority to make treaties, & enter into alliances? And what egregious stupidity to flatter themselves with the prospect of causing a defection among the people by requiring a sight of the unpublished Articles which every man of common sense will naturally suppose are kept from public view for wise and political reasons? This ridiculous[4] belief of the Congress's acting against the Sentiments of their Constituents and of the probability of dividing the People, which I suppose is infused into them by the DeLanceys in New York[5] (who have had a ~~espel~~ principal hand in instigating the British Claim of taxation) is sufficient to delude that ever-credulous, and self-destroying Nation for another year; or will at least

---

[1] Wat Tyler's Rebellion in 1381 was a popular uprising against taxation. After King Richard II granted concessions, Tyler was killed, the insurgents subdued, and the concessions revoked.

[2] "pop" written over other text.

[3] *Rivington's Gazette,* July 4, 1778, printed George Johnstone's speech in the House of Commons in which he asserted that when the Americans "are recovered from the phrenzy of fear which has so long distracted them" they will "compare their present state and condition, with that mild and equal government under which they lived" and choose to return to the old relationship.

[4] "c" written over other text.

[5] Livingston's major political competition before independence came from the New York DeLancey family who now were active Loyalists. Livingston's analogy here is that the DeLancey faction had undermined the 1768 nonimportation agreement by a selective polling

continue till some other blockhead fabricates some other chimera equally absurd and nonsensical. Have not those Gentlemen totally forfeited all pretensions to the Character of public persons commissioned to treat with Congress by acting the part of Incendiaries, & endeavouring to excite Insurrections against Government?

I think I may depend upon the Intelligence from Staten Island, that no flour or bread has been served out to the British Troops for[6] some days; & the French Admiral will entirely deprive them of Fish, which in the Season of it, used to subsist two thirds of the City. I doubt whether the Count will be able, without running too great a hazard to bring up his larger Ships; or whether his 64^s will be sufficiently <u>puissant</u> to cope with the Enemy. By barely continuing where he is, they must be ruined; & whenever the British Fleet leaves S^t· Helens, the Brest Squadron will undoubtedly start. Indeed I am under no great apprehensions of a British fleet__ The poor Wretches in the Metropolis will not chuse to part with their wooden walls__ Nor is their navy manned. And let but the Monsieurs talk about flat-bottom'd boats, & all the cits are as much as their wits end, as our fair Lady was, or pretended to be, at the sight of a spider or Caterpillar.

If those Englishmen were not so confounded proud, I should really think it best for them to ask our pardon, & petition Congress for leave to go home without molestation, upon promise of their good behaviour for the future without any Security, as none but a mad man would be bound for their keeping their promise any longer than it was[7] in their power to break it. I am with great Esteem & unfeigned Affection

Dear Sir / Your most humble Ser^t

Wil: Livingston

SOURCE: RC, HL Papers, ScHi; addressed below close "The honble Henry Laurens Esqr"; dated "Morris Town 22^d July 1778"; docketed by HL "Govr· Livingston / 22^d· July 1778 / Rēcd 26th–"; noted at top of first page "(private)". Copy (19th century), HL Papers, ScHi.

---

of citizens in 1770. If the Carlisle Commission were to succeed they too would need to divide the people and convince them to act against their own best interests. *Livingston Papers* (Prince), II, 397n.

[6] "for" written over other text.

[7] "was" written over "is".

FROM COMMISSIONERS AT PARIS
Passy, France, July 23, 1778

Sir,

      We have just received a Message from Monsr. Le Comte De Vergennes, by his Secretary, acquainting Us; that Information is received from England of the Intention of the Cabinet there, to offer (by additional Instructions to their Commissioners) Independence to the United States, on Condition of their making a separate Peace, relying on their Majority in both Houses, for Approbation of the Measure. M. De Vergennes, upon this Intelligence requests, that we would write expressly to acquaint the Congress, that tho' no formal Declaration of War has yet been published, the War between France and England is considered as actualy existing from the time of the Return of the Ambassadors; and that if England should propose a Peace with France, the immediate Answer to the Proposition would be, our eventual Treaty with the United States is now in full Force; and we will make no Peace but in Concurrence with them. The same Answer it is expected, will be given by the Congress, if a separate Peace should be proposed to them. And we have given it as our firm Opinion, that such an Answer will be given by you, without the least Hesitation or Difficulty, tho' you may not have been informed before, as you now are, that War being actually begun, the Eventual Treaty is become fully and compleatly binding. We are with great Respect, Sir,

      Your most obed^{t.} & most humble Servants.

B Franklin
John Adams__

SOURCE: RC, PCC (Item 85), DNA; addressed above salutation "Hon^{ble:} Henry Lawrens Esqr. / President of Congress."; dated "Passy July 23^{d.} / 1778."; docketed "Letter from / B. Franklin / J. Adams / Paris July 23. 1778 / Read March 5. 1779" and "The eventual Treaty is / become actually in Force"; noted "(Duplicate.)". Copies (2), HL Papers, ScHi.

FROM THE MARQUIS DE LAFAYETTE
White Plains, N.Y., July 23, 1778

Dr Sir

I have receiv'd your favor by M^r de vienne, and will do myself the honor of answering some few lines, as I am just setting of for a little journey which I like very well, and which you will know[1] the particularities off by his excellency's letters.[2]

I am entirely of your opinion, my good friend, about the[3] granting of high Ranks to stranger gentlemen in this very crisis where national officers think themselves some what injur'd by new arrangements__ no body in the world may have a higher respect than ↑this↓ I entertain for those virtuous men who leaving the plow for the sword turn'd out ~~at~~ ↑under↓ the greatest Risks, under the greatest disavantages, and by theyr noble conduct brought the Revolution to this glorious period__ a thing may be added with the most candid ~~illegible~~ truth, that I know few[4] officers whose merits may be Compar'd to the merit and talents of some of your country-borns__ one parker, one steward, silly, buttler, ↑h.↓ lewingston[5] ↑&c.↓ would be reputed among the most distinguish'd officers of any army in the world

~~let~~ These reflexions I will heartly make with Mʳ laurens, but never with the president of Congress,[6] as I think it Consistent with my duty, with my love for my country, and my sense of the confidence her sons have trusted upon me, to reccommend as warmly, and forward as speedily as possible the advancement of all the frenchmen in our service. I Confess I have been surpris'd and in the same time pleas'd to see Mʳ de vienne honour'd with the commission of a colonel; I will also be pleas'd to see Mʳ Touzard a major but nothing more because at lenght no body would accept of a captain's commission.

You will be[7] also troubl'd by me for Mʳ de Lesser who came over with me, who then wanted to be a brigadier general and wants

---

[1] "know" written in left margin.

[2] General Washington informed Congress that he had decided July 21 "to put two Brigades under marching orders....for Rhode Island...both under the direction, for the present, of the Marquis de la Fayette." George Washington to HL, July 22, 1778, PCC, Item 152, Vol. 6, p. 183ff.

[3] "t" written over "g".

[4] "few" written over other text.

[5] The American officers Lafayette recognized—colonels Richard Parker, Walter Stewart, Joseph Cilley, Richard Butler, and Henry Beekman Livingston—had all participated at Monmouth. *Lafayette Papers* (Idzerda), II, 113.

[6] HL on May 11 had instructed Lafayette "to write every thing you intend for Congress quite distinct from private intimations & commands to me." *HL Papers*, XIII, 285-286.

[7] "ll" and "b" written over other text.

again the same Rank. he is a good officer, he distinguish'd himself last war at Marbourg, and I beg you would Remember that I Reccommend him to the <u>president of Congress</u> for the succès of his enterprise upon the Rank of General.[8]

There is a thing I now particularly Reccommend both to the <u>president and to my friend</u>   M^r ~~Captin~~ Capitaine one of my family has got the commission of a captain of engeneers. he has since been ~~very~~ useful to the country by his Drafts of the Susquehana. you Rembember that I did object a little to his being made <u>an engeneer</u> because I foresaw what would happen. The <u>corps du genie</u> Can't help Considering him as an officer of theyrs who is to do duty with them__ Mr Capitaine was in the Marshal of broglio's family, they made me a present of him and I attach'd him to serve to me not only in america and in war but also to stay in the family in peaceble times__ such an officer I ca'nt spare, and I will employ him to make plans of our positions and battles for gāl washington, for me, and also for the king who will be glad to have an exact draft of gāl washington's battles__ the only way of getting him out of the Engeneery is to have for him a commission of Major in the line; he is now in my family but I want to have him entirely my supern. aide de camp. ~~that~~ I do'nt speack to any body about that affair, and as I have it more at heart than any other business of that Kind I want to have that obligation to your frienship__ I Even confess I wish to have it soon done to Avoid ~~different~~ any compromise.[9]

farewell, my dear sir, I have been much longer than I thought or even I ought__ I hope we'll ~~illegible~~ find the Red birds at home, and then we schall take care of them__ the Count d'estaing has ~~illegible~~ ↑desired↓ to add his land troops to any detachement I would Command

You see this letter is a private one, and the greatest part of it must be only <u>entre nous</u>. adieu, my good friend, with the highest Regard and most sincere affection I have the honor to be dear Sir
        Your most obedient servant
                            the Mis de lafayette

SOURCE: RC, HL Papers, ScHi; no address; dated "White plains 23^d july 1778"; docketed by HL "Marquis delafayette / 23 July 1778 Rec^d 26th.".

---

[8] Despite recommendations from Lafayette and de Kalb as early as July 1777, Chevalier Jean Thevet Lesser never obtained an American commission.

[9] Michel Capitaine du Chesnoy remained with Lafayette. He received a brevet commission

TO JOHN BURNET[1]

Philadelphia, July 24, 1778

~~Dear~~ Sir

I received much satisfaction by learning from M^r· Zahn that you continued at Mount Tacitus. I hope I shall find you there or in some other of my Plantations where you shall think you may be most serviceable__ my return to my own Country hardly depends upon my will; my interest and my inclination call loudly for it, but already I have received several applications requesting me not to leave Congress so early as the first of November, which day I had lately named. I will not finally determine until I shall have seen our public affairs two Months further advanced, in the mean time if leisure can be found at Mount Tacitus I desire about five thousand square feet of Cypress may be provided, and shingles sufficient to cover an House of about 50 feet square, there must also be a large quantity of boards and plank for inside work, and also flooring boards of the best Pine. I mean to build a log House such as I have seen and lived in, at York Town, where they are neat, wholsome, durable and built at a very moderate expence__ M^rs.[2] Zahn will speak to you on this subject and you will be governed in your proceedings by his advice and direction.

Except one visit of the Gout last Winter I have enjoy'd my usual good health ever since I left Carolina. That stroke of the Gout was extreamly severe, confined me a month and kept me lame near three months. You must have heard from time to time all public occurrences in this part of America up to the middle of the present Month, what follows and the newspapers which you will find inclosed with this, will give you a pretty full Account of the present state of Affairs.

The French fleet which lately arrived on this Coast is now lying off Sandy Hook, unfortunately there is not water enough on the Bar for their large ships, otherwise the whole English squadron

---

of major in November 1778 before returning to France with the Marquis and returned to America in 1780 as a member of Lafayette's staff. *HL Papers*, XIII, 187n; *JCC*, XII, 1097.

[1] John Burnet had a history of preaching to slaves and, it was feared, provoking them to insurrection. Admonished first in August 1773, he was arrested in July 1775 in St. Bartholomew Parish and brought before the Council of Safety in Charleston. He was dismissed upon his "solemn Promise of more circumspect Behaviour for the future" and sent to Georgia where HL offered him a position. *HL Papers*, X, 231-232; XIII, 392.

[2] The clerk erroneously wrote "M^rs." rather than "M^r·".

at New York would fall into their hands, these are at present block'd up, and the French fleet have taken a great number of Prizes some of them armed ships, and some with gold and silver and valuable Cargoes.

General Washington has now an Army of upwards of 20,000 Men all in high spirits and I hope we shall soon learn of his having accomplished some important Act__ every one whose opinion I have heard, say, if general Lee had done his part at the battle of Monmouth, Sir Henry Clinton would have been reduced to circumstances little, if any thing, better than those which Burgoyne experienced last Year. The Generals' trial before a Court Martial is not yet ended.__

While I was at York Town I lived in a stile much below that of my Overseers, All the room I had for my Office and lodging, was not near so large as the Hall at Mount Tacitus, more than once I have been obliged to dine upon bread and cheese and a glass of Grog__ here I fare much better, but in both places I have found hard work enough, and at so enormous an expence as would astonish you to hear of__ but thank God there begins to be ground for hoping we shall obtain an honorable Peace before another Year expires__ this however is not to be relied on, we ought therefore to persevere in every endeavour to oppose and repel the Enemy

The cruelties of the English, exercised upon our People who were their Prisoners is not to be parallel'd in History of Civilized Nations__ nor indeed are they exceeded by the practices of the barbarous Indian Allies of our Enemies.__

The Indians have scalped and butcher'd and burnt many of our inhabitants__ these means were cruel and severe but death soon ended all pain.__ The English have starved our People, suffer'd them to lose their limbs by frost and ↑to↓ linger out a miserable life for many days and weeks, have refused to let us cloath and feed them__ they have compelled our friends to drink unwholsome water, when good water was in plenty wasting before their Eyes, they have smother'd them in Prison Ships, killing every night five, six, and more, have kick'd beat and abused, have loaded Officers with Irons and a thousand other savage Acts they have been guilty of__ sometimes murdered the Masters of families, burned all the houses, goods and provisions and left poor helpless Women and infant Children exposed to the rigor of frost, snow and rain without food or covering__ a volume might be filled with Accounts of their barbarities__ in several instances of which even General Howe and General Clinton have been directly concern'd. But thank God their hands are now bound up, they are confined within their Lines at New York__ from whence deserters come into our Camp 6, 8, 10 of a day, lately a Cornet of Horse and a Captain of their new Troops deserted and came over to General Washington.__ If time permitted I would give you further information, but I have many other Letters to write by this conveyance, I must therefore close this, assuring you I continue.

      Your friend And Humble Servt.

With respect to y^r. wages, whatever M^r. Zahn does will meet my approbation.__

SOURCE: LB, HL Papers, ScHi; addressed "~~William Smith~~ ↑John Burnet↓ / Mount Tacitus" and by HL "by Durst"; dated "24th July".

FROM GEORGE WASHINGTON
                  White Plains, N.Y., July 24, 1778

Dr Sir

      I had yesterday the pleasure to receive your favour of the 18th Inst with the inclosure and packets, which you mentioned.

      I should have been sorry, if you or Monsieur Gerard had found the smallest difficulty in recommending the packets for the Count D'Estaing to my care; and I am happy to inform you, that they will meet with a speedy and safe conveyance to him by an Officer, who has set off for Rhode Island.

      It is very pleasing as well ↑as↓ interesting, to hear that prizes are already finding the way into the Delaware. The event seems the more agreable, as that Navigation but yesterday as it were, could scarcely contain the Enemy's fleet and their numerous captures, which were constantly crouding in. Happy change! and I should hope, that the Two prizes which have entered will be succeeded by many more. The want of information on the one hand of Philadelphia's being evacuated, and the countenance which our armed Vessels will derive from the French Squadron on our Coast, must throw several into our possession.

The second Epistle from the Commissioners, of which you have so ~~obligelengly~~ ↑obligingly↓ favoured me with a Copy, strikes me in the same point of view that it did you.[1] It is certainly puerile__ and does not border a little on indecorum, notwithstanding their professions of the regard they wish to pay to decency. It is difficult to determine, on an extensive scale, thō part of their design is tolerably obvious, what the Gentlemen would be at. Had I the honor of being a Member[2] of Congress I do not know how I might feel ~~on~~ ↑upon↓ the occasion; but it appears to me, the performance must ~~fill them~~ ↑be received↓ with a sort of indignant pleasantry ~~notwith-standing the~~ *~~illegible~~* ↑on account of it's manner on the *~~illegible~~* one hand, and on the other↓ as being truly typical of that confusion, in which their Prince and Nation are. ↑on the other↓ ~~I will be done upon the subject~~.

By the time this reaches you, I expect the Mess̄rs Nevilles[3] will be in Philadelphia. From the Certificates ~~which~~ these Gentlemen have provided, if I may hazard a conjecture, they are in quest of promotion, particularly the Elder. How far their views may extend, I cannot determine; but I dare predict that they will be sufficiently high. My present intention is to tell you, and with a ~~confidential~~ freedom I do it, that Congress can not be well too Cautious on this head. I do not mean or wish, to derogate from the merit of Mess̄rs Nevilles. The opportunities I have had, will not permit me[4] to speak decisively for, or against it. However, I may observe from a certificate, which I have seen, written by themselves, or at least by one of them & signed by Genl Parsons[5] ↑probably thrō surprise or irresolution,↓ that they are not bad, at giving themselves a good character; and I will further add, if they meet with any great promotion, I am fully convinced it will be illy borne by our own Officers; and that it will be the cause of infinite discontent. The

---

[1] HL described the July 11 letter from the British commissioners as "more puerile than any thing I have seen from the other side, since the commencement of our present dispute, with a little dash of insolence, as unnecessary as it will be unavailing." HL to George Washington, July 18, 1778, Washington Papers, DLC.

[2] "M" written over "m".

[3] René-Hippolyte Penot Lombart de Noirmont de La Neuville and Louis-Pierre Penot Lombart, Chevalier de la Neuville.

[4] "me" written in left margin.

[5] Brig. Gen. Samuel H. Parsons's letter of June 28 "in favour of the Chevalier de la Neuville and Major Noirmont de la Neuville" was read and referred to the Board of War on July 28. *JCC,* XI, 724-725.

ambition of these men (I do not mean of the Messrs Nevilles in particular, but of the Natives of their Country ↑and Foreigners↓ in general) is unlimited and unbounded; and the singular instances of rank, which have been conferred upon them in but too many cases have occasioned general ~~complaint~~ ↑disatisfaction↓ and general ~~disatisfaction~~ ↑complaint↓ . The feelings of our own Officers have been much hurt by it, and their ardor and love for the[6] service greatly damped. Should a like proceeding still be practised,[7] it is not easy to say, what intensive murmurings and consequences may ensue. I will further add, that we have already a ~~good~~ full proportion of Foreign Officers in our General Councils and should their number be encreased, it may happen upon many occasions, that their voices may equal if not exceed the rest. I trust you think me so much a Citizen of the World, as to beleive that I am not easily warped or led away, by attachments merely local or American; Yet I confess, I am not entirely without 'em, nor does it appear to me that they are unwarrantable, if confined within proper limits. Fewer promotions in the foreign line, would have been productive of more harmony, and made our warfare more agreable to all parties. The frequency of them, is the source of jealousy and ↑of↓ disunion. We have many__ very many deserving Officers, who are not opposed to merit wheresoever it is found, ~~and who are~~ nor insensible of[8] the advantages derived from a long service in an experienced Army__ *illegible* ↑nor↓ to the principles of Policy. Where any of those principles mark the way to rank, I am persuaded, they yield a becoming and willing acquiescence; but where they are not the basis, they feel severely. I will dismiss the subject, knowing with you, I need not labour, either a case of Justice or of policy.

I am Dr Sir / with sentiments of very warm regard & esteem / Yr much Obliged & Obedt Servt

G: W__

PS.

The Baron Steuben will also be in Philadelphia in a day or two. The ostensible cause for his going, is to fix more certainly with

---

[6] "this" altered to "the".
[7] "e" written over "i".
[8] "of" written over "to".

Congress his duties, as Inspector General which is necessary: However, I am disposed to beleive, the real one is, to obtain an actual
command in the line as a Major General; and ~~it is probable~~ he ~~will~~
↑may↓ urge[9] a competition set up by Mons[r.] Neville for the Inspector's
place, on this side the Hudson, and a denial ~~of~~ ↑by↓ him of his the
Baron's authority, as an Argument to effect it, and ↑the granting him
the ~~place~~ Post↓ as a mean of satisfying both. I regard & I esteem the
Baron, as an assiduous__ Intelligent & an experienced Officer; but
you may rely on it, if such is his view and he should accomplish it,
we shall have the whole line of Brigadiers in confusion. They have
said but little about his rank as Major General as he has ↑not↓ had
an actual command over 'em; But when we marched from Brunswic,
as there were but few Major Generals and almost the whole of the
Brigad[rs] engaged at the Court Martial, either as Members or
Witnesses, I appointed him pro tempore and so expressed it in
orders, to conduct a Wing to the North River. This measure thō
founded in evident necessity and not designed to produce to the
Brigadiers the least possible injury, excited great uneasinesss and
has been the source of Complaint. The truth is, we have been very
unhappy in a variety of appointments, and our own Officers much
injured. Their feelings from this cause have become extremely
sensible, and the most delicate touch gives them pain. I write as a
Friend and therefore with freedom. The Baron's services in the line
he is in, can be singular, and the Testimonials he has already
received are honorable. It will also be material to have the point of
the Inspector Generalship now in question between him & Mons[r]
Neville adjusted. The appointment of the latter it is said, calls him
Inspector General in the Army ~~under~~ ↑commanded by↓ Gen[l] Gates,
and under this, as I am informed, he denies any Subordination to
the Baron & will not know him in his official capacity. There can be
but one head.[10]
        Yr̄s

                                                        GW

SOURCE: Draft, Washington Papers, DLC; addressed below postscript "The
Hon. H. Laurens"; dated "Camp near White Plains July the 24[th:] 1778";
dated below postscript "24[th.] July 1778."; noted "Private". Copy (19th
century), HL Papers, ScHi.

FROM RALPH IZARD

Paris, July 25, 1778

Dear Sir

The Treaties were received by the Spy on the 9th Instant. I am glad to find that the 11th & 12th Articles of the Treaty of Commerce appeared to Congress in the same light that they did to me. The Committee for foreign Affairs in their Letters to the Commissioners here of 14th & 15th May, made nearly the same observations that I did to Dr. Franklin in my Letter on that subject.[1] I have not however the satisfaction of knowing whether the part that I have acted has been approved of; or even whether any of my Letters have got to your hands, as I have not been favoured with a line from you since your arrival at Congress. I shall not complain, but follow Dr. Franklin's maxim in his Letter of 29th January; which is "to suppose one's friends right, till one finds them wrong, rather than to suppose them wrong, till one finds them right."[2] It is possible that my Letters to you, & yours to me may have been lost, or stolen. The scandalous tricks that were plaid with Mr. Lee's Letters, & the public dispatches that were sent by Folgier, will justify any suspicion.[3] I shall take it for granted that if you have written, your Letters are miscarried; or if you have not written, that you were prevented by business of greater importance. It is however very unfortunate; & you can not but be sensible how mortifying it must be to me who have been engaged in distress, & trouble in consequence of my doing my duty to the public, not to find attention, & support from a quarter where I had every reason to expect it. I had just written thus far, when Mr. Adams sent me your Letter of 19th. May, which was enclosed to him; & I thank you heartily for the very friendly expressions contained in it. You mention that you intended to write to me more fully by the same opportunity; but as that Letter is not come to hand, I suppose it was

---

[1] Ralph Izard to Benjamin Franklin, Jan. 28, 1778, *Franklin Papers* (Labaree), XXV, 536-538.

[2] In addition to stating his opinion on the articles concerning export duties on molasses from the French West Indies, Izard complained of Franklin's failure to send him a copy of the treaty. Franklin replied on January 29 that he would "explain to you when I have the Honor of seeing you" the reasons for not "giving it a full Answer now." He offered the maxim Izard paraphrased here "which has thro Life been of Use to me and may be so to you in preventing such imaginary Hurts." *Franklin Papers* (Labaree), XXV, 538, 539.

[3] John Folger delivered a packet of "dispatches" from Paris to Congress in January 1778 that had been secretly opened and replaced with blank paper. *HL Papers*, XII, 281-283, 384-386.

too late for the conveyance. I am very anxious to receive it, & hope to find by it that my proceedings have met with your approbation.

The ratification of the Treaties by Congress has put the Ministry and the whole Nation into as good spirits as our Countrymen were put by them. Except the parts which I have mentioned to you, they seem to be very fair, & equitable; & I really believe if a certain Gentleman had thought less of his infallibility, they might have been made unexceptionable.[4] The Ministry made no objections to the alteration respecting the Melasses; & I most sincerely wish that Congress had not in their hurry past over the other Articles, which I am convinced will occur to them when perhaps it may not be so easy to get them altered as at present. The war in Germany is already begun. The King of Prussia finding that his negotiations proved fruitless, has invaded Bohemia; & that unhappy Country, the constant seat of misery, will in all probability experience more calamities than ever. The wisdom of the Congress, & the valour of our Countrymen will, I hope, soon remove the war from our Continent; & I pray to God that the blessings of Peace may be at no great distance. I can not help expressing to you my astonishment upon reading the account given of the interview between the Commissioners here, & M[r.] Gerard on the 16[th.] December, printed in the York-Town Gazette of May the 4[th.].[5] The part which I allude to is the following. The French Plenipotentiary speaking of the King says__ "He should moreover not so much as insist that if he engaged, in the war with England on our account, we should not make a seperate Peace for ourselves, whenever good, & advantageous terms were offered to us." This account, I understand was given to Congress by the Commissioners, & therefore it must be presumed to be true. How then can it be reconciled with the 8[th.] Article of the Treaty of Alliance? Suppose England should offer to acknowledge the Liberty, Sovereignty, & Independence of America, upon condition that she should make a seperate Peace. The question is, can we in honour do it? Monsieur Gerard, Royal

---

[4] Probably a reference to Silas Deane.
[5] This appeared in a May 4 "Postscript" to the *Pennsylvania Gazette* May 2, 1778, which was published in York, Pa.

Syndic of Strasbourg, & Secretary of his Majesty's Council of State informed the Commissioners on the 16th. December, <u>by order of the King</u>, that the only condition his Majesty should require, & rely on would be this. "That we, in no Peace to be made with England, should give up our Independence, & return to the obedience of that Government." The 8th. Article of the Treaty of Alliance declares directly the contrary; although the second says expressly "Le But essentiel, & direct de la presente Alliance defensive, est de maintenir efficacement la Liberté, la Soverainté, et l'Independence des Etats Unis." I most ardently wish for Peace; at the same time the preservation of our national Honour must be attended to. The virtue, & wisdom of the Representatives of our country in Congress will be shewn, if this question should ever be agitated.

You will find by my Letter to the Committee of this day's date that the situation of affairs have not allowed me yet to go into Italy.[6] My own inclinations, if they alone had been consulted, would have carried me there long ago. Mr. Wm. Lee was right in going to Vienna. That Court acts from it's own opinions, without control; & might possibly have been prevailed on to receive him publicly. The event has not proved answerable to our wishes. The conduct of the Empress Queen has certainly been occasioned by a resentment against the Court of France for not contributing, contrary to their own interest, to the aggrandizement of the House of Austria. A resentment so ill founded, & unreasonable may perhaps not continue long; in the mean time however, it is exceedingly provoking to me, as I am living at the public expense, without having it in my power to fulfil the objects of my Commission. Perhaps indeed my having been in Paris may not prove altogether useless; & I hope the papers which I have transmitted to you may not be thought unworthy of the attention of Congress.

After having had the facts stated to them relative to the situation of affairs in Europe they will judge what instructions are

---

[6] Izard, who had been selected commissioner to the Tuscan Court in May 1777, realized after receiving a discouraging letter from Abbé Raimondo Niccoli, the Tuscan minister to the French Court, that his proposed embassy would be impractical. He enclosed a copy of the Abbé's letter in a Sept. 12, 1778, dispatch to HL in which he "lamented exceedingly that the Situation of affairs has not admitted of my going into Italy." *HL Papers*, XI, 542; Abbé Raimondo Niccoli to Ralph Izard, July 28, 1778, HL Papers, ScHi; (translation), PCC, Item 89, p. 102ff; Ralph Izard to HL, Sept. 12, 1778, HL Papers, ScHi.

proper to be sent to me. If they are positive; at all events they shall
be followed. If discretionary; I shall act to the best of my judgment.
You are so good as to assure me in your Letter of 19$^{th.}$ May that you
will upon all occasions have at heart my honour, & interest; & that
you will by every opportunity keep me acquainted with the state of
affairs. I feel very sensibly these friendly assurances, & promise you
that amidst the troubles, & vexations in which I have been engaged
I derive considerable comfort, & satisfaction from them. You say
nothing of your Son: I heartily rejoice at his promotion. He must
have informed you that he was very desirous of going into the
Prussian Army. I dissuaded him from it, & advised him, if he was
determined upon becoming a Soldier, to take Marshal Saxe, & the
Chevalier Foland's Commentaries upon Polybius[7] into his hands, &
to go to America, where an ample field would be open to him. I am
happy to find that he has had no cause to repent of his having
followed my advice. My Wife offers you her Compliments & joins me
in desiring that they may be presented to him. We have heard
nothing very lately from his family in England. By the last accounts
M$^{rs:}$ Laurens was well & the child very much improved. I am Dear Sir
       With great regard, & attachment / Your most Ob$^{t:}$ humble
Serv$^{t:}$

Ra. Izard.__

P.S. D$^{r.}$ Franklin has not attempted an answer to my Letter of 17$^{th.}$
June.[8]

SOURCE: RC, PCC (Item 89), DNA; addressed below close "His Excellency
/ Henry Laurens Esq$^{r:}$"; dated "Paris 25th July 1778"; noted "Copy__". Copies
(2), PCC (Item 102, Item 105), DNA. Copies (2), HL Papers, ScHi. Extract,
HL Papers, ScHi.

---

[7] Maurice, comte de Saxe, *Reveries, or Memoirs upon the art of war, by Field-marshal Count
Saxe...Translated from the French* (London, 1757) and Jean Charles de Fulard, *Commentaries on
Polybius* (1727).

[8] A copy of the June 17 letter and other related correspondence was enclosed with Izard's
June 28 letter to HL. Izard wrote to Franklin April 25 reminding him that "You have repeatedly
given me the strongest assurances that you would justify your conduct to me in writing." The
letter was carried by Izard's secretary John Julius Pringle who reported the following day that
Franklin gave only an oral reply that Izard should provide a more particular request. The June
17 letter was a long detailed review of Izard's grievances. It appears that Franklin made no
written reply. *HL Papers*, XIII, 524-530; PCC, Item 89, p. 63ff; *Franklin Papers* (Labaree), XXVI,
342-343, 355-358.

FROM WILLIAM LIVINGSTON

Morristown, N.J., July 25, 1778

Sir

I had the honour of your Favour of the 22ᵈ instant respecting the Affair of Mr Marmajoy[1] accompanied by a Letter from himself from Princetown; in answer to which I sent him the original of which the inclosed is a Copy,[2] which I think is all I can do in the present Situation of that affair. Whatever can farther be done by me for his relief consistent with Law, Congress may depend upon being done with the greatest vigour & alacrity___ I have the honor to be with the greatest regard & esteem

Your most humble / Servant

Wil: Livingston

SOURCE: RC, HL Papers, ScHi; addressed on cover "To / The honourable Henry Laurens Esqʳ / President of Congress / Philadelphia"; addressed below close "The honourable / Henry Laurens Esqʳ / president of Congress"; dated "Morris Town 25 July 1778"; docketed by HL "Govʳ· Livingston / 25 July 1778". Copy (19th century), HL Papers, ScHi.

FROM JONATHAN TRUMBULL, JR.

White Plains, N.Y., July 25, 1778

Sir__

The Time is arrived when the two Armies__ Southern & Northern are conjoined__ by this Event the <u>Northern Department</u> seems almost to be annihilated__ my Resolutions respecting my Conduct on this Occasion are of equal Date with my Expectations of the Event__ in this Situation, considering myself as a Supernumerary Officer, & it being utterly inconsistent with my Ideas to hang as a dead Weight upon the Public__ or to be a drone in the Hive of

---

[1] Anthony Marmajou was an owner of the schooner *St. Louis*, George Ross, whose crew mutinied against its captain on July 6. Marmajou placed newspaper notices (in both French and English) offering a reward of five hundred pounds for anyone with information leading to the pirates and his vessel with its cargo. *Pa. Packet*, July 23, 1778.

[2] William Livingston sympathized with Marmajou but informed him that as governor he had no judicial power in this case. William Livingston to Anthony Marmajoy, July 25, 1778, HL Papers, ScHi.

the Cōmonwealth, I think myself justifiable in a Resolution to request, that Congress will be pleased to suffer me to resign my Employment which I hold under them, & to discontinue my Services for the Public.__ In the present Concentration of the Armies, Colᵒ Palfry,[1] with proper Assistants, may easily conduct the Payment of the Troops, with Addition of the little Business now remaining in the Northⁿ Department__ so long as I could consider myself necessary to the Public Service, notwithstandᵍ some unhappy Feelings, I have acted with a Degree of Contentment__ in other Circumstances now, I shall feel myself happy to retire.__ This Request I now beg leave to make, in full Confidence, that Congress, adding to the Circumstances I have mentioned, the Consideration of my havᵍ in the prime of Life, and under an early very mortifying Mark of <u>Neglect</u>, (the Sting of which my present Situation is not calculated to abate) almost <u>given</u> the Continent a three Years of my Services in the <u>worst of Times</u>, cannot but consent that I should <u>now</u> retire from public Service, and seek some other Employment in the more private Walks of Life.__

I forbear to trouble your Excellency any further__ begging you will be pleased to lay my Request before Congress, & waiting an early Answer__[2] with highest Respect for the Honᵒ Congress__ & most perfect Esteem I have the Honor to subscribe

Your Excellency's most Obedient / & very humble Servant__

Jonᵃ Trumbull Junʳ PMG
Northⁿ Department
PS: The Troops of my Departᵗ have their Pay to 1ˢᵗ June__ whatever Money I may have on Hand, I suppose may be delivered over to Colᵒ

---

[1] Lt. Col. William Palfrey was appointed paymaster general of the Northern Department April 27 1776. Heitman, *Continental Officers.*

[2] HL presented Trumbull's letter of resignation and Congress accepted it on July 29. Upon receiving HL's notification that his resignation had been accepted, Trumbull observed that Congress had misinterpreted his reason for quitting the office by only noting his comment on the combining of the Northern and Southern armies. "Whether this partial Caption was designed to cast an odium on me__ or that it is intended to keep out of sight my real Reasons, which were sufficiently hinted at & which might be tho't perhaps to convey some Idea of a Sense of Injury from Congress__ I will not pretend to decide." HL to Jonathan Trumbull, Jr., July 30, 1778, L.W. Smith Collection, NjMoHP; Jonathan Trumbull, Jr., to HL, Aug. 3, 1778, Jonathan Trumbull, Jr., Papers, CtHi.

Palfry__ Mr Peirce[3] who brings this has Directions to wait an Answer__

The Death of my Brother the late Com^ry Genl[4] ↑the News of which has just reach^d me↓ __ forms an additional Reason for my leav^g the Army__

SOURCE: RC, PCC (Item 78), DNA; addressed below close "His Excellency H: Laurens Esqr"; dated "White Plains 25th July 1776__"; docketed "Letter from J Trumbull Esq / paym^er of Northern depart / ment July 25. 1778" and "Copy of the Settlement / of his accounts at the / Auditors office". Copy, Jonathan Trumbull Jr. Papers, CtHi.

TO THÉVENEAU DE FRANCY

Philadelphia, July 26, 1778

Dear Sir

I thank you for your favor of the 15th·, particularly for those Polite and kind marks of your friendship for me which you are pleased to express, and shall endeavour to merit the continuance of your Esteem.

The favorable Events which you allude to make a proper impression upon my mind. I view them as Harbingers to an honorable Peace, and the Universal acknowledgment of American Independence; but a Man who has paid some attention for fifty years to the continual fluctuation of Human Affairs, feels not those raptures from the appearances of good Fortune which had been wont to seize his Heart between the Stages of 20[1] and 40__ perhaps a moderate degree ↑of anxiety↓ for[2] permanizing present advantages may appear to younger Men an alloy of Happiness. I feel as if led by it into the ~~very~~ ↑true↓ Sphere.

Many days have past over since I heard any thing from the

---

[3] John Pierce of Connecticut was assistant paymaster general at this time and would rise to the position of paymaster general in January 1781. Heitman, *Continental Officers*.

[4] Joseph Trumbull died July 23, 1778. *HL Papers*, XII, 340n.

[1] "20" written over "tw".

[2] "of" altered to "for".

Fleet or from His Excellency General Washington__ Count d'Estaing has been making Prizes in great numbers and of great value in sight of the Enemys ~~fleet~~ ↑squadron↓ safely anchor'd behind Sandy Hook extreamly chagrined at finding his own Ships drew too much Water to admit his coming nearer to them. The Newspaper which I shall here inclose will further inform you. I can add nothing on this head but that M[r.] Gerard and myself conjecture the Admiral is gone to Rhode Island. the choice of le Sieur Gerard for the Minister Plenipotentiary, displays the Wisdom of His Most Christian Majesty's Councils__. I will venture to say in one word France does not contain a Man better fitted for the People among whom he is to reside, with whom he is to Negociate, than is this Gentleman, nor have I a lower opinion of the Competency of Mons[r.] Gerards' Abilities for Negociating nor[3] of his Integrity.

The Letter which you sent for ↑to↓ the Commercial Committee was deliver'd to me by that Board and immediately presented to Congress. The House order'd it to be returned to the Committee, and that they should after full consideration make a special Report.[4] This happened yesterday Morning, Congress did not rise 'till near four o'clock P.M. this is Sunday, consequently the Report cannot be made before tomorrow, but considering the business which we have to transact with M[r.] Gerard I rather think nothing will be done in your Affair before Wednesday; to prevent anxiety therefore to yourself and perhaps some expence I submit to your Servants importunity to return, and you may be assured of hearing from me by a special Messenger without the loss of one minutes time after I shall have received the commands of Congress. And, if I form a right judgment from the sentiments of particular Members you will be convinced that Congress have in view nothing short, or that you can

---

[3] "n" written over other text.

[4] Congress resolved on August 1 that the cargoes of four vessels previously intended for John Ross be consigned to the Commissioners at Paris who were to settle Ross's accounts and then pay the balance to Roderigue Hortalez & Co. "as they judge proper." Another vessel, the ship *Virginia*, which also contained a cargo of tobacco "on public account" was to be consigned directly to the French firm. *JCC*, XI, 738-740. When HL sent Francy a copy of the resolves, Francy noted in his response that HL had chosen not to comment on the resolves and that the phrase "(as they judge proper) Seem to destroy all the good effect whch might have been expected of what precedes." HL to Théveneau de Francy, Aug. 3, 1778, PCC, Item 13; Théveneau de Francy to HL, Aug. 14, 1778.

in our present Circumstances require in favor of Monsr·
Beaumarchais, and in fulfilment of the Contract lately entered
into__ some Gentlemen who were at my House last Evening discovered much displeasure at the Orders which you say have been given
for consigning public Cargoes to M^r· Ross__ [5] I will not trouble you
with my own opinions or conjectures it would be altogether improper to do so since you are acquainted with my sentiments, and
more especially as your complaints are now before the proper
Tribunal and will very soon receive an Answer. I trust a satisfactory
answer.

I am glad you have made no purchases on my account I have
found it necessary to go into very large expences since my return to
Philadelphia for such Articles as I had[6] requested you to procure,
and the extravagant prices demanded for every species forbid
laying in double stocks__ but I would except the article of Claret
which you say is good, therefore, if it can be purchased at a price not
exceeding 30 or 32 dollars per dozen bottles, as ↑&↓ you find a good
opportunity for transporting it soon I request you to send me four
of five boxes, containing as I compute 20 dozen little more or less.
I have now an house almost as elegant as that in which I have enjoyed
the company of my friends at York Town. I shall be happy to see M^r·
Francy and to pass an opinion on his Claret.

Within the present Cover you will find two Letters for
yourself which are all that have come to my hands in your absence__
one for Versailles from Baron de Kalb two for Martinique and one
for the Cape transmitted to me by Marquis de la Fayette. for all these
I request you to procure safe and speedy passages.

Your Dispatches for Baron Steuben and Captain Landy shall
be sent forward this Morning.

I have the Honor to be / With great Respect &c.

SOURCE: LB, HL Papers, ScHi; addressed "M^r· De Francy / Williamsburg /
by James Dobbin"; dated "26th July".

---

[5] John Ross, who had gone to Europe as an agent for Willing, Morris & Co., had been hired
by the American Commissioners at Paris to obtain clothing and arms and to ship them from
Nantes. Congress was sending the public cargoes to pay for the suppplies he had purchased
which exceeded the commissioners' credit. *HL Papers*, XII, 203; *Adams Papers* (Taylor), VI, 28-
29, 80.
[6] Clerk altered "have" to "had"; HL interlined "had" for clarity.

TO JOHN LAURENS

Philadelphia, July 26, 1778

My Dear Son

Members of Congress and Citizens in general are under uncommon anxiety to hear from His Excellency the Commander in Chief__ and to learn something further than we know, of the present position of Count d'Estaing's fleet__ you know very well how I feel, we are not new acquaintance__ improve the present moment; events will be produced in due course.__ This maxim smooths much the path through Life.

Doctor Scudder is not a Free Mason,[1] you have had many escapes, but I submit it to your wisdom and Philosophy whether it be necessary to tempt the fates or to brave them, and to your friendship whether a person so dear and so much beloved, is not entitled for the sake of his Connections to ordinary protection.__ I shall never be surprised until I hear you have in one instance attended to the preservation of your Life by means which the bravest Man on Earth would not blush to adopt.

From Charlestown I learn they had lately captured Bachop a second time, and with him or in company with him in another Privateer which had long infested our Coast the very infamous Osbourne__ [2] General Howe had advanced on his march towards East Florida as far as the Bank of St. John's, the Season of the Year will not allow me to entertain very sanguine hopes of his success although the Enterprizing, never failing Colonel Williamson with 1000 of his own trusty Men were with him. I had intended to have written you a full sheet but the patience of Le Chevalier Failly who has been waiting above two hours in the Parlour must be near expiring. I have been all that time producing this scrap, six words at a time between interruptions.

P.S.

I send in the Packet with this, four Letters for yourself and sundry for Head Quarters and the Camp. I am sorry nothing lies on

[1] Dr. Nathaniel Scudder, who had returned to Congress from his Monmouth County, New Jersey home July 24, apparently informed HL of JL's daring battlefield exploits. *Delegate Letters* (Smith), X, xix; *HL Papers*, XIII, 536n.

[2] Peter Bachop and George Osborne, captains of the privateer sloops *Tonyn's Revenge* and *Ranger*, respectively, had been captured with their vessels and jailed in Charleston June 22, 1778. *HL Papers*, XIII, 484n.

me for paying my Respects to the General. I have no public commands and will not be so unkind as to take up a moment of his time with Ceremony__ but I love and pray for him.__ There is a Letter in the Packet for his Excellency the General from Don Juan De Miralis who appears to be a worthy old Castilian__³ I have much of his company.⁴

SOURCE: LB, HL Papers, ScHi; addressed "Colonel John Laurens / Head Quarters / by the Chevalier Failly"; dated "26ᵗʰ July".

FROM JOHN ADAMS

Passy, France, July 27, 1778

I thank you, my dear Sir for your kind Congratulations, on the favourable Appearances in our American Concerns, and for so politely particularising one of the most inconsiderable of them, my Safe Arrival in France, which was after a very inconvenient Passage of forty five days.¹

Your Letter to Mʳ Izzard, I had the Pleasure to send to him immediately, in Paris, where he resides, the Court of Tuscany being so connected with that of Vienna, as to discourage hitherto his Departure for Italy. He did me the Honour of a Visit Yesterday, when we had much sweet Communion ⌐as the Phrase is⌐ upon American affairs.

---

³ First "i" written over other text.
⁴ Don Juan de Miralles, ostensibly a Cuban merchant but actually a Spanish secret agent, landed at Charleston in April and proceeded overland to York where he arrived June 9. He remained close to Congress and dispatched intelligence to Madrid until his death in April 1780. *HL Papers*, XIII, 113n; *Delegate Letters* (Smith), X, 82n. For more on Miralles and other Spanish agents in America see Cummings, *Spanish Observers*.
¹ Adams recorded many of the events of the *Boston*'s crossing in his diary. They sailed from Marblehead, Mass., February 18, sighted Bourdeaux March 30, and landed April 1. He noted rough seas, seasickness, foul conditions aboard the vessel, and sea chases both as the pursuer and the pursued. Adams wrote HL immediately to report his arrival "after a most dangerous, and distressing voyage." The vessel conveying the letter was captured and word of his arrival did not reach Philadelphia until early July. Adams, *Diary*, II, 274-293; John Adams to HL, April 1, 1778, PRO, HCA 32/473; *Delegate Letters* (Smith), X, 218-219.

Your other Letter to your Daughter in Law, I have forwarded by a
safe Opportunity. You may depend upon my conveying your Letters
to any of your Friends with the best by the best Opportunities and
with Dispatch. The more of your Commands you send me the more
Pleasure you will give me.

War is not declared. that is no Manifesto has been published. but
each Nation is daily manufacturing Materials for the others Manifesto, by open Hostilities. In short, sir, the two Nations have been at
War, Since the Recal of the Ambassadors. The King of France, has
given orders to all his Ships to attack the English, and has given vast
Encouragement to Privateers.

The K. of G.B. and his Council have determined to Send Instructions to their Commissioners in America to offer Us Independency,
provided We will make Peace with them, Seperate from France.
This appears to me to be the last Effort to seduce, deceive, and
divide,— They know that every Man of Honour in America must
receive this Proposition with Indignation. an immaculate Virgin
would scarcely feel more Grief, more shame, more Horror, from
↑an↓ attempt made upon her chastity, by an old Debauchee, in a
public assembly. But they think they can get the Men of no Honour,
to join them by such a Proposal, and they think that the Men of
Honour are not a Majority.__ What has America done, to give
Occasion to that King and Council to think So unworthily of her.__?

The Proposition is in other Words this__ "America, you have fought
me untill I despair of beating you__ you have made an Alliance with
the first Power of Europe, which ↑is↓ a great Honour to your
Country and a great Stability to your Cause. So great, that it has
excited my highest Resentment, and has determined me to go to
War with France.__ Do you break your Faith with that Power, and
forfeit her Confidence, as well as that of all the rest of Mankind
forever, and join me to beat her, and ↑or↓ stand by neutre and see
me do it, and for all this I will acknowledge your Independency,
because I think in that Case you cannot maintain it, but will be an
easy Pray to me Afterwards, who am determind to break my faith
with you, as I wish you to do yours with France"__

My dear Countrymen I hope will not be allured upon the Rocks by the Syron Song of Peace.__ They are now playing, a sure Game.__ They have run all Hazards, but now they hazard nothing.

I know your ~~Avocations are~~ ↑Application is↓ incessant, and your Moments precious, and therefore that I ask a great favour in requesting your Correspondence, but the Interest of the Public as well as private Friendship induce me to do it.

I am with great Esteem your Frd & / sert.

SOURCE: LB, Adams Papers, MHi; addressed "Hon. H. Laurens Esq. / President of Congress."; dated "Passy July 27 1778".

TO WILLIAM SMITH[1]

Philadelphia, July 28, 1778

Dear Sir

I had the pleasure of writing to you a public Letter, in which was intimated, that agreeable to your request Congress had accepted your resignation of your seat at the Navy Board.[2]

It is time that I should cancel the Account which I stand indebted to you, for this purpose you will find inclosed one hundred and seventy seven dollars, which you will be pleased to pass to my Credit.

General Washington joined by General Gates is now with a very respectible Army at White Plains. Count d'Estaing finding it impracticable to enter with his large ships Sandy Hook, sailed the 21st Instant for Rhode Island. His Excellency the Commander in Chief has made large Detachments to reinforce General Sullivan, who will soon have upwards of five thousand Men. In the mean time it is said ~~G~~ the object in view, General Pigott and his Garrison are

---

[1] William Smith (1728-1814), who had served in Congress during the last three months of 1777, was the Marine Committee agent at Baltimore. HL carried on both private and public correspondence with Smith, who obtained personal goods for the president. *Delegate Letters* (Smith), VIII, xviii, 559; HL to William Smith, April 28, 1778, HL Papers, ScHi.

[2] Congress appointed William Smith a commissioner of the Navy Board in the Middle Department May 9. He requested permission to resign July 17 because he could not maintain his private business after the Board moved from Baltimore to Philadelphia. Congress accepted the resignation on July 22. *JCC*, XI, 484, 710; HL to William Smith, May 9, 1778, PCC, Item 13; Smith to HL, July 17, 1778, PCC, Item 78, Vol. 20, p. 225ff.

withdrawn and safely arrived at New York__ be it so, we shall know where to find them__ the Evacuation of Philad^{a.} and Rhode Island, the Battle of Monmouth, and the Arrival of a French fleet will operate more powerfully to ends of Peace upon the minds of our Enemies than Governor Johnstones' profer'd Gold wrought upon Congress.

The Indians Westward and Northward are exceedingly troublesome. We are beginning to be very serious with them.

I have been told of a new, neat, light English Carriage for sale at Baltimore in the hands of a Mr. Hopkins or Hopkinson,[3] and I am in great want of one__ Bringhurst of Germantown who had built one for me having refused to deliver it at the price agreed for without any better reason than that of a higher offer in these times from somebody else.[4] I request you Sir, to do me the favour to enquire for this carriage, inform me of particulars of the fashion, colour, lining &c. &c. and the Gentleman's lowest price in a Bill of Exchange or in paper Dollars.

Ɨ Have[5] ↑you↓ received a further supply of good Wines and Brandy and at what prices be so kind as to inform me which will oblige

Dear Sir / Your Respectful & Obed. Servt.

SOURCE: LB, HL Papers, ScHi; addressed "William Smith Esqr. / Baltimore"; dated "28th July".

FROM SILAS DEANE

Philadelphia, July 28, 1778

Sir

I had the honor of receiving on the 4th. of March last in a Letter from Mr. Lovell, (copy of which I now enclose),[1] the orders

---

[3] William Smith replied August 5 that he could not locate the carriage about which HL enquired. He did, however, offer other suggestions. William Smith to HL, August 5; HL to William Smith, Aug. 25 and Sept. 12, 1778.

[4] For HL's continuing frustration with John Bringhurst see *HL Papers*, XIII, 238, 251

[5] "H" written over "h".

[1] James Lovell to Silas Deane, Dec. 8, 1777, conveyed Congress's order of the same date. PCC, Item 103, p. 111; *JCC*, IX, 1008-1009.

Congress announcing my recall, and directing my immediate return.

This was the first and only intimation I ever received of the resolutions of Congress on the subject; I immediately complied with it and left Paris the first of April, with hopes of arriving in season to give Congress that intelligence, which in the order for my return they express their want of.

Unfortunately my passage has been much longer than I expected, and I but now begin to find myself recovering from the fatigues of it; yet my desire of giving Congress, as early as possible, an account of the State of their affairs in Europe when I left France, as well as the peculiar situation, in which my recall has placed me personally, has induced me to address them through your Excellency to solicit for as early an audience as the important business in which they are engaged will admit of. I have the honor to be with the most sincere respect &c.

(signed) Silas Deane

SOURCE: Copy, PCC (Item 103), DNA; no address; dated "Philadelphia 28th.

FROM JOHN LEWIS GERVAIS

Charles Town, July 29, 1778

Dear Sir,

By chance I learned that Mr Muckenfuss was to Set out early to morrow morning for Philadelphia ~~illegible~~ if I had had a little more time__ I should have troubled you with a long Letter, but I must make it short now for fear he may got to bed & I miss the oppertunity if he should rise to soon, to morrow morning for which I should be very sorry as I have several Letters for you received by the way of Bermudas which I shall Inclose, as also the last news papers__ Copy of Letter from Colonel Williamson & Mr Baillie, & some Cherokee talcks sent by Col: Hammond's desire with his respectful Compliments__ [1] I wish Congress could prevail on the North Caro-

---

[1] The packet of enclosures Gervais mentioned here has not remained intact. The copies of the Indian talks dated June 19 and 24, 1778, that HL received are in Henry Laurens

linians to be quiet, & not to disturb the Cherokees at this time__ I think the Mankillers talck one of the best Indian talcks I have seen__ Mr Hammond says he made him blush when he adressed him as one of the Commissioners that concluded the peace__ [2] I will be obliged to you to shew them to M^r_ Drayton__

Your favour of the 23^d_ June I received in bed where I was confined with a Cramp or Rhumatism I dont know which__ the news papers I distributed as you desired__ Since I received another paper of the 27th_June,__ I go about again it is now near three Weeks I have been confined__

I had also the honor to receive General Robedeau's Letter as soon as I go abroad I shall make the necessary enquiries

From all that we have seen I hope we may look for an honourable peace before next Spring.__ We have an Account of an Action that should have happened in the Jersies the 28th_ June, & ended to our advantage we wait for a Confirmation of it impatiently

General Howe returned here two days ago from his Southern expedition__

I wrote to you a few Lines this Month by Mr Carson of St Eustatia__ by which I informed you of the loss you had sustained by the death of Pompey & Tom peas in coming from Wright Savannah__ Scaramouch is to go Patroon I shall endeavour to persuade him to be honest M^{rs}_ Gervais respect wait on you and I am with a true attachment

Dear Sir Your affectionate / humble servant

John Lewis Gervais

PS Mr Belanges delivered me the two Letters which you'll find open, as he mentioned they were only Letters of recommendation, I

Correspondence, Collection 356, PHi. The letter from Andrew Williamson has not been identified but probably contained information like that included in his of July 20 to John Wells, Jr. Wells provided HL a long extract from Williamson's letter. John Wells, Jr. to HL, Juy 29, 1778. James Bailie's letter may have been his June 20 to Gervais in which he reported information about HL's southern plantations and slaves as well as the demands placed on HL's resources by American commanders during the East Florida expedition. HL Papers, ScHi.

[2] In the Indian talk dated June 19, 1778, the Cherokee chief Man Killer, or Outacity, noted that his nephew had been murdered by white people from North Carolina. He pointed to LeRoy Hammond, one of South Carolina's representatives at the signing of the Treaty of DeWitt's Corner in May 1777, and reminded him "the beloved white men of whom you were one...promised that if a Cherokee man was killed the murderer should dye for it." Indian Talk, June 19, 1778, Henry Laurens Correspondence, Collection 356, PHi; . O'Donnell, *Southern Indians*, pp. 57-58.

thought it would be necessary to see the Contents with respect to him. And am glad to find Mr Laurens is in France[3]

SOURCE: RC, Gervais Papers, in private hands; no address; dated "Charles Town 29. July 1778 / at Nine oClock__ at night."; docketed by HL "John L. Gervais / 29 July 1778 / Rec^d. 20 Aug^t.".

FROM RAWLINS LOWNDES

Charles Town, July 29, 1778

Dear Sir__

Our Expedition against Florida is at an end. Genl. Howe is arrived in Charles Town and part of his Troops the remainder are on their way, such as are able to travel, for many are Sick, and many are dead: Col^o. Williamson with the Militia under his Command from this State, I expect will recross Savanah River at Zublys Ferry[1] to Morrow on their return,; he has had the good fortune to be healthy and expects to bring back every Man he carryed out, owing in a great measure to his provident Care in supplying them properly and abundantly with all Necessarys, for while the other Troops, at some times, were obliged to eat bad rice without Meat, and at other times, Meat without either Rice or Salt, Williamsons Camp abounded with good fresh Flour and fat Beef and Bacon, and a Seasonable allowance of Rum, the difference therefore is not to be wondered at. Genl. Howe says his object was to Succour Georgia in iminent danger of being overrun with the Enemy from Florida aided with the disaffected from Carolina, and to chase the Enemy from that State, that having effected this, no other object important enough to justifye his progressing, in the then Situation of his Troops, presented itself with any probability of success or advantage, and therefore he returned.

---

[3] One of the letters recommending Louis Belanges (Bilanges) was from James Laurens, April 24, 1778. *HL Papers*, XIII, 181.

[1] The Rev. John Joachim Zubly began advertising his ferry over the Savannah River in 1769. The ferry crossed the river from the Georgia side near Ebenezer, about 22 miles above the town of Savannah, to a site on the South Carolina side about three miles above Purrysburg. *HL Papers*, VII, 120n.

Williamson having required from the General some Artillery and one hundred Regulars to manage them, and as a Condition on which he would proceed demanded that, if the General retired, the Command might devolve on Col⁰· Pinckney, And Gov'· Houston insisting that Brigadier Scriven a Militia Officer might have the Command, which not being Acceded to, therefore he Returned__

Governor Houston I beleive finding he had waded out of his depth, and certainly perplexed and Embarrassed with a good many difficulties and humours; his proposal not being Acquiesed in in Scrivens taking the Command, he therefore returned, and so they all returned, seeing and feeling at last all those impediments and Obsticles which ought and might have been foreseen at the begining of the expedition. Gen¹· Howe no doubt will send to Congress, the proceedings of the Council of War, and a particular Account of his progress, therefore it will be unnecessary to trouble you with them here, only observing, what I took the Liberty to say to Gen¹· Howe, that if his object was only to chase the Enemy from Georgia, it did not appear to me, to be a work of that difficulty as to require so much time__ the expence of this expedition will be very great, and much inhanced by the loss of horses &c. no doubt it will be a Continental Charge.

The Letters of Marque you sent me are all disposed of, every thing that carries a Gun, is Sollicitous of being in fortunes way, and taking out a Commission, which makes great demands upon me every day, and their obtaining them free of all expence gives a greater Scope to these speculative Genius's.__ I expect also, as soon as the whole Corps are returned and a little refreshed and rested that I shall be called upon to Issue Commissions on the late establishment of Congress respecting the Army, in which case I shall not have near blanks enough, and there is a great Impatience in the Gentlemen to have their Commissions in the Course of promotion. I have heard many Gentlemen express their uneasiness and apprehensions at holding Commissions Signed by M'· Hancock dated at different periods, when that Gentleman was not President, from whence some fears arises in their mind concerning their Legality in Case they should fall into the Enemies hands and the fact be proved that, at the time their Commission Issued M'· Hancock was not Empowered Officially to do any such Act. It is my Duty to represent any matter from whence any danger even by possibility may Arrise.

I have lately seen a Commission Issued by Gov$^{r.}$ Caswell of N$^{o.}$ Carolina to a Colonel Carriol a French Gentleman to Command a Regiment on Continental establishm$^{t.}$,[2] the Commission is Signed by the Gov$^{r.}$ himself, and I think runs in the name of the Congress__ this mode would effectually obviate the Impropriety and danger Suggested. I am just returned from a Visit to General Howe purposely intended to make the necessary enquiry concerning Capt Senf, agreeable to your request: General Howe Apologizes for not giving me an Ans$^{r.}$ to my Lett$^{r.}$ on that head, wrote him immediately after I had been favoured with your Commands, by saying, the Conveyances from Camp were so hazardous & precarious that he could not trust them. He now tells me that he has questioned Capt Senf on the matter, who says that he knows nothing of his own knowledge of Burguynes Treaty being Violated in any respect, that he has heard charges and Imputations of such a breach attributed to him, but does not recollect from whom, that he Cap$^{t.}$ Senf was taken Prisoner by the Americans previous to the Treaty, and Burgoyne's Surrender. Cap$^{t.}$ Senf will be in Town in a few days, and I shall make it my business to see him upon the Occasion, and if any information can be obtained that can strengthen or Corroborate the Charge you may depend Sir it shall not be delayed.[3]

A Sloop from Jamaica which Sailed out of that place in Company with a fleet of 104 Vessells under Convoy of the Southampton Capt Garnier, was lately brought into Charles Town by the Sailors (all Americans) seven in Number,[4] who took the Command, near Augustine where she was bound from the Captain & Mate and Conducted her in here together with M$^{r.}$ James

---

[2] Colonel Chariol, "a French Gentleman," received a commission from North Carolina in April 1778 to raise a regiment "composed of French Sailors and other natives of France, or the French West Indies." The North Carolina Assembly disbanded the regiment Aug. 19, 1778, because Chariol could not attract enough recruits. *State Records of North Carolina*, XII, 603, 692-693; XIII, 119-120.

[3] HL's pursuit of John Christian Senf's statement concerning the disposition of British and German regimental flags after the Saratoga Convention is discussed in *HL Papers*, XIII, 322, 478, 508-509. Senf's affidavit on the matter is printed in this volume as an enclosure with Rawlins Lowndes to HL, Aug. 16, 1778.

[4] The sloop *Dolphin*, John Roberts, sailed from Bluefield Bay, Jamaica, June 25, and was commandeered July 20 by American sailors who previously had been taken prisoner by the British. They arrived at Charleston on July 25 with the vessel and crew, James Jamieson, his wife Rebecca, their four children and Mrs. Margaret Bennet. The cargo consisted of 80 Hogsheads of rum and "other articles which are in great demand." *S.C. General Gazette*, July 30, 1778; *S.C. Gazette.*, July 29, 1778.

Jameison (and his Family) who was owner & going to reside in Augustine__ Jamieson was sent off the State last Fall, as his Principals and Practice did not at all Coalesce with our measures; he is now here without being Guilty of Treason, which a voluntary return would have subjected him to;[5] I shall send a Flag to Augustine in a few days with him and other Prisoners perhaps Bachop, but Osborne I fancy must abide a little longer with us to answer some Charges of a Criminal Complection not warranted by either Law Civil or Martial. pray Sir does the Enemy exchange our People whom they Capture in Ships of War indiscriminately with other Men or do they require Prisoners in the like Situation in Exch[a.] because both Bachop & Osborne and their Crews were in Armed Vessells purposely Equiped, and if the Enemy insist on Similarity of Circumstances as conditions in their Cartels, or lay us under any difficulties in exchanging our People we ought to know it, that our Conduct may be regulated thereby.

We have had reports for some days past from different Quarters of a general Ingagement in the Jerseys on the 28[th.] June and we are Impatient for the Confirmation. God grant that every Circumstance may Concur to bring ab[t.] a speedy Peace on the grand Basis of Independance now impossible to be relinquished, and I am happy that Events seem to open a prospect to that desireable end.

I congratulate you Sir on your Return to Philadelphia The Transitory possession of that place by the Enemy will be no great Subject of boast, but the Recovery of it must Assuredly place our Affairs on a much better footing

One John Mills a Man of Suspicious Character from his frequently appearing and disappearing in this Town has lately been taken up and Committed to our Goal.[6] he introduced himself to

---

[5] James Jamieson arrived in Charleston in May 1768 and worked briefly with HL who described him as "good natured" and "sensible" but lacking "diligence" and "application". Against HL's advice, Jamieson entered a mercantile partnership with Maurice Simons in February 1769. He married his partner's sister Rebecca in May 1773. Jamieson and 81 other prisoners—chiefly the captured crews of the privateers *Tonyn's Revenge* and *Ranger*—sailed for St. Augustine August 8 on the *Oakhampton* packet cartel. Jamieson's wife and children remained in Charleston. *HL Papers*, VI, 242, 384; VII, 261; *Gazette of the State of S.C.*, Aug. 12, 19, 1778.

[6] Probably John Mills who claimed to have come to America from Scotland in 1766 and to have arrived at Charleston by 1775. Banished in 1778, he returned during the occupation to act as Justice of the Peace, Notary Public, and organist at St. Philips. At the evacuation he went to East Florida and to England in 1785. Loyalist Transcripts, LVI, 213-220.

one Hutchinson at Camden who was Selling off his Estate in order to leave the Country to avoid taking the Test Oath,[7] he concluding from this Circumstance that Hutchinson was on the other side of the Question, as was really the Case offered him some Bills of Exch[a.] telling him that he was in the Service of Gen[l.] Howe, was employed to make discoverys in the different States, had procured plans of our Fortifications, and was furnished with Bills of Exch[a.] to raise Money for the Service of the King in the various trusts Com̃itted to him: This Story raised a Confidence in Hutchinson and left him no doubt of the goodness and Sufficiency of the Bills; he bought them and paid a very good price; but a day after some of his Friends suggesting to him that the Bills might be forgery's, he was Alarmed, pursued Mills who had left Town abrubtly, and coming up with him at Monks corner discovered that Mills had spent a good part of his Cash, had him apprehnd– and reveiled the whole transaction, and Mills now lies in Goal to be prosecuted on his own Confession as a Spy__ One Sett of the Bills are dated Philadelphia Oct[r.] 6[th.] 1777 drawn by Daniel Shaw on Mess[rs.] Champion & Dickenson Merchants in London[8] payable to the said John Mills for Eighty Six Pounds Sterling and Indorsed by Apthorp & C[o.]__[9] The other Sett are dated Jan[ry.] 4[th.] 1778 at Philadelphia, drawn by Joseph Shaw on the same persons in favour of M[r.] John Mason for £126 Sterling and indorsed by Daniel Grant. The Opinion I have formed on this matter is, that Mills affected these Connections the better to impose on the Credulity of Hutchinson and induce him to beleive that his Bills were genuine and good, as without that foundation he could not expect to get them off, and he knew he could not procure any one here to endorse them: As he is no fool, I cannot on any other Principal Account for his revealing himself and his Employment in a matter

---

[7] John Hutchinson, a native of Ireland, arrived first at Philadelphia in 1766 and at Charleston in 1774 where he set up a hop shop. He obtained land on Jackson Creek in the Camden District near Winnsboro. He remained loyal, fought with the British forces, and left South Carolina at the evacuation of Charleston. His loyalist claim for losses in South Carolina included a 750-acre plantation with house and mill in Camden District, six slaves, and livestock totaling £1,471 sterling. Loyalist Transcripts, LV, 272-282.

[8] Champion and Dickinson were among "the leading merchants exporting to Boston" on the eve of the American Revolution. Lawrence Henry Gipson, *The British Empire before the American Revolution*, XII, 134-135. The firm is last listed in the London Directories in 1794.

[9] Possibly the firm of Charles W. Apthorp in Boston.

[10] John Dorsius, a former Continental agent, had furnished wagons to transport six

of such Concern [*illegible*] & to a mere Stranger, one that he had never seen before, and trusted his Life in the hands of an Obscure Person such as Hutchinson ↑is↓. If you can Sir without much difficulty come at any knowledge respecting these Bills from the drawer or Indorser if they are known, I am desired to request you will be pleased to do it__ it may tend either to fix the guilt of forgery on Mills, or to Acquit him of the Imputation__ As to his being a Spy, true or false, he is his own Accuser, and that is the highest Evidence, from whatever motive it Arrises.__ I have been the more particular in troubling you in this Affair in order to furnish a Clue if possible to lead to some discovery. some of your Attendance may trace something out__

I had just now a Messaze from Mr. Dorcius desiring payment of a demand he has against this State for Supplying some French Gentlemen on their Journey to Congress with Cash &c^a_10 knowing we had formerly advanced a large Sum to Mr Dorcious for the use of the Continent which he was to repay & did not__ I mentioned that Circumstance to his Clerk but he very readily answered me that Mr Dorcious had placed the money he received from our Treasury to the Credit of the Continent and they were still in his Debt__ I just give a hint of this as it is so recent, because from every thing I have heard and understood I had reason to believe Mr Dorcious was greatly in Debt to the Continent, and Mr Livingston had often Complained he could not bring him to any Settlement__ indeed my Dr Sir it makes my head ach to see how the publick Treasure is wasted misapplied and how difficult it is to bring those Concerned to a proper reckoning__

Hearing that Muckinfuss is going to Congress with some Expresses of a private Nature I have taken the Opportunity to pay my Respects to you and to Assure you that I am with Unfeigned Regard

Dear Sir / Your Most Obed^t Servt.

Raw^{s.} Lowndes

P.S.
I beg my Respects to the Chief Justice.

French officers from Charleston to Philadelphia. John Dorsius to Secret Committee, Aug. 26, 1777. PCC, Item 78, Vol. 7, p. 113.

SOURCE: RC, Kendall Collection; addressed below close "His Excy Henry Laurens Esqr-"; dated below close "Chas. Town / 29th. July 1778__"; docketed by HL "Presidt. Lowndes / 29 July 1778 / Recd 19 Augt. / Ansd. 21st__". Copy (19th century), HL Papers, ScHi.

FROM JOHN WELLS, JR.

Charles Town, July 29, 1778

Dear Sir

Capt. Baddeley[1] having just informed me, that he sends Muckinfuss Express to Congress, I eagerly embrace the opportunity to do myself the honour of writing you__ I have but little time, as the Express will set out this Evening or early to morrow Morning; but I shall devote all the leisure moments I can catch, till his departure, to apprise you of our domestick occurrences__

In a former letter, I gave you reason to imagine little good would result from our southern Expedition__ I shall write you pretty fully on that head__ but I must ~~remind you,~~ ↑premise__↓ it is in confidence__

Whether or not there ever was any Expedition intended from East Florida against Georgia, is a matter in dispute__ My own opinion is, there was not__ At the same time, it was the policy of the Enemy to encourage ~~such an opinion~~ ↑a contrary one↓, as it would put us to an immense expence to collect a force to resist them, greatly injure our Army, and distract our attention__ If this was really their intention, they have certainly accomplished it at a very cheap rate__ We have got 2 small armed vessels, ~~are taken~~ ↑one of them↓ formerly belonging to ourselves, & retaken a Prize Brig, & got possession of a demolished Stockade Fort. In the latter, to be sure, we got 13 swivels, & some baggage & Clothing__ a mighty compensation for an Expence at least equal to 1500,000 dollars__ The expence is but a trifling consideration, compared with the loss

---

[1] John Baddeley (1751-1786), a Charleston merchant, was a captain in the Charleston Regiment of militia. Baddeley was captured in the fall of Charleston, paroled, then confined aboard the *Torbay* prison ship May-June, 1781. He later served three terms in the General Assembly. *Directory of the S.C. House,* III, 48.

of brave men, who might have lived to render signal services to their Country, had they not been led into those baleful regions, at this sickly season__ I have a long letter from Col. Williamson dated Camp at Great Sitillee, 20 July, wherein he tells me, that the Continental Troops at their arrival in May last at Fort Howe, amounted to at least ~~17~~ 1200 effective men__ and on 14 July they could not parade 300 men fit for duty, on their return from St Mary's. The Georgia Militia & Minute men were about 750; but they have been ~~also~~ reduced by desertion and sickness to about one half. The Militia under Col. Williamson were originally 930 effective, about 50 of which were ailing, but none had died, & he was almost certain of carrying them all home alive.__ He attributes the health ~~to~~ of those under his Command, to their being constantly in motion, when the weather would permit__ thier having abundance of good wholesome flour and thier having, in very hot or rainy weather a gill of rum dealt out to each, & half that quantity when the weather was moderate__

Here we are told, there were no fewer than four Commanders in chief__ Gen. Howe__ Governour Houstoun__ Col. Williamson__ and Commodore ↑Bowen↓__ [2] The first claimed the chief command, in virtue of his Continental Commission__ The second being lately appointed Captain General of the Georgia forces, in his opinion gave him a rank superior to that of ~~the~~ a Continental Major General__ Col Williamson commanded the Carolina Militia, & endeavoured to accommodate all differences__ & Commodore[3] Bowen commanded in the naval department__ I shall here give you an extract from the Colonel's Letter to me__

"I continued my march to join the Governour of Georgia, who had advanced to St. Mary's, at the pressing instance of General Howe. On the 11th July I arrived on the banks of that river, & next day ~~the~~ crossed it, with the troops under my command. It was here

---

[2] The Georgia Assembly named Oliver Bowen "Commodore or Commander" of the Georgia navy in January 1777. The Georgia navy was actually an adjunct of the state's army in which Bowen held the rank of colonel. During the East Florida expedition Bowen claimed that because the state's regiments had been taken under the Continental establishment he answered not to the state but to the Continental command. After the expedition the Georgia executive council suspended him for contempt. Coleman, *American Revolution in Ga.*, pp. 111-112; John Houstoun to HL, Aug. 20, 1778.
[3] "ado" written over "and".

I was first certainly informed of the differences that subsisted between[4] the Governour & General. I proposed a meeting at some place, where an open conference should be held, in order to accommodate & amicably put an end to this dispute; and in order that the sentiments of the Army should be more fully known, the Field Officers of every regiment should also be summoned to attend__ We all accordingly met on the 12th, when General Howe fully opined to the Meeting the state of the Continental Troops, and his intention of immediately returning from East Florida, whose Climate had been so fatal to the army. In this opinion he was supported by all his field officers__ To divert his attention from that resolution, I offered, on his assisting us with a train of Artillery["] [it must have been a very small one][5] "and about 100 of his men capable of managing it, either to proceed under his Command or, if he did not think it an object of ~~im~~ sufficient importance to go himself, Col Pinckney's, as far as St John's__ which must have bounded our operation; as we could not secure the command of the river. Unfortunately the Governour of Georgia and his Council of War dessented[6] from this proposal, ꝉ having resolved that on Gen. Howe's granting the artillery and men requested of him, these, with the detachment from my troops and the Georgia Minutemen & Militia, should proceed on the enterprise, under the command of a Brig. Gen. Screven, of their Militia, a man probably brave but without experience. This Circumstance afforded Gen. Howe an excellent apology for[7] putting his resolution of retreating into execution__ He accordingly embarked with some of his troops & baggage from Fort Tonyn, and sent the rest by land, the 15th inst. As our situation and want of artillery rendered us incapable of under-taking any opperation of more consequence, than to convince the Enemy we were ready, and only soght an opportunity to fight them, the Governour & myself agreed to detach from our different brigades, a strong party to scour the country. I accordingly sent off for that purpose 326 Choice[8] troops, and the Governour about 140,

---

4 "b" written over other text.
5 Square brackets used by Wells.
6 Wells wrote "dessenting" then interlined "ed" without cancelling "ing".
7 "f" written over "p".
8 "C" written over "t".

under the Command of Major Pickens,[9] whose activity and diligence on former occasions, justly entitled him to this mark of notice; especially as it fell to my share, on drawing lots with the Governour, to appoint the officer to command the party. He proceeded 20 miles towards St John's, but finding the bridges all broke down, and large trees felled across the roads, to impede our troops advancing, and having also received certain intelligence that the Enemy's sole intention was to harrass our troops on the march, and then retreat across St John's, he judged it most advisable to return. One of his small parties fell in with the two McGirths,"[10] (Schovolites from St Mark's Parish) "and some Indians, whom they immediately fired upon__ The Enemy secured themselves in a swamp, leaving 4 horses & some other articles, which fell into our people's hands. This small rencounter has disappointed the Enemy hanging on our rear, and trying to carry off Horses, as they no doubt intended, and enables us to retreat without molestation"__

I must here observe that the Colonel needed not to have sent Major Pickens to gain the Knowledge he mentions, as Col.[11] C.C. Pinckney, in a Council of War, urged those very arguments for an immediate Return Northward__ If the Militia think or affect to think the Regulars were rather averse to proceeding, from an ↑ill grounded↓ apprehension of danger, the latter are up with them, as they ascribe the keenness of the former to proceed, to no other motive whatever but a desire for plunder__ At any rate, & let the matter be viewed in whatever light you please, all parties I seem to answer in heartily condemning Gen H who they say is totally incapable of any Command__ And if I can depend on what I every day hear, it would appear, that removing him from Carolina would ↑be↓ highly[12] acceptable to the Army; nor would one think, very disagreeable to himself__ It is not improbable but you may hear from other quarters on this subject__ I am told W.H.D. has sent a Copy of a certain General's letter written on the resignation of a

---

[9] Andrew Pickens.

[10] Daniel McGirt, son of a prominent Camden merchant, was a notorious Loyalist who fled to East Florida and whose irregulars had by 1779 become comparable to the backcountry bandit gangs of the 1760s. Rachel N. Klein, *Unification of a Slave State* (Chapel Hill, N.C., 1990), p. 98.

[11] "C" written over "M".

[12] "highly" written over "be".

brother General Officer, which the latter says is very different from what he was told__ and that Copies of it are handed about, with remarks & annotation__[13] So that, what with one thing and another, the Person alluded to, has certain enough in his hands__

The accounts we hear from the North afford a most pleasing Contrast to what I have been just writing. I am in great hopes authentick intelegence of the defeat of Sir Henry Clinton, will be received before my Paper is published__

Inclosed I send you Timothy's, Crouch's & my ~~own~~ latest Papers__[14] also two Sheets of Dr Ramsays Oration delivered July 4th__ The whole will be published next Monday[15]

The Papers are sent regularly by the Post, & I hope ~~reaching~~ are received in the same manner. The last Letter I was honoured with from you is dated 31 May; since which I have received two Pennsylvania Gazettes which you were kind enough to send me__

You will be pleased to shew Mr Walton the Extract I have[16] given from Col. Williamsons letter, and any other part of this you ~~please~~ may think proper__

As far as I know, R.W.P's ~~voyage~~ ↑going↓ to Augustine, ~~was undertaken be~~ arose from leave being granted to George Ancrum junʳ and George Cooke ~~having obtained Leave~~ to go there in the Cartel__ He, the day before the Cartel sailed applied for & obtained

---

[13] Gen. Robert Howe's Aug. 28, 1777, letter to Congress reported Gen. Christopher Gadsden's resignation of his Continental commission. The letter was presented and accepted in Congress Oct. 2, 1777. Gadsden received a copy of Howe's letter from William Henry Drayton June 27, 1778, annotated it, and sent it with his July 4 reply to Drayton. *Writings of Christopher Gadsden* (Walsh), pp. 134-144.

[14] Peter Timothy resumed the *S.C. Gazette* in June 1778 after publication had been halted by the Jan. 15, 1778, Charleston fire. Mary Crouch, widow of Charles Crouch who had previously published the *South=Carolina Gazette and Country Journal*, established the *Charlestown Gazette* in July or August 1778. John Hammond Moore, *South Carolina Newspapers* (Columbia, S.C., 1988), pp. 44, 50, 56; *HL Papers*, XII, 333n; XIII, 162.

[15] Wells announced in his August 6 number of the *S.C. General Gazette* that he had, at his printing office in Tradd Street, David Ramsay's "Oration on the Advantages of American Independence; spoken before a Public Assembly of the Inhabitants of South Carolina, on the second Anniversary of that glorious Æra." Ramsay, a native of Lancaster County, Pa., had attended the College of New Jersey, studied with Dr. Benjamin Rush, and graduated from the College of Philadelphia before opening a medical practice in Charleston in 1773 or 1774. He partcipated in the whig politics of the day and associated most often with radicals such as Christopher Gadsden, to whom he dedicated the oration. Arthur H. Shaffer, *To Be An American, David Ramsay and the History of the American Consciousness* (Columbia, S.C., 1991), pp. 12-16, 20-22, 50-52.

[16] "v" written over "g".

leave to go in her, in order to settle some Concerns the ~~Company~~ House he was a Partner of, had there__ Mr Ancrum went in quest of some Clothes taken by Powell's Privateer__ They were ↑taken↓ on board a schooner, coming from Georgetown__ Mr Cooke went to collect or settle some debts__ Ancrum got his Clothes, Cooke got his business settled not altogether to his satisfaction__ I know not what success Powell had__ However Report has said he obtained a protection for any vessel he might be on board, but I can not think Tonyn could give any such thing__ Be that as it may he is among those "compelled to depart the State" & sailed in a schooner with Dr Skene, George Ogilvie, George Duncan, Edward Oats &c about 10 days ago for St Eustatius[17]

I have the honour to be Dr Sir, with Respect / Your most obedient servant

Jno Wells jun^r

SOURCE: RC, Kendall Collection; no address; dated "Charlestown 29 July 1778"; docketed by HL "John Wells 29 July 1778. / Rec^d 19 Aug^t-".

TO ALEXANDER WRIGHT[1]

Philadelphia, July 30, 1778

Dear Sir

I have been honor'd with your favor of the 11th Inst. and beg you'l accept my thanks for the two Letters from my youngest Son you are not pleas'd to intimate any thing respecting your own present circumstances. I know your delicacy, and therefore without

---

[17] Robert William Powell, George Ancrum, the younger, and George Cooke were all well-known Charleston merchants. Though an early supporter of the Whigs in Charleston, Powell abandoned them; Cooke remained loyal to the Whigs until the British occupation in Charleston; and Ancrum apparently remained steadfast throughout the Revolution. *Directory of the S.C. House,* III, 582; *HL Papers,* V, 599n. The *S.C. Gazette,* July 15, 1778, listed the following as passengers aboard the schooner *Trail,* John Hayes, which sailed July 14 for St. Eustatius: Dr. James Skeene, George Duncan (wine merchant), Edward Oats (vendue master), Hugh Pollock (saddler), Thomas Harper (silversmith), Thomas Inglis (merchant), John Coram (shopkeeper), the Rev. Edward Jenkins, Henry Reeves, and Robert William Powell (merchant). George Ogilvie was not included on the list.

[1] Alexander Wright, second son of Georgia Royal Governor James Wright, had worked in HL's counting house in the 1760s. He remained loyal and fled S.C. for much of the Revolution. His wife and three sons remained in S.C. *HL Papers,* V, 516.

an application I am prompted by my friendship and Regard to request you will let me know by the earliest opportunity if by any means I can contribute to your happiness.

At present I think it necessary to transmit a Certificate which you will find here inclosed.[2] It has at least the quality of Innocence, and may possibly be of use. I request you Sir, to intimate to Captain Pond[3] that he will find me disposed to render him every service which I may with propriety in our respective circumstances and that I shall be glad to hear from him.

If on your return to South Carolina you shall take this City in your way, I beg you will do me the favor to call first at my house in Chesnut Street, nearly opposite the State House, and that you will there think yourself at home and look for no other lodging. I believe you will meet as good Bed and Board as at any Inn in Philadelphia and no where a more hearty welcome.

I am with great Regard / Your Affectionate Humble Serv.

SOURCE: LB, HL Papers, ScHi; addressed "Alexander Wright Esq. / Norwich, committed to the particular care / of Dodd"; dated "30th July".

TO GEORGE WASHINGTON

Philadelphia, July 31, 1778

I Am this minute favor'd with Your Excellency's very obliging Letter of the 24th.

The British Commissioners, for, in the Act of one, there is good ground for charging the whole, having by various means attempted to bribe Congress have ↑and thereby↓ offer'd the highest

---

[2] The clerk copied the following enclosure below the text: "I Certify that Alexander Wright Esq. Citizen of the State of South Carolina obtained Permission in writing to leave that State and to proceed from thence to Europe on his own private concerns when I was Vice President of that State. That he had always acted with propriety and was held to be a friend to the liberties of the United States of America. / That Mr. Wright is a Man of Probity and Honor and possess'd ↑of↓ a large landed Estate in So. Carolina. / Philadelphia 30th July / 1778".

[3] William Pond, master of Le Despenser packet, plied the Charleston-Falmouth route in the 1770s. Pond and his vessel were captured by the Nancy and another American privateer earlier in the summer of 1778. HL Papers, XII, 40; Documents of the American Revolution (Davies), XIII, 324.

possible affront to the Representatives of a virtuous, Independent People, are in my humble opinion rendered wholly unworthy of the further regard of Congress in their Ambassadorial character.

Viewing them in this light I have been from the first reading of their last Address[1] under that kind of anxiety which ↑had↓ possessed my Mind when there was some cause ↑for↓ apprehending that General Burgoyne and his Troops would have slipt thro' our fingers into New York or Philadelphia, an anxiety to which I am a stranger, except upon ↑in↓ such momentous occasions concerns.

I have for several days past urged my friends to move Congress to ↑for a↓ Resolve that they will hold no conference with such Men, setting forth their ↑assigning↓ reasons in ample, decent terms__ ↑to↓ transmit the Act by a flag to the Commissioners, and make them the bearers of their own indictment; they will not dare to withhold the Resolve of Congress from their Court. Thence it will soon descend to the Public at large, and expose themselves and their Prompters to the just resentment of a ↑deluded and↓ much injured people Nation, whose deplorable circumstances I must confess deeply affects my heart. These ↑Commissioners↓ will be also held up in scorn at every Court in Europe, and finally be transmitted to Posterity in Characters which will render ↑mark↓ their Memory with Infamy.[2]

I am not ↑commonly↓ tenacious of my own Ideas, but in the present, as in the former case alluded to, I feel as if I clearly perceived many good effects which will be produced by a proper Act on our part__ justice is due to our own Characters, to the present age of[3] America and future Generations will with much satisfaction

---

[1] Carlisle Commission to HL, July 11, 1778.
[2] HL interlined the following note at this point: "☛ See a paragraph at foot to follow this." The paragraphs, in the clerk's hand, are:
"An immediate display of the intended bargain and sale will discourage the impudent, polemic Writers on American Affairs in London, or, invalidate their bold assertions and give force to the declarations of Congress.
"If we leave the story to be related by ↑after↓ Governor Johnstone's departure from this Continent, he will confidently deny the fact and how few in the World will be thenceforward well informed? Attack him Letters in hand upon the spot, his guilt will be fix'd from his own confession, for he cannot deny."
[3] "of" written over "if".

~~read~~ ↑dwell in↓ history ~~of~~ ↑upon↓ the transactions of Congress with these corrupt insidious ~~Commissioners~~ Emissaries.[4]

If a predilection to my fellow Citizens when standing in competition with strangers, of no more than equal merit, be criminal, I must own myself not free from guilt.

From habit I am disposed to give countenance to strangers, and I have besides, endeavoured, for obvious reasons, to be civil to such French gentlemen as have called upon me, hence my conduct had been mistaken, and I discover'd at a certain time that my friends had expressed doubts whether my courtesy had not been carried to excess__ I had the happiness soon to convince them that good manners and plain dealing were not incompatible__ upon this occasion I intreat Your Excellency will excuse the freedom which I take of sending with this, extracts of Letters written by me in answer to applications from foreign Gentlemen for employment and promotion in the Army; the same sentiments have always governed my replies in private oral importunities, I have carefully avoided amusing or flattering any of them.

I have often regretted the hesitation and indecision of our Representatives; on some occasions, and perhaps as often, their precipitancy ↑on others↓ respecting foreign Officers__ as a free Citizen I hold myself warranted to speak with decent freedom of ↑the conduct of↓ those whom I have appointed my attornies, respectful animadversion tends to produce reformation.

From the fluctuations which I allude to, have sprung, ~~many~~ to speak in the mildest terms, many inconveniencies, Your Excellency's experience may call them Evils.__ The dilemma to which we are now reduced in the case of the elder Lanuville, is one instance; if encouragements, tantamount to promises are of any weight this Gentleman must receive a Brevet to rank Brigadier General the middle of ~~this~~ ↑next↓ Month__ at his first arrival he

---

[4] On August 11, Congress issued a declaration on the conduct of George Johnstone in his attempts to bribe Robert Morris and Joseph Reed. With a series of resolutions Congress explained its position that "the conduct of the said George Johnstone, Esq. in the aforesaid particulars, unavoidably effects his colleagues in commisson and unfavourably impresses the mind, so that full confidence cannot be placed in them." A resolution "that Congress will not, in any degree, negotiate with the present British commissioners in America, for restoring peace" failed by a seven to three vote. HL and the majority of the South Carolina delegation voted for the resolution. *JCC*, XI, 770-774.

presented a Memorial in which was set forth the vast expence which had attended his voyage and journey to York Town. He solicited the grade abovementioned or ↑or↓[5] an immediate negative; intimating that in the latter case he would return to his ~~illegible~~ ↑own↓[6] Country__ a direct Answer was not return'd, he was amused from time to time: an increase of expence ~~had~~ ↑and the plea of flattering hopes↓ strengthened his claim. At length he was put into a state of probation. Certificates which he produced of his ~~behav~~ abilities and assiduities in the character of "<u>Inspector of the Northern Army</u>" were ~~illegible~~ expressed in terms somewhat higher than merely favorable__ I eyed the Paper signed by General Parsons with some degree of jealousy as I read it, but it did not become me to paraphrase, and it passed unnoticed by every body else.[7] On this ground I have said, he must obtain the[8] Brevet in a few days; you would smile Sir, if I were to repeat the principle upon which the delay is founded. This Gentleman is now gone ↑with an intention↓ to act as a Volunteer in the suite of Marquis de la Fayette, and if I understand him, he means soon to return to France.

The Younger de lanuville your Excellency is informed has obtained a Brevet to rank Major,__ what title had he to this promotion? Were I to draw ~~him~~ ↑the Gentleman↓ into comparison with Major Gibbs[9] and many other worthy Officers, I should answer, none. But ~~illegible~~ ↑he has↓ only a Brevet. Your Excellency is appriz'd of the restrictions on that kind of Commission by an Act of Congress of the 30th of April[10] and I trust the good sense of my Countrymen will lead them to reflect and distinguish properly, and to make some allowances.

---

[5] Interlineation by HL.

[6] Interlineation by HL.

[7] Chevalier de la Neuville presented a June 21 certificate from Gen. Samuel H. Parsons which noted the inspector general of the Northern Department's industry, diligence, military knowledge, manners, decency, and modesty and concluded that he had performed duties "with uncommon assiduity and unremitted application." La Neuville also offered a July 24 endorsement from Gen Horatio Gates who recognized his "diligence and ability". PCC, Item 41, Vol. 5, p. 328ff.

[8] "this" altered to "the".

[9] Caleb Gibbes, the captain of General Washington's guard, had been promoted to the rank of major July 29. HL to Caleb Gibbes, July 30, 1778, PCC, Item 13; *HL Papers*, XIII, 461n.

[10] The April 30 restriction limited officers "who shall be honored with a brevet commission" to the same rank they previously held and clearly stated that the brevet rank only applied on special "detachments from the line, and in general courts martial." Further the officer was not entitled to any additional pay from such brevet promotions. *JCC*, X, 410.

Your Excellency will discover in one or more of the extracts the strong desire of French Gentlemen for printed Commissions. I dont know what peculiar advantage they might have had in view, but in opposition to them and even to some attempts here, I have always confin'd myself to the mode of a simple Certificate in pursuance of the Resolve of Congress referr'd to in each case.

In the first conversation I had the honor of holding with Mons[r.] Gerard; with a view of learning what reception those French Gentlemen had met, who had return'd some 8 or 9 ↑eight or nine↓[11] months ago, murmuring and dissatisfied to France; I took occasion to signify my concern for the disappointment which some of them had suffer'd, and in honor of Congress made brief recitals of Commissions granted to many French Officers now in the Army, observing that it had been impossible to gratify the wishes of every one for promotion. M[r.] Gerard reply'd, His Court had seen with pain so many Frenchmen applying for permission to resort to the American Army, and that very few had receiv'd encouragements; the Court were sensible that crowds of foreigners pressing for Commissions would tend to embarrass Congress, that since his arrival at Philad[a.] he had been solicited in many instances for recommendations, every one of which, he had refused to listen to, and added, I might rest satisfied, Congress would never be troubled with Petitions under his auspices. In this sensible declaration methinks I discern sound Policy, be that as it may it will in some measure relieve Congress__ I most earnestly wish our noble friend the Marquis could be persuaded to adopt the determinations of Mons[r.] Gerard.

Very soon after I shall have the pleasure of conversing with Baron Stüben, his pursuits in the journey to Court will be known to me. I shall be equally explicit on my part and your Excellency shall be as candidly informed, if it ~~shall~~ ↑should↓ shall appear to↓[12] be necessary.[13] ~~to troubl~~

---

[11] Interlineation by HL.

[12] Interlineation by HL.

[13] Baron von Steuben intended to resign as inspector general and seek a field commission. He had been given a temporary command in early July because of a shortage of field generals during Charles Lee's court martial, but on July 22 Washington ordered him to resume his office as inspector general. Von Steuben accepted the staff position when it became obvious

On Thursday the sixth of August Congress will receive Monsr· Gerard in his public character. Your Excellency will find within copies of the intended Address of the Minister and Answer of the Representatives of the thirteen United States of America__[14] speaking as a Citizen I cannot forbear disclosing to you, Sir, that there is a reluctance in my Mind to acknowledgments of obligation or of generosity where benefits have been, to say the least, reciprocal__ this opinion has not been form'd since I ~~had~~ read the Address and Answer, as I am warranted to say from the Extract of a Letter to Monsr· Du Portail.[15]

After hours of disputation shall be exausted ~~in discussion~~ the point will remain moot.__

Among other Papers I take the liberty of inclosing copy of a curious performance of M^r· Maduit which is believed to be genuine.[16] If he is not delirious in the present time, his friends must conclude that he was raving from 1774 to the commencement of the present Year, time employed by him in dinning the Coffee houses with his cries against the Inhabitants of these States and against their Claims, down with America!__ I will not further presume on Your Excellency's moments but to repeat that I continue with the most sincere and respectful attachment and the highest Esteem.

Sir / Your Excellency's &c.

SOURCE: LB, HL Papers, ScHi; addressed "General Washington / White Plains / by Ross"; dated "31st July".

---

that Congress would support Washington's decision and more clearly define von Steuben's authority over all other inspectors in the army. Congress approved the new instructions for the Inspector General Feb. 18, 1779. Palmer, *Von Steuben*, pp. 190-196; *JCC*, XIII, 196-200.

[14] On July 16 Conrad-Alexandre Gérard sent Congress a copy of the speech he intended to give at his official reception. An answer prepared by a committee composed of Richard Henry Lee, Gouverneur Morris and John Witherspoon proved to be unacceptable to Congress and a second committee Joseph Reed, Francis Dana, and John Witherspoon "brought in a new draught, which was taken into consideration and agreed to" July 30. *JCC*, XI, 695, 730, 733, 753-757.

[15] In his letter of May 20, 1778, to Louis DuPortail, HL had strongly opposed DuPortail's view that America should acknowledge its "obligation" to France. *HL Papers*, XIII, 334.

[16] Israel Mauduit, a prosperous London woolen-draper and frequent unofficial colonial agent, anonymously published a handbill in London in March 1778 calling for British recognition of American independence. Mauduit was believed to be an unofficial spokesman for the North administration. Robert J. Taylor, "Israel Mauduit," *The New England Quarterly*, XXIV (1951), 208-230.

FROM CAESAR RODNEY

Dover, Del., July 31, 1778

I verry lately Received your favour, of the tenth Instant, Concerning the Confederation, which is the first application of Congress, on this head, to the General Assembly of this State and is the reason assigned me, by several of the members, why it was not taken into Consideration heretofore—The General Assembly of this State will, by adjournment, meet in this place the tenth day of August next, when I shall Lay your letter before them as Requested. I Shall urge them to as Speedy a determination as its Importance will admit of, and will cause their Resolutions thereon to be Transmitted to the Delegates of this State to be laid before Congress.[1]

SOURCE: Printed in Ryden, *Caesar Rodney*, p. 278; no address; dated "Dover July the 31st 1778".

FROM MATTHEW CLARKSON

Philadelphia, August 1, 1778

Sir

At the time Congress were pleased to honor me with the appointment of <u>an Auditor of Accounts of the main Army</u>, I was possessed of the Commission of Marshal of the Court of Admiralty for the State of Pennsylvania, which I still hold. My duty in that Office now claims my attention. I am therefore constrained to tender a resignation of the other, which I beg Congress will be pleased to accept, with my most grateful acknowledgements for their past favors.

I have the honor to be with ↑the↓ most perfect esteem, / Sir / Your most obed.t. serv.t.

Matth Clarkson

---

[1] The Delaware legislature did not determine to empower its delegates to ratify the Articles of Confederation until late January 1779. Thomas McKean, the state's sole delegate, signed for Delaware Feb. 23, 1779. Jensen, *Articles of Confederation*, p. 197; *JCC*, XIII, 150, 186-188, 236.

SOURCE: RC, PCC (Item 78), DNA; addressed on cover "His Excellency Henry Laurens Esquire / President of Congress.__"; addressed below close "His Excellency / Henry Laurens Esquire"; dated "Philadelphia August 1ˢᵗ· 1778."; franked "On public service"; docketed "Letter from / Matthew Clarkson / dated Augsᵗ 1 1778 / requesting leave to / resign."

FROM JOHN SULLIVAN

Providence, R.I., August 1, 1778

Dear Sir,

I have the honor to transmit to Congress, the particulars of my Proceedings, since I receiv'd General Washingtons Orders, to co-operate with the Count Destaign against the Enemy, on Rhode-Island.__[1] At that time my Magazines were empty, but few Troops, and scarcely any Boats to effect an embarkation, I immediately wrote to the several New England States, calling upon them in the most pressing Terms, to supply me with Men and Provisions,[2] and I have the pleasure to assure you, that their exertions exceed my expectations;__ The Magazines will be sufficiently large, to supply the number of Troops I shall have, and with the standing Forces in this department, the several Quotas of Militia, and the Reinforcement from the Grand Army, I make no doubt, I shall have a Force sufficient, with the assistance of the French Fleet & Army, to ensure me Success. I have collected a great number of Boats, and the Carpenters are indefatigable in building more, so that I think, I may venture to assure you, that I shall have a Number sufficient to transport my whole Army at the same time. On the 29ᵗʰ· Ultimo, the

[1] Washington's first orders to General Sullivan concerning the French fleet were included in his letter of July 17 in which he informed Sullivan of the fleet's arrival. Washington noted that no specific plan had been determined but that Rhode Island appeared to be a likely area for the first joint action. He directed Sullivan to apply for 5,000 men from Rhode Island, Massachusetts and Connecticut, to "establish suitable Magazines of provisions" and to "make a collection of Boats." Washington also ordered him to "engage a number of Pilots" to assist the French fleet. *Washington Writings* (Fitzpatrick), XII, 184-185.

[2] In preparation for battle in Rhode Island, Sullivan requested reinforcement troops from Rhode Island, Massachusetts, New Hampshire and Connecticut. *Sullivan Papers* (Hammond), II, 97-98, 102, 107, 110-111.

Count's Fleet arrivd, and anchor'd off the light House in Naraganset Bay, the next morning, two Ships, one of Sixty four Guns, and the other of fifty, were sent up the western Passage, between the Island of Connecticut and the Main, with a view, to capture two Frigates, that lay in that Channel between Prudence,[3] and Conanicut, but they on approach of the Ships, turn'd the point of the Island, and stood into the Harbour of Newport. Upon this Island, the Enemy had two Regiments of Anspach and Colonel Fannings Corps of New-York Volunteers[4] encampd. A small Battery fird upon the fifty Gun Ship as she pass'd, but She return'd it with a Broad side, which effectually silencd the Battery and before the Sixty four passd, they blew up their Magazine, and the three Regiments decamp'd and crossd over to Rhode-Island. Two ~~Regiments~~ Frigates were likewise sent round to Seconnet Point, to block up the eastern Channel in this River, the Enemy had two Gallies, and the King Fisher Sloop of War, which upon the approach of the Frigates, were set on fire and blown up.__ The Destruction[1] of the Sloop, and the Gallies, is a very capital advantage to us, as there is nothing now to obstruct our Landing, but a Battery upon the Shore, which can be easily silenc'd by the French Shipping.__ This disposition of the French Admiral, will convince your Excell^y· by a Survey of the Map, that the Enemy are compleatly block'd up; And my Preparations are in such forwardness, that ~~I expect~~ I shall doubtless, be able to make a Landing in the course of next week. In the interim,

    I have the honor to be, with the / greatest respect, / Y^r· obed^t· humble Servt

Jno Sullivan

SOURCE: RC, PCC (Item 160), DNA; addressed below close "The Hoñble / Henry Laurens Esqre·"; dated "Head Quarters Aug^t· 1st· Providence ↑1778↓"; docketed "Letter from gen^l Sullivan / Providence Aug. 1. 1778 / Read 10.".

---

[3] "Providence" altered to "Prudence".

[4] The 1st Regiment Anspach-Beyreuth, commanded by Col. F.A.V. Voit von Salzburg, and the 2nd Regiment Anspach-Beyreuth, commanded by Col. F.J.H.W.C. von Seybothen, had been sent to Newport, R.I., in July 1778. The King's American Regiment, under Col. Edmund Fanning, also had been sent to Newport in July. Katcher, *British Army Units*, pp. 88-89, 108.

FROM J. ROCQUETTE, T.A. ELSEVIER, & P. TH. ROCQUETTE

Rotterdam, August 3, 1778

Sir;

What preceeds is copÿ of our Last respects to you of the 21ˢᵗ april this goes bÿ our Intimate Friend Mʳ· Izard,[1] of charles Town, who passes hence to America by way of our Islands; Give us Leave to remind our house in your most valuable protection, and to Congratulate you upon the Eminent Post you occupy in Congres. we'll be very happy to be Employ'd by itt, and if we can render to you, or any of your friends any Services here, we'll be proud to receive yʳ· or theyr Commands, be assured of our readiness to Execute them.

Severall parcells of Tobacco are arrived by way of our Islands, which made the prices drop virginia Sells now 11 $1/4$. a 11 $3/4$ maryland 11 $3/4$ a 12 $1/2$.~ Rice 44 ß[2] Indigo according to quality.

Tho there is no ↑publicy↓ declaration of warr yett publish'd between France & England nevertheless the hostilities that continue to go on on both Sides make every body look upon warr[3] as declared. Severall men of warr have been taken on both Sides, Privateers of Both Nations are at Sea, and make as much prises as they Can, there has nott yett been an action between the Two Eminent fleets, that are at Sea butt itt is Generally Expected we'll Soon receive accounts of a battle between them

We remain with respectfull regards / Sir: / Your verÿ humble servants

J. Rocquette T.A. Elsevier, & P.Th. Rocquette

SOURCE: RC, Gratz Collection, PHi; addressed on cover "To / Henry Laurens Esqʳ· / at / Charlestown / South Carolina"; dated "Rotterdam 3ᵈ August 1778"; docketed by HL "Roquette Elziver & / Roquette 21 Ap 3 Augs / 1778 Recᵈ· 22 Janʸ 1779".

---

[1] Walter Izard (175?-1788), the youngest son of Ralph Izard (d. 1761) and Rebecca Blake, returned from Europe in November 1778. Rogers, *Evolution of a Federalist*, p. 82; *Directory of the S.C. House*, III, 375-376.

[2] Symbol may stand for barrel.

[3] "w" written over other text.

FROM JOHN RUTLEDGE

Charles Town, August 3, 1778

Sir__

The Bearer, Baron de Randerode de Thuilliers,[1] arrived, with Monsr. Britigny & other Officers, from France, last Summer, at this Town, in their way to Philadelphia, where they purposed offering their Services, in the military Line, to Congress__ They embarked, from hence, for Virginia__ He says, they were taken, on their Voyage, by the Carysfort, & carried to St. Augustine__[2] that his Fellow-Passengers are still Prisoners there, but that, he having thrown overboard his recommendatory Letters, not wearing a military Garb, & affecting the Character of a Trader, was permitted, after being detained for several Months, to go to St. Domingo, from whence he went to N^{o.} Carolina, & from thence he came hither, thinking it necessary to obtain a Line, from me, to Congress, to signify that I had seen the Letters which he says he destroyed__ I wish, that I c^d recollect, more perfectly than I do, the Substance of 'em, However, I remember, they were from Dr. Franklin, to Genl. Washington, & the Secret Committee, or Board of War, & mentioned this Gentleman's being well recommended to him, as an Officer of Experience & Merit__[3] Probably M^{r.} drayton may recollect more of the Matter than I can, as he had, & read in Council, the several Credentials, & Letters, which Monsr. Britigny & his Officers brought with them.

I have the Honour to be with great Respect Sir / y^{r.} most hble Servt.

J: Rutledge

SOURCE: RC, Americana Collection, NSDAR; addressed below close "The Hoñble Henry Laurens Esq. / Presid^{t.} of the Congress"; dated "Cha^{s:} Town August 3^{d:} 1778"; docketed "J. Rutledge Charlestown / 3^d August. 1778 / Rec'd 11th October".

---

[1] Baron Randrode de Thuillière had been mentioned by Rutledge in a November 1777 letter. He had a two-year leave from the Deux-Ponts regiment in which he had served as a captain since 1769. He did not obtain an American commission and returned to France where he rejoined his regiment. He returned to America with Rochambeau and fought in Rhode Island in 1780. *HL Papers*, XII, 35; *Franklin Papers* (Labaree), XXIV, 148n.

[2] The Marquis de Brétigney and several other French officers were captured on their voyage northward from Charleston in November 1777. *HL Papers*, XII, 17n.

[3] Benjamin Franklin's June 11, 1777, letter introducing Thuillière to George Washington

FROM GEORGE WASHINGTON

Headquarters, White Plains, N.Y., August 3, 1778

Sir

I do myself the honor of transmitting to Congress a copy of a Letter from General Knox, and of sundry observations and remarks on the Ordnance establishment of the 11th of Feby, which I received about the time we marched from Valley Forge. These would have been transmitted before, had it not been for the moving state of the Army and a variety of other Objects which engrossed my attention. We have found by experience, that some inconveniences have resulted from the Establishment, which I conceive, have proceeded principally from the total independence of the Commissary General of Military stores, on the Commanding Officer of Artillery. It seems some alterations are necessary and what they shall be, Congress will be pleased to determine.[1]

It is not without reluctance that I am constrained, to renew my importunities on the subject of the Committee of Arrangement. The present unsettled state of the Army is productive of so much disatisfaction and confusion and of such a variety of disputes, that almost the whole of my time is now employed, in finding temporary and inadequate expedients to quiet the minds of the Officers and keep business on a tolerable sort of footing. Not an hour passes without New applications and New complaints about rank__ and for want of a proper adjustment of this and many other essential points__ our Affairs are in a most irksome and injurious train. We can scarcely form a Court Martial__ or parade a Detachment in any instance, without a warm discussion on the subject of precedence__

---

noted that the French officer had experience and spoke both German and English. *Franklin Papers* (Labaree), XXIV, 147-148.

[1] Knox observed in his June 15 letter that under the ordnance establishment of Feb. 11, 1778, as head of the artillery department, he had been placed in the awkward position of not having command over the commissary general of military stores. He noted that in Europe and Britain, his counterparts had authority over the commissaries who furnished materiel for the artillery. Knox enclosed suggestions for altering the establishment in such a fashion as to allow him to "serve my country with reputation." A committee of Congress reviewed the issue and modified the plan so that the commanding officer of artillery could "arrange and direct all business of the ordnance department necessary to be done in the field." This alteration in the ordnance establishment was included in resolutions adopted by Congress Feb. 18, 1779. Henry Knox to George Washington, June 15, 1778, Washington Papers, DLC; *JCC*, XIII, 201-206.

and there are ~~now~~ several Good Officers now, who are forced to decline duty, to prevent disputes and their being commanded by Others, who upon every principle are their Inferiors; unless their having obtained Commissions before them from the opportunities they had of making earlier applications from local circumstances, should be considered ~~to give~~ sufficient to give them a superior claim. There are many other causes of disatisfaction on this head, but I will not enter into a minute relation of them. I sincerely wish, that the Gentlemen appointed or such Others as Congress may think proper to nominate for the occasion, would immediately repair to Camp.[2] The present opportunity is favourable for reducing matters to System and order__ and from painful experience I know, there is an absolute necessity for it.

I should also hope, that Congress will excuse me for mentioning again the necessity there is for appointing some Brigadiers. The Massachussets, by the resignation of General Learned wants One__ Pensylvania as General Hand is not here, has but One with the Army__ Maryland, which has Two large Brigades in the field, has only General Smallwood and the North Carolina Troops, since the departure of Gen[l.] McIntosh, have been without any. As I had taken the liberty upon a former occasion, to offer my sentiments to Congress and their Committee upon this subject, I should not trouble them now, if I was not more & more convinced that the service required promotions in this line. The frequent changes which take place among the Officers, where there are no Brigadiers, are attended with great inconvenience and detriment; and they are an effectual bar to the introduction of discipline. In such cases, the Officers know, that their command is but temporary__ always liable to cease__ and therefore they do not find them selves sufficiently interested to promote order and subordination;__ nor will the rest look up to them with that respect and deference which are essential. Every day's experience proves this__ and shews beyond question,

---

[2] Roger Sherman and John Banister, who were appointed to the Committee of Arrangement August 10, joined Joseph Reed at headquarters in mid-August. They worked with Washington for a month and formulated a plan which they offered as a report to Congress October 9. The plan to settle disputes over rank appeared in a series of resolutions approved Nov. 24, 1778. *JCC*, XI, 769; XII, 995, 1154-1160.

that the Affairs of a Brigade can never be in a right train without a Brigadier__ or some General to direct them. It is certain, these appointments at the first view will add a little to the list of expence, but in the end they will be a great saving__ and produce many important advantages.[3] We are also a good deal distressed at this time for Major Generals; however, as this arises more from the peculiar circumstances & and situation of many, which prevent them from duty in the line, than from a deficiency in the number appointed, I shall not add upon the occasion.

There is another branch of the Army which in my opinion calls loudly for the appointment of a General Officer__ and this is the Cavalry. For want of a proper regulating Head in this Corps, the whole has been in confusion, and of but very little service; whereas, under a right management, it might be most useful. The principal Officers in it do not harmonise, which circumstance with their disputes about rank would, were there no other Objections, effectually prevent the Corps from rendering the Public the services they have a right to expect__ and of which it should be capable. To promote any Gentleman now in it to a general command, would not be acquiesced in by the rest ([4]nor do I know that any of them wish it) and it would encrease their misunderstanding and of course disorder. I mean to draw all the Horse immediately together, when I trust they will be under the direction of a General Officer, appointed by Congress for the purpose. Who he shall be, will remain solely with them to determine. However, I will take the liberty to add, that he should be intelligent__ active__ attentive; and as far as I can judge, General Cadwalader or General Reed would fill the post with great honor and advantage__ tho it would seem from the seat the latter had taken in Congress and from his late appointment to the Council of Pensylvania, as if he had declined every military view. The abilities of these Gentlemen, as well as their

---

[3] Congress did not respond immediately to Washington's request for additional brigadiers. A November 24 resolution to create four brigadiers, one each for Maryland, Massachusetts, North Carolina, and Pennsylvania, was "postponed." On Jan. 9, 1779, Jethro Summer and James Hogun of North Carolina, Isaac Huger of South Carolina, and Mordecai Gist of Maryland were promoted to the rank. On May 12, 1779, Congress promoted William Irvine of Pennsylvania. *JCC*, XII, 1158; Heitman, *Continental Officers*, p. 10.

[4] Parenthesis written over dash.

Attachment are generally known__ and I am led to beleive that either would be as acceptable to the Corps, as any person that can be found;[5] indeed I have learned as much from two of the Colonels.

I have been waiting with the most impatient anxiety to hear of Count D'Estaing's arrival at Rhode Island, but as yet I have not been so happy. My last intelligence from thence is a Letter from Gen[l] Sullivan dated at 10 oClock in the forenoon of the 27th-; when he had no advice of the Fleet. He was in high spirits and from ~~which~~ the preparation in which matters were, he entertained the most flattering hopes of success in the intended Enterprize.[6] The Brigades of Varnum and Glover with Jackson's detachment would arrive, I expect on the 2[d] Inst.

As the Army was encamped and there was no great prospect of a sudden removal, I judged it adviseable to send Gen[l] Greene to the Eastward on Wednesday last; being fully persuaded his services, as well in the Quartermaster line as in the field, would be of material importance in the expedition against the Enemy in that Quarter. He is intimately acquainted with the whole of that Country__ and besides he has an extensive interest and influence in it. And in justice to General Greene, I take occasion to observe, that the Public is much indebted to him for his judicious management and active exertions in his present department. When he entered upon it, he found it in a most confused__ distracted and destitute state. This by his conduct and industry has undergone a very happy change__ and such as enabled us with great facility, to make a sudden move with the whole Army & baggage from Valley forge in pursuit of the Enemy__ and to perform a march to this place. In a word he has given the most general satisfaction and his affairs carry much the face of method and System.__ I also consider it as an act of justice, to speak of the conduct of Col[o] Wadsworth, Commissary General.

---

[5] Neither Joseph Reed, who was by this time a member of Congress and would be appointed to the Committee of Arrangement, nor John Cadwalader were willing to accept the command. Congress selected Cadwalader Sept. 10, 1778, but he declined September 19. On November 14 Congress directed General Washington to fill the command by transferring a brigadier from the infantry. Committee of Arrangement to HL, Sept. 7, 1778; PCC, Item 33, p. 263; HL to John Cadwalader, Sept. 12, 1778, Cadwalader Papers, PHi; John Cadwalader to HL, Sept. 19, 1778, Cadwalader Papers, PHi; *JCC*, XII, 897, 1158.

[6] John Sullivan to George Washington, July 27, 1778, Washington Papers, DLC.

He has been indefatigable in his exertions to provide for the Army and since his appointment our supplies of provision have been good and ample.[7]

August 4th.

At 7 oClock in the Evening yesterday, I received the inclosed Letter from Gen[l] Sullivan, with one addressed to myself, a Copy of which I do myself the pleasure of forwarding.[8] I am exceedingly happy in the Counts' arrival__ and that things wear so pleasing an aspect.__

There is another subject, on which I must take the liberty of addressing Congress,__ which is that of the Cloathier's department. I am perfectly satisfied, that unless this very important and interesting Office is put under better regulations and[9] under a different Head, than it now is, the Army will never be cloathed. M[r] Mease is by no means fit for the business. It is a work of immense difficulty to get him to Camp upon any occasion__ and no order can retain him there sufficiently long__ either to answer the demands of the Troops, or to acquire more than a very slight and imperfect knowledge of them. This of itself according to my ideas, would make him highly culpable__ but there are other circumstances. He is charged with inactivity, in not pursuing the best and all the means that present themselves, to provide Cloathing. His Agents too, who have been with the Army__ from inability or a want of industry__ or proper instructions from their principal, have been very incompetent to the purposes of their appointment. Besides these objections, M[r] Mease unhappily is represented to be of a very unaccomodating cast of temper, and his general deportment towards ↑the↓ Officers who have had to transact business with him, has rendered him exceedingly obnoxious. The constant and daily complaints against

---

[7] Jeremiah Wadsworth, a successful Connecticut merchant, had served as commissary general of the Connecticut militia in 1774 and had served under Joseph Trumbull as a Continental commissary from 1775 until Trumbull's resignation in August 1777. Congress selected him Commissary General of Purchases April 9, 1778, to replace William Buchanan. *Greene Papers* (Showman), II, 394n; *JCC*, X, 327-328.

[8] John Sullivan to HL, Aug. 1, 1778. John Sullivan to George Washington, Aug. 1, 1778, PCC, Item 152, Vol. 6, p. 209ff.

[9] "a" written over dash.

him, make it my indispensible duty to mention these points__ and it ~~becomes~~ ↑is↓ the more so, as I beleive both Officers and Men, particularly the latter, have suffered greater inconveniences and distresses, than Soldiers ever did before for want of Cloathing; and that this has not flowed more from a real scarcity of Articles__ than a want of proper exertions and provident management to procure them. It is essential that something should be done and immediately, to place the department on a better footing. We have now a great many men entirely destitute of Shirts and Breeches and I suppose not less than a fourth or fifth of the whole here, who are without Shoes. From the deficiencies in this line numbers of desertions have proceeded__ not to mention deaths, and what is still worse, the Troops which remain and see themselves in rags want that spirit and pride necessary to constitute the Soldier.[10]

I have been informed by Several Officers and by such as I can depend on, that many of the late Draughts are willing and desirous of enlisting during the War. I do not conceive myself at liberty to give direction on the point and therefore submit it to Congress to decide. However, if they can be engaged for the usual bounties allowed by the Continent, after proper precautions are taken to prevent fraud, I think the measure will be expedient. It is true our Affairs have an agreable aspect at present__ but the War may continue and we want men. A third of the time of some them, and a half in ↑the↓ case of others, is already expired; and as they will rise in their views and become more difficult in proportion as their service draws to a conclusion, if the step is considered adviseable, the sooner we attempt to enlist the better in all probability will the work succeed.[11]

---

[10] Congress took immediate action, appointing Samuel Adams, Roger Sherman, and Nathaniel Scudder a committee to examine General Washington's complaints. The committee's August 19 report recommended that Mease and his agents not be allowed to continue purchasing, that Washington appoint a court of enquiry into the conduct of the Clothier General, and that Mease be suspended pending the result of the investigation. Congress postponed consideration; however, Mease offered his resignation Sept. 19, 1778. *JCC,* XI, 768, 812-813, 937; James Mease to HL, Sept. 19, 1778.

[11] HL informed General Washington that on August 31 Congress had provided for the enlistment of militia drafts into the Continental service for a term of three years or the duration of the war. The bounty for these enlistees was set at twenty dollars. HL to George Washington, Aug. 31, 1778, PCC, Item 13; *JCC,* XI, 853-854.

I have the Honor to be / with great respect & esteem / Sir / Your Most Obed servt

G$^{o:}$ Washington

SOURCE: RC, PCC (Item 152), DNA; addressed below close "Hon$^{ble.}$ / Henry Laurens, Esq$^{re.}$"; dated "Headq$^{rs.}$ White plains August the 3$^{d:}$ 1778"; docketed "Letter from Genl Washington / White Plains 3^d & 4th Aug 1778 / Read 10." and "(Entered) / White plains 3 & 4 Aug: 1778 / Letter from Gen$^{l.}$ Washington / read 10th_ / Entered & Ex$^{d:}$". Copy, PCC (Item 169), DNA. Draft, Washington Papers, DLC. Copy, HL Papers, ScHi. Extract, Wadsworth Papers, CtHi.

FROM JOHN LAURENS

Providence, R.I., August 4, 1778

I thank you my dearest friend and father for your tender letter of the 26th Ult^o_ I was upon the point of writing to you the 22$^{d.}$ when I was ordered to fly with important dispatches to Gov$^{r.}$ Trumbull, General Sullivan and the Count d'Estaing__ I commissioned one of my friends to acquaint you of the circumstance,__ but perhaps the multiplicity of Affairs in which I left him involved, will have made him lose sight of the matter__ in 48 hours over the worst and in some parts the most obscure road that I ever travel'd, I arrived at Providence, had a conference with Genl Sullivan, and proceeded immediately with ~~the~~ Pilots provided for the french fleet, down to Point Judith__ Boats were soon provided and every thing put in readiness for boarding the Admiral as soon as ~~ever~~ he should announce himself by the firing of five Cannon__ here I waited in a very disagreeable kind of company 'till[1] the morning of the 29th for tho' the Squadron anchored off block island the preceding afternoon__ the haziness of the weather rendered them invisible to us__ in the morning when the fog was dissipated their appearance was as sudden as ~~the~~ a change of decorations in an opera house__ __

---

[1] "'till" written over "from".

Upon my delivering Genl. Washingtons Dispatches__ and Genl. Sullivans containing a plan of operations__ The Admiral informed me his intention had been to proceed immediately into the Main channel of Newport and attack[2] the Enemys batteries__ the day however began to be too far spent__ it was expedient to distribute intelligent Pilots ~~among~~ ↑in↓ the Squadron__ and in pursuance of Genl. Sullivans plan the main channel was blocked up with the Squadron__ a Ship of the Line was ordered up the West Channel__ & Two Frigates and a Tender up the East__ By consulting the Map you will find that there are three entrances to Rhode Island__ one on the east of Rhode Island between[3] it and the main__ called the Seakonnet passage__ one on the west, between it and Cononicut[4] Island__ which is the principal or main passage__ a third between Conanicut and the mainland, commonly called the western passage__ in the first Genl. Sullivan informed the Admiral there were two Galleys and one Small Frigate__ in the second two Frigates besides two Galleys and two or three frigates at Newport__ in the last two small frigates__ farther that he estimated the enemys land force including three Regiments posted on Conanicut at 7000 effective__

Genl. Sullivans plan founded[5] on these data__ was that the Admiral should detach a proper force up the eastern and western channels to take the enemys ships stationed in each__ to block up the main channel with the remainder of the squadron, so as effectually to cut off the retreat of their Ships, and to prevent the arrival of reinforcements. the French Ships in the eastern and western channels were afterwards to cover the passage of the American Troops from Tiverton and Bristol__ The Troops were not to amuse themselves with attacking the works in the northern part of the island__ but ~~to illegible~~ a sufficient detachment was to be left to be a guard upon the troops posted in those works while the main body was to advance rapidly to the attack of the ↑Fort &↓ redouts which immediately environ the Town of Newport__ at the moment of that attack the Count was to force the passage into Newport

---

[2] "attack" written over other text.
[3] "w" written over "e".
[4] "o" written over "a".
[5] "founded" written over "in".

harbour__ silence the enemys batteries. cannonade the Town__ and disembark his Marines and Land forces at the most proper place for seconding the American attack__

———

The Sagittaire a Ship of the Line, went up the western passage on the morning of the 30th. and was fired upon by a two Gun battery of 24 pounders which the enemy had on the west side of Conanicut__ the Sagittaire returned a broad side as she passed__ and we discovered from the Admirals Ship an explosion at[6] the battery, which induced us to believe that the enemy had abandoned it__

The Ship received two scratches in her hull__ and proceeded to her station__

The Aimable and Alemene Frigates accompanied by the Stanley (Prize) Tender__ went up the eastern passage__ upon their approach__ the enemy set fire to the Kingfisher 20 Gun Sloop__ and to the Lamb Galley mounting [*blank*] and sent the spit fire Galley mounting [*blank*] in form of a fire-ship__ The Count de Grace[7] commanded the boat which was ordered to tow the latter off__ she blew up soon after the Grapnel was fixed__ and the Gallant officer with his crew escaped unhurt__ an officer[8] who went on board with a party to extinguish the Flames of the Kingfisher had an escape equally providential__ she ↑her powder room↓ blew up while they were on board__ and they received no injury__ the hull drifted over to the main__ and her Guns will be saved__

———

From the enemys keeping possession of the island of Conanicut the Admiral concluded that it was an important post to them the battery which they had on the east side of it afforded[9] a cross fire upon the entrance of the harbour__ and the three Regiments there made it an object__ The Count therefore thought it essential that we should

---

6 "at" written over "in".
7 Etienne-Marc-Antoine, Comte de Grasse-Limermont was ensign of the frigate *Aimable*. Claghorn, *Naval Officers*, p. 354.
8 "o" written over other text.
9 "affo" written over other text.

make ourselves master of it__ ~~The objective / But as the Shipping~~ ~~[*illegible*] approach~~ The most effectual way of attacking it would have been by disembarking Troops on the West Side of it__ and sending a proper force of Ships up the main channel to run through the fire of the batteries at the entrance and take a proper position for cutting off the communciation between Rhode Island and Conanicut__ so as to prevent the enemys throwing across reinforcements__ but upon inquiry, it was found impracticable to anchor the Ships any where out of reach of the enemys batteries__ so that after running the Gantlet at the entrance the Ships w^d. have been exposed to a constant deliberate fire in the harbour__ these difficulties obliged the Count to renounce the[10] plan__ of sending Ships up the main channel__ for this duty__ It was then inquired whether the Ships might not ~~go~~ effect the business by going up the western channel, turning the north point of Conanicut and coming down the main channel__ by this means they would in the first instance avoid the cross fire at the entrance__ and might take such a position relatively to the ~~batteries~~ harbour as w^d. ~~discover~~ discourage the enemy from throwing across succours__ but the most experienced pilots informed us that to effect this detour the Ships must either have a wind which w^d. answer equally for going up the western and coming down the main channel__ or that after going up with a fair wind they would be obliged to beat down the main channel__ or lastly that they would be obliged to wait for a fair wind to bring them down from the North end of Conanicut__ The delay and uncertainty incident to the first and last put them out of the question__ the second was pronounced impracticable on account of the narrowness of the ↑m.↓ Channel above Newport__ which w^d. not allow scope enough for the Ships work^g. and missing stays w^d. be fatal in such circumstances__

It was determined therefore that ~~there~~ in order to gain Conanicut a body of Militia sh^d. be applied for, to make us equal to such a reinforcem^t. as we thought the enemy could spare__ Col Fleury and myself went by the Admirals desire to make application for this purpose__ in our way we learnt that some American Privateers had been on the island__ and that the enemy had

---

[10] "e" written over "is".

evacuated the battery which fired on the Sagittaire__ We met Genl. Sullivan on his way to the Fleet__ where he was going to have a conference with the Admiral and propose some changes in his plan__ he was received on board with the Guard of Marines, and the drums beating to arms__ and at ~~taking~~ his departure the Ship was manned__ and fifteen Cannon fired__

the evening of the 30th- the outer most Ships made signals of the appearance of a Fleet__ the Admiral got his Squadron in readiness for fight & chace__ but the fleet put about & escaped under the veil of night__ it proved to be 8 transports with wood from Long Island bound to Newport and convoyed by a Frigate__

On the evening of the 31st. The Admiral sent a party to reconnoitre Conanicut and discover whether the enemy had really abandoned all their batteries as was reported it was found that they had__

The next morning the Admiral landed in order to view the enemys batteries from the east side of Conanicut__ we found in the battery which fired on the Sagittaire two 24 pounders spiked__ and all their heavy Amunition__

from the battery on the E. end__ we had a distinct view of the Town Shipping__ and batteries the latter lost that respectablility which they had on paper__ the fire from the Ships of the Line must annihilate them in an hour__ The fort on an eminence ↑called Domine Hill↓ __ back of the Town; may require our heavy artillery and some Shells__ We have every reason to believe that we shall effect our landing on the island without opposition__ as the enemy seemed to have concentered their force in New Port__

   The Admiral has disembarrassed himself of his prisoners__ ~~and~~ sick and prizes__ __ he is in perfect readiness for acting his part and as anxious as a man can be__ General Sullivan has exerted himself to the utmost__ but the backwardness of the Militia called for from the Neighboring States__ the necessity of constructing Transport Boats, to supply the place of those destroyed by the enemy in their last descent__ and many other necessary prepara-tions which require time__ have delayed us till now__ and I find it impossible to tell you with precision on what day we shall be ready__

   I fear my dearest father that I have tired you with detail__ and that from a habit of speaking of our operations with my finger on the map__ I may in some places not have expressed my meaning fully enough but my time unluckily will not permit to remedy these inconveniences by writing a new Letter__ I am just come from the Admiral to see if it will be possible by any means to hasten our land operations__ The French Squadron will want a great quantity of provisions whether they winter here or return to France__ no biscuit is to be had here__

I am ever your most affectionate

John Laurens

Pennsilvania must furnish flower and bakers sh^d be employed there immediately.

It is reported that 20 Sail of Spanish Ships are on the coast pray who is Don Juan de Miralles__[11]

In the letter which I wrote you from black point I mentioned__ the Admirals intention to send his prisoners to Philadelphia__ some difficulties induced him to change his plan__ they are all landed here__ __

Deserters from Rhode Island__ say the Troops are in want of provision and look upon themselves as prisoners.

the Mq̄uis de lafayette with a division from the Grand Army is arrived__ and his men have had time to refresh themselves__

Genl. Greene is likewise arrived__.

Genl. Sullivans 1st. estimate of the Enemys land Force is too high__ they cannot be above have any above 5000 men__ and the Genl begins to think so himself__

SOURCE: ALS, Kendall Collection; addressed on cover "The honble / Henry Laur[ens] / Preside[nt of Congress]"; dated "Providence 4th August 1778."; docketed by HL "John Laurens / 4 Augt 1778__"; noted "Priv[ate]". Copy, HL Papers, ScHi.

---

[11] This postscript written in left margin.

TO RAWLINS LOWNDES

Philadelphia, August 5, 1778

Dear Sir

The date of my last private Address which went by Messenger Sharp is the 15th July.

I have now in view Your Excellency's several favors of the 28th May, 17th June and 6th July.

Nothing has been done in the ~~Army~~ arrangement since the return of Congress to Philad^{a.} and it appears to me that nothing will be done while ~~it~~ ↑the Army↓ continues migrative. I am very sensible Your Excellency will in the mean time have experienced much inconvenience and trouble from the demands of our local Continental Officers for Commissions. The terms in which our Carolinian Regiments were originally established, as far as I know, are singular, and entitle the Officers to claim all the benefits which were held up to them; and I am persuaded Congress will[1] not contend the point, when fully and clearly explained, but every attempt to this end has been overrul'd by the repeated reply "we cannot interfere in or consider these matters until the Army Arrangement is finished" from this consideration, and from that of the peculiar circumstances of the troops in our State. I am also persuaded that Congress will not censure[2] the Executive, should they advise Your Excellency to grant so many Commissions as shall appear to be absolutely necessary. I am farther confirmed in this opinion from the silence of the house when they were informed that Your Excellency had granted from necessity a few Commissions subsequent to the Act of the 31st Dec^{r.}[3] And therefore I shall inclose with this 20 signed Commissions, submitting these and my private sentiments to your Excellency's final determination referring at the same time to the Act abovemention'd compared with the circumstances of our Regiments.

The testimony from Captain Senff is extreamly wanted;[4] from the late humiliations of Great Britain I shall not be surpris'd

---

[1] "will" written over erasure.

[2] Word repeated for clarity in interlineation by HL.

[3] On Dec. 31, 1777, Congress had urged the state governments to stop issuing commissions to fill vacancies in their regiments because of an imbalance in the number of officers and privates. *JCC*, IX, 1073.

[4] HL had been asking for John Christian Senf's testimony concerning the Saratoga

to see by one of the first Packets a ratification of the Convention of Saratoga, immediately after which, the remaining troops will be hurried away; and from the repeated breaches of faith in the Ministers and officers of that Nation I shall be as little surprized to hear that those troops had immediately landed at New York or Charlestown; admitting the practicability and their opinion of the utility of such[5] an Act.

I am much affected by the relation of my fellow Citizens conduct in oppostion to your Excellencys' Proclamation of the 13th of June__ the Act of Congress upon which that Proclamation was founded was well intended, but it passed after much contention and proves to be the most unpleasing to the states in general of any determination of Congress within my experience. There is a distinction made by Tories between moral private honor and Political honor in the practice of which Men of the first Character have been detected and driven to a necessity ~~upon~~ ↑for↓ explaining in order to preserve some Character which has rendered every Man coming within the description suspicious in the highest degree. It would be tedious and probably unnecessary at this date to adduce particular proofs in the conduct of General Sir William Howe, Sir H. Clinton. Sir W[m]_ Johnstone, Governor Franklin and twenty etcetera. Nevertheless nobody here thinks your Excellency was faulty in pursuing the Recommendation of Congress in terms of the Proclamation and by advice of the Privy Council.[6]

I was well aware the embargo would press heavily on our State, and upon that occasion I desired to deliver my sentiments to Congress from the Chair. Your Excellency may rest assured I shall watch the earliest opportunity ↑for↓ recommending to Congress a revocation of the Act. In the mean time it may merit our attention

---

Convention since March. By coincidence, Senf gave his affidavit this day (August 5). Rawlins Lowndes enclosed Senf's statement in his letter to HL, Aug. 16, 1778.

[5] "s" written over "f".

[6] South Carolina's loyalty oath law was enacted March 28, 1778. All free males over sixteen years of age were required to swear allegiance to the state within thirty to sixty days, depending on their proximity to Charleston. The April 23, 1778, resolve of Congress recommended that the states enact laws or issue proclamations to grant pardons to citizens now willing to give up their loyalty to Britain. Lowndes issued a proclamation on June 5, in which he notified the populace of the April 23 resolution and extended the time for the South Carolina loyalty oath until June 10. Political opponents of the Lowndes administration provoked opposition to the proclamation. *HL Papers*, XIII, 437-439, 479-480.

whether other states pay that implicit obedience to <u>such</u> an Act of Congress as we do in South Carolina and our future submission with or without Remonstrance may be ~~illegible~~ warranted by the discoveries which shall be made[7]

The General Gazette of the 4th Aug[t.] will shew Your Excellency what respect has been paid to a ↑the↓ Resolve of Congress by this State. I am determin'd to introduce Vice President Bryans' Proclamation[8] into the house; Your Excellency shall be duly and as speedily as possible inform'd of the reception which my application shall meet with. My Countrymen will Act accordingly. I must do them the justice to say, they have hitherto acted with as much uprightness and fidelity in the common cause of the Union as any state of the thirteen. I will say nothing that shall appear to be invidious, altho' I have feelings against the expressing of which I can scarcely resist.

My Ideas relative to the views of the Court of Madrid was exploded at the time of reading the Treaties with France. I endeavoured to impress them upon the mind of my Colleague the Chief Justice, and now the Eyes of many Gentlemen begin to be opened[9]

Part of Your Excellencys' Letter from the words "<u>I am extreamly happy</u>" to the words "<u>I mean to the public</u>" I presented

---

[7] HL's June 10 circular to the states announcing the embargo enacted June 8 had reached Charleston June 27. Lowndes reported July 6 that "the Embargo was immediately published and enforced." Lowndes implored HL to "give the earliest intelligence when Congress shall see fitt to determine the Embargo." Rice that was ready for export had to be turned to the already glutted domestic market. The price of rice had been falling since early 1778 when, at its peak for this period, it soared to 80/ per hundredweight. In May shortly before the embargo it had fallen to 50/, and after the embargo was announced it dropped to 40/. The price firmed after this and by September John Lewis Gervais reported sales at 55/. Rawlins Lowndes to HL., July 6, 1778, Kendall Collection; *HL Papers,* XII, 86, 449; XIII, 274, 432, 433; John Lewis Gervais to HL., July 6, 1778, Gervais Papers, in private hands; John Lewis Gervate to HL., Sept. 21, 1778, HL Papers, ScHi.

[8] Vice President George Bryan, as chairman of the Pennsylvania Executive Council, issued an August 1 proclamation establishing an embargo as recommended by Congress. Pennsylvania, however, limited the embargo to thirty days rather than the November 15 termination determined by Congress. *Minutes of the Supreme Executive Council of Pennsylvania,* XI, 545.

[9] In May HL had expressed concern that the Bahamas and Florida were not included in the Franco-American treaties. They were, he believed, essential to the security of Georgia and South Carolina, and Spain coveted both. As early as June HL informed John Rutledge of the growing awareness among members of Spain's interest in these areas, but lamented that "our feelings however are generally proportioned to the distance from danger." *HL Papers,* XIII, 248, 393; HL to William Livingston, Aug. 21, 1778.

to Congress: 'twas extreamly approv'd of, and committed, instead of saying to the grave, I will only ~say~ intimate that no Report has been made thereon.[10]

Your Excellency "<u>would be very unwilling to change situations with me</u>" undoubtedly and for very obvious reasons__ nevertheless I have a thousand times wished most anxiously, and do at this instant ardently wish that you were here a Representative from South Carolina either with or without me. Yourself, Sir, and a few more whom I could name, without meaning to disparage the present Delegates or any individual of them, are extreamly wanted in General Congress. This remark excites very serious reflections in my mind, important, perhaps beyond your Excellencies apprehensions, but I feel a necessity for reserving a disclosure to a future opportunity. Happy shall I be to see such amendments in Public Measures as will render disclosure unnecessary__ I esteem the capture of Bachop and Osborne a fortunate stroke in favor of all the States. Georgia and South Carolina recieve the most immediate benefit.

It is now the 7th of August: what is written above is the product of four or five attempts in Minutes stolen from the hard service of the last three days. the Messenger has been and is detained for my Letters only, I must therefore hasten to conclude__

We have heard nothing late from General Washington or from Count d'Estaing, the Newspaper intimates the landing of 4000 British Troops from New York at Rhode Island, this is probably a mistake.

General Putnam from the Army informs me that Deserters were daily coming in, generally ten per day. A Green coat Captain[11] and a British Cornet of Horse among them.

---

[10] HL extracted this from Lowndes' June 17, 1778, letter, and presented it to Congress July 11. Lowndes explained the confusion in accounting caused by Continental and state agents' purchases for military supplies. Lowndes recommended that purchasing and accounting be put under state authority to avoid "clashing and interfering Jurisdictions." He also explained that local speculation in loan office certificates based in exchange advantages in Georgia currency "are certainly of no advantage here, I mean to the publick." *HL Papers*, XIII, 481-482; *JCC*, XI, 681-682.

[11] The British government had adopted a green and white uniform for all Loyalist or Provincial officers in 1776; after 1778, the provincial regiments adopted red coats. Charles M. Lefferts, *Uniforms of the American, British, French, and German Armies in the War of the American Revolution* (Old Greenwich, Ct., 1971), pp. 218, 225.

We do not yet know the result of General Lees' tryal.

I have been many days under that kind of anxiety which I felt during our debates on motion for detaining Lieut. General Burgoyne and his Convention troops, I then feared he would slip through our fingers[12] into this City__ now from an unaccountable delay on our part I dread losing the proper time for treating the British Commissioners according to their deserving. In the Acts and attempts of Governor Johnstone I charge the whole with having offered the highest posible affront to a virtuous, Independent Nation by attempting to bribe their Representatives in Congress. I have therefore much at heart a desire that Congress should resolve to hold no conference with such Men, to assign their reasons in ample decent language, and to transmit the Act by a flag to the Commissioners in New York, and make them the bearers of their own disgrace__ they will not dare to suppress the Resolve, they must lay it before their Court, it will soon descend to the public at large, and expose themselves and their Prompters to the resentments of a deluded and much injur'd People, whose deplorable circumstances I must confess affects me.__ The Commissioners and that group of Politicians who have led on the British Nation to ruin, will be held up and scorned at every Court in Europe, & their names will be branded with infamy in history.

If we leave this business to be transacted at our leisure, Governor Johnstone may in the mean time return to Great Britain, there he will confidently deny the fact, and charge Congress with a calculated forgery. I am for attacking him immediately Letters in hand, his guilt will be fix'd, for he cannot now deny.

I am not commonly tenacious of my own opinions, but in the present case I feel as if I clearly foresaw many good effects resulting from a proper Act on our part, I am therefore day by day urging my Colleague Drayton to force a Resolve for this purpose, which he has had in his pocket more than a fortnight.[13]

---

12 "g" written over other text.

13 William Henry Drayton's notes for a speech concerning the activities of George Johnstone, which he "had during many days waited for an opportunity of introducing," condemned the commissioner for his "plain, direct & base attempt to corrupt this honourable body." HL and Drayton and a majority of the South Carolina delegation voted for the motion that would have ended further negotiations with the Carlisle Commission because of Johnstone's attempts to bribe individual members of Congress. The motion failed. *Delegate Letters* (Smith), X, 424, 426; HL to George Washington, July 31; *JCC*, XI, 773-774.

The Captain Hawker, formerly the Instrument of Mr. Collector Moore at Charlestown, lately Commander of the British frigate Mermaid is now in Goal with his Officers and Crew under the law of retaliation, I have lost or mislaid a Note which he sent to me a few days ago, but from my Answer which your Excellency will find among other Papers the purpose may be gathered__ he has address'd Congress in a Memorial[14] signed by himself and his Officers praying[15] for enlargement on parole__ this has found able advocates and as strong an opposition, Mr. Drayton is firm against it.[16]

This instant we hear two articles of intelligence of some importance__ a Gentleman from New York says, a fire had happen'd in that City which had consumed upwards of 200 houses, among which were some store houses full of Kings' stores, and that five store ships with their lading were also burnt.[17]

That Admiral Byron with four British Men of War and supposed Cork fleet were on the coast, the Admiral had sent a frigate before him, the frigate or her barge had been up to the city, Sir Henry Clinton had confer'd with the Commander, and that a thousand hogsheads of Water ~~had been~~ ↑were immediately↓ filled and ship'd

We shall soon learn particulars of these crude accounts__ I believe neither of them are groundless, and begin to have some

---

[14] "Letter to the President" was interlined over "Memorial".

[15] An asterisk at this point refers to a note at the bottom of the page: "He does not pray, but after asserting his humanity to American Prisoners and referring to Governor Johnstones' Letter, says, he shall acknowledge an enlargement on parole an indulgence."

[16] Capt. James Hawker's Royal Navy frigate *Mermaid* ran ashore in Maryland July 5, during an encounter with d'Estaing's fleet. He, with 1st Lt. Jonathan Stoddart and 2nd Lt. Thomas Dickinson, sent a memorial to HL seeking better treatment and provisions. They claimed that American prisoners they had taken and held on the *Mermaid* had received good treatment. HL had known Hawker as early as July 1766 when the captain began a sixteen-month tour on the Carolina station. Daniel Moore served as the British Collector of Customs at Charleston during the same period. HL had several complaints against Moore for his extortionate fees and seizures of vessels. The conflict between the two reached a climax on Sept. 2, 1767, when in an altercation HL tweaked Moore's nose. Captain Hawker, a witness to the incident, claimed HL was at the head of a group of a hundred men who meant to attack and possibly kill the collector. Patrick Henry to HL, July 19, 1778, PCC, Item 71, Vol. 1, p. 179ff; James Hawker, et al. to HL, Aug. 2, 1778, PCC, Item 78, Vol. 11, p. 313ff; *HL Papers*, V, 254, 287-288.

[17] *Rivington's Gazette* reported Aug. 5, 1778, that sixty-four dwelling houses, several mercantile stores, and two sloops had been destroyed in a "tremendous fire" which broke out on Cruger's wharf the morning of August 3. Gov. William Tryon reported to Germain in a September 5 letter that "the perpetrators of the conflagration are still unknown." *Documents of the American Revolution* (Davies), XV, 198.

fears I may properly say, rather strengthned than beginning that the British fleet will be an overmatch for that of our Allies[18] in this Quarter__ there is also a rumour that we have taken Rhode Island out of the hands of the Enemy; this I regard only as report.

A discovery having been made of frauds in the Accounts of the Deputy Commissary General of Military Stores, he was arrested and committed to Goal; there, he made some confessions and charg'd the Commissary General, hitherto a Gentleman of very fair character, as a tempter and accomplice. Congress had directed the Board of War to arrest and safely keep him also__ the Board proceeded not with proper vigor and wrote such a letter to the house as is deem'd a disobedience of Orders and an high insult. The adjusting this troublesome affair will much retard business of the greatest importance__ it has already cost us two days, stagnated correspondence with the Board, and is not ended.[19]

I will trespass no longer upon Your Excellencys' time but to repeat, that I Am with very great Respect and Regard / Sir / Your Excellencys' Obed.t. Serv.t.

P.S.

While I was signing to the preceeding Page, Mons.r. Girard very politely transmitted to me the Treaty of Alliance, general & defensive between the King of France and the "Laudable Helvetique Body" or Swiss Cantons concluded the 28th May 1777 sign'd by the King on one part, and by Deputies from the thirteen Cantons and eight ↑seven↓ free States in Alliance with them, on the other. This was sworn to or finally ratified the 25th of August following, until this event France had not acknowledged the Independence of the Helvetic Body but in all their former correspondencies had treated

---

[18] "Ally" altered to "Allies".

[19] After the deputy commissary Cornelius Sweers was arrested on suspicion of fraud in June 1778, Sweers attempted to exonerate his conduct by implicating the commissary general, Col. Benjamin Flower. Congress ordered the Board of War to arrest Flower, but the Board balked at the order because Flower was ill and Sweers' charges were the sole evidence against Flower. Congress held the Board guilty of disobedience, but exonerated Flower after an investigation concluded on Aug. 24, 1778. The case against Sweers stretched out over the next several years and he ultimately was ordered to make restitution. *JCC*, XI, 751, 791, 831-834; Risch, *Supplying Washington's Army*, 433; PCC, Item 41, Vol. 9, 48ff; Item 42, Vol. 7, 87ff; Item 149, Vol. 1, 349ff.

with them as parts of the German Empire_[20] an annecdote known to very few in Europe or America.

I view this, an Act preparatory to acknowledging the Independence of America. although I will not hazard my conjecture with the Minister.

With this Treaty M^r. Girard sent me a ponderous and beautiful silver Medal struck upon the above occasion. On one face the Kings head encircled Ludovicus XVI Franc. et Nav. Rex._

on the other_   FŒdus
                Cum Helvetiis
                Restauratum
                Et Stabilitum
                MDCCLXXVII

and ornamented by a Garland or wreath of Olive Branches.

The States are / Zurich / Berne / Lucerne / Ury / Schwitz / Underwald le haut / Underwald le bas / Zug / Glaris Évangélique / Glaris Catholique / Basle / Fribourg / Soluire / Schaffouse / Appenzell / Abbé de Saint-Gall / Ville de Saint-Gall / Villais / Mulhause / Bienne

I have also just learn'd that upon the appearance of the French fleet near Rhode Island, the Enemy set fire to the Kings Fisher Man of War and two of their Gallies and abandoned them. The vessels were totally consumed_ some of their regiments which had been stationed on Connecticut side also retired into the Garrison at Rhode Island, where they are now about 5000 strong_ we now know where they are. When the Marquis de la Fayette shall have joined General Sullivan, an immediate attack will be made_ we may expect to hear somewhat important in a few days.

I sincerely condole with Your Excellency and M^rs. Lowndes your experience Sir, will point out the true way of softening and reconciling every stroke of Providence.[21]

---

[20] France's previous alliance (1715) had included only the Catholic cantons of Switzerland which were forced to acknowledge France's supremacy. The alliance of 1777 included both the Catholic and Protestant cantons and ended French supremacy. William Martin, *Switzerland: From Roman Times to the Present* (London, 1931; reprint, New York, 1971), pp. 101-120.

[21] Lowndes had apologized in his July 6 letter for not responding quickly to his last from HL. He explained that he had been mentally and physically incapacitated by an attack of gout and the death of two of his children within one week. Rawlins Lowndes to HL, July 6, 1778, Kendall Collection; Vipperman, *Rawlins Lowndes*, p. 208.

Papers inclosed to Mr. Lowndes__

> Copies of Letters from G.W. 14th, 17th. and 22nd July
> Mr. Maduits Paper
> Account of forces in England and Scotland
> The Answer to Captain Hawker
> Report of Treasury, sums advanc'd to staff officers
> Mr. Girards' Address to Congress
> The Presidents' Answer
> His Most Christian Majestys' Letter to Congress
> Twenty Army Commissions

The damage by fire at New York is ascertained to be confined to 120 houses including Stores. a great quantity of Wine, and a very large quantity of Kings' stores destroy'd__ only two Vessels burnt which happen'd to be aground.

The Account of the Arrival of Byrons' fleet is groundless.

SOURCE: LB, HL Papers, ScHi; addressed "President Lowndes / S^{o.} Carolina" and by HL "by Durst"; dated "5th August". Copy (19th century), HL Papers, ScHi.

FROM WILLIAM SMITH

Baltimore, Md., August 5, 1778

Dear Sir,

I Am now to acknowledge receipt of your very obliging favors, of the 23^{d.} & 28th Ult^{o.} with one hundred & Seventy Seven dolars, inclosed in the latter, which is[1] to your credit, leaving A Small balance in your favor.__

I have made every possible inquirey after the carriage you mention and cant find there is any such in this Town.__ A Mr. Hudson[2] of this place, purchased an English post Coach, this

---

[1] "is" interlined.
[2] Possibly Jonathan Hudson, a business associate of Robert Morris in Baltimore. *Delegate Letters* (Smith), XI, 13n.

Summer at Wilmington, which was imported for M^r· Montressieur the British engineer[3] & now lays at M^r· John Irwins at the head of Elk, for sale. M^r· Hudson says it is quite New, & very elegant & light. harness for Two horses only. No Box, the driver to ride. the Linnings a light Color, & painting the Same

One of the Cusshings lost. and one light of glass broke. the price £800. Curr^y·. he will not Sell for Sterling. If you think from the description & price it will Suit, it may perhaps be best to Send a Judge down to head of Elk to view it__

I am extreamly Sorry for your Sake as well as my own there is not a drop of good wine or Brandy for sale in this place. though we have arrivals almost every day, yit none of them have Bro^t· any of these good things

I am with greatest esteem / & Respect / Dr Sir y^r· M^o / hble Servt

W. Smith

P.S. a Boat from Charles Town arrived here Two days past. She left that place this day week brings no News__ Says there is no Cruisers off the Coast, that She Saw.__ that the expedition Against Augustine was dropd__

SOURCE: RC, Kendall Collection; addressed on cover "The Honble / Henry Laurens Esqr / Prisident of Congress / Philadelphia"; dated "Baltimore August 5th. 1778"; franked "Free"; docketed by HL "W^m· Smith Es¯q / 5 Aug^t· 1778 / Rec^d· 10^th_".

REPLY TO CONRAD-ALEXANDRE GÉRARD

August 6, 1778

Sir,

The treaties between his most Christian Majesty and the united states of America so fully demonstrate his wisdom & magna↑ni↓mity

---

[3] Capt. John Montresor (1736-1799), a military engineer who had served in America as early as 1754, incurred the displeasure of Sir Henry Clinton and returned to Britain shortly after the British command changed. "The Montresor Journals," ed. G. D. Scull, New-York Historical Society, *Collections*, XIV (1881), 3-6.

as to command the reverence of all nations. The virtuous citizens of america in particular can never forget his beneficent attention to their violated rights; nor cease to acknowledge the hand[1] of a gracious providence in raising them up so powerful and illustrious a friend. It is the hope & opinion of Congress that the confidence his Majesty reposes in the firmness of these states will receive additional strength from every day's experience

This Assembly are convinced, Sir, that had it rested solely with the most Christian King, not only the independence of these states would have been universally acknowledged but their tranquility fully established. We lament that lust of domination, which gave birth to the present war and hath prolonged & extended the miseries of Mankind[2] We ardently wish to sheath the sword and spare the farther effusion of blood, but we are determined, by every means in our power, to fulfil those eventual engagements, which have required positive & permanent force from the hostile designs, and measures of the common enemy__[3]

Congress ha[ve] reason to believe that the assistance so wisely & generously sent will bring Great Britain to a sense of justice and moderation; promote the common interests of France and America and secure peace and tranquility on the most firm and honorable foundation. Neither can it be doubted, that those, who administer the powers of government within the several states of this unison, will cement that connection with the subjects of France, the beneficial effects of which have already been so sensibly felt.

Sir, from the experience we have had of your exertion to promote the true interests of our country as well as your own, it is with the highest satisfaction Congress receive as the first minister from his most Christian Majesty a gentleman, whose past confidence↑duct↓ affords a happy presage, that he will merit the confidence of this body the friendship of its members and the esteem of the Citizens of America__

In Congress

Henry Laurens president

---

[1] "hand" written over other text.
[2] "nk" written over other text.
[3] Symbol between words interpreted as paragraph break.

SOURCE: ADraft, PCC (Item 25), DNA; no address; dated below close "August 6 1778."; docketed on first page "N 51" and "Reply" cancelled; docketed below close "Sieur Gerard's speech / to / Congress and / the reply of Congress".

TO BENEDICT ARNOLD

Philadelphia, August 7, 1778

Sir

Congress are much interrupted in the course of business in their Sessions at the State House by the beating of Drums & noise of the Soldiery at the Guard House. will you be so obliging as to give the necessary order for preventing in future the inconvenience complained of.[1]

I have the honor to be with / great Esteem & Regard &ca

SOURCE: LB, PCC (Item 13), DNA; addressed "General Arnold / Head Quarts. Philada."; dated "7th. August.".

TO JOHN LEWIS GERVAIS

Philadelphia, August 7, 1778

My Dear Friend

I am compel'd as usual to refer you for news to His Excellency the President, and to News papers which will accompany this.

Since my last of the 15th Ulto. I have received your obliging favors of the 2nd and 6th of that Month.

I am well satisfied of ↑with↓ your determination respecting Monsr. Jaussaud;[1] I have a long Letter from Mr. Delagayé but tis French, and I have not yet read it.

---

[1] The following day General Arnold replied that he had "given orders to prevent it in future." Benedict Arnold to HL, Aug. 8, 1778, PCC, Item 162, p. 140.

[1] In his letter of June 26 Gervais mentioned that the Chevalier de Jaussaud had arrived with a letter from John Delagayé and sought money from Delagayé's account. Gervais, after consulting Gabriel Manigault, advanced £500 currency and concluded "I shall be glad to hear it is all right." Later Gervais repeated the information and sent a copy of Jaussaud's receipt. *HL Papers*, XIII, 518, 539; Receipt from the Chevalier Jaussaud, July 1, 1778, HL Papers, ScHi.

Your Packet to Colonel Laurens is gone after him, perhaps it may overtake him at Rhode Island[2] where he is sent by his General with private orders and Messages to General Sullivan and probably to Count d'Estaing. I am glad he is found useful and to be trusted with important charges.

I tell you my dear friend, our situation which you say "is certainly much more promising" is not what you believe it to be; don't start when I say, it is deplorable. I am sorry for Pompey and Tom. you judge right with respect to Cuffy and March.[3] M[r.] Bayley & all the rest of my affairs are under your direction and controul whatever you have done, or shall do respecting those affairs will meet my thanks. If you have paid M[r.] Blundell, & dead loss of the sum will be sustained.[4]

Dispose of Lewis Roux as you shall judge most for his advantage, consistently with his inclinations, and also with his circumstances. I cannot expect to see him before the middle of December.[5]

The Act of Congress in favor of Tories reformed was well intended but has produced no good effects,[6] indeed from experience I am now of opinion that the most honest men amongst them do not hold themselves bound by any promises made to the most honest Men among those whom they stile, Rebels; the latter, therefore, are guilty of falling in the extreme when they trust them__ it is you know, Sir, I had formerly more charity for my neighbours & for Mankind in general. It is but of late that I have learn'd of the distinction establish'd by our Enemies between moral and Political honor, however, I do not say there is not one of the persons called Tories whom I would not rely upon. There are

---

[2] "Providence" written above "Rhode Island".

[3] Gervais reported that HL's slaves Pompey and Tom Peas had died of fever and that he intended to give Doctor Cuffee and March "a well deserved Correction." After the punishment Doctor Cuffee was to be sold at vendue and March to be put under strict supervision at Mepkin. *HL Papers*, XIII, 539-540.

[4] As executor of Elias Ball of Ashepoo's (d. 1758) estate, HL also controlled some funds of the estate of Samuel Ball, against which Charleston merchant Nathaniel Blundell had made a claim. *HL Papers*, XIII, 540.

[5] HL had overseen the education of Lewis Roux since his father Jean Daniel Roux had died in July 1773. *HL Papers*, XIII, 540-541.

[6] Congress, on April 23, 1778, passed a resolution recommending each state issue a proclamation offering a pardon to any Loyalist who would surrender before June 10, and that the patriots "receive such returning penitents with compassion and mercy." *JCC*, X, 381-382.

certainly exceptions. Captain James Willings' expedition will end as I prognosticated in the beginning of it. These States will incur a heavy debt, loss of lives, and receive no kind of benefit from it,__ It was the project of a private Member without the knowledge of Congress__ a Member who has done and does what he pleases.[7]

The name of new hope is very applicable to a Plantation whose buildings and improvements have been burned and destroy'd.

Bachop certainly promis'd me he would never bear Arms against America, provided he was allow'd to return to S^t· Augustine on his Parole, but I presume he has been regularly exchanged__ even in that case from repeated declarations which he made to me he is very criminal for cruising upon our Coast__ pray has he repaid the money I advanced him?[8]

Your President is not unpopular in Congress. I am sorry he is so, as you say at home. A sound conscience shields the Mind against all attacks of tongues and Pens.

I am rejoyc'd to learn of M$^{rs.}$ Gervais's perfect recovery. I salute her and the children with my best Respects__ I grieve for your friend the elder M^r· Trapier.[9]

Well but Sir! surely such full tables as I perceive mark'd in your letter of the 6th of July is not a proof of unpopularity.

If Monsr· Galvan is looking for promotion, he takes the wrong road.

You will be inform'd by His Excellency the President my Ideas about the Embargo__ this was also a well calculated and well design'd Act of Congress, but abuses are creeping in. I shall be as attentive as possible, and upon the earliest discovery ring an Alarm. I beg you will present my best Compliments to M^r· and M$^{rs.}$ Manigault. I hope to find time for writing to my worthy old friend next week. Remember me also to every other friend, and be assured I remain, with the highest esteem and affection

Dear Sir &c.

---

[7] James Willing, who had led an American expedition down the Mississippi River in early 1778, was the brother of Thomas Willing, Robert Morris's former business partner. The "private Member" to whom HL referred was Robert Morris. *HL Papers*, XIII, 541n; Cummins, *Spanish Observers*, pp. 54-88; *Delegate Letters* (Smith), X, 399n.

[8] Peter Bachop, who had been captured in July 1776 but paroled with HL's assistance, was again captured June 22, 1778, after he returned to privateering. *HL Papers*, XI, 215n; XIII, 484, 542.

[9] Gervais had reported the death of Paul Trapier, Jr., in his July 2 letter. *HL Papers*, XIII, 543.

P.S.

Have you sold my last years' Indigo? and for how much__ If you have not purchas'd ↑the↓ Negroes woolen cloathing yet, delay a Month or so, or until I write again on the subject

M^r· Drayton two days ago told me a story which almost surpris'd me, that General Gadsden has again ↑indeavour'd to↓ injure me, by a groundless charge or insinuation, that I had presented the Letter, intimating the resignation of his Commission, either improperly in the manner, or at an improper time. all[10] his suspicions ~~had~~ ↑have↓ been equally unjust, but it has not always been in my power to prove it, as I shall do in the present case. His resignation was tendered to Congress the 2nd of October by M^r· Hancock. I was order'd in the Chair the 1st· of November. It is true I said nothing upon the occasion; neither did any Member in the house, except those who said, "accept it," "accept it," I was not one of them. I should have been very cautious had it been put to a vote, even of giving my voice ~~for or~~ against it. 'Tis probable I should have withdrawn upon such an occasion__ the risk of offending would have been equal on either side__ When M^r· Gadsden was in the service I now am in, he knows, I endeavoured to assist and serve him & God knows I never attempted to undervalue or depreciate him__ if he had had any foundation for censuring me, he should have communicated his complaints directly to myself or have reserv'd them to be communicated at my return, instead of such generous procedure, he has, according to his custom, stabb'd me in conversations and private letters. It was by mere accident I learn'd his discourteous, injurious, attempts, from M^r· Drayton, and this, as I said above, but two days ago. I wish you would read every word of this to General Gadsden; it will keep up a consistency in all my conduct towards that Gentleman.[11]

SOURCE: LB, HL Papers, ScHi; addressed "Colonel John L. Gervais / Charlestown" and by HL "by Durst"; dated "7th August".

---

[10] "all" written over other text.
[11] William Henry Drayton told HL of the charges Gadsden had made but did not show him the letter. In September HL reported that Timothy Matlack gave him "a long Letter which he receiv'd from Mr. Gadsden." It was a copy of the letter Drayton had received from Gadsden. Moses Young, HL's clerk, made a copy which is now in the HL Papers at the South

TO JOHN WELLS, JR.

Philadelphia, August 7, 1778

I hope to send your Ephemeris[1] two days hence by Capt. Paine__. Please to apply to His Excellency the President and request him to communicate to you from my dispatches all such Articles as His Excellency shall think proper to be published, not meaning to bar a communication by any other paper which may be coming abroad earlier than Yours. This is all fair with respect to the Printer and due to the Public.[2]

I am &c.

SOURCE: LB, HL Papers, ScHi; addressed "John Wells / Charlestown / by Durst"; dated "7th August".

TO JACOB CHRISTOPHER ZAHN

Philadelphia, August 7, 1778

Dear Sir

I am indebted for your very obliging favor of the 13th of June, which I had intended to answer in all its parts with that respectfulness and attention which is due to it, but that is now impossible. I have not many minutes allowed for writing this. permit me then briefly to say, your Ideas and mine with respect to slavery appear to me, from your expressions, to accord.[1]

Carolina Historical Society. Gadsden accused HL, "the greatest and most inveterate Enemy I have in the World," of laying his resignation before Congress without comment or ceremony at a time which was not conducive to a fair hearing. Christopher Gadsden to William Henry Drayton, July 4, 1778, HL Papers, ScHi; HL to John Lewis Gervais, Sept. 10, 1778.

[1] Wells, who published the *South Carolina Almanac*, had asked HL to obtain David Rittenhouse's ephemeris or astronomical calculation for 1778 and 1779. *HL Papers*, XIII, 440-441, 484.

[2] Wells published the following items which HL had sent to Rawlins Lowndes in the *S.C. General Gazette*, Sept. 10, 1778: Louis XVI's letter to Congress; Gérard's address to Congress; HL's reply as president of Congress to Gérard; Israel Mauduit's handbill; and a report of the New York fire. Peter Timothy published in the *S.C. Gazette*, Sept. 10, 1778: Gérard's address, HL's reply to Gérard, and a report of the New York fire.

[1] HL's opposition to slavery suggests that Zahn was likewise inclined, though both men were slaveholders.

We shall, I hope, talk this matter over before Christmass to our mutual satisfaction. In the mean time, let it suffice to repeat my thanks for all you have done for me.

Inclosed with this you will receive the latest Newspapers, and also a letter to Mr Burnet which you'l be pleased to peruse, and then seal and deliver it.

Count d'Estaing's arrival at Rhode Island, obliged the Enemy to burn the King Fisher Man of War and two of their Gallies, and to call in all their out Posts__ they are now about 5000 strong in Garrison on the Island, these will soon be attacked by General Sullivan, aided by the French fleet and about 3000 French Troops. The Army of the Allies will then amount to about 8000 commanded by some of our very best officers. We must with patience wait the event.

General Washington closely hems Sir Henry Clinton within his lines upon New York Island, except such of them as come off as deserters; these are seldom less that 8 or 10 a day.

I have hopes we shall be in a state of Peace in a few Months. Neither the French nor English had declared War the 28th of May, although hostilities are committed by each party against the other as effectually as if War was actually declared.

The general voice of England from the latest Accounts appear to be for declaring these States Independent__ and those very Men who had hurried the People of that much deluded Nation ↑into ruinous measures↓[2] were paving the way for reconciling the minds of the Public to an event which one year ago they affected to treat with scorn.

Adieu, Good Sir, I wish you health and all happiness and am with great Respect

Your Most Obed^t Servant

P.S.

Please to let Mr Burnet have the perusal of the Newspapers

SOURCE: LB, HL Papers, ScHi; addressed "Christopher Zahn / Charlestown / by Durst"; dated "7th August".

---

[2] Interlineation by HL.

REMONSTRANCE FROM
CARLISLE COMMISSION

New York, August 7, 1778

By The Earl of Carlisle, Sir Henry Clinton, William Eden Esquire and George Johnstone Esquire His Majestys Commissioners Appointed with Sufficient Powers to treat, consult and agree upon the means of quieting Disorders now Subsisting in certain of the colonies Plantations and Provinces of North America.__

Upon a Representation from the Commander in Chief of His Majesty's Forces That the Troops lately serving under Lieutenant General Burgoyne, notwithstanding the Solemn Convention entered into at Saratoga, in which it is stipulated That the said Troops should have a free Passage to Great Britain, are nevertheless under various pretences still detained in New England: The following Remonstrance against the unjust Detention of those Troops, and requisition for their immediate Release on the Condition annexed to the Article by which their Passage to England is Stipulated are now Solemnly made to the American Congress.__

Whereas the means that have been devised by mankind to mitigate the horrors of War and to facilitate the Re-establishment of Peace depend on the Faith of Cartels, military Capitulations, Conventions and Treaties entered into even during the Continuance of Hostilities. From whence all nations have agreed to observe such Conventions, as they revere the Sacred Obligations of Humanity and Justice, And as they would avoid the horrid practice of Retaliations which however justly due to the Guilty, in such cases but too frequently fall on the Innocent.__

And Whereas upon these Considerations, all breach of Faith even with an Enemy, and all attempts to elude the force of Military Conventions or to defeat their Salutary purposes by Evasion or Chicane, are justly held in detestation and deemed unworthy of any description of Persons assuming the Character or Stating themselves as the Representatives of Nations.__

And Whereas it was Stipulated in the Second Article of the Convention entered into at Saratoga between Lieutenant General Burgoyne and Major General Gates "That a free Passage be granted to the Army under Lieutenant General Burgoyne to Great Britain, upon Condition of not serving again in North America during the present Contest. And the Port of Boston is assigned for the Entry of Transports whenever General Howe shall so Order."

His Majesty's Commissioners now founding their Claim on this Article join with the Commander in Chief of His Majesty's Forces in a Peremptory Requisition That free Entrance into the Harbour of Boston be given to Transports for the immediate Embarkation of the said Troops and that they be allowed to depart for Great Britain in terms of the said Convention. And the said Commissioners in order to remove every supposed difficulty or pretence for delay in the Execution of this Treaty arising from any past real apparent or Supposed infraction of it by word or writing on the side of either Party, hereby offer to renew, on the part of Great Britain all the Stipulations of the Convention and particularly to Ratify the Condition Annexed to the Second Article above recited by which those Troops are not to serve again in America during the present Contest.__ And This Requisition is now sent To the American Congress for their direct and explicit Answer.__[1]

Given under our hands at New york the 7th. day of August 1778.__

Carlisle
H Clinton
Wm. Eden
Geo: Johnstone.

SOURCE: RC, PCC (Item 57), DNA; addressed below close "To His Excellency / Henry Laurens Esqre / The President, and other / The Members of The / Congress at / Philadelphia"; docketed by HL "British Commissioners / Remonstrance & requisition / on suspension of the im / barkation of Convention / Troops__ 7th. Augt 1778 / Read 12th_". Copy, HL Correspondence, 1762–1780, PHi.

---

[1] The letter and remonstrance from the Carlisle Commission was conveyed to HL by Gen. William Maxwell, who had received it under a flag. Maxwell informed HL that "both ends of the cover has been pulled out and I suppose the contents was read by some partys or persons in the other side." The document was read in Congress on August 12 where it was referred to a committee. No action was taken at that time. On August 26 separate declarations from George Johnstone and the other members of the Carlisle Commission along with a second copy of the August 8 Remonstrance concerning the Convention troops were sent to Congress where they were read August 31. Congress began discussions of the Carlisle Commission's "requisition...respecting the troops lately serving under Lieutenant General Burgoyne" on September 3. The following day Congress resolved to accept no ratification of the Saratoga Convention unless it came directly from Parliament. William Maxwell to HL, Aug. 8, 1778, PCC, Item 57, p. 328; George Johnstone Declaration, Aug. 26, 1778, PCC, Item 167, p. 9ff; Carlisle Commission Declaration Aug. 26, 1778, PCC, Item 167, p. 5ff; Carlisle Commission Remonstrance, Aug. 26, 1778, PCC, Item 57, p. 333ff; JCC, XI, 776, 855; XII, 876-878, 880-883.

FROM THÉVENEAU DE FRANCY
                              Williamsburg, Va., August 7, 1778
Honorable Sir.

I have been honoured by your two favours from the 26th & 28th july. I am very thankfull for the warm & friendly interest which you have taken in my demand to the honorable the Congress. I am in hope that at last Mr. de Beaumarchais's affairs Shall be put upon the best & most proper footing, as it is So easy to know at this time what he has done & if his claims are right. the two Gentlemen who were the better acquainted in france with all his Exertions are now in philadelphia;[1] when I Shall be there myself, I will certainly unmask those mean & low intriguers who Exerted themselves So much to prejudice Congress against one of their best friends.

I have read With a very great pleasure what you Says of our minister plenipotentiary; in a beginning of an alliance as this, it was of the greatest importance to Send a Gentleman Such as you describe Monsr. Girard to be: I knew that he had Some very great qualities, but the portrait which you make of him, is so flattering for this ↑Gentleman↓ that as I know you to be a Very good judge, it rises yet[2] my opinion With his regard.

I Expect with a very great impatience the answer of Congress about my representation; I am Sorry that my Servant would return Without bringing it; I had ordered him dispatch, but by no means to hurry you as he did; be pleased to receive my Excuses for it.

the Claret is not in Cases, & it Should be impossible to get bottles here to put it, but I have ordered four pipes of two hundred & forty bottles Each to be put in other tuns So that the heat Shall not hurt it neither the Waggoners drink it; I Shall Send them from here to Baltimore by water & from thence to philadelphia by land; of these four pipes, you will Command any quantity which you will be pleased to have. I hope you will find it good.

I have the honour to be with the greatest respect & most Sincere Esteem

Honorable Sir / Your Excellency's most Hble / & most obedient Servant

                                             De francy

---

[1] Silas Deane and William Carmichael.
[2] "yet" written over other text.

P.S. I take the liberty of inclosing you two letters for Messrs Deane & Carmichael as I have not their directions; will you be pleased to forward them.

SOURCE: RC, HL Papers, ScHi; addressed below close "his excellency the H^ble. Henry Laurens president of C. Congress."; dated "Williamsburg 7th august 1778."; docketed by HL "~~WL~~az^r· de francy / 7th· Augt 1778 / Rec̄d. 18^th___".

TO MESHECH WEARE

Philadelphia, August 8, 1778

Honorable Sir,

Since my last of the 12th July I have been honour'd with your favors of the 4th· & 17^th_ of that Month & am much obliged by the particular recitals of such Letters as Your Honor had received from me.[1]

Within this Inclosure be pleased to receive Sir an Act of Congress of yesterday Resolving that the expence attending the late abortive expedition against Rhode Island shall be a Public charge.[2]

I have the honor to be / With great regard & respect / Honorable Sir / Your most obedient / humble servant

Henry Laurens.
President / of Congress.

SOURCE: ALS, Meshech Weare Papers, MHi; addressed below close "The Honorable / Meshec Weare Esquire / President / New Hamshire."; dated "Philadelphia. / 8th August 1778 ". LB, PCC (Item 13), DNA.

---

[1] HL had been frustrated with the New Hampshire governor's failure to acknowledge receipt of correspondence from Congress and in an April 20, 1778, letter instructed him in the polite and proper procedure. *HL Papers*, XIII, 156.

[2] The abortive Rhode Island expedition of 1777 had been under investigation since late that year. The commission selected to review the events had reported March 27, 1778. Congress referred the report to a committee that reported August 7. Rather than assigning blame for the failure, Congress agreed to assume the cost and reimburse Rhode Island, Connecticut, and New Hampshire for the expenses of the failed undertaking. HL to Rhode Island Expedition Commissioners, Dec. 15, 1777, PCC, Item 13; *JCC*, X, 321-322; XI, 658-661.

FROM GEORGE WASHINGTON

White Plains, N.Y., August 9, 1778[1]

Sir

Mr. Fuhrer & Mr. Kleinsmit have lately left the British lines and come in to us.[2] The account they give of themselves is this__ That they had been first lieutenants in the Hessian Corps__ were taken prisoners at Trenton, resided during their captivity at Dumfries in Virginia__ were lately exchanged and have since resigned their commissions__ That having solicited permission to come out from the enemy and being refused, they determined to leave them at all hazards, and have now put their design in execution. The circumstances of their captivity are known to several Officers in our army.

They are desirous of entering into our service, observing that there ↑are↓ a number of German Officers in the same disposition with themselves, who will resign and join us, if they find that these meet with proper countenance. It appears to me, that important advantages may attend the encouraging a disposition of this nature, if it really exists, which is far from being impossible; from the influence it will necessarily have upon the soldiery, by increasing that spirit of desertion and discontent, which already prevails among them.__

Congress will best judge of the propriety of employing these Gentlemen. I have been thinking in what manner it might be done; and the mode least exceptionable, which at present occurs to me, is to authorise them to raise a Corps for themselves, by inlisting such German inhabitants, and such of the prisoners and deserters from the foreign troops, as may be willing to engage. The Corps at first as it is only by way of experiment need not be large; but may be afterwards encreased, as circumstances shall point out. This measure, I apprehend, cannot be attended with any material inconvenience and may be productive of utility.__ If the Gentlemen are employed at all it must be in a new Corps, as they could not be introduced into any of those already formed, without injuring the

---

[1] Dated from draft in Washington Papers, DLC.

[2] Ensigns Carl Frederich Fuhrer of Knyphausen's regiment and Carl Wilhelm Kleinschmidt of Rahl's regiment, who had been captured at Trenton, deserted on August 7 at White Plains, N.Y. Rodney Awood, *The Hessian Mercenaries from Hessen-Kassel in the American Revolution* (Cambridge, Eng., 1980), pp. 201-202.

Officers in them, and producing dissatisfaction, murmurs and resignations.__

I have sounded them on the plan here suggested and they seem to be very sanguine in it's success and anxious to undertake it. They expect some augmentation in ran[k] and indeed it seems necessary in order the more effectually to interest others to follow their example; but caution should be used not to carry the idea too far, because besides other weightly considerations, the higher the rank conferred on them, the more difficult it will be to provide for those, who may hereafter come to us and who will of course frame their expectations by comparison.[3]

I have the honor to be / With the greatest respect / Sir / Your most Obed^t Servt

G$^{o:}$ Washington

P.S

An additional grade to the rank they held in the corps they come from will in my opinion be sufficient.

SOURCE: RC, PCC (Item 152), DNA; addressed on cover "The Hon$^{ble.}$ / Henry Laurens Esqr / President of Congress / Philadelphis"; no date; docketed by HL "Genl Washington / no date Rec^d & Read / in Coñg 18 Aug^t / 1778__" and in another hand "(Entered) / Read 18. / Referred to the board of war". Draft, Washington Papers, DLC.

TO BARON VON STEUBEN

Philadelphia, August 10, 1778

Dear Baron.

You have done me the honōr of intimating more than once your sentiments respecting certain necessary attentions to a River defence. Will you be so good my Dear Baron, when you can spare

---

[3] Congress resolved on September 3 that Fuhrer and Kleinschmidt be authorized to raise a corps of German volunteers and that they be commissioned as captains. Congress then set aside the plan on Dec. 5, 1778. *JCC*, XII, 866, 1192.

half an hour for this purpose to communicate your Ideas, including
if you please your advice, in writing to[1]

Your much obliged / & Obedient humble / servant

Henry Laurens.

not written as / President of Congress

Can you without inconvenience stop at my House one minute to
morrow Morning in your way to that of the Minister Plenipotentiary?

SOURCE: ALS, Steuben Papers, NHi; addressed below close "The Honorable
/ Major Gen: Baron Steuben"; dated "Chesnut Street / 10 Augt 1778__";
docketed "Phil^a_ 10 Aug 1778 / H Laurens". LB, HL Papers, ScHi.

FROM JOHN SULLIVAN[1]

Portsmouth, R.I., August 10, 1778

Dear Sir

I have only time to inform your Excellency & the Congress
that the Count De Estaing & myself had fixed upon This morning
Day Break to make our Landing upon the Island preparatory to
which the Fleet came through Newport Harbor on Saturday night
& Silenced two of their Batteries The Enemy Supposing that we
Should Land in the Night & cut off the Communication between
the out posts & the Town Evacuated all their works on the North of
the Island & Retired to Newport Early Saturday Even^g I was informed of this Early in the morning ↑of yesterday↓ & to prevent
their Reoccupying the works I immediately threw the whole Army
Across & Sent word to the Count to Land his Men & Join us. but

---

[1] In an August 29 letter Steuben urged HL "to make the Warmest applications to Congress
for the Execution of so necessary a Scheme, the neglect of which may be productive of very
great Evils." There is no evidence that Steuben did more than recommend improved
defenses. Baron von Steuben to HL, Aug. 29, 1778, Kendall Collection.

[1] The *S.C.General Gazette*, Sept. 10, 1778, published an "Extract of a Letter from a Member
of Congress, August 16," which summarizes the events outlined in this letter. Although HL
sent copies of several Sullivan letters to Rawlins Lowndes in his letter of Aug. 11-20, 1778, HL
did not list this Sullivan letter as an enclosure.

before the ~~word~~ ↑Message↓ could reach him & before our Army was Compleatly over a British Fleet of twenty Nine Sail appeared Standing for Newport Close in with Seconnet Point. This prevented the Count from Sending me any troops he took them all on Board & this morning went out to Engage the Fleet but on the Appearance of the French Squadron they fled I Saw the Count in Chase of them ~~illegible~~ at Eleven of Clock This must Retard my movements Some Respects & Render our opperations more tedious if nothing worse The Circumstance was Exceeding unfortunate Even if it does not Delay the Count a Day I am very fearful it may work a Delay till a British Fleet of Sufficient force may arrive to put an End to the Enterprize Congress may Rest assured that I Shall Endeavour to Surmount Every Difficulty & Effect the Design of the Enterprize with as much Expedition as possible

I have the Honor to be my Dear / Sir Your Excellency's most obed Servt

Jno Sullivan

PS I have the pleasure to Inform Congress that great Numbers of volunteers have joined me General Hancock[2] is with me on the Island with ~~great~~ a Number of Gentlemen of the first Character.__

SOURCE: RC, PCC (Item 160), DNA; addressed below close "His Exc^y Henry Laurens"; dated "Portsmouth Rhode Island Augt 10 1778"; docketed by HL "Gen. Sullivan / 10 Augt 1778 / Rec⁻d & Read in Con / gress 15 Augt 1778__". Copy, HL Papers, ScHi. Copy, MWA.

TO RAWLINS LOWNDES

Philadelphia, August 11, 1778

Dear Sir

I had the honor of writing, to Your Excellency under the 5th and 7th by a Messenger from Don Juan de Mirallis, who had very politely permitted me to detain him as long as I should think

---

[2] John Hancock, who had preceded HL as president of Congress, was in the field with Massachusetts' militia, in which he held the rank of major general.

proper__ my public engagements the week last past had rendered it impossible for me to devote much time to private affairs, my letter was therefore performed piecemeal and not finish'd till the 10th.

My present Address will be deliver'd by Captain Pyne,[1] late of the Comet[2] State vessel of War, or, by lieutenant Martin of our [*blank*] regiment,[3] these Gentlemen will in company begin their journey for South Carolina some time today. They arrived here from imprisonment by the Enemy, and were destitute of Money and apparel; they apply'd to me for aid, and with the concurrence of all my present Colleagues, I supply'd out of the fund belonging to South Carolina, Captain Pyne 1000 Dollars, Lieutenant Martin 940 Dollars, for which sums your Excellency will find their several acknowledgements within this cover.

In my last Letter I suggested some apprehensions of receiving shortly a ratification of the Convention of Saratoga. Last night a paper pretended to be a Ratification signed by four of the British Commissioners and usher'd by a Letter of the 7th from Mr. Ferguson[4] their Secretary was sent to me by General Maxwell, the General had received it as he writes by a Flag which had come by an indirect and prohibited road. The whole affair it is to be presumed, is calculated for insulting Congress by a retort on their late resolution that "no Answer be given to the Commissioners letter of the 11th" published by Charles Thomson, Secretary of Congress. In this view it appears trifling with serious matters, admitting their character to come within that description__ and in what other light can it be viewed__ the Commissioners knew that Congress had resolved that the embarkation of the troops of the Convention should be suspended "till a distinct and explicit Ratification of the Convention of Saratoga shall be properly notified by the Court of Great Britain to Congress." And those gentlemen have ground for believing that Congress will not hastily depart from important Resolutions. Possibly they may now pretend that their powers from their Court are

---

[1] Capt. James Pyne.

[2] Ship's name written by HL.

[3] John Peter Martin of Charleston had enlisted in the German Fusiliers during 1775. He was captured while on a cruise in 1777 and held prisoner at New York until his exchange in March, 1778. Moss, *S.C. Patriots;* Receipt, March 12, 1778, catalog of Dawson's Book Shop, July 1943.

[4] Adam Ferguson to HL, Aug. 7, 1778, PCC, Item 57, p. 321ff.

tantamount__ admitting this they ought to have been "distinct and explicit".

What the determination of Congress will be after I shall have presented this paper is uncertain, in the mean time my fears are, that the motion and Resolve which I have so anxiously wish'd will not be effected, or, not with that grace and perspicuity which would have been produced by a deliberate consideration antecedally to the receipt of this outrer illegitimate Remonstrance & requisite__ Yesterday I again repeated to the Chief Justice, "you will by this unaccountable procrastination slip an opportunity of doing justice and honor to your Country"

Among other papers which will accompany this Your[5] Excellency will receive Copy of the Remonstrance and the Secretarys' letter; these papers contain nothing like a distinct explicit Ratification properly notified by the Court of Great Britain to Congress, and therefore I estimate the correspondence and the mode, a calculated Insult; and were I to direct, probably it is best I should not, I wou'd immediately return the whole, accompanied by a few proper lines from Charles Thomson to Adam Ferguson__ Nothing has happen'd during the present Contest so embarrassing to the Court of Great Britain as the Resolve of Congress on the suspension__ A conformity ~~to~~ ↑with↓ the terms will amount to an acknowledgment of our capacity to treat as a Nation__ any ~~illegible~~ ↑thing↓[6] below this will be to retain her claim upon us as Subjects in Rebellion, with whom faith, is not to be held but for the benefit of the Sovereign, as in the exchange of Prisoners; and even in that communication there have been many attempts on the part of our Enemy to ↑exercise↓[7] arbitrary and cruel impositions__ your Excellency will recollect a recent instance which occasioned the seperation of Commissioners at Germantown who had met for establishing a Cartel.

If the Court shall, from necessity, find her interest in ratifying the Convention in the terms prescribed by Congress, it will then be for us to consider the Articles and to enquire whether ~~each~~

---

[5] "Y" written over "y".
[6] Interlineation by HL.
[7] Interlineation by HL.

the whole ~~has~~ ↑have↓ been strictly comply'd with by the contracting powers, and thus, according to strict justice and sound Policy, which are inseperable the work will be to begin.

Admitting these Ideas to be just 'tis not to be doubted, ~~but~~ ↑that↓ the Court of Great Britain perceives ~~her~~ ↑the↓ dilemma[8] to which she is reduced by a few deeply designing words of her Marionnette, Lieutenant General Burgoyne, who has acknowledged ↑in Parliament↓ that he penned every syllable of his infamous Proclamation and, at the same time declared he had no intention to carry the severe threats contained in it, into execution__[9] she must consequently view the troops of Saratoga as prisoners of War, unless she will engage, in a tacit concession of our Independence, and for which, she ~~would~~ ↑will↓,[10] be in the judgment of all her European Neighbours__ no wonder therefore, that in this entangled situation her Ministers are persevering in *illegible* practices of ambi-dexterity__ and as little that I continue anxiously wishing for the attestations of Captain Senff.

I am now at the 16th. Mr. Martin has been detained by bad weather and sickness.

Your Excellency will read in the Penna. Packet of the 13th the declaration of Congress of the 11th__ this is the Paper Mr. Drayton had kept so long in his Pocket and which I had so often solicited should be brought forward__ I now regret that some previous corrections had not *illegible* been apply'd to it and that[11] the house was hurried in its passage without such amendments as at first view Your Excellency will see it stood in need of__[12] be this as it may, it contains matters of fact, and such as it is, the Commissioners may criticize words and Phrases but the whole group will not be able to explain away our meaning, nor do I ~~think th~~ believe that even a Man of Governor Johnstone's command of features will have Art enough smoothly to laugh off his feelings whenever this Act of Abnegation

---

[8] "d" written over other text.

[9] John Burgoyne spoke in Parliament May 26 and defended his employment of Indians in his Northern campaign. He claimed to have been "very popular with the Indians." The proclamation of June 24, 1777, "was penned by myself. The design was to excite obedience, first by encouragement, and next by the dread, not the commission of severity,—'to speak daggers, but use none.'" Cobbett's *Parliamentary History*, XIX, 1179-1182; *HL Papers*, XI, 447n.

[10] Interlineation by HL.

[11] "th" interlined by HL.

[12] "of" interlined by HL.

shall be brought on the Carpet in his presence on either side of the Water. I put it in motion the 13th and it is probable the Governor has receiv'd his first shock this Morning. He has been severely lampoon'd in New York as will be seen in another paper to be inclosed with this___[13] The Declaration and other unavoidable business fill'd up the Session of the 11th and barr'd the delivery of the Remonstrance and Requisition before the 12th it was then committed to a special Committee, a compliment which, in my humble opinion it did not merit.

It is now the 18th. Captain Pyne and Captain Martin having declared themselves quite ready I would not attempt to detain them. They began their journey this Morning I understand they are to halt at Baltimore a day and an half on business of their own___ there I hope to overtake them, otherwise this will go by the common Post and not arrive so early as I could wish.

Mr. Deane late one of our Commissioners at the Court of Versailles, has already been two Mornings engaged before Congress reporting from Notes and Memory his own transactions seperately ~~and~~ ↑as well as↓ conjunctly with his Colleagues and the state of our Affairs at different periods at that and other Courts in Europe, how many Mornings more the whole Narrative will consume is extreamly uncertain; hitherto he has been very little impeded by questions, when these Commence, the progress will be slow___ above two hours were employed some days ago in debate upon a motion that Mr. Deane should report to Congress in writing and the motion lost___ very much loss of time I foresee will be the consequence; in this debate I clearly discovered that my fellow labourers had as absolutely taken sides as it can be supposed Gentlemen are capable of in a <u>pure unbiays'd</u> ↑unbias'd↓[14] Assembly.[15] Were I to say as ever

---

[13] This lampoon of George Johnstone's attempt to bribe some members of Congress had him selling the "British Rights in America" for which "a seat in Congress will be taken in part payment, the rest in Continental money." *Pa. Packet*, Aug. 13, 1778.

[14] Interlineation by HL.

[15] Congress defeated the motion August 15 nine states to four. Of the thirty-two members voting, twelve including HL voted for the motion "that the narrative Mr. Deane shall give to this house, of his transactions in France, be in writing." Included in the twelve were the entire Massachusetts, Rhode Island, Connecticut, and New Jersey delegations plus Francis Lewis of New York. *JCC*, XI, 799–801. This is HL's first mention of the factional division in Congress that grew out of the disputes between Silas Deane and the Lee brothers. Despite his criticism of factional politics, HL would be drawn into conflict and join the opponents of Deane.

Attornies had taken at a Bar I might be charged in the modern term with aberation, nevertheless I have taken the liberty to recommend the fillet and scales of Justice to one of my worthy Colleagues who appears strongly attached to one of the parties,[16] no doubt from conviction that that side is right adding the reply which I had made to M^r. D. after he had related to me in private conversation his state of the case__ "Your Account Sir, appears to be ↑have been↓[17] very candidly deliver'd, but I dare not flatter you with promises; when I shall have heard the other side I will give my voice as reason[18] and conscience shall dictate". M^r. Deane thank'd me. I remark'd further to my Colleague that nothing short of a written and correct narrative ought to have been accepted by Congress__ that if M^r. Deane had acted, which I made no doubt he had, with that accuracy and perspicuity which become ↑is the duty of↓[19] a Gentleman in the Great trust of a Plenipotentiary, nothing could be easier than to render a detail in writing.

As it was incumbent on him ↑M^r. Deane↓[20] to transmit from time to time to Congress advices of all his proceedings, discoveries and observations, and as I could not entertain so degrading a sentiment as a belief of the contrary would involve, very little more than a fair transcript of his letters and Journals would be necessary for satisfying the fullest enquiry__ without assuming to myself any superiour knowledge I cannot help regretting that the Chair was a bar to the delivery of that opinion in public which arrived too late in priv friendly conversation after the question had been determin'd by a *illegible* majority of nine of thirteen States, thirty two Members present.

Gentlemen had reasoned upon the immense labour of reducing to writing occurrences of ↑in↓[21] three whole Years, that the work would procrastinate the business several months, that all that could be deliver'd in writing might in less time and with equal accuracy be related viva voce, those who have ↑had↓ not been much

---

16 Probably William Henry Drayton who became a member of the pro-Deane faction.
17 Interlineation by HL.
18 "r" written over "r" for clarity.
19 Interlineation by HL.
20 Interlineation by HL.
21 Interlineation by HL.

accustomed to business, and who lament the waste of time in almost all our proceedings, were captivated__ but the most curious objection, considering it was started by M[r.] Deanes' friends, was, that should a narrative in writing be demanded, that Gentleman might avail himself of the advantage of representing glossing &c. &c. as he pleas'd__ every unbias'd Man now, after reflection sees that the mode we have adopted will extend debates and often lead disputants into warm contests, wandering from the point.

Whose memory will retain all that has been and shall be related on different days at ~~distinct~~ ↑distant↓[22] times? Whose notes will quadrate with those of a friend on the other side of the question? Who will acknowledge the accuracy and precision of the memory or minutes__ of his opponent? ↑Will you↓[23] Call on M[r.] Deane to recollect what he had said and to decide?__[24] here is a field without limits for Oratory and wrangle and ~~final~~ ↑finally for↓[25] mutual dissatisfaction.

I have troubled Your Excellency thus minutely, because the subject is not minute, it is of the highest importance to our Union__ I have been long of opinion and have intimated my sentiments to my friends__ that there have been errors on both sides among our Commissioners__ Errors, probably not of the heart, and therefore I had wished that a veil had been judiciously drawn and that a wise seperation ~~should be~~ made of Gentlemen whose tempers when mixed in joint Commission excluded all harmony.[26]

Already we have made this unhappy discovery that our funds abroad are exhausted, our resources dried up, our credit lost in the West Indies, our Bills of Exchange which are pledg'd for ~~pay~~ the Interest of loans will go forward at the utmost hazard of dishonor__ my sentiments on foreign debt conducted in the manner and by the Men it has been, were declared without reserve to my friends in Charlestown some twelve Months ago, and from the present gloomy prospect it was, that I lately intimated to one of them that our Affairs were in a deplorable state, more so my Dear

---

[22] Interlineation by HL.
[23] Interlineation by HL.
[24] "?" written over "!".
[25] Interlineation by HL.
[26] "all harmony" written by HL.

Sir, than you can form an Idea of, ~~or~~ ↑& more so↓[27] than I ought just now to express__ the value of our Current paper Money is to be determin'd by the price of articles given in Exchange__ this comparison will sink it low indeed__ add to all this, the injudicious behaviour of people in general, who flatter themselves with persuations that our troubles are at end, and who act accordingly__ the cunning ones striving to depreciate the value of our Money in order to get as much of it as by all means they can obtain__ the simple, by an almost total neglect of measures essentially necessary to be continued and pursued by a Nation in our circumstances__ immediately after we had repossessed this City, General Washington in the spirit of a watchful and wise Commander in Chief, sent General Duportail with a letter to Congress recommending the immediate securing the River against insults from the Enemy, and for that purpose gave the General, who is principal Engineer ample instructions, we have been here upwards of seven weeks, I have repeatedly urged Congress to hear the instructions read, yet to this moment no step is taken__ [28] we are in danger of being routed again whenever two or three English ships of War shall be ordered up this River, and should Count d'Estaing be overpower'd or block'd up at Rhode Island, Congress will again be shamefully exiled, possibly in the absence of our Army, captured and all our prisoners retaken__ all these things Your Excellency and the state I have the honor of representing should know with proper reservations__ there are a thousand other things you are entitled to be informed of, which time and political propriety forbid in the present moment. Therefore I shall leave the subject after one sentence more__ I remember to have read or heard some where of a Chief Justice's recommending to a Grand Jury to present the King__ [29] permit me to ask my

---

[27] Interlineation by HL.

[28] George Washington's instructions to General DuPortail were dated June 30, 1778. *Washington Writings* (Fitzpatrick), XII, 134-135. Congress did not take action until August 21 after receiving a letter of the previous day from the Pennsylvania Council which requested a meeting with a committee of Congress to discuss "the subject of fortifying the river Delaware." Richard Henry Lee, William Duer, and Nathaniel Scudder were selected to meet with representatives of the Pennsylvania state government. *JCC,* XI, 825; *Pa. Archives,* 1st ser., VI, 710.

[29] A reference to South Carolina Chief Justice William Henry Drayton's April 23, 1776, charge to the Charleston grand jury. William M. Dabney and Marion Dargan, *William Henry Drayton and the American Revolution* (Albuquerque, N.M., 1962), p. 123.

Countrymen if it would be a greater outrage, to present their Attornies (I am in earnest Sir,) for neglect of duty__ why are not public Accounts adjusted? Why are not the proceedings of the Confederal Attornies published?__ I have by strife this day obtain'd a continuation in two volumes including 31st December 1776 which I send to Your Excellency by this conveyance__ half, even quarter diligence would have reached to 1st August 1778 in boards, and to the 19th where I am now in sheets__ for the correctness of these which I now transmit I will not be answerable, I know not how they are compiled nor if by any body corrected at the Press.__ 30

Major General Mifflin has taken one step on the line of presentment, and although, with submission to his better judgment I think his ground unfirm, yet it may hereafter prove to have been an happy Omen__ the first Commandment is the basis of true religion.31

Concerning the present Embargo, Congress have recommended to this State and New Jersey to take Measures for ensuring a strict observance, and for preventing infractions by evil minded Men on this extensive unguarded Coast and upon the numerous Creeks Bays and Inlets__ 32 the Commercial Committee have recommended to their Agent in Charlestown to dispatch two Vessels with Rice from that Port, I wont affront Your Excellency by intimating that this is no authority__ the motive for the Order is good, to save a faithful Confederal Agent at Hispaniola from absolute ruin by

---

30 John Dunlap's last volume of the Journals of Congress through the end of 1776 had been published at York earlier in 1778. The next volume, through 1777, Dunlap published later in 1778 at Philadelphia.

31 In June 1778 Congress resolved to investigate Thomas Mifflin's administration of the quartermaster general's office and call for a court-martial if warranted. In his letters to HL dated August 10 and 11, Mifflin requested that the investigation begin and that outstanding accounts from his time as quartermaster be settled. When Congress failed to respond quickly, Mifflin sent HL a curt note, to which the president replied the same day that Congress had taken no action. Mifflin on August 17 informed HL that he "was much hurt by their neglect of my letters" and sent his commission with a letter of resignation. Mifflin sent copies of the correspondence from August 10 to August 17 including his resignation to the *Pa. Packet* where it was published in the August 20 issue. *HL Papers*, XIII, 442; Thomas Mifflin to HL, Aug. 11, 12, 15, 17, 1778, PCC, Item 161, Vol. 1, p. 141ff; HL to Thomas Mifflin, Aug. 15, 1778, PCC, Item 13.

32 On August 14 Congress resolved that the Pennsylvania Council "be requested to station one of their gallies...near the mouth of the Cape May channel" to examine vessels to assure the integrity of the embargo. The governor of New Jersey was requested "to take the most effectual measures to enforce the due observance of the embargo" because Congress feared that the coasting trade along that shore could supply the enemy. *JCC*, IX, 788.

paying protested Bills drawn on our Account, but who brought the unhappy Gentleman into this dilemma↓?↑ I will not say a faithless Secret Committee, but I have no doubt of proving the fact when I get home. Thank God this is the 19th August and that I have strength enough to write on without dinner at 6 o'clock P.M__ a report from the Committee recommending a relaxation of the Embargo in the particular case abovementioned was offer'd two days ago and remains unconsidered__ break one link, the gap will be thirteen wide maugre any and all particular considerations.[33]

20th August

When I had written Yesterday as above, Muckinfuss came in and honored me with Your Excellency's favor of the 29th July which I shall endeavour to pay my respects to, before I lay down the Pen. In the mean time a few scraps of intelligence shall precede.

Count d'Estaing from a happy prospect of immediate Conquest at Rhode Island, has in my opinion been decoy'd, what may be the consequence respecting himself is uncertain, but Your Excellency will learn from General Sullivans' last letter of the 14th that our insulated Army were in danger of a Coup de Burgoyne. Who but my friend General Sullivan would have thought that Lord Howe came within ken of the French fleet merely for the benefit of running away from it?[34] Sandy Hook would have been a much more advantageous starting Post.__ The French ships are extreamly foul, the bottoms of the English Squadron quite clean, these may take or leave; even the immagination of gaining time for the arrival of a Reinforcement was good, the hope encouraged the risque, but I can hardly think Lord Howe as well as he knows the Counts' impetus

---

[33] The American Commissioners in France had refused the bills of exchange drawn on them by Stephen Ceronio "said to be your Agent in Hispaniola, but of whom we had no knowledge." Commissioners to Foreign Affairs Committee, Oct. 7, 1777, PCC, Item 85, p. 85ff. Ceronio appealed for relief to Abraham Livingston, the Continental agent in Charleston, S.C. Livingston forwarded Ceronio's letter to Congress. The Commerce Committee presented the Livingston and Ceronio letters on August 18. The letters were remanded to the Committee which then made a recommendation on August 19. Congress accepted the report by exempting from the embargo vessels loaded with rice on the public account "for the purpose of making remittances for supplies...." *JCC*, XI, 810, 815-816. The order paved the way for Livingston to ship rice cargoes to Ceronio from Charleston.

[34] Sullivan had anticipated that "some such event" like the British fleet's arrival and the French chase would "deprive me of the Counts Assistance, induced me to call out more Men than I otherwise shou'd have done." John Sullivan to HL, Aug. 14, 1778, PCC, Item 160, p. 150ff.

for fight, could have expected such sudden success to his stratagem. The storm which General Sullivan suffered in will have made a great indisposition of both fleets, and they may have since met by single Combabants___[35] the story of a number of ships of War and others in this River and the bay is not yet explained to us__ this draws forth another complaint, upon a conference with Monsr· Girard I pressed, weeks since for a regular daily Courier to and from the Capes and Lewis town either by land or water or both, the expence being for an essential service ought to have been no objection, nor indeed has that Article been the obstacle__ ~~this~~ ↑mere↓[36] inattention has kept us in ignorance three days, of vessels of War being in the River.__

Three hours of this Morning passed in debate whether Governor Franklin should be given in Exchange for Governor M^c·Kinly the previous question by aye and nay__ an Oration by S.C. Esquire[37] on the improvement of time with the life and characters of Elizabeth and Mary Qu. of Scots__ the comparative beauty of black Eyes and blue Eyes__ adjourned.__ Seldom a question upon a Million of Dollars, seldom an unquestionable demand for an hundred.[38]

The Confederation is now signed by Delegates from ten States as Your Excellency will see in a paper inclosed__ Delaware and New Jersey will probably be instructed when their respective Assemblies meet, Maryland 'tis said will not come in without she receives a doceur of Land, New York is not bound unless the whole

---

[35] As the British and French fleets maneuvered in the waters off Rhode Island a storm, which began the night of August 12 and continued through the next day, scattered the vessels and did serious damage to several. The French fleet sustained greater damage. During the relative calm following the storm several isolated actions took place when British and French vessels happened upon each other. The most remarkable of these encounters occurred when the 44-gun *Renown*, Dawson, came across D'Estaing's totally demasted flagship *Languedoc*. Only the arrival of other French vessels and nightfall saved the count's vessel. Tilley, *British Navy*, pp. 150-152.

[36] Interlineation by HL.

[37] Samuel Chase.

[38] John McKinly, the former governor of Delaware, had been captured in September 1777 during the British campaign before Brandywine. Sir Henry Clinton granted him a month's parole in order to help negotiate his exchange for former New Jersey governor William Franklin. McKinly was in Philadelphia and appealed to HL on August 20. HL presented the letter and Congress voted nine to two not to consider the exchange, HL voting with the majority. McKinly again addressed HL in September, noting that his parole would soon expire. On September 14 Congress voted nine to three to approve the exchange. HL and the South Carolina delegation voted against the exchange. JCC, XI, 816-817; XII, 909-913; John McKinly to HL, Aug. 20, 1778, Sept. 11, 1778, PCC, Item 70, pp. 655ff, 663ff.

confederate__ the decimal is therefore equal to, ↑a↓[39] o.

General Lee's tryal ended a week ago. The sentence of the Court Martial is on the road, and ought to have been a secret until Congress had approved or disapproved, but I have been pretty well informed he is acquitted from the charges for disobedience of Orders and shameful retreat,[40] and censured only for insolent letters to the Commander in Chief__ [41] the British Officers in New York, who were good judges of fact have passed quite a different Verdict. Governor Mc·Kinly assured me upon his honor, they aver he might have taken the whole party before whom he retreated. That his retreat astonished them and led some of them to suspect stratagem__ that animadverting on his term of "Check"__ Sir Wm·Erskine the best Soldier they have, replied, "Lee may call it a check if he pleases, but, by —— I call it a very handsome flogging, Gentlemen may be convinced now the Americans can and will fight."

By a return lately reported from the Board of War, it appears we have ample stores of Cannon, Powder, Balls Lead &c. &c. and are not deficient in Muskets__ and a Member of that Board promises a report in a few days which will demonstrate cloathing of all species for upwards of 40,000 Men__ and yet however strange near half our little Army have long been and are half naked.

A Schedule to be subjoined or inclosed will shew Your Excellency what papers are intended to accompany this & to which please to be referred.

And now in order to give Your Excellency some prospect of relief from a tedious Epistle, I turn to Your Excellency's favour above quoted.__

The sequel of the Expedition towards Augustine does not strike me in disappointment upon my Mind. I will say no more upon that subject at present.

Your Excellency will ↑have↓[42] received Commissions both Marine and Army and I will endeavour to transmit more of each by

---

[39] Interlineation by HL.

[40] At this point HL interllined "☞ (an error, see below)".

[41] Charles Lee's court-martial trial began July 4 and concluded on August 12. HL's information was incorrect; Lee was found guilty on each of these charges.

[42] Interlineation by HL.

Muckinfuss' return, all Commissions signed by the late President and dated on and after 1st November 1777 ought undoubtedly to be exchanged, the objections against them are good.

The Commission granted by Governor Caswell to Colonel ~~illegible~~ Carroll appears to me a bad precedent, nor will it I apprehend be regarded as a Confederal; were Commissions to be granted by the Executive power of each State, and regular immediate notice given to Congress of name rank and date, it would answer all the ends of the present mode and ~~safe~~ ↑save↓[43] trouble, but the law and practice being otherwise, I should suppose the instance in question will be deemed invalid.__ I can perceive much regulation is wanted in this branch, there is ground for believing that a great, very great number of Officers are receiving pay and Rations who have never been in a field of battle, who are scatter'd over the face of the Country on various pretences and many employ'd in their private occasions, who will also by means of Certificates and good swearing entitle themselves to half pay after the war. This circumstance leads into deep reflection upon the total derangement of every important department in the Union.

The Enemy do not exchange Seamen for any but Seamen of equal rank, and they treat all our Seamen whom they capture with a rigor and barbarity unheard of before the present contest, hence we have begun to retaliate, but our returns of severity bear no kind of proportion__ I would not advise to exchange Bachop and Osborne for any persons but Seamen of equal Rank__ there is no Cartel established__ I have already intimated the interruption__ but the Commissaries on each side proceed in exchanging Officer for Officer, Soldier for Soldier, Citizen for Citizen__ regarding Rank__ the Marine Exchange has been govern'd nearly by like principles, but capriciously and arbitrarily executed on the part of the Enemy__ after having by every species of cruelty exercised on our Seamen in order to compel them to enter into their service, under which thousands have died languishing miserable deaths, they have exchanged the emaciated survivors, for healthy well fed fellows, compassion for fellow Citizens on our part has induced us to submit to the injustice and inequality of the Exchange.

---

[43] Interlineation by HL.

I shall make enquiry of the Bills of Exchange vended by Mills and communicate to Your Excellency according to discoveries.

The conduct of the Committee under which Mr. Dorsius acted is misterious, I can say nothing of his own, but from them we can obtain no Accounts__ upwards of twelve Months since Accounts of their proceedings were order'd by Congress have elapsed__ about ten since Mr. Robert Morris desired to take the books into his own custody in order to settle them in a six Months leave of absence which he said he had obtained from his State, and eight Months he threatned to send them back to Congress, which they by no means forbid, yet to this hour we are without books and remain in total ignorance of the expenditure of $2^1/2$ Million of Dollars except that we know a very large sum has been shamefully squandered by a brother of Mr. Morris', supported by him after being fully informed of the infamous practices of his brother by the Commissioners at Paris.[44] This, my dear Sir, is another circumstance leading the Minds of Men who have devoted their time and their fortunes to the public service into deep and melancholly reflections.

I have always held a favorable opinion of Mr. Dorsius, nevertheless I would have no further exchanges of Money or Accounts take place between our treasury and him or his Successor of whom as an individual I have likewise a good opinion, without an express order or recommendation from Congress. Meaning hereby to deliver only my own opinion in answer to Your Excellency's enquiry. If the waste in the stream makes your heart ache Sir, the prodigality and profusion at the fountain would break it, and yet I believe it will be necessary to draw you there.

My Colleague Mr. Heyward informs me of his determination to return to South Carolina in a day or two,[45] Mr. Hudson is in Boston, Mr. Matthews sick__ I shall do myself the honor of addressing Your Excellency again by the conveyance of Mr. Heyward, and also of Muckinfuss__ in the mean time as I am now at the 21st I have an opportunity of adding the sentence of the Court Martial on

[44] Thomas Morris, Robert's illegitimate half brother, had been Congress's commercial agent at Nantes. He became notorious for both poor business habits and personal excesses. *HL Papers,* XII, 81.

[45] Thomas Heyward, Jr., last attended Congress August 20. He arrived in Charleston in mid September. *Delegate Letters* (Smith), XI, xxi; Rawlins Lowndes to HL, Sept. 22, 1778.

General Lee and copy of a letter from General Sullivan, to which I beg leave to refer, and possibly I may get in tomorrows' Packet__ I shall send this to Maryland hoping to overtake Captain Pyne and Martin, whose business at Baltimore they said would detain them till Sunday Noon the 23^d

I have the honor to be &c.

P.S. Your Excellency will do me great honor by communicating such parts as you shall think proper to the late Pres^t ↑to↓ Mr Gervais and to permit Mr Wells to extract proper parts of the papers inclos'd for publication.[46]

Schedule of papers inclosed Mr Lowndes.

1. General Lees' letter to the Commander in Chief & Answer 30th June
2. General Sullivans' Letter to the President, dated Providence 1st Aug.
3. Colonel Laurens' Journal dated Providence 4th Aug^t
4. Captains Pine and Martins' Receipts for 1940 Dollars
5. Adam Fergusons' Letter to the President 7th Aug^t
6. General Sullivans' Letter to Genl Washington 13th Aug^t
7. J. Morris to Governeur Morris Esqr 14th Aug^t
8. General Sullivans' Letter to the President 17th Aug^t
9. List of Members who have signed the Confederation
10. New York Lampoon upon Govr Johnstone
11. Sentence of the General Court Martial on General Lee.

source: LB, HL Papers, ScHi; addressed "President Lowndes / S^o Carolina / by Jones to Baltimore, there to be deliver'd Capt. Pyne."; dated "11th August". Copy (19th century), HL Papers, ScHi. Extract, HL Papers, ScHi.

---

[46] The lampoon of George Johnstone was printed in the *S.C. General Gazette*, Sept. 10, 1778.

FROM JONATHAN TRUMBULL, SR.

Lebanon, Conn., August 11, 1778

Sir

I received your Favour of the 19th. ins^{t.}, I had before the receipt thereof, and in good time, sent Vice Admiral De Estaing a Number of Pilots__

By a Letter from Providence of the 7th. ins^{t.}__ I have this intelligence__ "We shall probably land on the Island, on Sunday__ The Continental, are very well disciplind, & very Healthy__ A Company of Volunteers arrived Yesterday from Salem, composed of Ninty principal people of the place__ And this day I suppose Genl Hancock will arrive with a Number from Boston."__

Your Letter to Alex^r Wright Esqr. is returned he is sailed in a Flag for St. Augustine, designed to go into Carolina.__

I have taken Liberty to enclose sundry Letters hope may not be too troublesome__

Col^o Joseph Trumbull, after long and tedious illness, departed this Life the 23^{d.} instant__ a very grievous bereavment to me, and Family__ may it be sanctified to us__ and quicken us to be also ready.

I have the Honor to be, with great Esteem / and Regard / Sir / Your Obedient / hble Servant

Jon^{th;} Trumbull

SOURCE: RC, PCC (Item 66), DNA; addressed on cover "Honorable Henry Laurens Esquire.__ / President of Congress__ / at / Philadelphia__"; addressed below close "President Laurens__"; dated "Lebanon 11th. Augt. 1778"; franked "Public Service / Jon^{th;} Trumbull"; docketed "Letter from Govr Trumbull / Lebanon 11 Aug 1778 / Read 24".

TO GEORGE WASHINGTON

Philadelphia, August 13, 1778

Sir

Since my last of the 30th July I have had the honor of presenting to Congress Your Excellency's several favors of the 3^d, 4th and 7th Ins^{t.}

The transcript from the journal of Congress dated the 10th Ins[t.] and here inclosed will shew Your Excellency how those of the 3[d] and 4th were dispos'd of.

I likewise inclose with this, ~~two~~ ↑an↓ Acts of Congress dated the 10th, and ~~four~~ ↑three↓ dated the 12th Ins[t.] together with the declaration of the last mention'd date.

1. for adding two Members to the Committee of Arrangement
2. for permitting Colonel Knobeloch to act as a Volunteer in the Army, and for allowing him 125 Dollars per Month[1]
3. for allowing a compensation for horses kill'd in battle.
4. A Declaration That Congress hold it incompatible with their honor in any manner to correspond or have intercourse with George Johnstone Esquire one of the British Comm[rs.]
5. An Act of Congress of the 12th for sending the said Declaration to the Commissioners by a Flag.

Congress request Your Excellency will give directions for carrying this immediately into execution.

Yesterday I presented to Congress a letter from M[r.] Ferguson, Secretary to the Commissioners of the 7th Ins[t.] and the Paper refirred to in that letter. Copies of these I take the liberty of transmitting herewith, merely for Your Excellency's information

I have the honor to be / With the highest Esteem and Regard

---

[1] Prussian nobleman Baron de Knobelauch had petitioned Congress July 27, requesting a commission to serve in the Continental Army. A committee composed of Richard Henry Lee, Gouverneur Morris, and James Lovell was named to review his request and to confer with him. He was accepted only as a volunteer but allowed 125 dollars a month, two rations a day and forage for two horses. The baron persisted in his attempts to obtain a commission and when that proved impossible he sought compensation for his expenses. On Sept. 16, 1779, Congress awarded him 10,000 dollars "in order to defray his expenses to Europe, and those incurred during his residence in America." Baron de Knobelauch to Congress, July 27, 1778, Sept. 4, 1779, PCC, Item 78, Vol. 13, pp. 459ff, 545ff; *JCC,* XI, 725, 778-779, 850; XV, 1069-1070.

SOURCE: LB, PCC (Item 13), DNA; addressed "General Washington / White Plains" and by HL "by a Messenger from Monsr Gerard__"; dated "13th August". Draft and copy, Washington Papers, DLC.

FROM THÉVENEAU DE FRANCY

Williamsburg, Va., August 14, 1778

Honorable Sir.

I have received the resolve of Congress inclosed in your favour of the 3^d instant; I Shall not make any remark upon it, only I beg leave to observe that these last words (as they judge proper) Seem to destroy all the good effect which might have been expected of what precedes. your Excellency's Silence upon the Contents of that resolve, make me believe that you have observed the Same.[1] I Shall leave[2] that matter as it is now, Without Speaking of it; because none of the Vessels mentioned in the resolve is ready for Sea by this time. after having Wrote to the Committee, I Sent an officer of Le fier Roderigue to examine them, & he has found that the Ship Governor johnson wanted new masts & to be repaired, ↑& that↓ the Virginia ought to be Careened. the Snow Speedwell did Sailed three weeks ago & the brig Braxton was thunderstruck last week in coming down york river to join Le fier Rodrigue. I have not heard of the Brig Morris[3] this month past; She was ready for Sea then, & I Suppose has Sailed by this time, matter quite indifferent to me, as She is not Consigned to M^r. de Beaumarchais.

I am very Sorry that you did not Sent your letters for france by the express, as the fier Rodrigue Shall Sail to morrow if the wind is fair; She has been ready loaded from the 1st. instant & I expected nothing else to dispatch her than the answer of congress.

---

[1] In his August 3 letter HL enclosed the August 1 resolution which was based on a Commerce Committee report of that day. Four vessels, with cargoes totalling 1,007 hogsheads of tobacco, which were ready to sail for France were to be consigned to the accounts of John Ross who had purchased and shipped goods for the public. The resolution included a provision that "the commissioners of Congress at Paris" were directed to pay "the residue, if any, to the house of Hortalez & Co. as they judge proper." HL to Théveneau de Francy, Aug. 3, 1778, PCC, Item 13; *JCC*, XI, 738-740.

[2] "v" written over other text.

[3] The *Morris*, Benjamin Gunnison, arrived at Roscoff, Brittany, Dec. 14, 1778, after a passage of forty-two days. *Franklin Papers* (Labaree), XXVIII, 226.

Cap^{tn} Michel commander of the lyon 40 guns Ship, is now lying in potowmack where he is gone to take the rest of his freight he will be ready, I Suppose, in four or five Weeks time; it will be a very good opportunity for your letters.

I have the honour to be with the greatest respect & a high Consideration / Honorable Sir / Your Excellency's / the most H^{ble.} & / most obed^{t.} Servant

L. De francy

P.S. be pleased to forward the inclosed letters.

SOURCE: RC, HL Papers, ScHi; addressed below close "His Excellency the honorable Henry laurens president of Congress."; dated "Williamsbourg 14th August 1778."; docketed by HL "Laz. de francy / 14th. Augt 1778__".

FROM GEORGE WEEDON

Philadelphia, August 14, 1778

Gentlemen

I had the Honor of addressing You by Letter at York of 28th. May upon the Subject of my retiring from Service in Consequence of the late Arrangement in the Virginia Line of Brigadiers   Since that time I have not been favoured with your Answer and am informed my Letter was ordered to lie on your Table for further Consideration[1]   I am sorry to be thus troublesome at a time when Matters of greater Moment, no doubt, engage your Attention, but my reputation as well as my disagreable and expensive Situation demands something conclusive.

I could wish to avoid Censure, and after stating a few Facts in Justification of my Conduct in this Instance, shall only request what every Gentleman has a right to demand, and what I hope you will grant to one that has faithfully served You   Your Journals to which I beg to call your Attention for a Moment, will more clearly shew the Cause of my Uneasiness at present, than any thing I can advance and will I hope apologize for the Trouble I give You

On the 21st. of February 1777 You were pleased to promote

---

[1] George Weedon's May 27 letter was read in Congress May 28. Congress resolved "That the consideration thereof be postponed." *JCC*, XI, 544.

me with several others (as will appear by the resolve of that day) to the rank of Brigadier; And in Order to establish the rank of Genl. Woodford, who had resigned, and was at the same time promoted from a Citizen, to Brigadier Genl., it is resolved on the 22^d. of same Month, as follows

> In Congress Feby. 22^d 1777:
>
> On Motion that Col^o. Woodford who formerly held a Commission of Col^o. in the Continental Service, but resigned, take rank according to date of said Commission
>> Question put, passed in the Negative
>> Extract from the Minutes
>> Ch^s. Thompson

I would also beg leave to communicate an Extract of a Letter from General Woodford to me, on our being promoted, dated the 17th. of March 1777 in which he not only accepts his Appointment, but relinquishes all pretentions of precedence as follows

> I have heard within these few days of the late Promotions, let me with much Sincerity give you Joy, and assure You I shall serve with pleasure under my old Friend. I am Sir determined to disappoint my Enemies in their Aim, and if they had appointed me a Corp^l. I would have acted.

After this Public Acknowledgement of my Precedence not only by Letter under his own Hand, but by actual Service during an active and bloody Campaign, he again claims his relative rank; and to my very great Surprize, was favoured with a Letter from his Excellency Genl. Washington while I was in Virginia dated 29th. March 1778[2] inclosing the following resolution of Congress.

> In Congress 19th. March 1778
>
> Resolved That General Washington call in and cancel the Commissions of Brigadier Woodford Muhlenberg Scott and Weedon. And that new Commissions be granted them. and that they rank in future agreeable to the following Arrangement Woodford Muhlenburg Scott Weedon

Thus Gentlemen I am deprived of my Rank, which was taken by regular Succession, and perfectly consistent with the Usage of all Armies and which I had held more than a Year, without any reasons assigned or without my ever having an Opportunity of

---

[2] In this letter Washington expressed his sentiment that "the parties interested should acquiesce" in the decision of Congress. *Washington Writings* (Fitzpatrick), XI, 173.

stating Facts respecting it either to Congress or to the board of General Officers before it was determined on

That some Mistake has been the Occasion of this Injury to me I cannot doubt, nor can it be questioned that the Honorable Congress will so far revise these former determinations as to cause right to be done I therefore pray for a reconsideration of their resolve of the 19th of March last, that an Opportunity may be given of fixing the rank of the Officers by their determination, according to the usual practise of Armies, and those established rules which promote the Military Service I am induced to make this Claim to justify my Conduct to my Country, as in the present Arrangement I cannot serve

Or, If Congress pleases to continue me in the Line. till I can take an active part again with Propriety, I shall whenever that is the Case, be ready and willing to serve. My present Situation obliges me to solicit an Answer so soon as Leisure will permit,[3] And am Gentlemen

Your most Obed[t.] Serv[t.]

G Weedon

SOURCE: RC, PCC (Item 159), DNA; addressed above salutation "To the Honorable the President and Members of / Congress"; dated below close "Philadelphia Aug[t.] 14th 1778"; docketed "Geñ Weedon 14 Aug 1778 / Read in Coñg 18th- / passed on___". Copy, RPB.

TO JOHN SULLIVAN

Philadelphia, August 16, 1778

Dear General

I have lately been honored with your several favors of the 27[th.] July 1[st.] & 10[th.] Inst. which I presumed were all intended as

---

[3] Congress resolved August 18 to maintain the order of rank for the Virginia brigadiers that it had established March 19, 1778, and determined that George Weedon should be permitted to retire but hold his present rank and "be called into service whenever...the inconveniences he now labours under can be removed." Congress called him out of retirement June 16, 1780. *JCC,* XI, 807-808; XVII, 518.

Public, & therefore duly presented each to Congress__ I have received no commands from the House nevertheless I think an intimation of the receipt of your Letters will be acceptable. you will be so kind as to take it in this private address.

When you can find half an hours leisure, you will much oblige me by a general or detail Account as time may permit of the proceedings of the Allied Fleet & Armies at or near Rhode Island, although I must confess I have now some apprehensions that the late seperation was the period of our hopes of subduing the Enemy in that Quarter until quite new measures shall be taken__ I wish my fears that the Count de' Estaing is decoyed, may prove groundless__ the Enemy's seeming flight gives this alarm, were they in earnest to fly they might have taken, with much less danger, the start from Sandy hook__ but we must with patience wait events. If you are so good as to communicate Intelligence of public transactions for my private use I intreat You Sir, to mark each Cover (Private). this will enable me to make acceptable offerings to my freinds in the State I come from & on my part, besides the obligation which I shall feel, I will endeavor to make suitable retaliation. at present I have nothing to transmit but the last News Paper & to ~~assure~~ inform you that the British Commissioners have attempted to open a corre-spondence with Congress by means of a Remonstrance & requisi-tion, demanding the Prisoners of the Convention of Saratoga & offering to Ratify that agreement on the part of Great Britain I will not say which is the most glaring in this Act their Insolence or their folly.__ I can see however they have with all their supposed Cunning ensnared themselves & exposed their Court to further contempt__ they must either be possessed of powers "distinctly & explicitly" to Ratify & "properly notify to Congress" or they have no such pow-ers__ if they have, their weakness & folly will appear in with-holding or neglecting to declare it.__ if they have not their Insolence will be seen in the attempt to negotiate without authority & I may repeat, their "folly" in supposing they could amuse Congress by a stroke of Newmarket Jockeyship.[1] upon the whole these Wiseacres have

---

[1] HL implied that the members of the Carlisle Commission, like horsetraders, attempted to bring off a crafty or fraudulent bargain. The *OED* gives one definition of "Jockeyship" as "the practice of...trickery, artifice, adroit management for unfair advantage."

inadvertently given their Seal to the Act of Congress of the 8[th.] January.

I wish you all success & happiness & am with very great Regard & Esteem Dear Sir

Your obedient & very hum̃ / servt

Henry Laurens.

SOURCE: ALS, John Sullivan Papers, NhHi; addressed below close "The Honble. / Major Gen̄. Sullivan / Rhode Island.__"; dated "Philadelphia / 16[th.] August 1778__"; noted below signature "private". LB, HL Papers, ScHi. Copy, MH. Copy, MHi.

FROM RAWLINS LOWNDES

Charles Town, August 16, 1778

Dear Sir__

On the 12[th.] your Messenger Sharpe arrived here by whom I had the Honour of Receiving your favours of the 15[th.] of last Month. Much bad Weather and Consequential Impediments retarted his Journey, and prevented the expedition he used with his former dispatches__

God Grant the favourable Prospect of our Affairs by your last advices, may not be clouded or intercepted by any Cross or Malevolent Interposition; I had formed such Sanguine hopes from the route of the Enemy through the Jerseys, that I confess to you Sir, notwithstanding the exertions at Monmouth, I was greatly disappointed; nothing less than the total overthrow of S[r.] H. Clinton had possessed my Imagination from the first instant I heard he had Resolved on his decampment in that Course, and I was vain enough to flatter my self with an Affair a la mode Burgoyne, as the fashionable Phrase is.__ Moments are precious in the Situation of Count D'Estaign__ the Arrival of an English Fleet, before the necessary work is done, must give a very different appearance to things and greatly change the face of Affairs.

I find the Confederation is Signed, except by a few States__ There are certainly difficulties in accommodating and adjusting arrangements of so general a nature, to the private taste and relish of every individual, from this considerations many sacrifices ought to be made and Subordinate points either Relinquished or ~~omitted~~ ↑reserved↓ for a fairer opportunity rather than obstruct so Important and indispensible a work. Yet I think some very seasonable and reasonable amendments would hardly be objected to, were it not for the inconveniency of leaving the whole open to debate and procrastination. The Chief Justices objections to which he tells me you have Concurd shall be laid before the Assembly which meets the 1st. of next Month.[1]

Mr. Wells, or any of your Friends whom you may refer to me shall always have ready access to any Intelligence I may receive from Philadelphia, as I only Consider my self as the Medium of Conveyance to the Publick, and he is the best Channel for Circulation.

I have procured from Capt Senf who is Returned from Georgia, a Written Accot. under his hand of what he knows, or has come to his knowledge by information relative to the Affair of Saratoga, which I herewith Inclose agreeable to your desire, and which he says contains the whole of what information he can give.[2]

There is an appearance of a Storm Brewing up in the Creek Nation; my late Letters from Galphin and others give grounds to suspect Hostile designs from those People & I am afraid our wild expedition to Florida and impotant taunts, will have a bad influence on our Indian Affairs; these People and our own disaffected Inhabitants keep us continually at work to Counter-act their Plots and watch their movements; and let me add, that the Emoluments arrising to many, and the views of others of Sharing the Indian Lands renders a War with those People a desireable Object not considering or Caring what expence is incured or by what means it is defrayed considerations that very little Affect them; we are taking proper precautions to be prepared for the event, which may have a tendency to prevent it__ our expences from these Causes are intolerable.

---

[1] HL complained in his July 15 letter to Lowndes that William Henry Drayton, who agreed to write for the entire South Carolina delegation, sent official letters to South Carolina over his name. Apparently Lowndes received a letter from Drayton in which he suggested amendments to the Articles of Confederation which the South Carolina delegates ratified July 9. The Assembly journal is not extant for this period.

[2] HL had first requested this information May 17, 1778. *HL Papers*, XIII, 322.

You seem Sir to be well apprized of the Ill use that is made of the Indulgence granted to the English Islands of Bermuda and Providence, no doubt, but you receive frequent intimations of the Fraud and abuse daily Committed under that Sanction. some instances have ocured to me. We have a Sloop now in our Port the Master of which a few Months ago was Lieutenant Successively to two Privateers, taking our Vessells in Sight of the Town. this Man together with ~~the~~ ↑a part↓ owner of the Sloop went lately from St. Augustine to Providence there made a Sham Transfer of the property; and then comes boldly into our harbour to enjoy all the Priviledge of Citizenship and from hence perhaps means to return to St. Augustine with what intelligence and discoverys they may obtain, probably the Chief purpose of the Voyage__ I have ordered her to be Seized upon strong Circumstances of Guilt, but depending chiefly for Conviction upon their own Evidence. we shall never be safe while Spys may so easily obtain Licence to come amongst us, and impunity affords such encouragement to fraudulent trade and practices.

General Howe countenances the Opinion of the Officers who think themselves intitled to succeed to Vacancies which happened anticedent to the late establishment of the Army, altho' no Commissions have been Issued. As I had forbore to Issue any new Commissions, in Consequence of an express resolve of Congress of which I had the Honōr to write you of the 18th. April last, and having had no explicit answer on that head, but received from Congress Printed Papers containing an "Establishment of the American Army" passed in Congress the 27th. May 1778. with Directions to cause the same to be made publick and to send Copies thereof to General Howe and General Moultrie; I considered my self bound by that Arrangement, and not at Liberty to Create any Officers Supernumerary thereto, which I must have done had I admitted of the Officers claim and Genl. Howes Construction. Congress had in Idea a new Arrangemt. and reduction of Officers & Companies, in Consequence of which the Issuing of any more Commissions was prohibited__ the simple question then is, whether during that interval before the Establishmt. took place, those Vacancies which fell are to be filled up, notwithstanding that so doing will give a greater Number of Officers and Companies than the Establishmt. allows?

This Moment while I am writing this Lett^r· a Special Flag of Truce which I sent to Augustine to Accommodate M^r· Colin Mackenzie[3] a Prisoner of War in a very Ill state of health returned, the Master informs me that the Persious and one other Ship of War are now lying off the Bar of S^t· Augustine.

On Monday last the 10th· Instant we had a most violent Storm which lasted the whole day it began ~~and~~ from the N.E. alarmed the Town very much with the apprehension of a hurricane but the Wind shifting to the Northward and Northwest towards Night ↑it↓ abated, It was accompanied with a Flood of Rain; altogether have done great Injury to the Crops of every sort and the Weather continuing very Rainy since, as it was before the Country is hardly passable.

The Baron Holzendorf has just left me, he called to take his leave, being ready to Embark for Nantes; Monsr· Gerrards plan of Conduct in respect to those Gentlemen adventurers must releive you from many disagreeable applications and troublesome Visits. I was Compelled the other day by Baron Randron to trouble you with a few Lines, tho' I told him I could inform you of little else but of our having advanced him upwards of 800 dollars to Assist him on his journey to Congress.[4]

There is no doubt Sir but it will be very Acceptable to this State to have their Money lodgd in our own Treasury; I have not yet had an Opportunity of sending to the Gentlemen, through whose hands it is to come but will see after it soon__

I cannot close my Letter without indulging my self in the pleasure of Congratulating you Sir and my Country on the distinguished Vertues and rising Merits of a young Gentleman who is so great an Ornament to his Name & Country and affords such a just Subject for praise and Admiration, may you long enjoy him S^r and may his example Stimulate and give Ardor to publick Spirits & Pratriotism

I am with very great Respect / Dr Sir / Your Most Obed^t hum Servt·

Raw^s· Lowndes.

---

[3] Collin Mackenzie of St. Augustine had been sailing on Peter Bachop's privateer "for the Benefit of Sea-Air" when the vessel was captured. Capt. William Phillips transported him back to St. Augustine. *HL Papers*, XI, 215n; Peter Timothy to HL, Aug. 16, 1778.

[4] Extra space interpreted by editors as paragraph.

P.S. It is altogether unnecessary for me to Suggest to you that my Letters are not calculated for or intended for the Eye of Congress neither are they addressed to the President of Congress as such but to our worthy delegate Mr. Laurens__ should I not be able to write to Mr. Chief Justice, I must beg of you to present my Respects to him__ I have received from Bourdeaux a Pacquet directed to the Chairman of the Secret Commee of Congress;[5] by bad Weather the Cover has received some Injury ~~which obliged me to put it under a new Cover__~~

Sharp will receive thirty dollars from me at his request__ the Storm has produced some advantage it has already thrown two disabled Vessels on our Coast who surr[ender]ed themselves up to the Pilots one from Jamaica with 200 Hds. Rum bound to [*Scotland*][6]

[*Enclosure*]

Christopher Senf to Rawlins Lowndes
Sir,

Obedient to Your Excellency's Orders I have the Honour to give Your Excellency some little Intelligence about Genl. Bourgoyne's Army:

Every regular Regiment of Genl. Bourgoyne's Army brought their Colours along with them from Canada. Genl. Bourgoyne left One English & One German Regt. at Tienderoge in Garrison. His Line was also besides Avant Corps
(wich had No Colours)

{
5 English Regt,	pr. Regt.	2 Colours__	10 Colours
5 German Regt,	pr, Regt	5 "	20 "
	Sm,	30 Colours,	

I was told at Albany that by Genl. Bourgoynes Orders in the time of the Capitulation, by wich I was allready tacken prisoner all the

---

    [5] Francis Lewis of New York was chairman of the Secret Committee or as it was now more commonly referred to, the Commerce Committee.

    [6] The schooner *Revenge*, John Atkinson, and its prize the Schooner *Betsey*, were forced to put in at Charleston because of the storm as was the Schooner *Sally*, Samuel Wilkins, which had been enroute from Jamaica to Glasgow with a cargo of rum. *S.C. Gazette*, Aug. 19, 1778.

German Colours had been burnt and after they had capitulated some of the English kings Colours had been carried out of the Camp in some Officers Bagage__

All the Arms in Bourgoyne's Army have been continualy in good Order, (wich allways is to belief from a regular Army) I was told, that the Soldiers destroyed ↑them↓ in the time of the Capitulation &c &c.

I am with the greatest Respect / Sir / Your Excellency's / most humble & obedient Servant

Christ^{n,} Senf
Cap^{t,} Eng^{r,}

Charlestown / August 5^{th,} 1778.

SOURCE: RC, Kendall Collection; addressed on cover "His Exc̄y President Laurens. / Philadelphia"; dated below close "Cha$^{s.}$ Town Sunday / 16 Aug$^{st.}$ 1778."; docketed by HL "Presid$^{t.}$ R Lowndes / 16 Aug$^{t.}$ 1778 / Rec$^{d.}$ 23 Sept^{r}–". Copy (19th century), HL Papers, ScHi. The enclosure is in PCC (Item 78), Vol. 20, p. 299ff.

FROM PETER TIMOTHY

Charles Town, August 16, 1778

Honourable Sir,

The Express not having yet called upon me for my Packet, I embrace the Time to give you some Intelligence I have just got, in Hopes it may tend towards the Capture of a Copper-Bottom Ship, the fittest Vessels to be assigned for this Station.

William Phillips (the Santee Coaster, who you know very well)[1] is just returned from St. Augustine, whither he went with a Flag, to carry one Mackenzie of that Place home; being in the lowest State, and who came out in Bachop's Privateer for the Benefit of Sea-Air.__ He arrived off St. Augustine Bar on the 8th, where he found at Anchor, the Perseus Man of War of 20 Guns, with two

---

[1] Capt. William Phillips was master of the twenty-ton schooner *Dispatch*. *HL Papers*, X, 595n.

Victuallers a Ship and Brig,[2] which had nearly discharged their Cargoes.__ The Perseus had anchored there but the Evening before, piloted round by Capt. Mowbray[3] from St. Johns, whither she had been sent from New-York, and where she had lain during the whole Windmill Expedition from Georgia.__ Mowbray came out of the Perseus, and piloted Phillips in.__ The Gale we had here on the 10th was also felt there: The Perseus and Victuallers, and also the Otter Sloop of War of 18 Guns, which ~~illegible~~ likewise came anchored off St. Augustine Bar on the 9th, were obliged to slip their Cables; but all ↑had↓ returned on the 11th, except the Ship Victualler__ Several Vessels were driven ashore in the Harbour.__ The Otter had been as long at St. John's as the Perseus__ They left there Mowbray's Ship the George, and a Galley, made of a Brig. cut down.__ Elphinston[4] said, the Man who planned the Georgia ↑Expedition↓ ought to be hanged.__ It was reported the Number of our Back-Woods People in East-Florida amounted to 700, who were all kept at St. John's; where they must have an easy Time to be sure.__ On the 12th, the ↑Scooner↓ Oakhampton Packet ~~Scoon~~ belonging to M[r.] John Rose, another Cartel sent from hence on the 8th, with 82 Prisoners commanded by Capt. John Hatter arrived at St. Augustine. The Otter ↑having↓ chasing her, the Crew ↑had↓ taken[5] the Command, and 14 went for the Shore in the Boat; only 12 landed the two others were drowned.[6] the Perseus's Boat afterwards came up with the Scooner. On the 13th the Prisoners from Hatter were landed, amongst them Jamieson, (whose wife & 4 Children remain here). The same Evening, a very small Northward-built Sloop, having a Quarter-Deck, mounting 6 Guns, with Netting all around, full of Cohorns & Swivels, ↑very clean and having Top-

---

[2] The *Perseus*, George Elphinstone, a victualler, and the *Rose* privateer, Duncan, had passed the Charleston bar on June 25 en route to St. Augustine. *Pa. Packet*, Aug. 29, 1778.

[3] Capt. James (John?) Mowbray, who at one time sailed his schooner *Rebecca* as a privateer, had a commission from East Florida governor Patrick Tonyn to defend the province. Mowat, *East Florida as a British Province*, pp. 100, 114, 119.

[4] Capt. George Elphinstone, commander of *Perseus*, later participated in the siege of Charleston and received special recognition from Sir Henry Clinton. During the Napoleonic wars he was named commander in chief of the British Mediterranean fleet. Tilley, *British Navy*, pp. 169, 174, 185, 281.

[5] "took" altered to "taken".

[6] Timothy's report three days later said that fourteen of the British prisoners took command of the *Oakhampton* packet cartel and attempted to escape to the beach in the packet's boat. Two drowned during the incident. *S.C. Gazette*, Aug. 19, 1778.

sail Yards aloft↓ arrived at St. Augustine, from New-York. The 14th Phillips was dispatched and came away.__ While there he understood Capt.[7] Elphinston would cruize off this Bar. He asked Phillips if he had spoke with no Men of War, on the Passage; but he had ↑not↓ seen ~~none~~ ↑not↓ a Sail, either↓ in going or returning.__ No Prizes had lately been carried into Augustine; and there very few Prisoners; Elphinston had only 6 on board his Ship.

I thought it necessary to give you this Information, because, as the Winds at this Season set in from the N.E. if the Perseus cruizes a few Days here, she ~~cannot~~ may get to the Northward before you receive this Intelligence; and it is possible some Disposition might to intercept both her and the Otter before the can reach either New-York, Rhode-Island or Halifax__ A Couple of Cruizers, a Frigate and a Privateer ↑or State Vessell↓ coming this Way might do the Business; for they cannot lay the Hurricane Season on the Coast of Florida__ but they might go to New-Providence.__ I was so fortunate as to plan the ↑successfull↓ Expedition against Bachop & Osborn__[8] I wish this Hint might be as successful.__ Great Things may be done from hence by a fast-sailing Frigate or two. I have the Honour to be, Sir,

Your Excell[cy's]_ Most obed[t.] hum[e] Sev[t]

Pet[r.] Timothy.

It is probable Mowbray may come on a Cruize in his Ship after the Equinox, for he can now man her with Osborn & Bachop's Crews. She mounts 18 3-Pounders.

Capt. Elphinston said ↑Capt↓ Pine &c.,[9] ↑as they belonged to a State Vessell↓ will not be exchanged, ~~as they belonged to a State Vessel,~~ for Officers of Privateers only[10]

SOURCE: RC, Dreer Collection, PHi; no address; no date; docketed by HL "P. Timothy (no date sup / posed the 16 Aug[t.] 1778) / Rec[d.] 23[d] Sept[r]".

---

[7] "Ca" written over "El".
[8] Peter Bachop and George Osborne. See HL to John Laurens, July 26, 1778.
[9] Capt. James Pyne.
[10] This paragraph written in left margin.

FROM JOHN WELLS, JR.

Charles Town, August 16, 1778

Dear Sir

Your very obliging & agreeable Letter of the 18th ult. with the Papers, was sent to me last Thursday by his Excellency, who has just now apprised me, that the Express sets out on his Return tomorrow morning.

Allow me to[1] join in the ↑general↓ Congratulation, in the additional Renown Col. Laurens has gained by his Conduct in the Battle of Monmouth__ He has led the van, among his Countrymen, in the Career to military fame__ Indeed few here seem emulous of overtaking him in these paths of Danger__ Several Resignations are talked of Among them Col. Motte, Capt. Sanders, Capt. Cattell, Lieut. Gadsden &c__ [2] The Time of Danger in all appearance, being now past, & the manifest & great disadvantages, the private Concerns of many in the Army must sustain by their continuing in it, are the Causes assigned for their quitting the service. Poor Sanders has a still stronger one__ since he returned from the wild goose Expedition into East Florida, he has had a stroke of the palsy__ he is recovered at present, but I apprehend he will not long be free of another visit of that dreadful disorder__

Being a little indisposed, & there being much Rain to day, I have not been abroad__ I was a little ago informed that Phillips who carried Mr Mackenzie of Augustine thither, is returned; & that he mentions a vessel arriving there last week from New York, the news brought by which were kept secret__ I am also informed, that the ↑Prize↓ Master of a ~~Brig.~~ ↑Schooner↓ taken by a Jamaica Privateer, but compelled by the late dreadful storm to make this port, says he met with a Vessel that had escaped through Hell Gate from New York, the Master of which informed him New York surrendered on the 3d of this month. If this account be true, Peace must soon follow__ I am rather incredulous__ but it may be true__ The advantages attending such a capital stroke must be immense__ ~~one~~ ↑two↓ will certainly immediately follow it__ I mean Peace with

---

[1] "t" written over "j".

[2] Capt. Benjamin Cattell and Capt. Roger P. Sanders, both of the 1st S.C. Regiment, were the only two who resigned in 1778—Cattell on July 20 and Sanders on October 8. Col. Isaac Motte served until the end of the war and Capt. Thomas Gadsden, until his death during the siege of Charleston. Moss, *S.C. Patriots; Directory of the S.C. House*, III, 135-136.

Great Britain, and her acknowledging our Independence__

It has been much agitated here, if we can now conclude a separate Peace with G.B. For my own part, I cannot doubt but we may__ To say that France aided us with a view of relieving us from arbitrary sway, and as friends to the Rights of Mankind, may do well enough with the Populace, or those who do not give themselves the trouble of thinking; but with People of a different stamp must appear highly ridiculous__ She could have nothing else in view but reducing the power of her haughty rival__ & consequently ↑had↓ an attention to her own interest__ She has not been involved in a war on our account, but has declared it her self__ To you these reflections will very naturally rise__ I am therefore clearly of opinion, that we are not bound by any tie of honour to become principals or allies in any of her quarrels__ The prospect of being at peace, & free of all the European feuds, are among the chief advantages to be derived from Independence; and I cannot allow myself to[3] think ↑that↓ in the outset, we will be involved in any other war than the present, if it still subsists__

I was much amazed yesterday at hearing under the Exchange, Tom Tucker[4] inform a number of Gentlemen, that on friday being in Company with the President in a boat going to Fort Moultrie, his Excellency read a letter mentioning the British Commissioners had made an attempt to influence the determinations of Congress by bribery__ To what a low, contemptible situation has Britain reduced herself?__ It seems the President had not observed that paper when he furnished me with the intelligence published in my last ~~paper~~ Gazette

Our Assembly will meet in a fortnight__ The abuses of the late Vagrant Act will come under their immediate consideration__[5] they have been such as you can scarce credit__ I saw a letter lately

---

[3] "t" written over "s".

[4] Thomas Tucker (d. 1784) was a Charleston sea captain and ship owner. A patriot, he served in the Provincial Congress for St. John Colleton parish and as a commissioner to assist in planning the defenses for Charleston harbor. *HL Papers,* XI, 235n.

[5] South Carolina's Vagrant Act, passed March 28, 1778, provided that all men declared as vagrants "shall be liable and obliged to serve in one of the Continental regiments of this State." Because of objections like those mentioned by Wells, the act was amended by an Oct. 9, 1778, act which created a five-person appeals commission in each parish or district. Under the amended Vagrant Act any person condemned to service had the right to appeal. *S.C. Statutes,* IV, 410-413, 453-454.

from Ben. Huger, who is at present at the Cheraws gathering recruits furnished by the Magistrates, in pursuance of that law__ He complains much of the service he is on, & declares he would sooner go on a forlorn hope, than be assailed as he frequently is, with the Cries of Women & Children, imploring for the Liberty of the Husbands & Parents, who have been cruelly snatched from them, tried on frivolous pretences, & condemned as Vagrants, to serve in the Continental Regiments__ The best things may be abused__ & this Act, well intended, has afforded opportunity to the malicious to wreak their resentment on their less powerful neighbour__ The suppression of the liberty of the Press in June last, I am credibly informed, will become an object of parliamentary (if we may use that expression) enquiry__ In that Case, I will be called before the House, which in any situation cannot be very agreeable__ It is also said, that an attempt will be made to have an Act of Oblivion & Grace will be passed, with some few exceptions__ who these may be, I cannot tell; but I imagine John Stuart will be of the number__ [6]

Our Statute Book, if we go on as we have begun, will in size soon rival that of Britain__ It is pity more attention is not paid to the Composition; but that is a matter that is not much attended to ↑minded↓ here__ Indeed the abilities of the A.G. to whose province much of the framing the Laws ↑must fall↓ you are too well acquainted with, to expect any thing very elegant from that quarter__ [7]

I am much in want of Journeymen Printers__ None are to be had here__ I have abundant Employment for two more__ To good hands I would give Seven hundred Dollars a year, & perhaps 50 more which is certainly higher wages than they can get to the Northward__ I apprehend they are equally scarce there__ I have one very indifferent hand who has £1000 a year__ a Pressman who has £800__ and two Apprentices. I am under the necessity of being constantly at the Case myself, though I have much other business,

---

[6] The editors have found no record of an act of this nature.

[7] South Carolina Attorney General Alexander Moultrie (*ca.* 1750-1807) took the position in 1776 under the state's first constitution and continued in office until he was impeached and convicted in 1793 of embezzling state funds. The number and length of acts passed increased each year; in 1776 twenty acts filled twenty-three pages, in 1777 twenty-nine acts filled thirty-three pages, and in 1778, fifty-one acts filled sixty pages. In contrast, the legislature in 1769 had only eleven acts that filled eight pages. *HL Papers,* XI, 584n; *S.C. Statutes.*

which I must neglect__ I cannot think of ~~Desiring of~~ asking You to help me in ~~the matter~~ getting a Journeyman, as I am ~~illegible~~ really ashamed of having given you so much trouble already__

I did myself the honour of writing you by Muckenfuss about 10 days since__ He & the bearer are the most expeditious Expresses we have ever had here__ The latter is exceedingly obliging & attentive as far as I know, and I am in hopes you will keep him constantly in Employ[8]

The Augusta Rider came to town on friday Evening. He informed me, that just as he set out, Intelligence was received, of the Creeks breaking out & 1500 of them being collected together. He brought a letter from M[r] Galphin to His Excellency who I suppose will apprise you of the Contents__ I wish it may be a false Alarm__

The Prize schooner mentioned above belonged to Tom Savage & Ned Lightwood__[9] & was bound here from Bermudas__ I do not think there is a single Man of War within 300[10] leagues of our bar at present__ so that we have some reason to expect Goods will fall__

It is an ill wind that blows no body good__ The late storm has made havock among the Indigo Plantations at Winyaw, and low down santee, & at Long Bay__ There was every reason to apprehend that Staple would be overdone this year; but the ~~storm~~ effects of the storm, it is said will occasion a very considerable difference__ Unless a number of French bottoms come here, Rice will be lower__ it is @ 70/__ The late Embargo has many keen opponents here__ The Chief Justice has the Credit of that measure__ We are told G. Morris was very hard upon him, ~~at~~ ↑for↓ his first Motion in Congress & that he has continued a similar line of Conduct to him ever since__

As there must be French Dispatch Boats & frigates frequently arriving from Europe now, we may naturally expect to have a more regular chain of intelligence from that quarter now__ I have made several Attempts to have News Correspondents there; but hitherto without effect__

---

[8] Joseph Sharpe.

[9] Thomas Savage (1738-1786) and Edward Lightwood, Jr. (1736-*ca.* 1798) were Charleston merchants who shared interests in several vessels. *HL Papers,* IV, 517n; *SCHM,* LXXIV (1973), 201, 229.

[10] "3" written over "2".

By the post before last I sent you Dr Ramsay's Oration__ I now send another Copy__ It is not without many blemishes__ but as it is well intended should be read with Candour & Indulgence__ I have also sent 2 of my latest Papers__ s with some of Crouch's & Timothy's__ a I have likewise taken the liberty of putting some papers for our other Representatives in Congress, & the Printers under this Cover__

Your Garden suffered a little in the late storm__ the Pallisades or fence were blown down__ but I suppose your servant will inform you fully in that matter__

As any thing from this quarter must be interesting to you I have endeavoured to fill this sheet for your amusement__ I cannot say there is much, indeed any News, in them__ but such as they are, be pleased to accept of them from Dr Sir

Your much obliged and / most obedient servant

Jno Wells jun^r

SOURCE: RC, Kendall Collection; addressed below close "Hon. Henry Laurens Esqr / President of / Congress__"; dated "Charlestown 16th August 1778__"; docketed by HL "John Wells 16 Aug 1778 / Rec^d 23 Sept^r".

FROM JOHN LEWIS GERVAIS

Charles Town, August 17, 1778

Dear Sir,

Your favour of the 23^d June by the Express from Georgia I answered the 29th July per Mr Muckenfuss, your Subsequent Letter of the same date by the way of Maryland is not come to hand [*torn*] now the Copy before me I shall take the necessary Steps to lay an attachment on Mr Nutts effect__ he well deserves it.__

I Sold Doctor Coffee last Saturday to a Man in the back Country named Robert Hankinson.[1] for two thousand Pounds

---

[1] Robert Hankinson (d. *ca.* 1789), an Orangeburg District planter in 1778, served one term in the South Carolina General Assembly (1785-1786) representing the District between the Savannah River and the North Fork of Edisto River. At his death he owned his residential plantation, various tracts of land, partnerships in several mills, and twenty-one slaves. *Directory of the S.C. House*, III, 312-313.

Currency payable the first of next March with Interest from the date__ The Man is very good__ I remitted him the whipping that [torn]² by informing Mr Loveday [torn] Mentas, who were at Work on board of some Vessels in consequence whereof they were taken, I had them Severely punished__ Debat is Still in the Work house where I mean to keep him till I have an opportunity to Sell him, I don't think he will fetch more then £1500__ Coffee is Likely, & Younger & his fault was not so great, I was afraid Debat had gone in the Randolph__ I have sent March again to Mepkin with directions to punish him & to keep him at the hardest Labour he is able to perform

Mentas was rather sore from his whipping__ & as the Garden had Suffered by the Gale last Monday & required a little additional aid, I have kept him in Town till the Flat returns__ she is to carry wood till harvest, it sells briskly at £10 ℔ Cord__

The powder is at last taken out of the Brick houses I had sometime ~~ago~~ ↑before↓ ordered the necessary Stuff to be Sawed to repair the out buildings & the fences, to put them in order to be tenanted__ The Flat with part of the Stuff & Sam & his Boys came down [torn] Morning, she went back in the Evening & will be here again with the remainder by the end of the Week__ Sam keeps a particular Acc^t of the Stuff & the days work which I shall lay before the Assembly next Month as also an Account for house Rent & I hope they will pay it chearfully__ I expect [torn] thousand pound ℔ Annum [torn]³

With respect to the Negro Cloathing__ I believe we shall have blanketts enough, there is about 50. now on hand, & better then 400 Yard Cloth homespun & Negro Cloth__ I think there will be enough to Cloath 100. Negros__ there will remain ↑about↓ 160. to Cloath, which will take about 800 or 900. Yard French Negro Cloth which I am going to purchase immediately if Mr Manigault is of my opinion some of an inferior quality at £4 ℔ Yard for petty Coats, & some of a very good quality at £5.5. ℔ Yard, ↑for breeches↓ it will come high but I knew you would rather be without the Money

---

² This manuscript was cracked at the folds and a line of text lost at each of the [torn] notations here and below.

³ Apparently, only £232 was allowed in payment to HL for "Negro Hire on the Fortifica[tion]:" for service from Jan. 1 to Nov. 2, 1778. Auditors General Accounts, 1778-1780, p. 99, ScAr.

then that your Negroes should be Nacked__ I am very Certain, that Negro Cloth will be much higher in a Month or two__ and it is too late in the Season to write to France now & receive Cloth in time__ I would rather send for Linens; & the Sale of that Article will make up for the great Cost of the Negro Cloth, there would have been much more homespun had I been able to purchase Coten__ I hope they will raise a good Quantity this Year at Mepkin__ From what Mr Baillie [*torn*] purchase any Shoes; he tells me, that having more carefully examined the leather he had tanning he believed he could Span 220. pair Shoes__ this is a good Article & which would cost above £1000__ I have wrote to him if he can get no Shoemakers to make them up to send the Leather & I will get them made__

The President was so obliging to shew me the papers & Letters he had received. I am [*torn*] pleased with the whole, only I am [*torn*] reputation__ his "retrograde manoeuvre" was ill timed besides it seems by his own Letters he had not acquainted the Commander in Chief with it, to form a plan in consequence, but on the Contrary it appears beyond a Doubt his retreat was confused & in disorder, & without General Washington's excellent dispositions at in ↑that↓ instant might have ruined our Army__ I can't think he betrayed I would rather attribute it to pride, ↑that↓ he could not bear that a battle should be gained when his opinion had been against the attack__ however it might have been equally fatal:__

Long before the arrival of the express we had received Flying News of the battle of Monmouth, the arrival of Count D'Estaing & Monsieur Gerard, & were in daily & impatient expectation to receive a Confirmation of them__ The Court of Versailles seems to Act a part which must Secure to them the regard of the People of these United States__ I hope they ↑she↓ always will.

I congratulate you most Sincerely that our Friend Colonel Laurens. has been saved in the midst of [*torn*] & has acquired an Addition of Laurels__

his Embassy to Count d'Estaing is a great proof of the high opinion & confidence his General has of him__

I Confess I was glad you were at this Juncture at the head of America, but I wish it costed you a little less Money 50 Dollars a day is a large Sum, but in [*torn*] it don't cost you more__ Borrowing Congress, should not lay such a Tax on one Member of the Empire, they can't in honour avoid allowing an table to their President__

I am Sorry to Say for Mount Tacitus Mepkin &ca– we can't allow 50 Dollars a day at least last Years Crop__ Mount Tacitus ~~had~~ made 6. Casks Indigo I sold one for £1600. Five remain__ had I followed my own Inclination__ I should have Sold the whole at the same rate at Least at £4. ℔ lb but [*it was*] thought it would rise ↑to £5 Now↓ on the Contrary it is fallen__

Mrs Gervais best Respects wait on you__ she is healthy now__ I recommend the inclosed for Baron the Kalb to your particular Care, it was recommended to me by my Friend Mr. Plombard, he w^d make a good Consul here, he is much liked[4] Baron Holzendorff goes to Morrow__ he seems greatly mortified that you don't mention him in any of your Letters__ I am respectfully Yours

John Lewis Gervais

Permit me to join M^r· Drayton, & dire[*ct*] my Letter as every body thinks it ought to be to his Excellency[5]

SOURCE: RC, Gervais Papers, in private hands; no address; dated "Charles Town 17th August 1778"; docketed by HL "John L. Gervais 17 Aug 177[8] / Rec^d 23 Sept^r–".

FROM FANNY RADDON

Philadelphia, August 17, 1778

Sir

My husbands Ill State of health in new york makes me at this moment appear trou~~t~~blisom in Requesting your honours kind Interpositin with the honerible Congress to obtain a pass for that City if possible to Day I W^d not be thus Importunate Did I not fear the Wo^rst from his indispositon & my Own far Advancement Will not permit me many Days Hence to Bear the Fataguie of Traviling

Pardon the Intrusion

---

[4] J. Plombard was appointed French consul at Charleston on Oct. 12, 1778. *HL Papers*, XIII, 6n.

[5] Postscript written in left margin.

Believe me none will Entertain a more gratfill memory of Such a favour than your most Obed^t

Fanny Raddon

I pray the Liberty of a trunk & Bed

SOURCE: RC, PCC (Item 78); addressed on cover "The / Hon^bl Henry Larense / Esqr / Presindent of Congress"; addressed below close "To the Honble· Henry Laurinse"; dated "monday morning arch street near Second Street."; docketed "Fanny Raddon / __ Aug^st 1778" and "Permission & Passport to / go to New York".

FROM JOHN SULLIVAN

Rhode Island, August 17, 1778

Dear Sir,

Notwithstanding the Train of missfortunes (mentioned in my Letter of the 14th Instant,[)] sufficient in number and aggravation, to depress the Spirits of Fortitude & damp the ardor of Enterprize; I have by the interposition of Heaven & unabated Industry nearly recoverd from the deplorable Situation, of which, my last gave you but an imperfect Description. I have by sending for Supplies to different Quarters replenish'd my Magazine with Ammunition & my Stores with Provision. & by timely addresses to my Men, have exhilirated their Spirits, & reconcild them in equal Measure to the Vicissitudes of War.

Having not heard any thing from Count Destiang, and apprehensive of the bad Consequences of delay. I on the 15th Inst· marchd down in Columns (so disposed as to render forming the lines as familiar and easy as possible.[)] and I am happy in informing your Excellency that the Regularity and good order observ'd by the different Corps on their March excited Admiration in every Beholder, and infinitely exceeded my most sanguine expectations. I halted the Army in full view of ~~the~~ & within long Shot of the Enemy in hopes that they would thereby ↑be↓ temptd to meet us in the Plain, and become an easy Conquest. But the Event convinces me, that how contrary soever they may act to the dictates of Nature in other Instances, they implicitly obey her Commands so far as they relate to Self preservation

After disposing my Army in such a position as to effectually invest their Works__ I began my Approaches under Cover of Night, within two hundred & fifty yards of their lines this days' Fog favors my Operations & I promise your Excellency that by tomorrow (noon) I shall be able to keep up so warm a Fire upon them, as to render the Properties of a Salamander essentially necessary to their existence. And I think I may venture to assure your Excellency, that I shall have it shortly in my power, either to force them to an action, upon dissadvantageous and destructive Principles or reduce them to honorable Terms of Capitulation.[1] In full expectation of this desirable event,

   I have the Honor to remain / with great Respect, / Y^r· very hble serv^t—

        John Sullivan__

SOURCE: RC, N; addressed on cover "His Excellency Henry Laurens Esqre / President of Congress / Philadelphia"; addressed below close "His Excellency / Henry Laurens"; dated "Head Qu^{rs} Augt 17$^{th.}$ Rhode Island 78"; docketed by HL "Gen̄ Sullivan / 17 Aug. 1778 / Rec̄d 21st—"; noted on cover "The Express who carries this Letter must go night & day".

FROM JOHN LEWIS GERVAIS
           Charles Town, August 18, 1778
Dear Sir
   I omitted yesterday to inclose Copy of Mr Galphin's Letter concerning the Creek Indians, as I am told the Express is not gone I hope it will go by him.[1] I suppose Capt Stuart[2] prevailed with the Indians to go to war in order to make a diversion in favor of East

---

 [1] Two days later Sullivan issued his last optimistic report informing HL that he had erected several batteries within musket shot of the enemy's redoubt and planned an attack for later that day. He had not heard from d'Estaing. On August 20 Count de Cambis informed Sullivan that the recent storm compelled d'Estaing to put into Boston for repairs and that none of the French fleet would be available for the Rhode Island campaign. Despite appeals from Sullivan, d'Estaing proceeded to Boston with his entire force. John Sullivan to HL, Aug. 19, 1778, PCC, Item 160, p. 156ff; *Sullivan Papers* (Hammond), II, 237-238, 243-246.

 [1] George Galphin's August 10 letter to Gervais warned of John Stuart's activities among the Creeks and that "there were several gangs coming down upon our frontiers". Gervais added his own postscript in which he expressed his opinion that these "are the effects of our Southern Expedition." Gervais Papers, private collection.

 [2] Capt. Henry Stuart, John Stuart's brother, served as a special agent in the Southern Indian Department. *HL Papers,* XI, 157n.

Florida I hope as the little Capenter[3] wishes "we shall humble that proud Nation" we have nothing else upon hand now & no probability of an attack in Front, so that our whole force may be employed

Baron Holzendorff requested me to forward the Inclosed__ he has suffered greatly by waiting for dispatches from Congress. & he waited so long that I believe he was much embarrassed__ But he found a friend, between us Mr Plombard has advanced him 1280 Dollars.__ it is all gone to 10. or 12 half Joes which he carries with him & got at the high exchange of 4^1/$_2$. for one__ his Passage & Stock cost him above £800 And notwithstanding this Loan he has not been able to pay the 400 Dollars you lent him__ he told me he is to send ↑200↓ Exemplars of his Military books to M^r· Wells & to pay it with part of the proceeds If he was really made to think dispatches for the Court of France were to be sent after him & by that means has incurred a great expence in waiting for them, I think for the honor of the United States Congress should make him some Compensation__ I believe his Ameri[can] Jaunt will not add to his Fortune, I am sorry for him, in my opinion he deserved a better Fate__[4] Mrs Gervais M^r & Mrs Manigault & Mr. Owen desire me to present their respects to you, & I am with a sincere attachment

Dear Sir / Y^r affectionate & / most obed$^{t.}$ Servant

John Lewis Gervais

SOURCE: RC, Gervais Papers, in private hands; addressed on cover "His Excellency Henry Laurens Esq$^{r:}$ / President of the Honourable / Congress of the United North / American States / Philadelphia / ℔ Express"; dated "Charles Town 18 April 1778__"; docketed by HL "John L. Gervais / 18 August 1778 / Rec$^{d.}$ 23 Sept".

FROM JOHN CHRISTIAN SENF

Charles Town, August 18, 1778

Sir

By this Opportunity I give myself the Honour to acquaint Your Excellency, that I am now returned again in very good Health

---

[3] The Little Carpenter or Attakullakulla was a Cherokee headman. *HL Papers*, XII, 198n.
[4] Louis-Casimir, baron de Holtzendorff, who had resigned from the army, was returning to Europe by way of Charleston. *HL Papers*, XII, 337n.

from East-Florida & Georgia to Charlestown. But I am very sorry, that I cannot send by this Express some little Plans. I bagg Your Excellency to excuse my Laziness, I certainly did not think, that this Express would go so soon. But by the next Opportunity I shall send Your Excellency the Plan of Fort Howe & Fort Tonyn__[1]

His Excellency the President Lowndes orderd my last Weeck to give him some Intelligence about Gen¹ Burgoynes Army__ according to His Order I gave to Him in writting about Collours & Arms, which I was told of at Albany, but I was not present in the Army at the time of the Capitulation.

I have taken the Liberty to stay a little time at Your Excellencys House with M^{r,} Loveday, till a little Room is repaired for my at Fort Moultrie.

Wishing You Health & Happiness I am with the greatest Respect / Sir / Your Excellencys / most humble & most obed^{t,} Servant

J^{n,} Christian Senf
Capt Eng^{r,}

SOURCE: RC, Laurens Collection, DLC; addressed on cover "His Excellency / Henry Laurens Esq^{r,} / President of the Honorable Continental / Congress / at / Philadelphia"; dated below close "Charlestown / August 18^{th,} 1778."; docketed by HL "Cap$^{t.}$ Senf / 18$^{th.}$ Aug$^{t.}$ 1778 / Rec$^{d.}$ 8$^{th.}$ Novem.~~".

FROM JOHN HOUSTOUN

Savannah, Ga., August 20, 1778

Sir

My long absence from town, and the confused Situation of publick Matters with Us, owing to the incessant Alarms we have had for these three Months past, must be my apology to your Excellency for my long, and otherwise unpardonable Silence. whilst I consider

---

[1] Fort Howe, formerly Fort Barrington, was located at the first landing on the Altamaha River. The East Florida Rangers captured and burned it in March 1778. Fort Tonyn, constructed in 1776, twenty-five miles up the St. Marys River, remained the main British outpost on the northern Florida frontiers until retreating Loyalists burned it in June 1778. Searcy, *Georgia-Florida Contest*, pp. 37, 76.

the Ills which fall on Individual States, and perhaps on few more sensibly than this, I cannot refrain from offering my most hearty and unfeigned Congratulations on the Train of auspicious Events which have taken Place on the great and general Scale. We may now begin to look up for the Harvest of all our Labours, and prepare for the Enjoyment of that which, as we have had Valour enough to acquire, I hope we shall have Virtue enough to preserve till Time shall be no more.

Before this comes to Hand your Excellency will no Doubt have heard of the Movement and Proceedings of a large Body of Continental and Militia troops to the Southern Frontier of this state.

After marching there at a very considerable Expence and Fatigue, we found that the Enemy acknowledged our Superiority and had drawn in the Garrison from Fort Tonyn. We viewed the Fort abandoned and in Ashes. a Militia Party under Genl Screven had a Slight Skirmish with the Enemy, in which we had one Man killed and four wounded and then to my great Surprize I found that the Continental Forces were resolved upon a Retreat. the particular Reasons which induced this Measure I am unacquainted with, further than what the inclosed Paper informed me and will your Excellency.[1] but I must observe that I did and do totally dissent from the Opinion of all those who sounded the Retreat. and I am happy in being able to say that a more unpopular Manuœvre never was attempted than this. ~~was~~ among all Ranks and Orders of the Militia who were present and saw for themselves. I pay great Deference to the Advice of Gentlemen whose Duty requires they should be conversant in Military Matters, but to acknowledge that I thought the whole Georgia Brigade, with the greater Part of that of S^o Carolina added to near 2000. hearty determin'd Militia Men who considered they were conquering the Enemy's Country to defend their own, insufficient to penetrate East Florida and subdue every thing short of the Castle, would be doing too great Violence to my own Judgment, and in fact saying what I did not believe. I therefore, altho' no Military Man, must retain my own opinion which is that we ought to have prosecuted the Enterprize; and altho' we did stop

---

[1] The enclosures to which Houstoun refers here and below have not been found.

short of reducing the Castle, yet breaking up the rest of the Province would be a considerable Point and have made some recompense for the enormous Expence of our Armament. But when I consider the Favor which a great Number of the Inhabitants of East-Florida bear our Cause__ the probable Disaffection among the Soldiery__ the Scarcity of Provision__ the intollerably bad Water within the Walls__ the small Prospect of Reinforcements__ the dying Hope of their Schemes of Tyranny__ the Desertion of their Indian Allies which happened on the appearance of our Army, and which is clear Proof of the Opinion of that People, I really am sanguine enough to think it is at least within the Possibility of Events that the Castle itself would have surrender'd or might perhaps have been betrayed into our Hands. the best Accounts do not make the regular Force in East-Florida above 700 strong, and we know the greater Part of them are raw Recruits chiefly taken or enlisted from Dr Turnbull's Grecians[2] who were ever more disposed to our Cause than the British.

your Excellency will find that great stress in the Failure of this Expedition is laid upon the Season__ but had we set out before the Campaign was open'd to the Northward, how easy a Matter would it have been for the British Commander to have spared a Reinforcement, and had them back again Time enough for himself. It is also worthy of Consideration how we should at any other Season have grazed and supported our Cattle, and whether it is not probable, that reflecting how many of our People are badly cloathed and without Blankets, the Winter would not be more fatal to their Healths than the Summer__ besides the Men who went upon this Business were not brought from Mountains of Snow, nor c^d they experience any sensible Difference between the Climate of South Carolina or Georgia, and that of East-Florida; and I dare venture to affirm there is not one in ten of them but what follows his Plough the hottest Day in Summer in the two former States. how the Continental Troops came to be sickly is not for me to determine, nor do I wish to impute Blame to any Man. the Militia altho' many of them out for three Months constantly, were not so,__ the former had all tents and the latter none, yet the whole Loss of the Militia by

---

[2] Greek, Corsican, and Italian immigrants who had settled as servants indentured to Dr. Andrew Turnbull at New Smyrna had fled north to St. Augustine in 1777 where many joined the Loyalists. *HL Papers*, V, 231n; XIII, 191n.

natural Deaths was in my opinion less than if they had staid at home. the Georgia Division lost three and Col: Williamson I beleive about as many.

Your Excellency will perceive by the inclosed Paper that it was deemed improper if not impracticable to carry the Gallies into S^t. John's River upon two Accounts. the one respecting Amelia Narrows and the other in regard to the Enemy's Force in the river. As to the former we had with Us near 200. able bodied Negro Men principally intended for this very Business, and it is the opinion of those best acquainted with the Pass that admitting there was no assistance by[3] white Labourers, <u>that Strength</u> could have completed the whole, whilst we were marching from S^t. Mary's to S^t. John's Rivers. however of this Passage I beleive ~~yourself~~ your Excell^y. yourself has some Knowledge__ if not, Information may easily be had. As to the Latter the Accounts were various__ some making the Enemy to have as many forty Pounders in the river as our Gallies had Swivels, and others declared there was nothing there that could stand before or injure our Force__ for in Addition to the four Gallies belonging to this state we had a very fine one belonging to South Carolina, besides several Flats (and might have had more) carrying very heavy Metal, and a Sloop of 14 Guns.__ I am of the latter opinion, and indeed subsequent Events have shewn this to be the Case, for since the Capture of Osborne & Bachop by the Vessels out of Chas. Town which happened before our Retreat, a small Schooner from Sunbury not larger than a Pilot-Boat has ravaged the whole Coast of East-Florida__ She has already bro^t. in a tender of much more than her own Force__ taken by stratagem without firing a Gun, and two other Vessels.

The tender[4] being immediately mann'd by our People yesterday came into Sunbury with great Part of Dr. Turnbull's Plate and Furniture together with his B^r. and 32 of his Negroes taken off his Plantation on the Misquitoes,[5] and the People on Board declared they saw or heard of no Force either in S^t. John's or any other of the rivers, but that they are fitting out two or three Privateers at S^t. Augustine. I was so fully persuaded of the Practicability and

---

[3] "y" written over other text.

[4] "tender" written over other text.

[5] This privateer had been a tender to the *Perseus* (Elphinstone) man of war. After the raid at New Smyrna, St. Augustine authorities sent two vessels in pursuit. Both, the sloop *Otter* and

Propriety of the Gallies going into S^t· John's River (and of that opinion were the Captains as I have been since informed) that I should without Hesitation have ordered them there, but the Gentleman (Oliver Bowen Esqr·) whom the state had appointed to the Command of them, with the Title of Commodore altho' I believe never has or recognized by Congress as such,[6] just then, when upon S^t· Mary's and not before, chose to find out he had no immediate Connexion with the state nor was he (altho' holding no Continental Appointment) any way subject to the Authority, and therefore agreeably to his own Inclination immediately retreated, leaving all the Militia Troops who were out both of this state and South Carolina, in the Enemy's Country with the rivers S^t· Mary's__ Satilla__ Alatamaha &^c &^c__ all open by entering into which with a few armed Boats or small Vessels the Enemy might have effectually cut off our Retreat. I shall forbear to mention many other Circumstances in this Business which altho' I wish your Excellency (from my firm Persuasion of your regard and Attention to this poor little state) to know *illegible* may be unnecessary at this time.

indeed I should not have been thus troublesome or tedious, well knowing how deeply engaged in more weighty Concerns you must be, but that I fear Misrepresentation may creep into the relation of this late expensive and unprofitable affair

I am informed Commodore Bowen means to set out for Congress in a few Days, tho' I do not beleive it as I have not learnt he has as yet obtained Leave of Absence for that Purpose. he has had none from the state and I think ought not to go without. the Gallies are certainly on the Continental Establishment, but I realy think they will be of little Service to us unless confined to and made Subject to the orders of the state for whose Benefit they were built and whose Protection they are. Nor can I suffer myself to think Congress ever had an Idea to the Contrary.

I flatter myself that if Congress can find Leisure to call for and examine the whole Circumstances attending this Expedition

---

schooner *George,* were lost during the chase off Cape Canaveral. *S.C. General Gazette,* July 15, 1778; E.P. Panagopolous, *New Smyrna* (Gainesville, Fla., 1966), p. 165.

[6] Oliver Bowen sought a naval commission from Congress in October 1779. The Marine Committee recommended he be granted a captain's commission "Provided Mr. Bowen shall on receiving such Commission resign his Commission of Major in the army of the United States." The report is docketed "passed in the negative Nov^r· 8. 1779." Marine Committee Report, Oct. 27, 1779, M332, Roll 6; *JCC,* XV, 1193, 1215, 1277.

there will be no Difficulty in their allowing the Expence as a Continental Charge. and I would wish that such state of Facts as they may require be laid before them on Oath. there are many Considerations which place our Situation in a very particular Light. We are the southern Barrier to all the other States__ the late Expedition was not deliberately and from Choice taken up, but arose from a Necessity imposed on us ~~illegible~~ ↑by↓ the Insurrection of a large Body of disaffected Persons out of another State__ their Irruption was sudden and violent, and any Measures to prevent their making a Continental Impression depended on Expedition, whereby there was no time left to consult Congress or obtain their Approbation before the Expence was contracted. there are many more reasons which may be urged for this Relief to an Infant-State already half-reduced by its Southern Neighbour, which like a Canker is daily eating it up. your Excellency knows we have not now a Settlement South of Sᵗ· John's Parish, and how soon the Enemy may follow Us as they find we have retreated, as far as the River Agechee, is with me Matter of Speculation.

I shall not longer dwell on this Subject than just to mention that we returned with a most ample store of Provision. in all near 700. Steirs were brought back with Us. about 1000 more were engaged for us__ 600 of them actually on their Way to our Camps. As to Rice there could be no Scarcity of that __ between 3 & 400 Barrels arrived in Sᵗ· Mary's the Day before we retr↑e↓ated.

We had great Plenty of Rum and almost every other Necessary that could be desired. From all which it is evident our Retreat did not arise from a Deficiency of either Men__ Provision or Necessaries, and with me I assure you not from Inclination.

Col: Williamson of whose Candour and Soldierly Conduct no Man can entertain too high an Opinion, and to whose Services this State is much indebted was a witness to the whole.

I fear, Sir, the Effects of our Failure in the Expedition will be severely felt by this State. the Creek-Indians look'd on with eager Expectation and from every Account were determined as usual to take the strongest Side. Mʳ· Galphin now informs me that Eight Towns have declared for War against Us, and since the 12ᵗʰ· Instant, 24 Persons have been killed by them in what are called the Ceded-Lands of this State__ So that in Addition to other Misfortunes we may consider ourselves as fairly in for an Indian War.

I have had the Honor to receive several Dispatches from your Excellency which I had it not in my Power before particularly to acknowledge the Receipt of. I now inclose you a List of the Acts of Congress which have come to hand, and have opposite to each marked what has been done in Consequence thereof. I take this Method because my absence from Town occasionally threw the Management of Matters into other Hands, and I find Congress were not advised of the Proceedings had upon their Acts. in future, Sir, the most punctual and strict attention shall be paid to every Matter transmitted by you and falling within my Line. our Assembly is to meet on the Second Tuesday in October when I persuade myself no Recommendation to them from Congress will wait a Day to be adopted.

I have the Honor to be with / the greatest Regard. / Sir / your Excell^ys. most Ob^t. / & very h̄ble serv^t.

J. Houstoun

SOURCE: RC, PCC (Item 73), DNA; addressed on cover "His Excellency / The President of Congress."; addressed below close "His Excellency / H. Laurens Esqr. / Pres^t. of Congress."; dated "Savannah 20th. August 1778."; docketed "Letter from gov^r Houston / Aug 20. 1778 / Read 6 Oct^r. / Referred to / Mr Drayton / Mr Telfair / Mr Marchant".

FROM GEORGE WASHINGTON
White Plains, N.Y., August 20, 1778

Dear Sir

I am now to acknowledge my obligations for your favor of the 31st. Ult^o. & for its several Inclosures.

The conduct of Governor Johnstone has been certainly reprehensible__ to say no worse of it__ and so I think the world will determine.__ His Letters to Messrs. Morris and Reed are very significant and the points to which they conclude quite evident.__ They are, if I may be allowed so to express myself, of a pulse-feeling cast, and the offer to the latter thro the Lady, a direct attempt upon his integrity.__ When these things are known, he must share largely in public contempt__ and the more so from the opposite parts he has taken[1]

I am sorry you troubled your self with transmitting me copies & extracts of your Letters to the French Officers, in answer to their applications for Rank.__ Your word, Sir, will always have the fullest credit with me whenever you shall be pleased to give it upon any occasion; and I have only to regret that there has not been the same degree of decision and resolution in every Gentleman, as you have used in these instances.__ If there had, it would not only have contributed much to the tranquility of the Army__ but preserved the rights of our own Officers.__ With respect to Brevet Commissions, I know many of the French Gentlemen have obtained nothing more.__ That these were intended as merely honorary__ and that they are not so objectionable as the other sort; however these are attended with great inconveniencies, for the instant they gain a point upon you, no matter what their primary professions and engagements were, they extend their views and are incessant in teasing for actual command.__ The reason for their pressing for printed Commissions in the usual form, in preference to the Brevits you give them is obvious.__ The former are better calculated to favor their schemes as they import an idea of real command__ and of consequence afford them grounds for their future sollicitations for the purpose.__ I am well pleased with Mons[r.] Girards declaration__ and if he adheres to it, he will prevent many frivolous & unwarrantable applications; for finding their pursuits not seconded by his interest, many of the Gentlemen will be discouraged, and relinquish every[2] hope of success.__ Nor am I insensible of the propriety of your wish respecting our friend the Marquis.__ His Countrymen soon find access to his heart and he is but too apt afterwards to interest himself in their behalf, without having a sufficient knowledge of their merit__ or a proper regard to their extravagant views.__ I will be done upon the Subject.__ I am sure

[1] Elizabeth Ferguson, wife of Loyalist Hugh Henry Ferguson, arranged a meeting with Joseph Reed during which she verbally conveyed George Johnstone's offer of wealth and high position in exchange for his influence in Congress. Reed had already received a letter from Johnstone which solicited his assistance and strongly suggested a reward for his efforts. William B. Reed, *Life and Correspondence of Joseph Reed* (2 vols.: Philadelphia, 1847), I, 381-393; *HL Papers*, XIII, 462.

[2] "relinquished" changed to "relinquish ev".

you have been severely punished by their importunities as well as myself.__

The performance ascribd to M^r· Mauduit is really curious as coming from him, when we consider his past conduct.__ He is a sensible writer__ and his conversion at an earlier day, with many others that have lately happened, might have availed his Country much.__ His reasoning is plain & forcible and within the compass of every understanding.__

I have nothing new to inform you of.__ My public Letter to Congress yesterday contained my last advices from Rhode Island.__ ³ I hope in a few days from the high spirits and expectations of General Sullivan, that I shall have the happiness to congratulate you on our success in that Quarter.__

I am Dr Sir / With the most perfect / esteem & regard / Y^r· Most Obed^t & Oblg^d / Ser^t·

G^O: Washington

SOURCE: RC, NNPM; no address; dated "Head Quarters Aug^t· 20th· 1778"; docketed by HL "Geñ Washington / 20 Augt 1778 / Rec̄d 25th·". Draft, Washington Papers, DLC. Copy (19th century), HL Papers, ScHi.

TO WILLIAM LIVINGSTON

Philadelphia, August 21, 1778

Dear Sir

I was honor'd with Your Excellencys' very obliging favor of the 3^d Instant on the 12th, not a day has since passed without an earnest desire in my Mind to pay my respects to it, but other employment obliged me day by day, to say, "tomorrow."

We have nothing new from Spain, I mean new to me, Gentlemen not only smiled, but laughed at my Ideas expressed while we were reading the Treaties with France, that the Spaniard had his Eye upon the Florida's and Providence, in order to secure the streights of the Gulph. My conjecture was founded on seeing the bawble of Bermuda thrown in to us, and not a word said of

---

³ Washington's August 19 letter enclosed a copy of General Sullivan's August 17 letter. PCC, Item 152, Vol. 6, p. 269ff; Item 160, p. 153ff.

Bahama__ I have lately received strong confirmation of my suspicions__ the Post of S^t. Marks having been withdrawn by the English, a Spanish Guard I suppose from Pansacola succeeded them, these had a conference lately with our friendly Creek Indians, and in the course of their Talks intimated to the Savages that Spain would soon be repossess'd of that Post and adjacent Country__ a venerable Don who lately din'd with me let the Cat a little further out__ speaking of the late abortive expedition against S^t. Augustine, a Gentleman observ'd in French that East Florida would be a great acquisition to South Carolina and Georgia[1], my good friend Don Juan, either unwarily or supposing I did not understand, replied with much gravity, "and also for Spain". I drank a glass of Ale with the Don.[2]

This I really mean Sir, as a secret, and if we keep it so, the discovery may be apply'd to good purposes when we come to treat in earnest.

I am afraid our present Commissioners are not appriz'd of the immense value to our whole Union of S^t. Augustine and Bahama, and that too many of us here, view the possession in a light of partial benefit__[3]

If the lampoon of New York hurt Governor Johnstone, W.H.D.^s declaration will ↑not↓ be received as an healing plaister; this thing by the bye, was sadly hurried up; I had been for a fortnight anxiously soliciting my friend out of doors to introduce an Act or Resolve to the same effect, but thro' delay, we were necessi↑t↓ated to accept of a stiff performance without time for a proper amendments.

Your Excellency may not have seen the late Remonstrance and requisition of Governor Johnstone and his Colleagues. I shall inclose with this a Copy of that, and of M^r. Adam Ferguson's Letter which usher'd the Paper, calculated as I presume to retort upon Congress for the late publication signed Charles Thomson. It is

---

[1] The marquis de Brétigney, who had been held prisoner at St. Augustine, submitted a plan for the capture of the British post which he enclosed in a letter to HL. Marquis de Brétigney to HL, Aug. 18, 1778, HL Papers, ScHi; de Brétigney's plan, PCC, Item 78, Vol. 3, p. 31ff; and a translation in HL Papers, ScHi.

[2] Don Juan de Miralles, in a report to the Ministry of the Indies in Madrid, noted that when he dined with HL on August 16, the conquest of St. Augustine had been discussed and that he had spoken directly to HL about Spanish interests in the area. *Delegate Letters* (Smith), X, 487-488.

[3] HL inserted a crosshatch to indicate a new paragraph. Emendations here and below by HL.

impossible they can conceive that Congress will admit their Commission for quieting disturbances, founded on a special Act of Parliament as sufficient authority for making a "distinct and explicit Ratification of the Convention of Saratoga"__ or, that it contains "a proper notification by the Court of Great Britain to Congress."

Congress have committed their paper, an honor which in my humble opinion it is not entitled to.

The Act of the 8th of January has exceedingly embarrassed the wise Men in the East, a conformity with the terms will Amount to an acknowledgement of our capacity to treat as a Nation, any thing below, will imply a continued claim upon us as Subjects in rebellion, to which we will not subscribe, hence the Court perceive the dilemma to which she is reduced by a few cunningly designed words dropt from the pen of her ~~illegible~~ ↑Marionnette↓ Lieutenant General John Burgoyne Esquire, who has acknowledged in Parliament that he, solely, penned his infamous Proclamation, and in the same moment declared, he had no intention to carry his threats into execution__ and it is not to be wondered that in such circumstances they instruct their present minions to try the effect of a little ambidexterity.

Your Excellency must know more than I do of the affairs of the fleets and Armies, late of Rhode Island and New York. My last Accounts were very unpleasant.

Colonel Boudinot will inform you Sir, the sentence of the Court Martial on General Lee, I presume Congress when they have approved or disapproved will order the tryal to be publish'd[4]

I Am / With high Esteem &c.

P.S.

I have been long out of humour with the too comprehensive term "Continental," and have a strong inclination to coin "Confederal." Confœderal if Your Excellency has no objection, it shall pass.

SOURCE: LB, HL Papers, ScHi; addressed "Governor Livingston / Jersey / by Mr. Witherspoone"; dated "21st Augt.". Copy, (19th century), HL Papers, ScHi.

---

[4] That same day Congress ordered "That 100 copies of the proceedings of the court martial of the trial of Major General Lee, be printed for the use of the members." The copies were printed by John Dunlap in Philadelphia. *JCC*, XI, 826; XII, 1287.

FROM WILLIAM LIVINGSTON

Morristown, N.J., August 21, 1778

Dear Sir,

I am sure you are not dead, or I should have seen it in the Papers, for I doubt not the demise of a President, especially of so respected a One as M^r: Laurens would make as much noise in the Prints, tho' of a very different nature as the Reception of a foreign Ambassador. To what then am I to ascribe your unusual Silence if not to the very Reception of this Ambassador, & for which I intend shortly to be revenged both upon You & Monsieur Gerard by troubling You with a visit in Philadelphia__ [1]

I am much pleased with the Declaration of Congress against Governor Johnstone__ A Step of this kind I have wished for & expected ever since I saw the publication of his Attempts to bribe__ He has certainly forfeited all right to be treated ~~to be treated~~ with as a public Person, by his villainous manoevres of private Corruption, & I think such attempts in an Independent State, as well as the Joint Machinations of all the Commissioners to spirit up the People against Congress, are a Species of treason for which, according to the usual practice of Nations, the Perpretrators are punishable by the municipal Laws of the Country notwithstanding their public Characters__

I doubt not the Declaration will reflect great Honor on Congress thro' all Europe; & in England will be matter of Astonishment; as I am sure they have no Conception of the Possibility of withstanding a Bribe in a Country where nothing is done without it__

In hopes of your Reformation in the punctuality of your private Correspondence, (the only Article in which you want mending) I am with the highest Esteem & Affection

Dear Sir / Your most humble St

Wil: Livingston

P.S: I think the History of the present War, & the rise & Progress of the Contest which occasioned it, ought for the Honor of America

---

[1] The Trenton, N.J., *Gazette*, Sept. 9, 1778, reported that William Livingston had passed through Trenton on September 5 en route to Philadelphia and again on September 8 after having visited with Gérard, the French ambassador.

to be undertaken by a number of able hands in Concert, & by public encouragement__ I know that every Body thinks himself capable of writing History who can put together a Collection of facts__ And if this deserved the Name of History almost every Body would indeed be able to write One__ But experience must convince us that for One Robertson we have had at least fifty Oldmixons__[2] As a Composition of this kind well executed, (And our Country affords Men competent to the task) would propagate the Glory of America thro' every Quarter of the Globe & inspire our latest Posterity with Emulation of the Renown of their Ancestors;__ I cannot but think that as many dollars as are stolen from the Continent in one week by a Set of worthless Rascals, who enrich themselves by public plunder, would be as usefully expended in the encouragement of such a work__ I wish You would think of the matter, & favor me with your Sentiments on the Subject__

SOURCE: RC, HL Papers, ScHi; addressed below close "The Honorable Henry Laurens Esq[r] / President of Congress__"; dated "Morris-Town 21[st:] Aug[t]- 1778__"; docketed by HL "Gov[r.] Livingston / 21[st.] Aug. Rec̄d 25th / Answ[d.] 1[st.] Sept[r.]". Copy (19th century), HL Papers, ScHi.

TO JOHN LEWIS GERVAIS

Philadelphia, August 22, 1778

My dear friend

You shall hear from me by Muckinfuss, at present let me refer you for News and Newspapers directed to you, to our friend the President__ who I know will use my opinion upon the various subjects which I have touched__ with his wonted discretion and wisdom.

I had not heard of Col[o.] Laurens from the 4th Instant till the

---

[2] Although a second edition of John Oldmixon's *History of the British Empire...* was issued in 1741, William Robertson's *The History of America* largely supplanted Oldmixon when it was published in 1777. Macaulay, for example, found Oldmixon "more distinguished by zeal than either by candour or by skill." Samuel A. Allibone, *A Critical Dictionary of English Literature and British and American Authors...* (3 vols.: Philadelphia, 1870), II, 1453.

advice from M^r· Morris,[1] therefore had concluded he had been with Count d'Estaing in order to tempt his fortune on Sea

Sullivans' Letter looks very like a Burgoynade.[2] I wish happier consequences respecting us may attend.

Adieu___

SOURCE: LB, HL Papers, ScHi; addressed "John Lewis Gervais Esquire / Charles Town / sent by Jones to Baltimore, there to be given to Captain Pyne"; dated "22 August".

FROM JOHN LAURENS

Rhode Island, August 22, 1778

My dear Father___

I have just had the satisfaction of receiving your kind letter of the 13th- the relation of what has passed since I last had the pleasure of writing___ will not ~~in general~~ amuse you___ but ~~as~~ it is necessary that you sh^d· know it & I will be exceedingly brief___ according to the first plan proposed by General Sullivan, the American forces were to land on the east side of Rhode Island, under cover of the fire of three frigates stationed in the eastern channel for that purpose___ A[1] Signal was to be given immediately as our boats should begin to cross___ and another when the descent should be effected___ upon the latter, the french troops were to disembark on the east side of

---

[1] Maj. Lewis Morris (1754-1824), the nephew of Gouverneur Morris, wrote his uncle August 14 from Rhode Island where he was serving as an aide-de-camp to General Sullivan. He mentioned that the "advanc'd Corps of the Army is commanded by one of the best officers in the service of the States, Col^o· Laurens the Son of my very good friend the President of Congress." He further noted that Count d'Estaing did not want any Americans "on board the fleet till after the reduction of the Islands." J. [L.] Morris to Gouverneur Morris, Aug. 14, 1778, HL Papers, ScHi.

[2] Although neither of Sullivan's letters of August 17 to HL and George Washington were listed among HL's enclosures in his letter to Rawlins Lowndes of Aug. 11-20, 1778, the reference here is apparently to one of those letters. In each letter, Sullivan made the identical boast about his position against the British forces on Rhode Island: "...by to-morrow noon, I shall be able to keep up so warm a fire upon them as to render the properties of a Salamander essentially necessary to their existence." See above for Sullivan to HL. The Sullivan-Washington letter is in PCC, Item 160, p. 153ff.

[1] "A" written over "the".

the island, and a junction was to be formed as speedily as possible__ but the[2] ambition of an individual and national pride discovered insuperable obstacles to this disposition__ The Mq̄uis de la fayette aspired to the command of the french troops in conjunction with the flower of Gen[l] Sullivans Army__ in a visit which he had paid to the fleet he prevailed upon the Count d'Estaing to write upon this subject__ The Count intimated in his letter a desire that some good american troops sh[d] be annexed to the french__ adding that if the command of them were given to M[r] de la fayette, it w[d.] be a means of facilitating the junction between the troops of the two Nations, as he was acquainted with the service of both__ and that in case any naval operations sh[d.] require his[3] (the Counts) Return[4] on board the Squadron, the Mq̄uis w[d.] naturally take the command in his absence which w[d–] prevent many difficulties that w[d.] otherwise arise on that account__ The Mquis strenuously contended that a considerable detachment of select troops ought to be annexed to the French__ that the pride of his nation would never suffer the present disposition to take place, as by it the french batallions w[d] land under cover of the American Forces and play a humiliating secondary part The Arguments against gratifying him in his request were these__ General Sullivans Army contained a very small proportion of regular troops__ it was necessary that a main body capable of resisting the enemy force, should exist__ as a contrary conduct w[d] expose either division to a total defeat or a vigorous attack from[5] the enemy__ The Mquis however seemed much dissatisfied, and his private views withdrew his attention wholly from the general interest__ [6]

On the 8[th–] Gen[l.] Sullivan received a Letter from the Admiral__ in which he says that the disposition for disembarking is militarily inadmissible__ that the American Generals were now for the first

---

[2] "t" written over other text.

[3] "his" written over "this".

[4] "Re" written over other text.

[5] "from" written over other text.

[6] JL's observations seem to be accurate. Lafayette's interest in a joint Franco-American command in the Rhode Island campaign was prompted by his personal preoccupation with obtaining glory for himself and France. The marquis himself noted that his "fantasies" about leading French troops to victory over the British in America "made my situation a delicate one." He understood that the Americans would find it "irksome...to see the beautiful scenes of a play performed by foreign actors." *Lafayette Papers* (Idzerda), II, 129-134.

time furnished with an opportunity of discovering the value which they set on the french alliance, by the number and composition of the troops which they w^d· annex to the french__ it was not for him to point out the number but he w^d· be gladly be have it in his power to give an account both to the Congress and his King of the American detachm^t· which should be sent to him__ [7] Genl Sullivan In consequence of this Letter it was determined that Jacksons Regiment,[8] and as many good Militia as in the whole w^d· amount to 1000 men sh^d· be sent under the command of the Mǭuis.__ The tardiness of the militia and[9] the impossibility of completing the transport boats so soon as was expected, & the slow arrival of the heavy Cannon, had obliged Genl· Sullivan more than once to procrastinate the attack__ he had fixed on the 9th· and for the reasons mentioned in my last the Count was to force his passage with the Squadron on the 8th· The Genl· found it impossible to keep his word__ and wrote to appoint another day on which[10] he declared he w^d make his descent at all events__ the Count however had made his arrangements and entered the harbour on the 8^th_ a thundering cannonade was kept up between the batteries and Ships as they Passed__ the injury to the latter is not worth notice__

9th· Genl· Sullivan received intelligence both from Deserters and Inhabitants that[11] the enemy has evacuated all their redoubts and batteries on the North part of the Island he took the hardy resolution of availing himself of this move and threw his whole Army across__ [12] this measure gave much umbrage to the french officers__ they conceived their troops injured by our landing first__ and talked like women disputing precedence in a country dance__ instead of men engaged in defending the pursuing the common interest of two great Nations__

[7] Count d'Estaing to John Sullivan, Aug. 7, 1778, *Sullivan Papers* (Hammond), II, 183-184.

[8] Col. Henry Jackson's regiment, organized in Boston in the spring and summer of 1777, was one of the Sixteen Additional Continental Regiments authorized in January 1777. It had been detached from the main army and sent to the Eastern Department July 22, 1778. Wright, *Continental Army*, pp. 215-216.

[9] "and" written over other text.

[10] "w" written over "he".

[11] "that" written over other text.

[12] An asterisk at this point refers to a note at the foot of the page: "an officer was sent immediately to give the Admira[l] notice of it__".

Admiral Howes fleet appeared in the Offing

10th. The French Squadron passed the batteries of Newport, (receiving their fire and returning broad sides___) without receiving any damage by reason of the distance___ and gave chace to the British Fleet___ On the 11th. Such a Storm of Wind[13] and rain arose as filled[14] us with anxiety for the french[15] Squadron___ The Army suffered much during the bad weather for want of Tents.___ and on account of the impossibility of crossing the ferry___ which circumstance reduced our magazines to a low ebb___

On the 15th. The Army moved to a position for commencing its operations against the enemy___ and some works were thrown up the same night for its security.

On the Evening of the 16th. a Battery of protection and its communication were begun___ the next morning as soon as our unfinished work could be discovered the enemys batteries began to fire on it___

our works have been carrying on every night since___ and as long as day light lasts there is generally a slow firing kept up on each side; without any effect worth mentioning___ on account of the great distance the method that has hitherto been pursued, will prove very tedious if continued___

20th. The French Squadron appears, and terminates much anxiety___

The Admirals Ship and the Marseilles were dismasted in the Storm___ the former totally dismantled ↑& without a Rudder___↓ was attacked by a british fifty Gun Ship___ which she obliged to sheer off by bringing her stern Chasers to bear___ imagine the cruel situation of the Count to see his Ship thus insulted___ after having arrived in the midst of the English Squadron and preparing for a combat in which victory ~~must~~ was inevitably his___ but a most dreadful Storm of which we had no idea___ dispersed[16] every thing___

---

[13] "of Wind" written over "arose".
[14] "filled" written over "gave".
[15] "french" written over other text.
[16] First "d" written over "p".

I was going on but am called away upon the most important business A[17] Council of War On[18] board the french Vessels have determined that the Squadron ought to go immediately to Boston to refit__ I am going on board with a solemn protest against it[19]

Adieu

J Laurens__

SOURCE: ALS, Kendall Collection; no address; dated below close "22ᵈ."; docketed by HL "John Laurens / 22 Augᵗ 1778 / Rec̄d 31ˢᵗ.". Copy, HL Papers, ScHi.

FROM CAESAR RODNEY

Dover, Del., August 22, 1778

Honᵈ Sir

In my last I informed you that the General Assembly of this State were to Meet, by adjournment, on the Tenth of this Instant when I would lay before them for Consideration The Confederation and your Letter on that head__ The Assembly did not meet according to adjournment and therefore by the Constitution cannot Assemble unless Called by the President.__ However I shall meet the Privy Council at Newcastle on Monday the 31ˢᵗ of this Instant therefore if Congress think it Necessary and will advise me of it I will then issue Writs for calling the Assembly for that purpose previous to the Anual Election to be held on the first day of October, The Assembly then Chosen will Set on the twentieth of the same month__[1]

I have the Honʳ to be / Your Honʳˢ / Most Obedᵗ Humᵉ / Serᵗ

Caesar Rodney

---

[17] "A" written over "The".

[18] "O" written over "a".

[19] The protest of the General Officers at Rhode Island was not written until after the French sailed from Boston. JL, pursuing in a swift privateer, was unable to catch d'Estaing and returned with the document. It was then sent overland and delivered to the French commander by General Heath. The document expressed the frustration of General Sullivan and the other officers and served no other purpose but to insult the French. *Greene Papers* (Showman), II, 487-491.

[1] The Delaware Assembly met in October but dissolved "without having Compleated any one piece of business laid before them." The Assembly did not approve the Articles until January 1779. Caesar Rodney to HL, Nov. 4, 1778; Jensen, *Articles of Confederation*, p. 197.

SOURCE: Copy, Rodney Manuscripts, DeHi; addressed on cover "The Hon^e·
Henry Laurens Esquire / President of / Congress__"; addressed below
close "The President of Congress__"; dated "Dover August the 22^d· 1778.";
franked "public Service".

TO JOHN BEATTY[1]

Philadelphia, August 23, 1778

Dear Sir

You will oblige me very much, and enable Me to accommodate our friends by procuring and sending to me as early as
convenience will admit of, an Almanack or other Pocket book
containing the latest Army and Navy lists of the Kingdom of Great
Britain, the best approved Charts of North America, and two dozen
neat silver Table Spoons. The Amount of which shall be paid to your
Order on demand in Gold or a Bill of Exchange which will be
considered in the price.[2]

I Am / With great Regard &c

PS.

Be so good as to send the inclosed letter forward by the first
conveyance.

P.S.

This moment I have the honor of yours of the 20th Instant
and thank you Sir for your politeness.__ Sending me New York
Papers as early and as constantly as possible will be very obliging,
and I will with pleasure repay any expence, and endeavour to
retaliate the favor. Inclos'd will be a letter from F. Raveneau a
Marine prisoner in New York,[3] permit me to recommend him to
your attention__ not meaning to ask a partial favor nor to give you
unnecessary trouble.__

---

[1] On May 28, 1778, Congress named Maj. John Beatty of the 6th Pa. Regiment Commissary
General of Prisoners to replace Elias Boudinot. Beatty, himself a prisoner of war who had
been exchanged only three weeks before his appointment, was promoted to colonel when
he accepted the position. *JCC*, XI, 546; HL to John Beatty, May 29, 1778, PCC, Item 13;
Heitman, *Continental Officers*.

[2] "which will be considered in the price" written by HL.

[3] Probably Francis Raveneau who later commanded the ship *Peter*, which belonged to
Samuel and Robert Purviance of Baltimore. PCC, Item 196, Vol. II, p. 96.

SOURCE: LB, HL Papers, ScHi; addressed "Colonel Jn⁰· Beatty / Com. Genˡ· of Prisoners / Princetown"; dated "23 Augᵗ·".

TO JAMES GRAHAM[1]

Philadelphia, August 23, 1778

Sir

This moment your favor of the 10ᵗʰ together with letters for Mʳ· Johnston and Mʳ· Houston were delivered to me. These shall go forward in the course of the present week.

Were it as inoffensive Sir, without further enquiry to grant a free passage to yourself, I would with great pleasure remove the difficulties you complain of, and add every means in my power for the happy prosecution of your wishes, but your application is met by a question which you have not enabled me to determine; Is the Gentleman a Citizen of any of these States?

If Sir, you are a Subject of His Britannic Majesty, the moment you pass the line of usurpation, you will consider yourself and be considered, as in an Enemys' Country, liable to penalties common in such cases, unless you are guarded by a special licence from the Representatives of the good People of the Union.__ All therefore that I can at present contribute towards your relief, is to lay your Letter before Congress__ and you shall be presently advised of the result.

I write now, because I have an immediate opportunity and because as I perceive your Letter has been long on the road I would not hold you in more than unavoidable suspense.[2]

I have the honor to be &c.

---

[1] James Graham, a native of Scotland and a former Georgia planter, was the brother of John Graham the last royal lieutenant governor of Georgia. He married John Stuart's daughter Sarah in 1767, and soon after moved to London where he acted as his father-in-law's agent. He arrived at Charleston in October 1778 from New York under a flag of truce with Robert Williams and John Hopton aboard the cartel sloop *Adventure*. While Williams and Hopton were accepted as citizens of the state, Graham was forced "to proceed, in the same Vessel, whithersoever she may be destined." He went to Savannah and remained there until 1780 when he returned to London. *HL Papers*, VI, 419n; *S.C. Gazette, Oct. 21, 1778; Wilbur* H. Siebert, *Loyalists in East Florida, 1774 to 1785* (Deland, Fla., 1929), p. 71.

[2] Third "s" written over "d" and then interlined for clarification.

P.S.

Having since writing the above intimated to M^r· Telfair the receipt and contents of your letter, that Gentleman observed there were circumstances in your favor which he should urge to Congress.[3]

SOURCE: LB, HL Papers, ScHi; addressed "Ja^s· Graham Esq. at the house of Rich^d· Yates Esqr· / New York"; dated "23^d August".

TO JOHN LAURENS

Philadelphia, August 23, 1778

My Dear Son

I writ to you the 13th· Have not had the pleasure of hearing from you since yours of the 7th·

Variety of Reports occupy the attention of all Classes in Philadelphia. Count d'Estaing has beat Lord Howe__ Lord Howe has been beaten by a hurricane__ Lord Howe has drove Count d'Estaing__ the British Isis engaged and had nearly taken Languedoc__ the Renown flog'd the Languedoc &c. &c. &c.__ all these, and many supplementary particulars you know are in my regard, flying Clouds & I patiently wait for more solid Intelligence, and flatter myself with hopes of receiving such from your hand in due time.

If General Sullivan falls short of his views of the 17th his Letter will be christened a Burgoynade and be deposited with the Proclamation of the 23^d July 1777. My Compliments to the General and assure him of my better thoughts. I persuade myself of the honor of congratulating ~~him of his having~~ ↑with him upon his↓[1] giving M^r· Prescott[2] a <u>coup</u> de Burgoyne. Inclosed with this you will find three

---

[3] Graham's letter was presented to Congress August 24 and referred to the South Carolina and Georgia delegates. *JCC*, XI, 830.

[1] Interlineation by HL.

[2] Maj. Gen. Richard Prescott, who had been captured in July 1777 and exchanged for Charles Lee in May 1778, was the commandant at Newport until he was superseded by Sir Robert Pigot.

foreign Letters, which from the dates of my own I believe will convey to you nothing new.

I am &c.

SOURCE: LB, HL Papers, ScHi; addressed "Colonel John Laurens / Rhode Island / by Jos. Burwell"; dated "23 Aug^t.".

TO LACHLAN McINTOSH

Philadelphia, August 23, 1778

Dear General

I receiv'd the inclos'd letters two or three days ago from South Carolina.

The last intelligence from Rhode Island is seven days old. General Sullivan writes, that on the 18th he should make an assault on the Enemy, begirt within their lines nearest to Newport town that he hoped to necessitate General Prescott to come out and fight on very disadvantageous terms, or to Capitulate. General Sullivan had of all sorts 9000 rank and file, his right wing commanded by General Greene, his left by Marquis de la Fayette, Lieutenant Colonel Laurens commanded the advanced Party. As The Enemys' strength about 6500 including all their Seamen collected from 6 frigates, 2 Gallies, and a great number of transports &c. which Count d'Estaing had oblig'd them to burn and sink.

Count d'Estaing had been drawn out to Sea the 10th Instant upon the appearance of Lord Howes' Squadron close in with the Island, he fled upon the Counts' making sail and there was every appearance of stratagem for diverting our Allies from the seige of the Island, for gaining time in expectation of a Reinforcement under Admiral Byron and drawing us into an unequal ↑fight__↓¹__ on the 11th on 11th happened a very violent storm of Wind ↑continued to the 13↓ which had almost ruined our insulated Army__ General Sullivans' prospect was then cover'd by gloom; he apprehended the Enemy would take an advantage of his distress; and he had only to trust to his Bayonets, and as he express'd himself, "to conquer or

¹ Interlineations here and below by HL.

die." From Mr Prescotts' silence at so critical a time, I conjecture he is by no means so strong as 6500, or that he dare not trust his Men out of the lines and from under his Eye. The desertions from him of scores of Men almost every night, warrants the latter opinion.

How our floating friends and Enemies fared in that storm, or what is become of them, we know not with precision, a letter from a French Gentleman in the Camp to Monsr· Girard, reports that Count d'Estaing had taken one capital English ship and six frigates, or small armed Vessels.

A deserter from New York examin'd by me last night, and he is a very sensible Man, says, the Eagle had been driven on shore back of Long Island, that Lord Howe had saved his person and return'd in a Frigate, that three or four more English ships of the Line were likewise driven on shore and left, but whether the storm of wind or Count d'Estaings' cannon had been author of these disasters, he could not aver__ [2] upon the whole, it is reasonable to conclude the Enemys' fleet is scatter'd and much hurt__ that, of our friends we wait to learn the fate of, probably tomorrow will inform us, and I also expect to know tomorrow whether General Sullivan has succeeded according to his sanguine expectations, or has met with a Burgoynade.

General Washingtons' Army remained at White Plains hemming in Sir Henry Clinton and ordering rations for deserters who are continually coming in. I conjecture Sir Henry has not lost less than 400, since General Washington establish'd his Encampment.

Two Hessian Lieutenants lately deserted from New York[3] the brother of one of them is Aid de Camp to General Knyphausen I expect him every hour. I receiv'd an indirect message from him last night__ Deluded, wretched old England! Inclosed you will receive Copy of the sentence of the General Court Martial on General Lee. Observe I send this only for yourself. I have added a

---

[2] The *Eagle,* Admiral Howe's flagship, had not been driven ashore. The confusion over the plight of the *Eagle* may have stemmed from the fact that Howe, in an unorthodox battle strategy, had shifted his command to the frigate *Apollo* in an attempt at a better view and more maneuverability. During the storm he shifted his flag twice ending on the 50-gun *Centurion.* The British fleet had fared better than the French; most of Howe's command, including the *Eagle,* had returned to Sandy Hook by August 17. Tilley, *British Navy,* pp. 150-152; Ira D. Gruber, *The Howe Brothers & the American Revolution* (New York, 1972), pp. 315-318.

[3] Probably Ensigns Carl Frederich Fuhrer of Knyphausen's regiment and Carl Wilhelm Kleinschmidt of Rahl's regiment. George Washington to HL, Aug. 9, 1778.

Note or two on the paper. I have been assur'd by a Gentleman on whose word I rely that he has often heard the British Officers express their astonishment at the retreat of my old friend, and repeatedly say the party before whom he retired__ ↑expected nothing less than being every Man Captured.↓ Sir W^m_ Erskine, particularly, animadverting on General Lee's phrase of an "handsome check," said, "Lee may call it what he pleases but by —— I call it a handsome flogging. We had[4] not receiv'd such an one in America." My dear General I wish you all happiness; and am with great Regard,

> Your friend / And Most Obed^t· Servant

Whenever you write to me, carefully seperate private from Public.__ I beg Sir, you will deliver the Inclos'd to Monsr· de Cambray, and communicate the News. I would have written by this bearer but he would not wait, had I attempted to write to both, I should have lost the opportunity.

SOURCE: LB, HL Papers, ScHi; addressed "General Lachlin Mackintosh, Commandant / Fort Pitt"; dated "23 Aug^t·".

FROM JOHN SULLIVAN

Newport, R.I., August 23, 1778[1]

My Dear Sir

I have been honoured with Your Excellencys favor of the 16th Instant with the Gazette Inclosed. I most Sincerely thank you for the License you have given me to ~~illegible~~ Communicate Intelligence to yr Excellency by private Letter & also for your promise to Retaliate in kind. my Letters to General Washington Copies of which he is to Convey to Congress from time to time must have Informed you of the Return of the French Fleet The Loss ~~is~~ ↑it↓ Sustained, in the Storm & their Sudden Departure for Boston. This movement has

---

4 "d" written over "s".

1 Sullivan misdated the letter August 16. D'Estaing departed for Boston on August 22. On August 23 Sullivan polled his officers, who replied the same day. *Sullivan Papers* (Hammond), II, 248-263; *Lafayette Papers* (Idzerda), II, 147-148.

Raised ~~illegible~~ Every voice against the French Nation Revived all
their Ancient prejudice against the faith & Sincerity of that people
& Induces them most heartily to Curse the New alliance. these[2] ~~is~~
↑are↓ only the first Sallies of Passions which will in a few Days
Subside. I Confess that I do most Cordially Resent the Conduct of
the Count or Rather the Conduct of his officers who have it Seems
Compelled him to go to Boston & Leave us on an Island without any
Certain means of Retreat__ & what Surprizes me Exceedingly is that
the Count could be perswaded that it was necessary for ten Sail of
the Line to Lay in the Harbour to ~~illegible~~ attend one which is
Refitting. I ~~illegible~~ Beg[d.] the Count to Remain only twenty four
Hours & I would agree to Dismiss him but in vain. he well knew that
the original plan was for him to Land his own Troops with a Large
Detachment of mine ~~illegible~~ within their Lines under fire of Some
of his Ships while with the Rest I made an Attack in Front__ but his
Departure has Reduced me to the Necessity of attacking their works
in front or of doing Nothing They have Double Lines across the
Island[3] in two places at Near Quarter of a mile Distance The outer
Line is Covered in front by Redoubts within musket Shot of Each
other the Second in the Same manner by Redoubts thrown up
between the Lines beside this there is an inaccessible Pond which
Cover more than half the Front of the first Line a Strong Fortress on
Tommeny Hill overlooks & Commands the whole ~~Country~~ adjacent
Country The Enemy have about Six thousand men within these
works I have Eight Thousand one hundred & Seventy four__ with
this Force I am to Carry their Lines or Retire with Disgrace__ Near
7000 of my men are militia unaccustomed to the Noise of Arms
Should I throw my men by Stratagem within their Lines it must be
my Best Troops Should they be Defeated the want of Ships will
Render their Retreat impracticable & most of the Army must be
Sacrificed you will therefore Judge of my Feelings & of the Situation
which ~~illegible~~ my inconstant ally & Coadjutor has thrown me into my
feelings as a man press me to make the Desperate Attempt my
feelings as an officer Cause me to Hesitate. I have Submitted the
Considerations to my officers how they will Determine I know

---

[2] "there" altered to "these".
[3] "I" written over other text.

not__[4] I fear Disgrace will attend this Fatal Expedition Though it gave at first the most pleasing presages of Success

I think the New Manoeuvre of the Comissioners Exceeds any thing they have yet attempted. I trust they will Return to England with that Share of Contempt Such Infamous Conduct Deserves

your Brave and worthy Son is a fellow Sufferer with me in This Fatal Island. believe me my Dear when I Tell you That America has Seldom produced his Equal for Bravery or for Judgment

I have the Honor to be Dear / Sir with the Highest Esteem your / Excell^{cys} most obed^t & very Humble / Servant

Jno Sullivan

SOURCE: RC, Gratz Collection, PHi; addressed on cover "His Excellency / Henry Laurens Esqr / President of Congress / Philadelphia"; addressed below close "His Exc^y Henry Laurens Esqr"; dated "Camp before Newport Augt 16th 1778"; docketed "John Sullivan / 16$^{th.}$ Aug$^t.$ 1778"; noted on cover "Private / M Genl Sullivan".

FROM JOHN TEMPLE[1]

New York, August 23, 1778

Sir__

After Seven years absence from my Native country I arrived here with my wife & family on the third Instant from England, and

---

[4] Sullivan enclosed a copy of an August 23 letter to his general officers in a letter of the same date to General Washington. Sullivan concluded that "The Count De Estaing having abandoned us" only three choices remained. The American forces could continue the siege, they could attack, or they could retreat. He requested the officers' opinions on the best course and asked them to offer a plan to carry out whichever choice they made. The ten extant replies reveal that four officers (Gens. John Tyler, William Whipple, Nathanael Greene, and James M. Varnum) favored some type of attack; five others (Gens. John Glover, Lafayette, and Ezekiel Cornell with Cols. William Shepard and James Livingston) voted for a retreat; while one (Col. William West) suggested the siege be continued. John Sullivan to George Washington, Aug. 23, 1778, Washington Papers, DLC; *Sullivan Papers* (Hammond), II, 248-265; *Lafayette Papers* (Idzerda), II, 147-148.

[1] John Temple, a native of Boston, had been dismissed as Surveyor General of North American Customs in 1773 on allegations he had aided the American patriots in stealing letters belonging to Gov. Thomas Hutchinson. In April 1778 he was hired to work as a secret agent for the Carlisle Commission. Lewis Einstein, *Divided Loyalties: Americans in England During the War of Independence* (Boston, 1933), pp. 82-98. This request for a passport was his first contact with Congress.

now beg leave to solicit Congress for liberty to come to Philadelphia to pay my respects to them: General Clinton will on his part grant me all Necessary paper for that purpose, and I trust I shall readily meet with the like favor from Congress[2]

permit me, Sir to beg that you will present my particular compliments to the Members of Congress from Massachusetts Bay to all of whom I have the honor of being personally known, and that you will believe me to be with the greatest respect

Sir / Your most Obedient and / Most humble Servant

J. Temple

SOURCE: RC, PCC (Item 78), DNA; addressed below close "To His Excellency / Henry Laurens Esqr-"; dated "New York 23^d Augt 1778.".

FROM JOHN WELLS, JR.

Charles Town, August 23, 1778

Dear Sir

Having just now heard of a private Express that sets off for North Carolina, in a few hours time, I avail of myself of the opportunity to write you a few lines

We had[1] yesterday undoubted Intelligence from Mr Galphin of 7 Towns of the Creeks having commenced hostilities__ or rather that so many Towns had declared against us, & six of ~~illegible~~ the Georgia Back settlers killed. He seems to be of opinion, that we have rather a majority of the whole Nation in our interest, & ~~has~~ been assured by many of them that they will make reprisals at Pensacola & Mobille for whatever mischief the hostile Indians may do on our frontiers The matter merits the highest Consideration; and I hope measures will be adopted to severely chastise these foolish wanton disturbers of the publick tranquiliity. If Mr Galphin had a larger supply of Goods, he thinks he might even yet prevent a war__

---

[2] John Temple's request was read in Congress September 1 and rejected by a vote of ten nays, two ayes, and one state divided. A motion was made and passed that Temple declare the "State in which he means to reside, and obtain their approbation, previous to the granting of any passport". HL and William Henry Drayton opposed both motions making South Carolina the only state to oppose Temple's passport to a specific state. *JCC*, XI, 858-860.

[1] "have" altered to "had".

Gen. H. has wrote a Reply to M^r G's Remarks on the formers Letter to Congress, an account of M^r G's resigning his military commission. It concludes, I am told, with leaving him the alternative of making an acknowledgment as publick as his offence or another mode of deciding differences between Gentlemen, which he needs not to mention__ It is also said, a demand for a categorical answer has been sent__ Some think arms will decide the Contest; but it appears to me most probable, that a grey goose quill, dipt in gall & bitterness will be the one chiefly employed on the occasion__ ²

People, particularly the younger part here seem anxious to repair the loss the Community has sustained in its Inhabitants by the present war__ With this view, & perhaps with some others, several matrimonial connections are ta in agitation, & will speedily take place. Publick Rumour says the following: A. Rose to Miss P. Smith__ Lieut. Gadsden to Miss Fenwick__ Capt. Ladson to Miss Judith Smith__ Major Pinckney to Miss Motte, daughter of Jacob Motte__ Abrahaham Livingston, to Miss Polly Roupell &c &c &c__ ³

The Musketoes bite so hard & are so numerous, that I must conclude & am / most sincerely & respectfully / Yours

J Wells jun^r

Charles Morgan, is just now, Sunday morning, going out on a Cruize against two Jamaica Privateers that have taken several valuable Prizes on our Coast__ One had the assurance to cut Capt

---

² Christopher Gadsden had been the ranking South Carolina brigadier general when Robert Howe, a North Carolinian, assumed command of the Southern Department. Gadsden believed he should have been given the honor. In August 1777 his friends raised the issue in the legislature but he did not obtain that body's support. In a pique Gadsden resigned. In June 1778 he discovered that Howe had written Congress on the dispute the previous year. Copies of the letters were sent to Gadsden who penned a point by point reply that insulted Howe. Howe demanded an apology or the opportunity to obtain satisfaction. They met August 30 and "fought" a duel in which each man decided not to fire at his adversary. The affair gained wide publicity but did not resolve the problem for Gadsden who continued to complain about Howe's command. Bennett and Lennon, *A Quest for Glory*, pp. 56-61.

³ Alexander Rose married Margaret Smith, the daughter of Judge William Smith of New York, on Jan. 21, 1779. Thomas Gadsden married Martha Fenwick, the daughter of Edward Fenwick and Mary Drayton, on Oct. 16, 1778. James Ladson married Judith Smith, the daughter of Benjamin Smith and Mary Wragg, on Oct. 1, 1778. Thomas Pinckney married Elizabeth Motte, the daughter of Jacob Motte, Jr., and Rebecca Brewton, on July 22, 1779. Abraham Livingston died in 1782, unmarried. Ann Roupell was born in 1760 and died in 1785. *Directory of the S. C. House*, II, 568; III, 280, 412, 563; Edwin Brockholst Livingston, *The Livingstons of Livingston Manor* (New York, 1910), pp. 535-536; *SCHM*, XIX (1918), 178.

Joseph Darrell's sloop out of Georgetown-River, below the fort__
One Boat did it__ & yet the sloop had some Carriage & Swivel
Guns__ [4]

SOURCE: RC, Kendall Collection; addressed on cover "His Excellency /
Henry Laurens Esq[r] / President of Congress / Philadelphia"; dated
"Charlestown 23 August 1778"; franked "Free."; docketed by HL "John
Wells / 23[d.] Aug[t.] 1778 / Rec[d] 29 Septem̄".

FROM LACHLAN McINTOSH
                                          Charles Town, August 24, 1778
Dear Sir
        I have at last Settled all my affairs here, and Expect to Sail for
Rotterdam this afternoon__ [1]

I have left for the Maintenance and Education of my Children[2]
£17600 by the way of a deed of Trust to the following Gentlemen,
The Hon[able.] Henry Laurens, Col: John Laurens and John L: Gervais
Esq[rs.] &c: the Bonds for this Money I have left with M[r.] Gervais__

M[r.] Gervais having told me he had so much business of his own and
other People, Beged I Might get some other Active Person for my
Attorney, I therefore appointed Thomas Farr Esq[r.3] with you, and
Col: John Laurens my Attorneys, and delivered to M[r.] Farr the Power
of Attorney with twelve thousand Pounds in Cash, and Bonds to the
Amount of four thousand odd Hund[d.] pounds, more to be let at
Interest and keept, till he hears from you, Sir, and this Money I

---

[4] Two Jamaica privateers—the sloop *Gayton,* William Chambers, and the schooner
Revenge, Atkinson—had been cruizing off the coast near Charleston. On August 19, Chambers decoyed two pilots by pretending the *Gayton* was a prize bound for Georgetown. The
Gayton's boat also captured Darrell's sloop the *Little Robert.* The *Fair American* went out in
search of the privateers on August 23, but put back the same day "having sprung her
foremast." *S.C. Gazette,* Aug. 26, 1778.

[1] A Loyalist, former commandant of Ft. Prince George, and an old friend of HL's, Lachlan
McIntosh (Mackintosh) had had his plantations on the market since January 1777. *HL Papers,*
XI, 383n. The Charleston newspapers did not take note of his departure.

[2] McIntosh married Elizabeth Smith in 1765; their two sons Lachlan and Simon would have
been minors at this time. *HL Papers,* XIII, 537n.

[3] Thomas Farr, Jr., was a Charleston merchant and plantation owner. He has appeared
frequently in the *HL Papers. HL Papers,* XIII, 21.

intend to Answer any Money I intend or may take up on your Account, and indeed My All, having Sold my lands, and Negros, my house and lott in Chas town to rise this Money

No bills of Exchange or Gold or Silver to be had here I Carry with me some Indigo to Answer present need__

whatever part of the world I may chance to be, I will do Myself the Honour of writing you, And should the devine Providence open a Communication betwixt America and Great Brittain (which I pray God may soon be) I beg I may Have[4] the Happyness of hearing from you.

I Beg Sir youl please Apolygize and Excuse me to the young Colonel, your Son, for Appointing ↑him one of↓ My Attorneys as well as one of the Trustees for My Boys__

My Boys are left in town at Schooll and M^rs. Mackintosh Retires to the Country, this letter is left with M^r. Gervais to be forwarded to you Sir, as my two formers was, and I pray the almighty to Conduct, Prosper, and Preserve you, and yours, and Am with Most Sincere Respect.
                D^r. Sir your Most obliged and / Most obed^t Servant
                                        Lach: Mackintosh

SOURCE: RC, Kendall Collection; no address; dated below close "Chas. town / 24th. Augt. 1778"; docketed "Genl. M^c. Intosh / Charlestown 24th Augt. 1778".

TO WILLIAM SMITH
                                Philadelphia, August 25, 1778
Dear Sir
        The receipt of your favor of the 22nd recalled to my attention that of the 5th which through constant application to Public business had not received the respect due to it.
        I have this Morning dispatch'd M^r. Custer a Young Man out of my own house to view the Post Coach at the Head of Elk__ If he approves of it and has an opportunity he will write to you from

---

4 "H" written over other text.

thence, in order to prevent the disposal or removal of it until I shall have corresponded through your favor with M^r. Hudson on the great point, the price.

I am inform'd he purchas'd with the Carriage, Harness for four horses, and that there were too cushions, the whole for £250 Currency__ His demand therefore, after deducting one set of Harness and one Cushion, is enormous.

The Idea that every thing is cheap enough for the present will ruin me unless he takes care to lay a proper restraint. You would be astonish'd if I were to tell ↑you↓[1] the daily Amount of my expence. I nevertheless, my Dear Sir, thank you for the purchase of the Wine, and within this Cover remit a reimbursement in 134 dollars.

It is said a ship from Bourdeaux is in the Delaware. I am persuaded when it is known in the West Indies the River is open we shall have Vessels dropping in with all kinds of goods, hence I am induced to lay the restraint intimated above for a few days.[2]

Dunlaps' Packet will give you the current News of Philadelphia__ let me assure you not one word relative to the French and English Fleets deserves higher regard than as mere report__ the most authentic Account respecting them I received from a very sensible Man of the rank of Commissary who lately came in from the Enemy at New York. He says that on the 18th Inst. it was whisper'd among the British and Foreign Officers that Lord Howes' Squadron had receiv'd very great injuries; the Eagle, and 3 or 4 other ships of the line were driven on shore on the back of Long Island, but whether by the French fleet or by the storm, he could not positively tell but believe the latter, except the ragged and distrissed state of the Isis and that one frigate dismasted had got into New York all is conjecture. I expect this Evening or tomorrow Morning to receive regular Advices.

You will find within, Copy of General Sullivans' late letter, by no means let this be publish'd. I send it for your amusement and information. My hopes of success at Rhode Island without the

---

[1] Interlineations here and below by HL.

[2] A British vessel cruising at the mouth of the Delaware, the *Enterprise*, Squires, was reported to have turned away more than twenty vessels. *S.C. Gazette*, Sept. 16, 1778.

further aid of Count d'Estaing are exceedingly faint__ 'tis probable however, there will be much blood spilt. I not only dislike the vaunting of his Burgoynade Proclamation but another material circumstance which need not at present be intimated.

This instant I have a letter from the General of the 19th inclosed ↑inclosed in↓ one of the 21st from His Excellency the Commander in Chief. The 19th General Sullivan had advanced his Batteries within Musket shot of the Enemys' Redoubts, and intended to open upon them the next Morning__ they had kept an incessant fire on him two days without injuring a single Man__ Count d'Estaing not return'd.

General Washington writes

"By advices from an Officer of Rank and intelligence I am informed that 16 ships entred the Hook on the 17th. one having a flag, and that on that and the preceding day a heavy Cannonade was heard at Sea. ["]³ 'Tis nine o'clock I must repair to duty. Believe me to be

With very great Esteem and Regard / &c.

SOURCE: LB, HL Papers, ScHi; addressed "William Smith Esqr. / Baltimore / by Post"; dated "25th Aug^{t.}".

FROM CHEVALIER DU PLESSIS
White Plains, N.Y., August 25, 1778

Dear president

These three months, I longed Nightly to write you, but devoted as your whole attention to the important Concern of your Country, I certainly relucted to call off any part of it for an individual; (though nevertheless the individual is your good Child, (so is your expression) the Mad fellow and the good fr↑i↓end of your whorty son.)¹

---

³ George Washington wrote two letters to HL as president of Congress on August 21. The letter quoted here was the cover under which Washington conveyed letters from General Sullivan of August 19. Washington's "Officer of rank and intelligence" was "stationed with a party in Monmouth County." PCC, Item 152, Vol. 6, pp. 273ff, 277ff.

¹ HL enjoyed a fatherly relationship with some of the young French officers, especially those who had fought with or become friendly with JL. Du Plessis and JL fought valiantly and recklessly together at Germantown in October 1777 and later JL recommended him to HL. In April 1778 HL wrote a chiding but light hearted letter to Du Plessis when he lost his

but my thoughts are entirely Converted to Day, since I maintain that writting you I am serviciable to your Country, to yourself, and to Myself too; so is my proof, Monsieur le president is Continually Very busy for the Concerns of his station, that Constant application is prejudicial to his health, Consequently to his Country and to his fr↑i↓ends, therefore M^r le president must take some diversions but when he writes to Mr Duplessis, he laughs, he jokes, he jests upon his good Child, finally he sports, I Conclude that Mr Duplessis must write to M^r le president, and M^r le president Must answer to Mr Duplessis, and the all for the good of the Country.__ I Fulfill my task.

I congratulate you upon the last events, viz, the Arrival of the french fleet to help our good allies the united states, the Arrival of a french ambassador to the Congress, and the action at Monmouth, I can tell you that your good Child Commanded The Artillery at the right wing, which Artillery playing upon the British Column's flank, has been so successful ↑that↓ the british Column has been obliged to retreat his Excellency General Washington speaks Conspicuously of that Artillery in his letter to ↑Congress↓ in few days I hope to have a new matter to Congratulate you, (the Capture of the English Troops and Germans at Rhodis-land;) new reason to write you be certain that I shall profit of it.

you ask, from me in your Last letter, what I shall do, if the peace comes soon, go to France and be Vigneron, or go to Carolina and learn to make Rice & indigo &^c you are so Kind to add that you wish I Decide Myself for your Country, I cannot express my Gratitude for your Kindness but, Dear president, My heart tells me that I am the very good fr↑i↓end of America but I am born subject of the french King or King of france Consequent[ly], I ought ~~dead~~ ↑to die↓ his subject, my station for all my life is to learn and to try to Kill my brothers, so is my ~~Career~~ Career, am-I-not unworthy to ~~life~~ ↑live↓ in your happy Country with such sentiments? indeed I am sometimes shameful, but my passion for Glory, or Rather and more justly ↑told↓ for ~~illegible~~ ↑air↓ is stronger then my poor Reason.[2]

commission. In another letter in May HL suggested that when the war ended the French officer consider settling in South Carolina. *HL Papers,* XII, 306-307; XII, 205-206, 280-282.

[2] Du Plessis returned to France in 1779 where he was made major of chasseurs of the Vosges. In 1787 he was appointed commander of the regiment of Port-au-Prince in the West Indies. By this time he had become a political reactionary and fought against reform at St. Domingo where he was murdered by his own soldiers in 1791. Balch, *French in America,* II, 176-178.

I have given now matter enough to jest upon me, and ~~farrway~~ having fulfilled my intention, I end, and I have the honour to be with the affectionate Attachment, and unfeigned Respect, Dear president
Your very humble and / Most obedient servant
Le Ch^r de Mauduit Du / Plessis

present, I pray you, My respectful Compliments to Mr Gerard, I have not the honour to be acquainted with him, but by all what I have heard on the account of that Gentleman, I wish very much to pay him my respect.

SOURCE: RC, Society Collection, PHi; addressed on cover "To his Excellency / ~~illegible~~ / henry laurens / president of Congress / philadelphia"; dated "White plains Camp August 25, 1778"; docketed by HL "Monsr duPlaisis / 26 Aug. 1778 / Rec^d 31__".

FROM GEORGE WASHINGTON

White Plains, N.Y., August 25, 1778
Sir,
If it be practicable, and convenient for Congress to furnish me with some Specie (gold, as more portable, would be most convenient) valuable purposes I think would ~~illegible~~ result from it.__ I have always found a difficulty in procuring Intelligence by the mean of Paper money.__ and I perceive that it increases.__ The period is critical & interesting, and the early knowledge of an Enemys intention, and movements too obvious to need explanation

Having hinted to the Com$^{ee.}$ of Congress when at Valley forge this want I address this Letter to you <u>now</u> rather as a private than public one. because I do not wish to have the matter again mentioned if Congress hath been apprized of my wants & find it inconvenient to comply with them.__[1]

---

[1] Apparently the members of the Committee at Camp failed to convey General Washington's request for specie because Congress took no action and HL did not remember the topic being raised. HL to George Washington, Aug. 28, 1778.

I have the pleasure to inform you that Col[o.] Laurens was well on the 23[d.]__ I have had a Letter from him of that date.__[2] With great respect & regard I have the hon[r.] to be

Dr Sir / Yr. Most Obed[t.] H[ble] Serv[t]

G[o:] Washington

SOURCE: ADrafts, Washington Papers, DLC; addressed below close "To / The Hon. / Henry Laurens Esq[r.] / Presid[t] of Congress."; dated "White plains__ Aug[t.] 25[th.] 1778."; docketed "To. / The Hon. Hen: Laurens / 25[th.] Aug[t.] 1778.". Copy (19th century), HL Papers, ScHi.

TO WILLIAM MAXWELL[1]

Philadelphia, August 26, 1778

Sir

M[r.] Thomson Secretary of Congress, shewed me a Note Yesterday in which you enquired of him whether he had any dispatches for Head Quarters; this message I apprehend arose from your having receiv'd no Answer from me to your favor of the 8[th][2] which had accompanied a Packet from the British Commissioners__ I beg you will be assured Sir, my silence has not been the effect of disregard__[3] the practice of Congress is to receive public Letters from the President, and to make such order or no order as the house shall think proper. The President when there is an Order carries it into Execution, but he has the letter no longer in his custody. It is filed in the Secretarys' Office.

Upon Your letter there was an Order made, but directed to his Excellency General Washington which I transmitted immedi-

---

[2] In this letter JL condemned the French for "abandoning the American Troops" under Gen. John Sullivan "and reducing them to the necessity of making a desperate attack, or a precipitate Retreat." JL to George Washington, Aug. 23, 1778, Washington Papers, DLC.

[1] William Maxwell, colonel of the 2nd N.J. Regiment from Nov. 8, 1775, had been promoted to brigadier general in the Continental Army Oct. 23, 1776. His brigade included the 1st, 2nd, 3rd, and 4th N.J. Regiments. Heitman, *Continental Officers*.

[2] General Maxwell's August 8 letter conveyed a packet containing the Carlisle Commission's remonstrance of August 7. Maxwell noted that both ends of the packet's cover had been opened and that it had been delivered by an unusual route. PCC, Item 57, p. 327ff.

[3] From this point to the end of the following paragraph the text is cancelled in the letterbook.

ately,[4] and should have paid the same attention to General Maxwell.

Your Letter, Dear General together with the Commissioners Paper which is of a very extraordinary nature were referred to a special Committee who have not reported. Be assured of hearing from me immediately after I shall have received any Order from Congress.[5] In the mean time accept this as a private Correspondence intended to signify the respect and regard with which

I have the honor to be &c.

SOURCE: LB, HL Papers, ScHi; addressed "Brigadier General Maxwell / Elizabeth Town / New Jersey / by his return Messenger"; dated "26th Aug.".

FROM COUNT D'ESTAING

August 26, 1778

Sir.

My duty prescribed to me, to have the honor of rendering an account to Congress, immediately[1] on my arrival, of the orders which I had received from the King__ the letter which you did me the honor to write the 10th July had preceded the receipt of mine__ you addressed me the intelligence which was printed by order of your government and at the request of Mess[rs] Franklin and Adams__ [2] of the arrival of an english fleet of eleven Vessels of the line__ as well as the Manuscript List of the British Ships, which were then collected at New York__ this List announced five Ships of 64 Guns__ one of 70__ Six of 50__ two of 44. one Ship formerly of 64 guns__ besides a number of Frigates and other Vessels__ the importance and certainty of the intelligence of a fleet from Europe, were attested by the respectable names of those who gave it by the publicity of ~~illegible~~ Print__ a method doubtless adopted in order that this intelligence might come to me with the greater authenticity, and by Your Excellencys kindness in sending it me__ as well as by General Washingtons attention in annexing it to his first letter.__

---

[4] The order concerned the Carlisle Commission's remonstrance, not Maxwell's letter. *JCC*, XI, 776; HL to George Washington, Aug. 13, 1778, PCC, Item 13.

[5] HL informed General Maxwell on September 5 that he had "received no commands from Congress respecting your late Letter."

[1] "immediately" written over "it".

[2] "Adams" written over other text.

a piece of intelligence clothed with such forms and the certainty__ ³ independently of the Squadron, ~~being~~ announced__ of the enemys having collected their naval force already in America merited therefore the most serious attention on my part.

Previous to receiving this double notification__ I had been informed at the Capes of Delaware, where I drove the Mermaid Frigate ashore__ that the bravery of your troops, the talents of your General__ the declaration of the treaty concluded with his Majesty, and probably the intelligence of our destination__ had obliged the enemy to evacuate Philadelphia to collect their force after the defeat of Monmouth at New York__ I did not delay going in quest of them ~~any longer than~~ 'till the want of Water, so necessary after a long voyage, and refreshments then so ~~necessary~~ ↑essential↓ to the health of our crews__ should be supplied__ having anchored at night after being 87 days at Sea__ I weighed the next morning__ the strongest of our frigates was dispatched at the request of Mͬ Deane to protect this ancient Deputy, and the Minister plenipotentiary of the King, from Cruisers which were said to be in the River__ and to convoy two such interesting personages to Congress__

I set sail at the same time that the Chimere did__ and indulged myself in the hope which the Pilot taken at Delaware had given me__ he promised that he would carry the Squadron within Sandy hook__ it is very convenient watering there__ this was placing me almost before New York__ it was giving me an assurance that I should soon meet the united Forces of Admiral Howe__ the time spent in sounding, the doubts, the Fears and finally the total Refusal of this pilot by keeping me out in the road__ reduced me to a dilemma, which can be expressed only by those who have felt it__ No one came to me from the Shore__ this part of New Jersey had not the reputation of being the best affected to the good Cause__ The Surf presented us only an inaccessible Shore__ and we were ignorant how far the Posts of the English, (who⁴ were in sight) extended__ they were supported by a whole fleet drawn up within the hook__ My humanity forbid me to order what appeared impossible__ circumstances required that I should reconnoitre the coast

---

³ "ty" written over other text.
⁴ "w" written over other text.

myself, and determined me to go almost alone in a boat__ by these means we discovered the communication of the River of Shrewsbury, the extreme difficulties of which cost me an officer, several Sailors, a quantity of rowing boats, and put L[t] Col Laurens in the most imminent danger of ↓being↑ drowned[5] ~~himself to~~ in bringing me General Washingtons Dispatches, and put him in a situation to prove that his patriotism and his Courage made him brave the most imposing dangers of the Sea, with the same firmness as the Fire of the English.[6] the small quantity of Water and refreshments which came to us through the difficulties and shipwrecks of Shrewsbury bar, were insufficient for the Consumption, or even the simple relief of the Squadron__ it was in this condition that the American boat charged with Your Excellencys Dispatches found me__ and delivered the printed advices of the expected Squadron, and detail of that which was in presence__ it appeared impossible to give a categorical answer in the face of our various wants__ my orders & prudence indicated the necessity of touching for refreshment__ Zeal without Success would have been counted imprudence, by those who weigh only the motives of actions__ As long as we retained any hope of penetrating to the Enemys fleet, the General Officers and Captains of the Kings Squadron were regardless of the dangers of an anchoring Ground where our Cables were wearing__ where the English never make any Stay__ where in case of a Storm, Ships are inevitably cast on shore__ and where one lately changed the isthmus of the hook into an island__ both Officers and Crews were kept in spirits, notwithstanding their wants, and the fatigues of Service__ by the desire of delivering America from the English Colours, which we saw waving on the other side a simple barriere of Sand, upon so great a crowd of Masts__[7] the collection of Pilots procured by the care of Cols Laurens and Hamilton destroyed all illusion__ these experienced persons unanimously declared that it was impossible to carry us in__ I offered in vain a Reward of 50,000

---

[5] "drowning" altered to "drowned".

[6] JL reached the French fleet July 16 just south of Sandy Hook at the Shrewsberry River estuary. D'Estaing lost one officer and four sailors when several rowboats were upset in the strong current while attempting to obtain food and fresh water. JL narrowly escaped drowning when crossing the same treacherous waters when he was being conveyed to d'Estaing's flagship. Massey, "A Hero's Life," pp. 267-268.

[7] "M" written over "sh".

Crowns of my own money to any one who would promise ~~to~~
success__ all refused__ and the particular Soundings which I ~~had~~
↑caused to be↓ taken myself too well demonstrated that they were
right__ All that zeal and the most attentive activity can do, was
~~employed by the~~ put in practice by the orders of Lt Col Laurens, to
conquer the impossibilities of the Shrewsbury ↑River↓ passage__ its
difficulty depending upon the least wind from the Sea, left us
without communication with the land for whole days__ the small
detachment which we had there, was so much the more hazarded__
we were finishing the four months biscuit which we brought from
Europe__ Our Water was consuming__ and we had blocked the
English Squadron at New York for eleven days__ when the opinion
of General Washington authorised by the Congress to treat with me
on Military Expeditions was found conformable to my orders and
sentiments__ he pressed me to sail for Newport__ It was feared that
the Garrison would be withdrawn__ but at that very moment
General Preston[8] was gone to reinforce it__

   the strong appearances of a storm would have constrained
us to have quitted that anchoring ground__ even if the expedition
of Newport had not engaged us to it__ We took seven days to make
the voyage and during the two first, we felt all the anxiety that was
natural in our circumstances, in open Sea with so little water in the
hold__ the moment of our arrival off point Judith was that in which
the arrival of the pilots ought to have facilitated our entrance into[9]
Newport. the Signal was given to the Squadron which was waiting
for them in the order of forcing the passage__ when Genl. Sullivans
first Letter informed me that he was not ready to act, and desired
that the attack should be suspended__[10]

I did not hesitate to do it__ altho one of the principal ~~operations~~
advantages of maritime operations is to astonish by their rapidity__
and delay multiplied obstacles, and deprived us of the hope of

---

[8] Richard Prescott.
[9] "at" altered to "into".
[10] General Sullivan did not receive notification of the French fleet sailing for Rhode Island
until July 24. On July 25 he addressed a letter to d'Estaing apologizing "that our Situation
renders it uncertain whether we can co-operate the Moment of Your Arrival." When d'Estaing
did arrive this was the first letter he received from Sullivan. Massey, "A Hero's Life," pp. 269-
273; *Sullivan Papers* (Hammond), III, 640-644.

securing the Vessels of War and Merchantmen__ which had the time to take precautions for burning when they were useless for defence__

My frequent correspondence with General Sullivan, while it proves all my condescension__ and the extreme desire that I had of conforming to his views__ offers a sincere State of the embarrassments of the Kings Squadron as well on account of Water as provisions__ My hopes deceived with respect to these two articles growing more and more important__ a failure of means which were thought possible thro'[11] the excessive zeal of the Americans__ some false Steps taken at the request of people of the Country, who imagined the movements of large Ships, as easy as the evolutions of the smallest barks__ did not hinder, after the eastern passage was cleared and the greatest part of the british frigates burnt, the destruction of the rest, as soon as we had forced on the 8th of ~~April~~ ↑Aug.↓ the middle passage under the fire of different batteries of the Enemy. the next day but one was the day agreed upon for the combined descent__ the Scorbutic persons which I had on shore, the increasing number on board__ induced me to me to ask Genl· Sullivan for a Wing of his Army, in order to give some consistence to our disembarkation__ my thousand land troops were reduced to a very few__ the Marines and Sailors that I was forced to add to them__ were going to leave our vessels disarmed__ I was in hopes of assembling for the first time, these different[12] and very small Corps__ the Island of Conanicut was the place chosen for giving them a form which they were absolutely destitute of__ they were landing when Genl· Sullivan sent me word, that he had not waited for the day appointed__ that the English astonished to see me force the entrance of their port had abandoned the North part of Rhode Island__ and that he had made his descent there__ I was assured that he had not then more than two thousand men__ and that his situation required prompt succour__ a little surprised I did not hesitate to go and join him myself__ knowing that there are moments which must be eagerly seized in war__ I was cautious of

---

[11] "thro'" written over other text.
[12] "different" written over other text.

blaming an overthrow of Plans__ which however astonished me__
and which in fact merits in my opinion nothing but praise__ Altho'
accumulated Circumstances may have been able to render the
consequences very melancholy__ the french Soldiers and Sailors
who were about landing on Conanicut & those who had been
debarked an hour__ received orders to follow me on Rhode
Island__ the Kings Ships were going to be left disarmed, the
destruction of the Shipping at Newport rendered this Step rather
less imprudent, when the Fog by dissipating, discovered to us Lord
Howes fleet approaching the entrance of the port and turning to
windward in the great Road__ we counted fourteen Ships with two
tiers of Guns, many frigates, Bomb Ketches, Fire-Ships, and about
thirty Six Sail__ however unexpected, miraculous and surprising
General Sullivan found the appearance of this fleet as he has since
done me the honor of informing me in his letter of the 10th August,[13]
its existence was not less certain__ nothing had announced it to me;
not the least intelligence of the dispositions and ~~illegible~~↑departure↓
of the English had reached me__ the Surprise was complete__ and
the day perfectly well calculated upon our projects__ the enemys
Spies had served them superiorly well__ for they arrived the morning after my entrance into the port__ two of our Ships were out__
two others at the north end of the west Channel__ our only three
frigates at a distance and in the eastern Channel the eight Ships with
which I had forced the middle Channel between Rhode island thick
set with english batteries__ and the island of Conanicut which I
could not occupy without disarming my Ships__ and which by its
extent ~~afford~~ afforded means of landing the troops which the
English brought and establishing batteries. Such was our maritime
disposition__ We should shortly have been between these fires
drawn so near together, our Ships would have been battered from[14]
the land by a deliberate fire__ and we should in a little time have had
to combat a Squadron so well protected, and provided with Ketches,
Fire Ships and all the means which ensure the greatest superiority
over Ships which are[15] altogether destitute of them__ and which are

---

[13] Letter not found.
[14] "from" written over other text.
[15] "were" altered to "are".

forced to receive at anchor and between two lands such an unequal Combat__

The Separation of the Squadron, and the position in which our excessive condescension had put us__ did not extort the least complaint against Gen¹ Sullivan, the fruitless hopes he had always given us on the subject of Water and provision__ persuaded us that he had flattered himself with all that he promised__

The Errors relative to the ~~illegible~~ disposition made at his request__ and the soundings of the communication between the East and West Channel, were attributed by us to the Skippers whose report he had credited__ the anticipation of his projects ~~illegible~~ one while¹⁶ precipitated, at another retarded, appeared to us the effect only of circumstances__ and we doubted not, but as he was as little instructed relative to the ~~illegible~~ movements of the enemy as we were ourselves__

if my General Officers and Captains gave me to understand that the painful and dubious Part of acting on the defensive, had been occasioned by my too great complaisance__ they did not prepare themselves with the less ardour__ when a North Wind so rare at this Season restored us on the morning of the 10ᵗʰ Augᵗ· that activity which we had lost only for twelve hours__

The Uncertainty whether this wind would be sufficient to carry us out or might not leave us under the English Batteries__ whether their Squadron reinforced by the arrival of the Cornwal of 74 Guns__ one of Byrons Squadron; might not have been still more strengthened by the arrival of a greater number__ whether the number of Ships that we were going thro the fire of the batteries to meet__ was not far superior to ours__ and whether the Masts of our Ships which had suffered in going in by the enemys Cannon, were capable of resisting the present Sallys and would not by their fall deliver up several dismantled Vessels__ nothing could balance the hope of joining the enemys Squadron__ our cables were cut in order to expedite the matter__ We underwent and braved the fire of all the batteries,__ which¹⁷ had been augmented and were better served__ each Ship made its way ~~defi~~ filing one after another__ their

---

¹⁶ "one while" written in left margin.
¹⁷ "which" written over "they".

astonishment was proved by the haste with which they ~~fled~~ cut their cables and fled__ whatever could be ~~done~~ ↑attempted__↓ to join them was put in practice for two days, we did not lose them at night, altho our light Vessels all remained in the eastern Channel of Rhode Island__ and the next day after five OClock in the afternoon__ the English Rear Guard was going to be attacked__ the enemys line formed was constrained to prepare for Combat__ we had [*illegible*] every assurance of Victory__ that day was ~~p~~ about to be that of America__ every thing would have become easy__ the Enterprise acquired a facility which it had lost__ when a Storm destroyed [*illegible*] hopes which were so well founded__

The complete[18] ~~The~~ dismastment of the Languedoc, which happened the next morning, the failure of her Rudder, this Superb Ship left alone and become an immoveable Mass liable to be attacked in whatever point the enemy should choose, incapable of presenting her broadside, & having[19] nothing more to defend her than Six Stern ~~Chasers~~, or four bow Chasers__ were circumstances which w^d have rendered her after the destruction of the Crew__ and my death__ the prey of an English Ship which engaged her with more advantage than perseverance__ The Marseillois of 74 Guns, less unfortunate, because having her main-mast and Rudder safe, ~~illegible~~ she still had it in her power to luff and bear away__ and consequently to use her broadside,__ with which she repulsed a more serious attack of one of the british Admirals__ The Separation of the Cesar of 74 Guns who[20] engaged in a hot and bloody Combat, the fruits of which she was prevented from reaping by the approach of several of the enemys Ships__ are maritime Events which Courage teaches to support and repair__ and which no Combinations of Judgement, can foresee or prevent__ those which employed my mind as soon as we were a little reunited, made me consider the Delaware as the most leeward Road__ and consequently the least difficult to gain__ with Jury Rigging, and a Yard hung with Carriages which served to steer us__ the firmness, the wisdom of the depositaries of the authority of the United States, their Justice, the interest which our good-will and the contradictions that we had just experienced, would have inspired them with, promised ~~in the neig~~ near

---

[18] "The complete" written in left margin.
[19] "had" altered to "having".
[20] "which" altered to "who".

the Congress and Your Excellency every kind of Consolation__
Boston by the wood which its vicinity furnishes, seemed on the other
hand, the place where our losses could be most expeditiously
repaired__ it was that where the general voice of the Squadron
counseled me to go__ but Sir I did not think myself at liberty to
choose; Your troops had landed on Rhode island, it might be
essential to their safety to inform them of our condition, and of the
indispensible necessity to refit, which was a consequence of it__ it
was in vain represented to me that their descent contradictory to
our convention, must have been followed after our Departure by a
proper Retreat, if our concurrence was necessary__ and that if it was
not or Gen¹· Sullivan could do without it, it was dismasted and
rudderless fruitlessly multiplying the difficulties of going to Boston,
as well as the extreme want of water and biscuit__ I had made a
verbal promise as I was setting Sail, to an Aide de Camp of the Mq̄uis
de la fayette that I would return__ my word was sacred__ I considered nothing but the duty which I had enjoined myself__ it was
~~fulfilled__~~ accomplished__ but your troops having notice given
them, if they thought it necessary to retreat__ or being assisted by
the disquiet which the appearance of the Squadron would occasion
the enemy__ it became necessary for me to confine all my attention
to the preservation of the Squadron, and restoring it to a condition
to act__

I was no longer at liberty to depend on the deceitful hopes
of watering and getting provisions__ I could not consider the masts
of Frigates which were mentioned to me__ as a resource for 80 and
74 gun Ships__ the pretention of finishing in two days a Siege, the
batteries of which without any real effect were still so distant from
the points which they battered__ did not appear to me well founded

Advices ~~from~~ of a Squadron from Europe given in a public Channel,
sanctioned by the names of Messʳˢ Franklin and Adams,[21] confirmed by different ways, by the arrival of one of the Vessels
belonging to it, at New York__ by the deposition of two french Ships
which[22] discovered an English three decker__ the profound ignorance of what became of Lord howes fleet__ which had an opportunity of reassembling while I was at Sea, and which the frigates

---

[21] The Franklin-Adams circular letter, dated Paris, May 18, 1778, warned that a British
squadron of eleven vessels was en route to America. See HL to Richard Caswell, July 9, 1778.
[22] "which" written over other text.

found stationed at Block Island, assert had reassumed their first design__ that of attacking us as soon as we should enter the port__ this movement which would have ensured our inactivity and Separation__ had nearly been too advantageous to him, for him to lose sight of it__ The picture which I drew of it in the beginning of my Letter Sir was not exaggerated__ our position with one Ship less, and two capital Ships dismasted would have been still more critical__ a north wind would not have extricated us as on the first occasion__ no risque would have hindered a second attempt__ it would certainly have been ~~happy~~ ↑successfull↓ for Admiral howe__ to consent to facilitate it for him, would have been as imprudent as culpable on my part__ The Soldiers counted in our armament are no longer sufficient__ the Quarter Deck Guns of the Protector, on board of which Ship I sh^d hoist my flag, in case of an engagement before the repair of the Languedoc__ it was a considerable Squadron and not a feeble Succour of Land Troops that the King thought useful to America__

the intention of His Majesty is not that I should do unnatural things, and that his Ships should be abandoned to add a few men to your numerous Armies, his prudence has foreseen that particular expeditions might exist, in which our naval force being in perfect Security and inactive for a little time__ it might be useful to land what was not wanted on board__ it was on this account that the Squadron had when about to sail, one thousand Soldiers substituted to an equal number of Sailors which ~~we~~ are ~~without~~ wanting to us__ tis in this principle that supposing the English fleet would not quit New York without first receiving a reinforcement,__ I was ready to debark even some companies of Sailors to aid the 12000 men under General Sullivan__ what I might do[23] on the first supposition, will appear certainly impossible to the equity of Congress__ whenever the Vessels are called upon to fight__ they are out of condition if deficient[24] in the number of men__ their quarter decks are unfurnished__ and the least debarkation would on account of our losses and Sickness ~~rendered~~ have left[25] the upper tier ~~illegible~~ ↑destitute↓ of hands to serve it__

---

[23] "d" written over "t".
[24] "d" written over "h".
[25] "have left" written in left margin.

It is with the noble confidence that I owe to the allies of the King, that I take pleasure in rendering them the account which I owe only to His Majesty__ but it would be wounding the dignity of his Crown, if I answered assertions and forms of which I do not complain__ Passion dictated them, this is perhaps a proof that Reason did not__ We presume that they were inspired by the Masters of small barks, who scarcely knowing the bottom over which they sail__ in order to avoid being blocked up, prefer the narrow Channels of Newport to the entrance of the banks of Boston__ and who are ignorant of maritime positions, and what determines the strength or weakness of Squadrons__ such men blinded by local and personal interest, which renders every thing excusable in their eyes__ have found means to surprise for an instant the opinion of some General Land Officers, whom we shall profess to esteem <u>Always</u>, altho we are fully persuaded that they have neither the knowledge nor experience necessary to decide despotically of the possibilities of an element which is not theirs__ we think that they will one day regret having accused their most faithful allies, by a kind of juridical protest, of the unhappy consequences of a Storm which snatched us from the arms of Victory, and the effects of two dismastments[26]

these two effects of hazard forced us from a farther share in the attack of Newport__ we should have supported otherwise as long as possible, altho it was not commenced at the instant of our arrival, and was afterwards a little inconsiderately__

To add to the raising of a Siege the Sacrifice of a Squadron, which at least would have become totally useless, by the manner in which it[27] would have been blocked, between the Channels, of which the two islands, remain the enemys__ would have been an increase of Misfortune__ it appeared to me a duty of the first order, to go almost beyond the bounds of possibility in coming dismasted and rudderless, to inform our allies ourselves of our situation__ to risk every thing was not abandoning them__ it was[28] giving them the power of deciding ~~the~~ for a retreat or a continuance of the attack__

---

[26] Several lines left blank as though JL was leaving space for something he was having trouble translating.

[27] "it" written over "she".

[28] "is" altered to "was".

it was not being responsible for the part which they should ask to navigate thus for this only end appears according to the Protest, and even to prejudiced eyes ~~are~~ a thing without example__ that of passing thro' the fire of the Batteries in a port, to go and attack a Squadron which came to seek us; is likewise a military action not much repeated__ The Kings Squadron wants no models, needs no sollicitation to undertake what honor and duty inspire__ Moderation which is the bond of Nations whom mutual inclination and interest unite__ and will ever unite__ hinders us from answering Complaints otherwise than by ~~illegible~~ participating the just chagrin which causes them__ and by making every effort to repair by an unshaken Constancy the injuries of fortune__

The Expedition[29] Sir with which we shall ~~illegible~~ take in our water__ that which we shall use in refitting__ and all the means which we shall employ to replace our biscuit, which is totally consume__ will depend upon the succours which we shall obtain__ I am going to sollicit them with that earnestness, which arises from a desire of employing the totality of our forces for the defence and utility of all the Americans, <u>without any exception whatever</u>.

I entreat you to be so good as to lay before Congress the sincere expression of all these Sentiments__[30] and the homage of the account which I have the honor of rendering them__ I flattered myself that I should have answered by success to the printed advices of the expected Squadron__ I have unfortunately been able to do it only by Attempts, they prove at least our Zeal and perhaps our Boldness.

I have the honor to be / Sir / Your Excellencys / most obed^t & most hble Serv

Signed / Estaing

SOURCE: Translation, Washington Papers, DLC; no address; dated "26th August 1778"; docketed "Copy of Admiral / Estaings Letter to / Congress__ 26th Augt 1778."; noted below close "Copy__ / Estaing.". This translation is in the hand of John Laurens. RC (French), PCC (Item 164), DNA. Copies (French), PCC (Items 111, 114), DNA.

---

[29] "Ex" written over "Pr".
[30] For Congress's response to d'Estaing, see HL to D'Estaing, Sept. 10, 1778.

FROM THE MARQUIS DE LAFAYETTE

Rhode Island, August 26, 1778

My dear Sir

I have been a very long time without hearing from or writing to you, the hope of telling som agreable news, the uncertainty of our situation, have alwaïs stopp'd my penn__ and if I did not write as soon ~~as soon~~ as the french fleet came back from the poursuit of the ennemy, and went to boston, it is because I did not like to afflict my friend's heart by the horrid picture of what I have seen upon this island__ but truth urges me to speack, I fear you would be prevented by false relations, and I must therefore trouble you with this letter. I will not go back to give the account of what has been done on our part before the admiral went after the british fleet__ but I may assure you upon my honor, that he was not at all influenc'd ~~up~~ by any behaviour of any body, tho some try to insinuate it, and that he did consider the whole as you and me would have done.

it is useless to say that <u>we americans</u> are a little indebted to france__ it is useless to Repute upon the advantages the fleet has already afforded to these coasts upon a military as well as a civil point of wiew__ six frigattes one of them was a check for a whole state have been burnt and destroy'd__ the Coasts clear'd__ the harbours oppened__ the british army and navy kept together philadelphia evacuated upon the intelligence of that fleet &c. &c. I may add that the fleet was ask'd for America by the Count destaing himself, which circumstance I heard by a third person, and I give you under the law of secrecy.

when after that storm which took a vay from his hands all the advantages of a gain'd victory, which put him in the most *illegible* schatered Condition, when he came back to Rhode island (because he had promis'd to come back) I was sent on board by gāl Sullivan__ I found him more distress'd than any man I ever saw, by the idea that he would be some weeks out of the possibility of serving america__ I am a witness that he did every thing to convince himself and convince others that they could stay__ but the orders of the king, the Representations of all his Captains, the opinion of all the fleet even of <u>some American pilots</u> made t it necessary for him to go to boston. indeed, my dear Sir, in such circumstances as he was, which are too long to be explain'd how could he help it?

Now, my dear friend, I am going to hurt your tender feelings by a picture of what I have seen___ forgive me for it___ it is A lover of America who speacks to you with indignation against a parcel of his ~~town~~ adopted countrymen. I hope such a thing would never be the case with the french nation I have the honor to belong to___ but then I would speack plain to french men, as I do now to an american.

Could you believe that forgetting any national obligation, forgetting what they were owing to that same fleet, what they were yet to expect from them; the people on this island treated them as a person one would not treat his ennemies. discoures which I have seen myself ~~obl~~ almost oblig'd to Revenge were publickly heard___ many leaders themselves finding they were disappointed abandonn'd theyr minds to illiberality and ungratefulness___ but it is useless to aflict your vision by so ugly a picture; I schall however add that the french hospital (so told one gentlemen to be depended upon) has been treated in the most inhuman way since the fleet has lost some Mâsts and has been oblig'd to go to boston.[1]

that affair, I consider, my dear Sir, I do consider upon a much more extensive point of wiew___ our external and internal ennemies will take a great advantage of that piece of ungenerosity some have been guilty of upon this island___ it would be a great pity that some Rascally discontents schould alter the union and confidence Ready to be establish'd between the two nations___ I see one only way of Repairing those evils which is this.

that Congress to settle the minds of the people, make a fine Resolve for approving of what has pass'd and presenting theyr thanks to the admiral, that Orders be immediately given to furnish them with provisions, biskett, and all the things they stand in a schoking want off___ that as soon as they are Repair'd which will be in three weeks new plans be entered into immediately for begining again the expedition of newport, and afterwards taking or new york

---

[1] In his August 25 letter to General Washington, Lafayette included in his litany of complaints against the American treatment of the French at Rhode Island—"I am more upon a warlike footing in the american lines, than when I come near the british lines at Newport. Nay, many vorthy characters, gentlemen to be entirely depended upon, assure me that the french hospital was abandonn'd as soon as the Fleet went off, and that they could not find any body who would give them what they wanted. However they have been now sent to Boston, and by a french man who met them I am inclin'd to think they will be very unhappy all the Rout." *Lafayette Papers* (Idzerda), II, 152.

or hallifax, or S^t augustine &c.__ I Confess this last ~~expedition~~ operation would please me extrenelly as we are going upon the winter season, and it would be a great service to the southern states I would beg leave to advise that a courier be sent immediately from Congress to boston__ for you know the bostonians. I think I schall be oblig'd to go there myself by the common desire of all the general ofices__ however disagreable it is to me, to be absent two days and an half from the army, my zeal is such that I will chearfully go there and execute my commission to know when the Count may join us, and engage him to come as soon as possible The latter I am sure he will do for I never saw a man so well dispos'd to serve us with all his power. the american boys will stay upon this island and wait for events, so it has been decided by a Majority of votes.

farewell, my dear Sir, forgive the hurry of my letter__ I am urg'd to write it by the love of my Country, of America, and the desire I have to see them well connected together__ the sincerity of my sentiments, and the frankness of my heart do'nt want Apology__ you may show some parts of my scribbling to any member of Congress you will think prudent and proper. farewell, my good friend, with the highest regard I am

Your affectionate

the Mis de lafayette

SOURCE: RC, HL Papers, ScHi; no address; dated "Rhode island the 26 august 1778"; docketed by HL "Marq. delafayette 25 Aug 1778 / Rec^d- 3^d. Septem__".

TO JOHN HOUSTOUN

Philadelphia, August 27, 1778

Dear Sir

I should not have remained so long in arrear for Your Excellency's obliging letter of the 9th of June, had I not flattered myself with hopes that long before this day the circumstances of Georgia would have been introduced as a subject demanding the consideration of Congress__ but it has happened otherwise; to account for the probable reasons would be extremely unpleasant, and perhaps at this time equally improper; nevertheless 'tis my duty

Sir, as a fellow Citizen to suggest to you in that, as well as in the character of supreme Magistrate of a State, that in my humble opinion we cannot fairly ascribe the dormancy of this, and of very many other momentous concerns, to want of leisure.

I see with grief the return of our Troops from East Florida without that success which Your Excellency had hoped for. This unhappy circumstance will add to the distresses of Georgia, and increase her cries for relief.

While S[t.] Augustine remains in possession of the Enemy Georgia will be unhappy, and her existence as a free and Independent State rendered very doubtful. South Carolina too will be continually galled by Rovers and Cruizers from that pestiferous Nest__ another expedition must therefore be undertaken at a season of the Year which will not outvie the Bullets and Bayonets of the Enemy, in the destruction of our Men.

I have before me a Plan for reducing East Florida which I will have the honor of communicating to Your Excellency very soon;[1] in the mean time I am constrained to say, that unless the several States will keep their representation in Congress filled by Men of competent abilities unshaken integrity, and unremitting diligence, a Plan which I very much fear is laid for the subduction of our Confederal Independence will, by the operations of masked Enemies, be completely executed; so far I mean as relates to all the Sea Coast, and possibly to the present generation. Were I to unfold to you Sir, scenes of venality, pecculation, and fraud which I have discovered, the disclosure would astonish you, nor would you Sir, be less astonished, were I by a detail which the occasion would require, prove to you, that he must be a pitiful Rogue indeed, who, when detected or suspected, meets not with powerful advocates among those, who in the present corrupt time, ought to exert all their powers in defence and support of their friend__ plundered, much injured, and I was almost going to say, sinking States__ dont apprehend Sir that I colour too highly, or that any part of these intimations are the effect of rash judgment or despondency; I am

---

[1] The Marquis de Brétigney's scheme for the capture of St. Augustine came under cover of his August 18 letter to HL, in which the marquis sought the chance "to serve against a place in which I have been so cruelly treated." The memorial is in the PCC, Item 78, Vol. 3, p. 47ff. A translation of the cover letter and the memorial are in the HL Papers, ScHi.

warranted to say they are not; my opinion, my sentiments are supported every day by the declaration of Individuals; the difficulty lies in bringing Men collectively to attack with vigour a proper object. I have said so much to you Sir as Governor of a State, not intended for Public conversation, which sound policy forbids; and at the same time commands deep thinking from every Man appointed a Guardian of the fortunes and honor of these Orphan States.

Colonel McClean who will do me the honor to bear this Address to Your Excellency, is well acquainted with the present state of our Arms.__ Copies of two letters from General Sullivan which will accompany this, will shew that, of his particular and important department as it stood eight days ago__ every hour I expect further intelligence. Had he been successful, and as expeditiously so, as his sanguine hopes had marked out, I should have received the important tidings the day before Yesterday.

Not a word that has been said or printed respecting Count d'Estaing's and Lord Howe's Fleets merits confidence. An Engagement, and a smart one too, there has undoubtedly been, but who was victorious, and what losses each Party sustained are unknown in this City__ this fact only, that the British Fleet had greatly suffered, and had carried in no Prizes four days ago, is ascertained; and from the following Paragraph in General Washington's Letter of the 21st, there is ground to hope, that many of Lord Howe's original shew of Ships at Rhode Island have been detained by his Rival, or lost in the late storm.

By advices from an Officer of rank and intelligence who is stationed in view of the Sea, I am informed that sixteen Ships entered the Hook on the 17th, one having a Flag, and that on that and the preceding day a heavy Cannonade was heard at Sea. This days Packet may afford Your Excellency more intelligence.

I will trouble you Sir no further at present, but to repeat that I am, with very great regard and esteem[2]

---

[2] The British found this letter after the fall of Savannah (Dec. 29, 1778). A copy, now in the Public Record Office, was made in Georgia and certified authentic by Lieutenant Colonel Prevost, April 14, 1779. A copy was conveyed to New York where it appeared in *Rivington's Gazette,* May 5, 1779. Meriwether Smith, one of HL's opponents in Congress, introduced a motion to ask HL to read the letter and verify its authenticity. HL refused, was upheld by a

Sir / Your Excellency's / Most obedient & most / humble
servant[3]

Henry Laurens.

SOURCE: CopyS, HL Papers, ScHi; addressed below close by HL "His
Excellency / John Houston Esquire / Governor & Commander in Chief
/ of Georgia__"; dated "Philad[a.] 27th August 1778"; noted "(Copy)" and by
HL "Private". LB, HL Papers, ScHi. Copy, CO 5/182, PRO. Copy (19th
century), HL Papers, ScHi.

TO JOHN SULLIVAN

Philadelphia, August 28, 1778

Sir

The Letter of the present date which will accompany this,
was written this Morning & waiting for the Messenger when I
attended Congress, while I was there, a Letter from General Washington of the 25[th.][1] was brought & ushered a Copy of yours to His
Excellency of the 25[th.]__ Geñ. Green's sensible & spirited Remonstrance to Count d'Estaing; the Count's Letter of the 21st to you__
the Protest of Officers at Camp before New Port of the same date,
and your Questions to[2] the General Officers & Commandts: of
Brigades,[3] these Papers having ↑been↓ read & considered, the
House adopted two Resolutions, 1 for requesting Baron Stüben to
repair to Your Head Quarters in order to contribute his advice &
assistance, & ↑2.↓ for preventing the publication of the Protest.[4]

---

majority, and brought a motion which condemned Smith's action as "irregular, unprec-
edented, and full of dangerous consequences" as well as "derogatory to the honor and dignity
of Congress." *JCC,* XIV, 592. A more moderate substitute motion was offered by Thomas
Burke and accepted. The animosity between HL and Smith's faction, which included
Thomas Penn, William Henry Drayton, and Silas Deane, spilled over in the press. A series of
accusatory and defensive letters were printed by the participants in the *Pa. Packet,* May 20, 25,
27, 29, June 1, 1778. JCC, XIV, 588-589, 590-595, 610-613.
   [3] Close by HL.
   [1] The correct date was August 23. "25[th.]" was altered to read "23[d.]" in the president's
letterbook. PCC, Item 13.
   [2] "to" interlined.
   [3] The enclosures are in PCC, Item 152, Vol. 6, p. 289ff.
   [4] Congress, in an attempt to avoid public criticism that might undermine the alliance with
the French, ordered "That the contents of the said letter and papers" forwarded with

I flatter my self with hopes that before the Act in which these Resolves are included & which will be here inclosed shall have reached you, a Glorious conquest or a safe & honorable retreat will have been effected.

I have the honor to be / With great Regard & Esteem / Sir / Your obed.ᵗ & huṁ servt

Henry Laurens.
President of / Congress__

SOURCE: ALS, Peter Force Papers, DLC; addressed below close "The Honorable / Major General Sullivan / Rhode Island."; dated "Philadelphia / 4 oClo.⁀ P.M. 28ᵗʰ August 1778."; docketed "Henry Laurens Esqʳ / Augᵗ 28ᵗʰ⁻ 1778". LB, PCC (Item 13), DNA.

TO GEORGE WASHINGTON

Philadelphia, August 28, 1778

Dear Sir

I am indebted for Your Excellency's favors of the 20ᵗʰ and 25ᵗʰ, the former receiv'd three days since, and the latter while I was in Congress this Morning; this takes my immediate attention__ I feel convinc'd that had Your Excellency named a sum in Gold and apply'd for it to Congress, an order for the Amount would have pass'd without hesitation__ but from circumstances which I have more than a few times observed to attend Motions made from private Letters by Gentlemen of Merit and influence transcending far, any that I presume to claim I feared on your Account Sir, to hazard a question in the present case__ there is a jealousy in the Minds of Men as unaccountable and unreasonable, as it is unnecessary to add a word more upon the subject; to contribute, however, towards forwarding Your Excellency's labours for public good, and from a melancholly conviction of the policy and necessity for constantly prosecuting the measures for which Gold in the present

---

Washington's August 25 letter "be kept secret." Washington was also ordered to "take every measure in his power that the protest of the officers of General Sullivan's army against the departure of Count D'Estaing be not made public." *JCC*, XI, 848-849.

critical moment is wanted, I have pack'd up a few pieces, the particulars noted below, which had been lying by me altogether useless and which do not comprehend my whole stock; these may possibly be of immediate service and ↑I may↓ [1] be reimburs'd when Congress shall order a supply, which I am persuaded will be in the instant of Your Excellency's demand; be this as it may I intreat Your Excellency will permit me to insist upon the receipt and application of this mite. I do not presume to offer it to General Washington but as a loan to our Country who will repay me amply even by permitting my endeavours to serve her.

I do not remember that ever an application was made by the Camp Committee of Congress. I am more inclined to believe those Gentlemen relied on each other and that neither of them attempted the business, but I may be mistaken. I shall without waiting for a dispatch from Your Excellency to Congress which I ~~will~~ ↑would↓ wish to receive seperately from all other business, and with permission to deliver or return it as occasion may require, consult a few friends on the point, and if they approve the Measure prevail on one of them to move ↑under a proper introduction↓ for 2 or 300 Guineas to be remitted to Your Excellency for public service. If more hundreds are necessary Your Excellency will be pleas'd to signify it, and even thousands.[2]

I return Your Excellency my hearty thanks for the kind intimation respecting my Son, or as I now hold him, my worthy fellow Citizen, Lieut. Colonel Laurens, which came the more acceptably as full three weeks had elapsed since the date of his last Letter.

I am / With the most sincere Esteem & Regard / Sir / Your Excellency's much Obliged / Humble Servant

Two double & six single Joannes		Contain'd in a Packet to be
Two Doubloons	Returned	deliver'd by Messenger
Two Pistoles		Jones
Eleven Guineas		

---

[1] Interlineations here and below by HL.

[2] Washington did not have to apply because the following day Congress ordered 500 guineas be issued and "transmitted to the Commander in Chief, to be laid out for the public service." Washington acknowledged receipt of the coin from HL and the specie from Congress in a September 4 letter. He also made arrangements to return the coin HL had sent. *JCC,* XI, 851; George Washington to HL, Sept. 4, 1778.

P.S.   Baron Steuben was much surpris'd at the Act of Congress requesting him to repair to Rhode Island, and seems to be very apprehensive the measure will be displeasing at Head Quarters.   I had been directed ↑during the sitting of Congress↓ to communicate the Intelligence receiv'd from General Sullivan to Mons.^{r·} Gerard, and to confer with that Gentleman.   I found at my return the Resolves on the Table.[3]

SOURCE: LB, HL Papers, ScHi; addressed "General Washington / White Plains / by Jones"; dated "28th Aug.^{t.}".

FROM JOHN WELLS, JR.

Charles Town, August 28, 1778

Dear Sir

Hearing just now of this vessel going to Philadelphia, & that she sails this Evening or early to morrow morning, I gladly embrace the opportunity of writing you a few lines & sending my last News paper__

About 10 minutes ago I saw a letter from N Low at South Quay,[1] mentioning that Gen. Washington had retaken Fort Washington, & summoned Clinton to capitulate__ also that the Count D Estaign had taken 80 Prizes__ if true, New York must be ours long ere this__ I have more reliance on this than in general on intelligence from that quarter, as the writer is well known here__ The Letter is of August 9th.__ Pray Heaven it may be so, then we shall be rid of war's dire alarms, & the villains in England who have ruined their Country will fall victims to the rage of an incensed, injured nation__

Many think seriously, or perhaps affect it, of the late ~~Commotion~~ Outrages of the Creeks__ A letter I have from Augusta,

---

[3] HL conveyed the resolve requesting von Steuben's assistance in Rhode Island to Washington in a public letter without comment. Because Washington neither wished to risk von Steuben in the Rhode Island action nor have the Congress send advice or advisers to generals under his command, he kept the Inspector General at White Plains. *JCC*, XI, 849; HL to George Washington, Aug. 28, 1778, Item 13, PCC; von Steuben to HL, Sept. 1, 1778, NNPM; Palmer, *Von Steuben*, pp. 196-197.

[1] Although in error, the reports of "Mr. Nicholas Low at South Quay in Virginia" were published in the *S.C. Gazette*, Sept. 2, 1778.

confirms me in the opinion, it is not of such importance but the <u>auri et agri sacra fames</u>[2] may induce ma↑n↓y to encourage the belief of a contrary ~~opinion~~ ↑one↓ __ No terms should be kept with the perfidious Race, if the accounts we have are true__ [3] Fire & sword are the only arguments ~~to use with~~ that can avail with them__ and though harsh in the execution, are eventually the most humane measures that can be adopted__

You may be assured I shall let slip no opportunity of writing you__ Your attention to me demands my warmest acknowledgments I hope to merit the Continuance of it, & am

With Regard, and the greatest Respect / Your most obedient servant

Jno. Wells jun^{r}

SOURCE: RC, Kendall Collection; addressed on cover "His Excellency / Henry Laurens Esqr / President of Congress / Philadelphia"; dated "Saturday Evening August 28th 1778"; docketed by HL "John Wells 28 Aug^{t.} / 1778 Rec^{d.} 29 Sept^{r.}".

TO JOHN LAURENS

Philadelphia, August 29, 1778

I had the pleasure of addressing you last Sunday & of hearing since by a kind intimation from your General that you were then well, but I have not receiv'd a line from you later than the 7th.

I should not have troubled you just now had not an odd circumstance of this Morning rendered it in some degree necessary.

A Monsr. Galvan lately a Lieutenant in the second South Carolina Reg^{t.} call'd on me and requested with very little Ceremony introductory Letters in his favor to His Excellency the Commander in Chief, and to Major General Sullivan. I had heard from Mr. J. Rutledge that Galvan had resign'd his Commission upon Colonel Motts' refusing him a furlough for making a Campaign and seeking promotion in

---

[2] The violent longing for gold and land.

[3] According to one account, John Stuart sent "500 scalpers" to East Florida. The Indians "purposed to spare no man, woman or child, that should be left alive by the British troops." *S.C. Gazette*, Sept. 16, 1778.

the Army now at White Plains__ with great candour and I am sure no less politeness and civility I lamented to the gentleman that he had committed so great an error, assuring him that I could give him no hopes of promotion, and producing many instances in order to convince him that he was spending his Money and time in a fruitless pursuit__ he would then be content he said to act as a Volunteer, but press'd for Letters to the Generals, from which I attempted to excuse myself by remarking that I had receiv'd repeated informations of the inutility and even troublesomeness of supernumerary Gentlemen Volunteers in the Army, that therefore I could not, consistently with my own honor and with that respect which is due to General Washington add the slightest weight to his present burthen

Mr. Galvan continuing to importune I prevail'd upon myself to say there was one Gentleman in the Army with whom I might take liberties. I had a Son who I understood was in good Credit there, to him I would give a recommendatory letter, the Gentlemen reply'd he should be glad of an acquaintance with my Son, but he knew he had no Command in the Army, and then demonstrated that he had as little command of good manners by abruptly retiring.__ Mr. Silas Deane sat impatiently during this dialogue, fearing that I should have acquiesc'd in Mr. Galvans' intreaties; immediately therefore after he had turned his back, Mr. Deane informed me of some very naughty tricks this young French Adventurer had play'd in Paris, which he discover'd from my Conversation I was ignorant of. You will therefore be on your guard__ Galvan speaks perfect English, is well read, and can behave like a Gentleman in all exterior deportment when he is not chagrined by disappointment.[1]

When I was at York town I sent Letters which I had receiv'd thro' Governor Johnstone from my friends Mr. Oswald and Mr. Manning either to Your General or to yourself for perusal. I request you, my dear Son, return them as soon as you can.

I need not tell you that I have written in great haste and

---

[1] This letter was left open and forwarded through headquarters for the commander's perusal. Being thus forewarned of Galvan's attempt, General Washington informed HL "This Gent^{n.} (if he may be so called, Monsr. Galvan) waited on me a few days ago, and met with þ reception due to his merit & conduct to you." George Washington to HL, Sept. 12, 1778.

under many interruptions nor that I shall be glad to receive a two and twenty days Epistle from you.

I pray God to protect you

SOURCE: LB, HL Papers, ScHi; addressed "Colonel John Laurens / Rhode Island / by Captain Josiah Stoddard"; dated "29th Aug.t.".

TO GEORGE WASHINGTON

Philadelphia, August 29, 1778

Dear Sir

I did myself the honor of writing to Your Excellency Yesterday by Jones, to which I beg leave to refer.

This Morning upon inquiry I was confirmed in my belief that the former Camp Committee had made no application to Congress for Gold or Silver to be deposited in Your Excellencys' hands for public uses, wherefore I suggested to two or three Members the necessity and utility of establishing such a fund__ and prevailed upon one of the Gentlemen to move the House for that purpose; the motion was accepted, and without a pause, the sum of 500 Guineas voted, these I shall presently receive and if possible convey them to Your Excellency under the protection of Captain ~~Stod~~ Josiah Stoddard of the light Dragoons.[1] I have just receiv'd new addresses to Congress from the British Commissioners at New York__ Governor Johnstone in graceless and almost scurrilous terms without exonnerating himself from the charges alleged against him submits to the decree of interdiction lately pronounced by Congress__ nor do the Gentlemen late his Co-adjutors so highly resent the proceedings on our part as to refuse to treat without the support of the Governors' name.

Your Excellency will judge best from their respective performances on the present occasion, Copies of which shall accompany this letter.

I take the liberty of inclosing with the present dispatches a Letter directed to Lieu.t Colonel Laurens under a flying Seal; and of requesting Your Excellency to peruse a paragraph contained in

---

[1] Capt. Josiah Stoddard of the 2nd Continental Dragoons.

it, w^ch· speaks of a Monsr· Galvan.

Monsr· Girard is exceedingly affected by the late determinations on the Water near Rhode Island and has communicated his sentiments to me with great candour.[2] Good accounts from General Sullivan will do more towards recovering him from a slight intermittant which really seiz'd that Gentleman immediately after he had received Monsr· Chouins' Letter than four ounces of Bark__ indeed I never saw people in general more anxious than my acquaintance are under the present suspense__[3] within the next two hours I make no doubt there will be fifty inquirers for news within this door.

I have the honor to be &c.

SOURCE: LB, HL Papers, ScHi; addressed "General Washington / White Plains / by Captain Josiah Stoddard"; dated "29th Aug^t·".

FROM RAWLINS LOWNDES

Charles Town, August 31, 1778

Sir__

I am induced thus Officially to trouble your Excellency on a matter wherein I apprehend this State is particularly interested, in order that no Priviledge or right legally appropriated to the State may be lost or impaired, either by non User or for want of a proper Representation, to the tribunal where these matters of dispute ought ultimately to be refered.

By Resolve of Congress of the 16th· Sep^r· 1776[1] it is provided "That the appointment of All Officers and filling Vacancies (except General Officers) be left to the Governm^ts· of the Several States &c"

The Office of Adjutant General of the Troops of this State, has within these few days become Vacant, by the Resignation of Col^o· Eveleigh:__ General Howe has filled up that Vacancy, by the

---

[2] For Gérard's Aug. 29, 1778, report to Vergennes, see *Gerard Despatches* (Meng), pp. 236-239.
[3] Final "s" written over "d".
[1] "6" written over "7".

appointment of Capt. Grimke[2] of the Artillery Regiment, one of his Aids de-Camp.

I have been applied to by Capt. Edmond Hyrne of the first Regiment for that post, and am very inclinable and desirous of giving him the appointm^t if it lies with me so to do.[3]

I have not seen, or do I know of, or beleive there is, any Resolution, or Act of Congress, which Cancels or Repeals the Resolve of the 16th. September above Recited, so far as relates to the Office now under consideration

Congress intrusts to the Executive powers of the State Blank Commissions, which are always Issued and filled up, by the President upon Application when any Vacancy Occur in the Line,__ And the Resolve is general and extends to All Offices and Vacancys,__ and Consequently Comprehends the Staff as well as the Line__ The Resolves are invariably transmitted to the President, undoubtedly for his Government and direction.

The late Arrangement of the Army,[4] makes some alteration in the Appointment of <u>some Officers</u> but leaves the, Adjutant General, subject to the former Regulation.

The President is empowered to remove Officers on the Staff, and in such Case to make temporary Appointm^ts to fill up Vacancys occasioned therby

I Conclude from these Circumstances, that I have sufficient Authority, and that the right of nomination of an Adjutant General of the Troops of this State is vested in me; And that, being possessed

---

[2] Robert Howe appointed Maj. John Faucheraud Grimké, with whom HL had fought a duel in 1775, acting Adjutant General of South Carolina "with the rank of Col^o. until the pleasure of Congress could be had." Later, when he had been informed "that there had been a difference between you and the Major," Howe wrote a personal note to HL apologizing and explaining that he had "never heard a word from Mr. Grimkée of any difference between you." Robert Howe to HL, Aug. 26, 1778, PCC, Item 160, p. 475ff; Robert Howe to HL, Sept. 5, 1778; *HL Papers,* X, 458-467, 492-497.

[3] Robert Howe's August 26 letter and Lowndes' August 31 letter were read in Congress and referred to a committee composed of William Duer, John Mathews, and Edward Telfair on September 29. The committee interpreted the Sept. 16, 1776 resolve to mean that the appointment of all officers and filling of vacancies (except general officers) should be left to the states. Because the Deputy Adjutant General for the Southern Department would serve in both South Carolina and Georgia, the Committee noted that disagreements could erupt if the appointment was made by one state. Both candidates were nominated and Congress elected Hyrne. *HL Papers,* XII, 62n; *JCC,* XII, 1137-1138.

[4] The new arrangement of the army had been approved by Congress May 27, 1778. *JCC,* XI, 538-543.

of blank Commissions, I could well justifye the Issuing one to Capt.
Hyrne, for that Office, acting in this respect under Authority of
Congress; And that Genl. Howe must at his Peril take notice of the
Appointment.__ I imparted to General Howe, by Message by his Aid
de Camp Capt Grimke, my Sentiments and Claim on this Subject
and desired, if he could invalidate them, or set up a better founded
right to the appointm^t, that he woud please to let me hear from him,
and I would desist from my pretentions__ three days have now
elapsed and I have not had any Answer__ it was my intention in that
Case to Issue a Commission to Capt. Hyrne, but on further Consideration, that the Service might not be Embarrassed or hurt, by any
altercation on the Subject, I have taken the Resolution to Submit my
self to Congress, not doubting but they will sustain, the right of the
State.

Independent Sir of the matter of right I can with the greatest
Confidence recommend Capt. Hyrne to the favour of Congress as
an Officer of great Merit and Attention, ~~and~~ who lately on the
Expedition to the Southward, in the Absence of Col^{o.} Eveleigh,
Acted at the Request of Genl. Howe, in the Office of Adjutant
General, to the Satisfaction of the Army__ And further that he was
a Captain in the first Regiment, when Capt. Grimke was only a Cadet.

I have the Hon^{r.} to be with very great Respect / Sir / Your
Excellency's most Obed^{t.} / and most hum Servt.

Raw^{S.} Lowndes.

SOURCE: RC, PCC (Item 72), DNA; addressed below close "His Exc̄y Henry
Laurens Esqr-"; dated below close "Chas. Town / 31st. Aug^{st.} 1778__";
docketed "Letter from Mr Pres^t Lowndes / S. Carolina Aug. 31. 1778 / Read
29 Sept^{r.} / Referred to Mr Duer / Mr Matthews / Mr Telfair". CopyS,
Kendall Collection. Copy (19th century), HL Papers, ScHi.

FROM JOHN SULLIVAN

Tiverton, R.I., August 31, 1778
Esteemd Sir,

Upon the Count Destiangs finding himself under a Necessity of going to Boston to repair the Loss he sustaind in the late Gale
of Wind, I thought it best, to carry on my Approaches with as much
Vigour as possible against Newport, that no time might be lost in

making the attack upon the Return of his Fleet, or any part of it to co-operate with us. I had sent Expresses to the Count to hasten his return, which I had no doubt woud at least bring part of his Fleet to us in a few days,[1] Our Batteries play'd upon the Enemys Works, for several days with apparent good Success. as the Enemy's fire from the outworks visibly grew weaker, and they began to abandon some of those next us; and on the 27th:, we found they had removd their Cannon from all the outworks except one. The Town of Newport is defended by two Lines, supported by several Redoubts connected with the Lines. The first of these Lines extends from a large Pond calld Easton Pond near to Tommeny Hill, and then turns off to the Water on the North of Wind-mill Hill. This Line was defended by five Redoubts in front; the Second Line is more than a quarter of a Mile within this, and extends from the Sea to the North side of the Island, terminating at the North-Battery. On the south, at the entrance by Eastons Beach, where this Line terminates, is a Redoubt which commands the Pass, and has another Redoubt about twenty Rods on the North. There are a Number of small Works interspersd between the Lines, which render an Attack extremely hazardous on the Land Side, without a naval force to co-operate with it. I however shoud have attempted carrying the works by Storm. as soon as I found they had withdrawn their Cannon from their outworks, had I not found to my great surprize, that the Volunteers which composd great part of my Army, had returnd, and reducd my Numbers to little more than that of the Enemy, between two and three thousand return'd in the Course of twenty four Hours, and others were still going off upon a supposition that nothing coud be done before the Return of the fleet. Under those Circumstances, and the apprehension of the arrival of an english Fleet with a Reinforcement to relieve the Garrison, I sent away all the heavy Articles, that cou'd be spard from the Army to the Main, also a large party was detachd to get the works in repair on the North end of the Island, to throw up some additional ones, and put in good repair, the Batteries at Tiverton and Bristol, to secure a Retreat in case of Necessity__ On the 28th: a Council was calld, in which, it was unanimously determined to remove to the North end of the Island, fortify our Camp__ secure

---

[1] On the evening of August 27, Lafayette rode to Boston to determine d'Estaing's intentions and to urge that at least a portion of his fleet return to Rhode Island. *Rhode Island History*, XXIX (1970), 30-31; *Lafayette Papers* (Idzerda), II, 155.

our Communication, with the Main, and hold our Ground on the Island, till we coud know whether the french fleet woud soon return to our Assistance. On the evening of the 28th: we mov'd with our Stores and Baggage which had not been previously sent forward, and about two in the Morning encampd on Bull's Hill, with our right extending to the west road, and left to the east road___ The flanking and covering Parties still further towards the water on right & left. One Regiment was posted in a Redoubt advancd of the right of the first Line; Colo: Henry B. Livingstones[2] with a Light Corps consisting of Colo. Jacksons detachment, and a detachment from the Army, was stationd on the east road. Another light Corps under command of Colo Laurens, Colo Fleury, and Major Talbot[3] ↑was posted on the west Road↓ . Those Corps were posted near three Miles in front, In rear of those, was the Picket of the Army commanded by Colonel Wade___[4] The Enemy having receivd Intelligence of our Movement, came out early in the morning with nearly their whole force in two Columns, advanced on the two Roads, and attackd our light Corps. They made a brave Resistance, and were supported for some time by the Picket. I orderd a Regiment to support Colo. ~~Laurens~~ Livingstone, another to Colo Laurens and at the same time sent them orders to retire to the Main Army in the best order they cou'd; they kept up a retreating Fire upon the Enemy, and retir'd in ~~good~~ ↑Excellent↓ order to the main Army. The Enemy advancd on our left very near, but were repulsd by Genl. Glover.[5] they then retird to Quaker Hill. The Hessian Column formd on a Chain of Hills running northward from Quaker Hill. Our Army was drawn up, the first Line in front of the Works on Bull's Hill, The second in rear of the Hill, and the Reserve near a Creek & near half a mile in rear of the first line. The distance between those Hills is about one Mile___ The Ground between the Hills is meadow Land, enterspers'd with Trees and small Cops of Wood. The Enemy began a Cannonade upon us about nine in the morning, which was returnd with double force. Skirmishing continued between the advancd parties untill near ten oClock, when the Enemys two Ships of War and some small armd Vessels having

---

[2] Col. Henry Beekman Livingston of the 4th N.Y. Regiment.
[3] Maj. Silas Talbot of the 1st R.I. Regiment.
[4] Col. Nathaniel Wade of the Massachusetts militia.
[5] Brig. Gen. John Glover of Massachusetts.

gain'd our right Flank and began a fire, the Enemy bent their whole force that way, and endeavourd to turn our right under cover of the Ships Fire, and to take the advancd Redoubt on the right__ They were twice driven back in great Confusion. but a third tryal was made with greater Numbers, and with more Resolution, which had it not been for the timely aid sent forward, woud have succeeded. A Sharp Conflict of near an hour ensued, in which, the Cannon from both Armies placd on the Hills, playd briskly in support of their own Party. The Enemy were at length routed, and fled in great Confusion to the Hill, where they first formd ~~where~~ ↑& where↓ they had Artillery and some Works to cover them; leaving their dead and wounded in considerable Numbers behind them. It was impossible to ascertain the Number of dead on the field, as it coud not be approach'd by either party, without being exposd to the Cannon of the other Army. Our party recover'd about twenty of their wounded, took near Sixty Prisoners according to the best Accounts I have been able to collect, Among the Prisoners is a Lieutenant of Grenadiers, The Number of their dead I have not been able to ascertain, but know them to be very considerable__ An officer informs me, that in one place he counted Sixty of their dead.[6] Colo Campbell came out the next day, to gain permission, to view the Field of Action, to search for his Nephew who was killd by his Side,[7] whose Body he coud not get off, as they were closely pursued__ The firing of Artillery continued through the day,__ the Musquetry with Intermission six Hours;__ The Heat of the Action continued near an hour, which must have ended in the ruin of the British Army, had not their Redoubts on the Hill coverd them from further pursuit__ We were about to attack them in their Lines, but the Men's having had no rest the night before, and nothing to eat either that night, or the day of the Action, and having been in constant Action through most of the day, it was not thought adviseable, especially as their position was exceedingly strong and their Numbers fully equal, if not superior to ours; ~~and~~ not more than fifteen hundred of my Troops have ever been in action before I shoud ↑before↓ have

---

[6] Sullivan lost 30 dead, 137 wounded, and 44 missing. The British had 38 killed, 210 wounded, and 12 missing. *Rhode Island History*, XXIX (1970), 32.

[7] Lt. Col. John Campbell and his 22nd Regiment of Foot, on "whom by their position the greater weight of the action fell," received special mention in Gen. Robert Pigot's official report on the action. *Documents of the American Revolution* (Davis), XV, 191.

taken possession of them Hill ↑They occupied↓ and fortifyd it but it ↑is↓ no defence against an Enemy coming from the South part of the Island, though exceedingly good against an Enemy advancing from the North end towards the Town and had been fortifyd by the Enemy for that purpose__ I have the pleasure to inform Congress that no Troops coud possibly show more Spirit than those of ours which were engagd. Col⁰ Livingstone and all the Officers of the light Corps behavd with remarkable Spirit, Col⁰ Laurens, Fleury, & Talbot Major Talbot with the Officers of that Corps behavd with great Gallantry__ The Brigades of the first Line, Varnum's, Glover's Cornells[8] and Greens behavd with great Firmness. Major General Greene who commanded in the Attack on the right did himself the highest honour by the Judgement and Bravery exhibited in the action. One Brigade only of the second Line was brought to action__ commanded by Brigadier General Lovell__ [9] He and his Brigade of Militia behavd with great Resolution. Col⁰ Crane[10] and the Officers of Artillery deserve the highest Praise__ I enclose Congress a Return of the Killed, and wounded and missing on our side & beg leave to assure them__ that from my own Observation the Enemy's Loss must be much greater__ [11] Our Army retird to Camp after the action, The Enemy employd themselves in fortifying their Camp through the night. In the morning of the 30ᵗʰ: I receivd a Letter from his Excellency General Washington giving me notice that Lord Howe had again saild with the fleet and receiving Intelligence at the same time that a fleet was off Block-Island and also a Letter from Boston informing me that the Count Destiang coud not come round so soon as I expected, a Council was calld and as We coud have no prospect of operating against Newport with Success without the Assistance of a Fleet it was unanimously agreed to quit the Island untill the Return of the French Squadron__ [12] To make a Retreat in the face of an Enemy, equal if not superior in number, and cross a River without Loss, I know was an arduous task,

---

[8] Brig. Gen. Ezikiel Cornell of the R.I. militia.

[9] Col. Solomon Lovell of the Mass. militia.

[10] Col. John Crane of the 3rd Cont. Artillery Regiment.

[11] For a return of casualties at Newport, dated Aug. 29, 1778, see PCC, Item 160, p. 178.

[12] General Washington informed Sullivan of the British movements in an August 29 letter in which he concluded "there can be no doubt, that every exertion is making to relieve Rhode Island__ " The Massachusetts Council wrote Sullivan on August 30 that despite their efforts "to persuade him to return immediately to Rhode Island & Cooperate with the army under

and seldom accomplishd if attempted. as our Centries were within one or two Rods of each other: I knew it woud require the greatest care and attention. To cover my Design from the Enemy, I orderd a Number of Tents to be brought forward and pitch'd in sight of the Enemy. and almost the whole Army to employ themselves in fortifying the Camp. The heavy Baggage and Stores were falling back and crossing through the day. At dark, the Tents were struck, the light Baggage and Troops pass'd down, and before twelve o'Clock the main Army had crossd with the Stores and Baggage. The Marquis de la Fayette arrivd about eleven in the evening from Boston, where he had been by request of the General Officers, to sollicit the speedy return of the fleet. He ~~illegible~~ was sensibly mortify'd that he was out of Action, and that he might not be out of the way in Case of Action, he had rode from hence to Boston, in seven hours, and returnd in six & a half, the distance near Seventy Miles. He returned time enough to bring off the Pickets and other Parties which coverd the Retreat of the Army. which he did in excellent order, not a Man was left behind, nor the smallest Article lost. I hope my Conduct through this expedition may merit the approbation of Congress.__

Major Morris[13] one of my Aids, will have the Honor of delivering this to your Excellency, I Must beg leave to recommend him to Congress as an officer who in the last, as well as several other Actions, has behavd with great Spirit and good Conduct, and doubt not, Congress will take such notice of him as his long Service and Spirited Conduct deserves__ I have the honor to be

Dear Sir, with much Esteem, / Your Excellencys most / obedient & very hble serv[t.]

Jn[o] Sullivan

P.S The Event has provd how timely my Retreat took place__ as One hundred Sail of the Enemy's Ships arrivd in the Harbour the Morning after the Retreat__

---

your Command" d'Estaing explained that he could not "by any means Justify himself in returning with his Fleet...untill he has supplied himself...made the necessary repairs & put his Fleet in a posture to meet the Enemy." They concluded "there is no Prospect of the return of the French Fleet or any part of it immediately." *Sullivan Papers* (Hammond), II, 276-277, 278-280.

[13] Maj. Lewis Morris, Jr., was an aide-de-camp to General Sullivan until June 1779 after which he served in the same capacity under Nathanael Greene. Heitman, *Continental Officers.*

I shoud do the highest Injustice if I neglected to mention that Brigadier Gen[l.] Cornell's indefatigable Industry in preparing for the expedition and his good Conduct through the whole merits particular notice. & Major Talbot who assisted in preparing the Boats__ afterwards servd in Col[o.] Laurens's Corps, deserves great Praise.

J. Sullivan

SOURCE: RC, PCC (Item 160), DNA; no address; dated "Head Q[rs.] Tiverton Aug[t:] 31[st:] 1778__"; docketed "Letter from Major gen / Sullivan. 31 Aug. 1778 / Read ~~3~~ 7 Sept. / Referred to the com[ee.] of / intelligence.__". Copy, HL Papers, ScHi.

FROM GEORGE WASHINGTON

White Plains, N.Y., August 31, 1778

Sir

I would take the liberty to inform Congress, that Col[o] Armand is come to camp with his Corps and has applied to me for Commissions for his Officers. By the Resolution for establishing the Corps it was to be officered out of the Foreigners then commissioned in our service, who were not, nor could be provided for in any of the Regiments.[1] Instead of this, there are only three Officers in his Corps, who before held any Commissions in our service, Viz Lieut Col[o] Vrigney & Captains Mereley & Shafner. The two last were only Lieutenants and are now appointed to Captaincies, contrary it seems to me, to the spirit and intention of the Resolution.__[2] As Col[o] Armand has departed from his instructions which must govern me, I am not authorised to grant the Commissions he requires__ and am therefore under the necessity of troubling Congress, with

---

[1] The Board of War recommended in a May 17 report and Congress resolved June 25, 1778, "That General Washington be authorized to officer this corps with such foreign and other officers of merit as at present hold commissions, and who are not already and cannot be annexed to other corps on the proposed arrangement of the army." *JCC*, XI, 642-645.

[2] Louis Cloquet de Vrigny came to America as an aide-de-camp to Lafayette and had been commissioned a lieutenant colonel on Feb. 2, 1778. Capts. Charles Markle (Merkle) and George Shaffner were both officers in Pulaski's Legion. *HL Papers*, XI, 9n. Heitman, *Continental Officers*.

the arrangement of the Corps, N° 1, as it now actually stands for their consideration & decision. The Colo founds his deviations from the Resolve upon some verbal intimation given him, that the part in question would not be insisted on.

I would also take the liberty to mention, that General Dᵘ Portail lately delivered me, a Memorial, in which among ↑other↓ things he represents, that he had made an agreement with Congress at his first appointment, that neither himself nor the other Gentlemen with him, should ever be commanded by any of the Engineers who had preceded them in our Army.__ I could not but answer, that the Commissions of Officers were the only rule of precedency and command I had to judge by; and while others held superior appointments, I must consider them accordingly in the course of service. He gave me the inclosed Letter to you upon the subject__³ and is extremely anxious to have the matter placed upon a certain footing; and no doubt it will be for the good and tranquility of the service that the claim be determined as speedily as possible one way or the other. At the same time I think it right to observe, that it can not be expected that Col° Coseiusko, who has been a good while in this line and conducted himself with reputation and satisfaction will consent to act in a subordinate capacity to any of the French Gentlemen, except General Portail.⁴

The frequent condemnations to Capital punishment, for want of some intermediate one between that and a Hundred lashes (the next highest under our present military articles)__ and the necessity of frequent pardons in consequence, induced me a few days ago, to lay the matter before a Board of Officers for them to consider, whether some mode might not be devised of equal or greater efficacy for preventing crimes and punishing Delinquents when they had happened, less shocking to humanity and more advantageous to the States, than that of Capital execution. The inclosed paper N° 3 contains the opinion of the Board upon the

---

³ Louis DuPortail's memorial is dated August 27 and was read in Congress September 3. PCC, Item 41, Vol. 8, p. 54ff; *JCC,* XII, 862.

⁴ Thaddeus Kosciuszko had been in charge of the construction of fortifications at West Point, N.Y. He was popular with the American officers but disliked by the French engineers, particularly Louis de la Radière. DuPortail's intent in writing to HL was to assure that Radière, his second in command among the French engineers, was not below Kosciuszko in rank. *HL Papers,* XII, 395n; PCC, Item 41, Vol. 8, p. 54ff; Louis DuPortail to HL, Aug. 27, 1778.

subject, with which with all deference I submit to the consideration of Congress__[5] and doubt not but they will adopt the expedient suggested, if it shall appear in any wise calculated to promote the service. I will only observe before I conclude upon this occasion that when I called the Board to consult upon the point there were Eleven prisoners under sentence of death and probably many more for trial in the different guards on charges that would affect their lives.

Since I had the honor of writing you on the 25 Inst, I have not received a single line from General Sullivan. The only intelligence I have from the Eastward is from Mon[r.] Pontjebeau.[6] This Gentleman left Rhode-Island the 27th and arrived about Two Hours ago in Camp. From him I learn that our people were still on the Island.__ That it was generally thought they had made effectual provision for a retreat in case of exigency.__ That in the evening of that day he met Mons[r] Preville,[7] an Officer belonging to the Languedoc, at Providence going with dispatch to Gen[l] Sullivan, who informed him that the French fleet had got into Boston. He further adds, that Mons[r.] Colonne,[8] who was in company with him at Providence and who had more conversation with M[r] Preville than he himself had, told him, that M[r] Preville said Count D'Estaing had sailed or was on the point of sailing again for Rhode Island with 10 ~~sail~~ ↑Ships↓ of the line and his Frigates.

I have the Honor to be / with great respect & esteem / Sir / Y[r] Most Obed[t] serv[t]

G[o:] Washington

P.S.

Your favor of the 20th only came to hand just now__

---

[5] General Washington posed the dilemma he faced in finding a suitable corporal punishment to a council of general officers August 20. The council, composed of Generals Gates, Stirling, de Kalb, McDougall, Parsons, Smallwood, Knox, Poor, Paterson, and Huntington, offered their opinion August 24. They suggested hard labor as an intermediate punishment. They further decided that prisons be established in each division to hold soldiers guilty of drunkenness and other offenses committed while intoxicated. *Washington Writings* (Fitzpatrick), XII, 343-344.

[6] Charles-Albert de More, chevalier de Pontgibaud (1758-1837) was a major in the Continental Army and an aide-de-camp to Lafayette. *Lafayette Papers* (Idzerda), II, 514.

[7] Washington may have been confused. Georges René Pleville was the naval officer from the *Languedoc;* chevalier de Preville was the naval officer in charge of the frigates which were to assist Sullivan in Rhode Island. d'Estaing to Sullivan, Aug. 4, 1778; de Preville to Sullivan, Aug. 9, 1778, *Sullivan Papers* (Hammond), II, 172, 186

[8] Capt. Louis St. Ange, chevalier de Colombe was one of Lafayette's aides.

SOURCE: RC, PCC (Item 152), DNA; addressed below close "Honᵇˡᵉ Henry Laurens Esqʳ·"; dated "Head Qʳˢ· White plains August / 31: 1778: 3 OClock PM"; docketed "(Examined) Letter from genˡ Washington / 31. Aug. 1778 / Read 3 Septʳ· / Referred to the board of war". Copy, PCC (Item 169), DNA. Copy, HL Papers, ScHi.

TO WILLIAM LIVINGSTON

Philadelphia, September 1, 1778

Dear Sir

Your very[1] obliging favor of the 21ˢᵗ reach'd me the 25ᵗʰ and has been ever since lying in my view, a scroll of the same date which I had the honor of writing will have inform'd Your Excellency that I was not dead I have not leisure for attending to a business which we ought to be least concern'd about.

More of my time than usual had indeed been engag'd in eating and drinking in that interval of silence which is so kindly pointed to in Your Excellencys' Letter, and as I made it a Rule never to neglect my Duty a faithful discharge had incroached largely upon hours which are generally passed on the Pillow, this excluded much of my ~~pleasu~~ satisfaction in private correspondence, but the honey Moon is over. We have slack'd into an easy trot again, and Mʳ· Gerard is an excellent sensible, sociable Neighbour, and conducts his visits without that formality which is an interruption to ~~business~~ ↑a drudging President.↓ __[2] I presented a day or two ago Governor Livingstons' Compliments to him, he longs to see you, and I Sir shall think my Paper correspondence realiz'd by the honor of Your Excellencys' company Upon my honor Sir I have many things to say which ought to be said and which I would attempt to say as properly as loudly were I not exactly in the station I am.

I do assure You Sir, our circumstances are truly deplorable I would touch gently on profligacy of time and treasure upon connivals or collusion, folly or tyranny especially when I meant to impute any or all of these to a person whose bottom of heart was good or where the innocent might suffer for the errors of the

---

[1] "ve" written over "fa".
[2] Interlineations here and below by HL.

mistaken, as soft a term as I can think of, but 'tis high time to pursue Measures for the protection of those innocents who are kept in an implicit belief that all is solid gold because of the much glistering__ a worm in one night destroy'd the Mansion of Jonah.[3]

M[r.] Deane late one of our Commissioners has been near two Months with us we know too much, and yet I almost fear we know nothing of our affairs in Europe, I do not mean hence to impute blame to M[r.] Deane, he has complain'd heavily to me in private of inattention on our part xxxxxxxxxxxxx[4] serious matters enter ↑entre-↓[5] nous.

Three hours my Dear Sir have I been writing not ↑studying↓ one second, what I should write, these two pages, perpetual influx of Personages of all sorts this Morning as if People had determin'd I should never write to Governor Livingston again, the finger now points to 9 I must fly to be in the way of my duty altho' experience has taught me I shall have squandired an hour and an half when I enter upon it.

For Your Excellencys' amusement entertainment and information I shall send with this__ Copies of a set of curious Papers which I have just receiv'd from Mess[rs.] le Commissioners who as the Merchants express have discarded one Partner and opened a house under a new firm__ [6] in the language of an old fellow I say, had my advice been followed, at York town, we should have preserv'd our dignity, given satisfaction to our Constituents, and ↑have↓ been free from the impertinent[7] attacks of these People__ M[r.] Johnstones' Declaration in particular cannot escape in New Jersey the correction it deserves, when the proper time shall come, of which due notice shall be given, it ought to be bated every where.

I go now to see whether we can with good grace recover the ground on which we stood on the late fast day 22nd of April.

---

[3] Jonah, 4:6-8. "n" written over other text.

[4] Laurens may be using the x's to indicate that he is omitting Deane's lengthy (and perhaps tiresome) protests.

[5] "enter" changed to "entre" and "entre" interlined above for clarity.

[6] George Johnstone was the "discarded...Partner" of the Carlisle Commission. He issued a declaration from New York on August 26 in which he thought "proper to decline acting as a Commissioner or otherwise interfering in any message, answer, agreement, negotiation, matter or thing that may regard the said Congress." He sailed for England on September 24. George Johnstone declaration, Aug. 26, 1778, PCC, Item 167, pp. 9ff; *Livingston Papers* (Prince), II, 426n.

[7] "impertinence" altered to "impertinent".

Adieu Dear Sir / I Am with much affection / And Respect &c. / Your Excellencys' / Obliged Humble Servt.

SOURCE: LB, HL Papers, ScHi; addressed "Governor Livingston / Jersey / by Ross"; dated "1st September". Copy (19th century), HL Papers, ScHi.

FROM CONRAD-ALEXANDRE GÉRARD

Philadelphia, September 1, 1778[1]

M^r. President will give me leave to Observe, that England will never think seriously of acknowledging your Independency whilst Congress will appear inclined to treat with Domestic Commissioners whose Powers and even Existence being founded on the Conciliatory Bills, The United States will be still reputed with reason as disposed to regard those Bills as[2] the Object of the Negotiation. It seems to me that it is turning the Back to the Object, and creating the greatest obstacles that can oppose your most sacred Interest. The Commission had neither Power nor Instructions, that is to say it had no more Existence from the moment you declared that you would treat only on the footing of Independance.

My zeal for the United States will Appologise for those Reflections.

SOURCE: Translation, HL Papers, ScHi; addressed on cover "A Monsieur / Monsieur Le President du Congrès / des Etas unis"; dated below text "Tuesday Morning."; docketed "Note from Monsieur / Gerard__". RC (French), HL Papers, ScHi.

TO CONRAD-ALEXANDRE GÉRARD

Philadelphia, September 1, 1778

My Dear Sir

You need not ↑to↓ have apologiz'd for the hints which you have so politely and kindly transmitted to me this Morning I feel

---

[1] Date supplied from HL to Gérard, Sept. 1, 1778.
[2] "a" written over "f".

myself happy that I cannot with respect to my own sentiments, add, necessarily.

At the receipt of the Commissioners first Address the Act of Congress of the 22nd of April instantly drew my attention my opinion and my advice was to have returned them all their Papers together with a Copy of that Act accompanied by a few necessary and proper lines from our Secretary intimating that Congress not being subjects to their Master were willing for the present to impute their conduct to pure mistake or something in these terms__ I trust we shall still recover our ground.

Believe me to be, / With the highest Esteem & Regard / Dear Sir / Your Obliged Humble Serv.ᵗ.

SOURCE: LB, HL Papers, ScHi; addressed "Monsieur Gerard, Minister of France / Philadᵃ / by M.Y."; dated "1 Septʳ.".

FROM JEREMIAH WADSWORTH

Philadelphia, September 1, 1778

Sir

When I was appointed to the office of Commissary general of purchˢ- private emolument did not opperate with me to accept it,

I hoped to answer the expectations of Congress and to have executed the trust without injuring my Country or loosing my reputation, I find I can do neither, and therefore intreat Congress will permit me to retire__

I do not propose to do so now in the middle of the Campaign but when the present year ends I beg Congress will be prepared to dismiss me__

Among the many reasons that induced me to ask a dismission are the following.__

When I entered into office the department was in a very unpromising situation and its Credit bad, I then informed Congress by their Committe, that to restore its Credit__ to furnish the necessary supplies and execute the business well; it was necessary to have always ready Money to purchase with of these truths the Gentlemen were satisfied and I believed measures woud be taken to enable me to restore the Credit of the department and furnish ample supplies on tollerable Terms__ but the Credit to which the department seemed to be restored is Vanished the purchaseing Commissaries are in such bad Credit that they cant buy the Articles ~~when~~ wanted in season or at reasonable rates, and the great difficulty in obtaining Money for the purposes of the Department makes it necessary always to buy on credit, and by this means private persons who have Money to purchase of the first hands engross the articles wanted and take unreasonable advantage of the ~~of the~~ publick and sell to them at a great advance: doing the publick business in this manner, if it wud be effectually done woud involve them in a mighty[1] and me in disgrace, but in this manner it can not be done and if under these circumstances I continue to hold my office I shall bring a train of Evils on my Country and on my selfe ruin__

I sincerely wish to render every possible service to my Country, and under all circumstances will contribute what may be in my power, to ward off impending Evils:[2]

I am with the greatest respect / Your Excelleny[s] most / Obedient & most / Humble servant

Jere[h] Wadsworth Com Gen P[s]–

SOURCE: RC, PCC (Item 78), DNA; addressed below close "His Excellency Henery Laurens Esqr"; dated "Philadelphia Sept[r] 1st 1778"; docketed "Letter from Col Wadsworth / Sept 1. 1778.__ / Read the same day.__". Copy, Wadsworth Papers, CtHi.

---

[1] Copy in Wadsworth Papers, CtHi, reads "mighty debt".

[2] Commissary General of Purchases Jeremiah Wadsworth wrote again in October to press Congress to consider his resignation. A committee concluded that because of his experience no one could perform the duties of that office better and recommended "therefore it will not be expedient to permit him to resign." In October 1779 Wadsworth again applied for permission to resign. Congress allowed him to retire Jan. 1, 1780. Jeremiah Wadsworth to HL, Oct. 20, 1778, PCC, Item 78, Vol. 23, p. 578ff; *JCC*, XII, 1024-1025; XV, 1200; Jeremiah Wadsworth to Samuel Huntington, Oct. 10, 1779, PCC, Item 78, Vol. 24, p. 125ff.

FROM GEORGE WALTON

Savannah, Ga., September 3, 1778

Dear Sir,

Recollecting the great and various Scenes of business in which you are necessarily involved,[1] I can but consider myself as much favored by your attention to me at York the 23 June last. Had not my letters miscarried, by some means or other, you would long before that Period have known that I was still above board in the United-States.[2]

I will not congratulate you on any particular event which hath taken place Since I had the pleasure of seeing you, but on the result of many_ the present great features of America. You have arduously and faithfully done your part in the business.

I confess to you, that I feel an almost irresistable inclination to be at Congress now; and nothing but my indispensible engagements at home, could keep me from it. Having attended almost two years in the worst of times, I seem to feel a right to be there in the hour of prosperity. I hope for the honor and Safety of the States, Congress is full and respectable_ It is certainly, as to future tranquillity, an important Crisis.[3]

We have had in this Country, Dear Sir, an expedition_ carried on without Co-operation, plan, or object. I went upon it with my Regiment; but I assure you I had no Share in the direction. When we got to Fort Tonyn_ General Howe, our Governor, The Commodore, Colonel Williamson and his field Officers and most of the field Officers in the other Corps, held a conference. The former said he never intended to go farther than St. Mary's; and his object being attained, he should return. The Governor said he always intended to cross St. John's. Colonel Williamson seemed to Steer between them. But the Commodore could not get the Gallies thro' Amelia Narrows. The truth is, that no part of any of the Corps was properly provided to have continued the expedition any farther. Thus it ended. The Enemy it is true was drove out of the State, and

---

[1] "n" written over "v".

[2] HL had been misinformed in February 1778 that Walton had died. In his June 23 letter HL explained that he had "lamented you as one numbered among the dead." *HL Papers,* XIII, 510.

[3] George Walton did not return to Congress until May 15, 1780. *Delegate Letters* (Smith), XV, 98n.

Fort-Tonyn in their Country, evacuated and distroyed; and this has been accomplished at an expence to this State of at least £150,000.

We are in great expectation of Admiral D'Estaing's fleet doing great things; but we are afraid that the delay, occasioned by his not being able to get into the Harbour of New-York, will give time for the arrival of Admiral Byron, which, with Lord Howe's fleet, will perhaps be an over match.

I beg you to beleive, Dear Sir, that I should consider it as a very great honor and happiness, if, in any moment of leisure, you would drop me a few intimations of what is going on in the great Council where you preside, or upon the theatre of War.

Being with much consideration & Confidence, I am, Dear Sir, your most Obedient Servant,

Geo: Walton.

SOURCE: RC, Kendall Collection; addressed on cover "To the Honorable / Henry Laurens, esquire, / President of Congress."; addressed below close "His Excellency / Henry Laurens, Esqr."; dated "Savannah, 3 September 1778"; docketed by HL "Geo Walton Esquire / 3d. Septem~ 1778 / Recd 16 Novem~__". Copy (19th century), HL Papers, ScHi.

TO JOHN BEATTY

Philadelphia, September 4, 1778

Sir

I had the honor of writing to you the 31st Ulto. by Messenger Ross.

This will be conducted by Josiah Tatnell Esqr. a Gentleman late of the State of Georgia decended from an Ancient and very respectable family in South Carolina, and himself no less respected in both those States, his political determinations excepted.[1]

Mr. Tatnal was lately made Prisoner of War by the Count d'Estaing's Squadron, the Honorable the Minister Plenipotentiary

---

[1] Josiah Tattnall (Josias Tatnell), a member of the Georgia Royal Council who was banished from the state in December 1777, had been captured on his way to England. After his exchange, he returned to Georgia in 1780 and remained at Savannah until the British evacuated in 1782. Palmer, *Biographical Sketches of Loyalists*, p. 847.

of France has permitted him by a writing of his hand subscribed and seal'd to go into New York in order to work his discharge by the releasment from thence of a Subject of His Most Christian Majesty in Exchange__ this paper and also a Copy of his parole M^r. Tatnal will produce for your inspection. Congress have directed me to give this Gentleman a Pass through Jersey, which he will also shew you, and as M^rs. Tatnal and a with a little family[2] are under his charge I request you Sir, to do me the favor of facilitating their passage.

Congress have also permitted Captain William Nicholls late Commander of the British Packet Eagle to go into New York for the like purpose of effecting a proper Exchange which you will prescribe and determine upon, and will also take Captain Nicholls' Parole and restrict the term for his absence in failure of his attempt, in which I would wish you to be very pointed, because from my particular application this indulgence has been obtain'd.[3]

Your Predecessor in Office the Honorable M^r. Boudinot will say much in favor of Captain Nicholls' conduct during his parole confinement within this State. I have known the Captain some five or six years, and have from thence a regard for him.

I Am with great Esteem & Respect / Sir / Your Obedient & / Most Humble Servt.

By Permission of Congress assembled at Phil^a. 3^d Septr. 1778 Josiah Tatnal Esqr. late of the State of Georgia a Prisoner of His Most Christian Majesty is to pass thro' New Jersey in terms of written subscrib'd and Seal'd Act of Egress granted to him by the Hoñble. the Minister Plenipotentiary of France residing at this City.

Captain Nicholls' Pass.

By permission of Congress sitting in Assembly at Philadelphia 3^d of September 1778.

---

[2] Josiah Tattnall had married Mary Mullryne, the daughter of John Mullryne, a prominent South Carolina and Georgia merchant-planter, and Claudia Cattell.. The Tatnalls had two sons born after 1762 at Savannah. *Directory of the S.C. House,* II, 488; *SCHM,* XIV (1913), 5, 6; XXIII (1922), 191.

[3] Nichols had been taken prisoner at New Castle by Capt. Harry Lee. *PMHB,* XXI (1897), 299.

Captain William Nicholls ~~is to pass unmolested~~ ↑late of the British Packet Eagle↓ now a Prisoner of War in this State is to pass unmolested from Philadelphia by the direct Road to Princetown in New Jersey or to ~~such other~~ ↑any↓ place within that State in which Col⁰· John Beatty, Commissary General of Prisoners holds his Residence and Office.

SOURCE: LB, PCC (Item 13), DNA; addressed "Col⁰· John Beaty Com. Gen¹· of Prisoners / Princetown / by Mʳ· Tatnal"; dated "4ᵗʰ Septʳ·".

FROM GEORGE WASHINGTON
White Plains, N.Y., September 4, 1778

Dear Sir,

I am your debtor for two Letters bearing date the 28ᵗʰ· & 29ᵗʰ· Ult⁰·__ The contents shall be the subject of a future address

Feeling my self interested in every occurrance that tends to the honor of your worthy Son; and sensible of the pleasure it must give you to hear his just plaudit, I take the liberty of transcribing a paragraph of General Greens Letter to me (giving some Accᵗ· of the conduct of particular Officers in the action on Rhode Island):

"Our Troops behaved with great spirit, and the Brigade of Militia under the Command of Gen¹· Lovel advanced with great resolution, and in good order; and stood the fire of the Enemy with great firmness__ Lᵗ· Col⁰· Livingston, Col⁰· Jackson, & Col⁰· H.B. Livingston did themselves great honor in the transactions of the day.__ But it is not in my power to do justice to Col⁰· Laurens, who acted both the Gen¹· & Partizan__ His command of regular Troops was small, but he did every thing possible to be done, by their numbers"[1]

Major Morris affords me too good an oppertunity of return- ing your paper parcel of gold, sent me by Messenger Jones, to pass by__ & therefore I embrace it__ a more particular acknowledgement of, and thanks for this favor, shall, as I have promised before, be conveyed in my next__ At present I shall only assure you__ & with

---

[1] Nathanael Greene's Aug. 28/31, 1778, letter extolling JL is in the Washington Papers, DLC. *Greene Papers* (Showman), II, 499-504.

the most perfect truth I can do it, that with every sentiment of regard and affection,

I have the Honor to be / Dr Sir, / Y^r· Most Obed^t· & Obligd / Servt·

G$^{o:}$ Washington

SOURCE: RC, CSmH; addressed on cover "The Honble· / Henry Laurens Esqr / President of Congress / in / Philadelphia / Favour'd / by / Maj^r· Morris"; dated "Whiteplains__ Sep: 4th· 1778". Copies (2), HL Papers, ScHi. Copy (19th century), HL Papers, ScHi. ADraftS, Washington Papers, DLC.

TO WILLIAM MAXWELL[1]

Philadelphia, September 5, 1778

Sir

I had the honor of paying my respects to you the 26th Ult^o· in a private Address, this is intended also as a private, having received no Commands from Congress respecting your late Letter.

The Executive Council of this State lately ordered Doctor Berkenhout who came from within the Enemy's Lines at New York thro' your Head Quarters into this City where he had remained some days without explaining himself or the nature of his errand to the Vice President of the State, the President of Congress, or to any Magistrate, to be apprehended and committed to Goal, where he now lies, under suspicion of being a Spy__ from the contents of a Paper found in his custody it appears he had a design of offering himself to Congress as a private Negociator for terms of peace consistent with Independence between these United States and Great Britain, and 'tis certain that upon his journey hither, he, in conversation with a Gentleman in Jersey assum'd the Character of Agent or Commissioner from the Court of Great Britain to Congress.[2]

---

[1] Brig. Gen. William Maxwell of New Jersey was the commander at Elizabethtown opposite Staten Island.

[2] Dr. John Berkenhout (*ca.* 1730-1791) was an unofficial agent of the British Ministry who had sailed from England with Mr. and Mrs. John Temple and arrived at New York in early August. During his medical studies at the University of Edinbugh he became acquainted with Arthur Lee, who had obtained a degree there in 1764. It was this connection with the Lees that

In a Letter to Congress written since he has been in confinement, in terms which appear to be extremely equivocal he claims no public Character, says, "he came hither under the sanction of a Pass from an American General," complains of the hardship of being imprisoned "in a Country which he had been taught to revere as the asylum of liberty" and "requests to be permitted to return from whence he came".[3]

Congress have declined interfering in this business, but I am particularly requested by a Gentleman of the Council to inquire of You, Sir, what were D[r.] Berkenhout's pretensions of business or Character when he apply'd to you for a pass and under what authority or permission he gained access to you

I have also to request you to inform me if you can possibly learn how many ships of the Line which lately went out of the Hook under the command of Lord Howe in order to divert our attack Count d'Estaing returned after the storm into New York__ a very sensible Man a deserter from the Enemy, assures me, the Eagle and 3 or 4 more capital ships were driven on shore on Long Island and totally lost, that Lord Howe returned in a frigate which bore his Flag, and hitherto I have seen no other names in the New York Papers of his Lordships squadron but the Isis, Renown, and Prescott, which gives an air of truth to the deserters narrative. This is an interesting subject if you will make the necessary enquiry and communicate the result together with every particular information

---

he believed would provide access to Congress. The Earl of Carlisle, hoping to make some progress after George Johnstone's indiscretions, sent Berkenhout to Philadelphia. As the commander at Elizabethtown, Maxwell was the first American authority to deal with Berkenhout, who told the general that he had important intelligence for Congress and obtained a pass through American lines on August 24. Reaching Philadelphia August 27, the British agent sought meetings with Richard Henry Lee and other members of Congress. He roamed the city unmolested until September 3 when an anonymous correspondent to the *Pa. Packet* inserted an item that called attention to reports reprinted from New York and London newspapers revealing that Berkenhout was on an agency. The Supreme Executive Council of Pennsylvania ordered his arrest and despite his protest to HL and others he was only released September 16 after giving a parole promising to return within British lines. Howard Peckham, "Dr Berkenhout's Journal, 1778," *PMHB*, LXV (1941), 79-92; John Berkenhout to Congress, Sept. 4, 1778, HL Papers, ScHi.

[3] Berkenhout denied connection with the British Ministry and claimed "The suspicions concerning me are not founded on the least shadow of evidence or probability." HL replied the following day that the Congress refused to take action in his case because it "is already and properly before the Executive Power of this State." John Berkenhout to Congress, Sept. 4, 1778, HL Papers, ScHi; HL to Berkenhout, Sept. 5, 1778, PCC, Item 13.

you can collect of the state of the British Fleet you will thereby render a favor which will oblige me very much, and of which I will embrace all opportunities for making proper acknowledgments.

I have the honor to be / With great Respect &c.

SOURCE: LB, HL Papers, ScHi; addressed "Brigadier General Maxwell / Elizabeth town New Jersey / by Mʳ· Tatnall"; dated "5ᵗʰ Septʳ·"; noted "Memᵒ· / Sent the Secretary's Letter to / Wᵐ_ Temple ↑Esqʳ·↓ under cover to Genˡ· Maxwell."

FROM SAMUEL ELBERT

Savannah, Ga., September 5, 1778

Sir,

I have the Honor to inclose you a Return of the present strength of the Continental Brigade in Georgia. I wish I could say that such Steps had been taken here, to make it as respectable, as sound Policy would have dictated. The times of Inlistment of the greatest part of the few Men we have left will shortly expire; and so great is their dislike to this service, that there is scarce an instance of one Man, who has been entitled to his Discharge, that could be prevailed on to engage anew. Should an Army be thought necessary for the defence of this State the next year, immediate and extraordinary encouragement should be given for Recruits, or we shall be in a very reduced situation.

The other inclosures will serve to explain the cause of my sending Captain Hancock,[1] of my Regiment, with this Letter.[2] He is a Gentleman of veracity, and can inform you of any ~~other~~ further particulars you may wish to learn. I hope Congress will find it convenient to send a sufficient sum of Continental Money for the purpose of paying the Troops, by return of this Conveyance, or

---

[1] Capt. George Hancock of the 2nd Ga. Regiment. Heitman, *Continental Officers.*

[2] Captain Hancock also carried a letter from Joseph Clay, the deputy paymaster general, who noted that Hancock "goes to Congress at the request of the Officers & Soldiers in this State...to Solicit their being pᵈ· in Contˡ· Currʸ." Clay noted that the condition of the soldiers was "truly distressing" and that the petitioners believed payment in Continental dollars would relieve their distress. Joseph Clay to HL, Sept. 9, 1778, Joseph Clay Letterbook, GHi.

nothing short of a Mutiny will take place among them; nor would a temporary supply, in my opinion, give entire satisfaction: And could this be extended to the Staff Department, I am convinced there would be a saving, nearly equal to one half, in the purchase of every thing necessary for the Army.[3]

An Hospital, well regulated, would be the means of preserving many Lives. At present, every Regimental Surgeon has his own, which occasions some abuses that it is impossible to prevent.

The Savages have, in the course of the last month, murdered upwards of twenty People on our Western Frontiers, which, considering their former trespasses of the like Nature is an insult that I hope will not be overlook'd with impunity.

M.r Gerardeau having resigned the Office of Dep: Comm.y: Gen: of Issues for this State, I beg leave to recommend M.r Mordecai Sheftall as a Person worthy of that appointment, who now does the Duty, until the pleasure of Congress be known.[4]

I am, with perfect respect, / Your Excellency's, / Most Obedient, humble Servant.

S: Elbert Col.º. Comm.dt:
Continental Brigade in Georgia

SOURCE: RC, PCC (Item 78), DNA; addressed below close "His Excell.y: Henry Laurens Esq:"; dated "Savannah the 5.th: September 1778__"; docketed "Letter from col Elbert / Georgia Sept 5. 1778 / Read 17 Nov.r 1778 / Referred to the board of war".

---

[3] The appeal was not read in Congress until November 17. In the meantime Congress, responding to a June 23 letter from Gen. Robert Howe requesting Continental money to establish a military chest, resolved on September 21 to provide $1,000,000 for Georgia. *JCC*, XII, 937-938; Rawleigh Downman and George Hancock to HL, Nov. 19, 1778, PCC, Item 78, Vol. 7, p. 225ff.

[4] John B. Girardeau was a prominent Savannah merchant and had been a member of the Georgia Council of Safety. Congress accepted his resignation because of ill health on October 28, but postponed confirmation of Sheftall's appointment. Sheftall served in the post until he was imprisoned by the British after the fall of Savannah. In addition to the $7,682 Congress awarded him for that service, he also received $20,000 in compensation for funds advanced to the army. *Revolutionary Records of Georgia* (Candler), I, 74; *JCC*, XII, 1069-1070; *Delegate Letters* (Smith), XV, 348-349.

FROM ROBERT HOWE

Charles Town, September 5, 1778

My Dear Sir

My publick letter will probably before this reaches you inform you that upon the Resignation of Col⁰· Eveleigh I had in orders appointed Major Grimkée (one of my Aids) to act as deputy Adjutant General with the Rank of Col⁰· until the pleasure of Congress was known. I did not intend to trouble you with a private letter upon this subject but, I was induced to do it by some Persons having since his Appointment informed me that there had been a difference between you and the Major and that you might Construe my having Appointed him as not consistent with that Respect, they had so frequently heard me profess for you, and that perhaps you would probably oppose his Confirmation__ As to the last of these, I was too well acquainted with the Generosity of your heart not to know, that you were incapable of suffering Private misunderstandings to have influence upon Publick Measures, and had I not been certain that the Persons meant both of us well, I could not have restrained myself from resenting the supposition as an imputation upon my Friend. As to the first Sir I should incur the censure of my own heart were I capable of an intentional Action which bore even the appearance of disrespect to a Person I so truly love and Esteem, but knowing (as I do) the liberality of your Sentiments, had I known that there existed any Personal Animosity between you and Mr Grimkée I am certain I should have been highly blamed by you had I upon that account denied to his Military Merit that Promotion it had a Claim to and which his having Acted so long as one of my aids I could not but have had an opportunity of being acquainted with more Especially as it is Officially incumbent upon a General to provide for his immediate Staff if they deserve it when an opportunity so fairly presents itself I have you may be assured never heard a word from Mr Grimkée of any difference between you, nor did I ever hear him speak of you with Respect. The office of Deputy Quarter Master General having become vacant by the Resignation of Col⁰· Huger, I have taken the liberty to recommend to Congress Col⁰· Stephen Drayton for that appointment,[1] may I Sir request the

---

[1] Congress elected Stephen Drayton deputy quartermaster general in the Southern Department, but selected Edmund Hyrne over John F. Grimké as deputy adjutant general. *JCC*, XII, 1137-1138; Rawlins Lowndes to HL, Aug. 21, 1778.

favour of your Interest in his behalf as an additional obligation to the many you have laid me under with every wish for your happiness and with Respect Esteem & affection I am Dear Sir

Your Obligd & ob[t] Serv[t.]

Robert Howe

As this letter will come by water I venture not to go into any subjects that could benefit the Enemy by falling into their hands I shall send a duplicate by land Excuse the haste I write in and kindly impute to it all inaccuracies.

SOURCE: Copy (19th century), HL Papers, ScHi; no address; dated "Charles town 5[th:] Septr 1778".

TO JOHN LEWIS GERVAIS

Philadelphia, September 6, 1778

My Dear Friend

My last was dated the 22nd Ult[o.] conveyed by Captain Pyne, since which I have received none of your favors. I must again beg leave to refer you to our worthy friend the President for news in General. I have sent him a Budget__ much of it ought to be confined within the knowledge of a few friends for the present.

Within the present cover I give you several of Dunlaps' Packets, Copy of a Letter from Your friend John Laurens of 1st September, and of one relative to him from General Washington, I know you will be glad to see these; if you think proper to publish the first in order to do justice to some characters of whom he writes don't <u>publish</u> his name.[1] I am sure he is as averse as I am to that sort of Newspaper Parade.

I was in great hopes to have sent you General Lees' trial at length, but 'tis not out of Press.

---

[1] JL's letter with details of General Sullivan's retreat in the Rhode Island campaign was published in the *S.C. General Gazette*, Oct. 8, 1778, as "Extract of a letter from an Officer in General Sullivan's Army, dated September 1, 1778."

You will read what I have written to His Excellency the President respecting the Embargo[2] and the Article of Rice an intimation intended for public good, to yourself, I say if you are disposed to purchase 4000 Barrels of very good Rice at the Current price as speedily as possible after you receive this I shall be glad to hold a moiety of the concern, you will be the best judge of quality, goodness of Barrels and convenience of Storage, I shall therefore not trouble you on these Points, nor do I mean to impose myself on you as a Partner unless it shall be quite agreeable to yourself and that you can pay for one half the purchase out of my own funds.

My next shall mark my sentiments respecting the shipping or otherwise disposing of the Rice.

A swift sailing Sloop or Schooner to run into Delaware with 2 or 300 Barrels immediately if you have general permission will probably make a good Voyage provided the freight is not too extravagant. I judge it will sell here at 40/ or perhaps 6 dollars per 112^{tb} if the Vessel be tight, you may dispose of as much rough Rice as will fill the hollows in stowage of the Cask__ but note 'tis not impossible that British Men of War may again appear in the Bay, and that there is no great hope of a back freight__ these circumstances you will duly consider.[3]

I shall also in my next talk seriously to you concerning my return. 'Tis high time, and yet when I reflect__ M^r· Heyward gone, M^r· Hudson absent, M^r· Mathews going, I feel a sensible pain at the prospect of leaving our State again almost unrepresented, but if my Countrymen are totally inattentive to their dearest Interests, the continuance of my feeble efforts to serve them will be in vain with respect to them, although it may work the ruin of my Estate.

I expect to hear from you such Answer as General Gadsden shall have given.[4]

---

[2] See HL to Rawlins Lowndes, Sept. 6, 1778.

[3] If Gervais had purchased rice about that time the price was £3.5 to £3.10 per hundredweight. By early December he reported that "Rice keeps up from £4.10 to £5. ℔ C^t." An embargo passed by the South Carolina Assembly in October remained in effect until January 1779. John Lewis Gervais to HL, Sept. 9, 1778, HL Papers, ScHi; John Lewis Gervais to HL, Dec. 3, 1778; Rawlins Lowndes to HL, Jan. 15, 1779, PCC, Item 72, p. 477.

[4] On September 9 Gervais reported "I have not seen Genl Gadsden yet but I shall take an opportunity to communicate to him the paragraph of your Letter concerning him." Apparently uneasy about approaching Gadsden on the issue, Gervais asked Rawlins Lowndes to intervene "which he had done, & says that General Gadsden will make an Apology__ I hope he will do it fully." John Lewis Gervais to HL, Sept. 9, 1778, HL Papers, ScHi; John Lewis Gervais to HL, Sept. 21, 1778.

My respectful Compliments to M^r· and M^rs· Manigault, M^rs· Gervais and all Friends. I continue with great Regard and Esteem, Dear Sir / Your Affectionate / H^bl· Servant

SOURCE: LB, HL Papers, ScHi; addressed "John Lewis Gervais Esquire / Charlestown / by Wilkinson to Muckinfuss at the Ship Tavern"; dated "6th September".

TO RAWLINS LOWNDES

Philadelphia, September 6, 1778

Dear Sir

M^r· Heyward left us so suddenly about the 10th Ult^o· it was impossible for me to pay my respects to Your Excellency by him. I writ the 11th ↑continued to the 21st↓[1] and my Packet overtook Captain Pyne the 23^d[2] at Baltimore which I hope will supply[3] that defect.

In that Dispatch I omitted to send Copy of the Decree of the Committee of Appeals on the case of the Brigantine Success,[4] because indeed I could not procure it in time from the Register__ it will now be found under cover with this among divers other Papers which will accompany it, as will appear by an inclos'd Schedule of the whole.

I am much dissatisfied with this determination, and have doubts concerning the respect which will be paid to the Decree in Charlestown. Certainly a very formal and solemn Verdict given there is intended to be set aside by the Judgment of a Court far inferiour to that of our Admiralty in every view__ besides the 280 Dollars to be paid in obedience to this judgment for the Costs and charges of Captain Arthur the law charges which I must pay here will

---

[1] Interlineations here and below by HL.

[2] "13th" altered to "23^d".

[3] "su" written over other text.

[4] Capt. George Arthur's brig *Success* was seized at Georgetown, S.C., by Edward Weyman in July 1777 for being in violation of a resolution of Congress prohibiting the importation of British goods. The South Carolina admiralty court upheld the seizure but Congress's Committee of Appeals issued a decision on Aug. 7, 1778, which reversed the state court. *HL Papers*, XI, 408-409; Records of the Supreme Court of the United States, No. 24, RG 267, DNA.

Amount I am inform'd to seven hundred Dollars and upwards.[5]

I have lately been call'd upon by three Persons who had made their escape or been exchang'd from imprisonment at New York, and who had been captur'd on Voyages from Charlestown whither they were desirous of returning, but could not proceed without assistance of Money. I have supply'd each of them, viz.

Lieu^t Richard Wells of the Comet	200 Doll^s
Captain Joseph Price of the Active	109
Captain George Leacey of the General Gadsden	350

Their several Receipts will be found within.__ I trust our State will suffer no loss from such unavoidable advance of Money to her distressed Citizens and in any case that I shall not incur censure__ indeed in every instance except that of Lacey I have had the concurrence and approbation of my Colleagues.[6]

The sundry Papers alluded to above, together with the printed Papers which I shall add, will give Your Excellency almost a clear knowledge of our public intelligence to this day, and therefore I will not be troublesome with repetitions.

Bad as General Sullivans' Case appears to be, and the appearance is bad indeed, I do with grief assure Your Excellency the state of our Treasury and finances, of our Loan-Office Certificates,__ our foreign Debts__ our waste of time & neglect of the most important concerns, are infinitely more alarming__ were I to indulge suspicions too well warranted from appearances, and the daily intimations which are given to me from different quarters, I should be provoked to say there are Berkenhouts' and Temple's, and more dangerous Engines than either in the vitals of our Union.

At this very instant the arrival of Major Lewis Morris Aid de Camp to General Sullivan is announc'd__ I must attend him.

Major Morris has deliver'd me Letters from General Wash-

---

[5] James Wilson had been engaged as South Carolina's attorney in the case. *HL Papers,* XIII, 39-40.

[6] Copies of the South Carolina naval officers' receipts to HL are in the Laurens Collection, DLC (Wells and Price) and the HL Papers, ScHi (Leacy). Leacy's receipt contained a history of his voyage. He was master of the *General Gadsden* when it sailed from Charleston to Amsterdam on Sept. 17, 1777. He was captured two days later by the *Galetea,* imprisoned at New York from Oct. 3, 1777, until his escape on July 26, 1778, after which he made his way to Philadelphia.

ington, General Sullivan &c. which will soon spread that joy which I myself feel, throughout an anxious City__ I will add to the pile of Papers a Copy of the Generals Letter__ the general anxiety was not without cause__ the Major's words in a whisper to me were "I do assure you Sir, we are indebted[7] to that good Man General Washington for our escape he gave us notice and press'd again our Retreat". The day following 5000 Men landed from New York at Newport__ Sir Henry Clinton said to be at the head of them__ when General Sullivan had determin'd to retreat he cover'd his design by a stratagem which compleatly deceiv'd the Enemy and happily effected his purpose. The Enemy were then at least equal in number Man for Man with himself__ the retreat of Major General Hancock and his Volunteers and of the Militia &c. who had followed his example had nearly ruined our cause, or to say the least reduced America to extreme distress__[8] we have cause to be thankful for an almost unparalle'd escape.

Major Morris informs me there are now upward of 10,000 British and foreign troops on Rhode Island and a fleet of British Men of War riding in parade in Boston Bay, this will probably however, end in parade furnishing M[r.] Rivington with small means for long vaunting Paragraphs.[9]

Will Your Excellency pardon me in my present haste for making this private letter a vehicle for conveying an Act of Congress of the 2nd Ins[t.] for relaxing the ↑general↓ Embargo in so far as to procure a supply of Vegetable Provisions for the necessary consumpt of the Eastern States.[10] I find the Embargo in this State is in existence and to run about fourteen days longer Peccadillo evasions excepted, whether it will be renew'd is a question, probably it may

---

[7] "b" written over other text.

[8] John Hancock, who had arrived from Boston at Sullivan's headquarters August 10 to lead the Massachusetts militia, only remained in Rhode Island until August 24. Sullivan informed HL that by August 27 the number of volunteers dwindled rapidly with "between two and three thousand return'd in the course of twenty four hours." They were unwilling to remain after the French fleet departed. *Rhode Island History,* XXIX (1970), 25, 28; John Sullivan to HL, Aug. 31, 1778.

[9] James Rivington's newspaper did not list the British forces in Rhode Island, but did include at this time a "State of the whole [British] NAVY...." *Rivington's Gazette,* Sept. 5, 1778.

[10] Congress resolved to recommend to "the legislative or executive powers of the State of Pennsylvania, and the states southward thereof" that they permit vessels to carry "flour, wheat, rice, corn, pease, or beans, for the eastern states" thus relaxing the general embargo that had been enacted June 8 to be in effect June 10 to Nov. 15, 1778. *JCC,* XI, 578-579; XII, 861-862.

be under the present relaxation which will answer every purpose to the 15th November.[11]

I am desired by the Honble. the Minister Plenipotentiary to encourage the exportation of Rice to the French West India Islands, ↑&↓ to Count d'Estaing's fleet, and I am persuaded small Cargoes will meet with good sales in this City__ which I intimate for the general benefit of my Countrymen that each may have timely notice and an option to adventure when the term of the present restriction shall expire. I am persuaded it will not be renewed this Year.

I have the honor to be / With the highest Esteem & Regard

Schedule of Papers sent Mr. Lowndes

No. 1. The Marquis de Bretigney's Memorial and Plan
2. General Sullivans' Letter to the Commander in Chief 21st Augt.
3. Dr. Berkenhouts' Letter to Congress 4th Septr.
4. Dr. Berkenhouts' unfinish'd Letter intended to R.H. Lee[12]
5. Dr. Berkenhouts' Letter to the Printer
6. Mr. Temples' letter to the President 23d August
7. Colonel Laurens' Letter to the President 22nd August
8. Declaration of the British Commissioners 26th August
9. Requisition by the British Commissioners 26th August
10. Governor Johnstone's Declaration 26th August
11. Dr. Fergusons' Letter accompanying the Declaration 26th Augt.
12. Resolves of Congress on the Declaration &c. 4th Septr.
13. Lieut. Richard Wells' Receipt for 200 Dollars 24th August
14. Captain Joseph Prices' Receipt for 109 Dollars 29th August
15. Capt. Geo. Leacey's Receipt for 350 Dollars 5th Septr.
16. List of British Men of War arriv'd at Sandy Hook the 28th of August with remarks on Lord Howes' Squadron & upon the reported loss of Admiral Byron
17. Decree of the Committee of Appeals at Phila. 7th Augt.
18. An Act of Congress of the 2nd September

---

[11] The Pennsylvania General Assembly ordered on September 4 that "the Embargo on provisions be continued for & during fifteen days from this date, & that a Proclamation be issued for that purpose accordingly." *Minutes of the Supreme Executive Council of Pennsylvania*, XI, 568.

[12] In a letter to the *Pennsylvania General Advertiser*, Dec. 16, 1778, Richard Henry Lee declared that Berkenhout "brought neither letter nor letters for me, nor carried any from me, altho both are insinuated." *The Letters of Richard Henry Lee*, ed. James C. Ballagh (2 vols: New York, 1911-1914), I, 458-459. The printed collection contains no letters to or from Berkenhout.

19. General Sullivans' Letter to the President 31ˢᵗ August
20. Return of the kill'd, wounded and missing in the Action on Rhode
    Island 29ᵗʰ August

SOURCE: LB, HL Papers, ScHi; addressed "President Lowndes / Charlestown
/ by Wilkinson to Muckinfuss at the Ship Tavern"; dated "6ᵗʰ Septem~".
Copy (19th century), HL Papers, ScHi.

TO CHARLES COTESWORTH PINCKNEY
Philadelphia, September 6, 1778

Dear Sir

Within this cover you will receive a schedule of sundry
articles which Mʳˢ· Morton late housekeeper to Mʳ· Middleton put
into my hands as your property & which I have sent forward under
the protection of Mʳ· Richᵈ· Wells Lieutᵗ· of the Brigᵗ· Comet whose
receipt is subjoined to the schedule.

I have transmitted the news of the day to His Excy President
Lowndes who I am persuaded will communicate to you all that is
desirable

I have the honor to be / &ca

SOURCE: LB, HL Papers, ScHi; addressed "Colonel Chˢ· C. Pinckney /
Charles Town / by Wilkinson to Muckinfuss at the Ship Tavern"; dated "6ᵗʰ·
Septem~". Copy (19th century), HL Papers, ScHi.

TO JOHN RUTLEDGE
Philadelphia, September 6, 1778

My Dear Sir__

I had the honor a few days ago of receiving your favor of the
18 July by Mʳ· Galvan; this Gentleman called on me for Letters of
introduction to Gen.~ Washington & Gen.~ Sullivan, which I
declined giving & stated the reasons for my refusal in terms equally
civil & candid, he discovered much chagrin at the disappointment
& retired in a manner which discovered he was angry.

M^r. Silas Deane happened to be present, & immediately after the young Gentleman had turned his back intimated to me that he had sat with impatience during the Dialogue, fearing I should have acquiesed it M^r. Galvan's importunity, that he knew this Gentleman's conduct at Paris, adding a detail of several particulars; the most important to our State is__ that Monsr. Beaumarchais & Monsr. Montieu[1] hold South Carolina Debtor for the Amount of the Warlike Stores imported there by Monsr. Galvan.[2]

I congratulate with your Excellency on the escape of our Army from the danger to which it had been exposed upon Rhode Island His Excellency the President will shew you Sir. particulars of this affair & all the papers of intelligence which I shall send to him by Muckinfuss.

I am happy in assuring you that Co^lo. John Laurens has not in any instance dishonored your recommendation. thank God he is well & generally esteemed a Man of as much virtue as personal bravery; I ought not to say less to a Gentleman who has been pleased to patronize a fellow Citizen so nearly allied to me.

A sensible shrewd Gentleman of a very considerable class of people called Tory. applied to me lately & engaged me in a private & Interesting conversation of a public nature, he requested at parting another opportunity of speaking to me__ I conjecture, these people know more than I minutely do of the designs & necessities of the British Court & that they are paving the way, by means of an Emissary, for making their peace.[3]

I have the honor to be &ca

SOURCE: LB, HL Papers, ScHi; addressed "John Rutledge Esquire / Charles Town / by Wilkinson to Muckinfuss at the Ship Tavern"; dated "6 Septem.~".

---

[1] Jean-Joseph Carrier de Montieu was a French arms manufacturer. *Franklin Papers* (Labaree), XXII, 463.

[2] Although South Carolina had paid Galvan £75,000 for arms and ammunition in October, 1777, this may indicate Galvan had not remitted the funds to Beaumarchais and Montieu. *HL Papers*, XII, 460n.

[3] Possibly John Berkenhout.

FROM JOHN WELLS, JR.
Charles Town, September 6, 1778

Dear Sir

I did myself the honour of writing you within these few days past, by a private Express to North Carolina, and a sloop for Philadelphia_ the latter is still detained by contrary winds_ I know not with certainty what conveyance this will go by; but I am informed several will occur in a few days_

Last friday I receivd a Packet of Newspapers & a Note of August 8th from you_ also a Packet of Letters from Mr Walton My poor brother Timothy had the mortification of announcing to the Assembly the sense you entertain of my attention in furnishing you with papers and intelligence. The President had sent his Despatches to the ~~Assembly~~ House, I am almost confident, before he had perused them with any degree of attention himself_ [1] The affair of the Riot of June 5th was then ~~before~~ under Considerations & some of the Persons concerned had their apprehensions_ These were removed, & they exulted not a little at your saying the Resolution of Congress, which occasioned the obnoxious Proclamation had met with an uncommonly general disapprobation throughout the states_ Mr Lowndes I firmly believe to be a man of inflexible integrity, & sincerely devoted to the interests of his Country_ Yet several Circumstances have concurred to make him very unpopular_ His attachment to Mr Gadsden, & his accepting of the President's Chair when vacated by Mr Rutledge, it is generally said, have gained him the ill will of that powerful family, which by their Opponents is stiled "<u>The Family Compact</u>" His issuing the Proclamation already mentioned, occasioned his being called a Friend to Tories, & some former parts of his Conduct, not according with the ideas of the Violent Party made many of them class him among those obnoxious People_ His frugality & Oecononomy follow him in publick life, & his strict investigation of accounts against the Publick, & his dealing out the publick money with a very sparing hand has given much offence to others_ Add to all this, the Civil & Military departments, particularly in money matters frequently clashing, ~~&~~ t has given rise to complaints against him from the Gentlemen of the Army_ His situation, from this representa-

---

[1] See HL to Rawlins Lowndes, Aug. 5, 1778.

tion of it, you may easily conceive, cannot be an agreeable one__ he has had Misfortunes of a domestick Nature also__ Yet this accumulated Weight of Distress does not appear to make him despond__ and his Countenance indicates a mind quite at Ease & satisfied with itself__

A Committee has been appointed by the Assembly to enquire into the affair of 5th June__ I have been summoned before ~~them~~ ↑it↓ __ You are possessed of what information I could give them__ It was with reluctance I mentioned names, & not till after their satisfying my scruples of its implying something like an informer, a Character the most detestable in my opinion that can almost exist__ From the Complexion of a Majority of the Committee I apprehend the Enquiry will end in fumo[2]

You will deserve the authentick Account of the late Duel__ Your Colleague W.H.D. is blamed by some as the occasion of it__ but I cannot see with what propriety if he sent the letter to Mr G. in consequence of his request__[3]

Since General H. has made his appearance in town, I cannot find the Rumours to his disadvantage, mentioned in a former letter are so current__[4] His Conduct on the occasion above mentioned may perhaps have some effect in preventing a revival of them__ For my own part, I cannot pretend to form any judgement, how far the late Expedition, or the Miscarriage of it (if what was evident long before, can be termed so) can be imputed to him But of the whole transactions I have no doubt you ~~have~~ will be possessed of full information from opposite sides__

Governour Houstoun appears much alarmed for the existence of the State of Georgia__ he is[5] confident of ~~an India~~ War with the Creeks__ & there ~~app~~ can be little doubt if hostilities are really

---

[2] "In smoke." The South Carolina Assembly's eight-member committee reviewing Rawlins Lowndes' June 5 proclamation was composed of five Charleston delegates—Edward Rutledge, Alexander Moultrie, William Moultrie, Owen Roberts, and David Ramsay—who opposed Lowndes. The three country members—Charles Cotesworth Pinckney, James Mayson, and Aaron Loocock—supported him. The Assembly postponed consideration of the committee's report and voted to extend the time to sign the oath thus upholding Lowndes. John Lewis Gervais to HL, Sept. 21, 1778; Vipperman, *Rawlins Lowndes*, pp. 215-216.

[3] It is not clear if Drayton sent the copy of Robert Howe's Aug. 28, 1777, letter to Congress at Christopher Gadsden's request. Gadsden did note in his July 4, 1778, rebuttal of it that he had "been long anxious to see Howe's letter to Congress." *Writings of Christopher Gadsden* (Walsh), p. 134.

[4] See John Wells, Jr., to HL, July 29, 1778.

[5] "is" written over "it".

commenced by them, but an attempt will at the same time be made from East Florida__ I hope & believe his apprehensions are premature__ In the present <u>myrative humour</u> of the British forces, I cannot think it would by any means ↑be↓ expedient to detach any part of our very small army from this State__ A Part of our Western Militia might be spared__ but they have ~~also fa~~ fared always so indifferently in Georgia heretofore, that it will be with reluctance they would go again__ beside the fable of the Shepherds' Boy & the Wolf is too applicable to our neighbours__ However should they be actually attacked, I hope ~~none~~ other Considerations but that of immediate Self Preservation will deter us from affording them effectual aid__

The Rice Planters, who are really to be pitied pluck up a little hope from some Expressions in your last letter__ Your Colleague W.H.D. I know not with what foundation, has ~~been~~ had the Embargo laid to his Door__ Notwithstanding it, we receive a little flour coastwise, and as it comes very opportunely, are not disposed to find fault with it__ It however adds strength to your opinion, that we are not the least honest people on the Continent__

A great deal of[6] money might be made by ~~a~~ Persons situated in Pennsylvania, & ~~possess~~ having good intelligence, by purchasing Prize Vessels & sending them here, where they ~~are~~ will be much wanted__ I sold at publick Vendue the week before last $3/4$ of a Bermudian Sloop, $3/4$ of her Cargo that cost 2200 Ps of Eight, & $3/4$ of the money (about 9000 Dollars) arising from the freight she had on board, from St Eustatius bound for Virginia, & the purchaser taking on himself the Risk from the West Indies, for Sixty three thousand Pounds__ The Sloop was 25 years old__ has 12 guns__ & was a fast sailer__ the $1/4$ of another Sloop alone I sold for £6,100 Six thousand one hundred Pounds__ If the Embargo is taken off in November, square sail Vessels of Burthen will sell high__ but new, & at any time handy Sloops & schooners will bring an immense Price__

All sorts of European, East-India, & West India Goods, & indeed every Necessary, Conveniency, or the most refined & delicate Luxuries of life sell at most exorbitant Prices__ Madeira Wine sells at £50 & £60 the dozen__ I do not live [i]n any other than a

---

[6] "of" written over "m".

frugal manner, Lieut. Col. Mackintosh[7] & a young man a Clerk to dine with me__ have 3 White Boys Apprentices,__ & 4 Negroes for the Business & House Work__ Yet the Mere eating & drinking exceeds the Rate of Three Thousand Pounds a Year, exclusive[8] of Clothing & House Rent__ It obliges me to be attentive & industrious to keep pace; especially as in our business the Charges are only doubled what they were twenty years ago__

We are impatient to hear of Count D'Estaign__ I have no doubt, from your Letter, that Byron is arrived__ What pity it is, that the Count did not arrive a fortnight sooner__ Should the Event be unfavourable to him, I am of opinion it will still operate to our advantage__ The British will be anxious to follow the blue__ they can do little or nothing with their land forces here__ anxious to repair in some degree their losses of treasure in their mad American war, Hispaniola or some other Considerable French West__ India settlement will attract their attention__ We will ~~be~~ thereby be releeved from a Land War, & there can be no doubt of Circumstances soon occurring to make them desirous of Peace with us even in the feeling of Independency__ This however is but a mere opinion formed on the present appearances of things__ which may have varried considerably by the time you receive this__

September 11th__

This goes by Post__ and as I have a little leisure shall write you a little more__

Last sunday Evening an old grudge between our & the foreign sailors broke out in a dreadful riot__[9] What was the immediate Cause of the Quarrel, is variously related__ but without prejudice, in my opinion the Foreigners began.__ Policy however say [torn] to the principal People, to throw the blame elsewhere__ Some who I should think might have known better, attributed it to a plot of some secret Traitors to create animosities between us & our

---

[7] Lt. Col. Alexander McIntosh (d. 1780), a St. David planter, commanded the 5th Cont. Regiment in South Carolina. During that time he also served on the Legislative Council and may have boarded with Wells while the General Assembly was in session. *Directory of the S.C. House,* III, 458-459.

[8] "exclusive" written over other text.

[9] On the evening of Sept. 6, 1778, between ten and eleven o'clock, small arms and cannon fire were exchanged in Charleston harbor between Americans on shore and French sailors from their vessels. One American and three Frenchmen were killed in the affair. Several lesser skirmishes during the prior two weeks had led to the riot. An investigation proved inconclusive. Rawlins Lowndes to HL, Sept. 7, 22, 1778; John Lewis Gervais to HL, Sept. 9, 1778.

Allies__ What gave weight to this opinion was one Johnson, an Irish man, ~~being~~ who had not taken the oath, being apprehended that night, while among the Militia with his musket, & pockets full of Cartridges__ Next morning, on his being examined before the Council, it appeared he had been on the Southern Expedition under Williamson, & that in his return to Town, the time prescribed for taking the Oath was elapsed__ He was discharged, his Case promised to be represented to the Legislature, & some kind of apology made for his Confinement__ The French Sailors on being driven to their Ship fired several pieces of Cannon loaded with Grape or Langredge__ Some Cannon being on the Wharf at Burn's, at which she lay they were soon loaded by the Sailors & 3 or 4 fired in return__ A Bermudian Sloop's guns being on shore on the Exchange Wharf, three[10] sailors procured powder for three of them which they fir'd in to[11] the French Ships Stern__ Some t of the American ↑or English↓ Sailors had now got Muskets__ Capt. Bell's (the Master of the French ship) Son with his servant, coming down to the Wharf were shot at by three villains;[12] the servant was killed on the spot, & poor Young Bell [*torn*] Youth[13] wounded in two places__ One Kennedy, formerly Mate of the armed Brig Polly, was the first Person, & the only one of our Sailors, killed__ four[14] or five of them were wounded__ Of the French, 3 were killed & 4 wounded__ The Militia were all under arms, & if[15] the first transports of[16] Rage they were in, had been allowed[17] vent, the Consequences would have been more bloody__ A French vessel very imprudently gave great offence by hoisting her Ensign & it was not till several Messages past, that it was pulled down__ On the whole, it appears to me to have been an quarrel arisen from the Aversion & Contempt [*torn*] entertain for those of other nations__ and if m a vigorous Police is not established in all the capital sea Ports, as there will now a greater [*torn*] of foreigners than could be heretofore Riots, of a

---

[10] "three" written over "sa".

[11] "to" written over "th".

[12] The French ship *Count de Narbonne* was lying at the end of Burn's wharf when the captain's son and a servant were fired upon by someone concealed behind a "heap of shingles" on the wharf. *S.C. General Gazette*, Sept. 17, 1778.

[13] "Y" written over other text.

[14] "four" written over "Three".

[15] "in" altered to "if".

[16] "of" written over other text.

[17] "allowed" written over "vent".

more serious nature may doubtless be apprehended__ Our Assembly have adopted the Idea__ & some kind of Riot Act is now under Consideration I wish the Devil had the beginners of the Disturbance, as, independent of other Considerations, it will occasion my loosing now & then a Nights' Rest, in doing Patrol-Duty in Town__ which is [*illegible*] to prevent the ~~Publick~~ Peace being again disturbed in such a manner__[18]

The Accounts from the West grow more serious & gloomy every day__

Wishing you health & happiness, & a speedy lasting & honourable Peace, I am, Sir,

With the highest Esteem & Respect__ / Your most obedient servant

Jn$^{o.}$ Wells, jun^r

I have received but one Philadelphia Paper by the Post__ The Sloop abovementioned sailed without my being previously apprized, otherwise should have wrote again by her__

It is said, I know not with what truth that the three sailors who fired on Young Mr. Bell were particular friends of Kennedy

SOURCE: RC, Kendall Collection; addressed on cover "To / His Excellency / Henry Laurens Esqr / President of Congress / Philadelphia / By Post"; dated "Charlestown 6th September 1778__"; docketed by HL "John Wells / 6 & 11 Septr / 1778 / Rec$^{d.}$ 28 Octob⁓".

FROM COMMITTEE OF ARRANGEMENT
White Plains, N.Y., September 7, 1778
Sir

Your Committee beg leave to sollicit your Attention to the Situation of your Country while destitute of a general Officer. Each Regiment having its own Colonel, & he only attending to the

---

[18] On September 8, Rawlins Lowndes issued a proclamation in which he offered a £1,000 reward for information about the "offenders." And, on September 12 the General Assembly informed him that they had "appointed a committee, to revise the laws relative to seamen, in the port of Charlestown, and to consider of ways and means to suppress riots in the said town." *S.C. General Gazette,* Sept. 17, 1778.

Concerns of his particular Regiment, a general Confusion & Neglect must take Place, for Want of an Authority which ↑can↓ extend
its Influence to the whole: & correct these Abuses, & that Profusion
of Expences, which hitherto has been incurr'd by this Corps. Nor do
we conceive it possible for the publick to derive the same Service
from them in their present State, that it would do if under the
general Direction of an active, & intelligent Officer__ The present
Colonels, tho Men of Merit, are upon such Terms with each other,
that it is probable the Appointment of either would occasion the
Loss of the other three;[1] there may also be other Reasons to
determine another Choice, & we can think of no Person so proper,
or so likely to be acceptable to the present Officers, as General
Cadwallader.[2] At least it is the Wish of the Committee that the
Experiment may be made__ the other Gentleman recommended
by the General having turn'd his Views to civil Life, & wholly
declining this Service now.__[3] If the Committee are so happy as to
meet the Opinion of Congress, with Respect to Genl. Cadwalladers
Appointment, they beg Leave to suggest the Expediency of immediately making the Choice, & leaving it to him to accept, or refuse;
as they have Reason to fear a previous Consultation will be more
likely to defeat, than advance their Views.

The Cloathing of the Army is also an Object of very great
Importance__ in the present State of Suspence with Respect to that
Department, we fear vigorous Measures are not taken either by the
States, or the Officers of the Department; & that when the Season
advances your Army will find itself suffering as it has done formerly.
If the Committee appointed on that Service, have made a Report,
we hope Congress will not delay the Consideration of it, as the
Consequences will be extremely prejudicial to the Service. It is an
Opinion universally prevalent here that the several States would
effect this Business with greater Oeconomy, & more Satisfaction to
the Army.__

We are to acknowledge your several Favours of the 30th. &

---

[1] Theodorick Bland commanded the 1st Regiment, Elisha Sheldon the 2nd Regiment,
George Baylor the 3rd Regiment, and Stephen Moylan the 4th Regiment of Dragoons.

[2] The committee's endorsement of John Cadwalader for the post confirmed Washington's
earlier recommendation. Cadwalader would decline the appointment. George Washington
to HL, Aug. 3, 1778; Cadwalader to HL, Sept. 19, 1778, Cadwalader Papers, PHi.

[3] Joseph Reed.

31ˢᵗ· Augᵗ· the former inclosing the Papers respecting the Cavalry, upon which we have not yet come to any Resolution but shall in a few days report to Congress the Allowance to be made them__ ⁴

As to any additional Encouragement beyond the usual Bounty of Twenty Dollars given to the new Recruits__ his Excellʸ has intimated his Opinion, that it will be best to keep it out of Sight at present & has communicated his Sentimᵗˢ· to Congress to this Effect.__ In which we concur.

I have the Honour to be with the greatest Respect & Regard Sir / Your most Obed. Hbble / Servᵗ·

Jos: Reed
Chairman

SOURCE: RC, PCC (Item 33), DNA; no address; dated "Camp at White Plains / Sept. 7ᵗʰ· / 1778"; docketed "Letter from the Committee / of arrangement at Camp / Sept 7, 1778 / Read 10.__ ".

FROM RAWLINS LOWNDES

Charles Town, September 7, 1778

Dʳ Sir__

If Accounts may be depended upon which have been received from the back Country, and from Georgia; and they are from the best Authority; an Indian War seems unavoidable. Many Murders have been Committed in that state, and every Appearance indicate War with the Creeks. We have strained every Nerve and exhausted every resource to supply them with Goods to secure their Friendship, in vain,__ The Frontier is abandoned and the Inhabitants in-forted, for their Protection, in many Places, and the panic is universal. The Assembly is now sitting and they have the matter

---

⁴ Capt. Josiah Stoddard and the officers of the 2nd Regiment of Light Dragoons on August 20 had requested "an allowance...towards defraying the enormous expences they were subject to" in maintaining their horses. Congress referred the matter to the Committee of Arrangement. On October 27, following the report of the committee, Congress granted officers of the Light Dragoons an additional 500 dollars, to be refunded if the officers left the service during the war. Josiah Stoddard to HL, Aug. 20, Oct. 20, 1778, PCC, Item 78, Vol. 20, pp. 283ff, 323ff; *JCC*, XII, 1066-1067; HL to Josiah Stoddard, Oct. 28, 1778, PCC, Item 13.

under their present Consideration. One expedition after another seems to follow as naturally as the Succession of Seasons and to produce only, a call for another__ Georgia looks up to us in dispair, and tho' her ill managem^{t.} Originates the Evil, she seems supine and Languid to a degree of stupifaction. This Conduct of our Indians compared with that we read of to the Northward, looks like the Result of some general preconcerted Plan, actuated by the same Councils, and calculated to favour, in point of time, the same Operations__ a General Effort perhaps to mend their Affairs, and if unsuccessfull to relinquish the undertaking__ we must make the best of it, and struggle through as well as we can__ looking up for an example and encouragem^{t.} to our brave partners Northerly. It will animate us much to hear some good News from you__ the disappointment of Count D'Estaign's not getting into the Harbour of New York troubled us greatly__ and now our hopes are fixed upon Rhode Island; if we miscarry there, whither shall our next hope be fixed? Keep off Byran[1] and all yet may be well. I tell you sincerely S^{r.} I cannot divest my self so far of former prepossessions as not to fear something from that Quarter.

Pray Sir, how stands the Law in regard to the Importation of Tea; we shall be glad to make any sacrifice that is necessary and a joint Affair, but I am apprehensive we may exclude our selves from some indulgences which our Partners are gratifyed in. it is Certain a poor, honest or At least unsuspecting trader who went to our Custom house openly and entered a Quantity of Tea had it Seized and Confiscated as a prohibited Commodity to the Emolument of the Officer.[2]

Congress I find does not think me <u>faulty</u> in Issuing the Proclamation in Obedience to their[3] Resolve; really my Dr Sir I should have been much surprized, if they had. it is however but a cold approbation for a very ready and Active submission to their Authority__ I could not know the measure was Contested, it came to me under no such disadvantage, neither was the reception it met with in the other States, an Argument either for or against my

---

[1] British Admiral John Byron, in search of d'Estaing, sailed for America with a squadron of fourteen vessels. Severe gales and fog played havoc with his command and he arrived off the coast of New England, August 17, with only his flagship the 90-gun *Princess Royal.* Tilley, *British Navy,* pp. 128-129, 146-147.

[2] Congress had passed the embargo on tea on Sept. 13, 1776. *JCC,* IV, 278.

[3] "their" written over other text.

Conduct, or sh^{d.} it, if known, have had any Influence on me in a point, when I was to Act Ministerially and Officially__ I draw Comfort from the rectitude of my own Intentions, and the approbation of my own mind, which to me is a better and surer Criterion of right than the Plaudit of Friends, or the Censure of Enemies.

I have reason to say the Embargo is not altogether made a rule of Action in all the States; indeed some Attempts have been made to infringe it here, but they have been detected and punished, so that the state is not blameable__ you will see by the Inclosed paper I have rec^{d.} from the Custom house__ [4] that in some other places attempts have been more successfull__ it is uncontrovertable that this Country is under peculiar difficulties on acco^{t.} of the Embargo__ but I assure you nevertheless there is no murmuring,__ ↑nor will be↓ unless infractions appear in other parts, to excite them, tho' we shall be glad, when the Safety of the whole, will admit of its being discontinued.__

Last Night about 10 o'Clock, we had a most violent Riot between the American and French Sailors, they proceeded to such lengths as to fire upon each other, the Americans from the shore & the French from their Vessells__ Canon from the Latter__ three persons were killed and several wounded__ and we expect a Repetition of the disturbance altho' we are taking all the precaution possible to prevent it

This is an Accidental Opportunity which I take the Advantage of to acknowledge the re^{t.} of your favour of the 7th. of August__ and to request you will be more liberal in your Commissions both Land & Naval__ the Establishm^{t.} of the ~~Navy~~ ↑Army↓ will require a great many & I suppose there can be no Objection so far as that matter appears to be fixed__ and as to the Naval they are already disposed of what I have received

I am with very great Respect__ / Sir / Your Most Obed^{t.} Servt

Raw^s Lowndes.

SOURCE: RC, Kendall Collection; addressed on cover "His Excy / Henry Laurens Esq^r__"; addressed below close "His Ex̄cy Henry Laurens Esq^r__"; dated below close "Chas Town 7th. Sep^{t.} 1778"; docketed by HL "Presid^{t.} Lowndes / (private) 7th Septem 1778 / Rec̄d 21st. Octob__". Copy (19th century), HL Papers, ScHi.

---

[4] Enclosure not found.

TO SILAS DEANE

Philadelphia, September 9, 1778

Dear Sir

I had the honor of presenting to Congress your Note of Yesterday, and have only to say, the House came to no determination thereon.[1]

I Am with great Regard &c.

SOURCE: LB, PCC (Item 13), DNA; addressed "The Honble. / Silas Deane Equire / Philadelphia / by M. Young"; dated "9ᵗʰ Septʳ·".

FROM JOSEPH CLAY

Savannah, Ga., September 9, 1778

Sir__

By this Conveyance I have sent you all my Acctˢ· to the 31ˢᵗ Ulto I know not whether I have been right in so doing, but never havᵍ received a line from any Board or Office giving me any Directions how to conduct myself I am totally at a loss to whom I shoud apply or with whom I shou'd correspond on the Business of my Office__ I have repeatedly seen matters that appeared to me improper but for want of knowing how far I was authorized to interfere have not been able to notice them__ unless I am can be properly supplied with Money & Instructed how to conduct myself it will be impossible for me to Execute the office[1]

We are again very much infested with Tonyns Banditti

---

[1] Silas Deane had completed his appearance before Congress August 21, and waited for their orders. On September 8 he implored HL to have Congress "reflect on the peculiar situation I have for some time past been placed in, and inform me if they desire my further attendance." On September 16 he was summoned to appear in two days. Before he could appear, however, Richard Henry Lee alerted Congress that William Carmichael would be arriving soon from France and would "in strong terms reprobate Mr. Deane's conduct both in his public and private character." Silas Deane to HL, Sept. 8, 1778, PCC, Item 103, p. 111ff; *JCC*, XI, 826; XII, 920, 927-928.

[1] On October 16, HL forwarded a resolution which "empowered and directed" Joseph Clay, as deputy paymaster general of Georgia, to pay "such sum or sums of money as may be wanting" to the commissary, quartermaster, and clothier general's departments. Clay's September 9 appeal, however, was not read in Congress until November 17. HL to Joseph Clay, Oct. 16, 1778, PCC, Item 13; *JCC*, XII, 1009, 1136-1137.

Stealing our Horses & Negros & doing ↑us↓ all the Mischief they can as Thieves two or three of them have been killed this last Week by our Scouts your Overseer who carry'd your Negro's to Florida is in Jaol here & will be hanged if sufficient Evidence can be pro-cured__ [2] all these Thieves claim the Priviledge of being prisoners of War as Soldiers in the service of the King of Great Britain & some of them have Commissioners__ however our Inhabitants seem determined that very few of them shall have in their power to claim the Priviledge by Killing them if Possible wherever they meet them they are mostly in small Companies of 5 or 6 Each We have ↑been↓ lately ~~been~~ much alarmed by the Creek Indians who murdered a Number of People in the Ceded lands but all seems to be quiet again this Country can never enjoy any tranquillity nor its inhabitants have any Security for their Property[3] till the Florida's are Reduced Tonyn with his Thieves & Stuart & his adherents with the Indians will always be annoying us__ I have only to add that I am with great ~~respect~~ regard & respect

Dr Sir / Your most Obed^t Servt

J: Clay

SOURCE: LB, Joseph Clay Letterbook, GHi; addressed "His Excellency / Henry Laurens Esqr"; dated "Savannah Septr 9th 1778".

FROM JOHN LEWIS GERVAIS

Charles Town, September 9, 1778

Dear Sir,

My last was of the 12 or 13th of last Month in answer to your favour of the 15^th_ July__ Since which I had the Honour to receive your Letter of the 7. August with several News papers for which I return you my thanks. The President also communicated me your Letter to him__ I am Sorry to find our affairs do not appear so

---

[2] George Aaron, HL's overseer at New Hope plantation, took five of HL's slaves to Florida in August 1776. He was captured while on a raid with some Florida Rangers and taken to Savannah as a prisoner of war. James Baillie, HL's overseer at Broughton Island, lodged a complaint to have him transferred from military to civil jurisdiction. *HL Papers*, XI, 224n; John Lewis Gervais to HL, Sept. 21, 1778.

[3] "Propriety" altered to "Property".

prosperous as one might have expected, I can't help thinking it must in some measure be our own fault__

I am glad I can inform you that I have not paid M^r. Blundell, & that I received the hint in time__

I mentioned I believe in my last Letter that I had only Sold one barrel of last Years Indigo at £4 p lb. it was kept by Mr Manigault's advice for a better price he was of opinion it would raise to £5. & perhaps it might, if the embargo on Rice had not been laid illegible, this has Stop'd trade greatly & it will not answer to ship Indigo only, the Loss is too great__ It sells now at £3.5 & £3.10 p lb. but there is very little demand__. it is probable it will raise again [next]¹ November or sooner if the embargo is taken of before that time__

I had bought the greatest part of Negro Cloath when I received your Last Letter viz.   132 Yard at £4.
                                102 ³/₄ Yd. at £5
                                400 ¹/₄ Yd. at £5.5.
which with about 400 Yards on hand Negro Cloth & homespun will be nearly sufficient, Last Year I desired Mr Loveday to make the Men's Jackets like Sailors Jackets ~~with~~ ↑which↓ saved about half Yard to each__ they are to be made in the same Manner this Year__ The above Negro Cloth would sell new at £5.10. to £6. p Yard__ & every body is of Opinion the price will be higher, If you should have an opportunity to procure some at a cheaper rate & get it here in time I would advise to send it ↑still↓ __ It would be of the same advantage to you, as if sent for your own people__ I think it would ↑at↓ least Sell for the price paid for what I have purchased__

The Boat under Command of Scaramouch is not returned from the Southward, I expect her daily__ I Suppose they are gone for another Load of Ruff Rice to Broughton Island__

I have let the Brick tenements at £1000. each. the Southern to John Sandford Dart,² the Northern to Arthur Peronneau's Widow,³ they think you would have Let them at a lower Rent, I tell

---

¹ Manuscript torn.
² John Sandford Dart, a Charleston merchant, was serving as deputy clothier general in South Carolina. *HL Papers*, X, 182n; XIII, 160n.
³ Arthur Peronneau (1735-1774), a Charleston merchant, married Mary Hutson on June 10, 1762. *HL Papers*, III, 31n.

them it is no more, then I pay & the former Rent was £450. as those were__ therefore I can't take less__ Sam[4] & his Boys are now repairing them__ I have not seen Gen[l] Gadsden yet but I shall take an opportunity to communicate to him the paragraph of your Letter concerning him__ Indeed since the meeting of the house a Committee on the Presidents Message, of which I am one has been kept very close to Business from Morning before the Meeting of the house, till Nine & Ten oClock at Night__ the objects under our consideration are the Georgia fruitless expedition, the Creek War a General Amnesty for past offences__ the Riot in Charles Town 5th June on the Presidents proclamation & the Expediency of prolonging the time to take the Oath of Allegeance to the State__ The President likewise notified the Treaty with the Court of france, for which we extend thanks, & requested to lay such parts of the Treaty of Commerce & alliance as had come to his hands before the house, [*torn*] the Creek people__ have [*torn*] agreed to the Report of the Com[e]. they approve the measures already taken by the President, for the defence of the Frontier & recommend to assist Georgia if requisition is made by that State & to take eff eventual measures to carry the War in the Creek Nation, if a treaty of peace by negotiation cannot take place__ Likewise to enquire, if our State or Georgia have been the Occasion of the War, in that case to make them ample reparation__ a General Amnesty unanimously rejected in the Com[e.]__ the Georgia expedition not taken under Consideration yet__ with respect to the Riot after two days examination of Witnesses & Debates__ Resolved not to report upon that part of the Message__ I believe unparlemantary__ And must be made to report__ Reported[5] A further time to be given to the Friends of America who through ignorance or inadvertence have not taken the Oath. recom[dig6] a Bill to be brought in for that purpose. to be taken in consideration to day by the house__

---

[4] HL had purchased "a Mulatto man named Samuel" from Charles and Susannah Lorimer for £1,200 currency on April 11, 1764. Although Samuel was described as a bricklayer, he was apparently well versed in other methods of construction. Sam and the gang of workers which he supervised were sent to HL's plantations as well as his Charleston properties on various projects. Sam died in November 1796. *HL Papers*, IV, 241; Henry Laurens, Jr., to Jonathan Lucas, Nov. 27, 1796, Miscellaneous Collection, ScHi.

[5] "Reported" written in left margin.

[6] "recom[dig]" written in left margin.

Last Sunday Night we had a great riot between the French & American Sailors with Canon & small Arms, three were ↑then↓ killed on the Spot & several dangerously wounded, I went down with the president upon the Bay__ where the balls wisseld round us__ the Militia & regulars were ↑all↓ called under Arms, & Artillery brought up__ but not made use of, & they were pacified about 11 oClock__ on all sides__ Information are now taking to find out if possible who were the Agressors, there has been an old Grudge for some time, & there had been several Skirmishes this fortnight past__ this last Riot seems to have been begun by the French Sailors, but I believe at first they were Ill used by our Seamen__ A Bill is ordered to be brought in for the better regulation of Seamen__ Some people suspect the Tories to have been at the bottom of this disturbance__ They are very troublesome in the back Country__ they have cut of several peoples ears particularly James[7] [torn][8] pleas__ also are [torn][9] Felder[10] has been robbed of every thing in his house, & then the house burnt, he was not at home, otherwise they swore they would put him in the Fire__ one of his Son's was very Ill used__ they also broke open Orangeburgh Goal & let out three prisoners__ This outrages are very alarming as much so as a Creek War__ I omitted to mention one part of the report on that head agreed to, that the best means to keep the Indians quiet would be the possession of Augustine & pensacola, & it is recommended to urge Congress Strongly for Aid to put the measure in execution__ and we expect Congress will pay the expense ↓of the War__↑

One of the Inclosed papers gives a full Acc.t of a duel between Gen.l How & Gen.l Gadsden__ [11]

M.rs Gervais thanks you for your kind remembrance she presents you

---

[7] James Pritchard, a magistrate in Orangeburg District, had his ears cut off in this incident. Salley, *Orangeburg County*, pp. 265, 274; Rawlins Lowndes to HL, Sept. 22, 1778.

[8] One line missing.

[9] One line missing.

[10] Henry Felder (1725?-1780) emigrated from Switzerland and settled in the Orangeburg District in 1735. He operated a store near Orangeburg Township that was destroyed by Loyalists when his house was burned on September 3. He represented St. Matthew parish in the Second Provincial Congress and served in the First and Second General Assemblies. He remained a firm patriot, held the rank of captain in the militia, and died at the hands of Loyalists who attacked his home again in 1780. *Directory of the S.C. House*, III, 228-229; *S.C. General Gazette*, Sept. 10, 1778; *S.C. Gazette*, Oct. 7, 1778.

[11] An account of the duel was printed in the *S.C. General Gazette*, Sept. 3, 1778.

with her best respects the Children are all well__ I am with the Sincerest attachment

Dear Sir / Your affectionate humble / Servant

John Lewis Gervais

SOURCE: RC, Gervais Papers, in private hands; no address; dated "Charles Town 9. Sept^r- 1778."; docketed by HL "John L. Gervais / Esquire 9 Sept^r- 1778 / Reĉd 21 October".

FROM ROMAND DE LISLE[1]

Georgia, September 9, 1778

Honorable Sir,

I embrace Captn- Hancock's Oppty going to Philadelphia to inform you that after coming to Georgia (to take the Command of the Artillery) with Ninety men I had inlisted at my own Expence, except one Thousand Dollars I receiv'd of General Putnam, Sixty four of the Men passed Muster, I am greatly Surprised Colonel White of the fourth Georgia Batt^n- should take upon himself to claim my Men under pretence of his having a power to take into his Batt^n- all the English Deserters;[2] In Consequence of his Behaviour I demanded a Court Martial whose deliberation was that my men should be restored to me, but General Howe did not ratify the Sentence__ I brought from the North Col. White's Battalion which I supplied with every Necessaries and kept in such order as to prevent any Complaints, I have gone so far as to advance part of their pay, but to my Sorrow I am not yet reimbursed I had taken a Resolution to return to you but the General prevented me in order that I should put the Artillery on the best footing possible, nothing being then in Order, and no more than fifty men in the three Companies under my Command, in Consequence of which Small Number I was under the desagreable Necessity of taking men out of

---

[1] Charles Noel Romand de Lisle had served as a major of artillery from Nov. 12, 1776, until April 12, 1777. While he was awaiting a determination on the appeal in this letter, he commanded the American artillery in the Battle of Midway Meeting House in Georgia on Nov. 21, 1778. Heitman, *Continental Officers;* Searcy, *Georgia-Florida Contest,* p. 162.

[2] Col. John White's 4th Ga. Battalion was composed largely of British deserters. Many of his men deserted during the East Florida campaign in the summer of 1778. White was wounded and captured by the British at Savannah on Oct. 9, 1779. He escaped but died of his wounds shortly afterwards. *HL Papers,* XIII, 437, 493; Heitman, *Continental Officers.*

different Corps to enable me to proceed on the last Expedition and that owing to Colonel White taking my men__ I know not what to think of the General respecting Col. White's Conduct, he gave me his word of honor that as soon as the Expedition should be over he would spend a few days to settle that Matter, but as soon as it was at an End he made his exit to Charleston and deigns not even give an Answer to Letters; prior to his Departure I put him in Mind of his promise but he said he'd have nothing to do in it.__ I have no reason to doubt but the Commandants of Brigades have already informed you of what I did to carry on the Expedition therefore will not trouble you with a Recital, I hope their Testimony will be sufficient to convince you of the warm zeal with which I act in your Cause and the Respect I pay to your Orders__

I dare flatter myself you will be kind enough to order either the House of Assembly of this State or the General to take and examine my Accounts, I am very positive your Justice will not Suffer a Stranger to carry on the war at his own Expence__

Prior to the Expedition I was the oldest field officer, the Promotion the General has made, makes me the youngest; it is three years since I am in your Service as Major, if I am to serve as such all my life, I will not repine, but only say that some men are born to be unfortunate and that I am one of them__ I will add Honorable Sir, that it would be necessary to augment the Corps of Artillery of one Company more and have the other three recruited, but the want of Continental Money makes this almost impossible, what I had I have laid out for the Troops, and am sorry to acquaint you that the Georgia Currency is so depreciated that more can be had for one Continental Dollar than for five of the Georgia emission, I have the Honor to be with unfeigned Respect

Honorable Sir, / your most humble, / and obedient Servant,

Romand delisle Major of / artillery Commandant

SOURCE: RC, PCC (Item 78), DNA; addressed on cover "Henry Laurens Esqr· President of þᵉ· / Honorable the Continental Congress / Philadelphia / pr· Favor of / Captn· Hancock__"; addressed below close "Henry Laurens Esqr· President of / the Honorable the Contl· Congress"; dated below close "9th· September 1778__"; docketed "Letter from Major Romand / de Lisle__ Georgia / Sept 9. 1778 / Read Novr· 17. / Referred to the board of war" and "Dec. / Wrote to Gen. Lincoln who / is to determine__".

TO COUNT D'ESTAING

Philadelphia, September 10, 1778

Sir,

I have the honor to inform Your Excellency that your Letters to me of the 8th July and 26th of August have been laid before Congress.[1]

The Trust reposed in Your Excellency by His Most Christian Majesty in your present Command is so high an Evidence of Your Excellency's proved abilities zeal and bravery as to secure your reputation against those injuries which the ill success of the best laid Plans sometimes brings upon less establish'd Characters.

I am to assure you Sir, that Congress, not admitting a doubt of Your Excellency's attachment to the joint interests of your Sovereign and of these United States, have readily concluded that Your Excellency has been influenced in all your aims for the general good since Your Excellency's arrival in America by a strict attention to Your Orders and to the peculiar state of your Squadron under the varying circumstances of time and place.

The People of America must indeed regret the failure of the late Expedition against Rhode Island; but certainly they will not omit to do just Credit to the Martial zeal of their Naval Allies which in pursuit of an hostile fleet was overborne by the power of a sudden and severe Tempest. From such an unfavorable casualty they will look forward, in hopes of Events more consonant to the wise intentions of His Most Christian Majesty, the Glory of his Fleets, and the security and Interest of the United States.

You may be confidant Sir, that every possible aid will be afforded to Your Excellency for the repair of your Ships. The most immediate and active Measures were taken to furnish your Squadron with all the supplies which Congress was at first informed were wanted. The true cause why you did not earlier receive them, was the difference between that facility with which ships move from one place to another, and the embarrassments of a distant land carriage. The Plan for furnishing Your Excellency's Squadron at Sandy Hook

---

[1] D'Estaing's August 26 letter was read in Congress September 9 and a committee composed of Richard Henry Lee, Samuel Adams, Gouverneur Morris, and James Lovell was chosen to draft an answer. The draft was presented the following day and Congress ordered the president to sign and forward it to the admiral. *JCC,* XII, 892, 897.

was rendered abortive by its removal to Rhode Island; and the Provisions ordered for this latter Place were afterwards to be transported by land to Boston.

The Public Officers are now diligently employed in forwarding to that Capital such supplies as Congress have been informed will suffice for the Squadron thirty days, and if more is required to be sent thither Congress will continue in the exertion of every practicable means to comply with Your Excellency's future Requisitions: but it is to be wished that the delay and expence of so long a land Carriage in victualling the Squadron could be prevented by its change of Harbour as speedily as possible to Chesapeak Bay or that of Delaware.

I have the honor to be / With the highest Esteem / & the most profound Respect / Sir / Your Excellency's / Most Obedient and / Most humble Servant[2]

> Henry Laurens.
> President of / Congress.

SOURCE: LS, Archives Nationales; addressed by HL below close "His Excellency / Count d'Estaing / Lieut⋅ General of the Armies / of His Most Christian Majesty / Vice Admiral of His Fleets / And Knight of His Orders."; dated "Philadelphia 10th September 1778". LB, PCC (Item 13), DNA. LB, HL Papers, ScHi.

TO JOHN LEWIS GERVAIS

Philadelphia, September 10, 1778

My Dear Friend

I had the honor of writing to you the 6th Instant by Muckinfuss to which I beg leave to refer, the opinion which I then intimated respecting the Article of Rice, I now confirm, more on your Account than mine; I am altogether indifferent respecting a Concern in any purchase you may think proper to make, except the wish ever uppermost in my mind to promote your Interest. I do not apprehend you will be a loser, should you venture to lay up even ten thousand Barrels, a small Cargo at Egg Harbour or Sinnepuxent will be in a fair way for Count d'Estaings fleet and for further Orders.

---

[2] Close written by HL.

I shall persevere in offering my opinion by every opportunity.

Within the present inclosure you will receive two Newspapers__ also a Copy of Count d'Estaings late letter to Congress and the Answer to it, which shew, that all at present is harmony, altho' I may ~~venture to~~ truly say, and say it with some concern, there is a cursed, unreasonable, impolitic jealousy resting in some Minds, what this observation alludes to will afford Annecdote when I shall have the happiness of seeing you at Ansonburgh__ you will shew these Copies to His Excellency the President, then be so good as to deposit them among my own Papers.

M^r. Timothy Matlack of this City has been so polite and generous as to put into my hands a long Letter which he receiv'd from M^r. Gadsden,[1] and if I understand him right he has hitherto shewn it to no other Person altho' the Author has intimated that it should be shewn to any body ~~and~~ ↑or↓ every body but me; It is highly probable you have seen or learned the Contents of that Letter; as M^r. Gadsden has ↑in this new instance↓ without the least ground, most injuriously and unjustly treated me, first, by what he has written, and aggravated in the second place by his manner of wounding an innocent Man in a secret manner, and at a time when such a stroke in the dark must be most affecting; and as he must feel conviction of his error, I expect from him an immediate and ample acknowledgment to each of the Persons to whom he has written, and to as many as possible to whom he has related such Articles contained in that Letter as respect my Character; even this, will fall far short of that justice which a vindictive Mind would demand, and which a generous Heart would, without prompting, express immediately upon discovery of so great a fault__ I am willing once more to sacrafice at the Shrine of Peace all that I might further with strict propriety exact from him.

You will, I am persuaded Sir, do me the honor to read all the preceding Page to M^r. Gadsden; be so friendly as to transmit me that Gentleman's Answer, which I hope you will obtain in a few plain, explicit Words.[2]

---

[1] A copy of this letter is in the HL Papers, ScHi. This is the copy that Richard Walsh identified and printed as Gadsden to William Henry Drayton, July 4, 1778, although it seems more likely that HL would have a copy of the letter addressed to Matlack. *Writings of Christopher Gadsden* (Walsh), pp. 134-144.

[2] Gervais apparently did not have the opportunity, or more likely, was unwilling to

M^r· Drayton, I find, has a Copy of that Letter, it was from thence he gave me the information which I formerly spoke of, but I had not known he was possess'd of the letter until I mention'd to him this of M^r· Matlack's__ M^r· Drayton expresses himself upon the occasion with much sorrow and concern on my Account. He is also vested with full powers "to make what use he pleases of it, <u>either in Congress or out</u>, but by all means to shew it to Heyward, Mathews and Hudson, and his old particular friends in Congress". Here it was calculated to ruin me among People with whom I live in the strictest harmony, and from whom I have the honor of receiving daily marks of friendship and respect I should have felt the blow, without knowing the hand from whose Art or power it had been struck__ but Alas poor Man! he mistakes his friends as egregiously as he does his Enemies. I do not, my Dear Sir, restrict you from reading the whole of this to M^r· Gadsden if you think proper, but I could wish whatever may be the Event ↑of↓³ this circumstance ↑it↓ may not be talk'd of abroad. I have written in great haste. The dictates of a Heart, honest, feeling, and disposed upon every occasion to pursue such Measures as may produce good effects ↑public & private.↓. My Compliments to each friend ennumerated in many former Addresses, and to all, if any, whom I may have inadvertently omitted.

God Bless you, and keep you in health and Peace.

H.L.

SOURCE: LB, HL Papers, ScHi; addressed "John Lewis Gervais Esquire / Charlestown / by Charles ~~Fish~~ Frisch"; dated "10th September".

TO RAWLINS LOWNDES

Philadelphia, September 10, 1778

I had the honor of writing to Your Excellency on the 6th which I sent after Muckinfuss[1] whom I had engaged to wait eight and forty hours__ business had crouded in upon me for the

---

confront Gadsden on this question and sought Rawlins Lowndes' intervention. While there is no direct response from Gadsden, Gervais reported that Lowndes "says that General Gadsden will make an Apology." John Lewis Gervais to HL, Sept. 9, 21, 1778.

[3] Interlineations here and below by HL.

[1] Michael Muckinfuss (d. 1779) had been a post rider since at least 1773. *HL Papers*, XI, 1.

preceding week in such quantity and numbers as to render it impossible for me to write while he remained in the City__ my Colleague M^(r.) Drayton had detained him five days. I have therefore paid Muckinfuss for the whole, 70 Dollars, which I charge to our State; had we sent a special Express which our variety of Intelligence seemed to call for, the expence would have been ↑ten times as↓ much ~~greater~~

By mere accident I have learned of an opportunity for Charlestown, and have half an hour allowed me to write.

General Sullivan writes the 3^d Inst.[2] that a perfect harmony subsisted between the Count d'Estaing and himself, this points at certain Circumstances which had happened upon the Counts' determination to go into Boston, ↑the knowledge of ~~which~~↓ which Congress had engaged to keep within doors, therefore I have not spoke of them to Your Excellency or any other friend and I think myself not yet releas'd.

The General adds that the British fleet in Boston Bay consists of 8 ships of the line, 10 frigates, one Sloop and a Schooner. They cannot lie there long without coming to blows with the French Squadron whose re-equipment is proceeding with great alcrity and whose Admiral is brimfull of desire for Action.

We are too ignorant of the State of our Enemy's forces in this neighbourhood both on land and water. I am endeavouring since I ~~see~~ ↑perceive↓ the public neglected to collect the fullest intelligence for their benefit.

General Washington the 4^(th) of September says "the desig↑n↓s of the Enemy as to their future movements remain yet entirely unfolded; but the expectation of their leaving the Continent is daily decreasing." The reasons which his Excellency assigns for the ground of this opinion appear to me as good premises for a quite contrary conclusion. M^(r.) Gerard concurs in my sentiments, therefore I am not very presumptuous in saying, that important point remains doubtful; in the mean time I am grieved by knowing from

---

[2] Gen. John Sullivan wrote to General Washington September 3, to assure him "that though the first Struggles of passion, on so important a disappointment, were Scarcely to be restrained" he was able "to restore the former harmony between the American and French Officers." Sullivan asked that a copy of the letter be sent to Congress and Washington enclosed it in his public letter of September 4. George Washington to HL, Sept. 4, 1778. PCC, Item 152, Vol. 6, p. 325ff, enclosure p. 333ff.

General Washington in the same Letter that our Army are again likely to suffer exceedingly for want of Cloaths and Blankets, yet we have been amused for Months past with Reports of Cloathing enough in the public Stores for forty thousand Men.__

The management of Provision is equally improvident, in a word, Sir, every complaint which I have lately made to Your Excellency of the deplorable state of our Affairs gathers strength from every days melancholly experience__ if Congress continues inert, the States will soon be alarmed by informations which will throw the whole into convulsions. I have written in the utmost haste, and under many interruptions and hear the person who is to conduct my Letter calls, and will not be detain'd.

I shall inclose certain Resolves of Congress approving the late conduct at Rhode Island,[3] and two of Dunlaps' Advertisers the Resolves may be published.__ I intimated to the House a Resolve of November last for enquiring into the causes of miscarriage of every Expedition &c. as a bar to hasty approbation and thanks but my sentiments were lost.[4] I have not time to expatiate on a subject which seems to require attention.

On the 5th Inst. a Member of Congress Mr. R. Morris declared in the house in a formal Address to the Chair that the Embargo was not regarded in Maryland, that flour was daily exported thence under, or under the Idea of, Tobacco. The Delegates of Maryland were present.[5] No Contradiction was intimated. No doubts of the fact suggested, and the matter passed over without notice. This is a simple relation of a fact which duty to my Country has prompted.

I have the honor to be &c.

---

[3] Congress passed a series of resolutions September 9 which gave that body's approbation to the retreat from Rhode Island. A vote taken to reconsider the approval of the retreat was defeated ten to two, with HL and South Carolina voting with the minority. *JCC,* XII, 894-895.

[4] After the resolutions approving the retreat from Rhode Island were passed a motion was made "That an enquiry be made into the causes of the failure of the late expedition against Rhode Island, agreeably to the resolution of Congress of November 28, 1777." The motion was set aside. *JCC,* IX, 976; XII, 895-896.

[5] Maryland's delegates present in Philadelphia on September 5 included Samuel Chase, James Forbes, John Henry, and George Plater. On September 11 Congress passed a resolution based on additional information "that several persons in the State of Maryland have eluded the embargo...by loading flour...and obtaining clearance for tobacco." HL informed the governor and council of the concerns of Congress. The governor replied that they would take "vigorous measures" to search Vessels sailing from Maryland ports. *JCC,* XII, 903; HL to Thomas Johnson, Sept. 12, 1778, MdAA; Thomas Johnson to HL, Sept. 17, 1778, PCC, Item 70, p. 277ff.

PS

I have prevail'd on this Messenger to wait a few hours for the benefit of my Colleague, if any thing important shall come to light[6] in the mean time__ your Excellency will be troubled with an additional Postscript

SOURCE: LB, HL Papers, ScHi; addressed "President Lowndes / Charlestown / by Charles Frish"; dated "10th Sept^r·". Copy (19th century), HL Papers, ScHi.

TO WILLIAM SMITH

Philadelphia, September 12, 1778

Dear Sir

I have been twelve days indebted for your favor of the 5th·

The Carriage which I so much troubled you about proved to be extremely dirty, damaged, and unfit for ~~use~~ my use.

The fellows who brought up my Wine tax'd me eight Bottles.

It has been acknowledged that a Member of Congress did give the Information respecting exportation of flour to the Eastern States, intending it only for the private information of your Governor and Council but that you my good friend opened the Letter and let the contents pass under the Eye of several Merchants and others, pray, between you and I, how stands this Mystery?[1]

General Sullivan, you see, made a safe Retreat and Congress have applauded him, this applause would have been in my humble opinion of no less value had it been founded on an inquiry in terms of our Resolution of November last__ it is known to very few, and I do not mean to depreciate General Sullivan's merit when I assure you the Union is indebted to that good Man General Washington for the escape of that part of our Army.

---

[6] From this point postscript copied by HL.

[1] Samuel Chase made the accusation which William Smith denied in his reply to HL. Chase himself disclosed information concerning the flour shortage in New England and the partial lifting of the embargo on August 24 to his business partners John Dorsey and Company. Dorsey immediately contracted for 7,000 barrels of wheat and 400 barrels of flour. Chase denied that he had given secret information but many of his contemporaries believed him guilty. James Haw, et al., *Stormy Patriot, The Life of Samuel Chase* (Baltimore, 1980), pp. 104-110; *JCC*, XI, 831.

The Newspaper under Cover with this will shew you W.H.D vs. British Commissioners,[2] and from a Copy of General Heaths' Letter of the 2nd Inst. you will see Lord Howe is determined at great hazards to attempt a further interview with Count d'Estaing__[3] what if Clinton with his 10,000 should from Rhode Island penetrate to Boston and the Troops of the Convention struggle to join him? Such an attempt would give us some trouble, and might end the War in their ruin__ four or five days will produce great and probably bloody Accounts.__ I write in haste & for your information, don't publish

I am with great regard &c.

SOURCE: LB, HL Papers, ScHi; addressed "The Honble. William Smith Esquire / Baltimore / by Ross"; dated "12th Septr.".

TO GEORGE WASHINGTON

Philadelphia, September 12, 1778

Sir

This will be accompanied by a Letter of the 9th, since which I have had the honor of presenting to Congress Your Excellency's favor of the 7th which the house were pleased to commit to the Board of War.

My present duty is to transmit to Your Excellency the undermentioned Acts of Congress which will be found within the present inclosure.[1]

---

[2] William Henry Drayton's September 4 response to the Carlisle Commissioners' August 26 declaration was printed in the *Pa. Packet,* Sept. 12, 1778.

[3] William Heath informed HL that British vessels had been reported off Nantucket and that Count d'Estaing had stationed his ships nearby and landed forces with cannon "on Hull, Georges Island &c. which Command the entrance...which will render it extremely difficult, if possible, for a Fleet, greater Superior in force, to enter." William Heath to HL, Sept. 2, 1778, PCC, Item 157, p. 194ff.

[1] A committee composed of Robert Morris, William Duer, Richard Henry Lee, and Henry Marchant was appointed September 8 to consider letters of August 31 from deputy commissary of purchases Ephraim Blaine and September 4 from deputy quartermaster general Henry Hollingsworth and George Washington in which each appealed to Congress for action to alleviate the severe shortage of wheat in the Northeast caused by the concentration of four armies (Washington's, Sullivan's, Burgoyne's, and d'Estaing's) east of the Hudson River. The

1. An Act of the 11th Septr. for removing if necessary the Troops of the Convention of Saratoga__ for obtaining Passports for American Vessels to transport Provision and fuel for the said troops__ for establishing Magazines of Provision the Eastern States__ for removing the Cavalry now with the Main Army to pl if their service can be dispensed with, to places where they can be best subsisted, and for reducing the number of Horses kept by Officers in the Army.

2. Duplicate of the Act of the 13th of January last refer'd to in the Act abovemention'd.

I have the honor to be &c.

P.S.[2] since writing the above I have been directed to transmit an Act of Congress of the 4th. Inst. Resolving that no Ratification of the Convention of Saratoga not equivalent to the terms prescribed in the Act of the 8 January last can be accepted which Act will be found inclosed with this & Your Excellency is requested to transmit it to the British Commissioners at New York__[3] & And this Instant the Secretary has bro^{t.} me an Act of the present date for regulating the purchase of forage & other purposes therein mentioned which will be also inclosed__[4]

By an unanimous ballot in Congress on the 10th Inst. Gen̄ John Cadwalader was appointed Brigad^r & Command^r of the

---

acts enclosed were passed in response to the committee's report. Ephraim Blaine to HL, Aug. 31, 1778, PCC, Item 59, Vol. 3, p. 195ff; Henry Hollingsworth to Board of War, Sept. 4, 1778, PCC, Item 78, Vol. 11, p. 321ff; Washington to HL, Sept. 4, 1778, PCC, Item 152, Vol. 6, p. 325ff; *JCC*, XII, 889, 901-903; E. Wayne Carp, *To Starve the Army at Pleasure: Continental Army Administration and American Political Culture, 1775-1783*, (Chapel Hill, N.C., 1984), p. 109.

[2] Postscript by HL.

[3] The resolve made clear that the position of Congress on British ratification of the Convention of Saratoga had not changed. Only ratification that was not subject "to the future approbation or disapprobation of the Crown or parliament of Great Britain, can be accepted by Congress." Washington conveyed the resolution explaining this position to Sir Henry Clinton Sept. 16, 1778. *JCC*, XII, 880-883; *Washington Writings* (Fitzpatrick), XII, 466.

[4] The committee appointed September 8 to consider Blaine, Hollingsworth, and Washington's letters continued to sit and make reports on the shortages suffered by the military in the east September 12. Resolutions in response to this report limited the purchase of "wheat for forage, except in the vicinity of camp, unless in cases of absolute necessity," ordered the commissary department to be careful not to purchase "the bad wheat and offals of wheat" that could not even be used for forage; and, recommended the number of "stationary teams" be reduced and that ox teams be used instead of horse teams when possible. *JCC*, XII, 906.

Cavalry in the service of the United States & on the 9th· a Brevet to rank ~~Lieut~~t· Colo granted to Maj Lewis Morris

SOURCE: LB, PCC (Item 13), DNA; addressed "General Washington / White Plains / by Dodd"; dated "12th Septr·".

FROM GEORGE WASHINGTON
White Plains, N.Y., September 12, 1778

Dear Sir,

A few days ago I wrote, in haste, a Letter to you by Major Morris, and took the liberty of returning the gold you were so obliging as to send me by Jones__ For your kind intention of forwarding that sum, and goodness in bringing Congress acquainted with my want of specie you will please to accept my sincere and hearty thanks__ These are also due to you for your polite attention in forwarding, for my perusal, the late exhibitions of Governor Johnstone, and his brethren in Commission__ That of the former is really a curious performance__ He trys to convince you, that he is not at all hurt by, or offended at the interdiction of Congress__ and, that he is not in a passion; while he exhibits abundant proof that he is cut to the quick, and biting his fingers in an agony of passion.

Your Letter to Colo· Laurens respecting Monsr Galvan was forwarded to Rhode Island while he was on his return from Boston, by which means he missed it__ This Gentn· (if he may be so called, Monsr· Galvan) waited on me a few days ago, and met with þe· reception due to his merit & conduct to you.__ The beginning of the next paragraph of that Letter, excited my curiosity to pursue it to the end, and to my shame, was reminded of my inattention to your favor of the 18th· of June, which coming to hand upon my March thro Jersey, and being laid by to be acknowledged at a time of more leizure, was entirely forgot till your enquiry after the Letters from Messrs· Oswald & Manning recalled it to my recollection__ I now return these Letters, together with Govr· Johnstones, & a tender of my thanks for the favor of perusing them.__ I am convinced that no apology can be more agreeable to you, in excuse for my neglect, than a plain narrative of the truth__ & this I have offered.__

I am sorry to find by your favour of the 29th. Ulto. that Monsr. Gerard was indisposed__ I hope his disorder was not of long continuance, & that he is now perfectly recovered.__ Having often heard this Gentleman spoken of as a wellwisher to, and promoter of the rights of America, I have placed him among the number of those we ought to revere__ Should you therefore see no impropriety in my (being a stranger to Monsr. Gerard) presenting compliments to him, I would give you the trouble of doing this, and of assuring him, that I could wish to be considered (by him) as one of his admirers.

With every sentiment / of esteem & regard / I am Dr Sir / Yr. Oblig'd & Affecte. / Hble Servt

Go: Washington

SOURCE: RC, Rosenbach Foundation; no address; dated "White-plains Septr. 12th. 1778."; docketed by HL "Gen̄ Washington / 12 Septem 1778__. / Recd 15th.". ADraftS, Washington Papers, DLC. Copy, Sparks Collection, MH. Copy (19th century), HL Papers, ScHi.

TO JOHN BEATTY

Philadelphia, September 13, 1778

I had the honor of writing ↑the 23d August↓ an Address to you private, and the 4th Instant another, public, to which I beg leave to refer.

This you will be pleased to receive as of the former Class, a Lady who has much importuned me to contribute my endeavours to effect the Exchange of her Husband a Prisoner in New York, has prevailed so far as to draw a promise from me tr to transmit a Letter which she lately received from the unhappy Captive, in order that you may know his name, and pay that degree of attention to him which is consistent with due preference. I shall inclose with the Letter an Advertiser of Yesterday as a very small compensation for the present trouble.

I Am with great Regard &c.

SOURCE: LB, HL Papers, ScHi; addressed "Colonel John Beaty, Commissary General of Prisoners / Princetown / by Charles Freeman"; dated "13th Septem.~".

TO WILLIAM GREENE

Philadelphia, September 13, 1778

Sir.

I had the honor of addressing Your Excellency the 5th. Inst. by Messenger Brown since which I have received & presented to Congress your favor of the 28th Ulto.

Within the present Inclosure Your Excellency will be pleased to receive the under recited Acts of Congress.

1. An Act of the 8th. Inst. for making up Clothing for the Army from materials in the Eastern States.
2. An Act of the 9th. expressing the high sense which Congress entertain of the Patriotic Zeal of the Eastern States demonstrated on the late Expedition against Rhode Island.
3. An Act of the 12th. for augmenting the Forces under Major Gen. Sullivan in Cases of great emergency__[1]

I have the honor to be / With very great Respect & Esteem / Sir Your Excellency's / Obedient & most hum servt

Henry Laurens.
President of / Congress.

SOURCE: ALS, R-Ar; addressed below close "His Excellency / Governor Greene / Rhode Island &ca."; dated "Philadelphia 13th. Septr 1778.". LB, PCC (Item 13), DNA.

TO JOHN LAURENS

Philadelphia, September 13, 1778

My Dear Son

I had last Evening entertained hopes of paying my Respects to you this Morning in full and proper terms, but after near nine hours drudging at this form, I find myself necessitated to submit to a bare acknowledgment of your favors of the 1st and 2nd Inst.__ you

---

[1] HL sent letters covering the same acts to the executives of Connecticut, New Hampshire, and Massachusetts. HL to Jonathan Trumbull, Sr., Sept. 13, 1778, PCC, Item 13; HL to Meshech Weare, Sept. 13, 1778, MHi; HL to Jeremiah Powell, Sept. 13, 1778, PCC, Item 13.

know, much more satisfactorily than I can express just now, the joy which the former must have afforded me. I congratulate with you on your safety, on your increased honor, on your enlarged Circle of honorable friends. You well know how to make the wisest use of these great gifts of Providence, and I think I feel your Heart swell with grateful thanks to God Almighty.

I earnestly wish to hear from you again, and I long to embrace you, consider my time for residence in this Country will expire the first of November. If I retire without seeing you, what a lump will be dragged from hence to Charlestown, and what a heavy hearted Creature shall I exhibit to our friends there.

Do you never think of your Brother? You know I postponed determinations respecting him upon an opinion of your own. I want much to see you on that important account.

I pray God continue to you his protection.

SOURCE: LB, HL Papers, ScHi; addressed "John Laurens Esquire / White Plains / by Dodd"; dated "13th Septr.".

TO WILLIAM MAXWELL

Philadelphia, September 13, 1778

Sir

I had the honor of addressing you the 13th[1] Instant since which I have received none of your favors.

I now write at the special request of the Honorable the Minister Plenipotentiary of France, and from my own feelings of the necessity of knowing the present state of the British fleet at New York, and if possible the number and strength of the whole Naval Power of Great Britain on this Continent from New York to Hallifax.__ I intreat you, Sir, attempt a proper enquiry and inform me as speedily as possible, whatever expence may attend the essay, shall be reimbursed with thanks.

I have the honor to be &c.

---

[1] HL had last written Maxwell on the 5th and 6th of September.

This will be accompanied by an Advertiser of Yesterday. A private Gentleman a friend of Yours has requested me to add two more with his Wishes that they may get speedily into New York.

SOURCE: LB, HL Papers, ScHi; addressed "Brigadier General Maxwell / Elizabeth Town / New Jersey / by Charles Freeman"; dated "13th Septem.".

FROM JAMES LAURENS

Le Vigan, France, September 14, 1778

My Dear Brother

my Last to you were of 20th: & 25th: June__ since that time I have been waiting with anxious expectation of being made happy by a Letter from your own hand but ~~my~~ ↑wishes are not↓ not yet gratified__ nor have I heard from any Person in Caro: since Mr Hawkins Left it__[1] the public Papers, however, have presented us with your name, on several occasions, & that has afforded us no small consolation, as we may reasonably hope you were in good health at the time of signing those Public Acts__ but when, when, my Dear Brother shall I have the happiness to be inform'd by yr. own hand of your welfare, & my Nephews & the cause of your Long Long silence__ I will endeavour to wait for it with patience not doubting but when that day arrives, I shall receive the utmost satisfaction__

I have defer'd writing you some weeks Longer than I intended, having been much engage'd & concer'd about the State of poor Jno. Petrie, who has been for some time past extreemly ill, & at this period, tho' well enough to come out of his Chamber & to walk on horseback for half a Mile, I fear he will scarcely recover his health, as he has too many sympto↑ms↓ of a confirm'd Consumption, however, his strict attention to a Milk diet, his youth & happy temper, & chiefly the favourable Climate where we find ourselves, makes ↑us↓ to hope & a Skilful Physician who attends him flatters us, that he may yet see health again__ it is with pleasure I can inform you that the rest of my family enjoy tolerable health__ the heat of

---

[1] Philip Hawkins and James Laurens had been partners in the firm Hawkins, Petrie & Co. Hawkins probably left South Carolina after the assets of the firm were divided among the partners in the fall of 1777. John Lewis Gervais had represented James Laurens in the division. *HL Papers*, XII, 13.

the weather before we Left Nismes the beginning of July was very disagreable, & M$^{rs.}$ Laurens fell back amazingly in her health. & I felt my old complaints__ but this wholesome Air[2] & exercise of Riding on horse back. have[3] restored us both so much that we have been at no period since we came to Europe better__ but ↑that I fear↓ may be of short duration as the confinement of winter is generally injurious to us both. my Dear Patsey & Polly are bless'd with the best health__

I mentiond to you in a former Letter ↑& duplicates↓ that M$^{r:}$ Bulman was about quitting his School & M$^{r.}$ Manning wrote me he was at a Loss where to place ~~him~~ ↑my nephew↓ & askd my advice__ [4] I have answerd him that unless he has a much better Sc↑h↓ool in Veiw, I think ~~he~~ Harry will be happy↑er↓ where he is ↑[(]N.B. the school is continued tho' M$^{r:}$ B. quits it)↓ till we shall have your instructions__ as he might meet with many insults at a School where he had no acquaintance, on account of his being an Americain__ I have always had a good character of Harry both from M$^{r:}$ Bulman & M$^{r.}$ Manning with regard his Learning & behaviour & I have great hopes that he will make a Valuable man in whatever ~~illegible~~ profession he shall act in__ we wait y$^{r:}$ directions in regard to his future plan__

A Mons$^{r:}$ Defleury a gentleman of S$^{t:}$ Hipolitte has address'd me, with an earnest request to forward the inclosed Letter thro' y$^{r:}$ hands to his Son, an officer at present in the Am$^{n:}$ service &[5] to pray you to render his son any services in y$^{r:}$ power__ adding "refuse not I entreat you Sir, this Grace, to a father & a Mother who have but this

---

[2] An asterisk at this point refers to the following written on the cover: "Vigan is ab^t 13 leag$^{s:}$ from Nismes in the Cevenne Mountains & is one of the most agreable situations we have met with in france. The Climate perfectly temperate, & free from Musquitto & buggs (w$^{ch:}$ together with the excessive heat & uncommon drought have renderd both Nismes & Montpellier intolerable & very sickly for two Months past)__ Here is besides plenty of good & Cheap Provisions, & polite, Civil inhabitants from whom we receive much courtesy__ as we travel merely for health it has proved a great happiness that we fell in with this retreat w$^{ch:}$ has ~~illegible~~ answ$^{rd.}$ our wishes__"

[3] "have" written over other text.

[4] *HL Papers*, XIII, 499-500; James Laurens to HL., June 25, 1778, HL Papers, ScHi.

[5] "&" inserted in left margin.

[6] Louis de Fleury, born Aug. 28, 1749, at Saint-Hippolyte, in Languedoc, was the son of François de Fleury and his wife Marguerite Domadieu. Major Fleury served as an engineer during the 1777 defense of the Delaware River and become a close friend of John Laurens, who hoped to engage "him as a Colleague, and Coadjutor in raising the famous black Battalion." Balch, *French in America*, II, 125-128; *HL Papers*, XII, 58, 63-65, 398.

only child__["]⁶ I never saw this Gentlemⁿ⁻ but he was strongly recommended to me⁷ by a good friend of mine in this town__ I promised to recommend to you the care of forwarding the Lettʳ⁻ & to communicate the purport of the Father's__ wᶜʰ⁻ is as much as I thought proper to undertake__

I Lately recᵈ⁻ a well wrote Letter from a Young Gentlemⁿ at present Nismes, who signs his Name Henry Laurens__ claims relationship with our family & gives me a Long geneology of his__ he acquaints me with his design to pass Soon to America to improve the patrimony that his Late Fathʳ (a Captain of Infantry) Left him__ he confidently calls for my protection in that Country as a relation to our family &cᵃ⁻__ I highly revere the name, but I doubt the alliance, & as this person produc'd no recommendation & I have no means of informing myself of his Character, I have only said to him that a Man of Merit can hardly fail to do well in America & wish him Success__ should he go there, there is no doubt he will find out his Name Sake & you will best judge what regard to pay him

My good friends Mʳ⁻ & Mʳˢ⁻ Delagayé⁸ of Nismes & Mʳ⁻ & Mʳˢ⁻ Wilkie⁹ of Marseille always desire to be presented in the Most friendly terms to you__ My dear Mʳˢ⁻ Laurens, Patsy, Polly & J. Petrie join me in the most sincere, wishes for your, & my dear Nephews health, & happiness & that our Country may very soon flourish in Peace within herself & with all the World__

I remain, with unalterable esteem, my Dear Brother's / very Affectionate friend & Servᵗ

Jaˢ⁻ Laurens

SOURCE: ALS, HL Papers, ScHi; addressed "Henry Laurens Esqʳ⁻"; dated "Le Vigan__ Cevennes__ Languedoc / September 14ᵗʰ⁻ 1778."; docketed by HL "James Laurens / 14 Septʳ⁻ 1778 / Recᵈ⁻ 25 Augᵗ 79".

---

⁷ "e" written over "y".

⁸ John Delagaye married Catherine Gaudie in St. Helena parish in 1737. He sailed from Beaufort, where he was a merchant, for London in 1769 and settled at Nimes. *HL Papers*, VI, 434n; IX, 595n.

⁹ James Wilkie, an Englishman, was a member of the Marseilles merchant firm of Sollicoffre Freres & Wilkie, whom HL visited in 1772 and from whom subsequently purchased wine and soap. *HL Papers*, VIII, 587, 625; *Franklin Papers* (Labaree), XXIV, 261n.

TO JOHN LEWIS GERVAIS

Philadelphia, September 15, 1778

My Dear Sir

I had the pleasure of writing to you the 10th Instant by M[r.] Frisch,[1] a chance opportunity, this will go by such another__ a M[r.] Whitney,[2] his short notice, and the extreme long sittings of Congress afford me very few minutes for paying my respects to private friends.

Inclosed with this you will find a Character of Joshua Brown, said to be imprisoned in Ninety six Goal, I intreat you Sir, interest yourself as speedily as possible in this Mans case, and if it may be done without offence to the laws of the Land obtain his enlargement and supply him on my Account with such Money as may be needful to help his return to Philadelphia. I need say no more on this occasion, you will take every necessary step for relieving a Man from suffering, if it has been brought on him from mistake of his Person, Principles or Conduct.[3]

The Subscribers to this Paper are all Quakers. There have been several little Addresses from these People to me which indicate a desire to be reconciled to the present ruling Powers__ and one of a very extraordinary extent to M[r.] Gerard which the Minister detailed to me last night, strengthens my belief__ I have promised one of the principal Persons of the Society a meeting for conferring on subjects which we have barely sketch'd, I am to point the time, but when shall I have leisure?

There are now strong Prognostics of an evacuation of New York by the Enemy, none stronger in my Mind than the advances

---

[1] Charles Frisch (Frish) served with the German Fusiliers of Charleston during the siege of Savannah in 1779. Moss, *S.C. Patriots.*

[2] Lebbeaus Whitney served 48 days as a horseman in 1779. Moss, *S.C. Patriots.*

[3] Joshua Brown, a Quaker minister from Little Britain in Lancaster County, Pa., set out in February 1778 to visit Quaker meetings in Virginia and the Carolinas. Along the way he was joined by Achilles Douglas of Virginia and Uriah Carson of North Carolina. When the three reached Ninety Six, they were arrested for refusal to take the oath of allegiance to the state. They also refused to give security to leave the state or cooperate in an effort to banish them to Europe. In July, after more than two months at Ninety Six they were sent to Charleston. In October 1778 the legislature authorized the president to release the Quakers from confinement and allow them to return to their residences. Brown returned to Pennsylvania some time in December 1778. "The Case of Joshua Brown for Henry Laurens Esq[r.] President of Congress," Sept. 12, 1778, HL Papers, ScHi; A.D. Bradley, "Joshua Brown, Prisoner for Conscience Sake," *Journal of the Lancaster County Historical Society,* LXXXI (1977), 25-29; Stephen D. Weeks, *Southern Quakers and Slavery, A Study in Institutional History* (Baltimore, Md., 1977), p. 187; *S.C. Statutes,* IV, 452.

which these friends are making. They have always been in the Secrets of the opposite Party, having Emissaries in each, and I am persuaded their Religious Principles will lead them to abide with the strongest, provided they may do so in Peace and free from persecution.__ The Policy of America will be to retain them after Independence is established in the enjoyment of all their ancient privilidges.

The Newspapers which you will receive under this cover together with Extracts of Letters from General Washington, General Heath, General Sullivan and Colonel Laurens will inform you the present Intelligence. I have not time to comment__ Lord Howe's leaving Boston Bay and appearing off Rhode Island is the only inexplicable Manouvre__ a few days will clear up doubts.

I have long predicted what has happened at Bedford,[4] and I dread such a stroke every hour in this River, the Enemys' great policy is to ruin our navigation, and here have we been sitting near three Months, and nothing done to prevent four frigates from destroying every ship and other Vessel accumulated at the Wharves of this City and laying the Town in ashes or under contribution of Money or Members of Congress.

Be so good as to communicate the inclosed intelligence to His Excellency the President, the late President, and other friends and all of it that is proper to the Public.

My thoughts are to return to my own Country early in November, but I am staggered when Mr. Mathews tells me that he must absolutely go home in that Month__ the remaining Representation will not be competent, for if one happens to be sick or absent, you will have no Vote.

Mr. Whitney calls and presses to be discharged.__
Present me as usual to all friends, and believe me to be
    With the utmost Regard &c.

---

[4] The British army that arrived at Newport after Sullivan's evacuation conducted an expedition along the Massachusetts coast September 4-6. Gen. Charles Grey, under orders from Sir Henry Clinton, destroyed numerous privateer and merchant vessels as well as large portions of New Bedford and Fairhaven. John Sullivan's September 10 letter reporting the attacks was enclosed with a September 12 letter from General Washington that had been read in Congress the previous day. Ward, *War of the Revolution*, II, 593; *JCC*, XII, 913.

M[r.] F. Kinloch[5] lately from New York brought me a message from M[r.] R. Williams whom he left 5 days ago in that City__ M[r.] Williams and ↑several↓[6] other late Inhabitants of S[o.] Carolina and Georgia were attempting a Voyage to Charlestown under a flag of Truce, 'tis probable therefore you will soon see them.[7]

SOURCE: LB, HL Papers, ScHi; addressed "John Lewis Gervais Esquire / Charlestown / by Lebbeaus Whitney"; dated "15th Septem.~".

TO WILLIAM READ

Philadelphia, September 15, 1778

Dear Sir

I don't know where your favor of the 5th has been detained, but it reached me no earlier than the present morning and unluckily half an hour too late for a conveyance to South Carolina of the letter to your Brother.[1]

Your returning health is a subject for congratulation. I hope the present temperate weather will confirm it in strength and vigor. When you have occasion for Money, draw on me without apology, and your Bills shall be honored, or, if it suit you better, I will transmit the sum necessary, by such hand as you shall direct.

The latest News from Charlestown is unpleasant, the shipping in the Harbour had suffered greatly in the late tempest which

---

[5] Francis Kinloch (1755-1826), a South Carolinian, had been sent to England for his education in 1768 and Switzerland in 1774 where he was a classmate of John Laurens. He returned to America in 1778 fearing his estate in South Carolina might be confiscated. He volunteered for service in the Continental army, was present at the Battle of Port Royal, wounded during the siege of Savannah, and taken prisoner at the fall of Charleston. He served one term in the Continental Congress (1780-1781) and several in the South Carolina legislature (1779-1780, 1787-1791). *HL Papers*, IX, 227n; *Directory of the S.C. House*, III, 402-405.

[6] Interlineation by HL.

[7] The cartel arrived in Charleston on October 9 with Robert Williams, Jr. (d. 1808) and his son Robert (b. 1761); John Hopton, HL's former clerk; and Georgians William Telfair, Charles Price, Jr., and James Graham. *S.C. General Gazette*, Oct. 15, 1778.

[1] William Read, a South Carolinian who had planned to offer his services as a physician at General Washington's camp, stopped at the Princeton General Hospital where Dr. William Shippen induced him to stay to assist with the troops wounded during the Battle of Monmouth and other clashes during the British evacuation through New Jersey. About the time he was ready to continue his journey to camp he was "seiz'd with a Putrid Fever & lay for many days in a deplorable situation." His letter of September 5 was addressed from Princeton and enclosed one for his brother, Jacob Read, which he requested HL "please forward...by first opportunity." *HL Papers*, XIII, 78; William Read to HL, Sept. 5, 1778, HL Papers, ScHi.

seems to have taken its course from the Gulph of Florida along Shore to Newfoundland, the Column was wide, since we find many Vessels were destroy'd by it an hundred leagues from the Coast__ in Charlestown 'tis said about 20 Vessels were lost or had suffered great damage in the harbor__ but this I apprehend will be trifling when compared with the loss of the Planters Crops of Indigo and Rice, of which I have not yet received accounts.

I have not receiv'd or seen a Letter for you since your departure, an Express Messenger from Charlestown has been some days due to me, I expect every day his appearance; depend upon it Sir, if he imposts any dispatches for you, they shall be immediately forwarded, and now that I know where to address, you may expect to receive from me the Carolina Gazettes when such come to my hands.

I am with great Regard &c.

SOURCE: LB, HL Papers, ScHi; addressed "Doctor William Read, General Hospital, / Princetown / by Isaac Fitsworth to be deliverd Mr· Humphreys"; dated "15th Septr·". Copy (19th century), HL Papers, ScHi.

FROM JOHN LAURENS

White Plains, N.Y., September 15, 1778

My dear father.

I avail myself of Col Bannisters[1] offer to have the pleasure of writing to you__ The intelligence which we have received since my last, confirm the idea of a grand move on the part of the enemy__ A British Matross who deserted the day before yesterday, declares that he assisted in embarking Artillery and Stores__ and says that five thousand troops are destined for the West Indies__ an accounts received some days since of taylors being employed in stripping Regimental Coats of their Linding and making up thin overalls and Waistcoats indicate an expedition to[2] a warmer climate, than any that in[3] the territories of the United States, in the approaching Season__ It is reported[4] that many Merchants are disposing of their

---

[1] John Banister, a Virginia delegate, was in camp as a member of the Committee of Arrangement. *Delegate Letters* (Smith), X, xxii.

[2] "to" written over "in".

[3] "i" written over "o".

[4] "reported" written over other text.

Wares by Vendue, at low rates__ I am not acquainted with the persons to[5] whom we are indebted for intelligence and therefore cannot be sure whether they are the dupes of reports circulated by the enemy or give us a relation of facts that may be depended on__ There appears to be no other object here for the enemy but the French Squadron__ nor elsewhere but the french Islands__ ~~and~~ either will require an exertion of their whole force__ and the latter perhaps will upon several accounts be prefered__ Some people are of opinion that they will aim first at the ruin of the squadron, and then direct their whole force against some french Island__ It ~~will~~ ~~illegible~~ is difficult to predict what measures will be pursued by men, who have been so excentric in their military operations__

If they had been vigorous the french Squadron might have fallen a sacrifice, and it would have been a tottering Stroke to the Marine[6] of France__ but their delay and the disposition which has been made by our General__ have I hope pretty well secured an object of such importance to the common cause__ It is to be urged in Excuse[7] for them, that Byrons fleet suffered by a storm & that the Crews belonging to it are in very bad health__ The division of Six ships under Rear Admiral Parker at New York, has been obliged to land, five hundred, some say a thousand men__ besides you know two of this fleet, (one of them the Admirals ship,) are said to be missing__ & one to have put back to Portsmouth__[8]

The Army will move from its present position to morrow morning__

God preserve you my dear father.

John Laurens.

Mr Galvan an officer in one of our Carolina Regiments brought me two Letters of very particular Recommendation from Bn de

---

[5] "to" written over "from".

[6] "Marine" written over "alliance".

[7] "E" written over other text.

[8] Admiral John Byron's squadron composed of fourteen vessels was separated during a gale and subsequent fog off Newfoundland. When Byron sighted the New England coast he was sailing alone. During the voyage each captain had reported numerous members of the crew incapacitated with "jail fever" (possibly typhus) or scurvy. Rather than New York, he sailed to Halifax to have his ship *Princess Royal* repaired. Admiral Hyde Parker the elder, *Royal Oak*, second in command in the squadron, had put in at New York with most of the other vessels. Byron arrived at Sandy Hook on September 16. The ship *Russel*, Francis S. Drake, returned to England because of storm damage. Tilley, *British Navy*, pp. 146-147, 153-154, 164-165.

Holdzendorff and Mr Reid__ ⁹ Some of our family informed me that in a Letter to me which I have not yet received, this ~~Gentleman~~ ↑Person↓ was mentioned in such a manner as excluded him from favor__ When he called upon me therefore, I did not introduce him to the General__ he found means however to introduce himself and ask the Generals protection__ The Genl· asked me in private whether this was not the person alluded to in your letter__ I told him he was__ the Genl· then left the room without taking any farther notice of him__ Galvan finding he had so little encouragement to stay__ ~~he~~ retired__ yesterday he came again and produced a letter which he said he intended to send to you__ ~~and~~ in which he desires that through my mediation he might¹⁰ be restored to your friendship__ and desired my leave to send it__ I told him he was the master to write that he pleased but that ~~it~~ I¹¹ should not confirm that in my letters to you__ he asked me the reason of the cold reception which the Genl· had given him__ I told him I must frankly inform him that we had all heard very serious matters to his disadvantage__ and besides that as his only object here was to serve as a Volunteer__ he might depend upon it__ that there was no opening for him__ he asked me whether I had received any Letter from you respecting him__ I told him I had not__ he desired to have an opportunity of justifying himself before the General__ but this I waved__ I was then called off for some business__ and he went away saying that he would call again__

SOURCE: ALS, Kendall Collection; addressed on cover "(Private) / ~~THis~~ Excellency__ / Henry Laurens Esqr- / President of Congress / Philadelphia"; dated "Head Quarters 15th Septem 1778."; docketed "John Laurens / 15th· Septem̄ 1778".

FROM WILLIAM HENRY DRAYTON

Philadelphia, September 16, 1778

D^r· Sir.

I cannot but frankly confess myself hurt at the manner & substance of your expressions to me, when I was in conversation

---

⁹ Louis-Casimir, baron de Holtzendorff and Jacob Read.
¹⁰ "might" written over "may".
¹¹ "I" written over "w".

with M^r· Adams upon the adjournment of Congress today: I should not have been hurt at either had you thought proper to have used them in private.

As it is your right to make any representation on my conduct, that you may think proper to be made, it is not possible for me to be hurt at your exercise of it; especially as I know, any such representation could proceed only from your sense of your duty to the public, & that if you make it, you will think it proper to furnish me with a copy of it.__ In a word the intention of this note is only to desire, that to the many marks of your friendship which I have received & feel, you will be so obliging as to add this: That when you differ in opinion with me, & think my conduct deserving of your disapprobation, you will reserve the subject for a private hour. You know I always communicate to you, my ideas & intended conduct, & that I always receive your advice with defference & as marks of your regard.[1] Being, D^r– Sir,

      Your most obed^t– & / most humble Ser^t–

            Wm H^y Drayton.

SOURCE: RC, Emmet Collection, NN; cover in HL Papers, ScHi; addressed on cover "His Excellency / Henry Laurens Esqr–"; dated below close "Sep. 16. 1778"; docketed "The Hoñble / William Henry Drayton Esqr· / 16th September 1778.".

TO WILLIAM HENRY DRAYTON[1]

            Philadelphia, September 16, 1778

Dear Sir__

     I am not ashamed, & particularly to you to acknowledge[2] a fault__ the declaration ~~which~~ you allude to was improper, ↑on my p[*art*]↓ as well in ↑the m[*ode*] of↓ address as in point of time__ chafed by the daily waste of the most precious moments of these

---

[1] The subject of the disagreement between HL and Drayton is unclear but Laurens apparently apologized. See HL to William Henry Drayton, [Sept. 16, 1778].

[1] Date and identification supplied by editors. This draft was written in response to Drayton's letter to HL of Sept. 16, 1778.

[2] "k" written over other text.

Orphan States, ↑& [*thrown*] ↑into the bargain↓ I was ↓when at liberty↑ hurried into expressions ~~of~~ ↑of↓ which a designing Man would have ~~h__~~ ↑avoided__↓ I am sure ↑upon this confession↓ you will forgive me & that you will not entertain a thought so injurious to me, as that I would make ~~any~~ ↑a↓ representation ↑in which your Name should appear↓ without your ~~knowledge~~ ↓privity↑__ I have no Idea of making any which can glance the least dishonor on you ~~which~~ ↑as↓ I shall explain when I have the honor of meeting you next which I wish may be in the course of the present day ~~in the mean time I solemnly declare most~~ ↑but further pardon me for says↓ with equal candor ~~confess~~ that I lament your being engaged as you are, if I ~~mistaken believe which may probably be the case~~ ↑am in an error↓ beleive me all that I have said to you on the subject at different times ↑has↓ arisen³ from a very sincere regard for your ~~honor~~, ↑your ~~self~~ ↑Character↓ in an extensive view__↓ ~~I am not afraid to say to a Gentleman of your candor & good sense that you do not appear competent to the particular point~~

SOURCE: ADraft, HL Papers, ScHi; no address; no date.

TO GEORGE WASHINGTON

Philadelphia, September 16, 1778

Sir

I had the honor of addressing Your Excellency under the 12ᵗʰ Insᵗ· by Dodd, and have in the mean time receiv'd & presented to Congress Your Excellencys' favors of the 11ᵗʰ and 12ᵗʰ.¹ In answer to the latter, I am directed to intimate, "That Congress highly approve of laying up Magazines of forage and Provisions at such places as Your Excellency shall judge proper for prosecuting an Expedition into Canada in the Winter, if the motions of the Enemy shall render the measure expedient." And Your Excellency is

---

³ "n" written over "s".
¹ HL was apparently confused over the dates of Washington's recent letters. The two public letters mentioned here were both dated Sept. 12, 1778. HL also received a private letter from Washington on that date. See above.

"desired to make every preperation of Cloathing, Snow Shoes, and other articles for this purpose which you shall deem necessary."[2]
I have the honor to be &c.

SOURCE: LB, PCC (Item 13), DNA; addressed "General Washington / by Isaac Fitsworth"; dated "16th Septr.".

TO JOHN LAURENS

Philadelphia, September 17, 1778

My Dear Son

My last was under the 13th Instant, I am now to thank you for your several favors of the 10th, 12h and 12th Inst. continue your intelligent correspondence by every opportunity I intreat you, and be as ample as circumstances will possibly admit of.

I shall upon every occasion pay particular attention to those brave officers whose names you have specified. It mortifies me exceedingly to see a Gentleman of Mr. Ternants' merit held in suspense without ability on my part to afford him any aid__[1] I can do no more than ask him to a Dinner and entertain him civily.

Can you, my Dear Son, appologize for asking me to supply you with common necessaries? You know nothing affords me more pleasure than acting the part of your Friend.

The first proper person going to Camp shall be the Bearer of Money, and probably of a Piece of Linnen. I presume you may get it converted into shirts with as much accuracy & expedition at Camp, as any where else.

---

[2] The letter alluded to enclosed a report Washington requested from a board of his officers appointed "to consider what would be the most eligible plan for invading Canada; in case our future prospects and circumstances should justify the enterprize." Congress approved the report on September 16. Report for a Proposed Canadian Expedition, Sept. 10, 1778, PCC, Item 152, Vol. 6, p. 355ff; *JCC*, XII, 919.

[1] Baron von Steuben had requested September 5 that Jean-Baptiste de Ternant, a volunteer, be appointed an Inspector of Light Troops and be given a lieutenant colonel's commission. Congress did not act on the request until September 25 when Ternant received the commission to date from March 26 and was transferred to become inspector of troops in South Carolina and Georgia. Baron von Steuben to HL, Sept. 5, 1778, PCC, Item 164, p. 146ff; *JCC*, XII, 904, 952; *HL Papers*, XIII, 37n; HL to Baron von Steuben, Sept. 17, 1778, NHi.

If I had been where you were treated with so much hospitality I should have been invited to accept the same sort of kindness, although the Person knows I hold him extremely cheap, because I have detected him in some mean, and even in some dishonest Acts, therefore, I am sorry it has happened that you are laid under any obligations, especially as I am told you are more indebted to the Creditors of the Person than to himself__ This is a disagreeable subject, but you know I hate Impostors, and I believe there never was a greater__ but dont misunderstand me, I never passed an angry word with the Man in my life; my present sentiments are not new, they are grounded in observation and conviction.[2]

Your friend F. Kinloch will probably[3] salute you in Camp this day se'nnight[4] another friend of yours R. Berresford[5] is in New York. I hope to obtain permission for his coming here in a few days, this indeed should have been done four days ago, but M^r. Kinloch had omitted till last evening to deliver me a message from M^r. Berresford.

M^r. Robert Williams, his son, and many other Carolina and Georgia Gentlemen are also in New York, among them M^r. J. Hopton__ [6] the Chief Justice assures me this young Gentleman and my old friend R.W. will meet the people in Charlestown full of resentment against them.

---

[2] Probably John Hancock at whose home JL stayed in Boston in early September. HL had made similar unfavorable comments about him in January 1778. *HL Papers*, XII, 270; Massey, "A Hero's Life," p. 286; JL to John Hancock, Sept. 12, 1778, PHi.

[3] First "b" written over "p".

[4] "night" written by HL.

[5] Richard Beresford (1755-1803) had been taken to England to study following his father's death in 1772. JL knew him both in Charleston and England where they read law at the Middle Temple. Beresford was returning to Charleston by way of New York to practice law. He, like some of the others returning at this time, may have been motivated by a South Carolina act passed March 28, 1778, which included a provision to double tax all absentees who had reached the age of twenty-one. He served in the military under Isaac Huger in Georgia in 1778, and was an aide to William Moultrie at the fall of Charleston. He served in the General Assembly (1782), was elected lieutenant governor (1783), and sat in the Continental Congress (1783-1784). *HL Papers*, IX, 47n; X, 11, 33; *Directory of the S.C. House*, III, 67-68; Rogers, *Evolution of a Federalist*, p. 83n.

[6] John Hopton (b. 1748), a former clerk in the firm of Austin and Laurens, established a mercantile partnership in Charleston with Robert William Powell and Samuel Brailsford in 1770. Hopton fled South Carolina in 1777, but lost a cargo of indigo he carried to privateers. He sought to return to South Carolina to settle his firm's accounts. Eventually he proclaimed his allegiance to England and left Charleston at the end of the occupation. *HL Papers*, I, 102n; VII, 176n, 250n; Loyalist Transcripts, LIV, 509-530.

M[r.] H. Peronneau[7] and his brother in law M[r.] Cooper[8] are both at New Providence waiting, no doubt, for the moving of the Waters. How very kind Great Britain has been to her Votaries. How very unkind these devotees, to themselves and their families.

Sir E.L. M[r.] Kinloch informs me is wretched and he will relate to you the melancholly Catastrophe of the unfortunate M.B.[9]

I again recommend to your serious Consideration the near approach of the 1st of November. I do not say that I shall leave Philadelphia immediately after its arrival, nor can I promise not to leave it on the 2[nd.] I have a duty to you, to your Brother, to your sisters, and some to myself which call loudly on me. My Country is like all other collective Bodies extremely easy when they can get a Man to serve them diligently and faithfully, be the consequence to himself what it may, even Ruin.

God Bless, ~~you~~ and keep you in health and safety.

P.S.

Inclosed you will ~~receive~~ find 2 Letters from England, and a Newspaper.

SOURCE: LB, HL Papers, ScHi; addressed "Colonel John Laurens / Head Quarters / by Isaac Fitsworth"; dated "17th September".

---

[7] Henry Peronneau (d. 1785) had been a treasurer of South Carolina from 1770 until his removal in April 1776. A Loyalist, he sailed from South Carolina in April 1777 to settle in England. He returned to Charleston during the occupation but left permanently with the British. *HL Papers*, XI, 328n; Loyalist Transcripts, LII, 505-532.

[8] The Rev. Robert Cooper had come to South Carolina from Wales in 1758, served as an assistant minister at St. Philips, and in 1761 became rector at St. Michaels Church. He refused to take an oath of allegiance to the new state and was dismissed in July 1776. He left Charleston in April 1777 but returned to become rector of St. Philips during the occupation. He was married to Henry Peronneau's sister Ann. Cooper sailed for England when the British evacuated and died there about 1812. *HL Papers*, XI, 232n; Loyalist Transcripts, LII, 658-590; *SCHM*, XXXVIII (1937), 120-125.

[9] Mary (Molly, Molsey) Bremar, the daughter of HL's sister Martha (d. 1769) and Francis Bremar, had been the ward of her brother-in-law Egerton Leigh. In 1774 Mary, probably as a consequence of a relationship with Leigh, delivered an infant who died shortly thereafter. HL, who had clashed with Leigh during the late 1760s over the latter's Vice Admiralty Court rulings, vilified Leigh and attempted to redeem his niece. She remained "a strange girl, discontented and flighty" and may have hastened her own death in December 1777 with laudanum. *HL Papers*, X, 13n; XIII, 500n; Philip C. Yorke, ed., *Diary of John Baker* (London, 1931), p. 428.

TO BARON VON STEUBEN

Philadelphia, September 17, 1778

Dear Sir__

Notwithstanding my promise which was really grounded on determination to pay my respects to you the 14th– this is the first moment I have been able to redeem for that purpose since my last of the 13th·__

I think it fortunate to your self that you did not proceed to Rhode Island,[1] it would have been on every account a disagreeable embassy.

The Commander in Chief having returned ↑to Congress↓ the report of the Committee on the Inspectorate with His Excellency's remarks & observations the whole is recommitted & will probably be soon reported on, but the House is so overcharged with business as renders it impossible even to guess at a time when it will be taken under consideration & concluded.[2]

My Man James having been sick for several days & no ↑other↓ person in my house knowing where to find your Servants, I can only hope that Mr· Peters[3] & Mr· Melcher[4] have done the needful, nevertheless I shall request Major Young while I am at Congress this Morning to make special enquiries & if there shall remain any room for my interposition, it will be immediately applied & you shall be further informed.

Nothing, I am extremely sorry to say it, is yet reported respecting Mr· Ternant, I am grieved to see this meritorious Officer kept in suspense.

---

[1] Von Steuben arrived at White Plains, N.Y. on August 31 and remained at headquarters until November 13, when he returned to Philadelphia. Palmer, *Von Steuben*, pp. 197-199.

[2] The committee, composed of Joseph Reed, Elias Boudinot and Samuel Chase, submitted a report on August 20 based on Steuben's ideas for reorganizing the Inspector General's office. Washington reviewed the report and concluded on September 12 that the "plan...is upon too extensive a Scale and comprehends powers so numerous and enlarged, as will naturally expose it to the jealousy and disapprobation of the Army." A new plan devised by the Committee of Arrangement was approved Feb. 18, 1779. *JCC,* XI, 737, 819-823; XII, 914; XIII, 196-197; *Washington Writings* (Fitzpatrick), XII, 438-444.

[3] Von Steuben had been forced to leave Philadelphia suddenly and as a consequence had outstanding accounts with a tailor and a saddler which he sent to Richard Peters, assuring that he would "take care to acquit them as soon as it is in my power" and that he wished "those good people might not be alarmed for their payment." Baron von Steuben to HL, Sept. 6, 1778, Kendall Collection.

[4] Von Steuben had requested that barrack master Col. Isaac Melcher gather "My whole Baggage, maps, plans, papers, &c...to order them immediately to Camp". Von Steuben to HL, Sept. 6, 1778, Kendall Collection.

Be assured Dear Baron my inclinations are warm for rendring you every service in my power, that I will embrace every opportunity of confirming this assurance, proving that I am with great truth,

Dear Sir / Your most obedient / & Most humble servant

Henry Laurens,

SOURCE: ALS, Steuben Papers, NHi; addressed below close "The Honorable / Major General Baron Stüben"; dated "Philadelphia 17th. Septem~ / 1778__"; docketed "Phila 17 Septr 1778 / H Laurens.". LB, HL Papers, ScHi.

FROM WILLIAM LIVINGSTON

Princeton, N.J., September 17, 1778

Dear Sir

I have very little faith in dreams; but whenever those unaccountable Visions of the Night make so strong an Impression upon the Sensorium as that I can recollect in the morning whole Paragraphs and Pages of what I dream't I read or heard while asleep I always commit them to writing for the sake of observing the difference between one's sleeping and waking Vagaries; And ↑as↓ the former with respect to myself may at this time of life be full as sensible & entertaining as the latter, I take the Liberty to send your Excellency my last Nights dream, which to prevent any suspicion of wilful defamation & recollecting that during the reigns of the roman Emperors many a poor fellow was capitally punished for dreaming about his Superiors, I shall communicate to no body but yourself__

Methought a little fairy ten thousand times as handsome as the most beautiful Tory ↑Lady↓ in Philadelphia with her top gallant Commode stood at my bed side (she must either have come thro' the keyhole or a broken pane of Glass as I am possitive the Door was locked) & delivered me a Paper with the Indentical Words contained in the enclosed & then instantly vanished without uttering a Syblable except "<u>But Virtue is its own reward</u>."

I am / With the highest respect / Your Most Obed Servt.

Wil: Livingston

Enclosure

FACTS.

The largest return of the army commanded by Major-General Sullivan in his attempt against Rhode Island, never amounted to ten thousand men; so that the militia of the eastern States which joined him could not have exceeded five thousand men.[1]

To join his Excellency General Washington in his pursuit of the enemy thro' New-Jersey, the firing of a tar-barrel, and the discharge of a cannon, instantly collected four thousand of our militia in the time of harvest, to co-operate with the grand army.[2]

The eastern volunteers, which composed great part of General Sullivan's army, returned home before his retreat.

The Jersey militia continued with General Washington till the enemy was routed, and their assistance no longer necessary.

General Sullivan seems rather to complain of the eastern militia's *going off, and reducing his numbers to little more than that of the enemy.*[3]

General Washington declares his deep sense of the service of the New-Jersey militia, *in opposing the enemy on their march from Philadelphia, and for the aid which they had given in harassing and impeding their motions, so as to allow the continental troops to come up with them.*[4]

---

[1] In mid August Sullivan reported that his forces numbered 8,174 including nearly 7,000 militia—but far less than expected because of the poor militia turnout from the Eastern states. The militia promised by Rhode Island amounted only to 1,128 instead of 3,000; by Massachusetts, 1,386 instead of 3,000; by Connecticut, 412 instead of 1,500. John Sullivan to HL, Aug. 16, 1778, Gratz Collection, PHi; John Sullivan to William Green, Aug. 18, 1778, *Sullivan Papers* (Hammond), II, 229.

[2] Approximately 6,800 New Jersey militiamen were mustered during the movement of the British army through the state after the evacuation of Philadelphia. *Livingston Papers* (Prince), II, 442n.

[3] HL in his frequent correspondence with Livingston may have enclosed copies or extracts from his Rhode Island dispatches. Sullivan had informed HL on August 31 that he had to forego any plans for a direct assault on the British installation after he "found to my great surprize, that the Volunteers which compos'd great part of my Army, had returnd, and reduced my Numbers to little more than that of the Enemy, between two and three thousand return'd in the Course of twenty four Hours."

[4] Livingston paraphrased the portion of Washington's July 1, 1778, report on the battle of Monmouth in which he wrote "that on the appearances of the enemy's intention to march through Jersey becoming serious, I had detached General Maxwells Brigade, in conjunction with the Militia of that State, to intercept and impede their progress, by every obstruction in their power, so as to give time to the Army under my command to come up with them." PCC, Item 152, Vol. 6, p. 147.

The honourable the Congress, by their resolve of the 10th instant, declare their *high sense* of the patriotic exertions made by the four eastern States on the late expedition against Rhode Island.[5]

But

By no resolve did Congress ever manifest *any sense* of the patriotic exertions of the State of New-Jersey in twice putting the enemy to rout, in their march through that State, with nearly their whole army.

Oberon, Chief of the Fairies.

SOURCE: RC, HL Papers, ScHi; addressed on cover "To / His Excellency Henry Laurens Esqr / President of Congress / Philadelphia"; addressed below close "His Excellency / Henry Laurens Esq"; dated "Princeton 17th. Sep[tr.] 1778"; docketed by HL "Gov[r.] Livingston / 17 Sept[r.] 1778 / Ans[d] 1 Octob". Copy (19th century), HL Papers, ScHi. The enclosure is printed in Theodore Sedgwick, Jr., *A Memoir of the Life of William Livingston* (New York, 1833), pp. 305–307.

FROM JOHN MORGAN[1]

Philadelphia, September 17, 1778

Sir

I take the Liberty of informing You that, by a Resolve of Congress Aug[st.] 9. 1777, on a former Memorial of July. 30th, preceeding, Congress concurred with the Report of a Committee upon it, that I was intitled to an Hearing, and that a Committee be appointed for that purpose.[2] No Committee, however, having been yet appointed

---

[5] Livingston quoted the resolve accurately but the date was September 9. *JCC*, XII, 894.

[1] Congress appointed Dr. John Morgan, who had established the first medical school at Philadelphia in 1765, Director General of the Continental Hospital Department Oct. 17, 1775. Unpopular, faced with a shortage of supplies and an abundance of enemies like Dr. William Shippen, Jr., Morgan lost support in Congress and was dismissed Jan. 9, 1777. The abrupt removal chagrined Morgan who bitterly sought to exonerate himself and traduce Shippen whom he believed responsible. Mary C. Gillett, *The Army Medical Department, 1775-1818* (Washington, D.C., 1981), pp. 19, 29-35.

[2] John Morgan's July 30, 1777, Memorial was read in Congress July 31 and referred to the Medical Committee which reported August 9. The committee found that he had been removed because of "the general complaints of persons of all ranks in the army" and "for the public good and safety." The committee judged his memorial to be "a hasty and intemperate production," but concluded "that he ought to be heard" and that a committee be appointed. Congress, in a resolve, approved the report. *JCC*, VIII, 593, 626; John Morgan Memorial to Congress, July 30, 1777, PCC, Item 41, Vol. 6, p. 19ff.

in pursuance of that Resolve, I have thought fit to present another Memorial & Petition to Congress for an Hearing. Relying on the Justice & Honour of the House to fulfill their Engagement, I beg you will be pleased to present it as early as possible.[3]

With the greatest Respect, I am / Sir / Your most obedient / & most humble Servant

John Morgan

SOURCE: RC, PCC (Item 63), DNA; addressed on cover "To / His Excellency / Henry Laurens Esqr / President / of Congress."; addressed below close "To his Excellency Henry Laurens Esqr President of Congress"; dated "Philadelphia September 17. 1778"; docketed "Septem^r 17 1778. / Letter of Doct^r Morgan / Read Septem^r 18__" and "Letter & memorial / of doct Morgan__"; and "J. Morgan / 17 Sep^t 1778__ / Letter & Memorial".

TO GEORGE BRYAN

Philadelphia, September 18, 1778

Sir

Mr Jackson[1] of Jamaica captured on his voyage from that Island bound for New York, where he was going to reside for the benefit of his health, and now a Prisoner of this State on Parole is desirous of going to South Carolina. I request you Sir, to enlarge his bounds and permit him to pass to that State. I will take proper means for holding him under such restrictions as that he shall be forthcoming if this State shall hereafter judge it necessary to demand his appearance.[2]

Mr Richard Beresford, a young Gentleman Native of South Carolina is now in New York and wishes to be permitted to pass to

---

[3] Morgan again appealed to Congress on December 29, but the issue was not brought to a conclusion until June 12, 1779, when Congress adopted a resolution that it was "satisfied" with Morgan's conduct as director general. *JCC*, XII, 1259; XIV, 724.

[1] Robert Jackson, whom HL later described as possessing a large estate in Jamaica and "allied by Marriage to one of the best families in South Carolina," obtained a permit to go to New York to try and work an exchange for himself as a citizen. HL to Lord Stirling, Nov. 5, 1778, PCC, Item 13.

[2] Although Jackson obtained permission to go to South Carolina in September, he was still in Philadelphia as late as November 1778. Pennsylvania Executive Council to Jacob Rush, Sept. 21, 1778, *Pa. Archives*, 1st ser., VI, 572; HL to Lord Stirling, Nov. 5, 1778, PCC, Item 13.

his own Country where he has a large Estate and where he means to become a Citizen__ I pray you Sir, grant him a Permit to come to Philadelphia on his way to Carolina, I shall write to Governor Livingston in order to obtain from His Excellency permission for Mr. Beresford to pass thro' New Jersey.[3]

I have the honor to be &c.

SOURCE: LB, HL Papers, ScHi; addressed "The Hoñble. / George Bryan Esquire Vice President of Pennsylvania / Phila. / by M.Y."; dated "18th. September".

FROM JOHN LAURENS

Fort Clinton, N.Y., September 19, 1778

I snatch a moment to present my love to my dear Father, and continue the recital of such intelligence relative to the enemys movements as we are furnished with__

Ld Howes fleet is returned to New York__ A[1] fleet of transports has likewise returned from the Eastward by way of the Sound__ presumed to contain Genl. Grays force returning from a successful sweep of Cattle and Sheep taken at Marthas Vineyard__[2] the intelligence in general seems rather to favor a West india Voyage, than any offensive operation against any part of our territories__ the extraordinary preparation of transports__ their being[3] so long[4] employed in wooding and watering__ the repeated accounts from various channels of troops being ordered for the W. Indies__ the return of Ld Howe and Genl. Gray__ the sickly condition of Byrons Crews__ and every days delay__ make me regard the expedition

---

[3] Pennsylvania authorities responded immediately, or HL believed they would, because the next day he wrote Beresford informing him that letters would be sent to General Maxwell and Governor Livingston "which will secure you against Arrest or Insult in the Journey thro' New Jersey" and requested Beresford stop at his lodgings in Philadelphia. HL to Richard Beresford, Sept. 19, 1778, HL Papers, ScHi.

[1] "A" written over "G".

[2] After Gen. Charles Grey's 4,000-man force completed its September operations along the Massachusetts coast they proceeded to Martha's Vineyard where between September 10 and 15 they destroyed vessels, damaged saltworks, took a forced collection from the inhabitants and carried off 300 oxen and 10,000 sheep. Charles Edward Banks, *The History of Martha's Vineyard* (3 vols.: Boston, 1911-1925), I, 371-383.

[3] "being" written over other text.

[4] "so long" inserted in left margin.

against the Squadron and Boston as less provable__ the keeping an army in Newport and New-York__ without any hopes of a successful forward Manœuvre, is keeping so many men inactive, and useless as to the general operations of the War__ France has her West india islands well garrisoned and provisioned__ G. Britain in hers is defective as to both these points__

I must finish abruptly and bid adieu__

John Laurens.

SOURCE: ALS, Emmet Collection, NN; no address; dated "Fort Clinton__ at Westpoint in / Highlands on the North River. / 19ᵗʰ Septemb: 1778"; docketed "John Laurens / 19ᵗʰ Septem⁓ 1778".

FROM JAMES MEASE

Philadelphia, September 19, 1778

Sir

Having learned that some uneasiness subsists & complaints been made respecting the department to which I had the honor of being appointed I beg you will please to inform the Honorable Congress that I request ↑the favour↓ of their choosing as soon as they conveniently can some suitable person for the Officer of Clothier General should the further continuance of such an Officer be necessary Although I have long wish'd (as the ↑inclosed↓ copy of a letter to his Excellency will evince)[1] to be freed from the execution of An office which I found very disagreeable on many Accounts & desire this may be veiwed as a resignation. Yet It is by no means my intention to embarrass the public service, & therefore will continue to Act untill the Honble Congress will be pleased to take illegible measures to render my service unnecessary which however I hope will be as speedily as possible__[2]

---

[1] In a letter to George Washington on Dec. 16, 1777, Meese had requested permission to resign because of ill health. PCC, Item 78, Vol. 15, p. 305ff.

[2] Congress did not act on Mease's resignation immediately. A committee expanded from the first selected Aug. 10, 1778, recommended in October that Mease not be allowed to make further purchases and that the clothier's department be reorganized with more responsibility falling on state agents. On March 23, 1779, Congress enacted a reform of the department but Mease was not replaced until James Wilkinson accepted the post in July 1779. *JCC*, XII, 937, 996-997; XIII, 353-357; Risch, *Supplying Washington's Army*, pp. 270-279.

I intreat you sir to believe & to represent to the Honble Congress, that this is not the dictates of passion ↑or↓ disgust, but the result of sentiments long entertain'd & that I have no design to aviod any necessary inquiry they may think proper. I flatter myself that all those I have[3] the happiness of being much known ↑to↓ will impute any defects there may have been in the execution my employ to a defect in judgment not to any error of the heart & that every Gentleman will be candid enough to make allowance for occasional failures in an department totally new & in which no line of conduct had been delineated & which required great supplies, without resources from whence they could be drawn with any certainty.[4] I have the honor to be with great respect & Esteem

> Your honors most Hble / & most Obed[t] Serv[t]
>   James Mease Cl[r] Gen__

SOURCE: RC, PCC (Item 78), DNA; addressed on cover "Honob[le.] Henry Laurens Esqr / president"; addressed below close "Honble Henry Laurens Esq[r] / Presid[t-]"; dated "Philad[a] 19 Sep[r] 1778__"; docketed "Letter from J. Mease / Cloathier gen[l.] 19 Sept[r] 1778 / Order to lie__".

FROM JOHN ADAMS

Passy, France, September 20, 1778

Sir I have the Honour to inclose the latest Gazettes, which contain all the News of Europe. The News from America by the Way of London, which is contained in the Courier de L'Europe of the fifteenth instant,[1] has raised our expectations and increased our Anxiety. We are not without Apprehensions that the Compte d'Estaing, may fall in with the combined Fleets of How and Biron.

The English are begining to elevate their Heads a little; and to

---

[3] "had" changed to "have".

[4] Some of the problems of the clothier's department may have been the result of wartime markets and prices over which Mease had no control. He did, however, with the help of his agents and others like Benedict Arnold, abuse the powers of his office for personal gain. In January 1781 Congress, with some prompting from Pennsylvania, recommend Mease be prosecuted. Risch, *Supplying Washington's Army*, pp. 428-429.

[1] The *Courier de l'Europe* was a French-language newspaper published in London and widely circulated in Europe. This number reported the arrival of some of Byron's squadron at New York, and the French fleet's sailing from Sandy Hook. *Adams Papers* (Taylor), VII, 58n.

renew their old insolent Language, both in Coffeehouses and in daily Papers. The Refugees from America, unable to bear the Thought of being excluded forever that Country, and Still less that of Soliciting for Pardon from their injured Countrymen, and returning to see established Principles, which they detest and Forms of government against which they have ever combatted, are Said to be indefatigable, in instilling hopes into the King and Ministers, that by persevering another Campaign, and Sending Twenty thousand more Men to America, the People will be worn out and glad to Petition for Dependance upon them. They flatter themselves and others with hopes that Spain, will remain Neuter, and that by intriguing in France, they can get the French Ministry changed, and then that they shall have little Trouble from this Quarter. Nothing can be more whimsical, more groundless, or ridiculous than all this.__ Yet it is said to amuse and please the credulous Multitude in that devoted Island.

Those who pretend to know the Bosoms of the Persons highest in Power in that Kingdom, Say, that they delight themselves with the Thought, that if it is not in their Power to reduce America, once more to their Yoke__ yet they are able to harrass, to distress, and to render miserable those whom they can not subdue. That they have Some little Compunction at the Thought that they shall be ranked in History with the Phillips and Alvas,[2] the Alberts and Gislers[3] of this World but this instead of producing Repentance and Reformation as it ought, engenders nothing but Rage Envy and Revenge.

This Revenge however, is impotent. Their Marine and their Finances are in So bad Condition, that it is with infinite difficulty they can cope with France alone even at Sea: and it seems to be the Intention of Providence, that they shall be permitted to go on with their Cruelties, just long enough to wean the affection of every

---

[2] A reference to the suppression of Protestantism in the Netherlands by the Duke of Alva (Alba) from 1567 to 1574 under the orders of Philip II of Spain. John Lynch, *Spain 1516-1598: From Nation State to World Empire* (Cambridge, Mass., 1991), pp. 387-403; Geoffrey Parker, *The Dutch Revolt* (London, 1977), pp. 105-142.

[3] A reference to Albert I of Austria who sent Herman Gesler to the Swiss canton of Uri as governor. Gesler's harsh tactics led to his death in 1304, just prior to a revolt of the canton. William Tell is said to have killed Gesler. Robert Comyn, *History of the Western Empire* (London, 1851), pp. 396-407.

American Heart, and make room for Connections between us and other Nations, who have not the Ties of Language of Acquaintance and of Custom to bind Us. I am, with the most perfect Respect, Sir, your most obedient humble servant

SOURCE: LB, Adams Papers, MHi; addressed "His Excellency President Laurens."; dated "Passi Septr 20 1778".

FROM JOHN LEWIS GERVAIS

Charles Town, September 21, 1778

Dear Sir,

My last Letter was of the 9th Instant p Mr Dumas with some News papers, but I forgot to forw$^{d.}$ the enclosed Letters, & therefore I am[1] particularly glad to meet so soon with another oppertunity.

Since that time I was honoured with your favour of the 22$^{d.}$ to which you was so kind to add the latest News papers__ The President laid the different papers accompanying your Letter before the Assembly, but not your Letter which he shewed to me__ General Sullivan was truly in a deplorable Situation the 14th Aug: And I think he has great merit in procuring Ammunition &^{ca} in so short a time as to be able not only to face the Ennemy on the 17th_ but to Act offensively__ I hope [*torn*][2] news particularly of the Fleets__

Considering that General Lee has been found Guilty of every Charge against him__ the Sentence is very mild; probably he will think otherwise, I wish he would resign__ His misconduct after being exchanged will look Suspicious to the Eyes of the World__

The boat returned here last Week from Wright Savannah with a Load of Corn & Clean Rice, the Rice was of the Year before last it sold at 55/ p C$^t.$ some of the Corn was damaged as they had very bad Weather indeed__ it sold at 20/. p Bushel,[3] I have now sent her to Mepkin for a Load of ↑last years↓ Ruff Rice, which is ↑partly↓ engaged at 15/. p Bushel. it is of an ordinary Quality & would not

---

[1] "a" written over "p".
[2] Two lines missing.
[3] Gervais noted at the bottom of the page: "That which was good sold from 35/. to 40/. p Bushel."

beat to advantage, Mr Ball[4] advised to sell it rather at 12/6. p Bushel than to have it beat__ The Boat did not go to the Alatamaha on Account of Intelligence that a Number of Indians were coming against the Frontiers of Georgia, & Mr Baillie judged it was not safe to venture__ I think he acted prudently as we have no Posts of Troops left near it & the Florida Scout is all over the Country, even make frequent inroads in this State & carry off Negroes & Horses. Mr Baillie writes me that George Aaron that Notorious Villain who robed & carried of your negroes is in Savanah Goal, he was brought in a Prisonner of War together with some more of the Florida Rangers__ he says he has lodged a Complaint against him & taken him out of the hands of the Military to be tryed by the Civil Law__

I also omitted in my last Letter to mention that I had not attached any property of Mr Nutt,[5] because the attach[ment] [torn][6] in a late motion of Alexander Rose against Greenwood & Higginson[7] for a sum due him by that house as also damages for protesting his Bills ↑a few years ago↓ when they had effects in hand he only recovered at the rate of Seven for one,[8] therefore Mr Manigault & Mr Owen as well as myself were of Opinion to postpone it till we heard from you after you should be informed of this Circumstance

I read to the President your Paragraph concerning General Gadsden; he told me he would mention it to him which he has done, & says that General Gadsden will make an Apology__ I hope he will do it fully__

I see our friend Colonel John Laurens is again with an Army to which we look for Success__ we had a report to night that Rhode Island was taken & the Troops made prisoners of War, by a person

---

[4] Elias Ball, Jr. (1744-1822), HL's nephew, supervised the overseers who worked at Mepkin plantation. *HL Papers*, XII, 84n.

[5] HL calculated London merchant John Nutt's debt to him to be with interest over £900 sterling on June 23, 1778. He directed his attorneys in Charleston to "immediately lay an attachment on Mr. Nutts' effects or property in the hands or books of any person in So. Carolina." *HL Papers*, XIII, 506-507.

[6] One line missing.

[7] William Greenwood and William Higginson comprised the leading London firm in the South Carolina trade on the eve of the Revolution. In 1790, Higginson, the surviving partner, claimed Americans owed the firm £295,891 sterling and won several awards against South Carolinians. *HL Papers*, I, 86n; Rogers, *Evolution of a Federalist*, pp. 250-251.

[8] While the rate of exchange between South Carolina currency and British sterling was stable at 7 to 1 prior to the Revolution, Gervais' comment indicates that S.C. currency had depreciated and that HL would be a great loser if he attached Nutt's property at this time.

said from Philadelphia in 22 days__ I hope we shall soon have a Confirmation of this good piece News__

Mʳ· Heyward returned a few days ago, he was in the house to day__ A report was brought in to day Concerning the Embargo, the purport of which is that Congress have no power to lay an embargo__ but recommend ~~that~~ ↑a Bill↓ ~~to~~ laying⁹ an embargo ~~may be laid~~ ↑on provisions↓ to the 15ᵗʰ₋ Novʳ· next, to be [*torn*]¹⁰ think it necessary__¹¹ The Committee on the Presidents Proclamation I believe will report to Morrow at last__ Never was a Business carried with more partiality, the whole Aim is to censure the president & to let the people get clear__ Whether the house will ~~yet~~ agree with the Committee is Uncertain__ There is but a thin house, & the Charles Town Members carry a great Sway Five are on that Com[*mittee*] [*torn*] Members__ they will have it just as they please__ [*torn*] to add a Member for each parish ↑to the Comᵉ↓; it was rejected__ In my opinion we shall have a new President before the end of the Month, unless the house reprobate the report.¹² We shall make a pretty figure in the Eyes of the World that we cant agree 6 Months with a Governor of our own chusing__ The Creeks Indians have killed 20 or 30. Inhabitants of Georgia last Month Col. Hammond & Colonel Williamson are marched to their relief I Inclose ↑Copy of↓ a Letter of Col. Williamson received this afternoon__¹³ which will best inform you with respect to Indian Affairs__ In my Opinion the Creeks will not be quiet till they are chastised__ an expedition to their Country ~~illegible~~ without loss of time would be attended with Success, be ~~illegible~~ least expensive in the End__ & keep the Choctaws,

---

⁹ "ing" inserted in left margin.

¹⁰ One line missing.

¹¹ On September 28 South Carolina enacted embargo legislation to prohibit the export of "all kinds of provisions" until November 15 "unless...the President, with the advice and consent of the Privy Council, shall...take off the said embargo, by proclamation." The same act included a section which extended the embargo on hemp, cordage, and salted beef or pork to Oct. 1, 1779, because of shortages in the state. *S.C. Statutes,* IV, pp. 447-448.

¹² The Assembly postponed consideration of the committee's report to the next legislature and Rawlins Lowndes completed the term which ended in February 1779. John Rutledge, whose resignation in March 1778 had brought Lowndes to the presidency, was elected. Vipperman, *Rawlins Lowndes,* pp. 216, 220-221.

¹³ An extract of Andrew Williamson's letter dated Sept. 17, 1778, "from Camp, 30 miles from Okonee river" was printed in the *S.C. General Gazette* Sept. 24, 1778. Williamson commanded a force of 530 men and reported that although he had spies and scouts out, "We have seen no enemy since our arrival in Georgia".

Chickesaws & Cherokees in respect__ Delay I am afraid will bring them all upon our backs next Spring__ It is idle to expect to be at peace with one part of the Nation & at War with the rest__ I prefer a War with the whole Nation, otherwise we shall have all the disadvantage of War & they all the advantage of Peace__

If Congress could be prevailed on to Countenance & give assistance in a well concerted plan [*torn*] to West Florida__ it would be the surest way to secure the Indians in our Interest__ the house have recommended to the president to apply or rather ↑urge↓ the Subject to Congress__

The boat came to Night from Mepkin with a Load of Ruff Rice, and I am in hopes it will sell at 20/ p Bushel__

Mrs Gervais presents her best Respects__ If you [*torn*]^14 Journey hither, if the further services of your Country detain you longer I shall chearfully continue my best endeavours__ for your Interest.

Mr Zahn expects to make a good Crop at Santee Mr Baillie & Springer,^15 give also good hopes__ I hope this Years Crop will help to bear your great Expences__ I am with great respect & affection

Dear Sir / Your most Obed^t. Ser^t

John Lewis Gervais

Names of the Comm^e on the proclamation

Edward Rutledge		Charles C. Pinckney
Alex^r Moultrie		Col. Mayson
Genl. Moultrie	Town Members	[*illegible*]
Col Roberts	in the majority	& yr humble Servt
Doctor Ramsay		names—the Minority

SOURCE: RC, Gervais Papers, in private hands; no address; dated "Charles Town 21 Septem^br 1778"; docketed "John Lewis Gervais dated / Charlestown. 21st Septr. 1778".

---

14 One line missing.
15 Casper Springer was HL's overseer at Wrights Savannah. *HL Papers*, VIII, 89n.

TO WILLIAM PALFREY[1]

Philadelphia, September 22, 1778

Sir

I had the honor of writing to you the 5th Instant[2] since which it does not appear by the Secretarys' List that Congress have received a Letter from you.

The present Cover will convey to you an Act of Congress of the 17th Instant for obliging Commanding Officers of Regiments, Regimental Paymasters, and Officers commanding Companies to account for Monies drawn for and received and not applied, agreeable to the Resolves of Congress the 6th February 1778.[3]

I have the honor to be &c.

SOURCE: LB, PCC (Item 13), DNA; addressed "William Palfrey Esquire, Paymaster General at Camp / by Owens"; dated "22nd Sept[r.]".

FROM SILAS DEANE

Philadelphia, September 22, 1778

Sir

In consequence of an Order of Congress on the 8[th.] of December 1777 for me to embrace the first opportunity of returning to America, and "upon my arrival to repair with all possible dispatch to Congress that they might be well informed of the state of affairs in Europe in that critical Juncture." I left Paris the first of April last, having received the order on the 4[th.] of March preceding, and arrived in Philadelphia, the seat of Congress on the 13[th.] of July following, ready at the pleasure of Congress to render such information as was in my power to give. In this situation I continued until the

---

[1] Col. William Palfrey, a former Boston merchant and aide to Generals Charles Lee and George Washington, had been appointed Paymaster General of the Continental Army, April 27, 1776. He held the position until 1780 when he was selected to be American consul in France. He was lost at sea en route to France. Wright, *Continental Army*, p. 32; Heitman, *Continental Officers*.

[2] HL's September 5 letter "inclosed an Act of Congress of the 3[d] Inst. for admitting proofs of back Rations, upon Oath and other circumstances in particular cases, and for regulating the pay of Brigade Chaplins." PCC, Item 13; *JCC*, XII, 863-864.

[3] *JCC*, X, 132-137; XII, 924-925.

15th. of August. when I received the Order of Congress to attend them on the 17th. on which Day and on the 21st. I had the honor personally to inform Congress generally of my public transactions under their authority from the time of my departure from Philadelphia in March 1776 until my return, in these audiences I particularly stated and explained the unsettled state in which the commercial transactions of the Commissioners in Europe were at my departure, and that as well from their nature and extent, as that even at my departure from Paris, many large orders were not compleated, and of consequence, neither the accounts or vouchers delivered; that the interval between my receiving my order of recall, and my departure in compliance with it was so short as to render it impossible for me to arrange those affairs, further, than to be able to give a general state of them, which I then mentioned generally, and added, that I was under the necessity of returning speedily to Europe, as well on Account of those, as of other important affairs left by my sudden departure in an unsettled state. At my last audience, I found and expected, that I should be called upon to answer Questions which might be put to me for the obtaining more clear and explicit information than what I had given of some particulars in my general narration, and I held myself in readiness to attend the pleasure of Congress for that purpose. In this situation my private affairs pressed my immediate departure from Philadelphia, and my public as well as private affairs in Europe, no less urged my departure from America. On the 8th. of September, I took the Liberty of reminding that honorable Body, that I was still waiting to receive their Orders if they desired my further attendance upon them, and my affairs daily pressing, on the 11th. of September I again reminded Congress of my waiting their pleasure, and took the liberty of mentioning the reasons which pressed me to be anxious for their speedy decision.[1] As Congress have not thought proper to make any reply to my Letters, nor to admit me to lay before them such further information as they may desire, and I am enabled to

---

[1] Deane's September 11 letter merely repeated his general complaint that "the situation of the affairs in Europe which I had been principally concerned in transacting...render it indispensably necessary on my part that I return as early as possible." And, "that if further intelligence is expected from me I may have an early opportunity of giving it." Silas Deane to HL, Sept. 11, 1778, PCC, Item 103, p. 112.

give, and as from the many weighty affairs upon their hands it is uncertain when I may be admitted, and as my affairs will not permit my longer continuance in Philadelphia, I take the Liberty of enclosing to your Excellency the account of the Banker, in whose hands all the public monies were deposited,[2] of which I gave you some time since a general State for your private information, and which I obtained from the Banker but a Day or two before my departure from Paris, with the view of giving all the information in my power on every subject to Congress in which they were interested which account, I expected in the course of my narration to have delivered personally to Congress. As to any other subject on which further information may be desired, I shall be ready to give it, whenever that honorable Body shall call on me for it, during the short time my affairs will permit me to tarry in this City I have indeed thought that some further information would be necessary, I have daily expected to be called upon for it, on this consideration alone, I have notwithstanding the pressing circumstances I have found myself in, waited with patience the Orders of Congress. I shall be happy if such information or any other service in my power, may be found agreeable and of use to that respectable Body and the United States to whom I have long since and ever shall be devoted. I have only further to request that honorable Body to be assured I shall ever retain a most grateful sense of the Confidence which they have heretofore honored me with, and consider it as the most honorable and happy circumstance of my Life, that I have had the opportunity of rendering important services to my Country, and that I am conscious of having done them to the utmost of my ability.

I have the honor to remain / with the utmost res / pect &c.

(signed) Silas Deane

SOURCE: Copy, PCC (Item 103), DNA; no address; dated "Philadelphia 22d Septemr· 1778".

---

[2] An account from Ferdinand Grand dated March 27, 1778, of "Money Received and Paid on Account of the United States of America" is printed in "The Deane Papers," ed. Charles Isham, New-York Historical Society *Collections* (5 vols. 1886-1890), XXI, 21-33.

FROM ROBERT HOWE

Charles Town, September 22, 1778

My dear Sir

My public Letters will Convey my opinion to Congress how essential the subduction of St Augustine is,[1] to the tranquillity both of this State and of Georgia of which, if Congress should be Convinced they will probably encourage an effectual expedition against it, to you therefore Sir as a friend whose attention to me and whose Services I never shall forget I take the liberty of addressing myself upon a Subject which relates merely to myself.

I flew to my Native Country when it was likely to become the seat of War, it fell to my lot to remain here (unwillingly I confess) when the War progressed Northwardly, but from a sense of Duty I submitted, you Sir know what a loss of Rank I sustained by being absent from the scene of immediate Action and I flatter myself also, know that nothing but an earnest desire to Sacrifice every private consideration to that public Cause in which I was engaged could have detained me a moment in a service, where I was deprived of that promotion which was my Right, & of which every Soldier of Sensibility cannot but be tenacious.

Now dear Sir if an Expedition against St Augustine should be undertaken, which long since believing to be absolutely necessary I endeavoured to prepare myself for, if after a great deal of private expense, to which I have put my self, to obtain an exact knowledge of its Strength and Situation, if after risquing the lives of Persons employed as Spies for this purpose, who were not insignificant Members of Society, and after every exertion and strenuous effort I have made, I should be deprived of the only opportunity which has offered in my department of serving my Country signally and of obtaining Fame, another elder in Commission than I am, should be sent up to reap those Laurels, and to avail himself of that information I have laboured to gather, it cannot but be supposed that I shall feel it sensibly__ You Sir whose sense of honour I know

---

[1] General Howe addressed Congress in two letters of this date; the one on the necessity of taking St. Augustine is Robert Howe to HL, Sept. 22, 1778, PCC, Item 160, p. 483ff. The other letter explained that the new arrangement of the army would not serve the Continental officers in his department, because they would often be outranked by militia officers, which "will give disgust to many respectable and experienced officers". Robert Howe to HL, Sept. 22, 1778, PCC, Item 160, p. 491ff.

to be delicate will feel for me in such a situation. You sir whose friendship & ~~illegible~~ kindness I have with gratitude experienced will I doubt not exert yourself to prevent a measure which will not only give malevolence an opportunity of reflecting upon me, but fix an indelible Stain upon me as a soldier, by implying that I had no talents adequate to Actual Service, Upon you therefore Sir, as a Friend (for so I know you[)] & for the sake of Justice I rely to guard me against a mortification & disgrace which I am conscious I do not deserve, and which for ever will wound the honour and peace of[2]

Dear Sir / Your most Obedient / Humble Servant

Robert Howe

P.S. You will please not to Communicate the Contents of this Letter unless you find it necessary

SOURCE: Copy (19th century), HL Papers, ScHi; no address; dated "Charles Town S°. Carolina 22 Sept. 1778".

FROM RAWLINS LOWNDES

Charles Town, September 22, 1778

Dear Sir

I have the Honor to inclose to your Excellency a Report of the Commͭee of the General Assembly, as agreed to by the House, the 8th. of September 1778 which was sent to me with a Message from the House the same day, "requesting that I would make the proper Application to Congress for their Assistance and Countenance to carry into Execution the measure recommended in the Close of the Report."[1]

---

[2] At this time Congress was reorganizing the Southern Department and on September 25, ordered General Howe to report to Washington's headquarters, and named General Benjamin Lincoln to replace him as the southern commander. Howe did not learn of the action until October 9, when he responded with anger and disappointment. "Have I not sacrificed my Fortune & Peace to the service of my Country!...How Sir have I deserved this disgrace?" *JCC*, XII, 951; Bennett and Lennon, *A Quest for Glory*, p. 87.

[1] The report was concerned with the danger from attacks by the Creek Indians, and the related fear that the Creeks would allow the "Worthless and disaffected" to establish a base on South Carolina's borders. The solution proposed by the Assembly was to mount another expedition against Florida. Extract from the Journal of the South Carolina General Assembly, Sept. 8, 1778, PCC, Item 72, pp. 469ff. The extract was read in Congress on Nov. 3, 1778, and referred to the committee considering a letter from Robert Howe of September 22 on the same subject. On November 10, the committee reported, and the Congress resolved, first

I do in Consequence thereof recommend this matter to the particular Attention of the Delagates of this State, as a measure of the first Importance to the Interest and Safety of the Southern department.__ The Vicinity of Augustine, the Annoyance they give to our Trade, the Assylum and Protection they afford to the disaffected from this Country, Georgia and North Carolina, and above all, the Influence the British Nation is allowed by means of that possession to preserve among the Indians, are powerfull motives to induce an undertaking for its reduction. General Howe from the experience he must have acquired, in his late expedition, must be Competent to the purpose of forming a proper plan for such and Interprize; he must know the adequate means, the former deficiencies, the obsticles and impediments, and accordingly, provide against every Contingency which Embarrassed and frustrated the execution of the former Ill Concerted, tho very expensive Scheme. I will recommend to him to digest a plan suited to this occasion and transmit it to Congress as I know, he is amongst those, who are very Sanguine, not only for the expediency, but the practicability of the measure.[2]

I intimated to your Excellency in my last, that a very great Riot had happened in Charles Town between the American Sailors, and those of other Nations; ~~three~~ ↑four↓ Lives were lost; one from among our People, and ~~two~~ ↑three↓ from the other side. every means were taken to procure an investigation of the first rise, and ↑the↓ progress of this Affair, in the most impartial unprejudiced manner; our endeavours have not fully answered our hopes or desires; I beleive the quarrel may be referred to that national prejudice and prepossession which keep these people at variance with one another, and excites them to mutual taunts and reproaches.__ Government has, and continues to do, every thing that can be done to Allay and quiet these disorders and ferments__ we keep the Militia under Guard every Night__ and the Assembly have

---

to inform South Carolina of the resolution of November 2 directing Gen. Benjamin Lincoln, the commander of the Southern Department, to attempt the reduction of East Florida; second, to approve the Assembly's investigation "into the causes of the Creek rupture"; and third, to authorize Lincoln to offer a land bounty to participants in the proposed East Florida expedition. *JCC*, XII, 1095, 1116-1118.

[2] Robert Howe to HL, Sept. 22, 1778, PCC, Item 160, p. 483ff. Howe's letters were read in Congress Nov. 2, 1778. *JCC*, XII, 1091.

it under Consideration to adopt some Regulations to prevent or to punish these Offences__ these People follow the impulse of Education and former propensities, they are not qualifyed for and accustomed to vary their mode of thinking or acting, according to different Circumstances and Situations; Occasional Conformity is a lesson they have not yet learn't, and will require some time to bring them over to it. I send your Excellency the Paperss, which will evince the intentions and desires of Governm[ts.] and how much they have it at heart to prevent, and discountenance any improper distinctions, or partial Connexions.__[3]

In Justice to the State I am induced to give you this information, because I have heard, by mere accident, that the French Gentlemen, without giving me any Notice of their intentions, have had a very general meeting, and have drawn up and transmitted to Mons[r.] Gerrard, a representation of this Case__ [4] notwithstanding they well know that no means were left unassayed to provide for their Safety and Security and to enable them to enjoy every priviledge and advantage in Common with the Citizen of our own State. I do not know the purport of their representation, but you may assure your self, there is in this State the best disposition to provide, every guard and Security that is due ↑to↓, or can be expected, from, the best of Friends

I have not for several days past, received any advices from the Indian Country; my last Acco[ts.] were, that Col[o.] Hammond had marched with Six Companys into Georgia for the Assistance of that state, and that the Indians had beset several of their small Forts, and had killed a party going to the Relief of one of them. intelligence concerning Indian Affairs, are generally so vague and contradictory, even from those most to be depended upon, that one is obliged to suspend their belief, and often the measures proper to be taken, untill a Concurance of testimony, or some clearer evidence, authenticates the facts. While the Enemy have the means of supplying these People plentifully with all they want, and we, with our utmost efforts, can afford them but a very scanty and irregular Trade, it is obvious,

---

[3] The *S.C. General Gazette,* Sept. 17, 1778, contained Rawlins Lowndes' proclamation offering a £1,000 reward for information about the riot and notice of the General Assembly's appointment of a committee to consider ways and means of suppressing riots.

[4] The representation has not been located by the editors.

in whose favour, the ascendancy ~~be~~ will be, and how uncertain and precarious ↑will be↓ our Interest with them or rather I should say, how Certain it is, that we shall have no Interest at all. M^r· Galphin is instructed in terms of the Report, ~~to~~ in Concert with Georgia, to negociate an accommodation, and we are preparing in the best manner we can against the event of his being unsuccessfull; Col^o· Thomsons Regiment is ordered on the Frontier on Savanah River, and detachments from the Militia are held in readiness to Act where they may be occasion for them. here Sir is a plentifull Source "for Debts and brown paper Dollars"[5]

Some very desperate Villains have lately committed cruel Ravages at and about Orangeburgh, cut off the Ears of one Prichard a Magistrate, and another Man; beat unmercifully Capt· Carmichael[6] and his Family, robbed, of a very considerable Value, old Felder a Member of Assembly and burn't his house; and have thrown all that part of the Country into a general Panick, and so intimidated the Inhabitants that those well affected, are detered from taking any steps for their own Security least, by so doing, they should bring upon themselves the resentment of these banditti, and share the fate of those who have so dearly paid for their displeasure. one hundred Men (from the Regulars) will be Stationed at Orangeburgh which I hope will recover the Spirits of our People, and encourage the Militia to go after these Publick disturbers; I have given orders, if they are come up with, to settle the point of Law, on the spot, for the Decission of the Courts does not seem to be an adequate remedy at this time.

Our Assembly are now setting, I laid before them an Acco^t· of what I had done respecting the Embargo on Provissions. various opinions on this measure; the Current seems to be against the right

[5] During the Revolution South Carolina authorized the creation of paper currency on several occasions. The three acts prior to Lowndes' comments were Oct. 19, 1776, when $80,000 in $1, 2, 4, 6, 8, and 10 denominated bills were created; Dec. 23, 1776, when $308,000 in $1, 2, 3, 4, 5, 6, 8, and 10 denominated bills were created; and Feb. 14, 1777, when $20 and $30 bills were created In each instance the currency was printed on "thick brownish paper" or "dark brown paper." The next emisssion under an act of Feb. 8, 1779 was $1,000,000 in $40, 60, 80, and 100 bills, printed on white and blue papers. Eric P. Newman, *The Early Paper Money of America* (Racine, Wisc., 1967), pp. 315-319; *Journals of the General Assembly and House of Representatives, 1776-1780*, ed. William Edwin Hemphill, Wylma Anne Wates, and R. Nicholas Olsberg (Columbia, S.C., 1976), pp. 158, 170.

[6] James Carmichael had been appointed a Commissioner of Public Roads in Orangeburg District March 16, 1778. Salley, *Orangeburg County*, p. 11.

of Congress, the Pensylvania Protest, in the very face of Congress, adds strength to the Opponents; nothing yet is determined upon, and the Embargo Subsists in full force, tho' I will not answer for private infractions. for my part, on a Comparitive view of advantages and desadvantages on both sides, I should be inclined to decide in fav^r of Congress; without her right is sustained, a general Embargo will be a rare Phœnomenon in the Political Administration of America. these matters ought to be cleared of all doubt and uncertainty, otherwise they will introduce contention and strife and a train of Ill Consequences: Is not the Confederation still under the controll Ꞓ of Congress? surely a matter of this magnitude ought not to be left undefined as a subject of future discussion.

A Flag of Truce is arrived from St Augustine[7] to demand Osborne and Bachop & their Officers, whom I had detained as a pledge for the Release of Pines and his Officers, confined at New York, not knowing they had obtained their discharge. we stood indebted to Augustine for two Masters of Vessells, Stephens[8] in a Continental Brig[9] and Dickinson in a Bermuda Sloop,[10] neither of any force ↑or very little↓ but both happened to have Commissions; for these the Govr has demanded Osborne and Bachop in exchange. I refered the matter to the Assembly, and they have considered them as being in Similar Circumstances, and advised their discharge; at the same time expressing great resentment against Govr Tonyn, for sending, as one of his Commissioners, a Mr Young, who is one of the proscribed of Georgia.[11] and in Consequence, desiring I would Confine to the Flag all the Persons who belongs to her, untill their business is transacted & then to send her packing__ she is also intended for Georgia__ but it is apprehended, Mr Yonge, from this Specimen of his reception here, will not like the hotter Region, and abide a fiery tryall there.

---

[7] The British cartel brig *Polly*, Capt. Stirrup, arrived in Charleston from St. Augustine September 16, with nine prisoners and two commissioners. *S.C. Gazette*, Sept. 23, 1778.

[8] "Stevens" altered to "Stephens".

[9] The Continental brig *Chance*, George Stephens, was taken in early February 1778 by HMS *Galatea*, Thomas Jordan. *Documents of the American Revolution* (Davies), XV, 44.

[10] Possibly the sloop *Bacchus*, Ichabod Dickenson, which arrived at Charleston about this time. *S.C. General Gazette*, Sept. 24, 1778.

[11] Henry Yonge, Jr., who was listed in the March 1, 1778, Georgia Attainder Act, had moved to East Florida. *Georgia Historical Quarterly*, XXXVII (1953), 271; Palmer, *Biographical Sketches of Loyalists*, p. 954; *Revolutionary Records of Georgia* (Candler), I, 328.

M^r· Heyward arrived here, very unexpectedly, a few days ago by whom I received your Excellencys Packet; Capt· Pines and Lieu^t· Martin are detained on the Road by Sickness.

M^r· Livingstone, before I received your favours, had called upon me, with a Letter wrote him by the Commercial Com͠me in answer to one he had wrote them on the subject matter of the Embargo, wherein he informed them of two Vessels Loaded with Rice which were detained at a great expence and not permitted to Sail. The Com͠mee without taking any Notice of the Embargo, give him positive orders to send the Vessells and Cargo forward to Cape Francois. This appeared to me pretty extraordinary, and produced, on my part, an absolute refusal. The Embargo is either Legal, or not Legal; in the former Case the ~~for~~ prohibition is general and unexceptionable; in the latter case it ought to have no operation, and every man should be on one footing__ I could not see or subscribe to, the reasons for a partial dispensation, to a positive Act, or could I take notice of any authority from Philadelphia, short of an act of Congress. M^r· Livingston therefore remains on the same footing with others, who heartily wish this restraint was taken of, whenever it can be done w^th· propriety.[12]

The Intelligence you[13] have Communicated to us respecting Rhode Island, like the heightening of a plot in a play, makes us more anxious for further advices, and a disclosure of the Sequel of that Affair__ indeed my hopes and fears alternately have their effect on my mind, and the Idea of Byron with his Fleet, like the Ghost, makes me start, from the fair prospect and flattering hope of Victory and Conquest. Muckenfuss's arrival is impatiently expected, who will put us out of suspense in this great Business

There is no accounting for the different Sentiments of Men in publick Assemblys__ the different impressions that the same Arguments will make__ why an Oral naritive should be prefered, to a Written one, as in the Case of M^r· Deane__ I sh^d· most certainly have joined you in that Question, and should have been surprized at ↑having↓ one Opponent__ if I had not long since ceased to be surprized almost at anything__

---

[12] HL had warned Lowndes that the Commerce Committee had acted without authority. HL to Rawlins Lowndes, Aug. 11, 1778.
[13] "y" written over "h".

I lately received a Letter from the Commander in Chief (Pieter Runnels) in the absence of the Govr· of S^t· Eustatius, complaining tha[t] a privateer belonging to Salem in New England, called the Scorpion commanded by Israel Thorndick__ [14] had violated the Neutrality of their State and Contemned the Law of Nations__ and requiring restitution of the Goods taken on board a Dutch Bottom, the Sloop Thomas, which by the said Privateer were bro^t· into this Port and Condemned as lawfull prize__ I have sent to S^t· Eustatious the proceedings of our Court of Admiralty where it seems the Condemnation was founded on several Circumstances of Fraud one of which was the Vessell having both English & Dutch Clearances & Registers__ and no discrimination between English & Dutch property__ The Complaint also sets forth that the Capture was made within less than a British Mile of Nassau Battery on that Island, which the Complainant alledges is Contrary to the Law of Nations & in breach of the Neutrality of a ffree port__ a Claim was put in here in behalf of the Dutch Claimants__ but they did not Appeal from the Sentence__

I am with very great Respect and Regard Dr Sir / Your Excellencys Most Obed^t· hume Servt[15]

Raw^s Lowndes__

P.S.

M^r· Neufville, whose Son, does me the fav^r– to take Charge of my Letters__ [16] has requested that I woud desire your Ex^cy to advance to his Son what money he may want in Philadelphia and he will lodge the Am^t· in the Treasury here__ as it will save him the Risque & trouble of carrying a considerable Sum with him__ & may also be a means of remitting so much to our Treasury, of the Money belonging to us__

RL.

SOURCE: RC, Kendall Collection; no address; dated below close "Sep^r· 22^d· 1778__"; docketed "President Lowndes / 22nd September 1778". Copy (19th century), HL Papers, ScHi.

---

[14] Israel Thorndike had previously served as captain of the Massachusetts privateer schooner *Warren*, early in 1777. *Naval Documents* (Clark), VIII, 613n.

[15] Lowndes wrote below the close "see postscript on 3^d· Sheet__".

[16] John Neufville (d. 1804), a Charleston merchant, had two adult sons—John, Jr. and Edward. Both were patriots who served in the South Carolina militia. *Directory of the S.C. House*, III, 525-526; Moss, *S.C. Patriots*.

FROM FIELD OFFICERS
White Plains, N.Y., September 22, 1778
Sir,

We beg leave respectfully to present to Congress, the humble Memorial of the Field Officers and Captains now with the Army. We can assure you it contains the general sentiments of your Officers, who directed us with great submission to lay it before you.

We have the honor to be with the highest respect, Sir, Your most obedient / and devoted servants

Dan[1] Morgan Col[o,1]
Oth H. Williams Col[l,2]
William Davies Col.[3]

Enclosure

Camp at white plains Sep[r.] 13th 1778___

We the Subscribers, Officers of the Continental Army, beg leave with all due diffidence, and respect, to Represent to the Honorable the Congress___

That we humbly conceive the Exclusion of Officers from the Army, without the imputation of a Crime or Regard to the Articles of war (which we consider as the law of the Army) without Regard to their past services or Sufferings and without regard to their Future prospects of acquiring an honest Subsistance has a Dangerous tendency is a Real Greviance, and without Redress Renders the Situation of an American-officer much more precarious and disreputable than any other who ~is~ has the Honor to serve where Liberty is not intirely banished, and that those who have been already discarded under those disagreeable circumstances Suffer great Mortification as well as Capital Injury Reparable only by the Ample Relief of Congress.[4]

---

[1] Daniel Morgan (d. 1802) was colonel of the 7th Virginia Regiment of Riflemen, known as the 11th Virginia until Sept. 14, 1778. He was promoted to brigadier general in 1780. Heitman, *Continental Officers.*

[2] Otho Holland Williams (d. 1794) had been colonel of the 6th Maryland since December 1776. Heitman, *Continental Officers.*

[3] William Davies was colonel commandant of the 10th Virginia, which had been the 14th Virginia until Sept. 14, 1778. Heitman, *Continental Officers.*

[4] Under the new arrangement of the army a consolidation of regiments resulted in the dismissal of some redundant officers. On Nov. 24, 1778, Congress accepted several recommendations in a report from the Committee of Arrangement, including provisions to give the displaced officers the right "to the first vacancy in any regiment of the State in their proper rank, after the officers belonging to such regiments have been provided for," and that they be provided one year's pay. *JCC*, XII, 1155-1156.

That the Honorable Congress have not made Any Provision for the Gentlemen of the Army, Adequate to the Sacrifice of Ease, health and property and the hazard of life itself in the Arduous service of their Country. That we Apprehend the Half pay Resolve is Incompetant in the term Contracting the Bounty of Congress, Limiting the Just rewards of our services, and is Clogd with A Clause Aquovical and Disgracefull making A temporary provision Conditional Upon the Officers Holding no place, Office, or post of profit under the State.[5]

Equovical Because it leaves Undetermined what is to be deem'd an Office of profit Disgracefull as it implies A suspicion that Officers, are either incapible or unworthy of being intrusted with such office,__

That the situation of Disabled and wounded Officers, and Officers Widows and orphans demands the Attention of Congress and require Particular Provision, that those Gentlemen, who unfortunately are Captivated by the Enemy are frequently left to languish under the severest Persecution and suffer the most pitiable distress for want of regular and Proper remittances of their pay.[6]

That the pay of Captains Lieu[ts.] Serg[t] Major, & Quarter Master serjeants, is unequal to their ranks and Insufficient for the[7] Duty of the respective Offices and that the pay of Subalterns in general is too Inconsider[able]__ [8] that we conceive it inconsistent with the Usage of Armies to give permanent Commands to Brevett Officers[9]
    That the Officers of Cavalry conceive themselves Subject to a great and unjust disadvantage in being Obliged to purchase horses for themselves at the very Extravagant prices they must give:

---

[5] The half pay establishment approved by Congress May 15, 1778, provided seven years half pay for commissioned officers who remained in service to the conclusion of the war, held no office of state for profit, took an oath of allegiance to the United States, and continued to reside in the states. *JCC*, XI, 502-503.

[6] Congress provided in the resolutions passed November 24 that officers held as prisoner, upon exchange, are entitled "in case of vacancy, to enter into the service of their respective State in such rank as they would have had if they had never been captured." And, that upon giving notice of the desire to return to active service the exchanged officer be allowed half pay "until entry into actual service." *JCC*, XII, 1157.

[7] "their" altered to "the".

[8] The pay scale suggested by the Committee of Arrangement and approved by Congress May 27, 1778, is listed in *JCC*, XI, 538-541.

[9] Congress resolved "That no brevets be for the future granted, except to officers in the line or in case of very eminent services." *JCC*, XII, 1158.

that the horses (for recruiting of which there is no Effectual Mode Established) are greatly Injured and the Service prejudiced for want of a Corps for the purpose of Expresses which would admit of the Cavalry being Employed in more Esential & Honorable Service__ That the want of Regiment[l] Foragemasters Subjects them to great Expence, inconvenience and Fatigue in Foraging at a great distance from the Army__

That the Cloathing department requires Severe Scrutiny and Exemp↑l↓ory punishm^t for the unpardonable Neglects and Gross abuse practised in it to the great prejudice of the Army; that the want of Cloathing Subjects the Officers of the Army to many distressing inconveniences, prejudicial to Military Appearance, Subversive of decency and Fatal to the lives of the Soldiery.__[10] That Several inconveniences arise from the present Establishment of the Medical department, as the sick in Camp for want of a Sufficient Number of Hospital Tents. lodge promiscously with the healthy Soldiers. The Regimental Surgeons are not Accountable for Neglect of duty to, or controlable by the Command$^g·$ Officers of Regiments, and Consider themselves not Amenable to Tryal by Court Martial;__ which is Subversive of Order, and prejudicial to the Sick.__ That the Corps of Artillery & Cavalry are not considered (and consequently not provided for with Necessaries) as belonging to any particular State, and for the same reason are deprived ↑of↓ the advantage of Recruiting in the same and in all of Receiving drafts to compleat their Corps.__

That the Irregularity of making payments to the Troops is a Disadvantage to discipline, injurious to the Soldiery & requires redress.

That we believe it is incompatible with ↑the↓ Humanity of Congress to Suffer the maimed & Wounded Soldiers no longer fit for duty to Roam Disolate through the Country depending for Subsistance on the Gratitude of the forgetfull populace, and therefore beg leave, to Suggest to Congress the Establishment of an Hospital Similar to that of Chelsea, for the Reception of Such as are incapable of serving in the Corps of Invalids.[11]

---

[10] The clothing department was currently under investigation. Clothier General James Mease had submitted his resignation September 19. *JCC*, 937, 996-997; James Mease to HL, Sept. 19, 1778.

[11] Congress authorized the creation of a corps of Invalids, June 20, 1777, to be composed of men not fit for regular duty, to consist of eight companies, "to be employed in garrisons, and

That in General the promises of Congress to grant Supplies & make provision of Necessaries, & Conveniences for the Army have not been Sufficiently Attended to, but on the contrary Supplies of Necessaries & Conveniences received have been so considerably deficient, that unfortunately many thousands have miserably perished & thereby the States have Sustained a Loss irreparable. We therefore with Submission recommend those & other Greviances of Less consequ^ence to the Consideration of the Honorable Congress, on whose candour Generosity and love of Justice, we depend for redress. Assuring them and the world of our unabated love of Liberty, inviolate Attatchment to our Country, Fidelity to the States in General & an unalterable Desire to Maintain A Glorious Independance.__

[*Signed by 90 officers*]

SOURCE: RC, PCC (Item 41), DNA; addressed on cover "His Excellency / Henry Laurens Esqr· / President of Congress."; addressed below close "His Excellency Henry Laurens Esqr·"; dated "Camp Sep^r· 22^d· 1778"; docketed by HL "Col^s· Morgan, Williams / & Davies__ Camp 22 Sept^r / 1778__ dd me with other / Papers by Mr Griffin / as from Mr Harvie who / had left them in his hands__ / in Cong: 19 Octob⁓ 1778__" and in another hand "Laid before Congress & Read / "Octr 20. / Ordered to lie on the table".

TO JOHN LEWIS GERVAIS

Philadelphia, September 23, 1778

My Dear Sir

Let me upon this occasion refer you to His Excellency the President for Intelligence, and for the security of my property in case of another visit from Sir Peter Parker to your friendship__ should the menaces of Governor Johnstone be attempted you will be exceedingly distressed, the earlier removals begin, the more likely to save something.

---

for guards...also to serve as a military school for young gentlemen, previous to their being appointed to marching regiments." And, they were to be "constantly employed in the recruiting service." Col. Lewis Nicola commanded the corps which was originally stationed at Philadelphia. While the corps never fulfilled its training function, it did valuable garrison duty at Philadelphia, Boston, and West Point. *JCC*, VIII, 485; Wright, *Continental Army*, pp. 136, 330.

Your Letters by Sharp are just come to hand but 'tis impossible for me even to read them 'till tomorrow.

I shall write again about the 25th.—

I pray God protect you all

SOURCE: LB, HL Papers, ScHi; addressed "John Lewis Gervais Esquire / Charlestown / S^{o.} Carolina / by Wilkinson"; dated "23^d September".

TO RAWLINS LOWNDES

Philadelphia, September 23, 1778

Dear Sir

Mr. Richard Beresford arrived at a late hour last night from New York and immediately called on me and delivered a verbal Message from Robert Williams Esquire.

Mr. Williams had been frequently in conversation with Governor Johnstone, at the last interview which happened on or about the 17th he discover'd, as he presumed, the design of the Enemy to detach part of their Squadron together with 10,000 Troops immediately after the Hurricane Season to South Carolina to land at Charlestown or at Port Royal, or both.[1] Governor Johnstone intimated the Conquest would be easily made, and the acquisition extremely beneficial by annexing South Carolina and Georgia to Florida, he particularly enquired who were the leading Men in South Carolina and other minutia which I have communicated to my Colleagues and to Major Butler[2] and whose advices will supply my deficiencies.

Mr. Williams intreats me to avoid naming him as my informant, hence Mr. Beresford did not enter upon his disclosure until he had with great form shut the Parlour door.

---

[1] Lord George Germain, in his orders of March 8, 1778, appointing Clinton as commander in chief, had focused in part on a campaign against Georgia and South Carolina which would mobilize Loyalist supporters. In his letter of Aug. 8, 1778, which Clinton received October 10, Germain again urged Clinton to mount a southern campaign. Savannah rather than Charleston would be the initial target for the British offensive. Paul H. Smith, *Loyalists and Redcoats: A Study in British Revolutionary Policy* (Chapel Hill, 1964), pp. 89-94.

[2] Pierce Butler had held a major's commission in the British army until 1773 and continued to be addressed as "Major". An active patriot, poor health limited his military contribution to that of an advisor during this period. *Directory of the S.C. House*, III, 108-114.

The Idea of secret, in this case, is truly ridiculous. M^r. Williams M^r. Hopton M^r. Graham and some others are going to Charlestown with a Flag of Truce.

I asked M^r. Beresford upon what principle Sir Henry Clinton had permitted these Gentlemen to go over to the Rebels, he replied with a smile, "a mark of extraordinary favor, certainly."

The announced enterprize is the most likely to succeed so far as to create a favorable diversion of any I can think of at this juncture of circumstances. It is the favorite Plan of General Grant[3] and 'tis not improbable Sir Henry will be glad of an opportunity to recover the honor he left in the Sands of Long Island[4]

Is it likely that Governor Johnstone would have communicated a design of such importance to M^r. Williams? How shall I account for M^r. Williams' betraying to me the confidence reposed in him. These are questions I have answered to my own satisfaction__ and submit them to Your Excellency__ M^r. Williams is exceedingly cautious I have received two Messages but[5] no writing from him.

All that Governor Johnston has said to M^r. Williams may have been calculated for amusement__ at the same time his Flag may cover two or more Engineers in Frooks and Trowsers and other dangerous instruments in disguise. Your Excellency will be governed by your own judgment and the best advice respecting the admission of either the Vessel or any individual contained in it higher than five fathom hole or Cumings Point and admitting her arrival whether she ought not to be detained, and the Officers and all the People belonging to her secured out of Charlestown.

I have written fully on this subject to His Excellency General Washington, and will have the honor of writing more fully than the present to Your Excellency in two or three days.

---

[3] Maj. Gen. James Grant, a former governor of East Florida with military experience in South Carolina, may well have promoted a Charleston centered southern campaign. At this time, however, he was preparing to launch a 5,000-man expedition to St. Lucia in the West Indies. Willcox, *Portrait of a General,* pp. 241-242, 253-254.

[4] During the British attack on Charleston in June 1776, Sir Henry Clinton commanded troops that landed on Long Island (Isle of Palms). The depth of the channel and the lack of boats kept them from crossing to Sullivan's Island and attacking the patriots who successfully held their fortified position there. Willcox, *Portrait of a General,* pp. 87-89; *HL Papers,* XI, 244-245.

[5] "u" written over "y".

I have ordered this Messenger Wilkinson[6] to ride night and day, and hope he will be in Charlestown on the 8th of October and be returned as expeditiously as possible.

I have the honor to be / With the highest Esteem and Regard

P.S.

This instant I have received repeated intelligence by escaped Prisoners from New York that the Enemy have abandoned Rhode Island, but I rely not upon such Reports.

SOURCE: LB, HL Papers, ScHi; addressed "President Lowndes, / Charlestown / So. Carolina / by Wilkinson"; dated "23d September". Copy (19th century), HL Papers, ScHi.

S.C. DELEGATES TO ROBERT WILLIAMS

Philadelphia, September 24, 1778[1]

Dear Sir

We thank you for the Intelligence by Mr. B___ he had a quick Journey and communicated your Message the moment of his arrival.

Fortunately we have there and in the neighbourhood so many Regulars and so many good Militia who always are held ready to join our own as will meet them with grace either in force or detachments___ but we will not boast, let them try again___ the Account is now $^1/_6$[th] of the distance on the way to C.T.

One article we anxiously wish to know, the number of ships of the line destined for the service, we mean ships of 50___ they know better than to risque larger___ it will be in our favor at this Season even to attempt 50's___ [2] the time when the Enterprize is to com-

---

[6] Samuel Wilkinson.

[1] Date changed from "22" to "24" in manuscript.

[2] The Charleston harbor bar stretched north and south several miles. The five passages through the bar were all shallow with only the "Ship Channel" deep enough to accommodate more than a sloop. When the British Navy returned in March 1780 to assist in Sir Henry Clinton's siege, no ship over 50 guns attempted to cross. Even the 44- and 50-gun vessels had

mence is another important article you omitted__ the services you have rendered your Country on this occasion will be properly acknowledged.

We understand by your two Messages that you are in such good Cr^t with the heads there as to leave no room to fear the miscarriage of this__ pray tell us when you expect to sail.

~~Your~~ ↑A↓ Letter directed to the President under Cover to Brigadier Maxwell will come very safe[3]

SOURCE: Copy, Misc. Mss. (Thomas Bee), DLC; addressed by HL "Delegates of So Carolina / to R Williams Esquire"; dated by HL "24 Septr 1778"; docketed "The Delegates of South / Carolina to R. Williams / Esq^r__ 24 Septr 1778.".

FROM SILAS DEANE

Philadelphia, September 24, 1778

Sir

Being informed that Letters from Mr Izard, reflecting on my Character and Conduct whilst in the service of the public abroad, have been read in Congress I have to ask that honorable Body to grant me Copies thereof.[1] and that I may be permitted to wait on Congress and to be heard in my vindication.[2] I have that regard for Mr Izard's opinion of my ability and disposition to transact public business which I ought to have, and am consequently easy on that subject; but facts asserted which affect either, call for an explanation. Those indeed which respect myself person-

---

to be lightened by removing guns, water casks, and supplies to negotiate the passage. Tilley, *British Navy*, pp. 176-179.

[3] Final sentence written by HL.

[1] Ralph Izard's letters to HL, dated Nov. 24, 1777, Feb. 16, March 1, April 1, and April 11, 1778, "of which he had informed Congress upon the receipt thereof and afterwards...all contained matters of private as well as public nature, and of which Congress declined to receive extracts" were read September 19. Congress answered Deane's request for copies by ordering that he "be furnished with extracts of all such parts...as relate to his public conduct." *JCC,* XII, 935-936, 949; *HL Papers,* XII, 81-82, 496-500; XIII, 65-67, 95-99.

[2] On September 26 Congress assigned the afternoon of September 29 for hearing Deane. In the meantime, however, they decided to take testimony from William Carmichael, who "had charged Mr. Deane with misapplication of the public money, &c." Deane's hearing was postponed and he did not begin presenting his testimony until December 22. *JCC,* XII 927, 955, 968, 1246, 1247, 1265.

ally, require none before Congress, nor will I trouble that honorable Body with the making any; but those which regard my Character and Conduct as a public Minister, and in so important a transaction as that of the late Treaties of Paris, call on me, as well in justice to the public as to myself, for an explanation which I am very happy in the having it ↑in↓ my power to give, as well as in the confidence I have, that Congress will neither delay nor refuse doing this justice to a faithful and greatly injured servant of theirs.

I have the honor to be &ᶜ·

(signed) Silas Deane

SOURCE: Copy, PCC (Item 103), DNA; no address; dated "Philadelphia 24 September 1778".

FROM JOHN LAURENS

Fredericksburg, N.Y., September 24, 1778

My dear Father.

I have received your kind favour of the 17ᵗʰ· inst:__

the information[1] which you give me relative to my hospitable acquaintance, gives me great pain__ I had conceived an esteem for him, and it afflicts me to find a new instance of the depravity of my species__

I am sorry that Kinloch did not return to America sooner__ his former sentiments on the present contest, give reason to suspect, if he is a convert, that success[2] on our[3] side, has alone Operated the change__ something[4] may be drawn in palliation of his conduct from the education he received, and the powerful influence which his Guardian had over him__[5]

Beresfords circumstances were peculiar, he has been uniformly a friend to his Country__

---

[1] "information" written over other text.
[2] "su" written over other text.
[3] "o" written over other text.
[4] "th" written over other text.
[5] Francis Kinloch's father died in 1767 and Governor Thomas Boone assumed guardianship. Kinloch was enrolled at Eton College in 1768 and at Lincoln's Inn in 1774. In 1776 he supported the monarchist position in debating the merits of Thomas Paine's *Common Sense* with JL, who defended republicanism. *Directory of the S. C. House*, III, 402-405; Massey, "A Hero's Life," pp. 138-144.

The approach of the period which you allude to, occasions the greatest anxiety in my mind__ the Public interest and my own lead me to wish that you may be continued in the august Assembly of the States__ I dread your being so remote from where my duty places me__ and see collected in one view all the painful consequences of it__ it was my intention at all events to have paid you the homage of my love in Philadelphia at the close of the present Campaign__ We are at present in a disagreeable state of suspense__ continued preparations in New York announce a very considerable embarkation__ our spies inform us that a council of war had been held, and continued for three days__ Lord Howe had certainly arrived__ Gen[l.] Grays troops had returned by way of the sound, and been relanded__ Admiral Byron in the Princess Royal of 90 Guns, accompanied by the Culloden Cap[t.] Balfour of 74 had arrived at[6] New York; illegible according to the Gazette of that place__ but I believe the truth was that they only arrived off the Hook__ they are since arrived at Newport where they are refitting__ it is probable that the Princess Royal could not get into port at N. York,[7] without taking out the greatest part of her Artillery__[8] accounts from various quarters__ inform us, that Lord Howe is preparing for England, and that Admiral Byron will take the Command__

the Arrival of the August Packet will in all probability determine his[9] operations__ the sickly state of his Crews__ and the damage which his Ships suffered in the storm; have rendered him inactive, here 'till the opportunity is lost for the only enterprise which remains for the[10] enemys combined land and naval force in America__

Nothing remains for them, but to garrison render the Garrisons of Quebec & Hallifax respectable__ (at the latter place, the Seventieth Regiment, the Duke of Hamiltons, and the Duke of Argyles highlanders, according to the N. York paper have arrived.__) to evacuate New York and Rhode-island__ and withdraw

---

[6] "at" written over "&".

[7] "at N. York," inserted in left margin.

[8] Byron, *Princess Royal,* arrived at Sandy Hook September 16, but "just as his flagship was about to enter the channel, a squall came up, brought down her fore topsail yard, and nearly ran her aground." At this point he gave up attempting to enter New York harbor and sailed to Rhode Island. Tilley, *British Navy,* p. 154.

[9] "his" written over "the".

[10] "the" written over "them in".

the flower of the[11] whole british infantry, which in their present situation, are useless as to the General operations of War__ The french have more Troops in the West india Islands, than are necessary for a mere defensive plan__ their magazines are well furnished__ the british on their parts are weak in both these respects in that quarter__ and I am convinced that the slightest demonstration there, would occasion the immediate removal of General Clintons Army__ Some think, that the british will keep possession of N.[12] York and Rhode island, to enable them to make better terms__

There is field for conjecture__ the british may at this moment be attempting a negotiation with France__ It ~~need is~~ can be neither her interest nor inclination to sacrifice her ally__ a general peace in this case would be the consequence__

__ but accident or the caprice of a minister, may disappoint the ~~best~~ most rational predictions, and give rise to events which at present appear the most improbable__

An unlucky affray has happened at Boston which gives us the deepest concern__ we are not acquainted with particulars any farther than that a quarrel arose between some American and French Sailors__ they proceeded from harsh words to more dangerous blows__ two valuable french officers who attempted to quell the riot, were much abused__ and one of them, the Count de S.t Sauveur it is feared will not recover__ Gen.l Greene informs us that the matter has been generally traced and found to originate with the convention troops__ the Sailors who were the immediate instruments were britons in the privateer service. If this is not strictly true, it is a story which policy w.d encourage__ [13]

Gen.l Greene in his first letter on the subject informs us that the french officers seemed satisfied that the mischief had been planned, by some artful hands in Bourgoynes Army__ but he since tells us that

---

[11] "thier" altered to "the".

[12] "N" written over "R".

[13] The Chevalier Saint-Sauveur was an army captain with d'Estaing's forces who died from wounds inflicted September 8 while trying to quell a riot at one of the bakeries established by the French squadron at Boston. In a letter of condolence to d'Estaing, Washington declared that an investigation of the riot had been "so far traced, as to leave no doubt that the plot originated with the convention troops, and that british Sailors in our service were the immediate instruments of their Malice...." *Lafayette Papers* (Idzerda), II, 180n; George Washington to Count d'Estaing, Sept. 29, 1778, *Washington Writings* (Fitzpatrick), XII, 517.

there are jealousies on the subject__

I saw very plainly when I was at Boston, that our ancient hereditary prejudices were very far from being eradicated__

A Serjeant Major who deserted from the 2ᵈ Battallion[14] of Highlanders gives Genˡ· Scott[15] the following intelligence__ that the 1ˢᵗ & 2ᵈ British Brigad[es] had received orders to hold themselves in readiness for embarking__ for the W. Indies__ that the Transports are lying in readiness to take them on board__ he has heard officers say that New York is to be evacuated__ another deserter asserts that four Regiments are already embarked__ &[16] that the horse transports as well as others are ordered to prepare for Sea__

I omitted to mention to you that Lord Howe was on board a frigate during the whole time that Count d'Estaing gave him chace__ this is a privilege allowed to Admirals for their personal security__ and is analagous to a Generals ↑placing himself↓ on a safe eminence to view an engagement__ but it could only be used in a desperate case and by a man of Lord[17] Howes established Reputation__[18]

For want of time to arrange my ideas, I have written you a chaos of intelligence which I fear you will hardly be able to reduce to any kind of order__

You[19] will not I hope quit Philadelphia, immediately after the first of next month__ a few days more must develop the enemys intentions, and may give me an opportunity of obtaining a furlough at a time when it will not be dishonorable to take one__ The Campaign in all probability will terminate very insipidly__ by the evacuation of N. York & Rhode Island__ and I shall have time enough to rejoin the army for the Canadian Expedition if it should take place__

Anticipating the happiness which I shall enjoy in embracing

---

[14] "Ba" written over "Di".

[15] Brig. Gen. Charles Scott of Virginia was stationed at Philipseburg Patent, N.Y. *Washington Writings* (Fitzpatrick), XII, 482n.

[16] "&" inserted in left margin.

[17] "Lord" written over "General".

[18] At the onset of the battle off the coast of Rhode Island, Admiral Howe had moved from his flagship the 64-gun *Eagle* to command from the frigate *Apollo*. Tilley, *British Navy*, pp. 150-151.

[19] "You" written over other text.

you, I commend myself to your love, and my dear father to Gods protection.

John Laurens.

Gen[l.] Scott informs us that a party of the enemy have advanced[20] ~~illegible~~ on this side Kings bridge__ another party have landed at Paulus hook and ~~illegible~~ advanced beyond Bergen__ from the description they are strong foraging parties__ and design to glean the Country previous to taking leave__

Our General has given orders to[21] parry any stroke which they may ↑possibly↓ meditate against our posts in the highlands__ tho' the possibility of such an enterprise is exceedingly remote; and their dispositions in this case would be void of common sense__

SOURCE: ALS, Kendall Collection; addressed on cover "(Private.) / His Excellency / Henry Laurens Esq[r] / President of Congress / Philadelphia__"; addressed below close "His Excellency Henry Laurens Esq[r.]"; dated "Head Quarters 24th September 1778."; docketed by HL "John Laurens / 24[th.] Sept[r] 1778 / Rec[d.] 28[th]_ / Answ[d.] 2[d.] October".

FROM LACHLAN McINTOSH

Pittsburgh, Pa., September 25, 1778

Dear Sir,

I rec[d.] ~~the~~ ↑Your↓ favor of the 23[d.] Ult[o.] ⅌ Return of the Express & thank you for the Intelligence it contained, which was realy an Act of Charity to one stationed so remote as I am, & accustomed ↑only &↓ almost Daily to hear the Commission of some Act of Savage Barbarity against our fellow Citizens without having it in my Power Yet to retaliate.

I am Sorry to hear Since, that General Sullivan has not Succeeded according to his Sanguine Expectations, but "Whatever is, is best."__ [1] I thought I could observe some of us were too much

---

[20] "advanced" inserted in left margin.
[21] "to" written over other text.
[1] HL's own motto. As an old friend, McIntosh had often heard Laurens use the phrase. *HL Papers,* IX, 157n

Elated already, & fear more from our Prosperity than adversity.__

I heartily Congratulate ↑you↓ on the growing & deserved Fame of your Son, who (Plantagenett Like) Distinguishes himself on every Occasion & in a Noble Cause, that of his Country & Humanity.__

The two Letters you forwarded were from Georgia, which gave Account of the Loss of some of ↑my↓ Negroes, by a Distemper which raged among the slaves in that state; but what I Lament most is the failure of the attempt upon Florida, Occasioned as I am informed by the Ambition of Individuals,[2] & that infernal Dæmon Discord its Natural Progeny, which rages more than ever in that unfortunate Little State.__ I hope their Conduct will be thoroughly Canvassed & enquired into.__ pray are we better Represented in Congress Yet, than by that insignificant Creature I Left at Yorktown?[3]

I have nothing yet from this Quarter worth Communicating to you,__ My Letter to the Board ↑of warr,↓ to which I begg Leave to refer you, will shew you my Present Situation, & General Lewis who accompanys the Express part of ↑the↓ way hurrys me to Conclude with wishing you every Happiness & am Dear Sir

Y[r.] most ob[t.] Hble Serv[t.]

Lach[n.] M[c.]Intosh.

Will you please to Present my Comp[ts.], to W.H. Drayton__ Mathews__ Heyward &__ Huttson Esq[rs.]__

SOURCE: RC, Kendall Collection; addressed on cover "(Private) / The Honourable.__ / Henry Laurens Esq[r.] / President of Congress / Philadelphia / ꝑ Express__ M[r.] John Gibson"; addressed below close "The Hon[l.] Henry Laurens Esq[r.]"; dated below close "Pittsburg 25[th.] Sept[r.] 1778"; franked "Lach[n.] M[c.]Intosh"; docketed by HL "Geñ McIntosh / Pittsburgh 25 Sept[r] / 1778 Rec[d.] 6 October / Answ[d] 18[th]_".

---

[2] "vid" written over other text.

[3] Edward Langworthy was the only Georgia delegate at York when Lachlan McIntosh left there in June 1778. By this time, Edward Telfair and John Walton had joined him. *Delegate Letters* (Smith), X, xvii.

TO RICHARD CASWELL
Philadelphia, September 26, 1778
Sir

I had the honor of addressing Your Excellency under the 5th Instant, since which I have received none of Your Excellencys favors.

This will convey an Act of Congress of the 25th for the immediate defence of South Carolina and Georgia to which I beg leave to refer.[1]

The apprehension which gave rise to this Act, springs from a private verbal Message sent to me by Robert Williams Esquire a Native of South Carolina, a Practitioner of the Law, a Man of good understanding, and of a very respectable general Character, possessor of a large Estate in that Country, but more attached to his private Interests, than zealous for the establishment of our Independence, and held to be a friend and favorite of the Ministers of Great Britain. This Gentleman's communication which I received three days ago imported that he had, on or about the 19th Instant, learned from Governor Johnstone that an attack by an Army of ten thousand troops, and a sufficient number of Ships of the Line was intended upon South Carolina at Charlestown and Beaufort-Port-Royal, or both; that Governor Johnstone obtained permission for him and several other unstaunch Carolinians to proceed to Charlestown under a flag of Truce.__ M[r.] Williams anxiously pressed a very ridiculous request "that I would not give him up as the Author of this important discovery"__ which strongly implies a degree of treachery and no less a degree of artifice.

Is it likely that Governor Johnstone would have informed M[r.] Williams the Plans intended by the Commanders of the British Land and Sea forces? It is possible he may have entrusted him with the secret for valuable considerations, the flag Vessel may contain

---

[1] A committee composed of William Henry Drayton, Joseph Reed, Richard Henry Lee, William Duer, and Samuel Adams had been appointed September 23 to review the intelligence HL had received "relative to the motions of the enemy." They reported the afternoon of September 24, and consideration continued until the following day after which Congress passed three resolutions. Virginia was requested to send 1,000 and North Carolina 3,000 men to South Carolina. Governor Caswell was, if he found "it consistent with the duties of his station," to march "at the head of the North Carolina forces" as a major general in the Continental army. And, the militia of South Carolina and Georgia were to be called and put on Continental pay. *JCC*, XII, 945, 948, 949-950.

skilful Engineers in the habit of Mariners, and she may Return with such intelligence as may greatly facilitate the meditated execution__ how shall we account for M^r· Williams' breach of confidence? only by supposing that in any event he means to secure his own Estate, and wishes to meet a more hospitable reception in Charlestown than his fears had indicated without this harbinger.

The recovery of South Carolina and Georgia is a project of the first magnitude to Great Britain in her present circumstances__ it is consistent too, with the declared intentions of her Ministers from the commencement of the present War, "that those Provinces should be the dernier resort"__ the subduing those States in the approaching November, unless in the mean time an ample aid shall be supplied by their Northern neighbours, will certainly be no difficult work__ the expected plunder of an abundance of Provisions, Merchandize, many thousands of Negroes, great quantities of Cannon and warlike stores, Horned Cattle, Sheep, Hogs, and Horses, an immense value of Indigo, and upward of 200 Sail of Ships & other Vessels appears to be a sufficient temptation to the Enterprize.

I have lately examined upward of 30 Deserters from Byrons' fleet, and many other Persons from New York, all of whom concur in opinion that an abandonment of that City and Port is intended, but none pretend to know whither the forces are to be transported; the most intelligent Person among these Informants intimated that the Enemy had contrived to circulate whispers of their designs so contradictory in terms, as to leave the truth undiscoverable, he had been much on board the Eagle, Man of War, and although he professed his ignorance in general, he had collected so much from various conversations as had induced him to believe the Enemy intended a complete evacuation of New York and Rhode Island; that Hallifax would be strengthened by one part of the Troops, the West India Islands by a second part, and the remainder cross the Atlantic for reinforcing Great Britain and Ireland.

A sensible Correspondent in General Washington's Camp gives me as his opinion, that the destruction of Count d'Estaings' Squadron will not be left unessay'd. If Your Excellency will have patience to hear my ↑private↓ sentiments, I will add, that Sir Henry Clinton is taking every necessary step for a sudden removal when he shall receive Orders from Whitehall, expected about this time by the August Packet, and there is no place more inviting than South

Carolina, an attempt ↑therefore↓[2] upon that State is most to be dreaded, especially as the Expedition may be made consistently with a voyage to the West Indies, consume but little time, and success be the means of securing a twelve Months food for the most populous of all the Islands, and for many Political considerations which will in a moment strike Your Excellency's Mind.

General Washingtons Camp was on the 19th Instant at West Point. We know nothing of transactions at Rhode Island except the return of Sir Henry Clinton to New York from thence and from thence the successful descent of General Gray upon Bedford and Marthas' Vineyard.

It is said that about 50 empty transports came out of Sandy Hook and steered southerly in view of Egg Harbor four days ago, and that the Enemy have landed about 5000 Troops at Hackinsack: these I regard only as Reports.

This instant came in two Seamen who left New-york the 21[st.] They say the Isis to which one belonged has lost upward of 50 Seamen by desertion. The other from the Conqueror reports near 100 Deserters from that Ship, both confirm the Accounts of intended evacuation__ the Packet was not arrived__ all the Men of War have lost Men in proportion, as these fellows aver. They add that the fleet in general were extremely sickly, provision extremely dear and scarce__ and repeat the landing at Hackinsack, and that the troops as well as Seamen were inclined to desert.[3]

I have the honor to be / With the highest Esteem & Regard / Sir / Your Excellency's / Most obedient & humble / servant[4]

Henry Laurens.

President / of Congress

SOURCE: LS, Franklin Collection, CtY; addressed below close "His Excellency / Governor Caswell / North Carolina__"; dated "Philadelphia 26th September 1778"; docketed "Letter from Presid[t.] / of Congress dated / 26[th.] Sep[r.] 1778. / inclosing an Act of / the 25[th.] request[g.] Aid". Copy, Nc-Ar. Extract, MH. Notation in LB, PCC (Item 13), DNA.

---

[2] Interlineation by HL.

[3] The 50-gun *Isis,* John Raynor, was being repaired at New York after doing battle with the 74-gun French ship *César.* The ship *Conqueror,* Thomas Graves, had sailed as part of Admiral Byron's squadron. A long and stormy crossing with a sickly crew probably resulted in a high number of desertions while the vessel remained at New York waiting for Byron's arrival. Tilley, *British Navy,* pp. 146-147, 151-152, 191.

[4] Close written by HL.

TO RAWLINS LOWNDES

Philadelphia, September 26, 1778

Dear Sir

Inclosed under Cover with this Your Excellency will receive a duplicate of a private Letter which I had the honor of writing to you under the 23ᵈ· by Wilkinson

I have not solid intelligence at present for adding much, and will not trouble your Excellency with recitals of flying Reports__ 'tis certain the Enemy are daily making signs of an intended general movement from New York, but 'tis unknown to us what is doing at Rhode Island__ I shall learn in a day or two from the Commander in Chief__ Your Excellency will perceive from the inclosed Copy of a Letter from one of the General's Secretary's to the Gentleman who officiates in that Character under me,[1] that nothing important was known four days ago at Head Quarters

The British Seamen desert daily from Staten Island &c__ I believe not less than one hundred are come into this City; I have examined many of them, but receiv'd no very interesting information

I shall have an opportunity of writing by Major Butler in two or three days, and again soon after by Lieut Colonel Ternant, and being anxious to send forward the public Letter which will accompany this I will not further detain Your Excellency than to repeat that I am with very great respect & Esteem

Your Excellency's Obedient & / Most Humble Servant

H.L

SOURCE: Copy (19th century), HL Papers, ScHi; addressed "President Lowndes / South Carolina"; dated "26 Septemʳ·".

TO JONATHAN TRUMBULL, SR.

Philadelphia, September 26, 1778

Honorable Sir

I beg leave to refer to my last of the 13ᵗʰ Instant by Mʳ· Dodd.

Yesterday Congress took under consideration a Report from the Marine Committee, and thereupon Resolved that the new frigate at Norwich be called the Confederacy, and that Seth Harding

---

[1] Probably a letter from John Laurens to James Custer or Moses Young, HL's clerks. No letter has been found.

Esquire be appointed to the Command of the said frigate,[1] the vote for Captain Harding was unanimous. I declared it accordingly, but[2] I perceive the Secretary has omitted to insert it in the Act of Congress which your Honor will find within this Cover__ Captain Harding is a Man of more dispatch than vanity, and will not wait the necessary time which an amendment will require, I commend him.[3]

I Am with the most sincere esteem & Regard / Honorable Sir &c.

SOURCE: LB, PCC (Item 13), DNA; addressed "Governor Trumbull / Connecticut / by Captain Harding"; dated "26th September".

TO GEORGE CLINTON
Philadelphia, September 27, 1778

Sir

On the 21st I had the honor of receiving and presenting to Congress Your Excellency's favor of the 9th Instant, and in answer I herewith transmit an Act of Congress of the 21st, duplicate of the Act of the 17th and Copies of the Sundry Papers which Your Excellency desired to be furnished with, in these I trust there will be found no deficiency, and I intreat Sir, you will be assured the late omission, of which you have justly complained was not the effect of inattention on my part.[1]

---

[1] Seth Harding (1734-1814) had a distinguished career in the Connecticut navy before his appointment to command the *Confederacy*. As captain of the ship *Defense* in 1776, he captured three British vessels which provided badly needed supplies for Washington's army. The next year his vessel, the *Oliver Cromwell*, captured two British ships. Governor Trumbull had written to Congress in support of Harding's appointment. Harding commanded the *Confederacy* from the spring of 1779 until he was captured two years later by the British. William M. Fowler, Jr., *Rebels Under Sail* (New York, 1976), p. 247; Claghorn, *Naval Officers*, p. 139; Jonathan Trumbull, Sr., to HL, Aug. 27, 1778, PCC, Item 66, Vol. 1, p. 10ff; *JCC*, XII, 951.

[2] "b" written over "p".

[3] Harding had waited impatiently in Philadelphia while the Marine Committee deliberated and made its recommendation. On September 24, he wrote to HL "to beg my business may be accomplished as soon as possible__" Seth Harding to HL, Sept. 24, 1778, PCC, Item 78, Vol. 11, p. 333ff.

[1] Governor Clinton wrote on September 9 to say that he read in the *New York Packet*, September 3, that the Court of Inquiry report on the 1777 loss of the Hudson River Highlands posts had been considered by a Committee of Congress and that no fault had been found with his actions. Because he was named in the inquiry and wished official exoneration, he requested that "certified Copies of the Report" be sent to him. HL was responding by order of Congress. George Clinton to HL, Sept. 9, 1778, PCC, Item 67, Vol. 2, p. 134ff; *JCC*, XI, 803-804; XII, 936.

All our Public Offices, which have hitherto been conducted as well, I presume, as circumstances in an infant State would admit of, now call for inspection and improvement, and none more than the Secretary's Office, from whence alone, according to the present Plan mode, I derive subject for every public Letter.[2] The Act of the 21st signifies the entire approbation by Congress of Your Excellencys' conduct as Commander of the Forts on Hudsons River, which I repeat with great pleasure in obedience to the Order of Congress, and from that sincere respect and esteem for your Excellency's Character with which I have the honor to be,

Sir / Your Excellency's Most Obed.t. & / Most Humble Servant

SOURCE: LB, PCC (Item 13), DNA; addressed "Governor Clinton / New York / by Dunn"; dated "27th Septr.".

TO GEORGE WASHINGTON

Philadelphia, September 27, 1778

Sir

I had the honor of writing to Your Excellency the 20th Instant by Colonel Hazen.[1]

This will be accompanied by an Act of Congress of the 25th Inst. for the immediate defence of South Carolina and Georgia, to which I beg leave to refer.

Congress have appointed Mr. John Ternant Lieutenant Colonel in the service of the United States, and Inspector of the Troops in South Carolina and Georgia to which I beg leave to refer and ordered that he be allowed the Pay and subsistence of a Lieutenant Colonel from the 26th March last.[2]

I have the honor to be &c.

---

[2] HL frequently criticized Charles Thomson, secretary to Congress.
[1] Col. Moses Hazen of the 2nd Canadian Regiment had been sent to Congress by Washington with a petition from officers interested in an invasion of Canada. Congress endorsed the plan on September 16. Hazen also used this time to gain support for his regiment which was "small and top-heavy with officers" and the target of reformers who sought to reduce or disband it as a savings for the treasury. On November 24 Congress voted to maintain the regiment. Allan S. Everest, *Moses Hazen and the Canadian Refugees in the American Revolution* (Syracuse, N.Y., 1976), pp. 61-64; *JCC*, XII, 919, 1159.
[2] Jean-Baptiste de Ternant, a French volunteer, had been appointed a subinspector March 28, 1778. He was captured at the fall of Charleston. *HL Papers*, XIII, 37n; *JCC*, XII, 952.

SOURCE: LB, PCC (Item 13), DNA: addressed "General Washington / by Dunn"; dated "27ᵗʰ Septʳ.".

FROM JOHN LAURENS

Fredericksburg, N.Y., September 29, 1778

My Dear Father

I have received your kind favor alluding to the verbal demonstration by which my friend Beresford was bamboozled___ and was indulged with the perusal of your Letter to the General, in which you treat the matter in its proper light.[1]

The Enemys' superiority by Water give them cruel advantages over us___

Baylor's Regiment of Horse has been surprized by a strong Party of the Enemy that surrounded them by coming up the North River___ a number of Militia shared the same fate few escaped___ the greatest part being taken Prisoners or killed___ several were butcher'd in cold Blood___[2] the Enemy are now in force on the Jersey side, and make a shew of advancing.___ General Lord Stirling is gone to take the Command of the two Brigades of Continental Troops and such Militia as shall collect to them___ General Winds[3] has already embodied six hundred.

The circumstances of the Enemys' collecting forage is equivocal, it may be either for Winter Quarters or Sea Store.___ The intelligence given by General Sullivan of the Enemys' being employed in building Barracks is against a move from thence___ but I

---

[1] HL's September 23 letter to General Washington, in terms like those he employed in his letter of the same day to Rawlins Lowndes, questioned the reliability of the intelligence Robert Williams conveyed by Richard Beresford concerning a British expedition to South Carolina. But HL admitted "the possibility of the design" and recommended preparations by Congress "as they ought if there was no ground for doubt." HL to George Washington, Sept. 23, 1778, HL Papers, ScHi.

[2] Lt. Col. George Baylor's 3rd Continental Light Dragoons was nearly wiped out by two British units under Gen. Charles Grey in a surprise attack at Old Tappan, N.J., the night of September 27-28. Thirty-six were bayonetted; forty captured; and only thirty-seven escaped. Baylor was among the wounded who were captured. Accounts of the "massacre" were published in the *Pa. Packet* by order of Congress. Ward, *War of the Revolution*, II, 616-617; *Pa. Packet*, Oct. 29, 1778.

[3] William Winds of Morristown, N.J., a brigadier general of the New Jersey militia posted at New Tappan about two and one-half miles from Baylor's forces, had learned of the proposed attack and had withdrawn his own troops without warning Baylor. Ward, *War of the Revolution*, II, 616-617.

am inclined to think his Intelligence ill founded.__[4] The Enemy may still meditate an Enterprize against Boston, which has been delayed till now by the sickly condition of Byrons' Crews, and the injury which he suffer'd from the Storm__ but I do not think it probable.

This Letter would be inexcuseable if I had not been writing the whole day, and snatched now a Moment when the Postman calls__ to scribble full speed, rather than be totally silent.

I Am my Dear fathers' / Most Affectionate

John Laurens

SOURCE: Copy, HL Papers, ScHi; addressed below close "His Excellency Henry Laurens / President of Congress"; dated "Head Quarters 29th Septr. 1778"; docketed "Copy of a letter from Colo. John / Laurens dated 29th Septr. 1778".

FROM JEREMIAH WADSWORTH

Philadelphia, September 29, 1778

Sir

Previous to the Resolutions of Congress of the 24th of August directing the purchase of 20,000 Barrels of Flour to be shipped to the New England States,[1] a number of Speculators had gone through the States of Maryland and Virginia and engaged a great part of the Wheat and all the Flour, even where the purchasing Commissaries had before been directed to purchase, they were out bid by private purchasers; who are more numerous in every State than any other Sett of Men, and have ready money which my purchasers are not possessed of__ I have not the least doubt but the total ruin of the Currency will soon happen and the Army disband for want of Food if immediate effectual measures are not taken to put a Stop to the practices of those miscreants the Monopolizers of Food__

---

[4] JL's views echoed those of Washington who had written Sullivan on September 27 that "there were many circumstances that led to a belief that an evacuation [*from New York City*] was intended." *Washington Writings*, (Fitzpatrick), XII, 510.

[1] The commissary general of purchases was ordered to purchase 20,000 barrels of flour "on the most reasonable terms" in Pennsylvania, Delaware, Maryland, and Virginia. *JCC*, XI, 831.

Immediately on the resolution of Congress to allow the New England States to carry out Flour by Water the price increased twenty five ⅌ Cent and the buyers were numberless and the price continued to increase when I left Maryland__ I am informed that permission is now given for the people of any State South of this to export Flour to New England__ if this permission would not be abused perhaps it would not wholey prevent our getting Supplies for the Army but neither Oaths or Bonds can bind Men who are not govern'd by honour or Conscience and I believe the Enemy will obtain as much of the Flour shipp'd for New England as the people of those States, and that a greater quantity will go to the Islands; as a hard northerly wind will be an excuse to bear away from this Coast for the West Indies and a protest Cancell the Bonds__

A Resolution of Congress of the 12th instant forbidding the purchasing of Wheat for Forage unless in cases of absolute Necessity will not relieve us as that necessity exists at this time and wheat is now actually purchased for Forage__[2] the other part of the same resolution directing me to Order no damaged wheat to be purchased forbids my purchasing any wheat in Virginia where it is all damaged by the Fly as is great part of the wheat in Maryland__ The Mills in Virginia are many of them destroy'd by the Violent Storms. and but little Flour is yet made and that principally in the hands of private persons who will Ship it__ and if Flour should be hereafter obtained it will be impossible to transport it to the Army as the Roads already very bad will soon be impassable with loaded Teams

The inclosed Letters and extracts will point out other Evils[3] which with what I have above mention'd appear to me to be Sufficient to prevent the Supplies for the army and Fleet being obtain'd, and shall not therefore add many others that occur as I wish to occasion Congress as little trouble as possible__[4]

I am / Sir, / Your most Obed^t humb^l Servant

Jere^h Wadsworth Com Gen Pur.

---

[2] *JCC,* XII, 906.

[3] Manuscripts not found.

[4] HL received letters with similar complaints from deputy quartermaster general Francis Wade and agent for the commissary of forage Owen Biddle about the same time. Francis Wade to HL, Sept. 28, 1778, PCC, Item 78, Vol. 23, p. 567ff; Owen Biddle to HL, Sept. 29, 1778, PCC, Item 78, Vol. 3, p. 197ff.

SOURCE: RC, PCC (Item 78), DNA; addressed on cover "His Excellency / Henry Laurens Esquire / President of / Congress___"; addressed below close "His Excellency / Henry Laurens Esq / President of Congress"; dated "Philadelphia September 29ᵗʰ· 1778"; docketed "Letter from col J Wads / worth Sept 29. 1778 / Read 29 Septʳ·- / Referred to comᵉᵉ· of col / Blaine's memorial & the / letter from Col H Hollinsworth". Draft and LB, Wadsworth Papers, CtHi.

FROM BARON VON STEUBEN

Fredericksburg, N.Y., September 31, 1778[1]

Sir

If I have returned no Answer to the two Last Letters you have favoured me with,[2] it was not to add to the Trouble of your continual Business by a less interesting Correspondence.__ With regard to the Inspection, I have nothing to say, but that I shall wait in a respectfull silence for the decision of Congress on that object If the Arrangements I have proposed for the Good of the Army are not accepted of, by having fulfilled a Duty I had[3] imposed upon me I have acquitted what I owed to myself, as Well as to all the Military.[4]

But, Sir, let us now drop this subject, & Examine a little the present Situation of our Military Affairs__ So happily[5] Escaped from a very critical one at Rhode Islᵈ· that the Enemy has no Advantage to boast of, Either on the fleet of our Allies, or our own Land forces. A storm has proved favorable to them, and rendered abortive our Enterprize. However, as it is Great to give the Enemy his due, We will fairly own that they and the Winds have hindered the Success of two important attempts which, had they succeeded, should have proved very fatal to them, the one on the Delaware (had the french fleet arrived a little sooner) & the last at Rhode Island__ The King of Prussia himself, in the Wars which I made with him would have

---

[1] Von Steuben dated this letter September 31; it is not clear whether the correct date should be September 30 or October 1.

[2] HL wrote to von Steuben September 13 and 17.

[3] "have" altered to "had".

[4] Congress did not adopt the reorganization plan for the inspector general's office until Feb. 18, 1779, and, because of General Washington's criticism, that plan did not provide the authority that Steuben had proposed.

[5] "i" written over "y".

reckoned that a happy Campain in which he would have Caused two such Enterprizes to prove ineffectual.

Now, our Plan is Entirely defensive__ A very difficult one in the Execution, & which often proves dangerous We must not lose Sight of two objects Equally important, tho' far ↑distant↓ from one another, I mean, the maintaining the North River & the opposing ourselves to any Enterprize the Enemy may make at the Eastward. In the Condition our army is in, inferior in Number to that We have to contend with, We must be Ready to resist any attempt whether at the East or West, And how shall we prevent that unhappy State of New Jersey to be pillaged and ransacked by the Enemy?__ Lord Cornwallis is there at the head of a Body perhaps of Six thousand Men, & Lord Stirling with Three Brigades, I shall not say how strong for fear of afflicting you. But pray, is that number Sufficient to oppose the forces of the Enemy? You will say that they will be joined by the state Militia__ But is it that same Militia America could boast of when she had yet no Enlisted Troops?__ Do they retain the same spirit which animated them at that Time? And now, if you take from our Army these three Brigades, & the two that are at Providence, what remains to us on this side the River? Pray, Sir, do not suffer yourself to be dazzled by the Accounts of the Strength of our Regiments and Brigades, at least a third part on them are unable to suffer the fatigues of a march, in this Season when Nights begin to grow cold & damp & that for want of Cloaths, Even of Shoes or Stockings. I dont fear displeasing you by laying the naked Truth before your Eyes, on the Contrary, I think it my duty not to Suffer you to be ignorant of the true state of our Army__ And now Examine the Land forces of our Enemies in this Country, their Numbers, food, cloathing and arms, their discipline & good order; Compare afterwards, and then tell me if you dont think our Case somewhat hazardous?__

How long will America suffer her Welfare to depend on the good or ill success of a day?__ Is it not certain that a greater loss will arise from the plundering of the Jersies, than it would have Cost to Keep the Regiments complete after the plan given by Congress? We should now have an Army of 40000 Men, and had We Even ten thousand less, would the Enemy dare Set their foot out of York Island?

An Army too numerous, I own, is Expensive, but the Contrary Extreme is dangerous. It was, I think, in 1776, that Gen[l] Washington had the glory to keep the field at the Head of an Army of 1800 Men__ I wish he mayn't have that glory again. Had a proper number of Soldiers been Raised, the War would probably at this time be at an End. In our present Situation the best principle I know of to procure a Solid and honorable peace, is, that the Warlike preparations should be Encreased to the double. Withal, Sir, if our Regiments are not completed, and put on an Equal footing, it is absolutely unnecessary to think of any Arrangement, Either in the Administration or Manœuvres, or Even of any Order or Uniformity in our Army.

You are not ignorant of Col. Baylor's Reg[t] having lately been taken by surprize__ The Consequence of a bad discipline. The service of the guards, piquets, & patrolls is totally neglected in our Army. Our Cavalry is without a Chief, without an Officer acquainted with the service__ Brave, it is true, but bravery never made an Officer.

Here is a long and woful Complaint on our Military Affairs, in which I do not Set them in a most advantageous Light, But were I to attempt to draw after Nature, I fear my picture would surpass all Likelihood.

Be persuaded, Sir, that you are the only person to whom I speak in such an unreserved manner, I know very well that whatever be one's Circumstances, the best is to put on a cheerful face, or as the French term it: <u>faire bonne mine à mauvais jeu</u>. But as I wish nothing more that the good of this country, it is the cause that makes me so anxious

Please to forgive the length of this Epistle to which I shall now put an End by renewing the assurances of the respectful sentiments with which

I have the honor to be / Sir / Your Excellency's / Most obed[t] & very humble serv[t]

Steuben

SOURCE: RC, Kendall Collection; addressed below close "His Excellency Henry Laurens, Esq, / President of Congress"; dated "Fredericksburgh, September 31st 1778."; docketed by HL "Baron Stüben / 31 Septem 1778 / Rec[d.] 7 Octob__ / Ans[d] 12th-". Copy (19th century), HL Papers, ScHi.

TO WILLIAM LIVINGSTON

Philadelphia, October 1, 1778

Dear Sir

I have been fifteen days indebted for your favor of the 11th: Ulto: and six for another of the 17th: believe me, Sir, I hold myself Your Excellencys debtor in every respect, and be pleased to apply this candid Declaration to the first and every kind paragraph of the former.

The entrance of Messrs. Kinlock and Jeffrey[1] was certainly very irregular, altho' I am persuaded their intentions respecting these States were to add two faithful Citizens to our numbers. I can vouch for the former, and must rely on the assurances of the other Gentleman__ I wish General Maxwell and the Magistrates in New Jersey whom it concerns would restrain all illicit importations from New York__ the Managers in that Garrison may now and then send us good goods in order the more effectually to impose counterfeits upon us__ I have faithfully executed your Excellency's commission by delivering the message to Mons Girard, who repeated, sentiments which he had expressed of your excellency's character before he had had "the honor of receiving your visit"__ we cannot say too much of this Gentleman's merits <u>out of his own hearing</u>.

I do'nt know any thing more troublesome than the conversation of those people who are eternally pestering one with recitals of their dreams this[2] does not however aim a blow at ↑against↓ all dreams↑__↓ within this exception I trust that a dream of my own which will appear in Dunlaps next packet will be viewed by your excellency__[3] I mention this because New Jersey is the Grand subject and you may be surprised at the presumption of any man the Governor excepted in dreaming about New Jersey the impressions of the visions alluded to were twice strongly made on my mind__ I regarded the second as an high command and determined it my duty to reveal the whole to that part of the world for whose benefit it seemed principally designed but I have given strict orders to my Herald to conceal the dreamers name, after this intimation your Excellency will be in that part of the Secret which I mean to go no ~~further~~ further.

---

[1] Livingston had written to HL on September 11: "Messrs. Kinloch and Jeffrey came with a flag from New York to Brunswick....The latter sailed not long since from Maryland with a Cargo of Tobacco for France." HL Papers, ScHi.

[2] "this" written over dash.

[3] See HL to the *Pa. Packet,* Oct. 3, 778.

Inclosed with this your Excellency will receive a copy of a New address from one of the Gentry at New York and of a sort of no-answer which Congress thought proper to return___[4] look sir at the date of the extract from Lord George Germain's letter, compare it with the dates of the late requisitions and remonstrances from Mess[rs] Carlisle & Company on the same subject. Is it not highly probable when those papers were fabricated the letter from whence this extract was made was in the hands of that Company?[5] Is it not therefore to be presumed they are now in possession of "a distinct and explicit ratification by the Court of Great Britain"[6] under special orders prohibiting the "due notification to Congress" until every Stratagem shall have failed? If it be true as I beleive it is that the French forces are scouring the British West India Islands and that Admiral Keppell has not beat the Brest Squadron our trouble-some inmates on this Continent must soon leave us in more quiet possession of our own beds.___

Adieu D[r] Sir &c.

HL.___.

SOURCE: Copy, HL Papers, ScHi; addressed "Governor Livingston / New Jersey"; dated "1[st:] October".

FROM JOHN HOUSTOUN

Savannah, Ga., October 1, 1778

Dear Sir

I did myself the Honor of addressing you in a publick Letter

---

[4] On September 19, Sir Henry Clinton wrote, under instruction from the crown, "that the Convention of Saratoga be fulfilled," and enclosed an extract of a letter he had received from Lord George Germain dated June 12, 1778. Congress ordered Charles Thomson to reply "Sir, I am directed to inform you, that the Congress of the United States of America make no answer to insolent letters." Henry Clinton to HL, Sept. 19, 1778, CO 5/96, PRO; JCC, XII, 964.

[5] Clinton received Germain's June 12 letter on August 18. The remonstrance from the Carlisle Commission on the subject of the Convention Army was dated August 26. This, however, was a duplicate of an August 7 letter which the Congress had not answered. HL was correct in believing that Germain's letter had arrived by the time the August 26 Carlisle Commission remonstrance was sent, but not before it was written. Documents of the American Revolution (Davies), XV, 139.

[6] HL's paraphrase of Congress's January 8 resolution under which Burgoyne and the Convention Army remained prisoners. JCC, X, 35.

on the 20th. of August, and therein gave you a full Detail of our Southern Expedition.

Since that time I am favor'd with your's of the 18th. July__ (private) and am happy to hear of the assistance you promise Mr. Telfair in bringing the affairs of our poor little State on the Tapis. the ready attention you have ever manifested to the Interest & Service of Georgia, of wch. the Inhabitants at large possess the most grateful Sense, assures us we shall never be unrepresented whilst you are in Congress, and therefore, Sir, we do upon all Occasions rest satisfied our Delegates may be furnished with the best Advice & assistance in the Conduct of their Business.

I assure you our Situation at present looks gloomy__ We seem to be encompassed with Enemies, and by no Means in a Posture within, to make any great Exertions. the predatory war that has taken Place between this state and East-Florida, has hurt us prodigiously we certainly in that petit Guere play a losing Game. whilst they have fine well-settled Plantations with Plenty of moveable Property on them to ravage, we have nothing to expect but here & there a Negro to be pick'd up in a Desert or pine-Barren.

a small Privateer out of Sunbury about five weeks ago brot. off all Dr. Turnbull's Negroes to the Number of thirty odd from his Plantation at the Musquitoes together with some other Effects. in Reprizal the People from Florida have since in armed Boats carried off 44 Negroes from the Island of Sapello, chiefly belonging to the Estate of old McKay.[1] the Enemy's Scouts by Land are constantly coming in upon Us and carrying off our Horses & Cattle. insomuch that there is scarce a good Horse left in the whole State. I am told Numbers have been shipt from St. Augustine to New-York.

the Creek Indians have broke with Us, and since the 9th. of August have killed & cruelly butcher'd upwards of thirty of our Inhabitants. they also drive off large Gangs of our Horses & Cattle, and what they cannot conveniently carry away, they shoot down. South Carolina gave Us the most ready & generous Assistance, and

---

[1] Patrick Mackay, a Scotsman and Indian trader, acquired Sapelo and Blackbeard islands from Grey Elliott in 1762 and became Sapelo's first large-scale planter. He engaged in farming around the northwest end of Sapelo until his death in 1776. Mackay's estate sold the island in 1784. Buddy Sullivan, *Early Days on the Georgia Tidewater: The Story of McIntosh County & Sapelo* (Darien, Ga., 1992), p. 80.

the active & intrepid Col: Williamson at the Head of 546 Men immediately crossed over, and is now upon our Frontier. as soon as this Force, added to our own appeared, the Indians retired, but I make no Doubt they will be upon Us soon again. M^r. Galphin thinks it is only a Part of the Nation that have taken up the Hatchet, and that the greater Part are still our Friends, but even suppose this to be the Case I do not see any Advantage we shall derive from it, unless such as are Friends assist Us in subduing the others, which I am told they refuse to do. M^r. Galphin's Labours have been immense, but I fear Stuart's Presents have got the better of them. whilst we have inculcated Neutrality, the Enemy (more Savage than their Allies) have adapted themselves more[2] to the Genius of the Indians, and paid them for Scalps, taken indiscriminately from Men Women & Children.

Should this War be prosecuted by them (wch. from every Appearance I think will be the Case) I do not know what will become of Us unless We are speedily & powerfully assisted.[3] but I shall tire you with Complaints and will therefore drop the Subject__ being sensible you and Congress will do every thing for Us you can.

We have been for some time past in anxious Expectation of some agreeable & important News from your Quarter, but as yet have had nothing certain, since the Arrival of Count D'Estaing.

I have the Honor to be / with the greatest respect / and Esteem. / Your Excell^y's. most Ob^t. / servant.

J. Houstoun

SOURCE: RC, Kendall Collection; addressed below close "His Excell^y. / H: Laurens Esqr.__"; dated "Savannah 1st. Octr. 1778."; noted "(private).".

FROM RAWLINS LOWNDES

Charles Town, October 1, 1778

Dear Sir

I neglected, by M^r. Neufville whom I troubled with a Lett^r. to your Excellency, to perform a promise I made to Capt. Hatter to

---

[2] "more" written over other text.
[3] "a" written over other text.

recommend to your Care a Letter from him to his Son, who he apprehends is amongst the Prisoners taken with Capt Hawker, and to Sollicit your good Offices in his favour as he is persuaded his Son, from Choice and Inclination woud rather take a different part from what he has hitherto done__ You will please therefore to receive herewith a Lett^r to Wm Hatter and also another to your self from the said Capt Hatter on that Subject, your humanity will sufficiently Interest you in the wishes of a Father for an only Son, and as I told Capt Hatter his best advocate would be found in your own breast.__ [1] The Notre Dame returned here yesterday having Landed Commodore Gillon at the Havanah, where the Commodore Meets with some difficulty in procuring a suitable Opportunity to proceed to France and has not received that warm profession of Friendship our Sanguine hopes had led us to expect from that Nation__ but on hearing of the Arrival of their Plate Fleet in Spain, their Civilities were encreased__ I send you a Lett^r inclosed in my packet from the Havanah__ [2]

__ This day came to Town from Beaufort the Capt of the Genl Moultrie Lett^r of Marque by Land, bro^t with him the Master of a privateer he has taken 14 Guns & 70 Men after a smart engagem^t in which the Enemy lost 12 Men killd & many wounded and was very much disabled the Genl Moultrie not at all hurt & only one Man dead of his wonds since the Action__ She was from Jamaica ab^t 3 Weeks had taken nothing__ a Boy the masters & one Smith also wounded__ [3]

Muckenfuss arrived last Tuesday by whom I was honoured with your dispatches__ the Retreat of Genl Sullivan was noble and deserves to be ranked amongst the highest Atchievem^ts of the present War__

---

[1] Capt. John Hatter commanded the privateer *Hope* and had been a prisoner at St. Augustine until his exchange in May 1778. *HL Papers*, XII, 275-276.

[2] The enclosure probably was the September 18 letter from Alexander Gillon, who explained that "Contrary Winds & bad sailing" on his voyage for France had induced him to turn south to Havana. He found the Spanish officials reticent in dealing with Americans but noted Cuba would be an excellent port to careen and refit vessels and, if permission could be obtained, an excellent market to sell ship lumber and naval stores. Alexander Gillon to HL, Sept. 18, 1778, HL Papers, ScHi.

[3] The *General Moultrie*, Newton, captured the Jamaica privateer brig *Wasp*, William Smith, after "an obstinate engagement of near two hours." The *Wasp* had 10 killed and 14 wounded; the *General Moultrie*, 5 wounded. *S.C. General Gazette*, Oct. 1, 1778.

many People were disappointed that we did not obtain Rhode Island I have the Advantage of most in not placing too much dependance on those uncertain Events so lyable to Vicissitudes in the very moment of Confidence__ Our Assembly is still sitting tho the House is [*freed*] of the most of the Country Members terrifed by the Sickness of Some & the Death of others__ You will see by the Inclosed paper what they have done in respect to the Embargo I am sorry the resolve of Congress had not arrived before the Ordinance passed that they might have provided for the law within the View of Congress but I hope it will still be done by a Clause tacked to some other Bill__ [4] I have heard nothing lately from Williamson in respect to Indian Affairs since I had the Honr. of Writing to you by young Neufville__

__ I was disappointed in not receiving a further Supply of Commissions for the Army the many Vacancies to be filled up by promotions resignations & Deaths required a Considerable number__ You will be pleased Sr. to excuse this Scrible performed by Candle Light which I am very unfit for and never undertake but in Cases of Necessity as this is not knowing of this Opportunity till since dark & the Messenger I expect every Moment to call for my Lettr. who it seems is going on the Business of the Marquiss De Fayette__ [5] I will trouble you no more than while I beg leave to Assure you that I am with very great Regard

D_r. Sir Your very hum Ser_t.

Raw^S. Lowndes.

SOURCE: RC, Kendall Collection; addressed on cover "His Excy Henry Laurens Esq"; addressed below close "Hoñble Henry Laurens."; dated below close "Thursday Night / 1st. Octr 1778"; docketed by HL "Presidt. Lowndes / 1st. October 1778 / Recd 7th. Novem__". Copy (19th century), HL Papers, ScHi.

---

[4] The legislature's action of September 28 prohibiting the exportation of provisions, hemp, and cordage until November 15 was extended by Lowndes own proclamation on November 19. *S.C. General Gazette,* Oct. 8, Nov. 19, 1778.

[5] Lafayette had purchased a ship, *La Victoire,* and cargo which had been consigned to John Splatt Cripps, a Charleston merchant. *Lafayette Papers* (Idzerda), II, 66n, 500; *HL Papers,* XIII, 343.

TO THE PENNSYLVANIA PACKET[1]
Philadelphia, October 3, 1778

> *"A virtuous woman is never solicitous to resound her chastity, although she feels a proper degree of resentment at being called a Whore even by implication."*

Mr. DUNLAP,

I HAVE very little faith in dreams, but whenever those unaccountable visions of the night make such strong impressions upon the sensorium as to leave whole pages of what I dreamt I had read or heard, it is my practice to commit them to writing early in the morning, and at my leisure to remark the difference between my sleeping and waking vagaries. I am an old man, and have been thought a good friend to American liberty, but too insignificant to be called on to carry a musket. I amuse myself with reading news papers, conversing with my neighbours about the times, applauding the young fellows who turn out chearfully against the common enemy, and encouraging such as appear a little timid.

I was last night under my pipe reading your packet of the 10th of September, some parts of which led me into deep reflection, and while I was taking a general view of public affairs, the conduct of each of the United States, and of their representatives in Congress, I fell asleep.

In this state of freedom from the cares of the world, a little fairy maid, ten thousand times handsomer than any Tory Lady in Philadelphia with her top-gallant-royal commode, stood at the foot of my oaken elbow chair, delivered me a paper containing the identical words here underwritten. She dropt a curtesy, said "Old man, Virtue is its own reward," and vanished.

"FACTS."

"The largest return of the army commanded by Major-General Sullivan in his late attempt against Rhode Island, amounted

---

[1] HL informed William Livingston on October 1 that he had prepared this account of his "dream", the impressions of which "were twice strongly made on my mind," for "Dunlaps next packet." The first impression was Livingston's "dream" which he sent enclosed to HL September 17. HL, by adding a different preface and conclusion, quotes or closely paraphrases Livingston's dream and thus the criticism of Congress's September 9 resolution extolling the New England states' militia actions in the Rhode Island campaign. William Livingston to HL, Sept. 17, 1778; HL to William Livingston, Oct. 1, 1778; *JCC*, XII, 894.

to ten thousand men; the Militia of the Eastern states who had joined him could not therefore exceed five thousand.

"The firing of a tar barrel and the discharge of a cannon collected instantly four thousand of the New-Jersey Militia, who joined and co operated with the army under His Excellency General Washington in his pursuit of the enemy through that state—And— *N.B.*—this was in the time of harvest.

"The Eastern Volunteers, who composed about one moiety of General Sullivan's army, took occasion to return home before the General's retreat, leaving him and the other moiety of troops on the island.

"The Jersey Militia continued with General Washington till the enemy was routed, and their assistance no longer necessary.

"General Sullivan seems to complain a little of the Eastern Militia's *going off and reducing his army to little more than the amount of those of the enemy.*

"General Washington declares his *deep sense* of the services of the New-Jersey Militia in *opposing the enemy in their march from Philadelphia, and for the aid which they had given in harrassing and impeding their motions, so as to gain time for his troops to come up with them.*

"Congress by their resolve of the tenth ult. declare their *high sense* of the *patriotic exertions* made by the four Eastern states on the late expedition against Rhode-Island.

"BUT,

"By no resolve have Congress ever manifested *any sense* of the *patriotic exertions* of the state of New-Jersey, whose Militia have twice put to the rout nearly the whole army of the enemy in their marches through that state."—

I had finished reading this paper, and was entering upon reflections in order to reconcile the conduct of Congress from a persuasion that they never willfully err, when my pipe dropped out of my hand; the clattering upon the floor startled and awoke me.

Now I am awake, let me, Mr. Printer, say what I should probably have dreamt had not the breaking pipe disturbed me.

From the sentiments which I entertain of the wisdom of Congress, I am perfectly satisfied the partiality implied in the fairy tale did not arise from a predilection in that august body to any particular state or states, but from mere inadvertency.—Inadvertence, howbeit the common failing of human nature, should not too often appear in the acts of those who are appointed guardians of an infant empire, and with the most profound respect for the FREE CHOICE OF THE PEOPLE, I claim the liberty of the press to inform them that all their proceedings in and out of doors are inspected by

AN OLD MAN.

[**] STATES, take the hint.

[**] And ye, British Commissioners know we are free.

SOURCE: Printed in *Pa. Packet*, Oct. 3, 1778.

FROM GEORGE WASHINGTON

Fishkill, N.Y., October 3, 1778

Dear Sir

Your favor of the 23ᵈ· Ult. came to my hands at Fredericksburg the afternoon before I left it for this place.__ I thank you for the transmission of Mʳ· Beresfords intelligence, tho I have not the smallest Idea that any thing more than a deception, is meant by it; and, that Mʳ· Williams is either a voluntary Agent, or the innocent instrument, for carrying it on.__ Yet, as the case may be otherwise, common prudence bids us guard against the worst.

A conclusive evidence against the measure with me, is, his speaking of the Force as a detachment only__ I am well convinced myself, that the Enemy, long e're this, are perfectly well satisfied, that the possession of our Towns while we have an Army in the field, will avail them little__ It involves us in difficulty, but does not by any means insure them conquest.__

They well know, that it is our arms, not defenceless[1] Towns, they have to subdue, before they can arrive at the haven of their wishes; and that till this end is accomplished, the superstructure they have been endeavouring to raise "like the baseless fabric of a vision"[2] falls to nothing__ But this, tho a reason operating powerfully with me, in deciding upon the point, is by no means the most weighty consideration in my Mind.__ A Measure of this kind, before the hostile disposition of France became so obvious, and before the French Squadron arrived upon our Coast, was probable, as their whole conduct was full of unaccountables; but to attempt now, to detach 10,000 Men (which is, I presume half their Army) and to

---

[1] "c" written over other text.
[2] Shakespeare, *The Tempest*, I, i, 148.

divide their Naval strength for Protection of it, would, in my judgment, be an act of insanity, & would expose one part, or the other, of both Land and Sea force, to inevitable ruin__ I therefore conclude, that they will transport their whole, or no part of their force there.__ And yet, I may find myself mistaken.__

As you have not acknowledged the receipt of my letter by Major (now Lt Col^o) Morris, by whom I took the liberty of returning the first Paper parcel of gold you were so obliging as to send me__ nor of of one of posterior date by Col^o Hazen, inclosing the Letters of Govr. Johnstone, M^r. Manning &ca. I am somewhat fearful that they may have been mislaid, and forgot, as these Gentlemen were charged with other business of more consequence__ [3] With every Sentiment of esteem, regard, and affection I am

Dr Sir Y^r. Most Obed^t. / & oblig'd H^ble. Servt

G^O: Washington

SOURCE: RC, PWAcD, Feinstone Coll., on deposit PPAmP; no address; dated "Fish-kill Octr. 3^d. 1778."; docketed by HL "Geñ Washington / 3^d. Octob^r. 1778 / Rec̄d 7th / Ans^d 10th.". ADraftS, Washington Papers, DLC. Copy (19th century), HL Papers, ScHi.

TO RICHARD CASWELL

Philadelphia, October 4, 1778

Sir.

My last Letter to Your Excellency was under the 26th. Ult^o. by Messenger Jones.

Within the present cover will be found two Acts of Congress Viz^t.

One of the 29th. Septem for enabling the States of Virginia & North Carolina to purchase certain Cannon now lying in North Carolina which had been imported on account of the United States.[1] And one of the 2^d. Inst. for extending the Present Embargo

---

[3] Washington's letter of September 4 delivered by Lewis Morris has no docket of receipt; Washington's letter of September 12 delivered by Moses Hazen was docketed as received September 15. See above.

[1] Because of a shortage of artillery, a plan had been offered to allow North Carolina and Virginia to use the recently imported cannon "until the further orders of Congress." The final resolution, however, provided that Virginia be allowed to purchase twenty-four and North Carolina twenty-five "dividing them equally as to weight of mettle." *JCC*, XII, 968.

on provision to the last day of January 1779 & for divers other purposes therein mentioned.[2]

Inclosed Your Excellency will also find extract of a Letter from a correspondent of mine in Camp giving a melancholy account of a late advantage gained by the Enemy over Colonel Baylor's Regiment of Horse & some of the Jersey Militia[3]

I have the honor to be / With very high Esteem & / the utmost Respect / Sir / Your Excellency's / Most obedient hum / ble Servant

Henry Laurens.
President / of Congress.

SOURCE: ALS, Governor's Papers, Nc-Ar; addressed below close "His Excellency / Governor Caswell / North Carolina"; dated "Philadelphia 4th· Octob˜ 1778__"; docketed "Presidᵗ Laurens / Philᵃ· 4 Octo. 1778.". LB, PCC (Item 13), DNA. Copy, Nc-Ar.

FROM JONATHAN TRUMBULL, SR.

Lebanon, Conn., October 5, 1778

Dear Sir

With great sincerity and satisfaction I beg leave to congratulate Your Excellency on the happy escape from danger of your son, in the late attempt on Rhode Island, and on the honor he has very justly obtained from the share he bore in the events of that Expedition, particularly in the memorable Battle fought on that Island__ With much gratitude to the Disposer of events, I also acknowledge the safety of my youngest son, who voluntarily, and without my approbation, shared the like dangers in the same expedition__[1]

I have none of your private favors to acknowledge, tho I have had my expectations__ Suffer me to ask your particular influence[2]

---

[2] In addition to the resolution to continue the embargo until the end of January 1779, Congress also included a recommendation to the "states to pass laws for the seizure and forfeiture of all grain and flour" that had been purchased or engrossed to take advantage of the high prices created by the embargo. *JCC*, XII, 974-979.

[3] The extract was from John Laurens's September 29 letter to his father. Governors' Letter Books, Nc-Ar.

[1] John Trumbull (1756-1843) served as a voluntary aide-de-camp to Gen. John Sullivan during the Rhode Island campaign. Shortly after the evacuation he left the service and sent "a descriptive letter to my father, a drawing of the field," and a sword he had taken from the battlefield as a trophy. *The Autobiography of Colonel John Trumbull*, ed. Theodore Sizer (New Haven, Conn., 1953), pp. 46-51.

[2] "influence" written over erasure.

on the subject of my Representation to[3] Congress__ an unnoticed[4]
Representation of like nature from my Son, was very grievous to
him__ It could not be pleasing to me__ I hope this will not meet the
like delay__ Were it not that your own good sense will dictate to you,
and your goodness will prompt you to make use of many considerations on this head, I could suggest a thousand things which might
be said on the score of that justice which I have fondly thought was
due to the merits of my Son, who I think has deserved honorably of
the Public, for his Public Services__ notwithstanding all the hard
treatment which he experienced__ the same justice which was his
due, while alive, is now due to his Relict and Heirs__ Your influence
in this determination will be peculiarly grateful to me__[5]

　　With much Consideration Respect & Esteem / I am / Your
Excellency's / most humble Servant

Jon^{th;} Trumbull

SOURCE: RC, Jonathan Trumbull, Sr., Papers, CtHi; addressed on cover
"Hon^{ble}_ Henry Laurens Esquire__ / Philadelphia / ⅌ M^r_ Brown /
Messenger__"; addressed at bottom of first page "Hon^{o.} President Laurens";
dated "Lebanon 5th. Oct^o 1778"; franked "Lebanon / Jon^{th;} Trumbull";
docketed by HL "Govr. Trumbull / 5 Octob. 1778 / Rec^{d.} 3^{d.} Ans^{d.} 10 Nov^{r.}";
noted "(Private)." Copy (19th century), HL Papers, ScHi.

TO ROBERT HOWE

Philadelphia, October 6, 1778

Sir

　　I have lately had the honor of receiving and presenting to
Congress many of your Letters, but I have nothing in Command
respecting you except the inclosed Resolutions of the 25th of
September, directing you to repair immediately to General

---

　　[3] "to" written over erasure.

　　[4] "an unnoticed" written over other text.

　　[5] Governor Trumbull sent a proposal for settling Joseph Trumbull's accounts the
following day enclosing William Hoskin's September 17 petition on the same subject. Both
were referred to a committee composed of Samuel Adams, Josiah Bartlett, Oliver Ellsworth,
and Richard Henry Lee on October 15. Because exceptions were made to the Committee's
report, the matter was recommitted November 2. The committee's recommendations were
not adopted until March 31, 1779. Jonathan Trumbull, Sr., to HL, Oct. 6, 1778, PCC, Item 66,
Vol. 1, p. 414ff; *JCC,* XII, 1011, 1091-1092; XIII, 395-401.

Washingtons' Head Quarters and Major General Lincoln to take the Command in the Southern Department.[1]

I have the honor to be &c.

SOURCE: LB, PCC (Item 13), DNA; addressed "Major General Howe / Charlestown / by Dugan to Baltimore, there to be deliver'd Col^o. Ternant"; dated "6th October".

TO RAWLINS LOWNDES

Philadelphia, October 6, 1778

Dear Sir

I beg leave to refer to my last private of the 26th. Ulto by Millet.[1] This will be delivered by Lieu^t. Colonel Ternant who is ordered by Congress to Act as Inspector of the Troops of the United States in South Carolina and Georgia__ this Gentleman has served as a Volunteer in the grand Army with the highest reputation__ South Carolina and Georgia will in Mr Ternant receive the acquisition of an excellent Officer, and each in turn experience in him a valuable Citizen__ his Conduct and manners will speak more in his favor than I can express

I shall do myself the honor of inclosing with this several Papers of Intelligence which with the informations Your Excellency will receive from Mr Ternant and such additions as no doubt will be made by my Colleagues will put Your Excellency in possession of all our present knowledge of public Affairs. In a Letter which I had the honor of writing to Your Excellency the 5th. Instant as President of Congress is contained a late Act for continuing the present Em-

---

[1] Congress recalled General Howe largely because of his continued disagreements with the political and military leaders in the Southern Department which undermined their cooperation. Governor Houstoun of Georgia, who refused to act in conjunction with Howe's Continental forces, blamed him for the failure of the East Florida expedition. Col. Andrew Williamson would not allow his South Carolina militia to be assumed under the Continental command. Personal animosity with Christopher Gadsden promoted by the South Carolinian's jealousy over Howe's command resulted in an August 30 duel. The final straw, according to North Carolina Congressman Cornelius Harnett, concerned "the little ridiculous matters he has been concerned in, in So. Carolina with regard to a female," which provoked the Georgia and South Carolina delegates to demand his recall. Benjamin Lincoln did not assume the command until Jan. 3, 1779, and Howe remained in the south until April. *JCC*, XII, 951; Bennett and Lennon, *A Quest for Glory*, pp. 85-101; *Delegate Letters* (Smith), XI, 252; *S.C. General Gazette*, Sept. 3, 1778.

[1] Joseph Millet. *HL Papers*, XII, 495n.

bargo, and for preventing engrossing Provision__ I shall not trouble you Sir with my opinions on the several branches of this Act but barely remark that when the power of Congress to lay an Embargo was made a question and the voices of each Member called upon__ there appeared fourteen in the negative, twelve affirmative__ six States affirmative, five negative. Of those six affirmatives, there were three States represented by Units[2] I am persuaded my Countrymen will Act on this great occasion as shall appear to be for the general good of these United States. If I may offer my sentiments Congress is not vested with sufficient power to lay a general Embargo and it would be dangerous to vest them with such power in our present system__ the recent Act I humbly conceive marks incompetency__ nevertheless I think it will promote the public good to restrain the exportation of Provision until January, and therefore I wish there could be a general restraint excepting of such quantities as should be found sufficient for re-equipping the fleet of Count d'Estaing, and a necessary supply to our fellow Citizens in the Eastern States under these indulgences and thro the artifices of cunning Men I fear the honest Citizen and fair trader will bear an heavy burthen__ so far as respects my own interest altho' I am persuaded the intended prohibition will in several States be evaded, and have doubts whether any regard will be paid to it in Pennsylvania and Delaware I am willing to submit__ Articles which the Enemy stand more in need of than either flour or Rice, I mean Tar, Pitch and Turpentine remain unrestrained. I offer'd on this head as many intimations as my situation in the Chair would permit, but without effect.

Inclosed Your Excellency will receive three Bills of Exchange particularized below, amounting to 50.000 Dollars a Draught out of the public Treasury here at the request of the Delegates for the use of South Carolina on Account of her general demand upon the United States__ the funds in the Treasury are so very low and the

---

[2] A copy of the Oct. 2, 1778, journal entry, in Charles Thomson's hand and signed by him, for the amendment to "continue the embargo and recommend it to the states to take measures for enforcing it" is in the HL Papers, ScHi. While the journal contains no record of a debate or vote on the issue of the right of Congress to lay an embargo, HL noted on the verso of the copy of the amendment "Votes Ay & No on the power of Congress to lay a gen̄: Embargo__ 2ᵈ· Octōb ☞ actually taken the 3ᵈ· late afternoon Octʳ· 2. 1778__" New Hampshire, Rhode Island, and Connecticut were the "three States represented by Units". The entire South Carolina delegation, HL, William Henry Drayton, and John Mathews, voted no.

daily demands on them so enormous we could not venture to ask for a larger sum___[3] The inclosed Note from Mons[r.] Gerard N[o] 1 I recommend to Your Excellencys particular attention Mr Ternant will deliver a Copy of General Lee's tryal so far as the Press is gone___ Congress will determine hereon in a few days

Bills___	Don Juan de Miralles 28[th:] Septr 1778 on Dan[l.] Hall and C[o4] at ten days sight	}	40.500
	Brown Platt and Russel 9th July 1778 on Maurice Simons[5] at ten days sight		7.500
	John Head[6] 26th June 1778 on Alex[r.] Rose Esquire[7] at ten days sight		2.000
			———
		Dollars	50.000
			———

I have the Honor to be / With great Esteem & Respect &c.
H.L

Schedule of papers inclosed viz

N[o]   1___Mons[r.] Gerard on Carolinas raising men in France
N[o]   2___ Extract of a Letter from A. Lee June 1[st.] 1778[8]
"   3___Sir H. Clinton's Letter to Congress with the Secy[s.] Answer 23[d.] Sept[r.] 1778.
"   4___Gov[r.] Livingstons Letter to the Pres[t.] 28[th:] Sept[r.9]
"   5___Copy of a Letter from Gen[l] Washington to the President 27[th:] Sept[r.10]
"   6___ Extract of a Letter from a Gentleman in Camp 29 Sept[r.11]

---

[3] Congress ordered "50,000 dollars, for the use of that State, which is to be accountable" on September 23. *JCC,* XII, 946.

[4] Daniel Hall (1750-1811), a Charleston merchant, whose wife Susannah came from the politically prominent Mathewes family of John's Island. *SCHM,* XVII (1916), 8-9n; XXXVI (1935), 70; LIII (1952), 15.

[5] Maurice Simons was a Charleston factor and merchant. *HL Papers,* XI, 201n.

[6] Possibly John Head, a Philadelphia merchant. *PMHB,* VII (1883), 495.

[7] Alexander Rose was a Charleston merchant and shipowner. *HL Papers,* XIII, 116n.

[8] An extract of Arthur Lee to the Committee for Foreign Affairs, June 1, 1778, which was highly critical of Silas Deane. PCC, Item 103, p. 1ff.

[9] Gov. William Livingston to HL, Sept. 28, 1778, which discussed British troop movements and a possible assault on New Jersey. PCC, Item 68, p. 403ff.

[10] Washington's letter included much of the same information found in JL's letter of the same date (see above), but also contained an extract of a September 17 letter from d'Estaing. George Washington to HL, Sept. 29, 1778, PCC, Item 152, Vol. 6, p. 387ff.

[11] JL to HL, Sept. 29, 1778.

[*Enclosure*]

Gerard on Carolina raising Men in France

It is reported that the State of South Carolina in sending some Gentlemen to France has instructed them 1st to purchase a certain number of Vessels, 2nd to raise a certain number of troops to be in the pay and immediate service of that State.

It is apprehended that this step executed by a single State in contradiction with the Plan of Confederation, could hurt in Europe the Idea of the uniformity of the Governments to rely on Congress for the exertion and application of the common forces and it might be misunderstood or misrepresented to the prejudice of the confidence and the consideration Congress has so justly acquired

If the concern for all what is conducible to the honor and Credit of the United States may apologize for a reflection offered on that subject, I should venture to say that the best method to prevent any inconveniences is perhaps to send immediate Orders to the Minister of the United States in France, to countenance the demand of South-Carolina.

Monsr Girard having received information as above communicated his sentiments I think it improper to apply to Congress before I am informed of the facts from Authority in South Carolina. I shall nevertheless consult my Colleagues, and Act by their advice. Monsr Girard treats the subject with great seriousness.[12]

Henry Laurens

SOURCE: Copy (19th century), HL Papers, ScHi; addressed "President Lowndes / South Carolina"; dated "6th· October". Enclosure, HL Papers, ScHi; dated below close "Philad^a· 6th· October 1778"; docketed "Monsr· Girard on Carolina / raising Men in France. / N^o· 1 / Submitted to His Excellency / the President and ↑Privy↓ Council / of South Carolina / Henry Laurens / Copy".

---

[12] Gérard's apprehensions concerning Alexander Gillon's mission to France for the government of South Carolina were well founded. Gillon was charged with procuring three frigates, totally fitted out for war, and took three captains, John Joyner, John McQueen, and William Robertson to command them. To obtain crews they would have to recruit seamen in Europe for the South Carolina navy. No reply from South Carolina has been found and the lack of an assembly journal for this time makes even the reception of Gérard's warning uncertain.

FROM PHILIP SCHUYLER

Fredericksburg, N.Y., October 6, 1778

Sir__

A variety of unforeseen Events retarded Major General S^t· Clairs Tryal which did not Conclude until Tuesday last on the next day his Excellency the Commander-In Chief Appointed a Court Martial for mine which sat on the three next succeeding days on the last of which they determined on the Sentence. In all probability the Sentence will be transmitted In the Course of this week, and altho my[1] defence has been Prolix Yet may I be permitted to hope that when Congress reflects I have already been near fourteen months deprived, either of that Command In the Army which my rank Intitled me to or of that attention ↑which I ought to have paid↓ to my private affairs If I had resigned or been dismissed, they will not suffer me any longer to languish In a Situation of all others the most painful and which Indeed I have Incessantly Experienced every moment of my tedious Suspension with a sensibility for surpassing my powers of Description.

I am Confident Sir that the Humanity of your heart will not permit You one moment to delay expediting the determination of the respectable body at which you preside whenever It shall be obtained__ [2]

I have the Honor to be with Great respect & Esteem
Sir / Your most Obedient / Humble Servant
Ph: Schuyler

SOURCE: RC, PCC (Item 158), DNA; addressed below close "Honorable Henry Laurens Esq^r__ &c."; dated "Fredericksburgh Octr: 6th 1778"; docketed by HL "Genl Schuyler / 6 Octob^r 1778 Reċd / & Read the 16th / ordered to lie on the / Table__". Copy, PCC (Item 170), DNA.

---

[1] "m" written over other text.
[2] Before his selection as president in 1777, HL had been a member of two committees investigating the loss of Ticonderoga and Mount Independence. Schuyler, who had evacuated Ticonderoga, was acquitted by a court-martial. General Washington sent a copy of the proceedings of the court-martial on October 6 and HL presented both the proceedings and Schuyler's inquiry to Congress October 16. Congress finally exonerated Schuyler of all charges on Dec. 3, 1778. *HL Papers,* XI, 417n; Washington to HL, Oct. 6, 1778, PCC, Item 152, Vol. 6, p. 395ff; HL to Philip Schuyler, Oct. 17, 1778, PCC, Item 13; *JCC,* XII, 1186-1187.

FROM SILAS DEANE

Philadelphia, October 7, 1778

Sir

In consequence of my Letter of the 24ᵗʰ· ult I had the honor of receiving the order of Congress of the 26ᵗʰ·, directing me to attend on the 29ᵗʰ· at three oClock afternoon, that day being assigned for my being heard; I was at the same time favoured with extracts from Mʳ· Izard's Letters. On the 29ᵗʰ· I was served with an order of Congress which postponed my being heard to some future time. On the 3ᵈ Instant an extract of a letter from the honorable Arthur Lee, dated Paris June 1ˢᵗ· 1778, was given me by order of Congress.[1] I have for some time past waited with the greatest impatience for an opportunity of being heard before that honorable Body, confident that my peculiar situation will excuse my impatience. I must without repeating what I have already had the honor of writing to you, once more urge for as early an audience, as the important business before Congress will admit of.

I have the honor to be &ᶜ·

(signed) Silas Deane

SOURCE: Copy, PCC (Item 103), DNA; no address; dated "Philadelphia 7ᵗʰ· October 1778".

TO SILAS DEANE

Philadelphia, October 7, 1778

Sir

I have had the honor this Morning of receiving and presenting to Congress your favor of the present date. The Order

---

[1] The extract Deane received of Arthur Lee's June 1, 1778, letter to the Committee for Foreign Affairs included Lee's damning comments about "accounts which Mr. Deane ought to have settled." Claiming irresponsibility and extravagance, Lee insisted "this sort of Neglect and studied confusion...have prevented Mr. Adams and myself, after a tedious examination of the papers left with Dr. Franklin, from getting any satisfaction as to the expenditure of the public money. All we can find is that millions have been expended and almost everything remains to be paid for." PCC, Item 103, p. 1ff.

of the House was, "to lie on the table" until the Examination of M^r·
Carmichael shall be finished.[1]

I Am with great Respect / Sir &c.

SOURCE: LB, PCC (Item 13), DNA; addressed "Silas Deane Esquire /
Philadelphia / by M. Young"; dated "7th October".

TO MESHECH WEARE

Philadelphia, October 7, 1778

Honorable Sir

On the 13th Ult^o· I had the honor of addressing you by
Messenger Dodd, and since that of receiving and presenting to
Congress Your Honors' Letters of the 19th August and 18th September.

My present duty is to forward two Acts of Congress viz.

1. of the 2nd Instant for continuing the present Embargo on Provision until the last day of January 1779, and for divers other purposes therein mentioned.
2. An Act of the 5th Instant for exchanging with Continental Currency such local Bills of Credit as have been received in the Loan Office of each State respectively.

These will be found within the present Cover.

I have the honor to be / With the highest Esteem & /
Respect / Sir / Your Honor's / Most obedient servant[1]

Henry Laurens.
President / of Congress

---

[1] William Carmichael, who had been secretary to the commissioners at Paris, appeared before Congress September 28 and 30 and October 5. He did not resume his testimony despite being scheduled to attend again on October 19. Carmichael's testimony proved to be less damaging than Deane's opponents had hoped. This occurred in part because Arthur Lee, Deane's greatest detractor, had alienated Carmichael, who renewed his friendship with Deane. *JCC*, XII, 927-928, 964, 970, 984, 1010; *Delegate Letters* (Smith), X, 651-654.

[1] Close by HL.

SOURCE: LS, Meshech Weare Papers, MHi; addressed below close "The Honorable Meshec Weare Esquire / President of New Hampshire"; dated "Philadelphia 7th October 1778". LB, PCC (Item 13), DNA.

FROM JOHN LAURENS
Fredericksburg, N.Y., October 7, 1778

My dear Father__

The M. de lafayette will not long have delayed after his arrival to open to you a Plan for introducing French Troops into Canada__ from the manner in which he explained himself to the General, he seemed to intimate a desire, that Congress wd sollicit him to bring about this business, as being sensible of its utility to the United States__ & he did not expect to succeed in any other way than by ~~peti~~ intrigues, petticoat interest &c he lays down ~~the~~ as self-evident that Canada cannot be conquered by American Forces alone__ that a French Man[1] of birth & distinction at the Head of four thousand of his Countrymen__ and speaking in the name of the Grand Monarque is alone capable of producing a revolution in that Country__ When he asked my opinion privately on the subject and asked me what I would say[2] if I were a member of Congress to such a proposition__ I replied, that I did not think Congress could sollicit[3] or even accept it__ because there did not appear a sufficient reciprocity in the benefits to be derived from such an expedition__ on the one side there would be an immense expense of transporting troops__ loss of valuable officers and Soldiers__ &c in[4] fine all the disadvantage__ and on the other all the Gain__ that he did well to say the[5] ~~must~~ Project could only take place by indirect means__ for a Minister ~~unless he~~ *illegible* would not in his cool moments__ deprive his Country[6] of so many Troops, with no other view than that of killing so many Englishmen and conquering an extensive

---

[1] "M" written over "of".
[2] "say" written over other text.
[3] "s" written over other text.
[4] "in" written over other text.
[5] "he" altered to "the".
[6] "Count" written over other text.

province for us__ that he was to reflect that France tho powerful in men, had an extensive Frontier to guard__ and ~~probably~~ in an European War w^d. not have to do with England alone__ this was my private opinion to the Marquis__ my still more private opinion is that we sh^d. not give France any new Pretensions to Canada__ it is a delicate Subject to touch on__ but I dare say that we agree in our Sentiments__ and that the Mquis will be thanked for his good intention__ and his Offers waved__ [7]

Our last intelligence, from Deserters belonging to different Corps, and who came out at different times__ confirms the ~~embarkat prepara~~ ↑intended↓ embarkation of ten Regiments for the W. Indies__ the 10th 45th. & 52 they say are drafted to complete those[8] Regiments__ and the Forage and Live[9] Stock collected in Jersey are destined for their use__

Genl. Scott writes that the enemy are very busy in embarking baggage, as may be discovered from an eminence, to which his parties go__ [10]

You will see the last unavailing effort of the Commissioners in their Manifesto__ [11]

Your most affectionate

John Laurens.

---

[7] Interest in an invasion of Canada came from several sources. Generals Horatio Gates and Jacob Bayley and Col. Moses Hazen had recommended such an enterprise in a September 10 report to Washington which he forwarded to Congress. James Deane, an Indian agent in upstate New York, on October 6 conveyed intelligence concerning pro-American sentiments among the Caughnawaga Indians in Canada who, with the French Canadians, hoped for "a speedy & joint attack upon Canada." Congress approved a "Plan of an Attack upon Quebec" later in October and sent it, with other instructions, to Benjamin Franklin to "lay substantially before the French minister." Franklin was further ordered to consult Lafayette, who was well versed on the important points of the proposed campaign. Report for a proposed Canadian Expedition, Sept. 10, 1778, PCC, Item 152, Vol. 6, p. 359ff; James Deane to HL, Oct. 6, 1778, PCC, Item 78, Vol. 7, p. 217ff; *JCC*, XII, 1042-1048.

[8] "those" written over other text, probably "them".

[9] "v" written over "f".

[10] Gen. Charles Scott's Oct. 6, 1778, intelligence report (from Fishkill) to General Washington revealed that the 10th, 45th, and 52nd British Regiments were ordered to complete the regiments needed on the 5,000-man expedition to St. Lucia that sailed from New York November 4, under the command of Commodore William Hotham. The quartermasters reported to New York September 22 to handle the embarkation of the baggage. Washington Papers, DLC; Katcher, *British Army Units*, pp. 33, 55, 59; Tilley, *British Navy*, pp. 121, 160-161.

[11] The Carlisle Commission issued its valedictory "Manifesto and Proclamation" on October 3. It blamed Congress for the continuing war, condemned the Franco-American alliance, and warned that this would be the final chance for a peaceful reconciliation. Peace was offered to the individual colonies rather than Congress whose authority the commission

SOURCE: ALS, Kendall Collection; no address; dated "Head Quarters 7th October 1778."; docketed by HL "John Laurens / 7 October 1778 / Answ[d.] 22[d.]".

FROM ROBERT HOWE

Charles Town, October 9, 1778

Dear Sir

I am just this moment informed that a Motion has been made & carried in the Committee "that I should be recalled from hence" that to add to the anxiety which I must feel at being called away when Service is likely to progress here; the motion for removing me was made by a Member of Congress immediately preceding those for Troops to be sent up to the Support of this place,[1] as if I was not worthy of being employed where Honor was to be obtained__ think Sir the undeserved mortification I must feel upon an Occasion like this__ And can Congress suffer it to be inflicted upon me! Have I not sacrificed my Fortune & Peace to the Service of my Country! have I not by the most unwearied diligence & with a Zeal which at least has some merit attended to the duties of my Station & by my every effort endeavoured to do my Duty! and shall I after being kept against my wish from the Scene of immediate Action, be recalled at that moment when this Country is likely to become the Scene of it__ How Sir have I deserved this disgrace? I am conscious I have not, & therefore can never believe that Congress can consent to Sacrifice so faithful a Servant

Upon you Sir I rely, upon your friendship I call, to avert from me so unexpected, so undeserved & so inexpressible a mortification & disgrace, which from my inmost soul I assert I have not de-

---

denied. Congress responded October 15 by declaring the manifestos "seditious papers" and refusing to recognize the flags of truce under which they were to be distributed among the states. The manifesto was published in the *Pa. Packet,* October 15, 1778. Weldon A. Brown, *Empire or Independence, A Study in the Failure of Reconciliation, 1774-1783* (Baton Rouge, La., 1941), pp. 284-289; *JCC*, XII, 1015-1016.

[1] According to the *Journals of the Continental Congress,* the September 25 resolution requesting the executives of Virginia and North Carolina to send 1,000 and 3,000 troops respectively to South Carolina was made during the morning session. Major General Howe's recall was the first order of business during the afternoon session. The next resolution concerned the appointment of Maj. Gen. Benjamin Lincoln to the command of the Southern Department. *JCC,* XII, 949-951.

served__[2] excuse the trouble of this Letter. I write in Haste & anxiety.

I am dear Sir with respect and / esteem your most ob^t· very hb^le_ Servt·

Robert Howe

SOURCE: Copy (19th century), HL Papers, ScHi; no address; dated "Charles Town S° Carolina 9th: Oct^r: 1778".

FROM WILLIAM LIVINGSTON
Princeton, N.J., October 9, 1778
Dear Sir

Our Assembly being dissolved by the Constitution and the Council of Safety expired by its own Limitation, I stand some chance of seeing my family at last; and perhaps the Devil and the Tories may so manage their cards at the ensuing Election, that I may have no avocation to leave it in future.[1]

I am much more pleased with the old mans dream <u>amended</u>, than I was with the original, & the conclusion I like extremely. With great Delicacy to Congress and putting a new plume in the cap of Liberty, the old Gentleman must escape the censure of the most severe.[2]

your Excellency has by this time seen (the last I know not whether I can say, considering that some people make more dying speeches than one, but) the second dying Speech of the British

---

[2] Howe, after reflecting on his removal from the southern command, wrote again on October 12 in an attempt to exonerate himself for the failure of the recent East Florida expedition. He had been "informed by one of my Friends, Congress conceives that, the Militia expedition into East Florida was under my Guidance & owing to my recommendation & request. This Sir I beg you to assure Congress was not by any means the case." PCC, Item 160, p. 495ff.

[1] The New Jersey Council of Safety's term, according to an act of June 20, ended with the conclusion of the legislative session October 8. The next general election was scheduled for October 13. Livingston was reelected governor by the joint meeting of the legislature October 31. *Livingston Papers* (Prince), II, 459n; 501n.

[2] Livingston recognized that in the October 3 letter from "an Old man" to the *Pa. Packet*, HL had made the same point concerning the undeserved praise Congress had lavished on the New England militias that he had in his "Dream" of September 17, but in more palatable terms. William Livingston to HL, Sept. 17, 178; To the *Pa. Packet*, Oct. 3, 1778.

Commissaries. Does not the very pomposity of the Vellum, and the grandeur of the types & Margin strongly operate towards your Conversion? No? Why then I am sure the matter will not.[3]

As I really cannot think them so great Blockheds as to flatter themselves after all their fruitless attempts of this kind, to do any Execution with this ridiculous harangue, I doubt not it is rather calculated for the meridian of London than that of America. For as the wise men in that Metropolis are fools enough to believe that such an address might be of service, their little fools here, must comport with the Sentiments of the great ones there in demonstration of their having exerted all their possibles. Thanks to their Excellencies however for the quantity of waste paper with which they have furnished me under the Denomination of proclamations, & the excellent tape which surrounded the several packets, of both which I stood in most lamentable need. Conceiving that they would afford very little Edification to the several Bodies in this State civil military & ecclesiastical to which they were directed, I have made prize of almost the whole Cargo without any lawful condemnation in the admiralty and with felonious intent of converting them to my own private use. His Majesty's aims however (having in days of yore heard so much about the Lords anointed) I cannot think of consecrating to the Goddess Cloacina;[4] but shall carefully separate them from the rest of the sheets & apply them to the embellishment of my little Grandsons Kite. And oh! for the vellum original signed & sealed with their Excellencies own proper hands & Seals! I will certainly lay it up in Lavender, that if I am hanged at last, my latest Posterity may know that it was thro' downright love of hanging after having refused so gracious and unmerited a pardon on repentance, with so grim frowning a lion at the top denouncing the royal vengeance in case of final contumacy__[5]

I am / Dear Sir / your Excellencys / most obedient & / most humble Sv^t

Wil: Livingston

---

[3] Livingston as the chief executive of New Jersey had received one of the thirteen original copies of the Carlisle Commission's October 3 "Manifesto and Proclamation".

[4] Although Venus was not normally associated with sewers, one of her aspects in Rome was Venus Cloacina—the goddess of drains (cloacae). P.M. Field, *Greek and Roman Mythology* (London, 1977), p. 161.

[5] Livingston under the pseudonym "Hortentius" paraphrased much of this paragraph in a letter to the *New-Jersey Gazette* which was published with the commissioners' "Manifesto and Proclamation." *New-Jersey Gazette*, Oct. 21, 1778.

SOURCE: RC, HL Papers, ScHi; addressed on cover "To / His Excellency Henry Laurens Esqr / President of Congress / Philadelphia__"; addressed below close "His Excellency Henry Laurens Esqr / President of Congress"; dated "Princeton 9 Oct 1778"; docketed "Governor Livingston / dated Princeton 9th Octr. 78 / Rec'd the 11th Oct^{r.}.". Copy (19th century), HL Papers, ScHi.

FROM ROBERT PRINGLE[1]

Williamsburg, Va., October 9, 1778

Dear Sir

I have taken the Liberty of inclosing a Letter to you from M^{rs:} Laurens to your Son, being ignorant of any other method of forwarding it to him. I left M^{rs:} Laurens ~~and~~ Mr. Manning and Family well in June last. With my Compliments to Col: John Laurens I Remain__

Your most obe^{t:} Servt.

R. Pringle

SOURCE: RC, Misc. Ms.: R. Pringle, NHi; addressed on cover "To / His Excellency Henry Laurens Esq^{r:} / President of Congress__ / Philadelphia"; dated "Virginia Williamsburgh / October. 9^{th:} 1778__"; docketed by HL "[R Pri]ngle 9 Octob~ 1778 / Recd.~ 26th..".

FROM WILLIAM READ

Princeton, N.J., October 9, 1778

Hon^d Sir

I had the honour of receiving your favour, & embrace this opportunity of paying propper attention to it__ I hope by this you have had good accounts from Ch^{s.} Town, & should be very happy to hear from or of my Brother as I have not enjoy'd that satisfaction

---

[1] Robert Pringle (1755-1811) returned to South Carolina after sailing from Nantes in July 1778. The son of Judge Robert Pringle (d. 1776) had been studying medicine at the University of Edinburgh. Waring, *History of Medicine in S.C., 1670-1825*, p. 277; *SCHM*, L (1949), 151.

since I left Home__ I thank you good Sir for your kind offer of forwarding any dispatchs, nothing could lay me under more lasting obligations than this, & your other kindly proffers of civility__

I was in hopes my indisposition would have left me, at the time I wrote you but I was not so lucky, it returnd with violence, & terminated in an imposthume of ~~illegible~~ my Arm which has rendred me for some time incapable of holding a Pen, & even at this time w^t difficulty__[1] Permit me here to congratulate you on the noble behaviour ~~of~~ & safety of your Son & my Country Man Col^l Laurens__ I have had the pleasure of hearing many Particulars & grieve at my incapability of being near him, methinks I could gladly lay aside my occupation & share with him the dangers of the Field__ unnoticed, & in a private station my share of glory would be small__ & who does not fight for honour? I have a thousand time repent'd not continuing in the Army, but I have not myself to blame the injunctions of a Father could not be surmountd__[2] be pleas'd ~~if~~ ↑when↓ it should fall in your way to make my respects to Major[3] Butler (who I hear is w$^t.$ you) & Mr Drayton__

I am w$^t.$ the utmost / respect__ Dr Sir / Your Obedient & most / Humb$^{e.}$ Servt

William Read

P.S. As an active scene is likely to commence near us, & I am only (as yet) fit for Hospital service I will joind the first Hospital that is formd__ pray sir when you shall do me hon$^{r.}$ of writing direct for me at Mrs Livingstons

Y$^{rs.}$ &ca.

W.R

SOURCE: RC, HL Papers, ScHi; addressed on cover "To / His Excellency / Henry Laurens Esqr- / President of Congress / fav$^{d.}$ by__ Mr Clarkson"; dated "Gen$^l.$ Hospital Prince-Ton / Octr 9th 1778"; docketed by HL "Doct^r W. Read / 9$^{th.}$ Octob~ 1778 / Rec$^{d.}$ 10th-". Copy (19th century), HL Papers, ScHi.

---

[1] A physician, Read had contracted typhus while attending the sick and wounded at the military hospital in Princeton. The abscess on his arm was related to the disease. HL to William Read, Sept. 15, 1778; Waring, *History of Medicine in S.C., 1670-1825*, p. 301.

[2] James Read, a member of the Georgia Royal Council and a Loyalist, requested that William not join the patriot military. William was offered a lieutenant's commission but deferred to his father's wishes. The elder Read died in March 1778. Jacob Read to HL, July 16, 1778; Waring, *History of Medicine in S.C., 1670-1825*, pp. 299-303.

[3] "Major" written over other text.

TO GEORGE WASHINGTON

Philadelphia, October 10, 1778

Dear Sir__

An accident which has very seldom happened to me in the course of thirty Years business, has deprived me of the honor of making an earlier & puts it out of my power even now of making a more proper acknowledgement of three of Your Excellency's favors which I remember to have been indebted for antecedent to the receipt of this of the 3ᵈ· Inst. which now lies before me.__ those, in removing my Desks & their Contents from one part of the House to a more convenient, I have mislaid among my private Papers, & after as much search at different times & particularly this Morning as the fleeting & pressing moments which I dare to borrow from public attentions have permitted me to make, remain undiscovered, although I am sure they are safe in a wrong class.

I recollect however & shall never forget a new obligation which in one[1] of them Your Excellency was pleased to lay on me by a very kind notice of my Sons behavior at Rhode Island & that you had returned the Gold which I sent to Head Quarters by Jones & also the Letters of Governor Johnstone Mʳ· Oswald & Mʳ· Manning.[2]

In the present circumstances of Great Britain, rendred deplorable by the waste of another Campaign on this Continent, by the loss of Dominigue in the West Indies[3] & of a great Marine battle at her own door,[4] it is exceedingly difficult to determine what will be her next step, although I do not think it is, to see the only measures remaining for her salvation. With respect to South Carolina, I cannot yet treat the Idea of an attack, as altogether chimerical, I am well warranted to say the British Administration held that State & Georgia in reserve, for a stroke of necessity which might at any time be made with success & they well know the immense value

---

[1] "e" written over "f".

[2] The three private letters from General Washington prior to the one dated October 3, were those of August 25 and September 4 and 12. HL remembered these particulars from Washington's September 12 letter.

[3] The British surrendered the island of Dominica September 7 to a French force led by the Marquis de Bouille, the governor of Martinique.

[4] The first naval battle between the British, commanded by Admiral Augustus Keppel, and a French force, directed by Admiral comte d'Orvilliers, took place off the coast of Brittany near the island of Ushant on July 27, 1778. Both fleets sustained considerable damage and between them suffered over a thousand casualties. No ships were captured or sunk and both fleets returned to port after the battle to make repairs. Dull, *French Navy*, pp. 120-122.

of those States & great things may be done by drawing their forces to one point__ they may indeed have stayed a day too late.[5] be that as it will, I have fully advertised my Countrymen, & if the alarm shall prove to have been unnecessarily sounded, their intermediate exertions towards a defence will do them no real injury.

Congress have ordered the proceedings of the Court Martial on Major Gen S[t.] Clair to be printed, & have appointed Friday the 16[th.] for considering & determining on those of the Cause on Major Geñ. Lee.[6] I have nothing further to offer at present Sir, but the repeated assurances of being with the highest sense of Respect & Obligation

Your Excellency's / Most obedient & Most / humble servant
Henry Laurens.

SOURCE: ALS, Washington Papers, DLC; addressed below close "His Excellency / General Washington."; dated "Philadelphia 10[th.] October 1778.".

TO BARON VON STEUBEN

Philadelphia, October 12, 1778
Dear Sir__

I thank you for your very obliging Letter of the 31[st.] Ult[o.] which reached me no sooner than five days ago.

I am in great hopes your arrangement for the Inspection will be a subject for the consideration of Congress this very Morning; it is so intended, but if it shall happen otherwise, ascribe the delay to unavoidable necessity for attending to some other business, or to any cause in preference to a disregard for you in Congress, where I perceive with great pleasure you are held in the highest Esteem.

A look into[1] the remaining parts of your Letter, would shock a feeble mind, yours & mine will from the melancholy description

---

[5] This sentence written between lines.

[6] Congress did not begin to consider the court-martial proceedings and sentence until October 24. On December 2 a motion was made to carry out the sentence but consideration was postponed. Finally on December 5, by a vote of five states yes, two states no, and four divided or abstaining, Congress upheld the court-martial. Both HL and William Henry Drayton voted to uphold. *JCC,* 1059, 1184-1185, 1194.

[1] "to" in-line insertion.

of our Military affairs receive no more than a proper degree of alarm, but alas, what can you & I do? what we alone cannot do, we must hope will be soon supplied by those whose duty & Interest it is to receive proper impressions from the warning which I shall under your sanction again & again repeat in their Ears.

I have desired Col⁰· John Laurens to consult you Sir, on some points respecting the late Massacre of Col⁰· Baylor's party. I am afraid indeed that unfortunate Gentleman was off his guard, but does his error warrant the Butchery which we are told the Cruel English exercised upon himself & his party? If this shall be proved ought we to suffer their guilt to pass with impunity? when & in what manner should retaliation be made? the Watch points to 9 oClock I must fly to my Post. Adieu Dear Baron be assured I continue in the most respectful & sincere attachment

Sir / Your obedient & most / humble servant

Henry Laurens,

SOURCE: ALS, Gratz Collection, PHi; addressed below close "The Honorable / Baron Stüben."; dated "Philadelphia / 12 Octob⁻ 1778__"; docketed "Oct 12. 1778 / H Laurens".

FROM SILAS DEANE

Philadelphia, October 12, 1778

Sir

I received your Letter of the 7ᵗʰ· instant, in which you informed me that mine of the same date, to you, was by Congress ordered to lie on the Table until the examination of Mʳ· Carmichael should be finished.

Though totally unable even to conjecture what relation the examination of that Gentleman can possibly have to those abusive and injurious Letters, wrote by Mʳ· Izard and Mʳ· Lee, yet as I had so often troubled Congress during a three months attendance with my repeated solicitations to be heard, I forebore repeating them until neither my health, my interest, nor my honor will permit me a much longer stay in america; I have therefore taken the Liberty of enclosing my answers to the Letters of those Gentlemen.[1] It pains me to be obliged to Answer at all, and it grieves me exceedingly to be deprived of the opportunity of doing it in person, I still hope to be indulged before I leave america. I have only further to inform Congress that I shall go into the Country tomorrow, for a few Days. that having engaged a passage in a ship which will sail for France sometime next month. I propose to leave Philadelphia in a few days after I return from the Country in order to embark, and shall esteem myself honored by Congress if they have any thing further in which I may be of service to my Country if they will favour me with their commands.[2]

     I have the honor to remain &c.

(signed) Silas Deane

SOURCE: Copy, PCC (Item 103), DNA; no address; dated "Philadelphia 12th. October 1778".

TO THOMAS JOHNSON[1]

Philadelphia, October 13, 1778

Sir

     I had the honor of addressing Your Excellency on the 7th Instant by Dugan,[2] since which I have not received any of your favors.

---

[1] Congress ordered that Deane "be furnished with extracts" of the letters from Ralph Izard "read in this house on the 19th, [September] as related to his public conduct." On October 3, Arthur Lee's June 1, 1778, letter to the Committee for Foreign Affairs was read in Congress which immediately ordered that Deane be supplied a copy. *JCC*, XII, 949, 980. Deane responded with the three enclosures to this letter each dated October 12 and directed to HL. In the first he answered Izard's charges. PCC, Item 103, p. 118ff. He replied to Arthur Lee's complaints in the second enclosure. PCC, Item 103, p. 130ff. And in the last he explained his position in support of Articles XI and XII of the Franco-American commercial agreement about which both Lee and Izard had raised issue. PCC, Item 103, p. 140ff.

[2] Congress did not dismiss Deane until Aug. 6, 1779. Delayed by business, personal matters, and a severe winter, he did not sail for France until June 20, 1780. *JCC*, XIV, 929-930; Coy Hilton James, *Silas Deane—Patriot or Traitor?* (East Lansing, Mich., 1975), pp. 85-90.

[1] The October 13 portion of this letter was a circular to the states (PCC, Item 13), to which HL added the October 16 continuation in his letters to each of the executives of the southern states to cover the act of that date. HL to Richard Caswell, Oct. 13, 1778, Nc-Ar; HL to Patrick Henry, Oct. 13, 1778, Vi; HL to John Houstoun, Oct. 13, 1778, PCC, Item 13; HL to Rawlins Lowndes, Oct. 13, 1778, PCC, Item 13.

[2] Cumberland Dugan, a Baltimore merchant and shipowner, had his vessel, the sloop *Friendship,* seized later that month by the Naval Officer at Baltimore for failure to obtain a permit. *HL Papers,* XII, 242; *Delegate letters* (Smith), XI, 287; *JCC,* XII, 1123.

Under the present Cover will be found an Act of Congress of Yesterdays date for encourageing true Religion and good Morals, and for the suppression of such Entertainments and diversions as have a contrary tendency.[3]

16th October 1778__

Sir__[4]

I beg leave to refer you to the above, which has been lying for the present conveyance, and now ↑to↓ inclose to[5] Your Excellency an Act of this date for preventing the spreading of seditious Papers in these States by the Enemy under Cover of Flags of Truce or otherwise, and for punishing Persons detected in attempts to disperse such Papers.[6]

I have the honor to be / With great Respect / Sir / Your Excellency's / Most obedient servt[7]

Henry Laurens.
President / of Congress

SOURCE: ALS, MdAA; addressed below close "His Excellency / Governor Johnson / Maryland"; dated "Philadelphia 13th October 1778"; docketed "16 Octr. 1778. / President of Congress with a / Resolve for preventing the / Spreading of Seditious Papers / &ca__ & a Resolve / for encouraging true Religion / & good Morals &ca." and on another leaf "Mr. Gresham / Mr. Smith / Mr. Chew / Mr. Hall / Mr. Wilson". LB, PCC (Item 13), DNA.

TO GEORGE WASHINGTON

Philadelphia, October 13, 1778

Sir

My last trouble to Your Excellency was dated the 9th by Messenger Dodd who was detained by bad weather and a little management of his own until Yesterday.

---

[3] JCC, XII, 1001-1002.
[4] Date and salutation by HL.
[5] "to" interlined.
[6] Congress appointed a commmittee, Gouverneur Morris, William Duer, John Mathews, Richard Henry Lee and Elbridge Gerry, on October 15, to consider the intelligence that the British were sending agents from New York to distribute the Carlisle Commission's recent Manifesto and Proclamation. The committee reported the next day that because the purpose of the Manifestos was "to stir up dissentions, animosities and rebellion, among the good people of these states" that the agents should not be "entitled to protection from a flag." The act HL enclosed was passed in response to this report. JCC, XII, 1013, 1015-1016.
[7] Close by HL.

Within the present inclosure Your Excellency will receive the undermentioned Papers

1. An Act of Congress of the 12th Ins$^{t.}$ strictly enjoining all Officers in the Army of the United States to see that the good and wholsome Laws provided for the preservation of Morals among the Soldiers be duly observed.[1]
2. Extract of a Letter from Governor Livingston dated the 2nd Instant, received this day.

Congress have directed me to request Your Excellency to give proper Orders for suppressing the evil complained of by the Governor.[2]

3. Copy of a Letter from Col$^{o.}$ Hartley dated Sunbury 8th October 1778.
4. An Act of Congress of this date founded on Colonel Hartley's Letter for preventing the Enemy from occupying a Post at Chemeong &c.[3]

SOURCE: LB, PCC (Item 13), DNA; addressed "General Washington / Camp / by Freeman"; dated "13th October".

---

[1] The October 12 resolution encouraging the states' to suppress theatrical productions, horse racing, and gambling was followed immediately by a second resolution to discourage "prophaneness and vice" among Continental soldiers. An October 16 resolution underscored this new concern for morality by providing for the dismissal of "any person holding an office under the United States" for participating in, encouraging, or attending the theater. This resolution was prompted in part by American officers not only attending but acting in productions in Philadelphia with the approval of a superior officer. *JCC*, XII, 1001, 1018; *Delegate Letters* (Smith), XI, 65-66.

[2] On October 13 Congress ordered Washington to take measures to prevent trade between American citizens and the British at New York. *JCC*, XII, 1005.

[3] Thomas Hartley's address to Congress described his retaliation against the Indians and Loyalists who had attacked settlements in the Wyoming Valley. Chemung, New York was the base for these attacks and Hartley described the post as "the recepticle of all villianous Indians & Tories." He asked Congress "to send a Connecticut Regiment" to govern Wyoming. Congress ordered the letter be transmitted to General Washington and that he take measures "for repelling the invasions of the savages on the frontiers of New York, New Jersey, and Pensylvania." Thomas Hartley Address to Congress, Oct. 8, 1778, PCC, Item 78, Vol. 11, p. 341ff; *JCC*, XII, 1005-1006.

FROM JOHN LAURENS

Fredericksburg, N.Y., October 13, 1778

My dear Father__

I should have been glad to have accompanied Mr Custis[1] Mrs Washingtons Son who is so kind as to take charge of this__ but I cannot be ready in less than a week or ten days__ The late bad Weather drove that detachment of the Enemy that was posted on Valentines Hill[2] into the City__ and they now confine themselves within Kingsbridge__ The Detachment[3] in Jersey from which there are daily desertions of two or three__ have not yet returned__ but they have contracted themselves__ and seem to be wholly employed in collecting and carrying off their spoil__ Deserters inform us that they have indiscriminately taken every kind of grain__ Indian-Corn, Stock & all____ One of the Vessels burnt by our parties__ had stalls fitted up for twelve horses__ and ample provision of Water__ for a sea Voyage__ We have repeated accounts of the Sickliness of Byrons Crews__ the report of their Disorder being contagious is without foundation, as well as that of the British fleets having put to Sea in quest of the French__

General Greene who arrived in Camp yesterday, gives us an account of Captain Barrys having lost his Frigate__ two days after he sailed from Boston he engaged a British 32 Gun frigate and had fought her with his usual bravery, and great prospect of Success__ his men and officers being sworn not to surrender__ when a 64 Gun Ship came up and put an end to the contest__ but not before she had given two or three such fires as Barrys Situation relatively to the british frigate allowed__ Our brave Captain then avoided violating his Oath by running his Ship on shoar at Seal Island__ and keeping up a fire from four Guns which he brought to bear in his Stern__ till he got[4] Out his boats &[5] some baggage__ he made his escape with eighty hands__ the rest were to shift for themselves by landing__ ten who concealed themselves have escaped since__ one an English-

---

[1] John Parke Custis, Washington's stepson, was apparently in camp to get Washington's dower release for the sale of several parcels of land in the Virginia counties of York and King William. George Washington to John Parke Custis, Oct. 10, 1778, Washington Papers, DLC.

[2] Valentine's Hill was located Just north of Manhattan, four miles above Kingsbridge. Ward, *War of the Revolution*, II, 880.

[3] "Deta" written over other text.

[4] "got" written over other text.

[5] "&" written over "so".

man remained on board and extinguished the fire which Barry put to the Ship in order to destroy her__ by which means she was saved and the enemy got her off__ [6]

If the Marquis de lay fayette goes to Europe it is probable that he will take a great many of his Countrymen with him__ [7] it is ~~probable~~ ↑almost certain↓ that many of them will be very Troublesome to Congress for Certificates__ Duplessis applied to me the other day to obtain him a furlough for Philadelphia__ and to give him a certificate of his having behaved well at the battle of Monmouth, that he might go and signify his design to Congress of retiring from Service__ I replied that he had no need of an introduction to the President if he had any business with Congress__ that he already had a most honorable certificate from them__ and that if he wanted a final certificate at going away__ the Commander in chief was the proper person to apply to__ the Commissions which Congress have bestowed so liberally have destroyed the value of Rank which is the ostensible Reward of Merit__ and have done great injustice to many brave & experienced officers who have found themselves on a par with[8] or but one remove from ↑some of↓ their Countrymen[9] who had no pretensions to rank of any kind__ The only reparation that can be made, and it is but a feeble one, is to be sparing in the Testimonials to be given at their departure__ and to make a pointed difference ~~in the~~ between those which are given to men of real merit__ and those which are the effect only of political management__

You will be so good as to excuse my mentioning these matters__ they have occasioned great disgust in foreigners con-

---

[6] Capt. John Barry (1745-1803), a native of Ireland who had resided in Philadelphia since 1760, joined the Continental Navy early in the war. When the *Raleigh* was pursued by the British frigate *Unicorn* under Sir James Wallace, Barry ran his vessel aground on Wooden Ball Island at the mouth of Penobscot Bay, evacuated most of his men, and left twenty-five behind to scuttle and burn the ship. Instead, they surrendered to the British. William Bell Clark, *Gallant John Barry, 1745-1803: The Story of a Naval Hero of Two Wars* (N.Y., 1938), pp. 163-171.

[7] This same date, Lafayette wrote HL requesting a leave of absence because "now sir, that france is involv'd in a war, I am urg'd by my duty as well as by patriotic love, to present myself before the king, and know in what manner he judges proper to employ my service." Congress approved Lafayette's leave on October 21, and placed no time limit or terms, allowing him to "return at such time as shall be most convenient to him." Lafayette to HL, Oct. 13, 1778, PCC, Item 156, p. 31ff; *JCC*, XII, 1034-1035.

[8] "w" written over other text.

[9] "tr" written over other text.

scious of their worth__ much uneasiness in our native Officers__ and have brought rank into disgrace__ __ in a few days I shall have an opportunity of speaking more fully on this subject & many others if you permit__ when I have the happiness of embracing you in Philadelphia__ I am anxious to receive a letter from you in the mean time__ and begin to count the hours which are to precede my Setting out__ My dearest friend and father Adieu.

John Laurens.

P.S.

The Purchasing Commissaries complain of the Scarcity of Flour__ some persons high in public office are accused of the detestable Crime of Monopolizing__ is there no means of bringing their Villany to light and expelling them from all Share of the peoples confidence__

SOURCE: ALS, Kendall Collection; addressed on cover "Private / His Excellency / Henry Laurens Esqr· / President of Congress / Philadelphia / favd by / J Custis Esquire__"; dated "Head Quarters 13th October 1778"; docketed by HL "John Laurens 13 Octob. / 1778. / Recd 19th· / Ansd· 22d·".

FROM RAWLINS LOWNDES

Charles Town, October 13, 1778

Dr Sir__

Your Excellency measured the time and distance, and the Heels of the Express with very great exactness, for he delivered to me his dispatches the 8th· Instant at about 12 o'Clock, just as you had Calculated. The Subject of your Intelligence was too Important and Interesting to have any part of it reserved to my own judgment, and therefore I Communicated your Letter immediately, with those from Mr Drayton, to the House then siting. On the ninth the Cartel from New York arrived with Mr· Williams & Son, Mr· Telfair, Mr· James Graham, Chas· Pryce Junr· and Mr· John Hopton. on the next days Evening Mr· Williams was permitted to come on shore and was examined on Oath before the Privy Council; he related the Conversation that passed between Govr· Johnson and himself. That when he left England he received Letters of Introduction from M^r· Leigh[1] and another Gentleman, to Govr· Johnson, hoping thro' that means to Facilitate his removal to Carolina__ That an Embargo at New York frustrating his original plan of procuring a passage in a Providence Vessel which he hoped for a Sum of Money he might prevail on to shape her Course for Chas· Town__ he resolved on the expedient of getting away in a Flag of Truce and for that purpose waited on Govr· Johnson, and Sollicited his Assistance, that in Conversation, without any reserve or Injunction of Secrecy or Confidence__ the Govr· asked him, who were the leading principal Men in Carolina for that, that province had made itself more Obnoxious to Government by its violent proceedings than any other of the revolted Provinces, and that it was absolutely Necessary the English should possess themselves of that Country, we must says he, "have that Province" M^r· Williams replyed, that he had not heard from Carolina or received a Single Line from any Person for more then 14 Months past, knew nothing of the state of Affairs there but from the publick prints__ that he imagined they were in a good Condition of defence, and as the English had failed before in their Attempt against it, he was of Opinion they could now make a greater resistance and be better prepared than they were when last attacked__ Governor ↑Johnson↓ said, as to that, it had been conducted wrong, the Ships should not have staid before Sullivans Fort, but have proceeded to the Town, Landed the Troops, and then it would have appeared which side would have acquitted themselves best,__ that 10,000 Men would have done the Business at once__ and besides, Continued he, Charles Town is not our only Object__ "we have Port Royall in View" Williams says this Affair made a great Impression on his mind, as he had, before he left England been informed, that Plans of Charles Town and Port Royall had been ordered to be laid before Ministry for their particular Consideration__ he thought it his indispensible Duty to Charge M^r· Beresford with a Message to your Excellency on the Occasion, that he might not be wanting in Duty to his Country, if the Event should shew, that Govr· Johnson spoke from a certain knowledge of a meditated design against us, & he requested, by M^r· Beresford, that his name might not be mentioned, for fear it might prove an obsticle to his

[1] Sir Egerton Leigh.

geting away__ he left New York on Sunday the 4th. Instant, says they speak there with the greatest Contempt of the American Army,: that 14,000 Men were sent into the Jerseys; that Govr. Johnson was Sailed for England__ that Admiral Byran commanded the Fleet, and that the price of provisions was greatly reduced since the Troops were gone to the Jerseys; and many other Articles of Intelligence which you must know e're this, whether true or false. finally Mr. Williams was discharged and permitted to take the Oaths, and is now one of us.__ Mr. John Hopton after an examination before the House respecting his having drank Success to the two Brothers,[2] in a Company, where the Kings health had also been drank, denying the same__ was also discharged__ The other Gentlemen are ordered to depart, but Circumstances coming to my knowledge which I think make in their favour I have sent a Message to the House, which I hope will induce a relaxation, if not a reversal of the order.__[3]

I have no doubt of the Conversation happening between Mr. Williams and Governor Johnson, but it appears to be a loose general discourse wherein the Subject relative to Carolina was introduced accidentally and Occasionally__ My fears are not so much excited from that Conversation, as they are from the nature of the thing and the great Importance of such an Acquisition to them as Carolina would be,__ their going to the West Indies merely to be in readiness to receive the Enemy, and to defend their Islands before they were attacked would in my humble Opinion be premature and bad policy__ they wd. spend and exhaust their strength before there would be occasion for their exertions__ they would fare badly receive no accidental or Illicit Supplys from private Friends, would be exposed to the danger of unhealthy Climates and Sickly Seasons and waste their Troops in an inactive tiresome expatation__ whereas in this Country they would Live well, have plenty of booty__ protect their Southern Provinces have safe and Comfortable Winter Quarters in a mild and healthy Climate__ And be ready whenever there is Occasion to Succour their Islands with vigourous, recruited & fresh Troops__ I am no General or do I pretend to be a deep

---

[2] Admiral Lord Richard Howe and Sir William Howe.
[3] William Telfair and Charles Price, Jr., were allowed to land in order to proceed to Georgia, but fellow Georgian James Graham was "obliged to return on board the cartel." *S.C. General Gazette,* Oct. 22, 1778.

Polititian__ but my Opinion is that an Army destined for the defence of the West Indies against an uncertain attack would be more advantageously posted in Charles Town for 6 or 8 Months to come, then they wou'd be on the spot__ Hence arises my fears of a Visit, that if they can venture to Subdivide their forces, Carolina rather then the West Indies will Attract their notice, and that such a plan would well Coincide with the measures for protecting their Islands__ I wish both my Politicks and my fears may be ↑ill↓-founded; I am not ambitious of another Opportunity of beating Sir Henry Clinton, neither have I so mean an Opinion of him as to think he will not improve upon the experience his former miscarriage gave him, and avoid the errors of that days Conduck__

I am happy in finding our delegates so watchfull and Attentive to our Interest and safety__ we shall do all we can for our own deliverance in Case of an Invasion, but we are so Encompassed with dangers, that no Assistance can be drawn from our Frontiers__ and if a Creek War should fall on our hands, which Mr Galphin and others, well versed in Indian Affairs, think unavoidable, you will judge Sir, what must be the fate of this Country, without very powerfull Aids and Succour.

I send your Excellency a Copy of the Report of the Commĩee agreed to by the House on this very Alarming Occasion I have only to Regret with all Humility, and Conviction of mind, that some Person more Adequate to the importance of the Charge, had not the Execution of it__ [4] & this naturally leads me Sir to Suggest to you, of my own mere Motion, the Propriety of having a Judicious, well chosen, approved Man amongst us to Conduct Operations on which so much depend.

Amongst the Letters bro^t. by M^r. Williams, are one directed for you, another for your Son, which I have the pleasure of inclosing herewith__ [5] all those bro^t. by M^r. Hopton being opened, led me to enquire of M^r. Williams by what means his escaped the same fate: He

---

[4] The enclosure was an "Extract from the Journals" copied by Peter Timothy, clerk to the General Assembly, dated October 12. The committee selected to review the intelligence concerning a likely British invasion concluded "that the Enemy mean to make an immediate and formidable Attack on this State." And, it recommended two thirds of the militia be immediately drafted, that the forts be put in a state of defense, that the fortifications at Charleston be repaired and supplemented, and that four months supply of rum and provisions for 10,000 men be procured. HL Papers, ScHi.

[5] The letter to HL was from William Manning, April 16, 1778, in which he recopied his April 11 letter. *HL Papers*, XIII, 103-105, 127-129.

tells me on his Application to Govr Johnson, and informing him that he had requested all persons who applyed to him to bring Letters, that they would not write on Politicks__ the Govr ordered his Seal to be put on the bag which protected them from all examination__ that he would have sent these Letters with others which he delivred to Mr. Kinloch for you but that Conveyance being precarious, and the Stile of the direction to you lyable to excite curiosity & Suspicion, he thought it best not to run the risque__

    Mr. Hopton says that there was almost a Certainty that 10 Batalions were in readiness to Embark and a Regiment of Horse__ that the Horses were newly shod with two Rows of Nails and that Transports were ready to take them in__ That every thing is kept very Secret at New York and no publications by Authority untill the transactions were known in England__ He does not think the present preparations are pointed at Carolina, the Shoeing of the Horses indicates a shorter voyage and different Soil: this may be Finesse.

    I do not find from any Intelligence which these Gentlemen have been able to procure, that any thing like an evacuation of New York is in Contemplation.__

I must beg Sir the favour of you to Convey to Mr Drayton my best respects and to crave his Pardon for not writing to him by this Conveyance__ My Comp^{ts.} also to Maj Butler

I am now ready for the Express but the poor Man is just gone from my house with a hot Feaver and tho' very impatient to be gone, I am afraid it will not be safe for him to undertake his Journey till he is better assured of his recovery

    I am with very great Regard and Respect / Dear Sir / Your Excellencys Most Obed^{t.} / and most hum̄ Servant

Raw^{S.} Lowndes.

The express being better called upon me this 15 and will set off tomorrow__

SOURCE: RC, Kendall Collection; addressed on cover "To / His Excellency / Henry Laurens Esq^r__ / President of Congress / Philadelphia"; addressed below close "His Excellency Henry Laurens Esq^r__"; dated below close "Chas. Town / 13th. Octr. 1778."; docketed by HL "Presdt Lowndes 13 Octob 1778__ / Rec̄d 5 Novem~". Copy (19th century), HL Papers, ScHi.

FROM CHARLES COTESWORTH PINCKNEY

Charles Town, October 13, 1778

Dear S^r:

I am exceedingly obliged to you for your favour of the 6th: of September, & for the trouble you have taken to preserve for me the Articles which I had left at Philadelphia. M^r. Wells was some days ago chased ashore, & informs me he landed them with the rest of the Cargo on North Island at the entrance of George Town Inlett, so that I shall receive them in a few days. We are now exerting ourselves to get our Fortifications in a proper state of Defence that we may receive with due respect & military honours the British Fleet & Army; & I assure you it will require our assiduous attention to repair our Forts & Batteries and to construct such others as will be necessary for us. No Person is more desirous of saving the public Money than myself; but in the timely & proper construction and repairing of Works requisite for our defence, and in particular conjunctures, a rigid Oeconomy is no Virtue. I however have the greatest confidence from the spirit which seems at present to animate our Countrymen that you will have no reason to blush for us in the hour of trial. If we should not be altogether so succesful as you could wish, it will not be for want of spirit & an utter detestation of the British Tyranny; and I declare I have not the least doubt but that if the Enemy should again pay us a visit, they will receive from our hands a more severe drubbing than we had the honour of giving them June Seventy Six__

I beg my Compliments to your Colleagues__ have enclosed Mathewes some Votes of our Assembly; and I remain with the greatest respect

Your most obed^t / humble Servant

Charles Cotesworth Pinckney__

Arthur Middleton has turned most insufferably Idle he has not attended the House of Assembly a single day during the present Sessions__ Our Friend Col Motte about three Weeks ago & before we received an Account of the intended Invasion of the Enemy, resigned his Commission; among other reasons on Account of his ill state of health__

SOURCE: RC, Kendall Collection; addressed on cover "His Excellency / Henry Laurens Esqr: / President of the Congress of / America./."; dated "Charlestown Oct^r: 13. 1778"; docketed "Cotesworth Pinckney / 13th. October 1778 / Rec^d. 8th. Novem.~ "; noted on cover "South Carolina / affairs". Copy (19th century), HL Papers, ScHi.

FROM JOHN LAURENS

Fredericksburg, N.Y., October 14, 1778

My dear Father

I have the pleasure of inclosing you a Copy of the London Gazette extraordinary__ the original we got from New York and sent by express to Count d'Estaing__ I heartily congratulate you upon what from Admiral Keppel's own State of the matter may fairly be interpreted an honorable advantage on the side of our allies__ and by the bye it is such a kind of victory as we sh^d wish for__[1]

I deduct from Keppels account the absurd and inconsistent gasconade of his suffering the French fleet to form without firing upon them__ for he himself tells you just before that the crippled State of some of his ships, and the consequent scattered State of his line__ gave[2] the French an opportunity of doing it__

I likewise deduct his pretence of the french fleets making off under cover of night__ he was to windward of the french__ and we all know that the british have very good night glasses__[3] all the rest is clearly against Admiral Keppel__ for the french line was always formed__ and his was ↑so↓ considerably broken__ as to drive him to the necessity of a very awkward retrograde[4] movement__ attended with great loss of time and remotion from his antagonist__ but I was not aware that I was commenting an affair, ~~on~~ which your superior judgement and experience of naval manoeuvres will penetrate and

---

[1] Under the heading "Victory, at Sea," the *London Gazette Extraordinary* of August 3 printed Admiral Augustus Keppel's report of the July 27 clash between the British and French fleets. Keppel said the French "had been so beaten in the Day, that they took Advantage of the Night to go off." JL's interpretation may have been based on the list of killed and wounded in Keppel's report.

[2] "g" written over other text.

[3] A nightglass was a short refracting telescope specially devised for night vision. It may have been a recent innovation, as the *OED*'s first citation is May 13, 1779.

[4] Third "r" written over other text.

expose more scientifically__ my zeal and joy will palliate my presumtion__ __

    I am / your most affectionate / and dutiful

John Laurens.

SOURCE: ALS, Kendall Collection; addressed on cover "His Excellency / Henry Laurens Esq / Philadelphia / fav^d. by John Parke Custis Esqr."; dated "Head Quarters 14th Octob 1778"; docketed by HL "~~Henry~~ John Laurens / 14 Octob. 1778__ / Rec^d. 19th. Ans^d. 22^d.__".

FROM JOHN WELLS, JR.

Charles Town, October 14, 1778

Dear Sir

    I am to apologize for not long before now acknowledging the Receipt of the Ephemeris & several Packets of Newspapers your Excellency has done me the honour to favour me with__ A visit of a vile fever called the Break bone,[1] which has been very rife here, and the late disagreeable sultry weather, occasioned it__ but as these excuses are now removed, past neglect shall be amply remedied by future attention

    Our attention for this week past has been chiefly engrossed by the intelligence from R Wms__ & by hi[s] arriving with Jn° Hopton, James Graham, Mr Telfer & Mr Price__ Williams & Hopton went through a fiery trial__ the former was ~~illegible~~ examined by the Privy Council & General Assembly__ the latter by the Assembly only__ Men's sentiments ~~of~~ underwent a most amazing change after they were heard__ they were <u>unanimously</u> allowed to become Citizens of this State A determination, which was not looked for, I beleive by ~~their~~ warmest advocates for the parties__ Generosity and Magnanimity overcame all obstacles__ & the claiming indulgence & forgiveness, if I may so ~~well~~ say, with the consideration of the happiness it would afford to their relations if they

---

[1] Beginning in 1777, and for several years after, South Carolinians suffered from the painful but not fatal infectious disease dengue. Symptoms included fever, headache, a rash, and severe joint pain; thus the common name applied to the malady was breakbone fever. Waring, *History of Medicine in S.C., 1670-1825*, p. 105.

should be admitted, made resentment & prejudice, yield to pity & Compassion__ Graham, I imagine will also be allowed to stay,__ the other two are to land & proceed forthwith to Georgia__

We have New York Papers to 3d October, which afford us later intelligence than any we have from Congress__ & I[2] regret for poor Baylors' fate__ such inhumanity calls aloud for retaliation__ What I have long dreaded, must soon happen__ No Quarters to be given or taken__ which however in the event may be the best policy for us__

I cannot help joining those who are of opinion we shall be visited this winter__ ie. before Christmas__ I thought so before Williams's intelligence was received__ Every measure is taking, on the supposition that they will be here__ What I chiefly dread is the Creeks, cooperating which appears highly probable__ In regulars we are very weak not exceeding 1300 fit for duty__ Even we should the Creeks break out, I think, indeed am confident we can have 2500 militia to oppose them, and 3000 militia in Charlestown, or wherever the Enemy may attempt to land, or rather where the previous dispatch may indicate they intend doing it__ this with our regulars, together with perhaps 2500 men we may have from Virginia & North Carolina, will form no contemptible force. If the Enemy really intend invading this state Beaufort may be first attacked, to draw our attention that way__ but the impracticability of the roads, will makes it ridiculous to imagine they will march hither__ some such thing may be attempted on Stono River, at the ferry from the Main to Johns Island &[3] thence to proceed to Ashly ferry[4] to get on the Neck about the Quarter house__[5] & that seems highly improbable, as they cannot have any Communication with the shipping, unless some Gallies or other small arm[ed] Craft should steal up in the Night to Ashly ferry__ something similar to which you may remem-

---

[2] "I" inserted in left margin.
[3] "&" written over dash.
[4] Ashley Ferry Town, sometimes called Shem Town or Butler Town, was located on the west bank of the Ashley River about twelve miles above Charleston on the road north from Jacksonborough. *HL Papers*, III, 79n.
[5] The Quarter House, an inn or tavern on a forty-acre tract once owned by HL's father, about seven miles north of Charleston on the Dorchester Road, was named for the fact that it was one quarter of the way to Old Dorchester or because colonial troops had been quartered there. *SCHM*, XIX (1918), 43-44.

ber was done in the North River previous to the reduction of Fort Washington__ for my own part, I envy men their military laurels, & wish I may be deceived in my expectations__ Should they come, I hope & believe, let the Event be what it may, our Endeavours & Exertions will not tarnish the reputation acquired in 1776__ I am certain there will be more men in arms, greater abundance of ammunition, & in my opinion more perfect unanimity of sentiment__ The dreadful state of those parts of the Continent ↑which↓ have become the seat of war, must stimulate every man to endeavour to prevent the possibility of this becoming a scene of rapine & desolution; which must be the Case, should the Enemy get a footing__ Besides, the uniform ruin that has attended all those who professed themselves friends to the British Tyrant, has cured many of their Toryism__ These Considerations induce ↑me↓ to be of opinion that Charlestown will be ours, maugre every attempt that the Ambition or Resentment of ~~the gene~~ Sir H. Clinton can suggest__

A small sailing & Rowing Boat, armed with swivels & carrying 15 or 20 men, has injured our trade much__ Several Coasters have been captured by her__ Mr[6] Nelsens' flyer Pilot boat was taken last week by her__[7] I am told Findlay who used to ply between this & Winyaw, commands the boat, which sails & rows amazingly fast__ Should he fall into our hands, he may chance to make his Exit on the leafless tree__ as he some time ago ran away with Tidymans' Schooner__[8]

Two vessels are arrived from Marseilles but in very long passages__[9] The Active & Minerva frigates have been both carried into the Cape__[10]

---

[6] "Mr" written over dash.

[7] "A privateer belonging to Goodrich (commonly called Gutridge) of Bermuda, commanded by Mr. Findlay, one of our old coasters," put ashore a group of prisoners on Bull's Island and sailed from there on October 10. S.C. Gazette, Oct. 14, 1778.

[8] William Findley had been the master of the schooner Dispatch owned by Philip Tidyman, and had been accused of illegal trading on the Santee River by the Committee of Safety in Georgetown in 1775. HL Papers, X, 594-596.

[9] The S.C. Gazette, Oct. 14, 1778, noted the arrival of four French vessels including the two from Marseilles.

[10] The Charleston press reported that the British sloop of war Active, William Williams, was taken by three French vessels near Puerto Rico while the Minerva, John Stott, was captured by the Concord, a French frigate at Cape François. S.C. Gazette, Oct. 14, 1778; S.C. General Gazette, Oct. 22, 1778.

The loss on board D'Orvillier's fleet, in the Action off Ushant, was said in France to exceed 700 killed__ that of the English was not known but thought to be much more__

A dreadful fresh has done immense damage on Santee & Pedee__ Col. Mackintosh lost most of his Crop ~~& the~~ live Stock, &[11] Indigo Vats &c &c__ [12]

Wishing you health & success, I am, / Dear Sir / With sincere respect & esteem / Your Excellency's most__ / obedient servant

Jn$^{o.}$ Wells jun^r

SOURCE: RC, Kendall Collection; addressed below close "His Excellency / Henry Laurens Esqr / President of Congress"; dated "Charles town 14 October 1778__"; docketed by HL "John Wells 14 Octob / 1778 Rec$^{d.}$ 5 Novem".

ADDRESS TO CONGRESS

Philadelphia, October 15, 1778

The president addressd Congress as follows

Gentlemen I informed you yesterday that I had received a letter from Mr Izard.[1] I have since perused it and find in ↑it↓ traits reflecting[2] highly on doct Franklin in his public character; I have observed in[3] this, the rule which guided me in the late case of M$^{r.}$ Izard's letters. I have ~~consulted no body I act according~~ communicated the contents of the letter and papers accompanying it to no body I have consulted no body, I act according to my own judgment unbiassed & impartial. M$^{r.}$ Izard's wish that these papers may be communicated to Congress appears to me to preclude option on my part. I therefore offer the letter and papers, if the house is pleased to receive & have them read I will deliver them to the secretary for that purpose. I have delayed offering these papers earlier in hopes of seeing a full house & had directed the absent

---

[11] "&" written over dash.
[12] Col. Lachlan McIntosh of South Carolina had advertised his plantations on "Patatoe Creek" and near Brachy Hill for sale in 1777. *HL Papers,* XI, 383.
[1] Ralph Izard's June 28, 1778, letter to HL is printed in *HL Papers,* XIII, 524-530.
[2] "l" written over "f" and "i" written over "l".
[3] "i" written over "o".

members to be summoned. I have not read any of the papers, the letter excepted.[4]

SOURCE: Rough Journal, PCC (Item 1), DNA; dated "Thursday Octr 15. 1778". Copy, Transcript Journal, PCC (Item 2), DNA.

FROM GOSUINUS ERKELENS[1]

Hartford, Conn., October 15, 1778

Sir

I have the honor to refer to þ letter of his Exellencÿ Govr Trúmbúll;[2] and take þ freedom to add: that 19 Months ago: I foúnd with pleasúre that One Certain nobleman at þ Coúurt of mÿ Coúntrÿ in the Hagúe by name the Baron Johann Teodore van der Capellen;[3] Member of their High Mightinesses had ~~illegible~~ with a publicq: Generoús and Noble Spiritt interested him self in so múch in favor of the United American State and their noble Cause that it had Such a happy effect that þ States never consented the reqúest of the Brittish Coúrt to assist them against þ Suffering Americans in giving up the Scotch Brigade then Stationd in Holland,[4]

The prospect of my States to come entirely in with these respected States gave me a great Joÿ on þ principle of Love for my own Coúntry as well as for this Coúntrÿ. I repaired to his Exellency

---

[4] After HL's address, Congress ordered Izard's letter "and the papers accompanying it be received and read," and then ordered the documents "to lie on the table for the perusal of the members." The enclosures, numbered one through six and containing sixteen separate documents, included Izard's correspondence with Arthur Lee, Benjamin Franklin, John J. Pringle, and John Thornton and other documents concerning the Franco-American negotiations. *JCC*, XII, 1011-1012; PCC, Item 89, p. 59ff.

[1] Gosuinus Erkelens, a Dutch merchant who had immigrated to America and settled in Chatham, Conn., wrote pro-American pamphlets with which he sought to stimulate support for the American Revolution in the Netherlands. Nordholt, *Dutch Repubilc and American Independence*, pp. 26-27; *Livingston Papers* (Prince), II, 451n.

[2] Gov. Jonathan Trumbull's letter introduced Erkelens and recommended his plan to send Col. Jacob Gerhard Dirik as an emissary to the Netherlands. Jonathan Trumbull, Sr., to HL, Oct. 16, 1778, PCC, Item 66, Vol. 1, p. 422ff.

[3] Joan Derek Baron van der Capellen (1741-1784), a Dutch philosopher and radical pamphleteer, was one of the most prominent champions of the American cause. Simon Schama, *Patriots and Liberators: Revolution in the Netherlands 1780-1813* (New York, 1977), pp. 61-67.

[4] The Scottish brigade had been stationed in the Dutch Republic since the Dutch War of Independence. Originally composed of Scots officers and 6,000 Scots troops, the brigade's

Gov Trúmbúll: and acquainted him of my plan: to send to M vd Capallen: a petition of thanks for the good he has done: at the same time to open þ Matter in dispúte between þ Americans and Great Brittain, in order that Holland should not labor: or Committ anÿ prœjúdicial affairs in ignorance Gov Trumbúll accepted and aproved múch ~~illegible~~ ↑of↓ the plan: and I proceeded with all þ papers and Letters prepared by Said Governor to Congress: þ plan being proposed to his Honor Mr: Hancock aproved múch of the Same: proposed þ Same in þ Honorable Congress. When: Richard Henry Lee; M: Morris and Wederspoon Esquires: Where apointed as a Committee to converse with me on þ Matter: When after fúll deliberation my proposition is been accepted by þ honle: Congress: When I sealed úp the different packetts: and delivered to þ Secreatarÿ M Paine to be send forward to M: Franklin in Paris to be send from there to Holland: I send a good many letters on þ Matter with an adition of a certain Pamplett which I ordered to let print in Holland in þ different Towns to open the eyes of my countryman: how cruelly in all aspect þ Brittish treated þ Americans: I have send these letters from time to time, and to my únexpressive sorrow: never received no answer: Which makes me úneasy: as I am restless to do good to this Country: by þ means of my own Coúntrÿ[5]

The Bearer Colonell Dirks offered and is bean inclined to go him self personally on this Bussiness: but Would not as an officer leave America in þ Middle of the War and distress. besides not being enough Acqúainted with þ tongue and þ political disputes; But howhever the Collonell is now fully determined to bring these Letters to Holland: he being of Such relations who are at Court: as will be necessarÿ for this Country to be acquainted with: and what will enable Coll: Dircks to be úsefúll in this affair.[6] I refer to

ranks had been depleted to approximately 1,800 soldiers of various nationalities. A 1678 treaty obligated the Dutch to send the brigade if England was at war with a third country. And there was precedent for calling the brigade during domestic upheaval. The Scottish brigade helped put down the 1715 and 1745 Jacobite uprisings. In October 1775 the British requested use of the brigade. Van der Capellen was one of the most vocal opponents of the transfer. Nordholt, *Dutch Republic and American Independence*, pp. 19-20, 26-27, 31-32; *Livingston Papers* (Prince), II, 492n.

[5] The editors have found no evidence of an earlier approval by Congress of Erkelens' plan or of the committee to which he refers.

[6] Jacob Gerhard Dirik (Diriks, Derick, Dirks), born in Deventer, Netherlands, and raised in the Dutch colony of Surinam, had been an officer in Westphalia before joining the American army as a volunteer in 1776. He served first as a captain in the 9th Pa. Regiment and

following Governor Trumbúll his letter. and he being readdy to go on his own risq and Expences: leaving his Ladÿ behind him: with a design to retúrn immediately: I feel confident that your Honor will ~~illegible~~ encourage his offers: and to give þ Colonell Such Powers: as will enable the Colonell to do what he will in Such a Station ↑be↓ in duty bound to; as his Commission in which he Served þ respective States: and his dismission in Such a Waÿ as I believe Generall Mufflin and other Gentleman of Caracter who will be able to inform your Honor about Coll: Dircks: and furthermore Such Authorisation as the Honorable Congress will find good:

I have þ honor to send a plan of negotiation between Holland and these States for twoo Million Pounds Lawfúll: that if Congress should aprove of the Same; and authorise Coll: Dircks in the tryall of Such negotiation; at þ Same Time by þ honorable Congress to have poincted oút the Waÿ of Secúrity for the Loan. When Coll: Dircks could introdúce ↑or execúte↓ the Same and on his retúrn here could bring the Same to a fúll execútion: When I would be glad being well acqúainted with Such bussiness to proceed personally to Holland or to staÿ here in order to be emploÿed by þ honorable Congress in Such an affair: I have þ honor to be well acquainted with his Exellency William Livingston Esq:[7] who can inform yoúr Honor aboút my Conection in Holland if yoúr Honor shoúld find þ proposed Plan of negotiation impracticable: shall be glad to return the Same to Coll: Dircks:__

I have the honor to remain with the most perfect esteem
Sir / Your Most Obedient / and Most humble Servant
                                        Gosuinus Erkelens

SOURCE: RC, PCC (Item 66), DNA; addressed at bottom of first page "Honorable Henry Laurens Esq"; dated below close "Hardford / 15th October / 1778.".

---

beginning in March 1777 as a captain in the 4th Cont. artillery. In May 1778 his petition to form an independent corps under Pulaski was denied. Congress did, however, grant him leave November 5, with rank of brevet lieutenant colonel in order to go to Holland to investigate the possibilities of a Dutch loan to the United States. Nordholt, *Dutch Republic and American Independence*, p. 33; *HL Papers*, XIII, 298n; Heitman, *Continental Officers; JCC*, XI, 509, XII, 1106.

[7] William Livingston became acquainted with Erkelens through his second cousin John Henry Livingston, a Dutch Reform clergyman. William Livingston to HL, Oct. 23, 1778.

TO GEORGE WASHINGTON

Philadelphia, October 16, 1778

Sir

I had the honor of writing to Your Excellency the 13th Instant by Messenger Freeman.

Inclosed Your[1] Excellency will be pleased to receive an Act of Congress of Yesterdays' date for removing from Massachusetts Bay to Charlotteville in Virginia the Troops of the Convention of Saratoga unless Sir Henry Clinton shall have complied with one of the requisitions of Congress in their Act of the 11th September last.[2]

Also an Act of this date in a printed Paper forbidding every Person holding an office under the United States to encourage or attend at Theatrical Entertainments.

I likewise trouble Your Excellency with an Act of the same date for preventing the spreading ~~of~~ seditious Papers in these States by the Enemy under the Mask of Flags of Truce or otherwise and for punishing Persons detected in attempts to disperse such Papers__ this, as I apprehend was intended to extend as a direction to Your Excellency, and to Commanders of seperate Departments, but upon a review I find it is not so comprehensive it is therefore offered at present as matter of information.

I have the honor to be &c.

P.S.

Your Excellency's favor of the 6th Ins[t.] & the Roll containing proceedings of a Court Martial on General Schuyler have been duly presented to Congress.

SOURCE: LB, PCC (Item 13), DNA; addressed "General Washington / By Brown"; dated "16th October".

---

[1] "Y" written over "y".

[2] Congress resolved on September 11 to apply to Sir Henry Clinton for passports which would permit American vessels safe passage for the purpose of transporting provisions and fuel to Boston for the use of the Convention Army. Failure to comply would justify Congress "removing the said prisoners to such parts of the United States as they can be best subsisted in." General Washington conveyed the resolutions to Clinton on September 16. The British commander refused to comply and Congress determined on October 16 to remove "all the prisoners of the convention of Saratoga to the town of Charlottesville...in the State of Virginia." *JCC*, XII, 901-902, 1016-1018; *Washington Writings* (Fitzpatrick), XII, 466; XIII, 119.

TO RICHARD CASWELL

Philadelphia, October 18, 1778

Sir.

I beg leave to refer Your Excellency to my late Letters of the 13[th.] & 16[th.] Inst. forwarded yesterday by the hands of Colonel Wood.[1]

Congress having received recent repeated intelligence of the Enemy's design to make an attack upon South Carolina & that an embarkation of Troops for that purpose had actually commenced at New York have directed me by an Act of the 17[th.] Inst. here inclosed, to request Your Excellency to forward with all possible expedition the 3000. Men requested to be sent to the aid of that State & Georgia in an Act of the 25th Ult[o.] transmitted in my Letter to Your Excellency of the 26[th.] & to make an addition of two thousand Men to the Number abovementioned[2]

I am also directed to assure Your Excellency that the necessary remittance of Money for payment of these Troops will be made in a few days.[3]

I have the honor to be / With great Esteem & respect / Sir / Your Excellency's / Obedient & most humble / servant

Henry Laurens,
President / of Congress.

SOURCE: ALS, Fogg Autograph Collection, MeHi; addressed below close "His Excellency / Governor Caswell / North Carolina."; dated "Philadelphia / 18[th.] October 1778."; docketed "President Laurens / 18. October 1778__". LB, PCC (Item 13), DNA. Copy, Nc-Ar.

---

[1] Col. James Wood of the 8th Va. Regiment had requested leave in late September to go to Virginia. *Washington Writings* (Fitzpatrick), XII, 530-531; Heitman, *Continental Officers*.

[2] Intelligence concerning the British "grand embarkation" came to Congress at this time primarily from the Earl of Stirling, the American commander in New Jersey. Congress may have been moved to further preparation for a southern invasion by his letter of October 13 which was read October 16. North Carolina Congressman Thomas Burke believed Congress overreacted "from the credulity of some Southern Gentlemen...and from the high idea of the importance of their country." John Mathews implied that the decision to send additional troops was contested well into the night and that Congress sat past 10:00 p.m. on October 17. Lord Stirling to HL, Oct. 13, 1778, PCC, Item 162, p. 527ff; Thomas Burke to Richard Caswell, Oct. 20, 1778, *State Records of North Carolina*, XIII, 244-245; *Delegate Letters* (Smith), XI, 70-71.

[3] On October 20, Congress approved resolutions to transmit $100,000 to Benjamin Harrison, Jr., deputy paymaster general in Virginia and $150,000 to William Blount, deputy paymaster general in North Carolina, to settle some previous accounts and "for the pay and subsistence of the Continental troops and levies recommended to be sent...to Charleston, for the defence of the states of South Carolina and Georgia." *JCC*, XII, 1026-1027.

TO RAWLINS LOWNDES

Philadelphia, October 18, 1778

Sir

I beg leave to refer Your Excellency to my late Letters of the 13th and 16th Instant sent to Governor Caswell by an Express Messenger with a request to the Governor to be forwarded immediately to Charlestown. Congress having received recent repeated intelligence of the design of the Enemy to attack Charlestown or some part of South Carolina, have directed me to request the Governors of Virginia and North Carolina to forward with all expedition the Troops requested for the aid of South Carolina and Georgia in their Act of the 25th Ulto. and also an additional number of two thousand from North Carolina, as Your Excellency will be more particularly informed by the inclosed Act of the 17th Instant.

One of the British Commissioner's Manifesto Flags of truce intended for this River, having on board three Packets, suppos'd to be intended for Delaware, Pennsylvania and Congress was by a violent Wind driven a few days ago on the Jersey shore and wreck'd. The Commander of the Flag vessel, said to be a Lieutenant of a British fifty Gun Ship,[1] a Midshipman and eight or ten Seamen escaped with their lives; these were seized and sent Prisoners to Philadelphia, and were Yesterday committed to the New Jail;[2] tomorrow I shall enquire more particularly into the history of their errand. There is among the Seamen a person who was formerly a skilful Pilot on the Delaware:[3] the hazard which this Man would have been exposed to, had the Vessel come safely in, would have been very great, it is therefore to be suspected that he was sent in order to discover what obstructions have been made in the River since the Enemy abandoned it, and 'tis not to be doubted that each of these flags will contain Spies and Emissaries. I must rely on my

[1] Lt. Christopher Hele of HMS *Preston* commanded the small party aboard the sloop *Hotham* which intended to deliver packets from the Carlisle Commission.

[2] HL made notes on a copy of pilot Abraham Whiltbank's October 20 testimony on this incident. Eleven seamen, Lieutenant Hele, Mr. Sanders (a midshipman), Whiltbank, and an unidentified woman survived. Two seamen drowned and all of the others, except the women, were "confined as prisoners of War." HL Papers, ScHi.

[3] Abraham Whiltbank of Sussex County, Delaware, remained loyal, migrated to Nova Scotia after the war and by 1790 resided in England. Harold B. Hancock, *The Loyalists of Revolutionary Delaware* (Newark, Del., 1977), pp. 105, 128.

Colleagues for the transmission of the News of the day which in my
circumstances I have not time to recite.

I have the honor to be &c.

SOURCE: LB, PCC (Item 13), DNA; addressed "President Lowndes / South
Carolina / by Patrick Maher from the Quarter Master."; dated "18th
October".

TO JOSEPH REED

Philadelphia, October 18, 1778

Sir

In obedience to the Order of Congress laid on me last
evening, I have written the Letter to Lord Stirling respecting Mrs.
Yard,[1] without postponing the matter on Account of the day.

When I reflect that on the 13th Instant I transmitted to
General Washington an Order of Congress "to take effectual
measures for preventing an illicit commerce between the inhabitants of these States and the Enemy in the garrison at New York,"[2]
and take into consideration the present Permit to pass Trunks &
Baggage from that place without examination, I feel a deep apprehension for the honor of Congress which will probably be called in
question by the Army in the first instance, and possibly by the good
people at large in these States eventually; nor am I without some
concern on your account Sir, should it hereafter happear that such
Trunks and Baggage had contained Merchandize. and had not
been fully explained to Congress when the Permit for free passage
was applied for. Pardon me Sir, for these suggestions, they flow from
the purest motives. You will determine in a moment whether they
contain any degree of propriety and will act as you shall judge
proper. I therefore submit the Letter to you under a flying Seal to
be sent forward immediately or detained for further reflection on

---

[1] Sarah Yard maintained a boardinghouse in Philadelphia across from the City Tavern at
which several delegates stayed. On October 17, Congress granted her the extraordinary
privilege of returning from within British lines to Philadelphia "without any examination" of
her trunks or baggage. HL's October 18 letter to Stirling was the pass for Mrs. Yard. Adams,
Diary, II, 115n; *Delegate Letters* (Smith), XI, 75n; *JCC*, XII, 1021; HL to Lord Stirling, Oct. 18, 1778,
MeHi.

[2] *JCC*, XII, 1005.

the subject matter. If you shall determine the former be pleased to close the ~~Message~~ Letter by a wafer.[3]

Believe me to be, Dear Sir, / With great Respect and Regard / Your Obedient & / Most Humble Serv.[t]

SOURCE: LB, PCC (Item 13), DNA; addressed "The Honble / Joseph Reed Esquire / Philadelphia / delivered by Mos. Young"; dated "Sunday 18th Oct[r.]".

FROM RAWLINS LOWNDES

Charles Town, October 18, 1778

Dear Sir

Having so lately had the Honour to write to your Excellency by Sam[l.] Wilkinson of the 13[th.] of October, that I have very little to say by this Messenger.

The Intelligence that I have from M[r.] Galphin and Col[o.] Hammond, is, that the Creeks have committed some fresh Murders in Georgia: That the greater part of the Nation is averse to a Warr and dispos'd to maintain the Peace with us, but that the powerful Influence of Stuarts presents operates strongly in reverse and while that Influence cannot be Counter-Acted or Suspended by an equal or superior force, it cannot be a doubt who will have the greatest weight and Ascendency in their Councils. The Cherokees, except a few called the Catlyees, appear to be fixed in their dispositions for peace with us, and M[r.] Hammond thinks may be prevailed upon even to take up the Hatchet in our favour.[1] All our preparations now will tend more immediately to wait the pleasure of Gen[l.] Clinton

---

[3] Joseph Reed, though not a member of Congress at this time, had supported Mrs. Yard's request for a pass and had gone so far as to draft a letter to Lord Stirling, the American commander at Elizabethtown, N.J. Reed's letter, dated October 17, explained her special priviledge was granted "for particular Reasons." HL obviously did not agree with Reed or Congress and realizing that Reed was one of the strongest supporters of Mrs. Yard in this matter left the decision of forwarding the pass to him. Joseph Reed to Lord Stirling (Draft), Oct. 17, 1778, HL Papers, ScHi.

[1] Col. LeRoy Hammond reported little success in negotiating with the Creeks to John Lewis Gervais in early October, but felt the Cherokees would assist the Americans if the Cherokee trade was well supplied with goods. LeRoy Hammond to John Lewis Gervais (extract), Oct. 11, 1778, PHi.

when we are Releived from the apprehension of his Visit I suppose our measures will be directed to other objects next in Importance. The passengers who Arrived in the Cartel from New York are all permitted to Land except Mr· Graham who is ordered to return in the Flag of Truce. they were all examined before the House, but he only did not give Satisfaction: Price and Telfair were directed to proceed forthwith to Georgia.

General Howes recall seems to have been unexpected by him__ he called upon me and I shewed him the Resolve & having a spare Copy he desired it and obtained it: as I was not directed Officially to Serve him with[2] a Copy, I told him so, and that I had no particular direction concerning him, other than was expressed in the Resolution so that I presume he will hold the Command till he is Superseded[3] by the Arrival of General Lincoln.__ the Removal from so easy a Birth, and so lucrative a one too, abstracted from other Considerations that must Affect delicate feelings, cannot be very agreeable__ 24 lb. of Beef ⅌ day at 10/. and 16 lb of Bread at 10/. the Currant price, ↑and the amount of his Rations↓ goes a great way in House Keeping and make a Considerable Sum ⅌ Annum besides little ditto's__

As Wilkinson set off so lately, I have detained this Express a few days as the Assembly were upon Adjourning, to see if I should have any Commands to Transmit to you. they adjourned yesterday leaving me only in Charge the Inclosed Report of a Commͤee agreed to by the House, which by Message I am desired to make the necessary application[4] to Congress upon, which thro' our Delagates, I now desire to do.__ ↑but↓ not being furnished with any of their Reasons in Support of the measure recommended, or being able to Suggest any good ones my self, I must leave it to the Delagates under the force and Sanction of the Report as herewith Transmitted.__ for Gods sake, my Dear Sir, releive me from the Continual Importunity I suffer for ↑want of↓ blank Commissions, which will now be more wanted ↑and in greater numbers↓, in Consequence of this Resolve of the Assembly[5]

---

2 A comma following "with" was cancelled.
3 Second "e" written over "i".
4 First "i" written over "y".
5 On October 9, the Assembly had extended its legislation "for compleating the Quota of Troops, to be raised by this State for the Continental Service." *S. C. General Gazette,* Nov. 12, 1778.

I am with the highest Respect, and the Sincerest Regard / Sir / Your Excellency's Most Obed$^{t.}$ / and Most hum̄ Servant

Raw$^{S.}$ Lowndes.

P.S

As I perceive Wells regularly sends you the papers, I do not for that reason trouble your Exc̄y with them__ but always give him Notice when an Express sets off__

SOURCE: RC, Kendall Collection; addressed below close "His Ex̄cy Henry Laurens Esq$^{r.}$"; dated below close "Cha$^{s.}$ Town 18$^{th.}$ Oct$^{r.}$ 1778__"; docketed by HL "Presid$^{t.}$ Lowndes / 18$^{th.}$ October 1778 / Rec$^{d.}$ 8$^{th.}$ Novem.~"; docketed "Rec̄d". Copy (19th century), HL Papers, ScHi.

FROM LACHLAN McINTOSH

Fort Pitt, Pa., October 18, 1778

Dear Sir,

I did myself the Honor of writing to you the 25[$^{th.}$] Ult$^{o.}$ by a M$^{r.}$ Gibson[1] who is not returned yet.__ in that I mentioned my receiving Letters from Georgia, which informed me of ~~illegible~~ Gen$^{l.}$ Howes disappointment in East Florida, & that he returned with the Continental Troops to Savannah, but that Houstoun Stayed behind with Col$^{o.}$ Williamson & the Militia I will be much obliged to you, if you can inform me by the bearer Capt. Stokeley,[2] if Houstoun & Williamson have done any thing, or the whole failed, with any particulars which may be Collected respecting that unfortunate Expedition.__

I am sorry to hear the Continental Troops of Georgia are so Miserably reduced Since I came away, & no prospect of Recruiting them.__ the Regiment of Horse which my Brother left in such good order, I am informed will hardly make one Troop without Horses

---

[1] Probably Lt. Col. John Gibson of the 9th Va. Regiment who had been recommended by Washington to HL in May 1778 as a man "who, from his knowledge of the Western Country and Indian Nations and language, is ordered to repair to Pitsburg." Washington to HL, May 28, 1778, PCC, Item 152, Vol. 6, p. 51ff.

[2] Capt. Nehemiah Stokeley of the 8th Pa. Regiment. Heitman, *Continental Officers*.

or Accoutrements.__³ the 4ᵗʰ· or White's Regᵗ· composed altogether of British Deserters & prisoners of Warr was certainly a great Imposition upon the Public, very few of them reached Georgia, & I am informed now they are almost all gone.⁴ the other three Regaments of Foot will not make above one, & I think should be all turned into the first, who have done the most service by far & attended with the Least Expence to the public.__ but this ↑is↓ only my private Opinion, & only to yourself.__ as I know that ungovernable Turbulent little state Acts altogether from Caprice & will do as they please, if these things are left to them.__ yet I am always anxious to hear every thing relating to it.__

I have wrote fully to the Board of Warr respecting the Circumstances of things here by Capt. Stokely which I request of you & Mʳ· Drayton to peruse with my former Letter to them, as I should be glad you were both informed of every part of my Conduct, & would be obliged to either of you to direct me at any times, where or how I could Ammend it.__

I am respectfully, Dʳ· Sir, / Your most obᵗ· Hble Servᵗ·
Lachⁿ· Mᶜ·Intosh.

SOURCE: RC, Kendall Collection; addressed on cover "(Private) / The Honourable__ / Henry Laurens Esqʳ· / President of Congress__ / Philadelphia / ⍦ Capt. Stokeley / 8ᵗʰ· Pennsylvᵃ· Regᵗ·"; addressed below close "Honˡᵉ / Henry Laurens Esqʳ·"; dated "Fort Pitt 18ᵗʰ· October 1778.__"; docketed by HL "Geñ McIntosh / 18 Octob. 1778 / Recᵈ· 30ᵗʰ__".

FROM GEORGE WASHINGTON

Fredericksburg, N.Y., October 18, 1778

Sir

I am honored with yours of the 9ᵗʰ⸱ inclosing a Resolve to extend the Embargo and to prevent forestalling provision. I hope

---

³ Col. William McIntosh commanded the Georgia regiment of Horse Rangers from its inception in early 1776 until his resignation in December of that year. He was replaced by Capt. John Baker. Before his resignation the regiment had about 300 men and in early 1777 the reorganized regiment consisted of twelve troops of men. Harvey H. Jackson, *Lachlan McIntosh* (Athens, Ga., 1979), pp. 41, 42, 49, 54-55; Wright, *Continental Army*, p. 314.

⁴ Col. John White of North Carolina was appointed commander of the 4th Ga. Regiment in February 1777. He recruited in Pennsylvania in late 1777. The regiment was composed

the latter will have the desired effect, for unless that most infamous practice of raising the prices of the necessaries of life can be stopped, it will be impossible for any Funds to subsist the Army.

Inclosed you have the Copy of a petition from the Refugees in New York to the Commissioners. You may depend upon the authenticity of it, as it is taken from a New York paper.[1] It should seem by this that they are extremely sollicitous and anxious to know whether New York is to be garrisoned, which implies a suspicion on their part, that it is to be evacuated.

All accounts since mine of the 14th. confirm the report of a very considerable embarkation. It is said to consist of ten British Regiments compleated to their full establishment, and their Grenadier and Light Companies added to them. This will make them amount to upwards of five thousand Men. They have not sailed.

I cannot say that I am satisfied, that a total evacuation of the City is intended this Winter, altho' many inhabitants near the lines, and several out of the City are of that opinion. I have set every engine at work to procure full intelligence of their designs and I hope to succeed. The current opinion of deserters and others is that the present embarkation is intended for the West Indies; some few have said that they have a design upon Charlestown.

I have the honor to be / with the greatest Respect & Regard / Your Excellency's / most obt. Servt.

G°: Washington

SOURCE: RC, PCC (Item 152), DNA; addressed below close "His Excellency Henry Laurens Esq:"; dated "Head Quarters Fredericksburg 18th: October / 1778:"; docketed by HL "Gen̄ Washington / 18th. October 1778 / Rec̄d in Cong.⁓ & / Read 22d__". Draft, Washington Papers, DLC.

---

largely of British deserters who turned out to be equally unreliable in the American service. Ten members of the regiment were executed on May 21 and 22, 1778, for desertion. *HL Papers*, XIII, 125, 437, 493; Heitman, *Continental Officers*.

[1] Hugh Gaines's *New York Gazette and Weekly Mercury* of Sept. 21, 1778, announced a meeting of "LOYAL REFUGEES" to be held the following day "to discuss matters in which they are highly interested." The *New-Jersey Gazette* picked up this item and suggested that the refugees feared that "New-York will shortly be evacuated" leaving them exposed to retaliation from the Whigs. This brought forth a reaction from James Rivington, whose newspaper denied that the city would be evacuated and threatened any patriots who fell into the hands of "refugees." *Rivington's Gazette*, Oct. 7, 1778.

TO COUNT D'ESTAING

Philadelphia, October 20, 1778

Sir

I have the honor of transmitting within the present inclosure, an Act of Congress of the 17th. Inst. expressing the high sense which the Representative Body [of][1] these States entertains of Your Excellency's zeal and attachment in the Cause in which the Arms of His Most [Chris]tian Majesty and those of the United States of America are mutually engaged. Also their perfect approbation of the conduct of Your Excellency & of the Of[ficers] and Men under Your Excellency's Command.[2]

Although Sir, no words of my own can give ene[rgy] to the language of the Resolves of Congress, I may [be] permitted upon this occasion to assure Your Excellen[cy] the present Act contains not only the opinion of Con[gress,] but, as far as I can penetrate, the genuine sentiments of each Member, & it is with particular satisfaction I do [so.]

I have the honor to be / With the highest Respect / and Esteem / Sir / Your Excellency's / Most obedient and / Most humble Servant

Henry Laurens
President / of Congress

SOURCE: ALS, Archives Nationales; addressed below close "His Excellency / The Count d'Estaing / Lieut. General of the Armies of / His Most Christian Majesty / Vice Admiral of his fleets & / Knight of his Orders. / now at Boston."; no date. LB, PCC (Item 13), DNA; dated "20th. October 1778".

TO CHARLES STEWART[1]

Philadelphia, October 20, 1778

Sir.

I have had the honor of presenting Your Letter of the 13th.

---

[1] Bracketed material here and below supplied from letterbook copy, PCC, Item 13.

[2] The resolutions commending d'Estaing "as a brave and wise officer" and extending Congress's "highest sense of his zeal and attachment" were made in large part to deflect some of the criticism made by General Sullivan and other American officers after d'Estaing decided to withdraw from the Rhode Island campaign. *JCC*, XII, 1021; *Rhode Island History*, XXIX (1970), 27-31, 34.

[1] Charles Stewart, formerly a colonel in the New Jersey militia, served as commissary general of issues from June 18 1777, to July 24, 1782. Heitman, *Continental Officers*.

Inst. to Congress & although no particular determination was had I have reason to beleive the House approve of your sentiments respecting M^r· Winship late dep. Comm^y· of Issues in the Northern department__² the vacancy which his neglect had made in that Office is now supplied by the appointment of James Gray Esquire³ who will deliver this & enter immediately upon the execution of his⁴ duty.

I am with great regard / Sir / Your most obedient / humble servant

Henry Laurens.
President / of Congress.

SOURCE: ALS, MH; addressed on cover "Charles Stewart Esquire / Commissary general of Issues / in the Northern department"; addressed below close "Charles Stewart Esquire / Commiss: General of Issues / Northern department:"; dated "Philadelphia 20th· Octob.⁓ / 1778__"; franked "On public service / Henry Laurens,"; docketed "Philadelphia Oct^r· 20. 1778. / from Henry Laurens Esqr· / President in Congress.__" and "Honble· Henry Laurens Esqr / President in Congress / 20 Oct. 1778". LB, PCC (Item 13), DNA.

TO LOUIS XVI

Philadelphia, October 21, 1778

Great, faithful and beloved Friend and Ally

The Marquis de la Fayette having obtained our leave to return to his Native Country¹ we could not suffer him to depart without testifying our deep sense of his Zeal, Courage and attachment.

---

² Stewart complained in his October 13 letter that the conduct of Ebenezer Winship, his deputy in the Northern Department, "has given cause to suspect...great want of attention." Stewart refused to extend any more money until the deputy delivered his unsettled accounts. Winship, who had served in the 5th Mass. Regiment before his appointment as a deputy commissary general of issues in August 1777, had submitted his resignation. Charles Stewart to HL, Oct. 13, 1778, PCC, Item 78, Vol. 20, p. 319ff; Heitman, *Continental Officers.*

³ Congress approved the appointment of James Gray, formerly a captain in the 3rd N.H. Regiment, to be deputy commissary general of issues in the Northern Department on October 19. Gray held the post until his resignation in November 1780. Heitman, *Continental Officers; JCC,* XII, 1023; HL to James Gray, Oct. 20, 1778, PCC, Item 13.

⁴ "h" written over "t".

¹ At his request Congress granted Lafayette a leave of absence on October 21. Lafayette to HL, Oct. 13, 1778, PCC, Item 156, p. 31ff; *JCC,* XII, 1034-1035.

We have advanced him to the rank of Major General in our Armies, which, as well by his prudent as spirited conduct he hath manifestly merited.

We recommend this Young Nobleman to Your Majesty's notice as one whom we know to be Wise in Council, gallant in the Field, and Patient under the hardships of War. His Devotion to his Sovereign hath led him in all things to demean himself as an American, acquiring thereby the confidence of these United States Your Majesty's good and faithful Friends and Allies and the Affection of their Citizens.

We pray God to keep Your Majesty in his holy Protection Done at Philadelphia the twenty first day of October 1778.

By the Congress of the United States of North America your good Friends and Allies

Henry Laurens.
President

Attest / Cha⁵ Thomson sec^y.

SOURCE: DS, Archives du ministère des affaires étrangères: Correspondence politique, Étas-Unis, V:133. DS, NHi. LB, PCC (Item 13), DNA.

FROM WILLIAM HEATH

Boston, October 21, 1778

Sir

Yesterday I received the Honor of yours of the 10th· Instant.[1]

I immediately Called for my File, and upon examination, find a Parole given ~~to~~ ↑by L^t↓ Col^o· Anstruther, and another by Capt· Willoe, the Former to go to Rhode Island ~~then~~ and New yorke the latter to Canada by the way of Hallifax both by express permission from the Hon Congress___[2] and a parole given a few Days Since ~~to~~

---

[1] HL requested that Heath make "a strict enquiry" into reports that officers of the Convention Army had been given or had purchased extensive paroles to New York. Persistent rumors led the appointment of a congressional committee of inquiry on Oct. 27, 1778. HL to William Heath, Oct. 10, 1778, Heath Papers, MHi; *JCC*, XII, 1065.

[2] On March 2, 1778, Congress resolved that Lt. Col. John Anstruther be permitted to go to Rhode Island on his parole to negotiate his exchange for Ethan Allen. No other exchange was to be accepted. Allen was exchanged for Lt. Col. Archibald Campbell and Anstruther's

↑by↓ Capt· England of the 47th Reg^t· on permission to go to New yorke^3 ~~and~~ in Company with and to return with the D^y Commissary of Prisoners^4 on a matter of Particular Concern to his Family ~~and~~ which Could not be Settled here, I have taken no other Parole, excep^t· when the Commissary ~~or~~ Quartermaster or Paymaster of the Troops ↑of the Convention↓ have had Occasion to go to Rhode Island or New yorke for the Purpose of Obtain'g Clothing & ↑&↓ necessaries ~~for money~~ or ↑for↓ the Settlement of the Public Acco^ts· in all which Cases the Officers who were Sent returned as ↑soon as↓ their Business was Compleated which never was any long Time__ indeed in the whole of my Conduct towards those Troops I have endeavoured to ~~Shape my Conduct in such manner as~~ ↑Consult↓ ↑act↓ ~~for~~ the Honor and Safety of my Country__ and most Strictly to observe the Instructions which have been given me__ Upon the Signification of the pleasure of Congress ~~If I mistake not upon an application of Lord Napier that they did not approve of~~ ↑on↓ the third of March, ↑last↓ that they did not ~~approve~~ think it expedient for officers to go within the the Enemys Posts to negociate exchanges when Such exchanges Could be effected in the Customary way, ↑By↓ I immediately ~~put a Stop to it in every instance tho~~ Communicated ↑it↓ to the Officers, and observed a ↑line of↓ Conduct Conformable thereto__ in every instance within my Knowledge__ ^5

on the 5th· of May I had the Honor to receive a Letter from his Excellency Genl Washington Observing that as the Ballance of Officers in the Hands of the Enemy was much against us He wished as many Exchanges as Possible might be effected with the Officers of the Convention,^6 after that at different Times the D^y Commissary Genl of Prisoners ~~repeatedly~~ informed me that Such and Such officers whom He named were ~~Sent~~ ↑Called↓ for by the Commissary

---

parole was revoked. Congress determined on March 3 that Capt. Samuel Willoe be given a passport to return to Canada under the restriction of the general parole given Canadian troops in the Saratoga Convention. *JCC*, X, 196, 213, 218; *HL Papers*, XII, 423-424.

^3 Probably the same Capt. Richard England who was on a list of officers proposed for exchange by Lord Rawdon early in 1779. Lord Rawdon to Joshua Loring, Jan. 10, 1779, PCC, Item 78, Vol. 3, p. 269ff.

^4 Joshua Mersereau.

^5 Congress had resolved on March 3, 1778, in response to an appeal from Lord Napier "and any other officer who may apply...that Congress do not think it expedient to continue to grant passports" to allow for the negotiation of personal exchanges. *JCC*, X, 219.

^6 Washington to Heath, May 5, 1778, *Washington Writings* (Fitzpatrick), XI, 349-351.

General of Prisoners, to be Sent in immediately, and Several officers were accordingly Sent in

These matters were Conducted by the D^y Commissary of Prisoners, and whether any Illicit measures have marked his Conduct is not within the Sphere of my knowledge, I recollect to have ↑heard↓ Someing of the kind hinted ~~antecedent to~~ ↑prior to↓ the date of your Letter, ~~as the D^y Commissary is now absent~~ and the enclosd is paragraph of a Letter from Governor Skeene to ~~Capt Masten~~ ↑Major Mersereau dated dated at N Yorke 27 Sep^t·↓ which was brought here in a Flag the last Evening__ ⁷ The D^y Commissary is absent__ as Soon as He returns I will make every enquiry ↑and as far as↓ in my Power ~~and~~ Comply with the Injunctions of your ~~Letter~~ ↑orders↓. Monthly returns of the Troops ↑of the Convention↓ are made to the Board war, ~~I request to be informed whether a Return different~~ a more particular One if Possible Shall be obtained__

In your ~~Letter~~ ↑favor↓ of 26th· June with which I was honored ~~in answer to my trouble of the~~ you were pleased to express your self on the ~~illegible~~ information given by two German officers that the Colours of the Reg^ts· ↑of ~~Convention~~ Foreign Troops ~~illegible~~↓ were Secreted in the Baggage as follows "Congress request you in the most effectual manner & by ~~every~~ all proper means unalarming to the present Commanding Officer of the British Prisoners to obtain further ~~acco^ts~~ accounts of any violation of the Convention of Saratoga and particularly if Possible to obtain the very Colours__ admitting they are carried off by Genl Burgoyne or destroyed before he left you a Search would prove fruitless & wear an ill aspect, but getting the Colours in hand will carry proof undeniable" I have been endeavouring in the most Secret manner to obtain further Intelligence but hitherto cannot I do not see what further step can be taken with respect to the Colours unless a Search be made for them which is a matter so delicate ↑unless there be a Certainty of Succeeding↓ that I dare not do it without directions for the purpose ~~as it will be deemed an infraction of the~~ and wish a ↑further↓

---

⁷ Probably Philip Skene (1725-1810) who had been appointed by the British as "lieutenant governor" of Ticonderoga and Crown Point in 1775 and later became Burgoyne's principal Loyalist advisor. Mark Mayo Boatner, *Encyclopedia of the American Revolution* (New York, 1966).

signification of the pleasure of Congress thereon,[8] I am Sorry to give you the Trouble of so long a Letter

and have the Honor to be / with the greatest est / your Honors / most Obt Hbble Se

W Heath

SOURCE: Draft, Heath Papers, MHi; addressed below close "Honble Henry Laurens Esqr"; dated "Head Quarters Boston Octr. 21st. 1778"; docketed "To Congress resp^g. Officers / going to N York on Parole / Com^y of Prisoners__ the / Colours &c, &c, / Octr. 21. 1778".

FROM LORD STIRLING

Elizabethtown, N.J., October 21, 1778

Sir

I have had the honor of receiveing your letter of the 18th. encloseing an Act of Congress of the 17th. "for permitting M^rs. Yard to return to Philadelphia with her Trunks and Baggage without any Examination."[1] I presume Congress is uninformed that there is in force a Law of this State prohibiting all Intercourse and Commerce with the Enemy, but under Certain regulations, and impowering any person whatever to Seize & Secure any goods wares or merchandize brought from within the lines of the Enemy. directs a process at Law for their Condemnation and orders them to be sold for the benefit of the Captors.[2] I could not therefore with any propriety Interfere in the Execution of the Laws of the State; But I

---

[8] The issue arose when Heath sent HL testimony from three German prisoners that the battle flags from the regiments that surrendered at Saratoga were being concealed and had not been destroyed or left in Canada. This was the same information HL sought from Christian Senf. His purpose was to strengthen Congress's position in the conflict with the British over both the interpretation and the implementation of the Convention of Saratoga. When Senf's August 5 affidavit arrived on September 23 it was referred to a committee. In his reply to this letter from Heath, HL made no further mention of the battle flags. William Heath to HL, June 6, 1778, PCC, Item 187, p. 152; HL to William Heath, June 26, 1778; *JCC*, XII, 945; Rawlins Lowndes to HL, Aug. 16, 1778, with Senf enclosure; *HL Papers*, XIII, 508n.

[1] *JCC*, X, 1021; HL to Lord Stirling, Oct. 18, 1778, MeHi.

[2] The Oct. 8, 1778, New Jersey "Act to prevent the Subjects of this State from going into, or coming out of, the Enemy's Lines, without Permissions or Passports" forbade the transportation of all goods except those to be consumed during the journey. *Livingston Papers* (Prince), II, 472n.

have prevailed on the Captors to Sell the whole without examination to Mrs. Yard for Six pence, altho' there is good reason to believe they would Sell for twenty thousand pounds. This the Captors do, out of the Respect they have for Congress, and from their great desire to Comply with every wish of that Honorable Body.[3]

Yesterday I detected the inclosed letter from J: Galloway to Mrs. Elizabeth Hylliard. by the Size & Shape of it he undoubtedly expected it would have escaped our Notice and have reached his Sister, the formal leave he takes of his Sister and this head Strong Country that will not be Saved by <u>him</u> indicates a general evacuation of New York; for he would never think of quitting his ground while he had the least hopes of reclaiming it.[4] other indications of the Same; are farther preparations for embarking more troops, are going on and they are now Actually dismantling and destroying their fortifications on Staten Island.

On its being intimated to me by Govr. Livingston that Congress was desireous to have the particulars of the Massacre of Colonel Baylors Regiment, I desired Doctor Griffith Surgeon and Chaplin to General Woodfords Brigade and who attends Colonel Baylor and the other wounded persons; to Collect all the Evidence he could of that Barbarous affair. I have Just now received his Collections on that horrid Subject: which with his letter to me you will find in this Inclosure.[5]

22^{d.} No Movements towards Sandy hook yesterday. I find the 5th. 40th. & 55th. Regiments on Staten Island are waiting the return of

---

[3] The New Jersey Act that forbade the transportation of goods through enemy lines provided that the militia or Continental forces who seized the property could keep it if the suspect was judged guilty of violating the act. HL responded to this letter by expressing his "admiration of the Liberality & obedience, displayed in the conduct of those persons who had captured Mrs. Yards Merchandize, by the gentle surrender of them." *Livingston Papers* (Prince), II, 472n; HL to Lord Stirling, Oct. 25, 1778, private collection.

[4] The letter from Pennsylvania loyalist Joseph Galloway (ca. 1729-1803) to his sister, Elizabeth Hylliard, Oct. 10, 1778, was written on a long, narrow strip of paper—folded many times so that its smallness would escape notice. Writing from New York, Galloway was saying goodbye to his sister before sailing for England. Galloway was bitter that Pennsylvania in particular had rejected his advice. PCC, Item 53, p. 135.

[5] Stirling enclosed a letter from Dr. David Griffith of Oct. 20, 1778, which was a report on the British attack on Colonel Baylor's regiment, and the affidavits which Griffith had collected from survivors of that attack. Griffith informed Stirling that "Congress was not misinformed respecting the Savage Cruelty" of the attack, in which the British commander, Maj. Gen. Charles Grey, had apparently ordered that no quarter be given. PCC, Item 53, p. 105ff.

detachmᵗˢ from those Regiments ~~in order~~ now on the Egg harbor expedition, in order to Embark;⁶ nothing Else retards it.⁷

I have no accounts from Count Polaski. I am ↑told↓ there was an Account at Prince Town Yesterday that he has gained some advantage over the Enemy, But if so Congress must be possesed of the Account.⁸

I am / with Great Regard & Esteem / Sir / your Most Obᵗ Humble / Servant

Stirling,

SOURCE: RC, PCC (Item 162), DNA; addressed on cover "The Honorable / Henry Laurens / President of Congress"; addressed below close "The Honorable / Henry Laurens. / President of Congress."; dated "Elizabeth Town October 21ˢᵗ 1778.__"; docketed "Letter from major genˡ / Lord Stirling 21. ↑Octʳ↓ 1778". Draft, Stirling Papers, NHi. Extract, PCC (Item 53), DNA.

TO GEORGE WASHINGTON

Philadelphia, October 22, 1778

Sir

Since my last Letter of the 16ᵗʰ by Brown, I have had the honor of presenting to Congress Your Excellency's favor of the 14ᵗʰ Instant.¹

---

⁶Each of the regiments did in fact embark for the south. The 40th and 55th sailed to East Florida in November and to the West Indies the following year. The 5th regiment was assigned to marine duty aboard Vice-Admiral Byron's fleet that sailed for the Caribbean in December. Katcher, *British, Army Units,* pp. 31, 51, 60; Tilley, *British Navy,* pp. 160-161.

⁷Paragraph indicated by spacing.

⁸The incident to which Stirling referred concerned the British attack on Pulaski's Legion near Little Egg Harbor, N.J. Several British naval vessels had been sent to the harbor because American privateers congregated there. After capturing ten privateers and destroying several buildings the expedition under army Capt. Patrick Ferguson and navy Capt. Henry Collins prepared to leave. Ferguson, however, gleaned intelligence about the strength and location of Pulaski's Legion from a deserter. With 250 men, Ferguson launched a surprise night raid on Pulaski's infantry early on the morning of October 15, inflicting heavy casualties. Pulaski reported to HL that the British "were so terrified" when he arrived on the scene with his cavalry that they "retired in so great a Disorder that they abandoned Arms accoutrements &ca." The British sailed shortly after, not because of Pulaski's action but under orders from General Sir Henry Clinton. Ward, *War of the Revolution,* II, 617-618; *Documents of the American Revolution* (Davies), XV, 225-226; Casimir Pulaski to HL, Oct. 16 and Oct. 19, 1778, PCC, Item 164, pp. 17ff, 38ff.

¹Washington's October 14 letter, which enclosed an account of the Battle of Ushant "as published by the British Admiralty Board," was read in Congress October 20. Washington to HL, Oct. 14, 1778, PCC, Item 152, Vol. 6, p. 399ff; *JCC,* XII, 1025.

Within the present Cover Your Excellency will receive three Acts of Congress of the 21st Instant.

1. for granting Monsr. de Vrigny such testimonial of his zeal and services as he is intitled to.[2]
2. for obtaining a Return of re-inlistments in the Army in pursuance of an Act of the 31st August last.[3]
3. for obtaining from Sir Henry Clinton a nomination of a proper Person for the Office of Commissary to the British Prisoners in the place of David Franks Esquire confined for a misdemeanor.[4]

To these I add a Paper containing information received from Abrām Whiltbanks lately from New York. I think he said he left that City this day fortnight_ his intelligence if true may not now be further important than to throw light upon other discoveries from that quarter which Your Excellency may have made.

I have the honor to be &c.

SOURCE: LB, PCC (Item 13), DNA; addressed "General Washington / by Jones"; dated "22nd October".

---

[2] Louis de Vrigny's October 21 letter of resignation contained a request for a "mark, that my Zeal and my Services have been attended with the approbation of the Honnourable Congress." He suggested "The Commission of a Collonel would be indeed an authentical and glorious testimony." He also asked for "full...pay and rations" for the period he served as a volunteer prior to receiving his commission. Congress ordered that Washington "be empowered and directed to give...such certificate and testimonial as his zeal and services may have entitled him to." Congress, however, denied both the promotion in rank and the extra pay and rations. Louis de Vrigny to HL, Oct. 21, 1778, PCC, Item 78, Vol. 23, p. 145ff; *JCC*, XII, 1033-1034, 1071.

[3] The resolve as recorded in the Journal noted that the enlistment report was to show progress "in consequence of the resolution of the 8 September." HL referred to the original act of August 31, in which Congress appropriated 120,000 Continental dollars for twenty dollar bounties to convince drafted troops to enlist for three years or the duration of the war. The act of September 8 merely empowered Washington to give an additional bounty of up to ten dollars for the same purpose. *JCC*, XI, 853-854; XII, 889-890, 1034.

[4] David Franks had been arrested October 21, accused of transmitting "by stealth" a letter to his brother Moses in London, that manifested "a disposition and intentions inimical to the safety and liberties of the United States." Congress released him in November to the jurisdiction of the state of Pennsylvania. Congress, in conjunction with his arrest, resolved that Franks no longer be permitted to exercise the office of commissary to the British prisoners after November 10. *JCC*, XII, 1026, 1032-1033, 1110-1111.

FROM GEORGE WASHINGTON

Fredericksburg, N.Y., October 22, 1778

Sir

I have been Honoured, in due order, with your favors of the 13 & 16 Inst;__ the former came to hand on Sunday Evening__ the latter today. The several matters, which are the objects of them, shall have my attention, as far as it shall be practicable.

With respect to the practices complained of by Governor Livingstone, the Extract from his Letter, transmitted by Congress, conveyed the first intimation ~~of~~ I had of them. I have written to Lord Stirling upon the occasion, and ~~directed~~ ↑requested↓ him to inquire into the matter & to report the result.[1] The party stationed in the Neighbourhood of Shrewsbury, was placed there ↑chiefly↓ for the purpose of gaining intelligence__ and under an Active & sensible Officer. I shall be sorry if his conduct ~~if con~~ is reprehensible, for having ~~sanctioned~~ carried on or sanctioned an illicit traffic with the Enemy; however I would observe without ~~any~~ ↑the most distant↓ intention of[2] decidiᵍ ~~upon the present~~ ↑*illegible*↓ ↑in this↓ case, that persons employed to ~~give~~ ↑obtain↓ information__ are frequently obliged to allow a certain sort of commerce__ as the most probable__ and indeed the only means, by which they can get ↑~~admission~~ access to the Enemy &↓ satisfaction in the points they wish.

Previous to the receipt of your Letter, inclosing a Copy of Colo Hartley's, I had determined and ordered another Regiment to march and co-operate with those under Colo Alden and Lieutᵗ Colo Butler, which have been employd on the frontiers of this state for some time.[3] It was intended that the whole should ~~march~~ go against the settlement of Anaguaga, with such Militia as might join; but

---

[1] Washington ordered Lord Stirling to investigate the allegations of illicit trade with the British in New York and "if you discover any improper connivance, or concurrence on the part of the officers at Shrewsbury, that you will take proper measures not only to prevent it in the future, but to punish the past." Washington to Lord Stirling, Oct. 21, 1778. *Washington Writings* (Fitzpatrick), XIII, 120.

[2] "of" written over other text.

[3] Washington had ordered Col. Philip Van Cortlandt's 2nd N.Y. Regiment to join Col. Ichabod Alden's 7th Mass. Regiment and Lt. Col. William Butler's 4th Pa. Regiment "in an expedition against Anaquaga." *Washington Writings* (Fitzpatrick), XIII, 94-95; Heitman, *Continental Officers*.

from the accounts received this morning, I have reason to hope__ that Lᵗ Colo Butler has already destroyed the Town__ ~~as the Oneidas had done that of Unindillo before, against which he was proceeding at the time.~~ I am now consulting Governor Clinton & General Schuyler, who are much better acquainted with the frontiers ↑in this Quarter↓ than ~~I can possibly be~~ ↑I am↓, upon the practicability of ↑an↓ expedition upon a larger scale, against Chemung. I dont know what will be the result; but I am apprehensive from the advanced season of the year and the daily encrease of the Rivers and Creeks__ it will be found ~~extremely difficult~~ ↑impracticable↓ ~~if not altogether~~ impracticable ~~in the execution~~ or at least extremely difficult in the execution.

I have written to General Heath to take immediate measures for carrying into effect, the intention of Congress, respecting the removal of the Convention Troops, in case Sʳ⸳ Henry Clinton has not furnished supplies of Provision and fuel, according to their Resolution of the 11ᵗʰ⸳ Ultᵒ⸳. The matter now rests upon this ~~atten~~ footing, as Passports have not been granted for our Vessels__ or any ↑answer↓ given to the application upon the subject. It will not be ~~im~~possible for me to send proper Guards from the Army to escort the ~~Prisoners~~ Troops on their march__ and therefore__ I have requested General Heath to employ a sufficient number of the Massachusett Militia to conduct ↑them↓ to Connecticut. I shall make a like requisition to Governor Trumbull__ and it will be necessary, that the several States in succession, through which they are to pass, be called ~~upn~~ ↑upon↓ in the same manner.[4]

With respect to seditious papers__ calculated to excite dissentions & mislead the people__ Congress may be assured__ that whenever they are sent from the Enemy by a flag and they come to my hands, I shall not fail to suppress them. I fear however, the avenues and channels in which they may be conveyed, are so various and so numerous__ that no exertions will be found sufficient entirely to prevent the evil, and ~~I am not certain that~~ ↑an↓ ~~ineffectual attempt by Authority, to suppressions would not involve would~~

---

[4] The Convention Army began its march south to Charlottesville, Va., on November 9. Three separate contingents left on successive days. The 623-mile march, with several interruptions for rest, inclement weather, or rivers to be forded, took fully two months. Each state through which they passed was directed to furnish guards and an average of 600 militiamen escorted them from border to border. The last troops arrived on Jan. 13, 1779. Dabney, *After Saratoga*, pp. 47-56.

~~not involve more disagreable Consequences than a free circula-~~
~~tion— especially with proper strictures—~~

Having mentioned the subject of seditious ~~and inflamatory~~
Papers_ I beg leave to observe_ that the Commissioners in their
late Proclamation and Manifesto ~~seem to~~ have touched upon every
thing to awaken the fears of the people. They have thrown out an
implied threat, to change the manner of ~~carrying on~~ the War to one
of a more predatory and destructive kind. They may have ~~been~~
↑done this↓ only ~~thrown out~~ in terrorem; but it is possible, ↑that↓ it
may be intended, as a serious principle of practice. It perhaps may
not be imprudent to guard against it, by fortifying our most valuable
and ↑most↓ accessible Seaports. Immediately after the Action of
Monmouth I sent General Portail to form a plan of fortification for
the ~~River~~ Delaware._ While he was in the execution of this_ he was
called away ~~by~~ at General Lee's instance as a Witness in his trial.
After this was over I thought it necessary, that he should turn his
attention to the Highland posts, and lately the possibility of an
Enterprize against the french fleet and the Town of Boston determined me to send him to that place to take measures for their
common security. ~~of the Town & Squadron~~ previous to this
↑however↓ he had sent Colo Laumoy to prepare the way, by taking
plans of the River and the Adjacent Country, near Philadelphia.
These points I deemed it material to mention_ and submit to
Congress the propriety, as Colo Laumoy is ↑not yet returned↓
↑*illegible* ~~Philadelphia~~↓ there, of their directing a number of Men, to
prosecute the defences._ [5]

October 23rd.

Congress, I make no doubt, will have heard from Lord
Stirling, or thrō some other Channel_ before this reaches them_
that a considerable fleet sailed from York on the 19th & 20th and put
to sea. According to advices, it consisted of about 150 sail_ includ-

---

[5]Gen. Louis Le Bègùe de Presle Duportail had been instructed as early as June 30, 1778, to plan defenses for Philadelphia and the Delaware River. Other activities diverted his attention and Congress was not forthcoming with funds to support the additional fortifications. Early in 1779, the state of Pennsylvania assumed responsibility and thereafter dealt with Duportail who submitted a report in May 1779. Pennsylvania followed his plan and improved the fortifications at Fort Mifflin and Billingsport. *Washington Writings* (Fitzpatrick), XII, 134-135; Walker, *Engineers of Independence*, pp. 199-200; *Pa. Archives*, 1st ser., VII, 201, 229, 366,400, 402.

ing transports & Ships of War. The account of the Troops on board is not known; but from the current of intelligence they are those mentioned in my Letter of the 18th- with some additional corps; and it is the general opinion__ that they are destined for the West Indies. There are many reasons in favor of this and among them__ the taking of Dominica by the French is a very weighty one. However, as Boston & Count D'Estaing's Squadron are capital Objects, and those only on the Continent to which we ~~could~~ ↑can↓ hope to afford succour; I thought it prudent and the part of caution__ to put three Brigades Viz__ Poor's__ Patterson's & the late Learned's in motion on the 18__ 19 & 21st ↑Inst↓__ which are ordered ~~for the present~~ to proceed for the present, as far as Connecticut River. Nixon's Parson's & Huntington's follow today ↑and are now on the march.↓. These movments will be attended with many great inconveniences, arissing more particularly from the difficulty of supplying flour; but as I have already observed, tho all reasoning is against an Eastern expedition at this time, especially with a Detachment, they are such as ~~would~~ could not be avoided.__ Besides advancing these troops__ I wrote to General Heath yesterday morning, to request ~~of the Neighbouring illegible~~ as many ↑of the Neighbouring Militia↓ as would make the whole number, comprehending those already assembled, Five Thousand__ which I trust with the other forces in the Eastern Quarter, will be sufficient to delay the operations of the Enemy, if they are going against Boston till we can give further__ and ↑I hope↓ effectual relief.[6]

I beg leave to inclose an Extract from a Letter of the 20th Inst. from Genl Hand, who is going to take the command at Albany, ~~whi~~ respecting the distressed Inhabitants of the German Flats.[7] In

---

[6]Washington ordered one division under Horatio Gates, composed of generals Enoch Poor, John Paterson, and the late Ebenezer Learned's brigades, to Hartford, Conn., and a second division under Alexander McDougall, made up of generals John Nixon, Samuel Holden Parsons, and Jedediah Huntington's brigades to augment them. Washington did this as a precaution but confided to Patrick Henry on November 3, that the rumors concerning a British thrust at Boston were intended "to perplex and confound the judgment." On November 17, he issued orders directing the brigades to other duty. *Washington Writings* (Fitzpatrick), XIII, 175, 195-196, 199-200, 270-272.

[7] Governor Clinton applied to Gen. Edward Hand for provisions for the German Flats settlement because General Stark had stopped providing them with supplies. Hand did not feel that he was "at liberty to continue that indulgence without particular instructions...." Edward Hand to Washington, Oct. 20, 1778, Washington Papers, DLC.

consideration of their sufferings__ and ↑of↓ the ↑great↓ importance of the settlement to us, I have consented to his furnishing
them with Provision, agreable to the propositions between him &
Governor Clinton, till Congress shall be pleased to decide on the
matter whether they are to be supplied at the expence of the
States__ or upon what other terms & for how long.__.

I have the Honor to transmit a Copy of Lieutenant Col°
Butler's Journal, which I just now received in a Letter from General
Stark[8] by which Congress will perceive ↑by this↓ that he has effectually destroyed the Settlements of Anaguaga & Unindillo__ and
returned with the Troops under his command to Schoharie.[9] I hope
their ↑destruction↓ will give some relief to the Frontier Inhabitants
of this & the States of Jersey & Pensylvania__ at least for this year__
as they were Towns places of Rendezvous for the Savages & Tories
who have ↑in↓ infested them__ and where they deposited a part of
their plunder.

We are again distressed for want of Money.__ The Military
Chest is quite exhausted__ and near three Months full pay due the
Army. ↑I wish↓ A Supply cannot ↑to↓ be too soon sent to the Pay
Master General as soon as possible.

I have the Honor &c

G°: Washington

PS.   I have written to Lord Stirling & requested him as he is much
nearer Congress than I am__ to transmit them information of any
↑material↓ occurrances that may come to his knowledge and respecting the movements of the Enemy.

SOURCE: Draft, Washington Papers, DLC; addressed below close "His Exc^y
Henry Laurens &c."; addressed at bottom of first page "His Exc̄y Henry
Laurens, Esq"; dated "Camp near Fredericksburg Octob 22nd 1778"; dock-
eted "To Congress / Octob 22^d & 23^d. 1778".

---

[8] A comma following "Stark" was cancelled.
[9] Lt. Col. William Butler's journal for October 1-16 had been enclosed in Gen. John Stark's
October 18 letter to Washington. Washington sent this copy on to Gov. George Clinton, who
at the general's request returned it. Clinton also received a copy directly from Butler. General
Stark sent HL a letter in which he summarized Butler's activities on the New York frontier.
Copies of the journal are in the Washington Papers, DLC, and the *Clinton Papers* (Hastings),
IV, 227-231; John Stark to HL, Oct. 22, 1778, PCC, Item 162, p. 213.

TO JOHN LEWIS GERVAIS

Philadelphia, October 23, 1778

Sir

I have the honor of transmitting within the present inclosure an Act of Congress of the 20th Inst. for appointing you Deputy Paymaster General in the State of South Carolina and for depositing in your hands for public services one Million Dollars.

From the Recommendation of the Delegates of South Carolina, Congress place the highest confidence in you, for the right discharge of the duties of your Office in all respects, I have therefore only to enjoin, in particular, frequent transmissions of Accounts, and Vouchers. of expenditures.[1]

I have the honor to be &c.

SOURCE: LB, PCC (Item 13), DNA; addressed "John Lewis Gervais Esquire / Charlestown / by General Lincoln"; dated "23^d October".

TO GEORGE WASHINGTON

Philadelphia, October 23, 1778

Sir

I had the honor of addressing Your Excellency Yesterday by Jones, and also of receiving and presenting to Congress Your Excellency's favor of the 18th with the Refugee Petition to the British Commissioners. This, I understand will appear in print tomorrow, and be prefaced by a private hand. Congress heard it read and paid no other attention to it.[1]

Inclosed in this Your Excellency will receive an Act of

[1] Gervais accepted the appointment without enthusiasm. He wrote HL "if you had known how Ill it Suits me, you would have declined the appointment on my behalf." He claimed other public affairs kept him too busy, that the pay was too low to hire an assistant, and that the one million dollars appropriated "will not last Long." On May 22, 1779, Congress combined the deputy paymaster offices of South Carolina and Georgia under Joseph Clay and relieved Gervais of the burden. John Lewis Gervais to HL, Dec. 20, 1778, Gervais Papers, in private hands; *JCC*, XII, 1027; XIV, 631.

[1] The "Refugee Petition" was printed in the *Pa. Packet* Oct. 24, 1778, and prefaced by an anonymous statement which attributed Great Britain's actions since 1763 to the "old maxim...that Providence makes those men crazy whom he wills to ruin."

Congress of the 22nd ordering Major General Gates to the Command of the forces in the Eastern District.[2]

I have the honor to be &c.

SOURCE: LB, PCC (Item 13), DNA; addressed "General Washington / by Thomas Crawford from the Quarter Master"; dated "23d October".

FROM JOHN LAURENS

Fredericksburg, N.Y., October 23, 1778

Accept my thanks my dearest friend and father for your kind letters of the 9th and 12th. and the money which accompanied them__ I have taken the farther liberty to draw upon you for twelve hundred and twelve dollars__ which from the various expence and ill-luck in which I have been involved, I was necessitated to do in order to avoid touching my pay__

I promise myself the pleasure of setting out for Philadelphia in three days__ at farthest__[1] The particulars of the enemys movements, and the Generals disposition in consequence will be transmitted to you in his official letter__ however improbable it is that the enemy may meditate any stroke against the French Squadron__ and Boston__ at this late season__ after having given us so much time to prepare ourselves__ and when their attention is so powerfully called another way__ the General prudently determines to leave nothing to chance__ all that I dread is the disadvantage of getting our troops late into Winter Quarters__[2]

I still continue to be of opinion that the british will be obliged to abandon a part of their possessions for the security of the rest__ Gibraltar and the W. India Islands togetheer with Halifax and Quebec__ require considerable reinforcements__ I cannot persuade myself that they will leave New York & Rhode Island feebly

[2] *JCC*, XII, 1038; HL to Horatio Gates, Oct. 23, 1778, Gates Papers, NHi.

[1] The exact dates that HL entertained JL in Philadelphia are not clear. John probably arrived in late October and did not permanently depart until mid-March 1779, when he set out for South Carolina. His stay had been extended because Washington came to confer with Congress and lodged at HL's quarters. Massey, "A Hero's Life," pp. 291, 300-301, 308.

[2] Washington had selected Middlebrook, N.J., for the winter cantonment by October 29 and arrived there by December 12. It remained the Continental Army headquarters until June 3, 1779. *Washington Writings* (Fitzpatrick), XIII, 179, 382; XV, 223.

garrisoned or to the protection of foreign Troops and new levies__

The stroke on the Island of Dominica by the Marquis de bouille was not wanted to awaken their fears for the West Indies__ and they have their dispositions to make not only in consequence of the measures taken to france__ but with a view to what may be meditated by the other branch of bourbon__ [3]

Conversing with you by letter will now yield to the greater happiness__ of personal embraces and the[4] unrestrained overflowings of my gratitude and love__

'till we meet I commend my dear Father to Gods protection and remain

Your most affectionate and / dutiful

John Laurens__

SOURCE: ALS, HL Papers, ScHi; addressed on cover "(Private) / His Excellency / Henry Laurens Esq[r.] / Philadelphia"; dated "Head Quarters 23[d] Octob 1778"; docketed by HL "John Laurens / 23 Octob 1778 / Rec[d.] 27[th.]".

FROM WILLIAM LIVINGSTON

Morristown, N.J., October 23, 1778

Sir

The Bearer Coll[o] Dirks a hollander has been in the Service of our States above two years. He is now bound to Holland with intent to return to America. I have no acquaintance with him nor with his Character. But of Mr. Erkelens from whom he has some proposals to shew you I have had the strongest Recommendation. D[r] Livingston a kinsman of mine who is a dutch Clergyman in the State of New york and a Gentleman of the nicest honour as well as strictest piety[1] knew him in the Netherlands and represents him as

---

[3] Even though Spain was excluded from the Franco-American Alliance, the French attempted to persuade the Spanish Bourbon King Charles III to enter the conflict against Britain. Spain offered to act as a mediator, but continued to negotiate with the French. In April 1779 the Convention of Aranjuez activated the provision of the 1761 Family Compact under which France and Spain were obligated to provide assistance if the other Bourbon monarchy were attacked. Dull, *French Navy*, pp. 9, 126-145.

[4] "the" interlined.

[1] John Henry Livingston (1746-1825), a second cousin of William Livingston, had a degree from the University of Utrecht and was ordained in Amsterdam in 1770. He served a

a man of Probity, & great Connections in Holland. He has long been sollicitous about giving his Country men a true Idea of our dispute with Brittain, on which Subject, he says, they, as most other Europeans, labour under the grossest Errors. He has for this purpose drawn up a kind of history to be presentd to Myn Heer Capallen a Gentleman of public Charactor, & of great weight & distinction among them; and who appears by a Speech of his which I have seen a warm friend to America, and to Liberty.[2] This Representation is to be presented by Coll⁰ Dirks, who, I am informed is a relation of Cappalens. I doubt not that some Dutchmen as well as some Frenchmen, by their ardent professions for the interest of America really mean to promote their own. And I am not easily taken in, by warm protestations. But as great things often rise from small beginnings, this may perhaps lay the foundation for some future advantageous acquaintance with their High Mightynesses, who I am confident will not shew any affection from Great Britain whenever it is more for their Emolument to express their zeal for America__

By the affidavits which I inclose your Excellency in my public Letter, you will find the Cruelty of the Enemy towards Collo. Baylors Regiment so fully proved, that your Constitutents will doubtless be for keeping you to your word of <u>Satisfaction</u> or <u>retaliation</u>.[3]

I am / Dear Sir / with the sincerest affection / Your most obedient / humble Serᵗ

Wil: Livingston

---

congregation in New York City until the British occupation. During the war he served churches in Albany, Kingston, Livingston Manor, Poughkeepsie, and Red Hook. *Livingston Papers* (Prince), II, 565.

[2] Baron van der Capellen's Dec. 16, 1775, speech, which was printed in several American newspapers, successfully opposed the British request to use the Scots brigade in the American war. Van der Capellen not only opposed the transfer of the troops but portrayed the American cause as a struggle for human rights. Baron van der Capellen's speech, Dec. 16, 1775, PCC, Item 78, Vol. 23, p. 89ff, with translation beginning on p. 109; Gosuinus Erkelens to HL, Oct. 15, 1778.

[3] Livingston's public letter of October 22 was his response to Congress's October 6 resolve, which HL had conveyed, "That Governor Livingston...use his utmost diligence in obtaining the best information, upon oath, of the treatment of the Lieutenant Colonel Baylor and his party by the enemy, who attacked them." HL had concluded that if the reports of atrocities were substantiated, "I apprehend suitable retaliation will immediately follow a refusal of satisfaction." Livingston enclosed eight affidavits. *JCC*, XII, 987; HL to William Livingston, Oct. 6, 1778, PCC, Item 13; William Livingston to HL, Oct. 22, 1778, PCC, Item 68, p. 413ff; Enclosure, PCC, Item 53, p. 113ff.

SOURCE: RC, MB; addressed on cover "To / His Excellency / The honourable Henry Laurens Esqr / President of Congress / Philadelphia / Favored by / Coll^o Dirks"; addressed below close "His Excellency / The hon^ble. Henry Laurens Esqr / President of Congress"; dated "Morris Town 23 Oc^r 1778"; docketed "Morris town 23^d. Octr. 1778". Copy (19th century), HL Papers, ScHi.

TO THE MARQUIS DE LAFAYETTE

Philadelphia, October 24, 1778

Sir

I had the honor of presenting ↑to Congress↓ your Letter soliciting leave of absence,[1] and I am directed *illegible* by ~~Congress~~ ↑the House↓ to express their thanks ~~to Your Excellency~~ for your zeal in *illegible* ↑promoting↓ that just cause in which they are engaged and for the disinterested services ~~which~~ you ~~Your Excellency~~ have rendered to the United States of America.[2]

In testimony of the high Esteem and ~~the great~~ Affection in which You~~r Excellency is~~ ↑are↓ held by the good People of these States, ~~and also~~ ↑as well as↓ in acknowledgment of your Gallantry and Military Talents display'd ~~acknowledgement of your Wisdom and Bravery displayed~~ on many signal occasions, their Representatives in Congress assembled have ordered an Elegant Sword to be presented to You~~r Excellency~~ by the American Minister at the Court of Versailles.[3]

~~I have the honor of transmitting within the present Cover~~ ↑Inclosed within the ↑inclosure↓ present Cover will be found↓ an Act of Congress of the 21st Instant authorizing these Declarations, and ~~further for~~ granting ~~Your Excellency~~ a Furlough for your return to France to be extended at your own pleasure.

---

[1] Lafayette to HL., Oct. 13, 1778, PCC, Item 156, p. 31ff.

[2] Congress upon the receipt of Lafayette's October 13 letter appointed a committee, composed of Gouverneur Morris, Richard Henry Lee, John Witherspoon, and Samuel Adams to consider it. The committee reported October 21, and HL was directed to write a letter expressing "the thanks of Congress" for the marquis' "disinterested zeal." A draft answer in Morris's hand, now in the HL Papers, ScHi, formed the basic text which HL edited to suit his own taste. *JCC,* XII, 1004-1005, 1034-1035.

[3] Benjamin Franklin, following the desires of Lafayette, had the marquis' own cutler craft the sword which had "Emblems on it, representing him, in all the most remarkable Situations he had been in in America." The sword was presented to Lafayette by William Temple

I pray God to Bless and Protect you Sir, ~~and~~ to conduct you in safety to the presence of your Prince and to the ↑re-↓enjoyment of your Noble Family and Friends.

I have the honor to be / With the highest Respect / & with the most sincere ~~attachment~~ affection[4] / Sir / Your ~~Excellency's~~ Most Obedient & / Most humble Servant

SOURCE: LB, PCC (Item 13), DNA; addressed "~~Major General~~ ↑The Right Honorable↓ / The Marquis de la Fayette, / Major General in the Army of the United States &c. &c. &c. / (delivered by Moses Young)"; dated "24th October". Copies (3), HL Papers, ScHi. Copy (in French), MH.

FROM GEORGE WASHINGTON
Fredericksburg, N.Y., October 24, 1778

Sir

The letter, which I had the honor of addressing to you the day before yesterday, would inform Congress of the embarkation and sailing of a considerable detachment of the enemy from New York; and of the measures I had taken, in expectation of__ and upon the happening of the event. Whether this will be succeeded by a further embarkation, or by a total evacuation of the posts, which they hold within the States, in the course of this year or the ensuing one, I cannot pretend to determine. But as it will be right and prudent in us to prepare for every contingency, I would, with the greatest deference, submit it to Congress, whether it may not be proper for them to call upon the States to provide Men in time for filling their respective Battalions before, or at any rate against, the opening of the spring, and in the same manner, as if there was a moral certainty that the War would be prosecuted with all possible vigor on the part of Britain.[1] Should this not be the case, or should any events cast up in the mean time to render Troops unnecessary__

Franklin at Le Havre in late August 1779. *JCC*, XII, 1035; *Franklin Papers* (Labaree), XXVII, 666; *Adams Papers* (Taylor), VIII, 380; *Lafayette Papers* (Idzerda), II, 303-306.

[4] Written by HL.

[1] Washington's letter was read in Congress October 31 and referred to a committee which had been appointed October 21 to prepare a plan for procuring reinforcements for the army. *JCC*, XII, 1034, 1084.

it will be easy to disband the levies, and to keep them from the field__ which on the other hand, our relaxations in not providing them, may subject us, at least, to many disagreeable consequences.

The General Return of the Infantry in the Month of September, transmitted to the Board of War by the Adjutant General, and to which I beg leave to refer, will shew Congress the whole amount of our reputed force at that time; but I am to observe, that large, very large deductions are to be made from it, on account of the Columns of sick and the men said to be on command. Many under the former description, particularly that of sick absent, are actually dead__ others unfit for service, and several, who have recovered, have deserted: nor will the latter afford more than one half of its number in time of Action, as various duties such as waggoning, distant Guards, Escorts &c$^{a.}$ employ a great proportion of those under this denomination.[2]

Besides the above deductions, Congress will perceive from the Return which I now take the liberty of transmitting__ that there are 4380 Drafts and others whose terms of service will expire during and by the close of Winter. For I am sorry to add that our exertions to re-engage the Drafts and old Soldiers, in this predicament, for the usual Bounty have proved so far ineffectual and without success. I have not tried what effect the additional Grant of ten dollars might have; but I fear, and it seems to be the opinion of all I have consulted upon the occasion__ that it would have but little if any influence. I know in the case of the Drafts and troops of one State, that the offer of twenty dollars on the part of the Continent, with a like allowance and an actual deposit of it by the State has been no temptation.

This general reluctance and refusal is founded in the unhappy depreciated light in which the Soldiery view the money, and their expectation of receiving immense State District and substitute Bounties__ Whether grants or bounties by Congress, bearing some proportion to those, to such as should inlist for the War would be attended with better success, I cannot undertake to decide. The experiment may be made, if they judge it proper, and if it proves an

---

[2] The general return for September 1778 showed Washington's Infantry to total 34,624, of which 2,255 were listed sick present, 4,015 sick absent, and 4,935 on command and extra service. Lesser, *Sinews of Independence*, pp. 84-85.

inducement to any extent, it will be an infinite saving in the end. I believe however, our surest and only certain aids will be derived from drafting__ which I trust may and will be done by the States on the recommendation of Congress, agreeable to the mode mentioned in my letter to their Committee, when they first honored me with a visit at Valley Forge. The exertions to recruit by voluntary inlistments may still go on, as both modes in all probability will not produce near as many men as may be found necessary__[3]

In the Case of the Carolina Troops, whose service is ending every day, the Officers say__ that nothing will induce them to inlist, unless they can be permitted to go home on furlough till the Spring. On this indulgence they seem to think, several might be engaged. The distance is great, and there will be some uncertainty as to their returning; besides it will be fixing a precedent for others. If Congress approve the plan, they will be pleased to inform me by the earliest opportunity.[4]

I am under some difficulty about cloathing the drafts and the old Soldiers whose service is expiring and will determine every day. As Congress have never expressed their sense upon the subject, and this is increased by a letter which I received some time ago from the Board of War, which respects particularly the drafts; I must earnestly request that Congress will fav^r· me with the speediest directions in the Case__ whether they are to be furnished out of the supplies coming on, equally with the other troops. At the same time I will take the liberty to offer it as my opinion, that however inconvenient ↑or expensive↓ it may be appear at the first view to cloath them, the measure will be necessary, and founded not only

---

[3] Congress attempted to increase reenlistment and recruiting by authorizing a bounty "not to exceed two hundred dollars" on Jan. 23, 1779. By March 9, however, Congress recognized that even a bounty of this size would not attract sufficient numbers and consequently repealed the January 23 act and resolved "that it be earnestly recommended to the several states to make up and compleat their respective battalions to their full complement by draughts, or in any other manner they shall think proper." *JCC*, XIII, 108-109, 298-299.

[4] Congress apparently did not respond to Washington's request for furloughs for the North Carolina troops. The 1st N.C. Regiment's November and December returns showed no men on furloughs. The September return counted 660 total in the regiment; by December that number had been reduced to 563. The 2nd N.C. Regiment's November and December returns listed four men on furlough. The September return counted 640 total in the regiment; by September that number had been reduced to 490. Lesser, *Sinews of Independence*, pp. 84, 88, 92, 96.

in humanity but sound policy. We have no prospect now of levying men in any other way, and if they are not cloathed, they will be exhausted by sickness and by death, and not doing it may prove an insurmountable Bar__ or at least a great obstacle to our obtaining future Aids__ tho' the Exigencies of our Affairs should be never so pressing. Yet, the Cloaths may be withheld as long as circumstances will permit, as an inducement for them to inlist. In the instance of the old Soldiers, who have not received the annual allowance of Congress, the point seems clearly in their favor. The Board suggested, that the drafts might be supplied out of the best of the old Cloaths, which might be given in by the troops on receiving new ones; but unfortunately there will be few of any worth.[5]

I have the honor to be / with the highest Respect & Esteem / Your Excellency's / most obed.[t.] Servant

G.[o:] Washington

SOURCE: RC, PCC (Item 152), DNA; addressed below close "Excellency Henry Laurens."; dated "Head Quarters Fredericksb.[g.] 24.[th:] Octob.[r.] / 1778"; docketed "A letter of 24 Oct.[r.] 1778 / from gen.[l] Washington / Read 31 / Referred. to the com.[ee] to / prepare a plan for pro / curing reinforcements &c__ / M.[r] Duer / M.[r] Sherman / M.[r] R H Lee / M.[r] G. Morris"; and "Entered page 44 / (Examined)". Copy, PCC (Item 169), DNA. Draft, Washington Papers, DLC. Copy, HL Papers, ScHi.

FROM GEORGE GALPHIN

October 26, 1778

My Dear Sir

Stuart at Last has prevaile[d] upon his frind[s] to Come against our frontier[1] the great present[s] he give them they were not prov of

---

[5] Washington informed Horatio Gates, who was assuming command at Boston, that his three brigades would be furnished new clothing only if any remained. The soldiers would be required to return their old clothing when obtaining the new. Gates and others "of the best Officers in the line" explained to the commander that the soldiers continuing in the service "looked upon it as an unjustifiable attempt to deprive them of what they had earned by their years service." Washington informed the Board of War that this plan proved "impracticable" and he "let the matter drop." *Washington Writings* (Fitzpatrick), XIII, 163-164, 198n, 245-246.

[1] Indian Superintendent John Stuart had instructions from the British government to have the Creeks ready to participate in a southern campaign. Stuart, however, had not yet received word as to when the British would begin the campaign and actually attempted to restrain the Indians during this period. O'Donnell, *Southern Indians*, pp. 75-77.

against them tho our frind^s when they Coul^d not Stope them they Sent us timely notis they were Rec$^{d.}$d by white men Each time tho they have not Disturbe^d any bod$^{y.}$ but upon the Cede$^{d.}$ Land as yeat I have not broke up my Setelme^t upon Ogeegee & all the Irish Setelme^{ts} in this State & Severell other^s the most of the people ni the Cede^d Land has wante^d an Indian warr Ever Since the Diferenc^e betwen ameraca & Englan$^{d.}$ & Di^d Everey thing in there power to bringe it on there was 4 or 5 of the Indian^s kill^d before there was one white man kill^d upon the fronteres the have run most of the good Land betwen the Line & the Ockane^s wich was Cause a neff to bringe on a warr with out any thinge Ell$^{s.}$ they have rate^d the Indian^s in their hunting groun^d & beat them

~~illegible~~ Ever Since the first Seteling of the Ceded Lan^d there has been a Deferens betwen the Indian^s & the Seteler^s the keep^t Steling of horse^s from one a nother & killing one another tho the Indian^s Di^d not at that time Disturbe any other part of the State by the a Count I have ha^d there is upwards of 30 people kill^d in the Ceded Land that is two many to put up with there was but two gaings Come out of the nattion the first gaing the people on ↑in↓ the frontiere ha^d 7 or 8 Day$^{s.}$ noti^s before they Came Down one of the hea^d men Came him Self to Let us no and ha^d his advice been folowe^d the might a kill^d a good many of them the next gange that Came we ha^d notis ten Day$^{s.}$ before they Came yeat they all return^d with Litell less on there Side it is Say^d there is 3 or 4 of them kill^d after the first gainge I sent up to the nattion to Deman$^{d.}$ Satisfettion you will Se the ans^r I rec^d a few Day$^{s.}$ a goe[2] I Sent of thre white men & Some Indian$^{s.}$ to Deman^d all the white men Die^d or Live that Come to warr with their Indian$^{s.}$ was the Indian^s to give us all the Satisfation we Disire tho I Do not Say they will it coud not pasify the mind^s of the people without a warr for the people in the Cede^d Lan^d Say$^{d.}$ if I was to Call the Indian^s Down to have any talke with them about a pease they woud Come & kill me & the Indian^s two all that Can be Don know is to to keep the Indian^s Divide^d till we are red$^{y.}$ for them by the Last a Count^s from the Creek$^{s.}$ there is but one Indian that has Left us there is not above 6 or 7 present in Stuarts Interest

---

[2] Galphin enclosed a "talk" from the Creek chief Tallassee King, dated Oct. 10, 1778. HL Papers, ScHi.

ha^d it not been for the Imprudence of Some of our one people it woud not been ni Stuarts power and all his present^s to have Set the Creek^s upon us it Shew^s pleinly for they have not as yet Disturb^d any part of the Setelrs but the Cede^d Lan^d Excep^d Some Strlagainge Indian^s that Lives at augistin that kill^d Some of our people Low Down I have meet with So much oposisan ni my affair that I wrote our govern^r I must Risine & that he woud apoyn^t Some bod^y Ells but he & the gent^m of the house of assemble Requste^d I woud not Risine till these troblesom times was over I Coul^d not Deny their request I have Don Every thinge in my power to Serve my Contery I have Stay^d upon the frontier^s for month^s at A time & mos^t 9 week^s as I new^d my presenes there was nissisery as the Indian^s was Daley a Comming Down at the Same time our Enemes ha^d Employe^d both white people & Indian^s to kill me our frend Indian^s propose^d retaliating upon florda for the murders Comite^d upon our frontiers the Say^d perhap^s that wood make Stuart Stope his frend^s from Coming hear I EnCorge^d them to try that they have made a begining as you will Se by the InClose^d talke Col^o Williamson is gon out to the Ceded Lan^d with 5 or 600 men to ↑Se↓ if he Can meet with any of the Enemey these Enemey I wont will be allway^s a picking at us till they get get a good Drubing we Can never put up with the Insultes we have rec^d from them without Leting them no we are there masters we Sartenly were the agressers in the begining but they have Care^d there resentment tow far I beleve when they ha^d Satsfattion they woud a Stop^t but Stuart & his Commesser^s keep^t puting them on our frind^s has Drove all the Commessers out of the nattion & has rat^d & Drove of the Disafecte^d traders Some of our frind^s has advise^d us to Sen^d up an armey & Cutt of the Disafacte^d Towns when these white men return^d from the Creks I shall Let you no by the first opertunity what a Count^s they bringe I Exepect Some Indian^s with them all my fear is that Some of ↑our↓ bad people will kill Some of our frind^s & that will bringe the hole nattion upon our back^s my Complmt^s to your Son

I am Dear Sir your Honr^s / most Obedn^t and Oblig^d huble / Servt

George Galphin

SOURCE: RC, HL Papers, ScHi; no address; dated below close "O^{br} / 26 1778"; docketed by HL "Geō Galphin 26 October 1778 / Rec^d 24 December__".

TO DON DIEGO JOSEPH NAVARRO[1]

Philadelphia, October 27, 1778

Sir

Your Excellencys' Letter of the 11th of March last address'd to Congress in favor of Don Juan de Miralles, I had the honor of presenting to the House__[2] the particular affection which you were pleased to express therein for Don Juan, has been justified by his honorable deportment during his residence in these States.

It cannot but be pleasing to your friendship to be told that the influence which Your Excellencys' Recommendations naturally convey, has, in this instance been rendered little necessary by the claims of the personal merit of Don Juan.

The United States of North America desire Peace and harmony with other Nations, and they particularly consider the prospect of a friendly intercourse between the Subjects of His Catholic Majesty and their own Inhabitants as a great branch of their future felicity.

The kind Prayer which you have made for our preservation we beg leave to retort in sentiments of the utmost cordiality.

I have the honor to be / With the highest Esteem & Respect / Sir / Your Excellency's / Most obedient & / Most humble servant[1]

Henry Laurens.
President / of Congress.

SOURCE: LS, PWacD, Feinstone Collection, on deposit PPAmP; addressed below close "His Excellency / Don Diego Joseph Navarro, Governor and Captain General of the Island of Cuba / &c. &c. &c. &c. / at / Havana"; dated "Philadelphia 27th October 1778"; noted "(Duplicate).". LB, PCC (Item 13), DNA.

---

[1] Don Diego Joseph Navarro Garcia de Valladares had been appointed captain general of Cuba in August 1776 and arrived in Havana in June 1777. He guided Spain's intelligence gathering in America and sent Don Juan de Miralles to observe the Congress. Cummins, *Spanish Observers*, pp. 61-72, 98-99.

[2] Governor Navarro's letter recommending Don Juan de Miralles to the "Most Illustrious Gentlemen" of the Congress had been read July 23. On October 26 the Committee of Foreign Affairs was ordered to prepare an answer. Don Diego Joseph Navarro to Congress, March 11, 1778, PCC Item 78, Vol. 17, p. 47ff; *JCC*, XI, 713; XII, 1061, 1068.

TO HORATIO GATES

Philadelphia, October 29, 1778

Sir

Your favor of the 13th. Inst. inclosing Letters from Lord Balcarras reached me the 27th. & was immediately presented to Congress.[1] the House had formerly heard with much concern that Officers of the Convention Troops had, contrary to orders, been permitted to go within the Enemy's Lines, & had ordered an enquiry respecting the Case, indeed it has been repeatedly said, that Gold had been given by several of those officers in purchase of furloghs, particularly that Lord Balcarras paid to some body One Thousand Guineas for this indulgence granted to him__ however groundless or otherwise this information may be, it is alarming at present. & therefore a further & more particular investigation is ordered.

The inclosed Act of Congress of the 27th. Inst. & the Act of the 21st. which is referred to will shew, in answer to Lord Balcarras's application the determination of the House.[2]

I have the honor to be / With the highest Respect / & Esteem / Sir / Your Most obedient / & most humble servant

Henry Laurens.

President / of Congress.

SOURCE: ALS, Gates Papers, NHi; addressed below close "The Honorable / Major General Gates / Danbury."; dated "Philadelphia 29th. October / 1778__"; docketed "Letter from the President / of Congress dated 29th Oct^{br:} / 1778__". LB, PCC (Item 13), DNA.

---

[1] Lt. Col. Alexander Lindsay, sixth earl Balcarres, of the 24th Regiment, sought to extend a temporary parole exchange for Col. Robert Magaw of the 5th Pa. Regiment, which would permit Balcarres to return to Britain. He informed Gates that he needed to return to assist with "family affairs connected with those of seven younger Brothers" which were in great disorder. Balcarres obtained his liberty in 1779 but Magaw was not exchanged until October 1780. Balcarres to Horatio Gates, Sept. 30, 1778, PCC, Item 154, Vol. 2, p. 19ff; *DNB;* Heitman, *Continental Officers.*

[2] John Beatty, the American Commissary of Prisoners, had written earlier on the subject of Lord Balcarras's appeal to be allowed to return on parole to England if an American officer would be afforded a similar privilege by the British. On October 21 Congress rejected the appeal, resolving only to accept "a general exchange of officers." On October 27 Congress simply referred to the act of October 21 in again rejecting the parole and appointed a committee to investigate the allegations that paroles had been granted for money. John Beatty, to HL, Oct. 19, 1778, PCC, Item 78, Vol. 2, p. 201ff; HL to John Beatty, Oct. 22, 1778, PCC, Item 13; *JCC,* XII, 1033, 1065.

TO CHEVALIER DE TOUSARD[1]

Philadelphia, October 29, 1778

Sir.

I have the [honor of transmitting][2] within this Cover an Act [of Congress of the 27th Instant] for promoting you to the [Rank of Lieutenant Colonel in the] American Army by Brevet & for granting you a Pension of thirty Dollars per Month during your life in acknowledgement of your Merit & in consideration of your misfortune in the loss of a Right Arm in the late Action at Rhode Island__ the display of your Courage & Gallantry upon that occasion has gained you the highest applause & insured immortal honor to your Name. Annexed to the Act you will receive the Brevet.

I intreat you Sir, accept my best wishes & be assured that my Esteem & Regard for you do not bear exact date with the affair at Rhode Island; Your Martial Spirit, your military talents, your services in the American Army, were known to me long before that event, I shall ever speak of them with pleasure & be one of your admirers.[3] in these sentiments I have the honor to be

Sir / Your most obedient / & most humble servant

Henry Laurens.

President / of Congress.[4]

---

[1] Anne-Louis, chevalier de Tousard (Touzard) (1749-1817) had entered the Continental army as a volunteer in the summer of 1777. He joined Du Coudray and was preparing to leave America after his death, but instead joined Lafayette in late 1777 when it appeared there might be an expedition to Canada. He lost an arm August 28 during the battle for Rhode Island. He returned to France and continued his career in the artillery. He served on Santo Domingo from 1786 to 1792. He was arrested in October 1792 and imprisoned in France until the next year when he returned to America. In 1795 he received a commission as a major in 1st Artillerists and Engineers and served in the American army until 1802. He rejoined the French army under Leclerc for the expedition against Santo Domingo in 1802 and was appointed French consul at New Orleans in 1805. Heitman, *Continental Officers; Lafayette Papers* (Idzerda), II, 56; André Lasseray, *Les Français sous les Treize Etoiles (1775-1783)* (Paris, 1935), pp. 439-444.

[2] Manuscript torn. Bracketed material here and below supplied from letterbook copy.

[3] Lafayette wrote HL on October 16, requesting promotions for his aides-de-camp and noting that Tousard lost his arm in a "dangerous and bold" attempt to capture two British field pieces. The letter was read in Congress the day Tousard was granted the commission and pension. Congress later failed to continue the pension and despite Lafayette's efforts in 1782, the French crown declined to assume the pension. Lafayette to HL., Oct. 16, 1778, PCC, Item 156, p. 51ff; *JCC*, XII, 1068-1069; *Lafayette Papers* (Idzerda), II, 198n.

[4] Noted below close "Being well-acquainted with the Hand of Mr. President Laurens, I do hereby certify that this Letter is all of his hand-writing, and therefore an authentic Paper. Given at Passy, this 21st Day of February 1779. B Franklin, Plenipotentiary from the Congress to the Court of France." The printed commission, signed by HL, certifying that Tousard's rank as a Lieutenant Colonel, dated Oct. 24, 1778, and certified by Franklin Feb. 21, 1779, is in the Tousard-Stocker Papers, PHi.

SOURCE: ALS, PHi; addressed below close "Lieutenant Colonel Touzard / Providence"; dated "P[*hiladelphia 29*th *October*]". LB, PCC (Item 13), DNA.

TO THE MARQUIS DE LAFAYETTE
Philadelphia, October 30, 1778

I had the honor of presenting to Congress the day before Yesterday the Letter which you were pleas'd to leave in my hands dated the 26th Instant. The House have directed me to repeat their assurances of their great Esteem and ↑Regard↓ for you, and that it is therefore with much regret and concern they are obliged to decline granting the advancements sollicited for Lieutenat Colonel Gimat, Major Noirmont and Captain Capitaine.[1]

I have the honor to be &c.

SOURCE: LB, PCC (Item 13), DNA; addressed "The Right Honorable / The Marquis de la Fayette, Major General &c. &c. &c / Camp / by ~~Colonel Gimat~~ William Hunter"; dated "30th October".

FROM WILLIAM KILLEN[1]
Dover, Del., October 30, 1778

Sir

Urged by the most ardent desire to do every thing in my power for the preservation and safety of the American States against the most unrightious attempts of Great Britain to oppress them, and at the same time to detect the base frauds and abuses committed by some persons acting or pretending to Act by virtue of authority derived from the Quarter Master or Commissary General

---

[1] Lafayette addressed three letters to HL on October 26. Each was related to his impending departure for Europe but none included recommendations for his three aides listed here. Lafayette, however, in an October 27 letter had thanked Congress for the recognition afforded Tousard and continued to press for promotions for Gimat, Noirmont, and Capitaine. Lafayette to HL, Oct. 26, 1778 (3), PCC, Item 156, pp. 39ff, 43ff, 47ff; Lafayette to HL, Oct. 27, 1778, PCC, Item 156, p. 52ff.

[1] William Killen (1722-1805), a Scots-Irish immigrant and prominent Kent County, Del. lawyer, had been a member of the Delaware Assembly and the Kent County Committee of Correspondence before being appointed the state's first chief justice (1776-1793). *Delaware History*, VI (1954-1955), 3, 93; *Appleton's Cyclopaedia of American Biography* (New York, 1900), III.

of the Continental Army within the Delaware State, I send you herewith some Depositions of sundry Persons whose credibility cannot be disputed taken before me.[2] By these Depositions and common Report it appears that the persons who are the objects of them have grosly betrayed the trust reposed in them for their own emolument, and I am well informed that one of them perhaps not worth a single shilling a Year ago, has lately made a very considerable purchase of real property for his own use in this County.__ The good People of this State for the greater part complain much of the oppression and abuses, nay, even Robberies committed upon them by this selfish tribe of Men, and I have actually issued a Warrant against one of them on a charge of the last mention'd Crime.

Tis with the deepest concern I acknowledge that disaffection to the freedom and Independence of America but too generally prevails throughout the Delaware State and the tyrannical practices of these offenders are not likely to remedy that evil.__ It is to Congress alone the injured People here look for redress of this and other grievances of a similar nature, which being obtained, and a security against the like Evils in future given, are, in my opinion the most efficacious expedient that can be adopted to reconcile the Inhabitants of this State to the true Interests of their Country.[3]

I have the honor to be / Sir / Your Excellency's / Most Obedient Humble Servant

William Killen Esq

P.S.
To determine what degree of Credit this letter may merit, enquire of the Chief Justice of Pennsylvania, Generals Read or Mifflin, who the Author is.

---

[2] The depositions are not in the PCC.

[3] Congress appointed a committee October 31, composed of Samuel Adams, Nathaniel Scudder, and Roger Sherman, to inquire into the abuses of the quartermaster general's department. HL informed Killen on November 1 that he would present this letter with the supporting enclosures to Congress the next day. Congress referred the letter and the depositions to the committee investigating the quartermaster department. On November 10, Congress appointed another committee including Gouverneur Morris, William Whipple, and Scudder, "to superintend" the commissary and quartermaster departments. On November 11 this committee addressed a circular to the states requesting that they "pass Laws for the prosecution & punishment" of Continental officials who "used the monies entrusted to them, in the engrossing of articles upon the public." *JCC*, XII, 1083, 1090, 1114-1115; HL to William Killen, Nov. 1, 1778, PCC, Item 13; *Delegate Letters* (Smith), XI, 202-203.

SOURCE: Copy, HL Papers, ScHi; addressed below close "His Excellency Henry Laurens."; dated "Dover in Kent County October 30th. 1778"; docketed "William Killen, dated / Dover in Kent County October 30th / 1778." and "Complains of the / aversion of the Inhabitants / of the Delaware State." and "The author of this Letter is / a Gentleman of the Law in / the Middle County of Kent in / the Delaware State, he is in a / Considerable Office (but what I / know not) under the rebel / State".

FROM CHARLES LEE

Philadelphia, October 30, 1778

Sir__

When it is considerd that I hold a high rank in the service of one of the most respectable Princes of Europe;[1] that I have been honored with the trust of the second command in your Army; that I have hitherto served with some reputation as a Soldier: that I now am charg'd, and have been try'd for the most heinous military crimes; add to the astonishment not only of myself, but I can venture to say of any Man in the Army who was present at the Court Martial, and of any Man not of the Army who has read the proceedings of this Case, been found guilty of these crimes__ when at the same time I am myself inflexibly persuaded that I am not only guiltless, but that the success of the 28 of June ought principally in justice to ↑be↓ ascribd[2] to me__ I say, Sir, when these circumstances are consider'd, it must be allow'd that my situation is extremely ↑in↓delicat[e] and somewhat awkward__ and that it's natural for me to wish, and reasonable for me to request that the Congress will no longer delay the final decision of my fate__ an additional Justn for requesting it, is that I find the Congress is every day growing thinner, and I confess I cou'd most ardently wish that the Congress was not only as complete as possible, but that if it was agreeable to the Mbrs of the

---

[1] During the Seven years War Charles Lee held a commission as major in the British army. In 1762 he fought with the British expedition to Portugal. Count William La Lippe, the grandson of George I and his mistress the Duchess of Kendall, commanded the Portuguese army. Lee led a daring and successful attack on the Spanish that won for him a colonelcy in the Portuguese army. Alden, *Charles Lee,* pp. 21-23.

[2] "ascribd" written over "be".

House, *illegible* that the People at large might ↑be admitted to↓ form an audience when the discussion is enter'd into of the justice or inequity, wisdom or absurdity of the sentence which has been pass'd upon me__ I do now, Sir, there[*fore*] most humbly but earnestly entreat that a day may be immediately fix'd for the final determination of this affair__ ³

and am, Sir, with the greatest / zeal and respect__ Your Most / Obedᵗ humble Servt__

Charles Lee

SOURCE: RC, PCC (Item 158), DNA; addressed below close "His Excellency Mr Laurens__"; dated "Philadelphia October þe 30ᵗʰ 1778"; docketed "Letter from Major genˡ / Lee Octʳ· 30: 1778 / Read".

TO JOHN McKINLY¹

Philadelphia, November 1, 1778

Sir

I Am extremely sorry to learn by your favor of the 29ᵗʰ Ultº· just come to hand that you have suffered further mortification by a delay of your Exchange; be assured Sir, neither Congress nor their President are on this account blameable, and that I will tomorrow transmit such instructions to the Commissary General of Prisoners as will remove every obstacle to your residence at home in freedom.²

I have the honor to be / With great Respect & Esteem &c.

SOURCE: LB, PCC (Item 13), DNA; addressed "The Honorable John Mᶜ·Kinley Esquire"; dated "1ˢᵗ November".

---

³ Despite receiving the proceedings of the court-martial on August 21, Congress did not begin to discuss the case until October 23. After numerous delays Congress approved the judgment on December 5. HL voted with the majority and with William Henry Drayton had opposed every effort to annul the court-martial's decision. Alden, *Charles Lee*, pp. 249-254; *JCC*, XI, 824-825; XII, 1059, 1195.

¹ John McKinly (1721-1796), the former governor of Delaware, was a prisoner of the British. HL to Rawlins Lowndes, Aug. 11, 1778.

² HL explained in his November 7 letter to Commissary of Prisoners John Beatty that McKinly's exchange had been "delayed by loss or miscarriage of the Act of Congress of the 14ᵗʰ of September which a particular friend of that Gentlemans undertook to convey." HL sent another copy and asked Beatty to "take the most speedy and effectual measures to carry it into execution." HL to John Beatty, Nov. 7, 1778, PCC, Item 13.

TO CAESAR RODNEY

Philadelphia, November 1, 1778

Sir.

I am just now honored with Your favor of the 27[th.] Inst. which shall be presented to Congress at their meeting to morrow.[1]

A budget of Manifestoes said to be from the British Commissioners was lately thrown up by the Sea on the Jersey Shore, it contained one Package marked Delaware supposed to have been intended for that State, another marked Pennsylvania, the whole number were brought to my House & by me laid before Congress. Congress would take no Cognizance of the Waif;[2] the Vice President of this State declined touching the bundle marked Pennsylvania___[3] if Your Excellency beleives that which was possibly intended for Delaware worth carriage, it shall be immediately transmitted.

I make no doubt Sir of your having heard that a Flag Vessel on board of which was a Lieut[t.] Midshipman & ~~fifteen~~ ↑thirteen↓ people of the Preston British[4] Man of War, had been wrecked some days ago on the Coast of New Jersey, two of the people were drowned, those who reached the Shore alive having no Credentials by flag or otherwise were conducted as Prisoners of War to the New Jail in this City where they remain.

I am directed by Congress to recommend to the State ↑of Delaware↓ to supply immediately a proper number of Representatives in Congress; for some considerable time past the State has

---

[1] Rodney replied in his October 27 letter that the Delaware government had "not, as yet, been honored with any Flags from the High & Mighty British Commissioners" but that they were "prepared to give them a proper reception." Caesar Rodney to HL, Oct. 27, 1778, PCC, Item 70, p. 671.

[2] Lt. Christopher Hele, whose unarmed sloop *Hotham* wrecked on the Jersey shore near Cape May October 10, carried three packets, one each from the British Commissioners to Congress, the Pennsylvania government, and "any principal person at Wilmington." HL to Rawlins Lowndes, Oct. 18, 1778; Christopher Hele to HL, Oct. 20, 1778, PCC, Item 78, Vol. 9, p. 397ff.

[3] George Bryan, Pennsylvania's Vice President, acted as the state's chief executive after President Thomas Wharton's death in May 1778. On October 16, the Pennsylvania Executive Council, with Bryan presiding, ordered state gallies to stop and detain any vessels that the British commissioners may have sent under a flag. The minutes of the Executive Council do not record their reaction to the package HL forwarded. *HL Papers*, XIII, 272n; *Minutes of the Supreme Executive Council of Pennsylvania*, XI, 595.

[4] "B" written over other text.

been almost wholly unrepresented, The Honorable Mr Vandyke having retired on account of the bad state of his health & the Honorable Mr Chief Justice McKean detained by unavoidable attendance on the duties of his Office[5] Also to request the State to give Instructions to their Delegates to Ratify the Articles of Confederation; New Jersey will accede in a few days, as Congress is informed by her Delegates & we hope Maryland will no longer delay__ the accession of these three States will perfect the foundation on which the happiness of our general Union [depends].[6]

Inclosed with this will be found Six Manifestoes by Congress, will Your Excellency be pleased to distribute by proper means to public view in your State__ Copies are sent to all the Posts of the Enemy.[7]

I have the honor to be / Sir / Your Excellency's / Most obedient humble / servant

Henry Laurens.
President / of Congress.

SOURCE: ALS, Gratz Collection, PHi; addressed below close "His Excellency / Cæsar Rodney Esquire / President of Delaware"; dated "Philadelphia / 1st Novem~ 1778."; docketed "A Letter / from / The President of Congress / dated Novr the 1st 1778". LB, PCC (Item 13), DNA.

---

[5] Delaware's three delegates elected in December 1777 were Thomas McKean, Caesar Rodney, and Nicholas Van Dyke. McKean attended intermittently during the last quarter of 1778. His was the only vote recorded for Delaware in Congress between Sept. 17 and Dec. 31, 1778. Rodney's election as president of Delaware in the spring of 1778 kept him from attending Congress. Delaware did not select delegates again until January 1779, when McKean and Van Dyke were reelected and John Dickinson replaced Rodney. Seldom during the first half of 1779 did the state have more than a single delegate and from February 25 to March 22 no one represented Delaware in Congress. *JCC*, XII; *Delegate Letters* (Smith), XI, xviii; XII, xvii.

[6] New Jersey ratified in late November 1779, Delaware on Feb. 22, 1779, and Maryland, the last state to sign, did so March 1, 1781. Jensen, *Articles of Confederation*, pp. 196-197, 238.

Bracketed material supplied from letterbook.

[7] In this October 30 "Manifesto," signed by HL, Congress condemned the British for their inhumane prosecution of the war. They declared, in conclusion, "that if our enemies presume to execute their threats, or persist in their present career of barbarity, we will take such exemplary vengeance, as shall deter others from a like conduct." *JCC*, XII, 1080-1082.

CONTINENTAL CONGRESS: RESOLUTION
Philadelphia, November 2, 1778[1]

The president having reminded the house that One[2] year is elapsed since he had the honour of being elected to fill the chair and expressed a strong desire to be relieved & that another be elected in his place; ~~and whereas the thinness of the house as well as sundry other considerations render it inconvenient to go into a new choice~~ ↑The house took the same into Consideration & ~~thereupon~~↓ & the House ↑being↓ satisfied with the whole conduct of the President[3]

Resolved That it is the unamimeous desire of this house that ~~the House being is satisfied~~[4] HL esquire continue for some time longer ~~as pres~~

SOURCE: Draft, HL Papers, ScHi; no date; docketed "Resolution, containing / the unanimous desire of / Congress that the President / continue in the Chair for / some time longer.".

FROM MARQUIS DE BRÉTIGNEY[1]
November 3, 1778

I request that it may be expresly declared in the Resolve of Congress, that I shall not be commanded by any Lieut. Colonel in the Army___

---

[1] In his notes on his resignation HL recalled that he "had frequently premonished Congress of his intention to resign the Chair on the 31st of October." When that day arrived he reminded the members of his intention and because it was a Saturday "humbly intreated them to make choice of some other Member to fill the Chair on the following Monday." Congress, unwilling to act immediately, deferred a decision until Monday, November 2. On Sunday November 1, HL obtained a copy of *Rivington's Gazette* of October 14, which contained a letter by "Verax" highly laudatory of HL but insulting to the other members of Congress who were characterized as "indigent," "worthless," and "desperate". Verax claimed only HL's "false sense of honour" kept him from leaving. Claiming to have been embarrassed by the scurrilous publication, on November 2 he accepted the unanimous request of Congress to continue in the chair. The resolution and his acceptance have been dated November 2 on the basis of HL's interpretation of the events. No record of his request to be replaced or the resolution to have him continue is in the journals of Congress. Henry Laurens Resignation, Dec. 9, 1778, note C.
[2] "One" written over other text.
[3] "& the...President" written by HL.
[4] Cancelled material by HL.
[1] Charles-François Sévelinges de Brétigney, who claimed the title marquis, came to America in September 1777 with "fifteen chosen Officers and what was necessary to Arm and

that I shall be made brigadier without passing thro' the grade of Colonel__

That previous to my departure for the Southward the formation of my Corps may be settled, and the necessary fund appointed, so that I may be able to have money for making French Recruits in Maryland & Virginia__

farther that my Corps which will be composed only of foreigners, may be upon the french establishment, and that the interior police of the Officers and Soldiers may be left to me.

I request[2] the nomination of my Officers, and that I may have the permission of taking four or five with me from this Country__

Finally I request admission into[3] the Council of War when the Colonels are called there__ [4]

De Bretigney

SOURCE: Translation made by JL, PCC (Item 78), DNA; no address; no date; docketed "Memorial from Marquis / de Britigny. / Read 18. Novr. 1778 / Referred, with report on / former memorial, to / Mr Drayton / Mr Williams / Mr Ellery / M^r M Smith / Mr Henry".

FROM CAESAR RODNEY

Dover, Del., November 4, 1778

Sir

Yesterday Evening I received your favour of the first Instant by Express__

I Suppose there can be little doubt that the Package Marked

Equip two hundred and thirty Men." His entire party was captured at sea in November 1777 while sailing north from Charleston and imprisoned at St. Augustine. He escaped in 1778 and began petitioning and memorializing Congress for a commission and to provoke interest in a campaign against St. Augustine. *HL Papers*, XII, 16-17; Marquis de Brétigney to HL, Aug. 12, 1778, PCC, Item 78, Vol. 3, p. 47ff; HL to William Livingston, Aug. 21, 1778; *Franklin Papers* (Labaree), XXIV, 96-97.

2 "re" written over other text.

3 "to" changed to "into".

4 In April 1779 Congress finally granted de Brétigney authority to form a corps of French volunteers as a part of the defense plan for South Carolina and Georgia. HL, at de Brétigney's request, wrote letters of introduction to John Lewis Gervais and John Laurens. He commended the French officer for "waiting upon Congress almost a whole Year in humble dependence, free from that inquietude which from almost all his Countrymen we have been witness of." *JCC*, XI, 808, 837; XII, 1183-1184; XIII, 117, 443-444, 445, 466; HL to JL, April 18, 1779, HL Papers, ScHi.

Delaware is filled with Manifestoes from the British Commissioners. if so. would not be at the trouble of Opening ↑them↓ for the Contents.

In my Letter of the 27th of October I informed your Excellency that I had laid before the General Assembly then Setting, the several Acts of Congress inclosed with your letters of the 7th and 13th together with the Confederation And that I Should take the Earliest opportunity, to make Congress Acquainted with their determination__ I am now to inform Congress and it is with Concern I do it, that by some means or Other in the Course of Yesterday and the day before, the Members of the House of Assembly have dispersed and thereby the House dissolved without having Compleated Any one piece of business laid before them__ It seems they had adjourned from Saturday to Monday that on Monday a Sufficient ↑number↓ did not meet to make a House, that on Tuesday the Others got impatient and went off__ but be that as it may this procedure of ~~theirs~~ theirs laid me under the Necessity of Immediately Calling the Privy Council to lay an Embargo for Thirty days, to take place at the Expiration of the present Act of Assembly. This is all we can do touching that business__ ¹ At the Meeting of the Council I intend Issuing Writs to call the General Assembly together on the fourth day of January Next__ but if Congress think their Meeting at a Shorter day Absolutely Necessary, Should be Glad² they would let me know it by the Ninth of this Month that I may then propose it to the Council__ ³

No New appointment of Representation in Congress for this State has been made. Mʳ· Vandike tels me he will attend Congress in a few days__ the Manifestoes of Congress shall be made public.

---

¹ Congress passed a resolution on October 2 recommending that the states take measures to halt "the wicked arts of speculators, forestallers, and engrossers" who were driving up the price of grain and flour. Among these resolutions was a request for the states to extend the embargo, due to expire November 15, until Jan. 31, 1779. HL forwarded copies of the resolutions to Caesar Rodney on October 7. *JCC*, XII, 974-979; HL to Rawlins Lowndes, Oct. 6, 1778; HL to Caesar Rodney, Oct. 7, 1778, PCC, Item 13.

² "Glad" written over other text.

³ HL replied on November 7 that Congress had requested "that Your Excellency will call the General Assembly together as early as possible." The following day Rodney answered that he expected the Privy Council to agree to call the Assembly and on November 13 Rodney noted "I have, by writ, called the General Assembly to meet at Dover on Monday the Twenty third Instant." HL to Caesar Rodney, Nov. 7, 1778, DeHi; Caesar Rodney to HL, Nov. 8, 1778, PCC, Item 70, p. 679ff; Caesar Rodney to HL, Nov. 13, 1778, PCC, Item 70, p. 683ff.

I am Your Excellencys / Obedient. and most / Humb^le Servant

Cæsar Rodney

SOURCE: RC, PCC (Item 70), DNA; addressed on cover "His Excellency Henry Laurens Esqr / in / Congress__"; dated "Dover Nov^r· the 4th 1778__"; franked "Public Service"; docketed by HL "Presid^t· Rodney / 4 Novem 1778 / Rec̄d 5th-" and "Read 6 / Resolved That the Govr be / desired to convene the Assembly / immediately". Draft, Rodney Papers, DHi.

TO THE MARQUIS DE LAFAYETTE

Philadelphia, November 5, 1778

I beg leave to refer you to what I had the honor of writing under the 30th Ult^o·

Your Letter to Congress of the 27th was duly presented and after mature consideration the House Resolved to make a gratuity to Lieutenant Colonel Gimat of five thousand Livres and two hundred Dollars,[1] to Monsr· Capitaine du Chesnoy a Brevet Commission ~~of M~~ to rank Major in the Army and two thousand four hundred Livres.[2]

To Monsr· Pontjebeau Eleven hundred & fifty Livres[3]

---

[1] In his October 27 letter Lafayette appealed to Congress on behalf of Jean-Joseph Sourbader de Gimat, "an old soldier in the french Service...who came here upon very disinterested principles." Congress postponed a resolution to promote him "to the Rank of Colonel by Brevet" on October 27. Gimat, disturbed by Congress's delay, wrote HL on November 5 that he would leave Philadelphia later that day and "that I renounce the rank of colonel which the marquis was pleased to ask for me, the only thing that I wish to know, it is, whether the honorable the congress is pleased to grant me the indemnity for my expenses or not." Congress responded by voting to present Gimat "an honorary certificate of his zeal and services," a 5,000-livre gratuity, and 200 dollars "to defray his expences to the port of embarkation." Lafayette to HL, Oct. 27, 1778, PCC, Item 156, p. 51ff; *JCC*, XII, 1068-1069, 1104-1105; Jean-Joseph Sourbader de Gimat to HL, Nov. 5, 1778, PCC, Item 78, Vol. 10, p. 121ff; HL to Jean-Joseph Sourbader de Gimat, Nov. 5, 1778, PCC, Item 13.

[2] Lafayette also recommended Michel Capitaine du Chesnoy, who had a captain's commission as an engineer in the Continental army. The marquis wrote that he "would have ask'd a commission of Major" when Capitaine first entered the service "but thought it would be better for his departure." Lafayette to HL, Oct. 27, 1778, PCC, Item 156, p. 52ff; *HL Papers*, XIII, 187n.

[3] Charles-Albert de Moré de Pontgibaud (b. 1758) followed Lafayette to America and joined him at Valley Forge in November 1777. He served as a volunteer and aide-de-camp until he returned to France with Lafayette in early 1779. He returned to America in August 1780 and fought under the marquis at Yorktown. Balch, *French in America*, II, 202-206; *Lafayette Papers* (Idzerda), III, 154.

To Mons.r de la Colomble Eleven hundred & fifty Livres[4]

Colonel Gimat has received the Bills for the sums granted to him___ for the several other sums ~~illegible~~ you will find the necessary drafts on the American Minister at Paris and also Major Capitaines' Commission inclosed within the present Cover and you will be pleased Sir, to make the proper distribution of these Papers.

The Treasury Board have repeated that they are unable to make any arrangement of the Papers which you left implying a demand on the Public for Money advanced in the Northern department; they have requested my assistance which I think can add little to their own discoveries, and that their labors must end in presuming on some given Amount which will be paid to your Order, and if it shall hereafter appear to have been less that is really due, Congress will immediately upon proper notification order the remaining Balance to be discharged.[5]

One thing still rests undetermined. a Nomination of a Person to whom you may apply in case of Doctor Franklins' death or other inability. I shall urge the House again this Morning on that point and ↑shall↓ have the honor, I trust, of informing you tomorrow of their Resolution.[6]

I Am / With the highest Esteem & Respect

SOURCE: LB, PCC (Item 13), DNA; addressed "The Right Honorable The Marquis de la Fayette / Major General in the Army of the United States / Boston / by Colonel Gimat"; dated "5th November".

---

[4] Louis Saint Ange, chevalier Morel de La Colombe, came to America with Lafayette and remained one of his party. He had received a commission as captain in the Continental army in November 1777. He did not sail to France until August 1779 and returned to America with Pontgibaud aboard the *Alliance*, Landais, a year later. *HL Papers*, XI, 586n; HL to chevalier Morel de La Colombe, Aug. 14, 1779, NNC; *Lafayette Papers* (Idzerda), III, 164.

[5] On November 7, Congress ordered "a warrant issue on the treasurer in favor of the Marquis de la Fayette...for three thousand seven hundred and eighty-seven and thirty-six ninetieths dollars, for sundry expences and disbursements in consequence of his appointment to command of the northern department, in February last." *JCC*, XII, 1110.

[6] Lafayette, who had been asked to deliver Benjamin Franklin's instructions as minister plenipotentiary to France along with a plan of attack on Quebec, had asked in an October 26 letter for alternative instructions in case "an ill state of health," or "if death itself, was to deprive his country of so valuable a citizen." *JCC*, XII, 1048, 1052; Lafayette to HL, Oct. 26, 1778, PCC, Item 156, p. 47ff.

TO GOSUINUS ERKELENS

Philadelphia, November 6, 1778

Sir

I had the honor of presenting to Congress your Letter of the 15th Ult⁰· together with a Plan for negociating a Loan in Holland which the House have duly considered and have directed me to return their thanks for your zeal in the service of the United States and to inform you that Congress have not yet prepared to ~~adopt~~ enter upon a Negociation for the Loan which you have suggested.[1]

The Plan according to your desire will accompany this__ Congress have granted a Brevet Commission of Lieutenant Colonel to Mr· Dircks.[2]

I have the honor to be &c

SOURCE: LB, PCC (Item 13), DNA; addressed "Gosuinus Erkelens Esquire / Hartford in Connecticut" and by HL "by Col⁰· Dirck"; dated "6th November".

FROM JOHN LAURENS

Philadelphia, November 6, 1778

Sir

As the approbation of the august Representatives of the united States is the first object of my ambition__ the mark of their good opinion in a Resolve of yesterdays date fills me with gratitude and as it was intended to confer on me an unexpected honor, would have afforded me the highest satisfaction, if I could have accepted it without injuring the rights of the Officers in the line of the Army; and doing an evident injustice to my[1] Colleagues in the family of the Commander in chief.__ Among the former a regular mode of rising is established which I have no desire to infringe__ the latter are my

---

[1] On November 5, Congress ordered HL to write to Governor Jonathan Trumbull and Gosuinus Erkelens informing them "that Congress are not yet prepared to adopt the scheme of a negotiation for the loan proposed." *JCC*, XII, 1106; HL to Jonathan Trumbull, Sr., Nov. 8, 1778, PCC, Item 13.

[2] Gosuinus Erkelens to HL, Oct. 15, 1778, *JCC*, XII, 1106.

[1] "my" written over "th".

seniors and from length of service as well as merit I humbly conceive have prior claims___[2]

Give me leave to assure Congress that I have not been an indifferent spectator of the convulsions which have been occasioned in our army by disputes of rank, and that I hold the tranquillity of it too dear to be instrumental in disturbing it.

The motion in my favōr yesterday, was made without my privity by an honorable Gentleman to whom I acknowledge myself much indebted for his kind intentions___ but from the considerations abovementioned I must entreat Congress will be pleased to suppress the Resolve and to accept my sincere thanks for the intended honor___

I blush when I reflect that on my account the attention of Congress has been for a moment diverted from the more weighty affairs of the Union___[3] and I beg the house will accept the assurances of ↑that↓ profound respect with which I have the honor to be their much obliged / and most humble / Servant

John Laurens

SOURCE: ALS, PCC (Item 165), DNA; addressed below close "His Excellency / the president of Congress___"; no date; docketed by HL "Lt. Colo. Laurens / Recd & Read 6th. Novr.". Copy, John Laurens Papers, ScHi.

---

[2] On November 5, Congress had resolved that JL "be presented with a continental commission of lieutenant colonel, in testimony of the sense which Congress entertain of his patriotic and spirited services as a volunteer in the American army, and of his brave conduct in several actions, particularly in that on Rhode Island, on the 29th day of August last." It further directed General Washington "to give Lieutenant Colonel Laurens command agreeable to his rank." Less than a month before, JL had complained to his father that "the Commissions which Congress have bestowed so liberally have destroyed the value of Rank which is the ostensible Reward of Merit." He may also have feared that his connection to the president had influenced that act. *JCC,* XII, 1105-1106; JL to HL, Oct. 13, 1778; Massey, "A Hero's Life," pp. 291-293.

[3] Congress received JL's letter the same day and respected his refusal of the commission, resolving "That Congress highly approve the disinterested and patriotic principles upon which Lieutenant Colonel J. Laurens has declined to accept the promotion conferred upon him by Congress." *JCC,* XII, 1106-1107.

FROM COMMISSIONERS AT PARIS
Passy, France, November 7, 1778
Sir

We have the Honour to inclose a Copy of the Declaration concerning the 11 and 12 Articles of the Treaty of Commerce, which we have received from his Excellency the Secretary of State for foreign Affairs, in Exchange for a similar one signed by us, in Pursuance of the Instructions of Congress.[1]

We have also the Honour to inclose Copies of a Correspondence with His Excellency M[r.] de Sartine, the Secretary of State for the Marine, concerning Cases of Rescues and Recaptures, that Congress may, if they judge proper, take some resolution on this Head. It Seems to be equitable that the same Rule should be observed by both Nations.[2]

We also inclose Copies of a Correspondence on the Subject of Negociation with the Barbary States. We do not find our selves authorized to treat with these Powers, as they are not in Europe; And indeed, we are not furnished with Funds for making them Presents.[3]

We have had the Honour of a Letter from the Auditor general, inclosing the form of Bills of Exchange to be drawn upon us for the Interest due upon Loan Office Certificates; and acquainting us that this Interest will amount to two Millions and an half of Livres annually.[4] when it was proposed to pay the Interest here, we had no Idea of so much being borrowed.

---

[1] Congress had resolved on May 5 to seek the deletion of Articles 11 and 12 of the Treaty of Commerce. On November 2, the American Commissioners and the French foreign minister Comte de Vergennes exchanged declarations, dated September 1, confirming the omission of the articles. *JCC*, XI, 459-462; *Adams Papers* (Taylor), VI, 172, VII, 116-120; PCC, Item 85, p. 201ff.

[2] The correspondence included the Commissioners' letters of September 10, 17, and 27, and Sartine's letters of September 16 and 21. At issue was whether French or American maritime law would apply in a case in which an American privateer—the *General Mifflin*—had retaken a French brigantine—the *Isabelle*—from a British privateer—the *Prince of Orange*. French and American maritime law differed on the percentages due the original owners and the captors after the sale of the prize and its cargo. The correspondence and a commentary on the issues is published in the *Adams Papers* (Taylor), VI, 398-400; VII, 22, 39-42, 46-48, 60-62, 82-83.

[3] The enclosures related to the 8th Article of the Treaty of Commerce which provided for French intervention in the Barbary States on behalf of the United States. Most are printed in the *Adams Papers*. PCC, Item 85, 175ff, 193ff; *Adams Papers* (Taylor), VI, 403, VII, 83-84, 86-88.

[4] John Gibson to Commissioners, Aug. 8, 1778. *Franklin Papers* (Labaree), XXVII, 234.

We shall pay the most punctual Obedience to these and all other Orders of Congress as long as our funds shall last; But we are obliged to inform Congress that our Expences on Prisoners being great, and being drawn upon by ~~the~~ Order of Congress from various Quarters, and receiving no Funds from America, we suffer the utmost Anxiety least we should be obliged to protest Bills. We have exerted ourselves to the Utmost of our Power to procure Money, but hitherto with little Success; And we beg that some Supplies may be sent us as soon as possible.

We are very unhappy that we are not able to Send to Congress those Supplies of Arms, Ammunition and Cloathing which they have ordered; But it is absolutely impossible for the want of funds; And M[r.] Beaumarchais has not yet informed us whether he will execute the Agreement made for him with you or not.[5]

We have the Pleasure to inform Congress that M. Mathew Ridley[6] of Maryland has made a Present to the United States of a valuable Manuscript upon naval Affairs, which he has left with us. We shall take the first Opportunity of a frigate to send it to Congress.[7]

We enclose to Congress Copies of a Correspondence between the Embassador of the king of the two Sicilies and us[8] which, as his Majesty is the eldest Son of the king of Spain,[9] is considered

---

[5] The Commerce Committee's letter of May 16 to the Commissioners enclosed the contract between Congress and Beaumarchais' agent Théveneau de Francy; instructions concerning the settlement of previous accounts; and an "Invoice of Articles" to be imported from France. The Commissioners wrote to Beaumarchais on September 10, but the issues remained unresolved. Commerce Committee to Commissioners, May 16, 1778, Commissioners to Beaumarchais, Sept. 10, 1778, *Adams Papers* (Taylor), VI, 127-128, VII, 20-22; *JCC*, X, 315-319, 356, XI, 505.

[6] "d" written over "b".

[7] Matthew Ridley described the book as "a Manuscript Book of the Commissioners of the English Navy, a few Years back" which contained "a very accurate description of the Dimensions, Guns, Men &ca. of most Ships then in Commission." Despite the Commissioners' assurances, the book is not listed among the papers of the Continental Congress. Ridley, an Englishman who had resided in Baltimore, returned to England in 1775 but spent most of the war in France. Matthew Ridley to American Commissioners, Sept. 29, 1778, *Adams Papers* (Taylor), VII, 85; Commissioners to Ridley, Oct. 22, 1778, PCC, Item 84, Vol. 1, p. 198; *HL Papers*, XIII, 410n; Richard B. Morris, *The Peacemakers* (New York, 1965), p. 317.

[8] Domenico Caracciolo to American Commissioners, Oct. 8, 1778, Commissioners to Caracciolo, Oct. 9, 1778, *Adams Papers* (Taylor), VII, 118, 122-123; PCC, Item 85, p. 234ff.

[9] Ferdinand I, King of the Two Sicilies, was the third son of Charles III of Spain. The Commissioners may have been confused because he followed his father to the throne in Naples when Charles succeeded to the Spanish crown in 1759.

as an Event indicative of the good will of a greater Power, altho' this is respectable.

It is of great Importance to penetrate the Councils of an Enemy, in Order to be prepared before hand against his Designs: We should therefore be happy to advise Congress of the Intentions of Great Britain as far as we can conjecture.

We have every reason to believe that the hostility of the Disposition of the British Court has no other Bounds than those of their Power. Their Threats, however, of large reinforcements and of russian Auxiliaries, are without foundation. The Interest of the King of Prussia and of the Empress Queen (who both choose at present to preserve decent Terms with Great Britain) to preserve a close Alliance between England and russia, we apprehend will prevent it. In short, we can see no Probability of Englands forming any Alliance against America in all Europe: or even against france. Whereas on the other Side, from the astonishing Preparations of Spain, the family Compact and other Circumstances; and from the insolent Tyranny of the English over the Dutch and their consequent resentment, which has shewn ~~him~~↑it↓self in formidable remonstrances, as well as advances towards a Treaty with us, there is reason to believe that if Great Britain perseveres in the war, both these Powers will be at length involved in it.[10]

The English, the last year carried on a very valuable whale fishery on the Coast of Brazil, off the river Plate in south America, in the Latitude thirty five south and from thence to fourty, just on the Edge of Soundings off and on, about the Longitude Sixty five from London.

They have this year about Seventeen Vessels in this fishery, which have all sailed in the Months of September and October.

All the officers and almost all the Men belonging to these seventeen Vessels ↑are↓ all Americans, from Nantucket and Cape Cod in the Massachusetts Bay, excepting two or three from rhode Island, and perhaps one from Long Island.

The Names of the Captains are; Aaron Sheffield of new-Port [blank] Goldsmith[11] and richard Holmes from long Island. John

---

[10] The following paragraphs relating to the British fishery were part of an October 30 letter the American Commissioners addressed to de Sartine. *Adams Papers* (Taylor), VII, 176-178.
[11] William Goldsmith.

Chadwick, francis May, reuben May,[12] John Meader, Johathan Meader, Elisha Clark, Benjamin Clark, William ray, Paul Pease, Buncker fitch, reuben fitch, Zebedda Coffin, and another Coffin,[13] all of Nantuckett__ John Lock Cape Codd__ [blank][14] Nantuckett; Andrew Swain Nantuckett, William ray Nantuckett.

four or five of these Vessels go to Greenland.__ the fleet sails to Greenland the last of february or beginning of March.

There was published last year in the English News Papers, (and the same Imposture has been repeated this year) a Letter from the Lords of the Admiralty to Mr. Dennis de Berdt in Coleman Street, informing M. de Berdt that a Convoy should be appointed to the Brazil fleet.[15]

But this, we have certain Information, was a forgery, calculated merely to deceive American Privateers, and that no Convoy was appointed or did go with that fleet, either last year or this.

for the Destruction or Captivity of a fishery so entirely defenceless; (for not one of the Vessels has any Arms) a single frigate or Privateer of twenty four or even twenty Guns would be quite Sufficient.

The Beginning of December would be the best Time to proceed from hence, because they would then find the whaling Vessels nearly Loaden.

The Cargoes of these Vessels, consisting of Bone and Oil will be very valuable; and at least, four hundred and fifty of the best kind of seamen would be taken out of the Hands of the English, and might be gained into the American Service to act against the Enemy. Most of the Officers and Men wish well to their country, and would gladly be in its Service, if they could be delivered from that they are engaged in. But whenever the English Men of war or Privateers have taken an American Vessel, they have given to the whalemen among the Crews, their Choice either to go on board a Man of war and fight against their Country, or to go into the whale

---

[12] Francis and Reuben Macy.

[13] Hezekiah Coffin.

[14] The Commissioners October 30 letter to de Sartine which included the same list had "Delano" in this blank—probably Nathaniel Delano whose brig *Fair Haven* had been taken May 19, 1776. *Adams Papers* (Taylor), VII, 177; *Naval Documents* (Clark), V, 331.

[15] Dennis De Berdt, Jr. (d. 1817) managed the London whaling operations of Robert Bartholomew and his associates. *Franklin Papers* (Labaree) XXVII, 515n.

fishery. So many have choosen the Latter as to make up most of the Crews of seventeen Vessels.

We thought it proper to communicate this Intelligence to the Congress, that if they find it proper to order a frigate, to take from the English at once so profitable a Branch of Commerce and so valuable a Nursery of Seamen, they may have an Opportunity of doing it; if not, no Inconveniences will ensue.[16]

We had the Honour to write to Congress on the 20 July, 17 of September of which we have sent Duplicates and Triplicates and to which we beg Leave to refer. By this Opportunity we shall send the News Papers which contain all the public Intelligence.

With great respect we have the Honour to be / Sir / your most obedient humble Servants__

B Franklin
Arthur Lee
John Adams

Post-Script.

We enclose a Number of Notes of Hand, fourty seven in number, which have been taken from our unhappy Countrymen who escaped from England, to whom we have lent Money, as they had no other way of Subsistance./[17]

SOURCE: RC, PCC (Item 85), DNA; addressed below close "The Hon. the President of Congress"; addressed at bottom of first page "The Honble. President of Congress"; dated "Passy, Novemr. 7. 1778"; docketed "Letter from B Franklin / A Lee / J Adams / Passy Novr. 7. 1778 / Read Feby 24.__" and "The Two Sicilies. / Morocco__". Copy, PCC (Item 105), DNA. Copy, PCC (Item 84), DNA. LB, Adams Papers, MHi. Copy by HL, HL Papers, ScHi.

---

[16] The Commissioners' interest in the southern whale fishery was sparked by an October memorandum from seaman Richard Grinnell, of Newport, R.I., who supplied much of the intelligence regarding the British fishery. He had sailed aboard New England whaling vessels in the South Atlantic, was captured by the British, and then sailed in the same trade from London with other Americans under British protection. *Franklin Papers* (Labaree), XXVII, 514-517; *Adams Papers* (Taylor), VII, 121-122. For more on the relationship between New England whaling interests and the British government during the war, see Joseph L. McDevitt, *The House of Rotch, Massachusetts Whaling Merchants 1734-1828* (New York, 1986), chapter 5.

[17] Congress ordered on Feb. 24, 1779, that the receipts be referred to the Board of Treasury for transmittal to the Marine Committee and the Committee of Commerce for "such of them as may belong to those respective boards." *JCC,* XIII, 247.

FROM JAMES LAURENS

Le Vigan, France, November 7, 1778

My Dear Brother

My Last was the 14th. Sepr. via Nantes__ w^ch: I hope will reach you__ I have but just time at present to acquaint you that my Dear Patty & Polly are in good health__ M^rs. Laurens & myself as well as for some time past__ that our Dear Jno. Petrie[1] after ab^t: 8 Weeks confinement, always full of patience, meekness & resignation, died (29th Ult^o.) in perfect peace & assurance of the Love & favour of God__ I could not, if I had time, describe within the bounds of my Letter the many amiable & excellent qualities of that truly pious Youth__ with all his infirmities he made a most agreable & Valuable Member in our family. particularly since we came to France__ our little Polly especially feels the Loss of such a[2] kind & Capable tutor as is rarely to be met w^th:__ but we chearfully submit to the Will of God, firmly perswaded that our dear young friend has made a most gracious Exit from a Life ↑of↓ weakness & Sorrow to a State of Everlasting Bliss

O' how we all Languish, to hear from my Dear Brother. when will that happy hour arrive, that we shall be informed by y^r: own hands of your Welfare__ & the reason of y^r. Long Silence? Ever since[3] June 1777__ We all unite in Love & respectfull Salutations to my Dear Brother & Nephew, & in Prayers to the God of all our Mercies for every Blessing of time & Eternity on you both__

Your sincere friend & very Affec^e B^r.

Ja^S: Laurens./__

SOURCE: ALS, HL Papers, ScHi; addressed on cover "Henry Laurens Esqr. / Charles Town / S^o: Carolina"; dated "Le Vigan 7th. Novem^r: 1778__"; docketed by HL "Ja. Laurens / 7th Novem̄ 1778__ / Rec̄d 25 Augt. 1779.".

---

[1] John "Jacky" Petrie (b. c. 1765) was one of the younger children of Charleston silversmith Alexander Petrie (d. 1768) and Elizabeth Holland (the sister of James Laurens's wife). Young Petrie had been sent to England in 1771. HL oversaw his education when he took his sons to England and the continent and enrolled Petrie at Geneva in 1774. Petrie left Geneva because of poor health and joined his uncle James Laurens who arrived in London in July 1775. He never fully recovered and remained an invalid until his death. *HL Papers*, VII, 458n; VIII, *passim;* IX, *passim;* XI, 513, 529; XIII, 499.

[2] "a" written in left margin.

[3] "c" written over "g".

FROM BENJAMIN LINCOLN

Williamsburg, Va., November 9, 1778

Sir,

I arrived here ↑on↓ the 5th. which was later than I expected, having been detained on the road from the injury I received in my knee from a fall from my carriage soon after I left Port Royal; and the same cause hath protracted my stay in this city; but, I trust, will not do it beyond tomorrow or next day.

No Militia are ordered from this State to South Carolina; I am informed by the Governour he hath sent the reasons forward why they are not.[1]

The[2] Congress will give me leave to suggest that the public interest apparently suffers here from the want of some person in the absence of the commanding officer in the Southern department, authorized to settle accounts and give warrants for the payment of sums due from the Continent to individuals for services which have been performed. Many such accounts are now, and have, for a long time, been open, and which, it will not be in my power, to close.

I have the honor to be / Sir, / with sentiments of / the greatest regard & / esteem your most / obedient servant

B Lincoln

SOURCE: RC, PCC (Item 158), DNA; no address; dated "Williamsburgh Novr. 9th. 1778"; docketed by HL "Williamsburg 9 Novr- / 1778 Recd. 20th- / Read

---

[1] Governor Patrick Henry informed HL that previous Virginia law had only provided for the state militia to assist neighboring states in cases of actual invasion. Recent legislation extended the power to "Cases of expected or apprehended Invasions" and preparations were being made to send Virginia troops to South Carolina. The Council, however, suspended the action "when Intelligence from Govr. Johnson of Maryland arrived, by which it Seems pretty certain the Enemy are gone northwardly." Patrick Henry to HL, Nov. 9, 1778, PCC, Item 71, Vol. 1, p. 188ff.

This brief paragraph replaced the following passage in the letterbook copy: "I am informed that on the first requisition of Congress to the State of Virginia for raising and sending to the aid of South Carolina one thousand of their Militia including the Continental troops in that state, The matter was laid before the Assembly, they came to a resolution that the Governor with the advice of Council be empower'd upon fuller & more explicit evidence that the enemy intended to invade South Carolina to march a body of Militia not exceeding three thousand to the assistance of that state, while for this purpose a bill was preparing, the second requisition from Congress was receiv'd, that made no alteration in the resolution of the House but the bill was compleated__ The troops are not yet order'd and the Governor appeared to me, when I conversed with him on the subject to doubt the propriety of ordering them forward untill more authentic evidence of the enemies designs were against Carolina should be obtain'd." Lincoln Papers, MHi.

[2] In the margin beside this paragraph HL noted "refered to Treasury / A.".

immediately / referred to Treasury / from A__". LB, Benjamin Lincoln Letterbook, MHi.

FROM WILLIAM LIVINGSTON

Trenton, N.J., November 9, 1778

Dear Sir

I hear an evil Report about you, which I am sure is the first that ever was heard. They say that your Excellency is about quitting the Congress. I hope that in so saying, they say the thing that is not. I dare say you wil[l] think of it more than once. Certain [I] am that you do not give out; and [as] certain that the Chance is against us in your Successor. And as for poor me, to whom the pleasure and honour of your Correspondence, and my local proximity to you while you continued at Philadelphi[a,] was no small inducement to take hold of the helm of the good Ship the New Jersey for another year,__ [1] as for poor me, I say, I fear the warm climate of South Carolina will soon cause an evaporation of your recently-contracted friendship; & the wide distance between us, a total Interuption of your Correspondence, But wherever you go, may God bless & preserve you, and be assured Sir, that (while he has any Memory at all) you shall never go out of the memory of

Dear Sir / your Excellencys / most humble Servant

Wil. Livingston

SOURCE: RC, Emmet Collection, NN; addressed below close "His Excellency / the Honble Henry Laurens Esq[r] / President of Congress__"; dated "Trenton 9 Nov[r] 1778". Copy (19th century), HL Papers, ScHi.

FROM WILLIAM LIVINGSTON

Trenton, N.J., November 9, 1778

Dear Sir.

I remember to have heard of a preacher who was a very close preacher but a very loose liver__ Having his example contrasted

---

[1] A joint meeting of the New Jersey Council and General Assembly reelected William Livingston governor for a third one-year term. *Livingston Papers* (Prince), II, 476n.

with his precepts, he answered, "<u>do as I say but not as I do</u>". I fancy his exhortations had little effect upon his audience__ Is it true Sir that Several members of Congress encourage Theatrical Entertainments after having recommended it to the United States to discountenance them?[1]

I have the honor to be with the Greatest respect d[r] sir &c

Wil Livingston

SOURCE: Copy (19th century), HL Papers, ScHi; addressed below close "Prest Laurens.__"; dated "Trenton 9. Nov 1778.".

TO JOHN BEATTY

Philadelphia, November 10, 1778

Sir

I had the honor of writing to you yesterday by Messenger ——— a light Horseman from Lord Stirling.[1]

Within the present inclosure you will receive the undermention'd Papers to which I beg leave to refer for your government.

---

[1] HL voted with a majority October 12, in approving a resolution that "earnestly recommended to the several states...for the suppressing of theatrical entertainments, horse racing, gaming, and such other diversions as are productive of idleness, dissipation, and a general depravity of principles and manners." A second resolution, approved the same day, "strictly enjoined" all army officers "to see that ...rules provided for the discountenancing of prophaneness and vice, and the preservation of morals among the soldiers, are duly and punctually observed." That very night, some officers attended the theater in Philadelphia. On October 16, Congress, claiming that frequenting of playhouses could divert the minds of the people from the important issues of defending their country and preserving their liberties, resolved "That any person holding an office under the United States, who shall act, promote, encourage or attend such plays, shall be deemed unworthy to hold such office, and shall be accordingly dismissed."

Immediately below the October 16 resolve as printed in the *Pa. Packet* was an "ANECDOTE." Lafayette had asked HL to join him at the theater. HL refused, replying that Congress had just passed a resolution recommending that the states "enact laws for the suppression of theatrical amusements" and that he could not act contrary to the wishes of Congress. "Ah! replied the Marquis, have Congress passed such a resolution! then I will not go to the play." *JCC*, XII, 1001-1002, 1018; *Pa. Packet*, Oct. 17, 1778.

[1] HL's November 7 letter, carried "by Lord Stirlings Messenger", informed Commissary of Prisoners Beatty that the committee considering James Dick's October 29 letter concerning the release of the British prisoners taken from the grounded sloop *Hotham* had not reached a decision. HL to James Beatty, Nov. 7, 1778, PCC, Item 13.

1. An Act of Congress of the 7th Instant for the temporary supply of British Prisoners.
2. Extract of a Letter from Sir William Howe to General Washington 19th January 1778 on the subject of supplies of Provision to American Captives in Philadelphia.
3. The Paper referred to by General Howe.[2]
4. An Act of Congress for enabling the Commissary of Prisoners to give an Answer to the peremptory requisition of Admiral Gambier in a Letter from Mr. Dick[3] for the surrender of Lieutenant Hale & others who were wreck'd in the Hotham Sloop
5. An Act of the 16th October for punishing by confinement Persons who shall presume under the sanction of a Flag to disperse the Manifesto of the British Commissioners calculated for stirring up animosities dissentions and Rebellions among the good People of these States. which you are to transmit to Admiral Gambier.

I likewise return Mr. Dick's original Letter__ I perceive the Secretary has only given me the Cover of Mr. Dick's Letter__ 'tis too early to mend the mistake this Morning; the Letter shall be in my next.__ I send you two of this days Papers.
    I Am &c.

SOURCE: LB, PCC (Item 13), DNA; addressed "John Beatty Esquire /

---

[2] The act authorized the American commissary of prisoners to supply provisions to British prisoners at the same rate American prisoners in Philadelphia had been supplied during Sir William Howe's occupation. The enclosure in Howe's letter to Washington provided a detailed list of the "Quantity of Provisions issued to one Man pr. Week at two Thirds Allowance according to the victualling Regulations agreeable to which the Prisoners in Philadelphia are victualled." It included 4 lbs. 10 2/3 oz. of bread, 2 lbs. 10 2/3 oz. of pork, 2 pints of peas, 4 oz. of butter, and 5 1/3 oz. of oatmeal. *JCC,* XII, 1111-1112; Sir William Howe to George Washington (with enclosure), Jan. 19, 1778, Washington Papers, DLC.

[3] The committee, to which James Dick's letter had been referred on November 5, reported and Congress ordered on November 9, "That Commissary Beatty be furnished with a copy of the resolutions of Congress on the subject of seditious papers circulated under the colour of flags" and informed that Congress believed the officer and crew of the *Hotham* were being held for good reason, and that "if any objections are made to it...they must be discussed and settled on national grounds." *JCC,* XII, 1103, 1113-1114.

Commissary General of Prisoners / Princeton / by Dugan"; dated "10th November".

TO WILLIAM HEATH

Philadelphia, November 10, 1778

Sir

Since my last address under the 22d. Octob.~ by Jones I have had the honor of presenting to Congress your sundry favors of the 13th. 21st. 29th. & 29th. of that Month.__ the first was Committed to the Committee on Ensign Brown's case who have not yet reported,[1] nor have the Board of War to whom the second was referred.

In answer to the general contents of the two latter I beg leave to refer you to an Act of Congress of the 9th. Inst. for indulging Major Harnage, Capt. Hawker Mrs. Reynolds her Children & servants as far as circumstances will admit of,[2] which Act you will receive under the present cover accompanied by an Act of the 21st. October for regulating the Exchange of Officers.__

I have the honor to be / With great Esteem & Regard / Sir / Your most obedient / & most humble servant

Henry Laurens.
President / of Congress.

SOURCE: ALS, Heath Papers, MHi; addressed below close "The Honorable / Major Gen.~ Heath / Boston."; dated "Philadelphia 10th. Nov~ 1778__"; docketed "From Congress". LB, PCC (Item 13), DNA.

---

[1] Ensign John Brown, under sentence of death from a general court-martial, admitted his guilt in a May 23, 1778, petition to Congress and begged mercy. He received a stay of execution pending a response from Congress. The committee that reviewed the case recommended on November 28 that Brown be released from the sentence and cashiered. Finally, on March 9, 1779, Congress pardoned Brown. *HL Papers*, XIII, 280-281.
[2] Maj. Henry Harnage and Capt. Earle Hawker, related to Harnage by marriage, had appealed to General Heath for relief from the order to move with the Convention Army. Heath had written specifically on behalf of Harnage. "If from good behavior here, I was to solicit a favor for any British officer of the Convention, I should find myself inclined to do it in favor of this officer." Mrs. Reynolds' husband had been killed Sept. 19, 1777, and she had two small children. Congress agreed to allow the officers "to continue on parole in the State of Massachusetts bay, with their families, upon their engaging to supply themselves" and gave Heath permission to issue "passes for Mrs. Reynolds, her children and female servants, to go to Europe, Rhode Island or New York." Henry Harnage to William Heath, Oct. 27, 1778, PCC, Item 157, p. 253ff; William Heath to HL, Oct. 29, 1778, PCC, Item 157, p. 221ff; *JCC*, XII, 1114.

TO JONATHAN TRUMBULL, SR.

Philadelphia, November 10, 1778

Dear Sir__

I intreat you will not blame me for the long delinquency on my part in our correspondence permit me to assure you Sir my silence originated in a sympathy arising from my particular love & regard for you; Your kindness & your knowledge of business will supply an apology for the rest.

I have now my Eye on your favor of the 5$^{th.}$ October__ I have learned enough of the services of our late freind in his Office of Commissary to know that the Public are much indebted to him & you may rely on me Sir, for doing every thing in my power to obtain suitable acknowledgements for the benefit of his family__ You have no doubt been informed by M$^{r.}$ Elseworth that a Report had been lately made on your Representation to Congress, that exceptions were urged to certain parts & that therefore the whole was recommitted__ the best influence on that occasion was to assure my freinds who were unacquainted with the merits of the late Mr Joseph Trumbull that he had been one of the best Servants of Congress, that I was persuaded, had he been continued in the Office of Commissary upon his own terms, the Public would have saved five Millions of Dollars or more & many hundreds of Soldiers, to prove this to the satisfaction of every reasonable person, will not be difficult to me. it requires only a retrospect to the circumstances of our Army at Valley forge during the last winter & ↑to↓ the amazing advance of every species of provision immediately ↑after↓ the Stores which he had amassed were consumed.

I cannot on this occasion bound my self by five Millions, the want of forethought & Industry in his Successor occasioned an advance of the price of provision & every other article kept pace with that__^{1} the Contrast of these Officers demonstrates the merit of the former, hence Sir, your requisitions & expectations on behalf of the surviving family do not appear to me ill grounded, nor do I believe there would be any great opposition, provided the Accounts were adjusted, or adjusted so far as circumstances will admit of, I

---

^{1} William Buchanan, who had replaced Joseph Trumbull as commissary general Aug. 5, 1777, lacked both experience and an adequate staff. He proved a failure in the post and resigned in March 1778. *HL Papers*, XI, 252n.

shall make an opportunity to day for conversing with M^r. Elseworth on this subject & do my self the honor of writing to you again very soon.

I perceive Sir, we were in equal danger on the 28th. Aug^t. & that we have each of us particular cause for thankfulness for the escape of our Children from dangers to which their Love of Country had exposed them;[2] My own, inform me what were your feelings while the event of that day remained unknown to us, & I am persuaded we have both learned, in all cases, under the severest pangs arising from apprehensions, such as I confess I felt on that occasion & in deep distress from real misfortunes to say "thy Will be done."

11th. I have conversed with M^r. Elseworth who informs me the Committee have reconsidered their late report & are prepared to deliver another Report to the House, I hope this will be done to morrow & that the issue will afford you satisfaction.

Congress seem to be now in earnest to proceed upon measures for realizing & appreciating our Paper Money we may make of this a fine spun theorem, but unless we strike at the Root, the cause of our immense emissions, the peculation of great public Officers, the practice of monopolizers &c &c, we may drudge on, the Evil will remain & our Country will be reduced systematically to destruction. in a word Sir, that Patriotism which we affected to say had led us into the present contest, is out of fashion & unless we speedily revive it, we shall experience a violent convulsion which will go near to ruin us, & which will at least bring us into universal disgrace, I lament the prospect.

Believe me to be Dear Sir / with the highest respect & Esteem / Your obliged & obedient hum / ble servant

Henry Laurens.

P.S. I beg my Compliments to Mr Jonathan Trumbull Juñ the Treasury I am told have informed him of his appointment to the

---

[2] Gen. John Sullivan's siege of Newport, R.I., in which JL and John Trumbull participated, reached its climax on August 28. Governor Trumbull had commented on the young officers' participation "in the late attempt on Rhode Island" in his October 5 letter to HL. *Rhode Island History*, XXIX (1970), 31-32; Jonathan Trumbull, Sr., to HL, Oct. 5, 1778.

Comptrollership, unanimously elected__ Salary 4000 Dollars ℔ Annum__[3]

SOURCE: ALS, Jonathan Trumbull, Sr. Papers, CtHi; addressed below close "The Honorable / Governor Trumbull / Connecticut."; dated "Philadelphia 10ᵗʰ⋅ Novʳ 1778__"; docketed "10 & 11ᵗʰ Novʳ⁻ 1778 / President Laurens / de Comy General Trumbull / &c. / rcᵈ⋅ 19ᵗʰ⁻ ℔ Mʳ Brown"; noted "Entᵈ in L. Book / N° 2. pag. 137.". Copy, HL Papers (19th century), ScHi. Copy, Force Transcripts, Trumbull Papers, DLC.

FROM GEORGE GALPHIN

November 11, 1778

My Dear Sir

I wrote you the other Day InClosg you Some talks the white men I Sent to the Creekˢ⋅ to Demand Sattisfation Sent me the InCloseᵈ talks by an Indian[1] I find our frindˢ⋅ Can not give us the Satisfattion we Demandeᵈ a warr is unavodable with our Enemis but it is our Enterest to keep them Divideᵈ till we are redey for them I beLeve we have Lost Some grounᵈ In the Creekˢ⋅ by Stoping the trade I noeᵈ it was ronge at the Same time but the people upon the frontierˢ thretᵈ to kill me & the Indianˢ⋅ two if I Seplyᵈ them InCloseᵈ is a Copʸ⋅ of an affadavᵈ⋅[2] you will Se what it Sayˢ it is harᵈ a manˢ Livig Shoulᵈ be thretenᵈ for Doing all in his power to Serve his Contry & our Enemis ofering a Large rewarᵈ⋅ for me Deᵈ or aLive[3] the Cedeᵈ Lanᵈ people may thanke them Selves for the

---

[3] On October 31, Elbridge Gerry nominated Jonathan Trumbull, Jr., formerly paymaster general in the Northern Department, to be comptroller of the Treasury. Congress elected him to the post on November 3. *JCC*, XII, 1077, 1085, 1096.

[1] Galphin enclosed two Indian talks, each dated November 4. The Creeks, Fat King of Cussita and Patucy Mico, both claimed to be friendly toward the patriots but noted British agent John Stuart's attempts to incite the Creeks against Galphin and the Americans. Fat King of Cussita to George Galphin, Nov. 4, 1778, Patucy Mico to George Galphin, Nov. 4, 1778, HL Papers, ScHi.

[2] In an affidavit taken Nov. 7, 1778, in the Orangeburg District by Justice of the Peace Richard Brown, John Pigg reported that he had heard Nathaniel Fulsom say that when the friendly Indians came down for their gifts from Galphin "he wou'd with a party of Men fall on them & Kill them & take their Presents...Kill and Scalp all the Indians and Half Breeds about Ogeechee and Likewise Kill and Scalp Mʳ⋅ Galphin". HL Papers, ScHi.

[3] Galphin claimed in a June 25 letter to HL that British officials offered a "500£ Rewarᵈ for me Deaᵈ or Live." *HL Papers*, XIII, 514.

Creeke warr as ↑it↓ never, ↑w^d↓ been in Stuart^s power to have Set them on us I beleve I menti^d to you before there was 5 Indian^s kill^d before one white man was kill^d upon the frontiers it will be an Exepensef warr but there may be Land^s got from them to pay a great part of it numbers of people in the Cede^{d.} Lan^d has run a great Deale of the Indian Land out that was a neff to Set them on us I thinke them that run it ought not to get a foot of it when it is got from the Indian^{s.}

it is reporte^d hear the king^s troop^s has Left Neue Yourke god Sen^d it may be true and that the french has tacke two Island^{s.} from the Englissh

   My Complimt^{s.} to your Son I am Dear Sir
   Your Excell^{y.} most Obed & Oblige^d humble / Servant
            George Galphin

SOURCE: RC, HL Papers, ScHi; addressed on cover "To / His Excell^{y.} Henry Larince / Esquire Presid^{t.} of the / Honur^{bl.} Continental / Congress"; dated below close "Nor / 11 1778"; docketed by HL "George Galphin / 11 Nov^{r-} 1778 / Rec^{d.} 21st. Decem̄".

TO JOHN SULLIVAN

            Philadelphia, November 12, 1778
Dear Sir__
  I have not had occasion to trouble you with a Letter since the 2^{d.} Ult^{o.} in the mean time your several favors of the 25th. Septr. 18th. 26th. & 31st. October have reached me & have in due course been presented to Congress. but at present I have no Commands from the House respecting their several contents.
  A Report from the Board of War on the article of forage lies for consideration, I shall endeavor to bring it forward this Morning & you shall as early as possible be informed of the event.[1]

---

 [1] General Sullivan wrote on October 26 complaining that his forage master could not find hay for the army's horses in Massachusetts or Connecticut unless he was willing to pay unreasonably high prices. He claimed that unless Congress intervened he would lose horses for lack of forage. Sullivan's letter had been referred to the Board of War on November 9. The Board reported its recommendation the next day; however, Congress did not act until November 30. Congress resolved that in "cases where forage...cannot be purchased...at

Major Talbot's capture of the Pigot armed Vessel afforded much satisfaction to Congress, his whole conduct in that affair is admired & applauded & I am persuaded that an occasion will be embraced for signifying the same to himself in terms of suitable honor.[2]

I have the honor to be / With very great Respect & / Esteem / Sir / Your most obedient & / Most humble servant

Henry Laurens.

President / of Congress__

SOURCE: ALS, IMunS; addressed below close "The Honorable / Major Gen: Sullivan / Providence."; dated "Philadelphia 12th· Novem̄ 1778__"; docketed "Honbⁱᵉ Henry Laurens / November 12 / 1778". LB, PCC (Item 13), DNA.

TO RICHARD CASWELL

Philadelphia, November 14, 1778

Sir.

I had the honor of writing to Your Excellency the 18th· Ultᵒ· recommended to the particular care of Governor Henry of Virginia. since which I have reꞓd. none of your favors.__ This will be accompanied by an Act of Congress of the 10th· Inst. recommending to the Governments of North Carolina South Carolina & Georgia to afford every necessary assistance to Major Gen̄: Lincoln for enabling him to subdue the Province of East Florida.[1]

---

reasonable rates, application be made to the executive or legislative authority of the State...for their interposition and assistance in procurring the necessary supplies". And, Congress recommended to the state governments "to take such measures, in aid of the forage masters...for the procuring sufficient quantities of forage, at reasonable rates." John Sullivan to HL, Oct. 26, 1778, PCC, Item 160, p. 197ff; *JCC*, XII, 1112, 1177.

[2] Maj. Silas Talbot of the 1st R.I. Regiment on October 24 used the sloop *Hawke* to capture the eight-gun British schooner *Pigot* with its forty-five man crew. Sullivan's October 31 letter enclosed Talbot's account of the action. Congress on November 14 recognized "the bravery and good conduct" Talbot demonstrated in the action and rewarded him with a lieutenant colonel's commission in the Continental Army. HL transmitted a copy of the act with the commission November 17. John Sullivan to HL, Oct. 31, 1778, PCC, Item 160, p. 207ff; Silas Talbot to John Sullivan, Oct. 29, 1778, PCC, Item 78, Vol. 22, p. 605ff; *JCC*, XII, 1132; HL to Silas Talbot, Nov. 17, 1778, PCC, Item 13.

[1] This November 10 resolution said that bounties would be granted to all forces that accompany General Lincoln to East Florida and serve "till the castle of St. Augustine is

Congress have Resolved that each Major General who shall go on the intended expedition, shall, in case of the reduction of that Province be intitled to a grant of three Thousand Acres of Land; each Brigadier to a grant of two Thousand &c__ [2]

I shall inclose in the Packet with this the two last News Papers which will inform Your Excellency of our Current intelligence. The Enemy's Garrison at New York continue to give tokens of a complete evacuation intended, but are slow in their motions, sullen & full of wrath.

I have the honor to be / With very great Respect & / Esteem / Sir / Your Excellency's / Obedient & humble servant

Henry Laurens.
President of / Congress__

SOURCE: ALS, Richard Caswell Papers, NcU (SHC); addressed below close "His Excellency Governor Caswell / North Carolina."; dated "Philadelphia 14th Novr· 1778". LB, PCC (Item 13), DNA. Copy, Nc-Ar.

TO PATRICK HENRY

Philadelphia, November 14, 1778

Sir

The last Letter which I had the honor of addressing to Your Excellency was under the 24th Ulto· since which, and for a long time before I have received none of your favors, and therefore Congress remain uninformed of the reception of many of their Acts transmitted to the State of Virginia

---

reduced" in "the same proportions of land as is allowed by the resolutions of Congress of 16th September, 1776." That resolution allocated 500 acres to colonels, 450 acres to lieutenant colonels, 400 acres to majors, 300 acres to captains, 200 acres to lieutenants, 150 acres to ensigns, and 100 acres to each non-commissioned officer and soldier. *JCC,* V, 764; XII, 1117.

[2] Calls for the conquest of East Florida came from various sources. Most recently a September 22 public letter from Gen. Robert Howe, read in Congress November 2, emphasized "the reduction of Saint Augustine, and the possession of East Florida to be as essential to the Interest of both So· Carolina and Georgia, and almost to the very existence of the latter." That day after considering Howe's letter, Congress concluded that if the enemy did not attack Charleston the "considerable force" which had been directed to assemble there under Benjamin Lincoln should "be directed to endeavour to reduce the province of East Florida." The Congressional action on November 10 to which HL refers here provided for the implementation of a Continental campaign against East Florida. Robert Howe to HL, Sept. 22, 1778, PCC, Item 160, p. 483ff; *JCC,* XII, 1091; 1116-1121.

Inclos'd with this Your Excellency will receive an Act of Congress of the 10th Instant for obtaining such of the Armed Gallies belonging to the State of Virginia as are fit for service on an Expedition intended against the Province of East Florida to which I beg leave to refer, and being persuaded the Government of that State will perceive in a moment the utility of this Measure, and the necessity for the utmost dispatch, there remains nothing for me to add to the recommendations of Congress.[1]

Your Excellency will also receive an Act of Congress of the 11th Instant requesting the Government of Virginia to suffer the immediate departure of the Vessels and Cargoes therein mentioned__ the Minister Plenipotentiary of France having given to Congress the most explicit and candid assurances that both are for the immediate use and service of His Most Christian Majesty's Fleet and Troops, and wholly unconnected with private trade.[2]

I have the honor to be &c.

SOURCE: LB, PCC (Item 13), DNA; addressed "Governor Henry / Virginia / by Hunter"; dated "14th November".

---

[1] Congress determined that the success of the proposed East Florida campaign depended in part upon the deployment of a blockade of armed galleys. The governors of Maryland and Virginia were asked "to direct such of their armed galleys...to proceed either in company, or otherwise...to Charleston...there to follow such orders as they shall receive from the commander in chief of the department, or from the officer appointed by Congress to command the galleys of the respective states employed on this expedition." During this service "they shall be at the expence and risk of the United States." Congress as an inducement agreed to allow the officers and men serving on these vessels to keep "the continental share of all property taken by the said galleys...agreeably to the resolutions of Congress relative to captures." And, the governors were authorized to grant a bounty not exceeding forty dollars to mariners entering the service for at least six months. Congress named Capt. John Barry "to take the command of all the armed vessels." *JCC*, XII, 1118-1120.

[2] The French minister, Conrad-Alexandre Gérard, wrote to HL and Congress on November 9 to explain that two vessels, the *Gentille*, George André, and the *Adventurer*, Joseph Tassis, with cargoes consisting of between 1200 and 1300 barrels of flour and 150 barrels of bread were loading at Petersburg, Va. The provisions had been purchased for d'Estaing's fleet. Shortages of wheat and flour had prompted the embargo on the export of provisions that Congress had recently extended until the end of January 1779. The need to supply the French squadron was one of the reasons given for the embargo. *JCC*, XII, 974, 1122; Conrad-Alexandre Gérard to HL, Nov. 9, 1778, PCC, Item 94, p. 34ff (translation on p. 311ff).

S. C. DELEGATES TO RAWLINS LOWNDES

Philadelphia, November 14, 1778

Sir

Inclosed Your Excellency will find a Resolve of Congress of the 10th Instant relative to an Expedition against East Florida. In this Resolve there is a Clause which not being so clearly worded as we wished, makes it necessary for us to inform your Excellency of what was the sense of Congress upon it, the Clause is as follows. "That if Major General Lincoln shall be of opinion that the Continental Battalions of the States of South Carolina and Georgia &c."[1] We conceived that this expression of the <u>Continental Battalions</u> tended to destroy by implication the Controul of the President of South Carolina over two thirds of the effectives of the Battalions of that State as vested by the Resolution of Congress of the 18th of June 1776 and an amendment was moved to clear up the ambiguity. But it being universally declared in Congress that the Resolution as it stood did not impair that controul and that no part of the Resolution of the 18th June 1776 could be effected by implication, or could be annulled but by expressions referring to that Resolution and annulling the whole or part of it, the amendment was withdrawn as unnecessary: and we hereby inform your Excellency of the sense of Congress upon the subject[2]

We are Sir with the highest Respect and Esteem / Your Excellencys / Most Obed[t] & Most Humble Servts

Henry Laurens
W H Drayton
Jn[o.] Mathews
Rich[d.] Hutson

SOURCE: Copy (19th century), HL Papers, ScHi; addressed "President Lowndes / So: Carolina"; dated "14th November".

---

[1] The clause continued "and the continental levies and recruits from the States of Virginia and North Carolina, will not be a sufficient force to proceed on the expedition against East Florida, he be authorized to engage a number of volunteers, not exceeding fifteen hundred, to serve during the continuance of the expedition, and that the volunteers so engaged by organized into such corps and commanded by such officers as Major General Lincoln shall approve of." *JCC*, XII, 1117.

[2] For more on the attempts by HL and Congress to avoid conflicts between Continental commanding officers and South Carolina and Georgia chief executives, especially Rawlins Lowndes, see *HL Papers*, XIII, 144, 158-159, 318, 384-386.

FROM THOMAS HARTLEY

Fort Jenkins,[1] Pa., November 14, 1778

May it Please the Congress

Since I had the Honour of Writing to Congress last. The Enemy have come down in Force, they have surrounded Wyoming; They have distroy'd Nanticoke Settlement and nearly all the Buildings on this side__[2] They approached this Garrison but the Commanding Officer Cap[t.] Forrester[3] Preserved so good a Countinance that the Enemy did not think proper to Attack him__ a Party of 50 Indians moved towards the Head Waters of Chilisquaque. I sent a Sufficient number after them__ I maintain the Posts on the West Branch: Fort Muncy[4] is so strong that with its present Garrison about seventy in number 1100 Men cannot take it at this season of the Year__ With all the Men I could collect (which you must well know it not many) I am moving towards Wyoming I have a months provisions of Flour with me__ One Feild Peice__ One Howitzer and a Swivel__ by which I shall Command the Waters which has fortunately rose considerably. I shall have the Country well reconnoitered as I go on__ and I shall push our ~~good~~ Fortune as far as we dare__ I am in hopes we shall make the Enemy face about__ cold Weather Stares them already in the Face.

on the 8th of November the Garrison was safe at Wyoming. they are in want of Flour but have plenty of Meat. Unless another Regement be immediately sent to Wyoming: (which from its situation must depend upon itself) The Frontiers of New York Pennsylvania and Jersey will soon give way__ if some Militia were sent up: this place might be made strong, so as to preserve the Communication to Wyoming: By Observing the Geography of this Country__ The importance of Wyoming to the States in General will be discovered.__ I cannot help mentioning one favourable Circumstance__

---

[1] Fort Jenkins was on the east branch of the Susquehanna River between the present towns of Berwick and Bloomsbury, Pa. C.A. Weslager, *The Nanticoke Indians—Past and Present* (Newark, N.J., 1983), p. 182.

[2] Nanticoke was located in the Wyoming Valley of Pennsylvania six miles south of the Wilkes-Barré settlement. *PMHB*, III (1879), 167.

[3] Capt. James Forrester of Hartley's Additional Regiment. Heitman, *Continental Officers*.

[4] Colonel Hartley ordered Capt. Andrew Walker to build Fort Muncy. Construction began August 2 and the Pennsylvania fort, located on the west branch of the Susquehanna River, was completed September 18. *Pa. Archives*, 1st ser., VII, 323-324.

That is "a Letter from me to Lieut^t. Col^o. Zeb: Butler fell into the Enemies Hands__⁵ in this I inform'd him that Congress had directed His Excellency Genl. Washington to send Troops to destroy Chemung and that the Board of War had ordered me to hold myself in readyness to cooperate with them["] I also told him that I expected to be soon with him. Our apparatus seems formidable, tho' we are deficient of Men__ I shall endeavour to conceal our Numbers. As I shall have the Country reconnoitered ten or 12 Miles before me as we advance__ I trust we shall not meet with any misfortune__ The Men I have are good__ and in high Spirits__ as I write under many disadvantages I must beg you will excuse incorrectness__

I am with the Greatest / Respect__ Your / Most Obed^t Hble serv^t.

Tho^S: Hartley.

SOURCE: RC, PCC (Item 78), DNA; addressed on cover "His Excellency H. Laurence / President of / Congress / By Express"; addressed below close "The Honble. Congress / of the United States / of America"; dated "Fort Jenkins Six Miles from / Nescopack Falls N. East Branch / of Susquehanna, Nov: 14th. 1778"; docketed "Letter from Col / Hartley Novr. 14. 1778 / Read 21.".

FROM GEORGE WASHINGTON

Fredericksburg, N.Y., November 14, 1778

D^r. Sir,

This will be accompanied by an official letter on the subject of the proposed expedition against Canada.¹ You will perceive I

---

⁵Col. Zebulon Butler of the 2nd Conn. Regiment, who had moved to the Wyoming Valley with Connecticut settlers in 1769, commanded patriot forces during the "Wyoming Massacre" on July 3, 1778. Heitman, *Continental Officers; PMHB*, III (1879), 120.

¹ General Washington's official response to the proposed Franco-American Canadian campaign for 1779 was negative. He listed numerous military, economic, and diplomatic reasons for his opposition. "The plan proposed appears to me not only too extensive and beyond our abilities, but too complex. To succeed__ it requires such a fortunate coincidence of circumstances, as could hardly be hoped and cannot be relied on." And, he concluded, "In whatever point of light the subject is placed__ our ability to perform our part of the contract__ appears to me infinitely too doubtful and precarious__ to justify the undertaking." George Washington to HL, Nov. 11, 1778, PCC, Item 152, Vol. 6, p. 451ff.

have only considered it in a military ~~point of view~~ ↑light;↓__ indeed I was not authorised to consider it in any other; and I am not without apprehensions, that I ~~shall~~ may be thought in what I have done__ to have exceeded the limits intended by Congress__ But my solicitude for the public welfare which I think deeply interested in this affair, will I ~~think~~ ↑hope↓ justify me in the eyes of all those who view things through that just medium.

I do not know, Sir, what may be your sentiments in the present case__ but whatever they are I am sure I can confide in your honor and friendship, and shall not hesitate to unbosom myself to you[2] on a point of the most delicate and important nature__ The question of the Canadian expedition in the form it now stands appears to me one of the ↑most↓ interesting that has hitherto agitated our ~~public~~ ↑national↓ deliberations__ I have one objection to it, ↑untouched in my public letter,↓ which is in my estimation, insurmountable__ and alarms all my feelings for the true and permanent interests of my country.__ This is the introduction of a large body of French troops into Canada, and putting them in possession of the capital of that Province__ attached to them by all the ties of blood, habits, manners, religion and former connexion of government. ~~It appears to me~~ I[3] fear this would be too great a temptation to be resisted by any power actuated by the ~~prevailing~~ ↑common↓ maxim of ~~fashionable~~ ↑national↓ policy. ~~to lay no particular stress on that spirit of ambition and love of dominion which the enemies of France have pretended to be peculiarly characteristic of that enterprising nat__~~ Let us realize for a moment the striking advantages France would derive from the possession of Canada;__ the acquisition of an extensive territory abounding in ~~those supplies pr~~ supplies for the use of her Islands ~~and~~ ↑the↓ opening a vast source of the most beneficial commerce with the Indian nations, which ↑she↓ might then monopolize__ the having ports of her own ~~whi independent on th~~ on this continent independent on the precarious good will of an ally__ ~~the infinite maritime benefits.~~ the engrossing the whole trade of Newfoundland whenever she pleased__ the finest nursery of seamen in the world__ the

---

[2] "to you" written in left margin.
[3] "I" written in left margin.

security afforded to her Islands__ ↑and finally,↓__ the facility of awing and controuling these states, the natural and most formidable rival of every maritime power in Europe. Canada would be ~~the most solid~~ ↑a solid↓ acquisition to France on all these accounts and because ↑of↓ the numerous inhabitants, subject to her by inclination, ↑who↓ would aid in preserving it under her power against the attempt of every other.__

~~illegible~~[4] France acknowledged for some time ↑past↓ the most powerful monarchy ~~of~~ ↑in↓ Europe by land, ~~and~~ able now to dispute the ~~superiority at~~ ↑empire of the↓ sea with Britain, and ↑if↓ joined with Spain, I may say certainly superior,__ possessed of New Orleans, on ~~illegible~~ our right, ~~with~~ ↑Canada on our left and seconded by↓ the numerous tribes of ~~sa~~ indians ~~illegible~~ on our rear from one extremity to the other, a people, so generally friendly to her and whom she knows so well to conciliate__ would, it is much to be apprehended ↑have it in her power to↓ give ~~the~~ law to these states.__

~~suppose~~ Let us suppose, that when the five thousand ~~thousand~~ french troops ↑(and under the idea of that number twice as many might be introduced:)↓ were entered the city of Quebec; they should declare ~~their~~ ↑an↓ intention to hold Canada, as ↑a pledge and↓ surety for the debts due ↑to France↓ from the United States or under ~~illegible~~ ↑other specious↓ pretences hold the place till they can find a bone for contention__[5] and ↑in the mean while↓ should excite the Canadians to engage in supporting ~~illegible~~ ↑their pretences & claims↓; what should we be able to say with only four or five thousand men to carry on the dispute?__ It may be supposed that France ~~ar~~ would ~~have reno~~ not choose to renounce our friendship by a step of this kind as the consequence would probably be a reunion with England on some terms or other; and the loss of what she had acquired, in so violent and ~~false~~ ~~illegible~~ ↑unjustifiable↓ a manner, with all the advantages of an alliance with us. This in my opinion is too slender a security against ~~a~~ ↑the↓ measure ~~which~~ to be relied on.__ The ~~fo~~ truth of the position will interely depend on naval events__ If France and Spain should unite and obtain~~ed~~ a decided superiority by Sea__ a reunion with England would avail

---

[4] One line of text canceled and replaced by "France...possessed" written in left margin.
[5] "or under...contention" written in left margin.

~~nothing~~ ↑very little↓ and might be set at defiance. France ↑with a numerous army at ~~the~~ command↓ might throw in what number of land forces she thought proper to support her presensions; and England without men, without money and inferior on her favourite element could ~~afford~~ ↑give↓ no ~~aid~~ effectual aid to oppose them. Resentment reproaches and submission seem to be all that would be left us. Men are very apt to run into extremes;__ hatred to England may carry some *illegible* into an excess of Confidence ~~against~~ ↑in↓ France; especially when motives of gratitude are thrown into the ~~latter~~ scale. Men of this description would be unwilling to suppose ~~that~~ France ~~was~~ capable of acting so⁶ ~~wicked and~~ ungenerous a part.__ I am heartily ~~wicked~~ disposed to entertain the ↑most↓ favourable sentiments ~~But but the faith or honor of any nation, who~~⁷ of our new ally ↑and ~~wish~~ to cherish them in others to a reasonable degree;↓ ~~but~~ ↑but↓ It is maxim founded on the universal experience of mankind, that no nation is to be trusted farther than it is bound by its interest; ↑and no prudent statesman or politician will venture to depart from it.↓__ In our circumstances ~~just launching into the great sea of politics~~ we ought to be particularly cautious; for *illegible* we have not yet attained ~~to~~ sufficient vigor and maturity to recover from the shock of any false step ↑into which ↓ we may ~~be~~ unwarily ~~betrayed~~ fall.

If ~~If~~ France should even engage in the scheme in the first instance with the purest intentions__ ~~she would be ↑might be↓ strongly tempted in the progress of the business to alter her intentions,~~ there is the greatest danger that in the progress of the business ~~perhaps~~ invited to it by circumstances and perhaps urged on by the solicitations and wishes of the Canadians, she would alter her views__ ~~But, Sir, there are symptoms which~~ As the Marquis ~~has~~ cloathed his proposition ↑when he spoke of it ~~to me↓~~ to me it would seem to originate wholly with ~~France~~ ↑himself↓; ~~but these are but I am not without strong suspicions,~~ ↑but it is far from impossible↓ that it had its birth in the Cabinet of France, ~~was~~ and was put into this artful dress, to give it the readier currency. ~~I hope I am mistaken; and that~~ I fancy that I read in the countenances of some people on this occasion more than the distinterested zeal of allies__ I hope I

---

⁶ "s" written over other text.
⁷ Cancellation written in left margin.

am mistaken and that my fears of mischief, make me refine too much, and awaken jealousies ~~which~~ ↑that↓ have no sufficient foundation.[8]

But upon the whole, Sir, to wave every other consideration; I do not like to add to the number of ~~the~~ ↑our national↓ obligations ~~my country~~ I would wish as much as possible to avoid giving a foreign powers new claims of merit for services performed to the United States, and would ask no assistance that is not indispensible. ~~and would endeavour to make~~

I am with the truest attachment and most perfect confidence

D[r] Sir / Your most Obed[t] serv

SOURCE: Draft, Washington Papers, DLC; no address; dated "Fred[g.] 14[th.] Nov[r.] 1778:"; docketed "To / His Excel[y.] H Laurens / 14[th.] Nov[r.] 1778.". Copy (19th century), HL Papers, ScHi.

TO LORD STIRLING

Philadelphia, November 15, 1778

My Lord

I had the honor of addressing Your Lordship the 10th Instant by Dugan and last night of receiving your favor of the 11th with two New York-Garrison Papers___ such parts of Your Lordships intelligence as I know will be acceptable to Congress shall be communicated to the House tomorrow, accompanied by a necessary hint respecting publication.[1]

---

[8] Neither the French minister Gérard nor the French military commander in America Admiral d'Estaing had instructions concerning the Canadian campaign. HL, who opposed the campaign on many of the same practical considerations as those presented by Washington, believed "the scheme...originated in the breast of Marquis delafayette, encouraged probably by conferences with Count d'Estaing." Lafayette, however, claimed "The idea was not Suggested by me, and I acted in the affair a passive part." Stanley Idzerda, the editor of the *Lafayette Papers,* concluded that the plan "seems to have been put together before Lafayette arrived in Philadelphia" and suggested "some members of Congress seemed always ready for another expedition against Canada." HL to George Washington, Nov. 20, 1778; *Lafayette Papers* (Idzerda), II, 192n, 195, 196n.

[1] Despite the fact that Stirling addressed his November 11 letter to "The honorable President of Congress, Philadelphia" HL apparently considered it a personal letter. The

The false representations contained in the Newspapers of the several attempts made on the part of the Commissioners for treating with Congress, their Account of the designs and desires of that body, equally false, discover in those Commissioners and their Coadjutors, a despair of Conquest, their business is[2] therefore to blind the understandings of the Nation whom they have reduced ~~with~~ to the verge of ruin and overwhelmed with disgrace.[3] This subterfuge will not long screen them, the Nation will be better informed, and misfortunes will give an edge to their resentments

If Sir Henry Clinton did actually proceed with the second Embarkation of Troops, I can think of no place upon the Continent so inviting to his Enterprize as Charlestown, South Carolina, he may with six thousand troops do much mischief in that Country, acquire much plunder, of Negroes and proper provisions for the West Indies, but he will meet hard blows, and from the Season of the Year, hazard a total disappointment.[4]

I shall inclose in the present Packet seven of Dunlaps' Papers, four of the 12th and three of the 14th Instant. I wish somebody in New York may be so wise as to send Common Sense to a friend in London, there is scarcely an American Commodity so much wanted as this, in that great Metropolis.[5] and Your Lordship shall hereafter be regularly supplied with the Advertisers.

I Am Sir / With the highest Esteem and Respect / Your Lordships &c.

SOURCE: LB, PCC (Item 13), DNA; addressed "The Right Honorable / The Earl of Stirling / Elizabeth Town / by White"; dated "15th November".

November 16 reference, to this and another letter of November 13, in the *JCC* "were read" is lined out. HL retained the letter among his personal papers. Lord Stirling to HL, Nov. 11, 1778, Kendall Collection; *JCC*, XII, 1134.

[2] "s" written over "t".

[3] Lord Stirling had enclosed two "New York-Garrison Papers" in his November 11 letter. HL's reference may be to *Rivington's Gazette* for October 28, which contains the Carlisle Commission's "Manifesto and Proclamation" of October 3.

[4] Lord Stirling had conveyed "somewhat extraordinary" intelligence concerning Sir Henry Clinton. "I have for two or three days past had some suspisions of it, and have it now reduced to a Certainty: and I believe he is on board the fleet which Sailed from Sandy hook on the 3d. Instant....he cannot be gone to the West Indies or to Europe for they still Call him the Commander in Chief." Lord Stirling to HL, Nov. 11, 1778, Kendall Collection.

[5] Lord Stirling had requested "two Sets of Dunlaps papers as often & as early as possible, they will enable ↑me↓ to get intelligence from N York in Exchange." Thomas Paine's "Crisis No. VII," dated November 11 and addressed "To the PEOPLE of ENGLAND," was printed in the *Pa. Packet* Nov. 12, 1778.

FROM JAMES GAMBIER[1]

Ardent off New York,
November 15, 1778

Gentlemen

When I made requisition for the immediate release of an Officer belonging to the King my Master, shipwreck'd in carrying a Flag of truce, an Act sacred, not only among all civilized Nations but held inviolable even among Savages, it was no more peremptory than the singular conduct of your Officer demanded, who under such circumstances (unauthorized, I was sure, by any liberal set of Men, whatever my sentiments may be on other parts of their conduct) could dare to put an Officer and his Crew into a common Prison.[2]

1st It was an undue advantage taken of the calamity of a Wreck! and that Wreck a Flag of truce!

2ndly. The Resolution on which the Congress now wish to justify themselves is subsequent in date to the fact of which they complain.[3]

3dly The Manifesto in question was addressed in the first instance to the Congress themselves, and ↑consequently↓ could not possibly be seditious.

This proceedure being against the universal Law of Nations and repugnant to the common dictates of Reason and humanity, I rely on the most ample redress from the Congress, in compassionate consideration of those innocent individuals who must suffer from retaliation.[4]

---

[1] James Gambier, a captain and commissioner of the Portsmouth Dockyard, had been promoted Jan. 23, 1778, to the rank of rear admiral. Appointed second in command to Lord Howe, Gambier arrived at New York May 23, 1778. On September 11 Howe resigned his command to him. George III, after reviewing Gambier's dispatches, concluded Gambier was unable "to cope with difficulties though most ready to point them out." On April 5, 1779, Gambier gave up the command and sailed for England. Tilley, British Navy, pp. 117-118, 138, 153, 161-162, 167.

[2] A reference to the capture of Lt. Christopher Hele and the crew of the royal sloop Hotham.

[3] Gambier's reference was to the October 16 resolution in which Congress "recommended to the executive powers of these United States, to take up and secure in safe and close custody all and any person and persons who, under the sanction of a flag" attempted to convey seditious papers. The Hotham had been taken on October 3. JCC, XII, 1015-1016.

[4] Gambier's letter was read in Congress November 25 and referred to a committee composed of John Witherspoon, Samuel Adams, and William Henry Drayton that had been selected November 5 to entertain Gambier's first complaint conveyed in Commissary Beatty's

I Am Gentlemen / Your Most Obedient / Humble Servant
James Gambier

SOURCE: Copy, PCC (Item 78), DNA; addressed below close "His Excellency Henry Laurens Esqʳ· / and others ↑the↓ Members of ~~the~~ Congress. Philadelphia"; dated "Ardent off New York 15ᵗʰ Novʳ· 1778"; docketed "Admiral Gambiers Letter to / the President dated Ardent / off New York 15ᵗʰ Novʳ· 1778".

TO PATRICK HENRY

Philadelphia, November 16, 1778

Sir

By Messenger Hunter[1] I had the honor of writing to Your Excellency under the 14ᵗʰ Instant.

Under the present Cover will be found two Copies of the undermentioned Acts of Congress viz.

An Act of the 26ᵗʰ August 1776 for establishing a Provision for Soldiers and Seamen Maimed or disabled in the service of the United States__ to which is subjoined a supplementary Act of the 25ᵗʰ September 1778 for the benefit of maimed and disabled Volunteers in the service of the States antecedent to the date of the first abovemention'd Act.[2]

An Act of the 26ᵗʰ September for organizing the Public Treasury, and for providing an House for the several Offices of Treasury.

17ᵗʰ

Your Excellency will also receive an Act of Congress of this date for holding throughout these United States a general Thanksgiving on Wednesday the 30ᵗʰ December next__[3] And three Copies

---

October 30 letter. The committee drafted a letter which HL signed and forwarded to the admiral on November 28. The letter denied the validity of each point he had raised. *JCC,* XII, 1103, 1163-1164, 1168-1169; HL to Admiral Gambier, Nov. 28, 1778, PCC, Item 13.

[1] William Hunter served as a messenger for President Laurens carrying letters dated October 28 to the Northeast and letters dated November 14 to the South. *PCC, Index.*

[2] The September 25 act provided "That all provisions and regulations contained in the said resolve of the 26th of August, 1776," extended to persons "who lost a limb or were otherwise disabled" in service to the colonies or the states, "since the commencement of hostilities on the 19th of April, 1775." *JCC,* XII, 953-954.

[3] The chaplains of Congress were directed on November 7 "to prepare and report a recommendation to the several states" for setting aside December 30 "as a day of general

of the Treaties of Amity and Commerce, and of Alliance eventual and defensive between his Most Christian Majesty & these United States__ I had the honor this Morning of presenting Your Excellency's favor of the 9th Instant to Congress, the House intreat Your Excellency will not delay the intended relief of Troops for South Carolina and Georgia, there is still great reason to believe an Embarkation has been made at New York intended at least for subduing the latter, and in order to distract our Measures they have prevailed on the Creek Indians to take up the Hatchet, these Savages have already made inroads upon Georgia and committed many Murders, my last advices from South Carolina express the apprehensions of Men best acquainted with the temper of the Indians, to be, an open and general War, this alone will involve both those States in deep distress, but I view the attempts on the Western as a prelude to the part which is designed to be acted on the Eastern frontier, and Lord Stirling writes to me from Elizabeth town under the 15th Ins[t.] that the whole of the 71st Regiment Highlanders__ two Battalions of Hessian Grenadiers, two Battalions of Delancys',[4] two of Skinners New Levies,[5] three Companies of the 64th and two of the 33[d] are actually embarked and only waited a wind to sail, as from a variety of circumstances he conjectured for the Floridas, under convoy of the Vigilant[6] and three Gallies__ this Navigation is exactly calculated for Georgia, either directly or by the route of S[t.] Augustine, and the number of Troops about 2500 will be far superior to the strength of Georgia with all the aid which South Carolina engaged in an Indian War can afford her.[7]

The dispersion of Byrons' fleet which Your Excellency will learn from the Newspaper which I have the honor of inclosing may

---

thanksgiving." The chaplains reported their recommendation on November 16 and on the following day Congress issued a proclamation in the form of a resolution. *JCC,* XII, 1110, 1135, 1138.

[4] Brig. Gen. Oliver DeLancey, a New York Loyalist, commanded a provincial brigade composed of three battalions. Two of his battalions (540 men) participated in the Georgia campaign and later saw action in the Carolinas. Katcher, *British Army Units,* pp. 84-85, 136.

[5] Brig. Gen. Cortland Skinner's New Jersey Volunteers contributed two battalions (733 men) to the British southern campaign. Katcher, *British Army Units,* pp. 93, 136.

[6] An asterisk here refers to the following note at the bottom of the page: "An old India Ship cut down. draws little Water & bears 24 Pounders."

[7] This Georgia expedition commanded by Lt. Col. Archibald Campbell sailed from New York November 27 and arrived at Tybee Island December 23. Coleman, *American Revolution in Ga.,* pp. 118-120.

occasion very great alterations in the Schemes & Plans of our Enemies, tis far from improbable that Count d'Estaing has carried off some of the scatter'd Ships, he sail'd in the critical moment for meeting them___8 nevertheless it appears to be essential to the general welfare of our Union that Georgia and South Carolina should be immediately reinforced, and that if possible East Florida be subdued. I submit these intimations to Your Excellencys' competent Judgment and remain with great Respect and Esteem,

    Sir &c.

SOURCE: LB, PCC (Item 13), DNA; addressed "Governor Henry / Virginia / by Millet"; dated "16th November".

TO CAESAR RODNEY[1]

Philadelphia, November 16, 1778

Sir

    On the 7th Instant I had the honor of addressing Your Excellency by Messenger Owen,[2] and on the 11th of presenting to Congress your Letter dated the 8th.

    My present duty is to transmit two Copies of the undermention'd Acts of Congress viz.

An Act of the 26th August 1776 for establishing a Provision for Soldiers and Seamen maimed or disabled in the service of the United States___ to which is subjoined a supplementary Act of the 25th September 1778 for the benefit of maimed and disabled Volun-

---

    [8] Adm. John Byron sailed from New York October 18 with the intention of blockading d'Estaing's fleet at Boston, where he had put in for repairs after the devastating storm of August 12-13. On November 2, another storm damaged and scattered Byron's fleet. While the British struggled into Narragansett Bay for repairs on November 4, d'Estaing sailed from Boston for the West Indies. Tilley, *British Navy*, p. 160.

    [1] This letter, with variations like the one of this date to Governor Henry printed above, was sent to each state to convey the acts mentioned. The text of each letter differed as HL included matters peculiar to that state. Each letter was dated November 16. See Catalog of Documents.

    [2] "Simon Owen from the Quarter Master's Office" was identified as the messenger in the President's Letterbook. HL to Caesar Rodney, Nov. 7, 1778, PCC, Item 13.

teers in the service of the States, antecedent to the date of the first abovemention'd Act.

An Act of the 26th September for organizing the Public Treasury, and for providing an House for the several Offices of Treasury.

17th You will likewise receive an Act of Congress for holding a general Thanksgiving throughout these States on Wednesday the 30th December next__ and three Copies of the Treaty of Amity and Commerce, and of Alliance eventual and defensive between his Most Christian Majesty and these United States for the information and use of the State of Delaware__ 18th.[3] Your Excellency's favor of the 15th. this Morning presented to Congress afforded the House much satisfaction, You Sir, & the privy Council have done your part Congress confide on the General Assembly to Co-operate with you for the benefit of the Union particularly by acceding to the articles of Confederation.[4] the State of Jersey have Resolved to Ratify we trust that Maryland & Delaware will not much longer be[5] delinquents.

I have the honor to be with / very great Esteem & Respect / Sir Your Excellency's Most Obedient servant

Henry Laurens.
President / of Congress.

SOURCE: LS, IHi; addressed below close "His Excellency Cesar Rodney Esquire / President of the State of Delaware"; dated "Philadelphia 16th November 1778"; docketed "A Letter / from / the president of Congress / dated Novr. the 16th. 1778.". LB, PCC (Item 13), DNA.

---

[3] From this point the letter was written by HL.

[4] HL may have been confused on the date of Rodney's letter and perhaps in the dating of this postscript. Rodney replied on November 13 to HL's November 7 letter, which conveyed a request from Congress that the Delaware Assembly be called to "attend to the Articles of Confederation." Rodney informed HL "that with the Concurrence of the Privy Council, I have, by writ, called the General Assembly to meet at Dover on Monday the Twenty Third Instant." No record of a November 15 letter from Rodney appears in the papers of Congress; however, the Journal does record that the November 13 letter was read in Congress November 19. HL to Caesar Rodney, Nov. 7, 1778; Caesar Rodney to HL, Nov. 13, 1778, PCC, Item 70, p. 683ff; *JCC*, XII, 1143.

[5] "be" written in left margin.

FROM ALEXANDER GILLON

Havana, Cuba, November 16, 1778

Sir

I did myself the pleasure to write you a few lines þe 18[th.] Sept[r.1] per Capt Hall of the Notre Dame since when have been occupied in trying to compleat my business here it wou'd be the height of injustice in me if I did not Aver that every Assistance was given me here that I expected or desired and with the surest expectations of a speedy Arrival I left this the 24[th.] past in Company with 2 Packets and a Merchantman bound to Spain but a few hours after we was out a Gale of Wind commenced that lasted 7 days and prevented hoisting any boat out to visit our Neighbours our Vessel suffered much part[y] when we was on the 29[th:] within a few minutes of being Shipwreck'd in the height of this Gale which forc'd us to cut away our Main topmast and all thereto belonging to heave 6 of our Guns over board to clear the decks and to try to get in here but we could not thus was kept out till the 3[d.] Instant when we return'd almost a wreck they rec[d.] us with much friendship and immdly favd me with the Needful to refit the Medley whereby she is now again ready to proceed once more and to morrow She with sundry vessels bound for Spain sail I have little doubt of getting safe tho it is winter and less doubt about succeeding in Europe where I will try to purchase so as to hurry out by May__ I am more and more Convinced of the Utility of this Port to America part[y] to the Southern States during our present War wherefore I again Assure you that every Continental or State Vessel whose Commander properly attends to the Method of this place without hurry will receive every attention and find it very Convenient to refit his Vessel here for which they should have a something to repay the Advances, I am happy in having had an opportunity of well knowing what is to be done here & in having experienced such attention to particularize wou'd be tedious to you thus will only say that for allowg disbts

---

[1] In this previous letter from "Reglé opposite to þ Havannah" Gillon noted that "Contrary Winds & bad sailing of þ Vessel" in which he had set out for France had forced him on a different course. While he waited for repairs to one of his vessels he took the "op[ty] of judging how Americans may be rec[d.] here & of what Utility this Port may be to us." And he concluded goods procured from Spain could be traded through Cuba, with spars, masts, and naval stores always acceptable in that market. Alexander Gillon to HL, Sept. 18, 1778, HL Papers, ScHi.

here on acct of Notre Dame and the Medley Bills have been rec^{d.} at Par on So Carolina or pay^{e:} in Phil^{a:} perhaps they may fall into the hands of friend from here who is now with you,[2] whose family has made my residence here Agreeable and thro his introduction have pav'd the way for others to fare better than formerly permit me therefore to crave your and Congress attention to him whilst with you or your Vicinity Nothing seems to be left undone towards me they even delivered me every American Prisoner here. if any thing is now wanting here it is an Agent to be Appointed by you here for your Business which Sanction wou'd be the Means of every American being readily Assisted here and no Expence to Congress the Major or Governors Adjutants now Actually are Agents for much is left to them therefore if you will permit me the recommendation I think such an Appointm^{t.} useful and no one so properly prepared for it as the Active and I may safely say Acting Agent here Mr Rafel de Luz Adjutant to the Governor and a Major in the Kings service whose friendship not a little Assisted me but if he or any other person is appointed by you it will be necessary that he is Confirm'd by his King__ Mr Lee I presume may easily settle that & as Mr Luz holds his Post for life that he is so attached to America, so capable for despatch I know none so fit for this important Post which if you deign to grant can do no harm but may much good. the[3] other Adjutant Don Diego de Barrera who also very much favoured me is willing to shew his Zeal by offering his service and proposes going your way wish he may be useful have craved him to Accept of a Letter to your Excelly to use in that case as you may think proper perhaps whilst I am in Europe & contracting for some Vessels may procure more if so and that thereby I can serve Congress they and you may freely dispose of me as I am determin'd to ransack every Corner in

---

[2] The "friend from here" was Juan de Miralles who had met Gillon at Charleston earlier in 1778, while traveling to Congress. Gillon had extracted a letter of recommendation from Miralles in case he called at Havana. It was largely because of this recommendation that the Captain General of Cuba allowed him to use Spanish facilities to make repairs. The cost of the repairs to the *Notre Dame* and *Medley* amounted to 14,424 pesos. Gillon's letter of credit on a Charleston merchant house was protested for lack of funds. The Captain General held Miralles accountable for Gillon's protested bill because the hospitality and services had been extended at his recommendation. Miralles who had his private funds in Havana attached to pay the bill, complained to HL but never obtained compensation. Cummins, *Spanish Observers*, pp. 140-142; HL to John Adams, Oct. 4, 1779, Adams Papers, MHi.

[3] Word repeated by copyist.

Europe but will procure the Needful & tho we are long from Home it cou'd not be help'd as no Vessel sailed from here for Europe since I arriv'd here till 24$^{th:}$ past please pres$^{t.}$ my best respects to Mr Drayton Mr Mathews and Mr Hudson, I am with all due respect
Your Excellencys / Most Obt & Most humble Servt
A. Gillon

SOURCE: Copy (19th century), HL Papers, ScHi; addressed below close "To His Excellency / Henry Laurens Esq$^{r.}$"; dated below close "Havana 16 Nov$^{r:}$ 1778".

FROM JONATHAN TRUMBULL, SR.
                                    Lebanon, Conn., November 16, 1778
Sir
      This Letter will be delivered by the hon$^{ble.}$ John Temple Esqr-__ He hath done and suffered much for the cause of this, his native and much injured country.__
      I had the pleasure of conversing with him, when returning from Great-Britain via New York to Boston, and now on his journey to Philadelphia.__ He is well acquainted with the public men and measures in the British Court__ He appears a warm and real friend to our American Liberties and independance__
      I recommend him to your regard, trusting he will meet the esteem and respect due to his services, sufferings and merit__ [1]
      I am, with great Esteem & Regard / Sir__ / Your obedient / hble Servant
                                    Jonth; Trumbull

SOURCE: RC, PCC (Item 66), DNA; addressed below close "Hon$^{ble.}$ President Laurens__"; dated "Lebanon 16th Novr 1778"; docketed "Letter from his excell^{y} / Gov$^{r.}$ Trumbull Nov 16 / 1778 / Read Dec$^{r.}$ 3 / Respecting J. Temple Esq$^{r.}$". Copy, Emmet Collection, NN.

---

[1] John Temple also carried letters of recommendation from the Council of Massachusetts, William Livingston, George Washington, and James Bowdoin. Council of Massachusetts to HL, Nov. 3, 1778, PCC, Item 65, Vol. 1, p. 356ff; James Bowdoin to George Washington, Nov. 7, 1778, PCC, Item 78, Vol. 3, p. 205ff; George Washington to HL, Nov. 23, 1778, PCC, Item 152, Vol. 6, p. 563ff; William Livingston to HL, Nov. 29, 1778, PCC, Item 65, p. 429ff.

FROM BENJAMIN WHITCOMB[1]

Rutland, Vt., November 16, 1778[2]

The Petition of Major Benj[a] Whetcomb, in behalf of himself and the Officers and Soldiers of his Corps; Humbly shewed,__

That your Petitioner by express order of Congress was Appointed & requested to Raise a Corps of Rangers, for the Service of the United States,[3] for which Purpose the Hon[ble] Gen[l] Gates, was Pleased to give incouragement that Pay & Cloathing should be at least equal to any Troops in S[d] Service;

That the Soldiers under your Petitioners command belonging to no Peculiar State have never had the benefit of Purchasing Cloathing & Provision in order to Maintain themselves & Families agreeable to provision made & granted by different States to Soldiers as an incouragement to list into the Service, Whilst at the Same time Money is very much depreciated & the Pay insufficient on that Acc[t:], Your petitioner being at a Great distance from Congress & head Quarters, begs leave to complain that altho repeated applications have been made to the General commanding at Albany__[4] for a Muster Master to muster my Corps, yet for a Twelve month past I have been unable to obtain that favour, on which Account I have been destitute of Pay during that time save a Small sum of Money which I have borrowed & divided amongst my soldiers to pacify[5] them__ at the same time being deprived of ~~co~~ cloathing, lately sending purposely to General Washingtons Head Q[rs.] and receiving not quite a full complaiment, said Cloathing was very much damaged particularly the Blanketts being rotten are intirely unfit for the fatiguing Service in which we are imploy'd, which deficiency alone renders my Corps in a Manner unfit for Service__

Your Petitioners having from the beginning acted the Parts

---

[1] Maj. Benjamin Whitcomb (Whetcomb) of the New Hampshire Ranger Battalion. Heitman, *Continental Officers.*

[2] Major Whitcomb dated the petition November 16, but both dockets call it November 11 and claim it was enclosed in Washington's letter of the 13th.

[3] Congress ordered the raising of "two independent companies", to be commanded by Whitcomb, on Oct. 15, 1776. They were organized at Fort Ticonderoga the following month. *JCC,* VI, 876; Wright, *Continental Army,* p. 200.

[4] Gen. Edward Hand replaced Gen. John Stark as the commander at Albany in late October 1778. Whitcomb probably meant Stark when he referred to the unresponsive commander. Hand took immediate action by forwarding the complaint to headquarters. Edward Hand to George Washington, Nov. 20, 1778, Washington Papers, DLC.

[5] "c" written over "s".

of Good Soldiers stand now ready to maintain the Interest, Dignity & Independency of the United States and with the remains of Life & spirit mean to assist in Percuring & defending the inestimable Priviledges, for which we have been contending in Conjunction, with Our breathern__

At the same time being involved and Surrounded with so great embarrassments that not only our-selves whilst exposed to the greatest danger & hardships in the Face of the Enemy__ are oppressed[6] but even our Wives & children Suffer unavoidable hardships and misery for want of the bare conviencies & necessaries of Life

Humbly beg that your Excellency in Congress will be Pleased to consider our Miserable situation and in wisdom grant reasonable relief to your Petitioners and their families also redress those evils which have nearly ruined us__ Or kindly dismiss us from the Service & disband the Corps that we may be enabled to make our-selves, & our families Situation more Tolerable[7]

And your Petitioners as in duty bound shall ever Pray__

Benj^a Whetcomb Major

in behalf of the Officers & Soldiers / of three Independent Companies / under his Immediate Command

SOURCE: RC, PCC (Item 41), DNA; addressed on cover "To / His Excellency Henry Lawrence Esqr- / President, and the Members of Congress / Petition of Major Benj^a Whetcomb"; addressed at top of first page "To his Excellency Henry Lawrence ↑Esqr↓ the President / and Members of Congress__"; addressed below close "His Exellency Henry Lawrence Esqr / the President & Members of Congress"; dated "Rutland on Otter Creek near Lake Champlain / 16 Novr 1778__"; docketed "Novem^r 11 1778 / Memorial from Major / Whitcombe / enclosed in Genl- / Washington's letter of 13. Nov^r / 1778__ / Read 30. / Referred to the Board of War" and "Novem^r 11__ 1778 / Petition memorial from / Major Whitecombe / enclosed in Genl Washington's / letter of 13 Novr 1778 / Read 30th / Referred to the board of war" and "4 Dec. 1778. acted upon. / vide Letter to Gen. Hand / of this date.".

---

[6] Written over other text.

[7] George Washington, reviewing the Whitcomb complaint, admitted "My information respecting the Corps...has hitherto been very imperfect, and even now I do not know the terms on which it was engaged." Washington ordered Gen. James Clinton "to send a proper Officer to muster the Corps–and also three companies which he calls provincials under his direction...both will be paid on his presenting proper Rolls." George Washington to HL, Nov. 23-24, 1778, PCC, Item 152 Vol. 6, p. 545ff.

TO SILAS TALBOT

Philadelphia, November 17, 1778

Sir

I feel a very high degree of pleasure in obeying the Orders of Congress by transmitting an Act of the 14th Instant for expressing the sense of the House of the bravery and good conduct of yourself and of the Officers and Men under your Command in taking the Armed Schooner Pigot, and for granting you a Commission of Lieutenant Colonel in the Army of the United States in acknowledgment of your Merit.

You will receive Sir within the present inclosure the Commission annexed to the Act, and will be pleased to signify to your Officers and Men the applause due to them on this occasion.

I intreat you to accept my best wishes that you may have many future opportunities of distinguishing your Character in the Annals of your Country, and that you will be assured

I Am with great Respect & Esteem / Sir / Your Obedient and Most / Humble Servant.

SOURCE: LB, PCC (Item 13), DNA; addressed "Silas Talbot Esquire / Lieutenant Colonel in the Army of the United States of America / Providence / by Dodd"; dated "17th November". Copy, MHi.

TO LORD STIRLING

Philadelphia, November 18, 1778

My Lord

I had the honor of writing to you on the 15th. & am now to thank Your Lordship for your favor of the 13th. which with that of the 11th. were read to Congress on Monday.

I perceive by Copy of a Letter which this moment reached me from General Washington & forwarded by Your Lordship, that Sir Henry Clinton was in the Garrison at New York on the 10th. unless he had written the original before his departure & anticipated a date the more effectually to conceal his absence from our knowledge.[1]

---

[1] In his November 11 letter Stirling informed HL "You will think it somewhat extraordinary when I assure you that Sir Henry Clinton is Absent from New York....I believe he is on board

In the present Packet I send three of Dunlap's yesterday's Papers & was going to say that I had nothing further to offer, but in the very instant M^r· Gerard conveyed to me by his Secretary the following intelligence which if authentic & the Minister is persuaded it is, will give a favorable aspect to the affairs of the Allies.

Count d'Estaing sailed from Massachuset's Bay in the Morning of the 4th· in a very strong gale of fair Wind & went safely to Sea, in the Evening of that day an Express from [*blank*] arrived at Boston with information that Admiral Byron's ffleet of 16 Sail of the Line which had been lying perdue,[2] had been overtaken by the Violent Storm which happened on the 3^d·__ the whole ffleet were dispersed the Sommerset of 64 Guns wrecked,[3] 40 of her Men drowned about 500. made Prisoners__ 4 or 5. large Ships were seen entangled among the Shoals & Rocks all their topmasts gone & several lower Masts; the topmasts tis natural to suppose had been struck; the Ships were if not already stranded were thought to be in the utmost danger.

deduct 5 from 16. 11 will nominally remain, but I would not insure them for a lower Præmium than two__ of that number, taking the chance of foundering smashing of Masts &c &c.[4]

We shall soon receive more special accounts of this fortunate circumstance, I am sure I should have received one as early as the french Minister & probably ~~with~~ more minutely, had we not (as I think unluckily & unnecessarily) superseded Major Gen̄ Heath, by which I have lost an excellent correspondent.[5]

I have the honor to be / Sir / Your Lordship's / Most Obedient & Most hum / ble servant

Henry Laurens.

SOURCE: ALS, Kirkland Collection, NNC; addressed below close "The Right Honorable / The Earl of Stirling"; dated "Philadelphia 18th· Nov^r· 1778".

the fleet which Sailed from Sandy hook on the 3^d· Instant." HL, however, was correct in doubting this intelligence. While Gen. James Grant sailed on November 3, with five thousand troops for St. Lucia, Sir Henry Clinton remained in or around New York City until he sailed for South Carolina in December 1779. Lord Stirling to HL, Nov. 11, 1778, Kendall Collection; Willcox, *Portrait of a General*, pp. 253-255, 300-301.

[2] Lying in wait or in ambush. *OED*.

[3] An asterisk here marked the following text for insertion: "said to have been In the West of Cape Cod".

[4] Two of Byron's squadron, the sixty-four gun *Somerset* and the sloop of war *Zebra*, ran aground and were destroyed. Tilley, *British Navy*, p. 160.

[5] Congress replaced Gen. William Heath as the Continental commander in the Eastern Department, headquarters at Boston, with Gen. Horatio Gates on Oct. 22, 1778, *JCC*, XII, 1038.

FROM SILAS DEANE

Philadelphia, November 19, 1778

Sir

I did myself the honor of writing to you on the 7th: of October last, and having since received a Letter from Mr. Williams, I send it enclosed to shew to Congress that the moneys, mentioned by Mr. A. Lee in his Letter of the 1st. of June last, to have been received by that gentleman, have in the opinion of two of the Commissioners been well laid out and faithfully accounted for. It gives me great pleasure to find that the Cloaths contracted for by Monsr. Monthieu, Messrs. Holker, Sabbatier Desprez that Gentleman and others, are on examination approved of and allowed to be the best of the kind, both as to the quality of the Cloth and the fashion they are made in, of any that have ever been imported; it is indeed a fortunate circumstance that out of near forty thousand Suits so few have been intercepted.[1] As Mr. A. Lee in his Letters has insinuated that the contracts for these Cloaths were made entirely by me, and has charged me with great extravagance in them, I beg leave to inform Congress that these Suits compleat, and delivered on board do not cost on an average thirty six Livres or thirty one Shillings and six pence Sterling the suit. I laboured hard to send over Shoes, Stockings and Shirts in proportion, and so far as it was effected, the suit compleat with Shoes, Stockings and Shirt, does not amount in the whole to forty shillings Sterling. These facts being known I am content to take on myself the merit or demerit of furnishing these supplies. I will make no comment on the dismission of a man of Mr. Williams known abilities, integrity and ecconomy and who did the business of the public for two per Cent, to make room for the Deputies of Mr. Wm: Lee who shares five per Cent with them,[2] nor on

---

[1] Congress ordered the American Commissioners, in February 1777, to contract for 40,000 uniforms and other military supplies. The Commissioners began making contracts immediately and by late April had agreements with Jean Holker who in turn contracted with Sabatier fils & Després for 10,000 uniforms. In August the same firm agreed to produce an additional 5,000. The contract with Jean-Joseph Carrier de Montieu, for 10,000 uniforms and other goods was concluded in early June 1777. This would account for as many as 25,000 of the 40,000 uniforms requested. *JCC,* VII, 92-93; *Franklin Papers* (Labaree), XXIV, 122-126.

[2] Benjamin Franklin's nephew Jonathan Williams, a Boston merchant, was serving as an agent at Nantes. He told Deane that two of the American commissioners in Paris had noted his generosity in charging only "2% Comn. when all the other Agents charge 5." Jonathan Williams to Silas Deane, July 22, 1778. PCC, Item 90, p. 583ff.

the still more unaccountable conduct of M^r· A. Lee in ordering Bills accepted by Messrs· Franklin and Adams to be protested.[3] It gives me pain to be forced to lay these facts before Congress, but cannot consistent with the Duty I owe my Country, nor with the Justice due myself to permit them and others of the like nature to remain longer concealed from public view, and examination. my Letter of the 7th· ult. covered observations on M^r· Lee's and M^r· Izard's Letters to Congress, to which am still without the honor of any reply; nothing would give me greater satisfaction, than to learn by what part of my public conduct I have merited the neglect with which my Letters and most respectful Solicitations for months past, to be heard before Congress, have been treated. I confess that I once flattered myself the services I preformed in procuring supplies, and sending them to the United States at the most critical period of their affairs, and in assisting to bring forward and conclude the Treaties, together with the honorable Testimonials from the Court of France whilst I had the honor of residing there, would have merited the approbation of Congress. and I now leave it with every person of sensibility and honor, to imagine what must be my disappointment and chagrin to find myself obliged at last to leave America without being informed if exceptions have been taken to any part of my conduct, or what they may be. thus situated though I can but feel most sensibly, yet a consciousness of the integrity and zeal which have ever guided and animated my conduct, and a sense of the important services I have been so fortunate as to render my Country, with the confidence I have that justice will yet be done me, support and will never permit me to forget or desert myself or my country, whilst in my power to be useful. I took the liberty on the 12th·

---

[3] Because he distrusted Silas Deane and most of the other diplomats and commercial agents, Arthur Lee did not sign off on bills presented to the American commissioners as perfunctorily as his colleagues might wish. Further, he did not like the fact that he frequently was ignored or consulted late on all types of matters, including those financial. In the context of this letter Deane may have been referring to an incident during the spring of 1778 when payment of Jonathan Williams' bills, drawn on the Commissioners, were held up because Lee protested that he had not been consulted. He also complained about the procedure that allowed an agent to send bills directly to the Commissioners' banker, rather than through them for approval. *Franklin Papers* (Labaree), XXVI, 228-229, 245.

instant in writing to Congress,[4] again to remind them of my being without any answer to my request, and having wrote already repeatedly, I will not trouble that honorable Body further on the subject of my being heard agreeable to what by their resolutions which recalled me, and since I hoped for, and had reason to expect, but praying them to accept my sincere thanks for the honor they did me, in appointing me their Commercial and political Agent in Europe, and afterwards one of their Commissioners to the Court of France, by which I have had an opportunity of rendering my Country important Services, I have only to repeat my former request, that orders may be given to their Minister at the Court of France, to have my accounts examined and settled immediately on my return thither, referring to my Letter of the 7th. on that head, and intreating for a speedy resolution on the subject. I have the honor to remain with the most profound Respect &c.

(signed) Silas Deane

P.S. since my writing the above I am informed that Letters have been received from the honble. Mr. Lee and read in Congress, which mention certain proceedings of Mr. Hodge, and that a sum of money had been paid Mr. S. Wharton by my Order without the knowledge of the Commissioners, and which I left unexplained and Accounted for.[5] I will only say here, that any insinuation of this kind is totally groundless, and makes me feel most sensibly what I suffer by not being permitted to be heard before Congress which I still solicit for.

SOURCE: Copy, PCC (Item 103), DNA; no address; dated "Philadelphia 19th. November 1778".

---

[4] Possibly the "Letter of 1 and 13th" read in Congress November 14, which in addition to reminding Congress that he awaited an answer, included enclosures on the Continental currency and a plan to equip a fleet "to defend the Coasts and Commerce of the United States." Congress ordered that the letter with enclosures be left on the table "for the perusal of the members." *JCC*, XII, 1132; Silas Deane to HL, Nov. 1-13, 1778, PCC, Item 103, p. 143ff.

[5] Arthur Lee's letters of August 7 and 11 were read in Congress November 18. The former included accusations, apparently well founded, that Silas Deane in league with others including Samuel Wharton used their inside information concerning the Franco-American negotiations to speculate in London stocks. *JCC*, XII, 1141-1142; *Franklin Papers* (Labaree), XXVII, 229-233.

FROM WILLIAM HEATH

Roxbury, Mass., November 19, 1778

Sir

I now do myself the honor to transmit to Congress the most accurate Returns & state of the Troops of the Convention that I can obtain, and hope they are such as will be satisfactory.[1]

The Lists of Officers contain all that were put under my direction, such as have been exchanged or are on Parole have a note made against their Names respectively.__ There appears to be a number of the latter; I beg leave to refer to my letter of the 21$^{st.}$ Ult$^{o.}$ for those whose Paroles are with me, to those mentioned should have been added Lieutenant General Burgoyne, Lieu$^{t.}$ Col$^{o.}$ Kingston[2] and Doctor Wood.[3] The other Paroles I conclude are in the hands of the D^y Com^y Gen$^{l.}$ of Prisoners, who sent the Officers in; he is not yet returned from executing the last exchanges, which prevents my sending any Returns or Reports from him. I think it will appear that Lord Belcarres and the other Officers who went on with him were to have been immediately exchanged, and that General Sir William Howe had given a sanction to it just before he resigned the Command in Chief of the British Army, but that before the exchange could be completed Sir Henry Clinton, having taken the Command, objected to & would not allow any exchanges of Officers of the Convention Troops to be made; I am credibly informed that this Resolution of Sir Henry's has caused no small dissension among the Officers. I take the liberty to enclose Paragraph of a Letter from Major General Phillips to me of the 6$^{th.}$ of June on the Subject of Exchanges.__[4] A great number of the Soldiers both British & German have deserted since the Troops have been in this State and cannot any other way be accounted ↑for↓ Some are probably in our

---

[1] The returns have not been located in the PCC.

[2] Lt. Col. Robert Kingston, Lt. Gen. John Burgoyne's adjutant general, had been included on a Feb. 28, 1778, list from Burgoyne requesting passports to return to England. *HL Papers*, XII 487-488; *Documents of the American Revolution* (Davies), XIV, 214, 289.

[3] Doctor Wood may have been Burgoyne's personal physician. Heath had been ordered to take these three paroles when Congress agreed to permit them to return to England. *JCC*, X, 218.

[4] Maj. Gen. William Phillips, the commanding officer of the Convention troops, had expressed his dissatisfaction with the way exchanges were being conducted. PCC, Item 157, p. 244ff.

own Army, some scattered through the Country & others gone to the Enemy.

The Troops marched from their Quarters in this State the last week: The Parole given by them heretofore being local, I took a new one for propriety of Conduct on the rout to Virginia. They set[5] fire to the Barracks in several places when they left them, but a timely discovery being made the fire was extinguished.__ They marched in very good order through this State; how it has been since I have not learnt.

In mine of the 19$^{th.}$ of June last I mentioned that the Ballance of the former Account of Supplies furnished the Troops, remained in my hands in Gold and requested directions whether I should send it on to the Treasury Board, or retain it until I received a further Sum; in a letter which I had the honor of receiving from you of the 9$^{th.}$ July you were pleased to observe, that, that part of my Letter relative to the Gold was committed to the Treasury, upon whose report I should receive further directions; I have never yet received any and therefore again request a signification of the pleasure of Congress, whether the Money shall be sent on to the Treasury, be paid into the hands of Major General Gates or otherwise as the Hon$^{le.}$ Congress may think proper. The Sum is something better than Three Thousand Pounds Lawful Money of this State as will fully appear by the Accounts (reference thereunto being had) which I did myself the honor to transmit the 19$^{th.}$ June.[6]

With every sentiment of respect / and esteem, I have the honor / to be / Sir / Your most Obedient / & very humble Servant

W Heath

SOURCE: RC, PCC (Item 157), DNA; addressed below close "Hon$^l.$ H Laurens Esq$^{r.}$"; dated "Roxbury 19$^{th.}$ Nov$^{r.}$ 1778."; docketed "Letter from Maj gen^l Heath / Nov$^{r.}$ 19. 1778 / with a list of Convention / troops, / Recd Dec$^{r.}$ 3 / Referred to the board of war".

---

[5] "e" written over "i".

[6] Heath's letter was read in Congress December 3. Because of information it contained about the Convention Army it was referred to the Board of War. *JCC*, XII, 1185.

TO GEORGE WASHINGTON

Philadelphia, November 20, 1778

Dear Sir—

I feel myself doubly honoured by your favor of the 14th. Inst. from the confidence of General Washington in the free communication of his sentiments & in the coincidence of his Ideas with my own, upon a question, on the wise decision of which the Inheritance, possibly the establishment, of the freedom & Independence of these States, seems to depend. The respect Sir, which I owe you, demands an immediate reply, & yet the variety of avocations in which I am engaged, do not afford me moments for arranging or expressing my thoughts suitably to the importance of the subject; I am nevertheless encouraged to proceed without hesitation from a conviction, that, were I to deliver my opinions at full length I should be obliged to borrow Your Excellency's words, which I have the honor of assuring you Sir, are in more than one Instance a repetitions of my own, & that in every other, one excepted, our sentiments on this momentous discussion exactly accord.

I beleive & upon good ground, the scheme for an expedition into Canada in concert with the Arms of France originated in the breast of Marquis delafayette, encouraged probably by conferences with Count d'Estaing & I also believe it to be the offspring of the purest motives so far as respects that origin, but this is not sufficient to engage my concurrence in a measure big with eventual mischiefs.

As deeply as my very limited time & faculties had suffered me to penetrate, I had often contemplated our delicate connexion with France, & although it is painful to talk of ones own foresight, had viewed & foretold fifteen Months ago the humiliating state to which our embrio Independence would be reduced by courting from that Nation the loan of more Money than should be actually necessary for the support of the Army & of our unfortunate Navy. I was one of the six unsuccessful opponents to the resolution for borrowing Money from France for paying the Interest of our loan Office Certificates—[1] we have in this single article plunged the Union into a vast amount of debt, & from neglecting to exert our

---

[1] In this Sept. 9, 1777, vote, as recorded in the *Journal*, HL was actually one of five members voting against the proposal. *JCC*, VIII, 725.

very small abilities or even to shew a leading disposition to cancel any part of the former demand against us, our Bills for that Interest are now floating in imminent danger of dishonor & disgrace_ fully persuaded of the true value of National honor I anxiously wished to support our own by a propriety & consistency of conduct & I dreaded the consequences of subjecting our happiness to the disposal of a powerful Creditor, who might upon very specious grounds, interpret National honor to our destruction_ I warned my friends against the danger of Mortgaging these States to foreign powers.[2] Every Million of Livres you borrow implies a pledge of your Lands, & it is optional in your Creditor to be repaid at the Bank of England with an exorbitant Præmium, or to collect the Money due to him in any of your Ports & according to his own mode whenever National Interest shall require the support of pretended National honor_ hence Your Excellency will perceive ↑what were↓ my feelings, when the propositions for subduing Canada by the aid of a french Fleet & Army were first broached to me_ I demurred exceedingly to the Marquis's scheme & expressed some doubts of the concurrence of Congress, this was going as far as I dared consistently with my Office or considering him as a Gentleman of equal honor & tenacity_ I trusted the issue of his application to the sagacity of Congress, the business was referred to a Committee who conferred with the Marquis, their Report was framed agreeable to his wishes, but the House very prudently determined to consult the Commander in Chief previously to a final determination, and although Your Excellency's observations are Committed, I am much mistaken if every Member in Congress is not decided in his opinion in favor of them_ If the prosecution of so extensive a project is from the present state of our Army & funds impracticable on our part, it becomes altogether unnecessary to discuss the point in a Political view. & I trust the Marquis will be satisfied with such

---

[2] HL's correspondence to his friends John Lewis Gervais, Lachlan McIntosh, and John Rutledge from late August through mid September 1777 was full of warnings, complaints, and lament concerning negotiations for a French loan. HL believed that the loan(s) would be ruinous to the economy and feared "the french under all their pretensions to kindness" would use the debt as a means to reestablish a claim in North America. He summed up his criticism in a September 10 letter to Rutledge in which he concluded "To borrow Money from a foreign power is to Mortgage our Soil." *HL Papers,* XI, 450-451, 456-457, 479, 499, 500-504, 505-507, 514-518.

reasonings in apology for our desisting from the pursuit of his favorite enterprize as our circumstances ~~will~~ dictate.[3]

The immense debts which we are involved in abroad & at home demand the most serious attention & calls for an exertion of the collected wisdom of all these States in order to secure what we have saved from the ravages of the Enemy, I am very short sighted, if there be at this time any encouragement for attempting ↑distant↓ conquests.__

I have been uniformly averse from every proposition which tended to dissipate our strength & to accumulate our debt__ events have confirmed my opinions, & at this Instant taking in view all circumstances I have doubts of the policy & more of the success of the pending expedition against East Florida.

Congress will probably recommend to the States to raise a Tax of near 20 Million the ensuing Year,[4] this I hope will have a good effect, by returning many of us to first principles from which we have been too long wandering this almost intolerable burthen will rouse & animate our fellow Citizens, they will probably send Men of abilities to investigate Causes, to enquire into expenditures & to call delinquents ~~delinquents~~ for unaccounted Millions to severe reckonings, they will do what they have hitherto shamefully neglected, pass necessary Laws for this purpose. this heavy Tax & the prospect of increasing impositions will shew our constituents the necessity for consolidating our strength, as well as the impropriety & danger of new expensive Military enterprizes__ Virtue & Patriotism were the Motto of our Banners when we entered this Contest, where is virtue, where is Patriotism now? when almost every Man has turned his thoughts & attention to gain & pleasures, practicing every artifice

---

[3] The Committee for Foreign Affairs on October 27 sent General Washington the resolve and plan for the joint campaign with the French against Canada and requested his observations. Washington's November 11 reply, read November 19, detailed the reasons for his opposition to the plan and was referred to a committee. Support for the campaign diminished rapidly and it was last mentioned Jan. 1, 1779, when a committee that had consulted the commander on the issue reported, concluding that "however desirable and interesting," the negotiations with France on this matter "should be deferred till circumstances shall render the co-operation of these states more certain, practicable, and effectual." Committee for Foreign Affairs to George Washington, Oct. 27, 1778, Washington Papers, DLC; *Washington Writings* (Fitzpatrick), XIII, 223-244; *JCC*, XII, 1147; XIII, 11-13.

[4] On December 16 Congress increased the amount to be raised by taxation "during the ensuing year" from ten to fifteen million dollars. *JCC*, XII, 1223-1224.

of Change Alley or Jonathan's__[5] when Men of abilities disgrace-
fully neglect the important duties for which they were sent to
Congress, tempted by the pitiful ffees of practicing Attornies__
when Members of that Body artfully start a point, succeed, & then
avail themselves of the secrets of the House, commence monopolizers & accumulate the Public debt for their private emoluments; I
beleive many such tricks have been acted, the particular instance
which I allude to cost these States a large Sum of Money without
putting the Criminal to the expence of a blush.__[6] When Men in
almost every important public department are actually concerned
in Commerce incompatible[7] with the strict duties of their respective
Offices, when the most egregious delinquents meet with support in
Congress & escape examination__ I am tired & fear tiring you Sir
with this horrible half finished picture, I will therefore leave it but
not before I add that the United States of America are in most
deplorable circumstances, that the acquisition of a foreign Minister
has fixed the Eyes of Europe upon them, that their weaknesses &
their wickednesses are no longer hidden, & that the States respectively are much to blame, & that without speedy reformation their
~~ruin~~ shame & ruin collectively will follow.

The disaster of Admiral Byron's ffleet & the successful departure of
Count d'Estaing's ~~illegible~~ are events much in our favor, that is to say,
if we are pleased to make a wise improvement of them but from
experience fearing the contrary I am almost tempted to wish they
had not happened. these fortunate circumstance will lull us to sleep
again, & while our Ally is gaining honor aggrandizement & the
highest national advantages we shall be sinking into a State little
better than tributary & dependent__ be this as it may, the World will
ever honor by acknowledging the virtues of the Man who from my
inmost Soul I beleive keeps us at this Moment from crumbling.

I have the honor to be With the / most sincere Respect &
Esteem / Dear Sir Your much obliged / & obedient humble servant
Henry Laurens.

---

[5] HL often railed against speculators who attempted to profit from the war. Jonathan's
Coffee House in Change Alley, opposite the Royal Exchange in London, in this context
represented a place where speculators would congregate.

[6] Probably a reference to Samuel Chase and his participation in a scheme with his business
partners in Baltimore to profit from confidential congressional plans concerning the
embargo. HL to William Smith, Sept. 12, 1778.

[7] "m" written over "p".

SOURCE: ALS, Washington Papers, DLC; addressed below close "His Excellency / General Washington."; dated "Philadelphia 20th. Novem̄ 1778"; docketed "His Excelly H Laurens / 20th. Novr. 78.".

FROM L.S. [1]

Philadelphia, November 20, 1778

May it please your Excellency

Among the many Causes of the depreciation of the Money of the United States [next to the superabundance thereof][2] I apprehend the Want of a greater Foreign Trade than that the Inhabitants of these States now have; is one of the most principle.__ to me it appears that the whole Trade of a Country like ours should be particularly attended to;__ If the Inland Trade be too great for the foreign, as now our case is, and an abundance of Money in circulation, The spirit of Speculation and engrossing will certainly encrease; and the Money will in proportion become less valuable, the necessaries of Life as well as the superfluities rise in Value, and the supporting of Families will become more and more expensive; Every person then who has Money & see's his Neighbour making a fortune by speculation, enters the List__ becomes a Trader__ neglects either his Farm or Manufactory, because he finds he makes more Money in his New business; and thus the evil like a growing Monster becomes daily more and more dreadful. And it is not within the power of any Legislature to stop the Torrent of this accumulating evil by any <u>direct</u> Laws against it, because the Wisest of Men heretofore have failed in effectually preventing engrossing &ca. As A in a corner may always given B for any goods whatever as much as he pleases, altho the Legislature should have limitted the price at half of that amount, and so on to C &ca. &ca.

My advice therefore to lessen the present, and prevent the further growth of this Evil of the depreciation of our Money is, Not to attack the Evil by attempting to make Laws for preventing forestaling &ca.__ but to attack it by an <u>Indirect</u> way. That is, To draw the attention of the Monied Men from an Inland Speculation to a

---

[1] The editors have been unable to determine the identity of "L.S."

[2] Square brackets here and below used by L.S.

foreign Commerce; to do which, I would have Congress to reccommend it to the several Legislatures of the different States to pass Laws for the Establishing within their respective States, for and on Aco^t of such State, a Public Insurance Office, for the Insuring of all <u>Vessels & Merchandize belonging to the Inhabitants of such State and bound to or from the same</u>, it being thus limited I have not the least doubt, but that it would answer better than if it was at the Risque of the United States, As the Commissioners or directors or Managers [or what they might please to call them] of such Insurance Offices would know or have some oppertunity of knowing not only the Vessels to be insured, but the Characters of the Captains, & Persons applying for having such Insurance made__ and thus avoid great frauds on the public, which might happen if carried on, On Account of all the States, when the subject of one State might get his property insured in another State at a distance, and where those that underwrote being Ignorant of the Person & þ^e Vessel might be imposed on.

Perhaps I may be told, this step is unnecessary, as there is already some private Insurance Offices established in some States and others may follow the example.__ To which I answer that in times like these, Private Insurance Offices do not, nor cannot answer the purpose so well as public ones, for if the Under writers make privately a fortune by obtaining from the Merch^t *illegible* Trader too high a Primium, it will be a proportionate Tax or Load on the Trade, And on the other hand, If the underwriter should accept of too small a Primium, he will suffer by it, perhaps <u>fail</u> in making good the Losses that may happen, which will discourage Persons from Adventuring further.__ I apprehend that Primiums for Insurance should be as low as possible to Encourage Adventurers to enter into Foreign Trade,__ And if a Loss to the State should arise thereby, I would venture to declare, That in the end it would not be equal to the Loss, which the public by the Continuance of the depreciation of our Money would experience__ beside, I contend it is just and right, That Losses occasioned by insuring Vessels & Merchandize at these times should be bore by the <u>State where made</u> and not by individuals, because the benefit arising from such regulations will, beside lessening the evil before mentioned, be the means of importing larger Quantities of foreign articles and of course come to every person at a more reasonable rate, Will encourage Ship Building, & with that, the immence appurtenant businesses thereto belonging, already known to your Excellency and too tedious to be here enumerated__ Will encourage Husbandry, as the Merchant will & must have <u>Produce</u> [where Specie is not to be had] for a remittance or for Payment of the Goods he may Import.__

I think I need say little more Than that the Dutch while they were Contending with Spain for their Liberties, had the whole time a foreign Trade, without which probably they would not have succeeded, a foreign Trade should at all times be encouraged in these States, but more particularly at the present, and as soon as the same shall be general, the people will be enabled without inconveniency to themselves to pay the <u>TAXES</u> which may be required, & so that in a few years to lessen the Circulating Money now with us__ I would however not be understood That Taxes should not immediately commence & continue till all þᵉ Paper is Sunk

I am your Excellency's / most Obedient and / most Humble Servᵗ·

L.S.

SOURCE: RC, HL Papers, ScHi; addressed at bottom of first page "His Excellency Henry Laurence Esqʳ·"; dated below close "Philadᵃ· November 20. 1778."; docketed "Letter of LS on a / foreign trade and the / expediency of establishing a / Public Insurance Office. / Philᵃ· 20ᵗʰ November 1778".

TO STEPHEN DRAYTON[1]

Philadelphia, November 21, 1778

Sir

I have been near two Months in possession of your favor of the 5ᵗʰ of September without power ↑to make a proper reply↓ until the present ~~moment~~ ↑opportunity↓ because Congress had ~~delayed~~ ↑not determin'd upon↓ the appointment of a Deputy Quarter Master General earlier than the 17ᵗʰ Instant.

---

[1] Stephen Drayton, a South Carolina planter and cousin of William Henry Drayton, resided in Georgia at the outbreak of the war, and served on that colony's Council of Safety before entering the military. Appointed acting deputy quartermaster general for the

Within the present Inclosure you will receive an Act of Congress of that date, by which you will be informed that you were then unanimously elected to the Office abovementioned and this Act will be your Warrant for proceeding in the execution of the Duties of your Appointment.[2]

I have had more than one conference with the Board of War respecting your Rank. The Board are of opinion that there is no Rank incidental to the Office, and therefore decline the insertion of Rank in a Commission. I have instanced the Commission of your Predecessor, to this I have been answered that there had been some management in that case unknown to Congress, and altogether improper. This opinion seems to be supported by referring to all the Deputy Quarter Masters in the other Departments, none of whom, as far as my knowledge extends have Rank in the Army as of right annex'd to the Office, altho' they are generally complimented with the title of Lieutenant Colonels. In the late Arrangement of the Quarter Master's Department, not a Commission has been issued from my Office, and I observe that the Commander in Chief directs to my Neighbour, commonly call'd Colonel Mitchell, "John Mitchell Esqr· Deputy Quarter Master General."[3] You will naturally ask, have Congress established no Rule in this Case? This shall be my enquiry, and if I discover that you are entitled to Rank, by Rule or established precedent, you may depend upon receiving a proper Commission by the next Messenger to Charlestown__ in the mean time I will endeavour to prevail on my Honorable Colleagues to move Congress for an appointment in your favor of Quarter Master General of the Southern Department. There appears at present an absurdity in the term of Deputy, when compared with the appointment of Major General Greene, & his power of appointing all his Deputies, from whom you receive no instructions, nor are you in any respect accountable to him under an appointment descending directly from Congress. I will not trouble you Sir, with further reasonings on

Southern Department in the fall of 1777, he was superseded by Francis Huger in December 1777. Huger, however, resigned in September 1778 in a dispute over rank and Congress named Drayton to the position. *HL Papers,* XII, 142; *Directory of the S.C. House,* II, 202-203, 205.

[2] *JCC,* XII, 1137-1138.

[3] John Mitchell of Philadelphia had been a colonel in the Pennsylvania militia before being appointed deputy quartermaster in April 1778. Upon the British evacuation, his office was placed in Philadelphia where he served as liaison between Congress and Quartermaster General Nathanael Greene. *Greene Papers* (Showman), II, 388n.

this subject, you will perceive my inclination from what I have already said to obtain for you all that of right appertains to your office. I know that heretofore Commissions have been shamefully prostituted, and I am informed that former Deputy Quarter Masters in several instances from favoritism and other vicious sources derived Rank; if this be true, I am too well acquainted with your Principles Sir, to suppose you would wish me to follow such examples__ the Army cried aloud against them, and the late Arrangement was intended to prohibit and abolish the practice.[4]

I have the honor to be / With great Regard / Sir / Your Obedient & / Humble Servant
P.S.

Upon further investigation I find that the Officers under General Mifflin as Quarter Master General were entitled to Rank, & Colo. Mitchell informs me that none of the Deputies of Major Genl. Greene in the present Establishment have Commissions. As Commissions have fm necessity been lodg'd in þe. hands of Governors presidents of States ↑and General Officers↓ & no returns ~~mad~~ made of the disposition of such Commissions, it has been hitherto impossible for the President of Congress or the Board of War to ascertain with precision an Army list__ this has occasion'd much clashing of Rank. We are now endeavouring to lessen the mischief, and if possible to remove it altogether.[5]

SOURCE: LB, PCC (Item 13), DNA; addressed "Stephen Drayton Esquire / Charlestown / So. Carolina / by Sharp"; dated "21st November".

---

[4] Congress did not change the designation and Drayton continued to serve as deputy quartermaster general in the Southern Department under Benjamin Lincoln and Horatio Gates. Personal crises, including his wife's death, during the summer of 1780 interrupted his service. He returned, however, in 1781 to resume his duties as deputy quartermaster under Nathanael Greene. *Greene Papers* (Showman), VI, 429-430; *Delegate Letters* (Smith), XVII, 349-350.

[5] Originally the quartermaster general and the deputy quartermaster general received the military rank colonel. Regular line officers complained and as part of the rearrangement of the army, Congress determined in May 1778 that thereafter no person appointed to the Continental Army's civil staff would as a result be entitled to any rank in the army. Risch, *Supplying Washington's Army*, pp. 46-47; *JCC*, XI, 554-555.

TO LORD STIRLING

Philadelphia, November 21, 1778

My Lord.

I thank you for Your Lordships favors of the 17 & 19th which came to hand late last Night_ it may be truly said that Admiral Byron has paid for his peeping, & I fancy we don't yet know the whole score, there seems to be about 6. or 7_ unaccounted Vessels of his squadron which I think consisted of 16 Capital Ships, if these have taken their Lodgings at Nantucket or gone to Winter with Count d'Estaing in the warmer latitudes, I am content.

Alas poor old England, I feel her approaching distress & pray that her Eyes may be opened before it be quite too late; who can dry eyed behold, a falling Kingdom, or a Kingdom in which there are thousands whom he personally loves, falling into great contempt & disgrace among Nations?

Your Lordship will find within, the Advertisers of the 19th & this date with duplicates say triplicates

I have the honor to be With very great / Esteem & Respect My Lord / Your most obliged & obed[t.] / servt

Henry Laurens.

SOURCE: ALS, Gratz Collection, PHi; addressed below close "The R[t] Hoñble / the Earl of Stirling."; dated "Philadelphia 21st Nov[r.] 1778"; docketed "From / President Congress / Nov[r.] 21. 1778".

TO JOHN ETTWEIN

Philadelphia, November 23, 1778

My dear freind.

Mons[r.] Gerard the Minister Plenipotentiary of France will be, provided he meets no obstruction on the Road, at Bethlehem on Wednesday the 25th Inst. about midday, this worthy Character merits regard from all the Citizens of these States, an acquaintance with him will afford you satisfaction & I am persuaded his Visit will work no evil or inconvenience to your community   Don Juan de

Miralles a Spanish Gentleman highly recommended by the Governor of Havaña will accompany M^r. Gerard, the whole suite may amount to six Gentlemen & perhaps a servant to each   I give this previous intimation in order that preparations suitable to the occasion may be made by M^r. Johnson at the Tavern,[1] & otherwise as you think expedient. My good wishes attend you all   I beg M^r. Okely will forbear with me a few days longer   I consider him as a merciful Creditor & when an opportunity presents I will pay him more in one Act than all my words are worth.[2]

Believe me Dear sir to be with sincere respect & very great affection your friend & most humble servant.

Henry Laurens.

SOURCE: ALS, PBMCA; addressed below close "The Rev^d. Mr Edwin / Bethlehem__"; dated below close "Philadelphia / 23 Novem⁓ 1778".

TO ARTHUR MIDDLETON[1]

Philadelphia, November 23, 1778

Dear Sir.

I hold my self always responsible to a Creditor & if my debt is greater than he is apprized of I think it mean to avail <u>myself</u> of little remissnesses on his part as a pretext for concealing a tittle of the Account, nor will I take advantage of my Lord because he is gone into a far Country, nor hazard my fame to be ranked with the cursed unaccountable, He to be accountable, family, the most numerous

---

[1] The innkeeper's name was actually Jost Jansen. A Norwegian who had been a sailor, Jansen served as landlord of the Sun Tavern in Bethlehem from June 1771 to April 1781. Construction on the tavern had begun in 1758, and it opened in 1760. Joseph M. Levering, *A History of Bethlehem, Pennsylvania, 1744-1892* (Bethlehem, Pa., 1903), pp. 279, 360-361.

[2] John Okely had written to HL in June 1778, appealing on behalf of "the United Brethren, amongst who I reside," for compensation for their losses. *HL Papers,* XIII, 444-445.

[1] Arthur Middleton, elected in February 1776, served in the Continental Congress from April 1776 until October 1777. *Directory of the S.C. House,* II, 456-458; *HL Papers,* XII, 19n.

& most infamous of all the tribes in the Northern & Eastern parts of our ununited States.

When about 13 Months ago you left York Town you were pleased to deposit in my hands five hundred & twenty Paper Dollars & said you would inform me from Fredericksburg how to dispose of them, this I esteemed an honorary procuration, & although you have failed of your promises to write, yet as I have heard of no supersedes I hold myself to be your true & Lawful Attorney in the State of Pennsylvania, in ~po~ virtue of my power therefore I have paid to M^rs. Middleton's Chesnut Street House keeper[2] one hundred & twenty five Dollars which the good Woman says ought to have been twenty five golden Guineas, I received from her several articles of your household furniture which she had saved from the claws of the Enemy, & profiting by her information, I have by a little address of my own & much adroitness of Mr James Custer squezd out a great many more from your late Landlady, the whole as James informs me falls short of M^rs. Morton's account__ & he is therefore ↑determined↓ to exercise his utmost skill for the recovery of the balance. You will receive ↑within,↓ his list of every thing I mean of the things referred to which are now in my possession or rather in his. pray order your Secretary Sir, to inform me what I shall do with them, poor as I am I have not a covetous eye upon a single article, the black silk Petticoat excepted, I think it will afford me a couple of very clever under Jackets, if you should hear that it has been destined to such service impute it to no other desires than those which this frigid clime ~illegible~ & the horrid price of quilted silk in these times naturally provoke. I have consulted our friend the Chief Justice on the propriety of selling all these articles except the one before excepted I forget what was his opinion, I will consult him again to day & pursue his advice, James has been continually on the look out for an empty Waggon going to our Country, had such an opportunity presented it would have been embraced even at some expence in order to have put your property into your own hands especially the finer articles & a straw Box & narrow deal Case which M^rs. Morton says contain Papers, these however you may be assured are

---

[2] Mary Izard Middleton and her husband had resided in Philadelphia from April 1776 until the evacuation of Congress to York, Pa., in September 1777. *Directory of the S.C. House*, II, 457; *Delegate Letters* (Smith), III, xxi.

as safe as you would wish them to be if they are full all your juvenile Billets doux.__ Don Juan de Miralles expects a Waggon from Charles Town this may afford me a proper conveyance, but should my new Landlady our old Landlady's daughter Allen again eject me under a pretence that she mistook our bargain for Rent because she has been offered more, I shall certainly order all the heavy articles to be sold at auction in preference to lugging them from House to House__ I fancy when you left York Town you had no expectation of hearing so long a tale of your ~~effects~~ deserted effects, I won't tire you with any more of it but say in a word I will do for you as I would for my self for upon my honor if you wanted an old black silk quilted Petticoat as much as I do & I had one to spare it should be at your service. You will also find under cover with this an Account from your Landlord, if he presses very hard for the paper part before I receive your Audit I must pay it, this seems to be implied in the surrender of your demeans which had been in his custody,__ for the Gold I must move to postpone.³

the state of ↑the Garrison at↓ New York, the disaster of Byron's ffleet, the escape of Count d'Estaing & the prospect of his running in triumph through the West India ↑Islands↓ are topics of our present conversation, you will read more extended accounts of each in the News Papers & this moment we learn by a Vessel ~~by a Vessel~~ from the West Indies of a second engagement between Monsʳ d'Orvilliers & Ad: Keppel in which the former 'tis said gained a victory. I wish this may be true.

I have the honor to be / With great Respect / Sir / Your obedient & most / humble servant

Henry Laurens.

source: ALS, Middleton Papers, ScHi; addressed below close "The Honorable / Arthur Middleton Esquire / South Carolina."; dated "Philadelphia 23ᵈ· Novʳ· 1778__"; docketed "Henʸ· Laurens / 23ᵈ Novʳ· 1778__".

---

³ Middleton answered HL seven months later and thanked him "for the trouble you have taken with my Trumpery, which I never expected to have heard of more." He noted that a Dr. Bond was among his creditors and "Mr [John] Lawrence (my Landlord) & Mʳˢ· Moreton (the Housekeeper) if I recalled right, by your Letter, are not satisfied." Middleton asked HL to discharge the accounts "out of the money in your hands." An undated note in the Arthur Middleton papers, in James Custer's hand, includes the comment that Dr. Bond occupied the house the Middletons vacated with the understanding that Arthur Middleton would pay to have it put in good repair. The inventory of repairs was assessed at £7.15.0 and paid in gold to John Laurance. The note also mentioned "Rent due...seventy five Pounds continental Money__" Arthur Middleton to HL, June 9, 1779, Arthur Middleton Papers, ScHi.

FROM PATRICK HENRY

Williamsburg, Va., November 23, 1778

Sir

I am Honoured with the Receipt of your Favour of the 14ᵗʰ· instant covering two Acts of Congress viz. one of the 10ᵗʰ· instant for obtaining from this State & Maryland, Gallies to attack East Florida another of the 11ᵗʰ for requesting permission to export from Petersburg in Virginia a Quantity of Flour & Bread for the use of his most Christian Majesty.

No Time has been lost in giving Efficacy & Despatch to both these Measures. Orders are Issued to the Naval Office to permit the Exportation of the Flour & Bread as requested.[1] I only wish that the French Gentlemen might be informed, that the Quality of ↑our↓ Flour this year is by no means equal to what it is in common Harvests, owing to the Weavil & other Accidents.[2]

In the Deliberation which was had on the Subject of furnishing the requisite Aid to attack Florida, the Council with myself, ever anxious to forward the Views of Congress, were not a little embarrassed. We have two Vessels called Ship Gallies drawing eight or nine feet water carrying about eighteen 3 or 4 pounders & one of them formed to use two heavy Guns in the Bow in still water with men, & about six smaller Gallies, calculated for Service in the Bay or rivers. The latter it is thought cannot without great Danger of Sinking, be sent to Sea. The former are therefore pitched upon to go on the Service required, if Congress think them fit. In the mean time Orders are given for them to be got in readiness which I'm informed w̶i̶l̶l̶ ̶h̶a̶p̶p̶e̶n̶ ↑may be↓ in three Weeks; and they will proceed to Charles Town unless they are countermanded by Congress.[3]

---

[1] On November 23, Governor Henry, with the advice of the Virginia Council, ordered permits for the *Gentille*, George Andre, and the *Adventurer*, Joseph Tassis, to sail from Petersburg with flour and bread for the French Navy. *Journals of the Council of Va.* (McIlwaine), II , 222.

[2] The size and quality of the wheat harvest in Maryland, Virginia, and North Carolina had been diminished by a wheat fly infestation. Conrad-Alexandre Gerard had informed Vergennes on July 25 that although provisions in general were "plentiful" in all states, there was a concern about "diseases which are attacking the grains of Virginia." *Delegate Letters* (Smith), XI, 354-355; Baisnée and Meng, "French Diplomacy," LVII (1946), 36.

[3] Governor Henry requested the Virginia Navy Commissioner to prepare the *Dragon* and *Tartar* for the expedition "there being no Gallies fit for the Service." *Journals of the Council of Va.* (McIlwaine), II, 222.

Besides these two Vessels there is the Ship Caswell belonging to this State Stationed in North Carolina to protect the Trade. She carrys about Guns 12, 9, & 6 pounders & 135 Men & draws about 5 feet Water. I write to Day to Governor Caswell to know if she can be spared,[4] & if possible to get hir added to the other two above described, for the expedition. When Congress were pleased to call for Vessels fitted for this particular Service, their Designs might have been answered if the Service had been explained. Not being favor'd with any such Explanation I have been obliged to proceed in uncertainty.

When General McIntosh was directed to begin his Operations on the Frontiers against the Indians I gave orders to 14 Counties beyond the Mountains to furnish him with any number of Militia he should call for. His Requisitions were sent to such of them as he chose long since. The Number of men sent to him, I know not. But a few Days ago three County Lieutenants appeared before the Council Board[5] & informed that their Counties & two others adjacent, were called upon by the General to send him 1,000 men immediately. These Gentlemen easily convinced the Executive, that it was impossible to comply with this Demand, because it would be the 20th December before the Men could be assembled at some rendezvous to begin the march, & that no Tents, Kettles, Horses, provisions or Necessaries were to be had for the Service: And because many of the Troops would have 400 Miles to proceed thro' a Country chiefly Desart, & utterly unfurnished with those Things which are essential to the Support of human Life at that inclement Season when the Snows are several Feet Deep on the great Ridges of Mountains, many of which lay in their Rout. Knowing therefore the utter impossibility of the measure, the Council unanimously concurred with me in judging it necessary to countermand General McIntosh's orders, & I have accordingly done so. The General shall

---

[4] Governor Henry wrote to his North Carolina counterpart on November 23, requesting the *Caswell* for the expedition, with the suggestion that one of the galleys could temporarily replace the ship. Richard Caswell agreed to the plan on December 1. *Official Letters of the Governors of Virginia* (Richmond, 1926-1929), I, 327-328; *State Records of North Carolina*, XIII, 309.

[5] The records of the Virginia Council do not give the names of the lieutenants, but the counties involved were Washington, Montgomery, Botetourt, Greenbriar, and Rockbridge. *Journals of the Council of Va.* (McIlwaine), II, 220.

be apprized of it as soon as possible, & will take his measures accordingly.[6]

I did myself the honor to inform you by Letter which I doubt from yours has not reached your Hands, of several matters respecting the marching of the Militia from this State to Charles Town, which was requested by Congress. When the requisition arrived here the Assembly was sitting. It became necessary to lay the matter before them as the Law gave the power of marching the Militia to a Sister State only in cases of actual Invasion. An Act was thereupon passed to enable the Executive to send out the Militia when <u>certain Intelligence</u> of an <u>intended</u> Invasion should be received. Just in the Instant when orders were going to be sent to put the men in motion for Charles Town, a Letter from Governor Johnston arrived, by which it was apparent the Enemy had no Designs on that place but it was said, meditated a Descent on the Eastern Shore. Upon this the Council thought with me it was proper to suspend the matter, & it has remained in that Suspense 'till the present Time.[7]

I send inclosed a List of sundry Acts of Congress received Since Sept last, most or all of which I thought I had acknowledged the Receipt of by particular addresses which I had the honor of send↑ing↓ you.__

The variety of Matter which the present occasion calls on me to mention will I hope plead my Excuse for the length of this Letter.

I beg to be presented to Congress in the most acceptable manner & in Terms expressive of that high Regard with which I have the Honour to be__

Sir / Y^r· mo. obed^t· & very hble Servt·

P. Henry

P.S.
I am looking out for a Messenger to carry your Despatches to Govr· Caswell__

SOURCE: RC, PCC (Item 71), DNA; no address; dated "W^{m}sburg Nov^r· 23^d· 1778__."; docketed by HL "Govr· Henry / 23^d· Nov^r- 1778 / Rec̄d 2^d- Decem̄ / Read 35^d__" and in another hand "Referred to the Marine / Com^{ee}·__".

---

[6] Letter not found.
[7] The militia was not sent to South Carolina at this time.

FROM JEAN-BAPTISTE TERNANT

Charles Town, November 23, 1778

Sir

In Spite of the ague & fever &c.__ I arrived at last in Charlestown on the 18th. inst, before any foreign ennemy had made his appearance, & so far I thought myself very lucky__ I have attended ever since to the cure of that terrible disorder with some kind of success; & as I was going to business after having had my appointment announced in the General orders &c. we received the desagreeable intelligence of the ennemy having landed to the number of 1200, on this side of Altamahaw river, & advancing very fast in Georgia__ [1] whatever may be the simple or complex design of the ennemy, as the distance between this town & Georgia is but small I have taken the resolution to set off immediately for savannha in order to offer my aid & services upon this emergency & afterwards return here, to fulfill the object of my mission.

your Excellency's friends have been very kind & polite to me; permit me to express my gratitude for your kind introductions, & assure that I am

with the greatest respect / your Excellency's / most obedient humble / servant

Ternant

source: RC, Laurens Collection, DLC; addressed on cover "his Excellency Henry Laurens Esq: / President of Congress. / Philadelphia"; dated "Charlestown Novemb. 23d. 1778"; docketed by HL "Coll. Ternant / 23d. Novr. 1778 / Recd 21st Decem".

---

[1] By mid November a force of some four hundred British Regulars, Rangers, and Indians, under the command of Col. Lewis V. Fuzer from St. Augustine, had moved north of the Altamaha and taken Sunbury. About the same time another smaller force under Lt. Col. Mark Prevost helped to prepare for the British invasion by raiding the areas around the Georgia settlements at Newport and Midway. The British invasion from New York commanded by Lt. Col. Archibald Campbell did not arrive off Tybee Island until December 23. Bennett and Lennon, *A Quest for Glory*, pp. 88-94; Robert Howe to HL, Nov. 24, 1778.

TO BENJAMIN LINCOLN

Philadelphia, November 24, 1778

Sir.

I have already written to you by this conveyance under the 16[th.] since which I have had the honor of receiving & presenting to Congress your favors of the 7[th.] & 9[th.] which are committed to the Board of Treasury for consideration & Report.

The injuries which you received by the fall from your carriage, I had heard of in much more alarming terms than your own account, I am rejoiced to learn, you were so well recovered as to be able to prosecute your Journey, I am in hopes the mild Climate of South Carolina will restore your strength.

Capt Barry having made some extraordinary demands on Congress, for allowance of a Table & a secretary, which the House have not determined upon, is detained here. I beleive Capt Barry to be a brave & active Seaman, but I am told by Gentlemen of the Marine Committee that the intended service is not pleasing to him, 'tis possible therefore he may wish to avoid it, & besides, you will find old Commanders in the two southern States who will be much mortified should he actually proceed & take the Command of them, consequences will arise which[1] will be disagreeable to you & which may prove detrimental to the service. I have suggested these sentiments to the Marine Committee, the determination of Congress will probably be known to morrow.[2]

Inclosed[3] with this be pleased to receive an Act of Congress of the 17[th.] Inst. for subjecting the Troops raised in the State of south Carolina to the same regulations as the other forces of the United States are under except in Cases governed by contrary stipulations; for explaining a Resolve of the 16[th.] September 1776 respecting the appointment of Officers on the general Staff & for appointing Capt

---

[1] "wh" written over "ma".

[2] On November 10 Congress, as a part of the plan to "reduce the province of East Florida" directed Capt. John Barry "to take the command of all the armed vessels employed on the intended expedition" and, "That he proceed...to the state of Maryland, in order to expedite the equipment of the galleys to be furnished by that state." The Marine Committee sent more particular orders November 20, including the combining of the Maryland and Virginia galleys into a single force. For whatever reason, as indicated by HL, Barry balked. The Marine Committee's report submitted December 2 was debated and recommitted, however, and Congress recorded no further action on the matter. *JCC,* XII, 1118-1120, 1184.

[3] "l" written over "o".

Ed. Hyrne ↑dep↓ adjut^t· gen: & Stephen Drayton Esqr- dep. Q M. gen. in the sothern department.[4]

I have the honor to be with great / Regard Sir Your obedient & most / hum servt

Henry Laurens.
President / of Congress

source: ALS, Berg Collection, NN; addressed below close "The Hoñble Major Gen. Lincoln / so Carolina."; dated "Philadelphia / 24th· Nov^r· 1778__"; docketed "President of Congress Novr 24__ 1778". LB, PCC (Item 13), DNA.

FROM ROBERT HOWE

Charles Town, November 24, 1778

Sir.

The letter by Col^o Ternant inclosing a Resolve of Congress by which I am recalled, has been delayed by the Illness of the Colonel untill a very few days since.

In obedience to that Order, I was just setting out when a Letter, a Copy of which I have the honour to transmit, arrived Express from Georgia,[1] the Imminent danger of that State, rendered very weak in the part assailed, by the necessity there had been for detaching a considerable number of the Regular Troops to the westward, to prevent the Ravages of the Indians, induced me to think that it was incumbent upon me to fly to the assistance of Georgia, with what Troops could be spared from hence, & that a short delay in my Setting out for the grand-Army, could be attended with no great inconvenience to the Service in that Quarter, and that the necessity I conceived Georgia to be in, would plead my excuse

---

[4] The November 17 resolution had been prompted by the continuing dispute between South Carolina governor Rawlins Lowndes and the Continental commander in the Southern Department, Robert Howe, over appointments. Congress determined that the Sept. 16, 1776, resolution upon which Lowndes claimed authority extended only to "regimental officers, and not to officers on the general staff." Rawlins Lowndes to HL, Aug. 31, 1778; *JCC*, XII, 1137-1138.

[1] The letter from Col. John White at Savannah November 21, contained the first news concerning the British preparations for invading Georgia. He estimated "The Number of the Enemy, by every Intelligence I have been able to collect, appears to be about 1100, five hundred of which, chiefly Horsemen, are come by Land." John White to Robert Howe, Nov. 21, 1778, PCC, Item 160, p. 503ff; Jean-Baptiste Ternant to HL, Nov. 23, 1778.

with Congress__ If Sir in this, I have thought wrong, I flatter myself that Congress, whose Candour I rely upon, will deduce the Action from the Motives and do me the justice to beleive, that my Conduct resulted from the firm persuasion I had, that I was promoting their Service, & consequently pursuing the Dictates of my duty which it will ever be both my Pride & pleasure to do__[2]

     In haste I am with the greatest Esteem & Respect.__ / Sir, / Your most Ob^t· / very hum^le Servant

                                Robert Howe

source: RC, PCC (Item 160), DNA; addressed below close "His Honor the President"; dated "Charles Town S^o· Carolina 24th Nov^r· 1778"; docketed by HL "Mj^r Gen~ Howe 24 Nov^r· / 1778 Rec^d_ 21^st_ Decem̃" and in another hand "Letter from Major gen R Howe / Charlestown nov^r· 24 1778 / inclosing letter of 21 from / from Col White. / notifying that Georgia is / invaded __ / Read 22 Dec^r· 1778__".

FROM JOHN ETTWEIN

                            Bethlehem, Pa., November 25, 1778
Honoured and Dear Sir,
     I received your Favour of the 23^d_, this Morning at 9. a clock, We are highly obliged to you for the previous Intimation of this high Visit, M^r_ Johnson prepared directly for their Reception and at 2. a clock they arrived Safe & Well. I should be glad if we could treat these Gentlemen agreeable to our Regard, we have for them, and the great Character they bear, but I can not promiss so much, yet we shall endeavour to please them & to make their Visit as agreeable to them, as the Season and Circumstances will permitt.

M^r_ Okely has seen what you wrote for him, I should be sorry for it, if he should trouble you good Sir with private concerns.

My Thankful Heart, for your great kindness to poor me and my

---

[2] Robert Howe remained in command of the Southern Department until he met Benjamin Lincoln at Purrysburgh, S.C., on Jan. 3, 1779. After that he took his time settling his affairs and started north on March 18. He arrived in Philadelphia April 26. Bennett and Lennon, *A Quest for Glory,* pp. 100-101.

Brethren, I cannot express, but I pray for your Happiness in all Respects and am in Truth
  Honoured Sir / your Humble & obedient / Servant
                                        John Ettwein

source: RC, HL Papers, ScHi; addressed on cover "To / His Excellency Henry Laurens / President in Congress / at / Philadelphia"; addressed below close "The Honorable Henry Laurens Esqr- / in Philadelphia"; dated below close "Bethlehem Nov^r- 25th- / 1778."; docketed by HL "Rev^d- Mr Edwin / 25$^{th.}$ Rec$^{d.}$ 26$^{th.}$ / Novr 1778__".

FROM JOHN HOUSTOUN
                          Savannah, Ga., November 25, 1778
Sir
    The Situation of this State at the present Moment is truly critical. On the 20$^{th.}$ Inst: a Body of the Enemy (supposed to be about 700) from East-Florida entered the State by Land, whilst another Body of between 4 & 500., attended with a small naval Force,__ came by water and landed on an Island called Colonel's Island, fordable at Low water, and opposite to the Town of Sunbury. these two Bodies, moving on in Concert, presently became Masters of the town of Sunbury, tho' not without some skirmishing in which we lost some valuable Men. the Fort however, at one End of the Town of Sunbury,__ still holds out, and I am hopeful will continue to do so untill we can afford it Relief. your Excellency knows the Predicament we have been ↑in↓ for some Months past, in respect to the Indians, which had in fact not only much diminished the Number of our Inhabitants in the General, but had particularly weaken'd the lower Part of the Country by drawing off the Troops and Volunteers, to the Westward, in opposition to the Indians. thus situated, and the Enemy's Expedition not having transpired, and their March exceedingly rapid, I must say their Success has exceeded even (as I conceive) their own Expectation.[1] they have marched thro' the whole Country, and are now advanced as near Savannah as within three Miles of Ogechee Ferry.[2] their Savage Warfare beggars De-

---

[1] "cta" written over other text. Possibly "Expedition" altered to "Expectation".
[2] The ferry across the Great Ogeechee River was above Hardwick about twenty miles west of Savannah.

scription, and brands their Names as well as their Cause with Infamy. not a House which they came across but was laid in ashes, and the plentiful well Settled Parish of St. John now presents one continued Scene of Horror Ruin & Devastation. even helpless women & infant Children were thought happy in having escaped with their Lives__ their Cloaths were refused them. By the extraordinary Exertions of General Screven of the Militia with about fifty Men, the Planters got off most of their Negroes, but vast Stocks of Cattle have fallen a Sacrifice. the General (whose Merit cannot be too much extolled) now languishes under five Wounds__ two of which he received after he fell. in short, Sir, when you read the History of the Conquest of Mexico, your Mind is season'd for the Tragedy of St. John's Parish. Col: Fuser[3] commands by Water, and Col: Prevost[4] by Land__ it was under the latter these Enormities were committed.

South Carolina as usual has ordered us the most ample & generous Assistance.__[5] if we can but maintain our Ground until that arrives, I trust we shall have full Satisfaction. I assure you, Sir, unless East-Florida is reduced, the Existence of Georgia, as a free & independent State is render'd very precarious. Your Excellency can have no Idea of our Weakness in the lower Part of the state, and whilst the Indians remain so troublesome not a Man will on any Emergence come from the back Country.

---

[3] Lt. Col. Lewis Valentine Fuzer of the 60th (Royal American) Regiment. Katcher, *British Army Units*, pp. 62-63.

[4] Lt. Col. James Mark Prevost of the 60th (Royal American) Regiment was the younger brother of Gen. Augustine Prevost, the commander of British troops in East Florida. After the British reestablished control of Georgia in early 1779 Lt. Col. Prevost served as lieutenant governor. Mowat, *East Florida as a British Province*, pp. 108, 122-123; Coleman, *American Revolution in Ga.*, pp. 119, 123-124.

[5] Upon receiving HL's letter of October 18, Gov. John Houstoun presented it to the Executive Council on November 19. The Council took the warning seriously and began to improve Georgia's defenses. They also sent an officer to Charleston to recruit sailors for the Georgia galleys. South Carolina military and civilian leaders responded to this invasion of Georgia because they believed it to be part of the larger British military plan that included the subjection of South Carolina as well. Gen. Robert Howe arrived at Zubly's Ferry on November 27 and applied to Gen. William Moultrie for more troops and supplies from South Carolina. *The Revolutionary Records of the State of Georgia*, ed. Allen D. Candler (3 vols.: Atlanta, 1908), II, 119; William Moultrie, *Memoirs of the American Revolution* (New York, 1802. Reprint, New York, 1968), I, 243-246; Searcy, *Georgia-Florida Contest*, pp. 159-164.

I have the Honor to be / with very great respect / Sir / y^r·
most Ob^t· hble s^t·

J. Houstoun

source: RC, Kendall Collection; addressed below close "His Excellency /
H: Laurens Esqr·"; dated "Savannah 25th· Nov^r· 1778."; docketed by HL "Govr
Houston 25 Nov^r· / 1778 Rec^d· 3 Jany 1779". Copy (19th century), HL Papers,
ScHi.

TO LORD STIRLING

Philadelphia, November 26, 1778

My Lord.

My last was under the 24th. since which I have been honored
with Your Lordship's favor of the 23d.—the packet which accompanied it is from Admiral Gombier, its contents, relate to Lieut. Hele
& others who were shipwrecked in a vessel on the Jersey Shore said
to have carried a flag in order to dispense Manifestos—The Admiral
is of opinion these people ought not to be confined, Congress have
a twofold reason for differing with him—These people have not
only called, but in every instance where it might be done as they
thought with impunity, treated us as Rebels—on the other hand
when it suited their Interest and purposes, they pretend to caput,
for they demand from us, refinements upon the practice of established Independent Nations—God be praised we are out of their
reach & I am persuaded our conduct will not be censored by any
Court of Europe, St James excepted, hitherto it has stood the Test.
& whenever it is brought into a fair of light of comparison even by
British historians, that of our Enemies will undergo severe strictures
of Condemnation.

Your Lordship will receive with this two of this Morning's
Advertisers which is all I have to offer except repeating that I am
with the highest Esteem & Respect

Sir Your Lordship's / Obedient & most hum / Servant

(Signed) Henry Laurens

source: Typescript, "William Alexander (Lord Stirling) Papers," Personal
Papers (Miscellaneous), DLC; no address; dated "Philadelphia / 26
Novem 1778".

FROM GEORGE WASHINGTON

Fredericksburg, N.Y., November 27, 1778

Sir,

I was yesterday honored with your favor of the 20th: with its several inclosures__ [1] Congress will be pleased to accept my acknowledgements for the communication of the treaties between his Most Christian Majesty and the United States__ The resolve respecting the exchange of Prisoners has been transmitted to Sir Harry Clinton, and I have appointed Commissioners if he thinks proper to meet his at Amboy the 7th. of next Month.__ [2]

I have the pleasure to inform Congress that the whole Army, one Brigade and the light Corps excepted is now in motion to the places of the respective cantonments for Winter Quarters. I have thought it prudent to delay this event, a while, to give time for the Convention Troops to make some progress in crossing the North river__ to prevent a possibility of accident. The third division passed this day and if no unexpected interruption happens the whole will be over the 30th. instant. When their passage is completed, the remaining Troops kept in the field will immediately retire to quarters.

The disposition for Winter quarters is as follows__ Nine Brigades will be stationed on the West side of Hudsons River, exclusive of the Garrison at West point, one of which, the North Carolina Brigade, will be near Smiths Clove for the security of that pass, and as a reinforcement to West Point, in case of necessity__ another, the Jersey Brigade will be at Elizabeth Town to cover the lower part of Jersey, and the other seven, consisting of the Virginia, Maryland, Delaware and Pensylvania Troops will be at middle

---

[1] HL wrote twice to Washington on November 20. A private letter primarily concerning the proposed Canadian Expedition is printed above. The public letter to which Washington refers here enclosed an act of November 17 calling for a general thanksgiving to be observed throughout the states, an act of November 19 concerning an exchange of Convention troops for American officers, and three copies of the Franco-American treaties. HL to George Washington, Nov. 20, 1778, PCC, Item 13; *JCC*, XII, 1138-1139, 1145-1146.

[2] Washington wrote to Sir Henry Clinton November 27, and named Cols. Robert Hanson Harrison and Alexander Hamilton as commissioners to meet Col. Charles O'Hara of the 2nd British Regiment and Col. West Hyde of the 1st British Regiment. Harrison and Hamilton reported December 15 that the meeting, delayed "by impediments of weather" until December 11, ended abruptly the next day when the British officers "objected to our powers, as not extending to the purposes they had in view." *Washington Writings* (Fitzpatrick), XIII, 348-349; *Hamilton Papers* (Syrett), I, 598-599.

Brook. six Brigades will be left on the East side of the River, and at West Point, three of which, of the Massachusetts Troops, will be stationed for the immediate defence of the Highlands__ one at West Point in addition to the Garrison already there, and the other two at Fishkill and the Continental Village__ the remaining three Brigades, composed of the New Hampshire and Connecticut Troops & Hazens Regiment, will be Posted in the vicinity of Danbury, for the protection of the Country lying along the Sound__ to cover our Magazines lying in Connecticut river and to aid the Highlands, on any serious movement of the Enemy that way.__ The Park of Artillery will be at Pluckemin. The Cavalry will be disposed of thus, Blands regiment at Winchester in Virginia__ Baylors at Frederick or Hagars Town in Maryland__ Moylans at Lancaster in Pennsylvania and Sheldons at Derham in Connecticut. Lees Corps will be with that part of the Army which is in the Jerseys, acting on the advanced Posts.

    This comprehends the general distribution of the Army, except Clintons Brigade of New York Troops Pulaski's Corps, and some detached regiments, and Corps, stationed at Albany and at different parts of the frontier, of which Congress have been already particularly informed. Genl Putnam will command at Danbury, Genl McDougal at the Highlands, and my own quarters will be in the Jerseys, in the neighbourhood of Middle Brook.

    This disposition appeared to me best calculated to conciliate, as far as possible, these several objects__ the protection of the country, the security of the important posts in the Highlands__ the safety, discipline, and easy subsistence of the Army. To have kept the Troops in a collected state would have increased infinitely the expence and difficulty of subsisting them, both with respect to forage and provisions__ To have divided them into smaller cantonments__ would have made it far less practicable to maintain order and discipline among them__ and would have put them less in a condition to controul and prevent offensive operations on the side of the Enemy__ or to assemble to take advantage of any favourable opening, which their future situation may offer, should they be obliged to weaken themselves by further detachments, so far as to invite an enterprize against them.

    By the estimate of the Quarter Master and Commissary General it appeared indispensible to have the principal part of the

Army on the ↑other↓ side of the North River. It was thought, impracticable to furnish the necessary supplies of flour for the whole on this side of the river, from the immense difficulty and expence of transportation in the Winter season, and from the exhausted state of the country, with respect to forage. As this subject has been already fully before Congress__ I shall not trouble them with a repetition of the detail.__

In order as much as possible to reduce the demand of forage and facilitate the supplies, I have given directions when the several divisions arrive at their cantonments, to send away to convenient places at a distance from them, all the horses not absolutely requisite to carry on the ordinary business of the army.

It is unnecessary to add, that the Troops must again have recourse to the expedient of hutting, as they did last year, but as they are now well clad, and we have had more leisure to make some little preparations, for Winter quarters__ I hope they will be in a more comfortable situation than they were in the preceding Winter.

With the highest respect & esteem / I have the honor to be / Sir / Y^r. Most Obet servant

G$^{o:}$ Washington

source: RC, PCC (Item 152), DNA; addressed below close "His Excellency / Henry Laurens Esqr."; dated "Head Quarters Fredericks / burg Novr 27th. 1778"; docketed "Letter from gen^l Washington / Novr 27. 1778 / Read Decr 3. 1778 / relative to the winter quar / ters of the army / Entered page 138 / Examined". Draft, Washington Papers, DLC.

FROM PATRICK HENRY

Williamsburg, Va., November 28, 1778

Sir,

Your favor of the 16th inst. is come to hand together with the Acts of Congress of the 26th. of August for establishing provision for Soldiers & Seamen maimed or disabled in the public Service__ of the 26th. September for organizing the Treasury, a Proclamation for a General Thanksgiving. & three Copies of the Alliance between his most Christian Majesty & these united States__

I lost no time in laying your Letter before the Privy Council & in deliberating with them on the Subject of sending 1000 Militia to Charles Town S°· Carolina. I beg leave to assure Congress of the great Zeal of every Member of the Executive here, to give full Efficacy to their Designs on every occasion. But on the present, I am very sorry to Observe, that Obstacles great & I fear unsurmountable, are opposed to the immediate March of the Men. upon Requisition to the Deputy Quarter Master General in this Department,[1] for Tents Kettles Blankets & Waggons, He informs they cannot be had. the Season when the March must begin will be severe & inclement, & without the forementioned Necessaries impracticable to Men indifferently Clad & equipped as they are in the present general scarcity of Clothes.

The Council as well as myself are not a little perplexed, on comparing this Requisition to defend South Carolina & Georgia from the Assaults of the Enemy with that made a few Days past for Gallies to conquer East Florida. The Gallies have orders to rendezvous at Charles Town, which I was taught to consider as a place of acknowledged Safety; And I beg leave to observe that there seems some Degree of Inconsistency in marching militia such a Distance in the Depth of Winter under the Want of Necessaries to defend a place which the former measure seemed to declare safe.__

The Act of Assembly whereby it is made lawful to order this march confines the operations to measures merely Defensive to a sister state & of whose Danger there is certain Information rec^d·

However as Congress have not been pleased to explain the matters herein alluded to, & altho a good deal of perplexity remains with me on the Subject, I have by advice of the Privy Council given orders for 1000 Men to be instantly got into readiness to march to Charles Town, and they will march as soon as they are furnished with Tents, Kettles and Waggons In the mean Time if Intelligence is received, that their march is essential to the preservation of either the States

---

[1] Col. William Finnie of Williamsburg had been appointed deputy quartermaster general for Virginia by Gov. Patrick Henry in 1775, and Congress named him deputy quartermaster for the state on March 28, 1776. He continued in that capacity until the end of the war. Heitman, *Continental Officers; Greene Papers* (Showman), III, 52, 83n; Risch, *Supplying Washington's Army,* pp. 31-32.

of S^{o.} Carolina or Georgia The men will encounter every difficulty & have Orders to proceed in the best way they can without waiting to be supplied with those necessaries commonly afforded to Troops even on a Summers march.

I have to beg that Congress will please to remember the State of Embarrassment in which I must necessarily remain with Respect to the ordering Gallies to Charles Town in their way to invade Florida, while the Militia are getting ready to defend the States bordering on it, & that they will please to favor me with the earliest Intelligence of every Circumstance that is to influence the Measures either offensive or Defensive__

I have the honor to be / Sir / y^{r.} mo: obed. & very / Hble Servant__

P. Henry
P.S.

The Dispatches to Govr. Caswell are sent by a safe hand

SOURCE: RC, PCC (Item 71), DNA; no address; dated "W^msburg Novr 28th 1778__"; docketed "Nov 28th, 1778 / Letter from his Exc^y gov^r / Henry of Virginia / Novr. 28 1778 / Read Decr 8. 1778 / Referred to Marine Com^e".

TO LORD STIRLING

Philadelphia, November 29, 1778

My Lord.

I had the honor of writing to Your Lordship yesterday; Will[1] you permit me now to ask a very great favor of Your Lordship, designed more for the public benefit than for my private convenience or amusement, that Your Lordship will endeavor to procure for me as early as may be, one or two Copies of Vatell's Law of Nations, I would rather have two than one; when I learn the cost of it or them, the amount in Gold or Silver shall be immediately remitted.[2]

---

[1] "W" written over "w".
[2] Admiral Gambier claimed in his November 15 letter that the actions taken by Congress in holding the officer and crew of the wrecked *Hotham* despite their carrying a flag of truce

Inclosed herein Your Lordship will find a Copy of Admiral Gambier's Letter & my answer, spoken of in my Official Letter of this date, 'tis highly probable both will soon be published, at present these Copies are intended for Your Lordship's private information & no further.

I intreat you Sir to pardon the liberty I have taken on the present occasion & beleive me to be with very great respect & Esteem

Your Lordship's / Obliged & obedient humble / servant
Henry Laurens.

source: ALS, NNPM; addressed below close "The Right Honorable / The Earl of Stirling / Elizabeth Town."; dated "Philadelphia 29th. November / 1778__"; docketed "From / President Congress / Novr. 29. —78"; noted "(Private)".

FROM THE MARQUIS DE LAFAYETTE

Fishkill, N.Y., November 29, 1778

dear Sir

Running very fast is not alwaïs the best way of arriving soon__ I am a very Melancholic exemple of that true saying, and a very severe fit of illness did put me very near of Making a greater Voyage than this of Europe__[1] I have been detain'd till this instant, and find myself able to set off to day for Boston.

I am under the Necessity of sending an express to Congress for several Reasons which are explain'd in my public letter__ it will be directed to you because I understand you have been prevail'd upon to act yet for some days as a president of Congress__ I dare

---

was a "procedure...against the universal Law of Nations." HL may have sought the work to support the position of Congress. Emmerich de Vattel, *The Law of Nations* was first published in English at London in 1760.

[1] In his memoir Lafayette noted that he "had been taxed by his travels and exertions" and before he left Philadelphia for Boston where he planned to embark "he had stayed up all night, had drunk freely, and worked very hard." He traveled through heavy rain while suffering with fever and finally stopped at Fish Kill, N.Y. where he was put to bed with "an inflammatory illness." Dr. John Cochran, Surgeon General of the Middle Department, treated him and after three weeks he recovered. *Lafayette Papers* (Idzerda), II, 17-18.

hope those gentlemen will not spend in deliberating a time which schould Much Retard my arrival in france__ I ardently desire the dispatches would be sent back to head quarters without loss of time, from where gāl Washington will forward them to Boston where they schall be expected with the greatest impatience[2]

I beg you would be so good As to send me several exemplaries of the gazette where our letters and the Resolve of Congress have been printed__[3] if they had not been printed what I Ca'nt Believe they Might be sent immediately to the press__ be so good, My dear Sir, as to order the express before going off to take the Commands of the king's minister, the Marine Committee, Mr̄s Moriss and Carmichall and the other gentlemen who Could want to write to me.

if Colonel john Laurens is yet in philadelphia I beg you to present him My best Compliments, and assure him how sorry I am to quit this Country without having the pleasure of embracing him.

I Confess, My good friend, that mr̄ du plessis's promotion increased my desires in favor of my dear mr̄ gimat.

Farewell, My dear Sir, do'nt forget Ɨ our friendship and Believe me for ever with the sentiments of the highest Regard and Sincerest affection

Your most obedient Servant

lafayette

source: RC, HL Papers, ScHi; addressed at bottom of first page "Colonel henry Laurens Esq. &c &c."; dated "Fish kills 29ᵗʰ November 1778"; docketed by HL "Marquis delafayette / 29 Novem̄ 1778 / Recᵈ· 3ᵈ· Decem̄ / Ansᵈ· 6ᵗʰ·".

---

[2] In his public letter of the same date, Lafayette listed four points for which he requested action. First, he had not received instructions "for what I was to do in case Doctor Franklin's death or illness." Second, he continued to lobby for Gimat's promotion. Third, he sought a resolve from Congress, that he could carry during the voyage, which would provide for his exchange for one of the Convention Army generals if his ship was taken on the high seas. And finally, he asked for a firm answer about "the Resolv'd expedition into Canada," so he could explain in France "if there will be an American cooperation." Lafayette to HL, Nov. 29, 1778, PCC, Item 156, p. 77ff.

[3] In his reply, HL recalled "no remembrance of the printing of the Letters you allude to." Congress ordered, on December 17, "That the resolutions of 9 September, and 21 October last, in favour of the Marquis de la Fayette, together with the letters written by the President in consequence thereof, and the Marquis's answer, be published." HL to Lafayette, Dec. 6, 1778; *JCC,* XII, 1227; *Pa. Packet,* Dec. 27, 1778.

FROM WILLIAM HENRY DRAYTON

Philadelphia, November 30, 1778

Dr Sir.

I am entirely of opinion that there is not only much more villany in the transaction of our public Affairs ~~can~~ ↑than↓ we can fathom, but more than we have any idea of. This Spanish Cargo discovers new wheels which have been running to private advantage under the guidance of public Agents.[1] What can be done!

I am glad De Francy is so sensible of the merit of your offer.[2] You will Pardon me when I tell you, that when you made it, I felt what your Son would have felt, had he heard you make it. It was an action worthy of you, greatly advantageous to the Public, & honourable to your Constituents. You took the lead in a Patriotic conduct__ but there are none who are able or have the virtue to follow it. I can only admire & applaud; Being with great respect

D^r- Sir, / Your most affectionate / humble Ser^t-

W^m H^y- Drayton.

source: RC, HL Papers, ScHi; addressed on cover "His Excellency / Henry Laurens Esqr-"; dated below close "Monday"; docketed by HL "Mr. Drayton / on Beamarchais' / affair &c / 30 Novr. 1778__"; note below docket: "which clearly shews that / Mr. Drayton had not been / deluded, altho he had been / tempted, until after my re / signation of the Presiden / cy__ the 9 Decem~__".

---

[1] HL's comments, on the cover of this document, "that Mr. Drayton had not been deluded, altho he had been tempted" and had not clearly sided with the Deanites until after HL's resignation helps shed light on the meaning of this paragraph. In "Spanish Cargo" Drayton is employing the term Spanish in one of its obscure eighteenth century uses to mean "mixed." He is critical of the public officials like Deane and Robert Morris who enriched themselves by mixing private cargoes with trade carried on in behalf of Congress.

[2] Théveneau de Francy, Beaumarchais' agent, had written to HL November 28, requesting that Congress "determine upon some measure immediately that a quantity of 2000 or 3000 Hog^{ds.} of Tobacco be provided to be remitted in Vessels which I expect every instant, & to order that this Commercial transaction may be at last established upon some regular plan." In his appeal Francy reviewed the contract between Beaumarchais and the Commercial Committee and noted that American debt had risen to more than £300,000 sterling. The letter, read in Congress later that day, was referred to a committee composed of Meriwether Smith, William Ellery, and Drayton. The editors have not located a response. Théveneau de Francy to HL, Nov. 28, 1778, PCC, Item 78, Vol. 9, p. 209ff; *JCC*, XII, 1168.

NOTES FOR A SPEECH TO CONGRESS
December 1778[1]

South Carolina, admitting a full Months time for preparation, & no alarms from the Indians, may bring into the Field__ 10,000 Men, one half of them badly clad & as badly Armed__

   should the Indians be in action or threatning the Inhabitants of the back Country will not leave their families exposed on that frontier__

in such Case 4 or 5 thousand is the most Militia that can possibly be collected for defence of the Sea Coast__

the Enemy by landing 2000__ at Winyaw[2] will meet little[3] or no opposition in plundering & ravaging all the Northern part

2000 more landed at Beaufort may act in the same manner to the Southward including all the Islands

   5000 with a few frigates may very easily take possession of Fort Johnson & Charles Town__ securing the mid-country.

   Fort Moultrie falls of course without firing a Gun against it. Plunder__

   not less than 50000 Barrels of Rice in three Weeks.
   immense quantities of Indian Corn Pease, Flour &c
   Indigo at least half a Million
   horned[4] Cattle Sheep Hogs &c
   10,000 Negroes__

   very great quantities of Merchandize__ 150 to 200 Sail
   of Ships & other Vessels for transporting the Provision
   & Negroes__ Warlike Stores &c.

---

[1] It is unclear when HL wrote these notes. His own notation indicates that he was concerned with "the danger to which So Carolina & Georgia were exposed in Decem 1778." But the points expressed could have been made at any time during the fall or winter of 1778, after the intelligence concerning a British invasion from Robert Williams about September 23 and before the report of British activity in Georgia that began in November and was received in Philadelphia in late December. *JCC*, XII, 949-950, 1021.

   HL wrote the following on the verso of the second page: "Notes, from whence I / remonstrated to Congress / on the danger to which / So Carolina & Georgia / were exposed in / Decem 1778__ / which I had often / done at former / periods__".

[2] "aw" written over other text.

[3] "i" written over "a".

[4] "horned" written in left margin.

We have no fleet to retake the place__ if we call foreign aid, it will be ineffectual__ because four fifty Gun Ships & six frigates within will bid defiance to the whole fleet of france.

Georgia will fall immediately or may be over run by the Troops from S[t.] Augustine & 500 Indians.

SOURCE: AD, Society of the Cincinnati Collection, DLC; no date.

FROM LORD STIRLING
                                    Elizabethtown, N.J., December 1, 1778
Dear Sir

I have to acknowledge the honor of haveing received your two letters of the 28[th:] & 29[th.]__ If the Event of the Battle your mention in the former should turn out to be, as it has been reported to you; it will be such a Check to the late lords of the Occean, as will not only lower their Crests, but put that Haughty Nation in the Utmost terror and Confusion, hitherto the Ballance between the two powers, has been kept up, by the one being Superior at Land, the other at Sea, If this Action at Sea, should give France but a Small Ballance in her favour, they will have both points in their hand, and poor Old England must Soon Sing piano[1]

Such an Event together with the disasters Admiral Byrons fleet has met with, the dismasting and Absence of most of their frigates on Convoys &c will give a fine oppertunity for our Trade to pass in Safety and will undoubtly have an Influence on our Stocks, and tend to bring the Whole Oeconomy of our Affairs into their Natural Channels, our Stocks are our paper Bills or Certifycate's, the Stocks of all Nations who Borrow under any denomination will rise or fall according to the Events of War; In our Scituation it will be more particularly so__ Such favourable Events as lately appear, will Command a General belief with Tories as well as Wigs that the Contention with Great Brittain will soon terminate in our favor to our Utmost Wishes. This makes me rise in hopes that the Spirit of Avarice of will be Gluted, and with all my Soul I wish it may be Smothered.

---

[1] More softly.

I offer this as some Consolation to your apprehensions in yours of the 24ᵗʰ· I wish I could offer more.[2]

In the public letter which accompanies this, you will find that I sent Capt Combs[3] this Morning with a flag to Carry your letter to Admiral Gombier and the Event of it, I sent the Captain in hopes that the Admiˡ would have detained him, I[n] which[4] Case I should have Complained to Sir Henry Clinton of the Infraction, and Should have informed him there was an [end] of all Intercourse or Truce on any busyness Whatever 'till the Captain was restored, and I belive the Knight of the Red Ribbon,[5] would have Complyed rather than loose his favourite Treaty on the 7ᵗʰ· at Amboy.[6]

I have this day wrote to Mʳ Elliot Superindent General[7] for three Copies of Vatells Law of Nations, and if they are to be had at New York I am sure he will send them; he lately applyed to me for a printed Copy of General Lee's Tryal, If one can be procured & you think it proper to be sent, I should be glad you would enable me to Oblige him, It will enable me to get any thing[8] from them in the literary way.

You may be Assured no other use than what you wish will be made of the Several enclosures you have been[9] so Obliging as to send me for my private Information.

With Sincere Esteem & Regard / I am Your Excellencys / Most Obedient and / Most Humble Servᵗ·

Stirling,

---

[2] HL's November 24 letter, from which late nineteenth century dealer catalog extracts are available, included the president's lament that the "Spirit of Virtue, Patriotism and Economy which we pretended to possess in 1775" had passed away. *Dodd, Mead and Company's Catalogue of Autographs and Manuscripts* (Philadelphia, 1893), p. 36.

Extra space interpreted as paragraph.

[3] Capt. John Combs of New Jersey returned and reported that "he was not permitted to proceed further than the sloop George at the Mouth of the Kills between Staten Island and Bergen Point" where the dispatches were received and forwarded to Admiral Gambier. Lord Stirling to HL, Dec. 1, 1778, PCC, Item 162, p. 551ff; John Combs to Lord Stirling, Dec. 1, 1778, PCC, Item 162, p. 555ff; Heitman, *Continental Officers*.

[4] "h" written over other text, possibly "a".

[5] Sir Henry Clinton had been invested with the Order of the Bath, symbolized by a red ribbon, on April 11, 1777. Willcox, *Portrait of a General*, pp. 137-138, 141.

[6] Negotiations for a prisoner of war exchange, to include Convention Army officers, was scheduled for December 7, at Amboy, N.J. George Washington to HL, Nov. 27, 1778.

[7] Andrew Elliot (1728-1797) served as superintendent general of police in New York City. He had served as customs collector before the Revolution and would be appointed New York's last royal lieutenant governor in 1780. *PMHB*, XI (1887), 129-150.

[8] "t" written over other text.

[9] "been" written over other text.

past 12 °Clo.

I dare not longer detain the Express or would myself Copy over the public Letter

SOURCE: RC, Kendall Collection; addressed below close "The Honorable Henry Laurens"; dated "Elizabeth Town Decem^r. 1: 1778__"; docketed by HL "Lord Stirling / 31^dst. Decem̃ 1778 / Rec^d. the 3^d / Answ^d. 5th"; noted "(Private)". Copy (19th century), HL Papers, ScHi.

TO PATRICK HENRY

Philadelphia, December 2, 1778

Sir

I had the honor of addressing Your Excellency under the 16th Ultimo, and on the 18th of receiving and presenting to Congress your favor of the 9th.

Within the present Cover will be found two Acts of Congress viz.

1. of the 24th November for ↑further↓ arranging the Army. 6 Copies.
2. An Act of the 30th for obtaining Forage for the Army of these United States.[1]

When I was about closing this Letter Your Excellency's favor of the 23^d Ultimo was brought to me, three days passed over before other important Affairs under consideration of Congress before the House would permit it to be received. Yesterday it was read and committed to the Marine Committee whence I hope it will soon be returned with a proper Report. I had with Colonel Smiths'[2] consent detained this Messenger from the 28th Ultimo to the 2nd Instant for the printed Arrangements, amused by the Printer with promises of having them finished much sooner, and from the 2nd to this day, from a prospect of receiving a determination from Congress re-

[1] HL sent brief cover letters enclosing these two acts of Congress to each state and Generals Benjamin Lincoln and John Sullivan.

[2] Meriwether Smith was sometimes called "colonel." Robert Douthat Meade, *Patrick Henry, Practical Revolutionary* (Philadelphia and New York, 1969), p. 106.

specting the Gallies without the intervention of a Report. This day the 6th, and Sunday too, I have had such a variety and quantity of Public business on my hands as has rendered it impracticable for me to add these few lines till 8 o'clock P.M. the whole detention nine days, for which I shall order Payment of the expences of Man and Horse.

I can assure Your Excellency from the best authority that in the Month of August the Court of St. James' applied to that of Madrid to use its influence in mediating between the former and the Court of Versailles. Spain listened and required the terms, these being disclosed, but I have not time to relate particulars, were highly resented by the King of Spain as an insult upon himself because they were inconsistent with the dignity of his good Ally, Spain was in the middle of September in motion with all her Armaments bespeaking the very near approach to hostilities.[3]

I have the honor to be &c.

SOURCE: LB, PCC (Item 13), DNA; addressed "Governor Henry / Virginia / by Thomas Ripley"; dated "2nd December".

TO SILAS DEANE

Philadelphia, December 3, 1778

Sir

On Tuesday I had the honor of ↑received and↓ presented[1] your Letter of the 30th Tuesday ↑Ultimo↓ to Congress and received direction from the House to intimate to intimate to you that the House having resolved to take into consideration as on this evening the state of their foreign Affairs such branches as you have been

---

[3] William Ellery reported to Gov. William Greene of Rhode Island on December 8 that HL told him that Conrad-Alexandre Gérard had informed him about the British attempt to gain Spanish mediation in their dispute with France. *Delegate Letters* (Smith), XI, 305; Conrad-Alexandre Gérard to HL, Dec. 8, 1778. For a discussion of the British attempt to engage the Spanish as mediators in 1778 see Dull, *French Navy*, pp. 114, 127-137.

[1] "ed" written over "ing".

particularly concerned in, would in due course become subjects of deliberation without any, avoidable or unnecessary, delay.[2]

I should have given you this information Yesterday had not the very long Sessions of Congress morning and evening together with very full employment in Public business in the interval rendered it impracticable.

I have the honor to be &c.

SOURCE: LB, PCC (Item 13), DNA; addressed "The Hoñble. Silas Deane Esqr / Philada. / by M. Young"; dated "3d. December / 10 o'Clock".

FROM JOHN LEWIS GERVAIS

Charles Town, December 3, 1778

Dear Sir,

Just now I learn at the Presidents that one Mr- Saxton sets off very early to Morrow Morning for Philadelphia, & that the Letters must be Sent to him this Evening__ By this oppertunity I acknowledge the receipt of your favours of the 6th Octr by Colonel Turnant & of the 28th Octr· by a Vessel from Philadelphia[1] with a receipt for three barrels of Apples, one I sent to our Friend Mr Manigault one, I divided between his Excellency the President & the late President, & on the third we Feast; with some of our Friends Mrs: Gervais returns you many thanks for this acceptable present, & wishes she had something nice to send to you__

My last was of the 14th: Ulto: & was to go by an Express of Mr Livingston which I hope will come to hand before this__

This day came to Town 8 Casks of Indigo, part of Mount Tacitus Crop__ I hope when the embargo is taken off it will fetch £3.15 or £4. ⅌ Pound

---

[2] Deane had complained that he was "still so unhappy as to be without the honor of any reply to the several letters I have wrote through you to Congress." The press of business abroad, he said, obliged him "most earnestly to entreat the attention of Congress to my situation and requests." The resolve stated "That after tomorrow Congress will meet two hours at least each evening, beginning at six o'clock, Saturday evening excepted, until the present state of our foreign affairs shall be fully considered." Silas Deane to HL, Nov. 30, 1778, PCC, Item 103, p. 163; *JCC*, XII, 1181.

[1] Neither of these letters is extant.

We have suffered a great Loss__ Our Friend William Brisbane died in Town last Saturday__ he was Sick ever since last September__ As this unfortunate Event has taken place, I am glad Mr̲ Baillie is at Wright Savannah.__[2] I hope by his attention & assiduity your Interest will not Suffer in that Quarter Casper[3] thinks he has made a tolerable good Crop ~~last~~ this[4] Year, if it turns out as well in thrashing as it appears in the Stalk__ I intended to have Sent the Augusta boat there before now__ but I thought it would not be prudent to send her away so far before we are sure, the Ennemy's Operations are not intended against us this Winter__ Since the apprehensions of an attack upon Charles Town appear less probable, I have been prevented by the real Invasion of Georgia, from St Augustine, who have had possession of Sunbury, & whose privateers have been on this Coast__ & ~~illegible~~ taken 12 or 15 Negroes on a plantation at Black point near Tybee,__[5] & Capt Osborn lately exchanged from here, was decoyed from his privateer on board of a Small State Vessel of Georgia__ but his Vessel was not taken, under these Circumstances I thought it would be imprudent to run the risque to Send the Boat to the Southward__ I sent her to Mepkin for a load of Ruff Rice, but as they had none beat yet she brought a Load of Fire Wood__ which is a good Article it sells from £14. to £16. ⅌ Cord__

Alto̲ we have a General embargo, on Acct̲ of the dreaded attack yet Rice keeps up from £4.10. to £5 ⅌ Ct̲

General Howe is gone to Georgia as also Col: Turnant & Capt: Senff__ By the last Accts̲ the Ennemy has retired from Sunbury to New port__[6] where[7] they were entrenching themselves__ they summon'd the Fort at Sunbury, the Commanding Officer refused to Surrender__ ↑they↓ did not get possession of it__ Brigr Genl

---

[2] William Alexander Brisbane, who resided on the New River in St. Luke Parish, acted as HL's agent for his southern plantations. James Baillie was one of HL's most trusted overseers. *HL Papers*, XI, 75n, 264-265, 458-459, 561-562.

[3] Casper Springer had been HL's overseer at Wrights Savannah plantation since 1773. *HL Papers*, VIII, 89; IX, 108, 416; XII, 85.

[4] "this" written in left margin.

[5] The unnamed plantation was probably on Black River, S.C., an area just south of HL's Wrights Savannah plantation and just north of Tybee Island.

[6] The area south of Sunbury, Ga., on the Midway River to the lower Newport River which contained an extensive network of rice plantations. David R. Chesnutt, *South Carolina's Expansion into Colonial Georgia, 1720-1765* (New York and London, 1989) pp. 83-124.

[7] "where" written over other text.

Screven of St. John's parish who was wounded in some Skirmish is dead of his Wounds__[8] they have burnt a great Number of plantations, but have not destroyed Sunbury__ I am of opinion they came in Search of provision, & perhaps in hopes of being joined by a great number of Tories or Indians. I wish the Conquest of East Florida, was determined upon, & measures taken accordingly,__ but it must not be done by halves, We must have the command of St John's river by a Naval force__ M$^{rs.}$ Gervais respect wait on you & I am Sincerely Your affectionate & / most Obed$^{t.}$ Serv$^{t.}$

JL Gervais

P.S. I have not heard how the Election has turned out for Charles Town__ I am told the poll was not finished to day at 12 oClock__[9]

SOURCE: RC, HL Papers, ScHi; addressed below close "His Ex^y Henry Laurens."; dated "Charles Town 3^d December 1778"; docketed by HL "John L. Gervais. / Esqr- 3$^{d.}$ Decem̄ 1778__ / Rec̄d. 3$^{d.}$ Jan̄ry 1779. / Ans$^{d.}$ 7th-".

FROM RAWLINS LOWNDES

Charles Town, December 3, 1778

Dear Sir__

M$^{r.}$ Saxton the Bearer this Moment called on me and informs ~~he~~ me that he sets out for Philadelphia to Morrow Morning very early and it is now 8 oClock at Night__ I shall therefore only give you a short Acc$^t.$ of Affairs in Georgia__ You have heard that that State was Invaded with an Armed Force from E. Florida; partly Rangers and Scoflety[1] amounting to ab$^t.$ five hundred Men who Arrived at Altamahaw and from thence proceeded by Land; the rest Regulars ↑ab$^t.$ the same number↓ who came by Water landed a few Miles S$^{o.}$ of the Fort at Sunbury, marched on the beach and entered

---

[8] Gen. James Screven of Georgia died from wounds suffered November 24, at the Battle of Midway. Searcy, *Georgia-Florida Contest*, pp. 161-162.

[9] The election for the South Carolina legislature had been held in late November. Some of the results appeared in the *S.C. General Gazette* Dec. 3, 1778, while those selected for Charleston, including HL, appeared the following week.

[1] Scoflety, a variation of Coffellite or Scoffellite—the terms used to refer to South Carolina backcountry Loyalists and Loyalist refugees in East Florida. The name originated from followers of Joseph Coffell (Scofel, Scophol, Scovil), a backcountry agitator and leader both during the Regulator movement and the Revolution. *HL Papers*, XIII, 114n.

the Town__ a little before they did so Co^lo. White found means to throw into the Fort some Regular Troops & a few Militia who Sustained the Fort and by the Acc^ts. last Rec^d__ the Enemy had retired from thence without doing any Mischief there and had formed a junction with the other Forces at New Port Bridge[2] where the whole were Intrenching themselves__ that part which came by Land had Skirmished with our People too weak to make any great resistance & had obliged them to retreat as far as Ogeche Ferry where they made a Stand__ and from whence the Enemy have retreated to New Port & joined their Regulars__ laying waste and destroying all the plantations and Effects that came in their way not Sparing the Meeting house at Medway with every mark of Ferocity & barbarity that can Characterize the Savage__ Col^s. Prevost and Fuser Command this Expedition, and Genl. Screvin is killed on our side, Shot several times after he had been Conquered__ Col^o. Prevost in a Lett^r. he writes to Col^o.- White in An^s to one sent him Apologizes for the Conduct of his People or rather the Irregulars disclaims having any hand in it but at the same time insists that it is a just retalitation and threatens that if he meets with any Opposition he shall revenge it by repetition__[3] he threatens also with Terifick words to bring the Indians ready at his command into the heart of the Country if they do not Surrender the Country untill the Disputes between England & America are adjusted and hopes they will attribute his demand to his desire of saving Lives, and avoiding the Calamity of War which the State will otherwise be Subjected to__ The suddenness and Rapidity with which this Incursion was made and the Consternation naturally resulting and the unprepared State in which Georgia was Surprizd has Occasioned their Efforts to be very feeble & inadequate to their danger and has given the Enemy great advantage over them and the Militia to the Westward are still very tardy & inert, whether from timidity or disaffection or both Causes I dont pretend to say but they have as yet contributed nothing towards the deliverance of their Country__ We have been endeavouring to aid them as well as we co^d. but the uncertainty of

---

[2] South of Sunbury on the Newport River.
[3] John White to James Prevost, Nov. 20, 1778; Prevost to White, Nov. 22, 1778. George White, *Historical Collections of Georgia: ....Relating to Its History And Antiquities, from Its First Settlement to the Present Time* (New York, 1854), pp. 524-525.

our own Security has dictated more Caution than was reconcileable to a Spirited and Effectual Succour and tho' we have been informed of this Event ever since the 21st ult^o.^ at Night and have used our utmost diligence none of our Force had crossed Savanah two days ago__ But by this time I please my self with the expectation that the most of them are approaching the Enemy as our last Account say our People were put not far from Purysburgh__ We have destined for the Aid of Georgia the whole of Thomsons Reg^t.^ out of which Certainly may be reckoned 350 Men__ Col^o.^ Hugers Detachment 180__ Col^o.^ Sumpter 130__ Col^o.^ Roberts detachm^t.^ 40.__ from Col^o.^ Beales Reg^t.^ of Militia 300__ Col^o^ Skirvings 240.__ [4] a number superior to that of the Enemy exclusive of the whole strength of Georgia and I flatter my self the next Acc^ts.^ will inform that the Enemy have precipitately abandoned their post if their plan is not Combined with an expectation of Reinforcem^ts.^ which may Arrive in the mean time their Naval force is Contemptable and yet S^r.^ with our utmost ingenuity and Efforts we have not been able to Equip a Fleet sufficient to face them for want of Men altho' the Town is full of Seamen__ they will not enlist, the Merchants retain their men in full pay expecting the Embargo to be taken of could ~~be~~ we have Succeeded in this Attempt we might have Atchieved great things__ but after spending £4000 in rendesvousing and giving 20 Dollars bounty besides we obtained 40 Men and so was obliged to relinquish the Scheme__ This State is now under an Alarm (fired yesterday) in order to enforce Obedience to Military Arrangements from the Penaltys Applicable at such a juncture__ [5] and Detachm^ts.^ from every Reg^t.^ are ordered to be Embodied & rendesvousd at different places adjacent to C Town to be prepard ag^st.^ the worst__ And the North Carolinians it is said are on their March so that we shall have a Military Shew and at least an expensive Camp[6]

Col^o.^ Williamson is in the Creek Country with a Considerable body of Men ab^t.^ 600 from Carolina besides what has joined him from Georgia, gone to the Oakmalgies after a Camp of disaffected

---

[4] Col. William Thomson commanded the 3rd S.C. Regiment, Col. Isaac Huger the 5th S.C. Regiment, Col. Thomas Sumter the 6th S.C. Regiment, and Col. Owen Roberts the 4th S.C. Regiment. Cols. John Beale and William Skirving commanded S.C. militia.

[5] "An Act for the better settling and regulating the militia..." provided a £100 fine for militia who failed to report to their companies in response to an alarm. *S.C. Statutes,* IX, 617, 674-675.

[6] "C" written over other text.

Creeks & Cherokees whom it is said their respective Nations woud be pleased to have set off__ this may be favourable to the Georgians at this time and Awe the Indians from taking any part with the Florida Troops__ Genl Howe repaird to Georgia on the first Intelligence of the disturbance without waiting to be accompanied with any Troops__ By the best Intelligence I can get the Georgia Batalions are extremely deficient__ our own are too much so__ I sh^d have mentioned that a large Number of Fat Cattell are ~~drawn~~ drove off by the Enemy from the Settlements in Georgia and perhaps their present post at Newport is intended to prevent a pursuit untill the drivers are out of danger__

I send you a Lett^r rec^d a few days ago from the Govr of Georgia directed for you__ and now S^r relying on your Indulgence & Candour to excuse the imperfections and inaccuracys of this Epistle wrote by Candle light & not in my power to read over and Correct__ I beg leave to Assure you that I am with unfeigned Respect and personal Regard

Sir / Your Most Obed hum Sev^t

Raw^S. Lowndes.

P.S
I had the pleasure of Writing Mr Drayton some days ago__

SOURCE: RC, Kendall Collection; addressed below close "His Ex̄y the President of Congress"; dated below close "Chas Town Thursday Night__ / 3^d Decem^r 1778."; docketed "Presed^t Lowndes 3 Decem̄ / 78 / R̄ed 3 Jany 1779.__". Copy (19th century), HL Papers, ScHi.

TO PHILIP SCHUYLER

Philadelphia, December 4, 1778

Sir

I had the honor of writing to you the evening of the 2nd Instant, to which I beg leave to refer.[1]

---

[1] HL had been appointed in August 1777 to the committee that investigated the charges against Generals Philip Schuyler and Arthur St. Clair stemming from the surrender of Forts Ticonderoga and Mount Independence. Both men were exonerated by courts martial in September and October 1778. Congress did not, however, review and approve the acquittals until December. HL Papers, XI, 417n; JCC, XII, 1186-1187, 1225-1226.

The business before Congress at the meeting which I had intimated totally obstructed the passage of that in which you had been from various untoward and unavoidable circumstances too long unhappily detained: at length on the following Evening Congress took under consideration the proceedings of the General Court Martial on the tryal of Major General Schuyler, and resolved that the sentence of acquittal with the highest honor be confirmed, ordered the Publication of the proceedings of the Court be pub~ lished and that the Resolution be transmitted to the Commander in Chief.[2]

It is with peculiar satisfaction Sir, that I now convey to you An[3] Act of Congress of the 3ᵈ Instant for these purposes, and I request you will do me the honor of believing that I Am with very great Respect and Regard

Sir / Your Obedient & most Hbˡ· Servᵗ·

SOURCE: LB, PCC (Item 13), DNA; addressed "Major General Schuyler / Albany / by Dunn"; dated "4ᵗʰ December".

FROM SILAS DEANE

Philadelphia, December 4, 1778

Sir

I have now to acknowledge your favours of 10 oClock last Evening and to thank you for the attention paid to my last Letter to you. Previous to receiving the intimation you have given me, "That Congress had resolved to take into consideration their foreign affairs, and that such branches as I had been particularly concerned in, would in due course become the subjects of deliberation", I had prepared to leave this City and had made my arrangements accordingly which will not be in my power to dispense with for any time.[1]

---

[2] General Schuyler had written October 30 and November 2 on behalf of the Oneidas. HL's December 2 letter informed him of the response Congress made in passing an act on November 30 "for supplying our friendly Indians with Cloathing upon moderate terms, and for securing the continuance of mutual Amity between the United States and those People." HL to Philip Schuyler, Dec. 2, 1778, Item 13; *JCC*, XII, 1177-1178; Philip Schuyler to HL, Oct. 30, Nov. 2, 1778, PCC, Item 153, Vol. 3, p. 364ff, p. 386ff.

[3] "An" written over other text.

[1] This may have been an opaque reference to his letter "To the Free and Virtuous CITIZENS of AMERICA" which he wrote in late November and knew would appear the following day. *Pa. Packet*, Dec. 5, 1778.

I take the liberty of mentioning this as I do not find in the intimation you have given me of the Resolution of Congress any time fixed for my attendance, and I take the liberty of repeating what I have before had the honor of writing to you, that my detention is extremely prejudicial to my private affairs, and so far as I am able to judge, in some degree so to those of the public which I have had the honor of being entrusted with, some of which require my presence at the settlement of them, as well on account of my own Reputation as for the interest of the United States. I have the honor to be with much respect &c.

(signed) Silas Deane

SOURCE: Copy, PCC (Item 103), DNA; no address; dated "Friday 4th December 1778".

FROM CONRAD-ALEXANDRE GÉRARD [1]

Philadelphia, December 4, 1778

Leave is begged from the hon Presidt of Congress to Submit him Some reflections upon a late conversation.[2]

The insinuation made was founded upon the consideration that the method proposed would be more Simple, more easy and more convenient than any other, and that besides the troubles, the expences, the dangers of the Sea and of the ennemy, the Spoiling of the cargoes &ca would be avoided.

The manner of executing this plan if adopted, could be very Simple and attended with no inconveniency. The Court Shall take upon herself to Satisfy the furnisher of the articles in question and

---

[1] Charles Thomson copied this note from Gérard, among others from the French minister, dated it December 4, and prefaced it with this explanation: "The president communicated to Congress another unsigned note from the Minister of France, relative to a plan he had proposed for discharging the debt due to Roderigue Hortalez & Co., alias, Beaumarchais namely by furnishing the french fleet in America with ~~such~~ provisions for the amount of which the court would procure them ↑United States↓ a credit with ↑R.↓ Hortalez & Co. The note was delivered in english in the words following." PCC, Item 114, p. 41.

[2] HL's undated notes on the suggestion by Gérard to reconcile accounts between the

Congress Shall receive his discharge for ready money in his accounts with the Court.

SOURCE: RC, PCC (Item 94), DNA; no address; dated below text "December 4[th.] 1778.". Copy, PCC (Item 111), DNA. Copy, PCC (Item 114), DNA.

TO SILAS DEANE

Philadelphia, December 5, 1778

Sir

I had the honor of presenting your Letter of the 4[th.] to Congress this Morning, the House have assigned Monday Evening for hearing you as you will learn from the inclosed Act for that purpose[1]

I am with very great Respect / Sir / Your most obedient servt.

Henry Laurens.
President of / Congress.___

SOURCE: ALS, Silas Deane Papers, CtHi; addressed below close "The Honorable / Silas Deane Esquire / Philadelphia."; dated "Philadelphia 5[th.] Decem̄ / 1778.". LB, PCC (Item 13), DNA.

United States and France arising from Americans provisioning Count d'Estaing's fleet, while obtaining military stores from Caron de Beaumarchais, place the date of this conversation at December 2 or 3. HL's notes also more clearly point out that such an accounting procedure would end the pretense of French supplies coming from private sources by the fact that such a measure would "be acknowledging that the Court of France had furnished those Stores." The French interpretation, however, differed in recognizing that while the military stores came from the national arsenal they had been purchased by Beaumarchais. HL also noted that he suggested "that M[r.] Girard should signify what he had said to me in writing in order to avoid mistakes." Henry Laurens: Notes on Military Stores, [January 1779], HL Papers, ScHi.

[1] On December 5, while Congress was approving Monday December 7 as the date for Silas Deane's next hearing, Deane's public letter "To the Free and Virtuous CITIZENS of AMERICA" appeared in the Pa. Packet. This publication, an attack on the Lee brothers and by implication those who supported them, proved to be the first shot in a partisan conflict that raged well into 1779. JCC, XII, 1192.

TO LORD STIRLING

Philadelphia, December 5, 1778

My Lord.

I am particularly indebted for Your Lordships obliging favor of the 1st. December. those of ↑public concerns under↓ the 29th. November & of the date first mentioned remain yet a secret to Congress, I mean the Contents, for I have day by day for some days past announced these & many other public Letters to the House.[1]

Your Lordship will justly conclude that the business which has obstructed the bare hearing the import of dispatches which for aught we know may be nothing less than the evacuation of New York Garrison or the reinforcement of that place by Ten thousand new troops, must be exceedingly momentous. I speak to you Sir as a Gentleman & fellow Citizen.

My last date to Your[2] Lordship is the 1st. Inst, I owe you News Papers of Thursday & this Morning two of each, together with ↑two↓ Copies of Geñ. Lee's & one of Geñ Sinclair's trials will be found in the Packet which will contain this.[3]

Congress have not yet decided on these Cases;[4] this Morning's Paper shews the determination on Major Gen. Schuyler's. Your Lordship will observe the coverings of Geñ. Lee's trial are of different colours, the Marble was published by order of Congress,

---

[1] Lord Stirling's letter of November 29, which contained intelligence concerning British troop movements, was read in Congress December 2, and his December 1 letter was read December 5. Lord Stirling to HL, Nov. 29, 1778, Kendall Collection, is docketed "Recd. 2d. Deceñ Read in Congress"; *JCC*, XII, 1188.

[2] "Y" written over "y".

[3] *PROCEEDINGS of a GENERAL COURT MARTIAL, held at BRUNSWICK in the State of New-Jersey, by order of his Excellency GENERAL WASHINGTON, Commander in Chief of the Army of the UNITED STATES OF AMERICA, for the trial of MAJOR GENERAL LEE. July 4th, 1778. Major General Lord Stirling, President* (Philadelphia, 1778). John Dunlap printed 100 copies for Congress and afterwards another edition was printed for sale. Evans, *American Bibliography*, No. 16140. *PROCEEDINGS of a GENERAL COURT MARTIAL, held at White Plains, in the State of New-York, by order of his Excellency GENERAL WASHINGTON, Commander in Chief of the Army of the UNITED STATES OF AMERICA, for the Trial of MAJOR GENERAL ST. CLAIR, August 25, 1778. Major General LINCOLN, President* (Philadelphia, 1778). Printed by Hall & Sellers. Evans, *American Bibliography*, No 16141.

[4] Congress confirmed the court-martial's acquittal of General Schuyler on December 3, but postponed consideration of the proceedings of Gen. Arthur St. Clair's court-martial until December 16, when the acquittal was confirmed. Later in the December 5 session Congress voted to uphold the court-martial's conviction and dismissal of General Lee. *JCC*, XII, 1186-1187, 1195, 1225-1226.

the blue I apprehend by Gen̄ Lee's order, I bought this of the Printer & have not had time to examine it. I am not conscious of any impropriety in requesting Your Lordship to recur to the Verdict of the Court on the second Charge which is founded on the 13th. Article of the 13th. Section of the Articles of War, & then to the 12th. Article of the same Section, had I the Articles before me I should score under the words & runaway & be strongly of opinion that the Copyist had, which is easy to imagine, inserted 13th. when 12th. had been the fact. but if this be arcanum & not a plain error, it would be highly impertinent to attempt to develop a single jot__ which is not my meaning.[5]

I believe the late Report of a second naval engagement; although we have received no further accounts.

I thank Your Lordship for the offer of kind consolation, but My Lord when Liberty is tottering on the verge of a precipice & her Salvation dependant upon an hypothesis, 'tis impossible that her Sons should suppress apprehensions. indeed My Lord the Baby Independence is asleep, the Nurse is gadding & the Wolf is at the Door, if the Gypsey does not return at this very instant the Innocent Child will be torn to pieces, for besides the danger from the Wolf there's a fox in the House & a Tyger approaching. believe me My Lord my mind is not of a gloomy cast, & ↑beleive↓ nothing more of my understanding than bare common sense & a very little penetration, those who would ruin us will readily subscribe to the latter.

I have the honor to be / With the highest Respect & Esteem / Sir / Your Lordship's / Obliged & Obedient servant

Henry Laurens.

SOURCE: ALS, Personal (Misc.), Henry Laurens, NN; addressed below close "The Right Hon̄ble / the Earl of Stirling."; dated "Philadelphia 5th. Decem̄ 1778."; docketed "From / President Congress / Decr. 5. —78"; noted below close "private.".

---

[5] Lord Stirling had presided at Lee's court-martial where three charges were presented. The court found Lee guilty on each point. The second charge, "Misbehaviour before the Enemy" claimed Lee had made "an unnecessary, disorderly and shameful Retreat." This violated article 13, section B of the Articles of War. *Washington Writings* (Fitzpatrick), XIII, 448-449.

FROM ROBERT H. HARRISON[1]

Elizabethtown, N.J., December 5, 1778

Sir.

I have the Honor to address you by command of His Excellency, who went from this place at four oClock this morning in consequence of advice received last night, that fifty two Vessels great & small, including a Bomb Ketch, with troops on board, had the day before yesterday moved up the North river as far as Cloyster landing_ and yesterday morning got under way and were proceeding further up. He proposed to make his first stage at Acquakanunch and to proceed as his future intelligence might require. He is much at a loss to determine the design of the enemy; but thinks it may either have respect to the Forts in the Highlands or to the Convention troops.[2] When he left Peeks Kill, the two Massachusetts brigades, on their march thither from Hartford were not arrived,[3] so that the troops on the spot were only the original Garrison of West point and Nixon's brigade, which lay near the Continental village; but without the most inexplicable delay, those must have reached their destination some days since. If so, and the Enemy should meditate a stroke against West point, they will probably fail in it, unless there should be something like a surprize. The[4] General also thinks it probable that the Maryland division were yesterday evening at the Clove;[5] Their instructions were to communicate with West

---

[1] Lt. Col. Robert Hanson Harrison (1745-1790), a Maryland native, was a lawyer at Alexandria prior to the war. He had advised George Washington on legal matters before joining the 3d Va. regiment in September 1775. Washington appointed him an aide-de-camp in November 1775 and secretary in May 1776. *Hamilton Papers* (Syrett), I, 195n; Heitman, *Continental Officers*.

[2] The object of this British force was to intercept the rear guard of the Continental forces as they escorted the Convention Army during its march southward to Virginia. They embarked the night of December 2 under the command of Brig. Gen. Edward Mathew but arrived after the Convention Army with its escort had crossed the Hudson River. The British force continued north to Stoney Point but returned to New York City after a few minor skirmishes. Closter Landing was located on the Hudson just above Manhattan and Aquaknunk Bridge, New Jersey was on the Passaic River southwest of New York City. *Documents of the American Revolution* (Davies), XV, 287-288; Dabney, *After Saratoga*, pp. 54-55; *Greene Papers* (Showman), III, 105-106.

[3] Both Gen. John Paterson's brigade, which took up winter quarters at West Point, N.Y., and Gen. Ebenezer Learned's brigade, that wintered at Fishkill, N.Y., had arrived by December 5. *Greene Papers* (Showman), III, 106n.

[4] "Th" written over "H".

[5] Smith's Clove was strategically located where the Ramapo River cut a valley through the southern New York Highlands. The reference was probably to Gen. William Smallwood's division that had been ordered to winter at Middle Brook, N.J. *Greene Papers* (Showman), II, 120-121; *Washington Writings* (Fitzpatrick), XIII, 346.

Point and reinforce it on an emergency. They were, in addition to them, directed, last night, by express to move immediately toward the forts, divested of baggage and Artillery, for the more speedy communication. The Carolina Brigade[6] has been some time stationed at the Entrance of the Clove. ~~illegible~~

One brigade of the Virginia Troops is at Pumpton__ and the other two were expected to reach Springfield yesterday. The Pensylvania troops it is supposed would be at Acquackinunch or in the neighbourhood of Paramus. These troops, immediately on receiving the present intelligence were ordered to halt__ and his Excellency is gone forward to regulate their movements, according to circumstances. The Brigade in this Town is ordered to hold itself in readiness.

If the Convention troops should be their object, it is probable the attempt will be too late to answer any purpose. The rear division was to cross the North river on Wednesday last; but must certainly have done it on thursday__ the front must be not far from the Delaware and the whole too far advanced to be subject to a rescue. Added to this, there is a pretty strong guard with each division. His Excellency, however, has sent on the intelligence to Colo Bland,[7] who directs their march, urging him to hasten them forward, with all possible dispatch. ~~and in case the danger of a rescue should become iminent, to act as necessity might require~~.

One Brigade of Connecticut troops was at Danbury__ the Other at Fredericksburg when we came away__ and Gen[l] Poor's was in full ~~force~~d march for the former and must long since have arrived.

I have the Honor to be / with the highest respect / Y[r] Excellency's / Most Obed sevt

Rob: H: Harrison Sec̄y

P.S. Your Ex̄[y] will excuse this hurried scrawl

source: RC, PCC (Item 152), DNA; addressed below close "His Excelly / Henry Laurens, Esq."; dated "Elizabeth Town Dec[r] 5[th.] 1778"; docketed

---

[6] General Washington ordered Col. Thomas Clark, on November 18, to "take post at the entrance of the Clove" with "the two Carolina Regiments." *Washington Writings* (Fitzpatrick), XIII, 282-283.

[7] General Washington placed Col. Theodorick Bland in charge of the removal of the Convention Army from Massachusetts to Charlottesville, Va., on November 5. *Washington Writings* (Fitzpatrick), XIII, 207-208; Dabney, *After Saratoga*, p. 52.

"Letter from R H Harrison / sec^y of Genl Washington / Decr. 5. 1778 / Read 7.__ / Entered page 147 / examined". Copy, PCC (Item 169), DNA.

FROM WILLIAM HEATH

Roxbury, Mass., December 5, 1778

Sir,

I am just honor'd with the receipt of Yours, private, of the 21st ultimo, ⅌ Mr Dodd, enclosing the Advertisers of 19 & 21st: for w^ch: and the many marks of honor & politeness confer'd on me, I beg you will be pleased to accept my warmest acknowlegements of gratitude and thanks.

As you are pleased to mention my particular Situation, and Major General Gates's taking the Command of this District, I cannot forbear just observing, that this measure has given me some uneasiness; Inasmuch as no mention has been made of me, or my future destination:__ ¹ be that as it may, I beg you will be assured Sir of my warmest affections, and most sincere Wishes for the honor and happiness of Yourself and Family.

With every sentiment of / Respect & Esteem, I have the honor to be, / Sir Your most obed^t hble Ser^t.

W Heath

SOURCE: RC, Kendall Collection; addressed below close "Honble / Henry Laurens Esqr,"; dated "Roxbury Decem⁓ 5. 1778."; docketed by HL "General Heath / 5th. Decem̄ 1778 / Rec̄d. 12 Jany. 1779." Copy (19th century), HL Papers, ScHi.

TO THE MARQUIS DE LAFAYETTE

Philadelphia, December 6, 1778

My Dear Marquis.

I most sincerely rejoice at your recovery from so dangerous a fit of sickness as you described yours to have been in your favor of

---

¹ General Heath remained in Boston until June 1779 when he rejoined the main Continental Army as commander of troops east of the Hudson.

the 29th. Ultimo I had been given to understand that you were but slightly indisposed by fatigue, your maxim Dear Marquis is just what unfortunately it is generally out of sight when we are in good health, & stand most in need of the application.

I have presented your public Letter to Congress & thence it has been put into the hands of a Commēe. who I hope will not delay to report as they are fully sensible of your anxiety to commence your Voyage & of the dangerous approaching Season of the Year.

I have at this Instant no remembrance of the printing the Letters you allude ↑to↓ & would rather say I will enquire to morrow than risque the loss of this opportunity by an immediate enquiry, I recollect to have applied to Congress for an order to print but forget the result.__ when Congress authorize me to write to you, the several persons you have named shall be duly notified of the Messenger's intended departure who is to conduct my dispatches.

Colonel Laurens ~~illegible~~ is still here & desires me to assure you of his respect & good wishes & he is equally mortified at the disappointment of meeting you at camp or on the Road when he was coming to Philadelphia.

There is a Comedy of errors between Monsʳ· Gimat & Monsʳ· du Plessis, each are jealous of an advantage which he supposes the other has gained while each remains in status quo Lieutenat Colonel nor would I advise these my Friends to be anxious for obtaining a Commission ~~for~~ in an order which by the late arrangement is abolished in the American Army. I have the honor of transmitting with this half a dozen Copies of the late arrangement which shews there is no grade between a Lieutenant Colonel & a Brigadier, now suppose colonel's Commissions were given to these Gentlemen what would be said in France by any person acquainted with this arrangement, either that the Commissions had been surreptitiously obtained or that Congress had given them a blank Paper to get rid of their continued importunity & both the arrangement & the importunity are well known at their Court & will from thence diverge to all parts of the Army.

I have been about four hours writing this Short Letter & yet every syllable has been written in haste & without premeditation, judge Sir, how often I have been interrupted__ I often mentally repeat Pope's words__

shut shut the door good John, fatigue I said.
tye up the knocker say I'm sick I'm dead.[1]

I will not yet take a final leave of my good freind I shall have the honor of addressing him once more before this week expires__ Congress yesterday confirmed the sentence of the General Court Martial on Geñ Lee. his Letter which you will read in Dunlap's Paper of the 3ᵈ Inst. will do him much hurt, it is exceedingly malicious & will be answered, the answer will be pointed, I judge so from my knowledge of the Pen, which I am told is to perform it.[2] he has certainly exposed himself to very severe strictures, but I will not interfere in these matters.

Mʳ· Dean's Letter which appeared in yesterday's Paper, astonished one of his best freinds, I have not read it, such of its contents as have been related to me lead me to think his silence would have discovered more wisdom__ you will find a Copy within.

Adieu my Dear Marquis beleive me to be with every sentiment of Esteem & Respect Your obliged & most obedient servant

Henry Laurens.

SOURCE: ALS, Archives du ministère des affaires étrangères: Correspondence Politique: Etats-Unis, supplement; addressed below close "The Right Honorable / The Marquis delafayette__"; dated "Philadelphia 6ᵗʰ· Decem~ / 1778"; noted "Private".

TO LORD STIRLING

Philadelphia, December 6, 1778

My Lord.

Yesterday I had the honor of transmitting a pretty large Packet to Your Lordship this will accompany one not very small, its

---

[1] Alexander Pope, "An Epistle to Dr. Arbuthnot," Vol. 4, p. 96, line 2. (Twickenham ed.)

[2] In his December 3 essay Charles Lee not only attempted to defend himself but also subtly criticized General Washington's leadership and military ability. The commander's strongest supporters including John Laurens and Alexander Hamilton wished to reply. John Laurens informed Hamilton that he had "collected some hints for an answer" but fearing he lacked the "facts and style to answer him fully," encouraged Hamilton to take up the pen "and put him for ever to silence." HL probably referred here to Hamilton; however, nothing appeared from him to answer Lee. Alden, *Charles Lee,* pp. 256-258; New-York Historical Society, *Collections,* VI (1873), 273; Massey, "A Hero's Life," pp. 294-295.

↑other↓ contents will be two Copies of the Treaties, last Night I received advice from France of the arrival of the Ratifications of Congress to the very great joy of the Court & people of that Kingdom Your Lordship is at Liberty therefore to dispose of these as you shall judge proper, they may form a good subject for Barter, but let us watch that fountain of falsehood & forgery Rivington.[1]

I am with the highest / Respect & Esteem / My Lord / Your obliged humble / servant

Henry Laurens.

SOURCE: ALS, Alexander Papers, NHi; addressed below close "The Right Honorable / the Earl of Stirling."; dated "Philadelphia 6th. Decem / 1778__".

TO GEORGE WASHINGTON

Philadelphia, December 6, 1778

Sir

I had the honor of writing to Your Excellency Yesterday[1] by a Messenger to Lord Stirling. This will be accompanied by an Act of Congress for taking eventual Measures for emancipating the Province of Quebec dated the 5th. Instant.[2]

---

[1] James Rivington, a London native, came to America in 1760 and opened printing and book shops in New York and Philadelphia. By the late 1760s, he had concentrated his business in New York. He began publishing a weekly newspaper in March 1773. By late 1774 Whigs considered his paper to be pro-British and he was forced to suspend publication from Nov. 23, 1775, until the British forces occupied New York. He began publishing *Rivington's New-York Gazette* again in October 1777, changed the name to *Rivington's New York Loyal Gazette* on October 18, and to *The Royal Gazette* on December 13. He became notorious among the patriots for printing rumors and propaganda such as his reports that Benjamin Franklin had died in Paris, that Robert Morris had left Congress in disgust, and that Washington had been killed or captured. Later, however, Rivington became a secret agent for the patriots and conveyed intelligence to the American command. *Rivington's New York Newspaper, Excerpts from a Loyalist Press, 1773-1783* (New York, 1973), pp. 1-27.

[1] HL informed Washington that Congress had confirmed General Schuyler's court-martial acquittal and had granted leave to Maj. Augustine F. Des Epiniers. HL to George Washington, Dec. 5, 1778, PCC, Item 13.

[2] The committee to whom Washington's November 11 letter, opposing an expedition to Canada, had been referred brought in a report that was accepted. Congress resolved that "nothing of great Importance can be attempted in that Quarter unless the Enemy should evacuate the Posts which they now hold within these United States." *JCC*, XII, 1190-1192.

The 4th Instant Congress resolved to promote Lieu[t.] Henry P. Livingston to be Captain in the Corps of Your Excellencys' Guard vice Captain Gibbes promoted. M[r.] Livingston having called on me for his Commission I have delivered it to him.[3]

The 5th it was resolved to lay aside the Plan for raising a Corps to be called the German Volunteers, in which a M[r.] Feuher and M[r.] Kleins↑h↓meit had obtained Commissions to be Captains; these Men deserted some Months since from the Enemy's Garrison at New York and I think came hither from Your Excellency's Camp; the Board of War in their Report on this head intimate as one reason for desisting from raising the intended Corps, the late bad behaviour of the two Captains abovenamed[4] which revived in my Mind that they had been upon their arrival at Philadelphia conducted to me by another pretended Deserter and Quarter Master in the Enemys' Army, a Jew, who has since been discovered to be a fellow of infamous character. He interpreted from them several pieces of intelligence respecting the Enemy which were altogether ground-less, and must have been calculated for sinister purposes I therefore esteem them suspicious and dangerous Persons, and have made these remarks in order to apprize Your Excellency in case of their appearance at Camp.＿ The same day Lieu[t.] John Carter having signified by Letter that he consider'd his promotion in Colonel Baylor's Regiment of Horse as inj irregular and injurious to other Officers in that Corps and desiring leave therefore to resign his Commission.[5] The House Resolved to accept his resignation, and also on the same day Congress resolved ↑as will appear by the inclosed Act↓ that the sentence of the general Court Martial upon Major General Lee be carried into execution.

I have the honor to be &c.

---

[3] Capt. Caleb Gibbes who had been appointed in March 1776 to command the Commander in Chief's Guard, a special unit that protected Washington, the army's cash and official papers, was promoted to major. Capt. Henry P. Livingston, who replaced him by this act of December 4, held the command until his resignation March 26, 1779. *HL Papers*, XIII, 139n; *JCC*, XII, 1188; Heitman, Continental Officers.

[4] The Board of War's report of October 20, which was read in Congress December 5, was accompanied by a letter from Richard Peters that noted "the character of the above mentioned Mess[rs.] Führer and Kleinschmitt induce an opinion that it will be impolitic to trust them or to put the public to the expense of raising the Corps." *JCC*, XII, 1193.

[5] John Hill Carter of Virginia had been a lieutenant in the 3d Cont. Dragoon Regiment since Oct. 12, 1778. Heitman, *Continental Officers; JCC*, XII, 1190; John H. Carter to HL, Dec. 5, 1778, PCC, Item 78, Vol. 5, p. 273ff.

SOURCE: LB, PCC (Item 13), DNA; addressed "General Washington / by Freeman"; dated "6th December".

TO RAWLINS LOWNDES

Philadelphia, December 7, 1778

Dear Sir

By this Sea Conveyance I shall not say much, because I think the chance of miscarriage is great, and because I mean to write again in a day or two by a safe hand out of the reach of Bachop,[1] if my Packet escapes the Enemy Your Excellency will receive four or five of the latest Newspapers, the most striking Articles in these are General Lee's and Mr Deane's Letters

The former has made neither Proselytes nor Advocates, the people in Carolina will see at the first glance how open he has laid himself and I am told he will be attacked in every vulnerable part by a Pen which possibly may not hurt his feelings while it displays truth to the World. Congress on Saturday last Resolved that the Sentence of the Court Martial against him be carried into execution, eleven States present, 6 Ayes 2 Nays. 2 divided, and 1 unrepresented__ Members 16 Aye, 7 No__ 1 excused not having read the Tryal nor heard the Debates, which deprived New Jersey of representation.[2] I shall send particulars by Land

Your Excellency will be so good as to recur to my Letter of the 11th. August. What might there have appeared trifling to many People will now be regarded as a well founded and well intended alarm, this Appeal to the People this rash unnecessary appeal I trust will this day be attended to in Congress, but as I am concerned in no intrigue ↑n↓or Cabal I am consequently ignorant of the designs of my fellow labourers__[3] the honor and interests of these United

---

[1] Peter Bachop, a notorious Loyalist privateer captain, frequented the waters off the South Carolina coast.

[2] Rhode Island, Connecticut, New York, Pennsylvania, North Carolina, and South Carolina voted their approval of the sentence while Massachusetts and Georgia opposed it. The New Hampshire, Maryland and Virginia delegations divided and New Jersey delegate John Fell was excused. *JCC*, XII, 1195.

[3] HL had devoted a large section of his August 11 letter to Lowndes to the inquiry into the affairs of Silas Deane.

States call upon every Delegate in Congress for support, if therefore other Men shall be silent, I will deliver my sentiments on this very extraordinary circumstance and I have in prospect the production of much good out of this evil

Your Excellency will receive among other Papers, Lord Stirling's discoveries of the Enemy's strength of Troops in America I believe the aggregate much overrated.

The Court of London in August last applied to that of Madrid for a mediation between the former and the Court of Versailles, Spain required an explanation by a specification of terms, and being informed that a revocation of the Duke de Noailles' declaration of March last would be expected,[4] the King of Spain heard the Proposition with much resentment as being inconsistent with the honor and dignity of his good ally, & therefore an insult upon himself. In September all the Spanish Armaments were in motion, predicting, perhaps only threatening, immediate hostilities

I have the Honor to be &c

H.L

SOURCE: Copy (19th century), HL Papers, ScHi; addressed "President Lowndes / South Carolina"; dated "7th. December".

FROM CONRAD-ALEXANDRE GÉRARD

Philadelphia, December 7, 1778

Sir.

I have had the honor of explaining to you the motives of my embarrassment on the subject of transmitting to my court ideas relative to certain persons strongly suspected of being emissaries of the Court of London__ as well as concerning the doctrine of the liberty, which it is pretenced the United States have preserved, of treating with that power separately from their Ally, as long as ~~the Kin~~ Great Britain shall not have declared war against the King my Master.[1]

---

[4] The Marquis de Noailles, French ambassador to Britain, announced the Franco-American treaties to George III on March 13, 1778. *HL Papers,* XIII, 290n.

[1] Gérard suspected John Temple of being a British agent. The French minister feared that

I signified to you how remote it was from my Character to rely on public Rumor or the reports of any individuals whatever, in a matter as serious as delicate__ __ and my desire that Congress itself would be pleased to furnish the means of forearming my Court and thro' it all the present or future friends of the United States,[2] in Europe, against the impressions which these ideas might produce. They appear to me above all dangerous relatively to England, where they will cherish the hope of sowing domestic division in the bosom of the United States and separating[3] them from their ally, by thus annulling the treaties concluded with him.

It appears in effect that as long as this double hope will subsists, England will not think seriously of acknowleging your independance, upon the footing expressed in the treaty of Paris.

Your Zeal Sir for your Country, and the preservation of harmony so happily established__ is too well known to me not to make me hope that you will render an account to Congress of this matter, which my anxiety for whatever regards the support of the Reputation of the Alliance makes me consider as very important.[4]

I am persuaded Sir that you will at the same time be so good as to inform Congress of the proof of firmness and attachment to the interests of the United States, the common cause and the alliance__ which the King my Master has given in rejecting the overtures which the Court of London has made through the Channel of Spain.

I have the honor to be with respectful Sentiments
Sir / Your most humble / and most obed[t] Serv[t]

(signed) Gerard

---

some members of Congress, including Samuel Adams, William Henry Drayton, and Richard Henry Lee, would be willing to ignore Article 8 of the Treaty of Alliance which forbade a separate peace with Britain. *Delegate Letters* (Smith), XI, 333-335.

[2] Comma written over dash.

[3] Second "a" written over "t".

[4] Gérard's letter was referred to a committee consisting of William Henry Drayton, Samuel Adams, Gouverneur Morris, William Paca, and John Jay. The committee's report, in Drayton's hand, was read in Congress Jan. 14, 1779. Upon consideration, Congress resolved unanimously "That as neither France or these United States may of right, so these United States will not conclude either truce or peace with the common enemy, without the formal consent of their ally first obtained." The resolve also condemned assertions or insinuations to the contrary. *JCC*, XII, 1197-1198; XIII, 61-63.

SOURCE: Translation, PCC (Item 94), DNA; no address; dated "Philadelphia 7th Decem 1778"; docketed "A memorial from / S^r· Gerard Minister of / France / Datd 6̶7̶ Dec^r· 1778 / Read Dec^r· 7. / refered to M̶^r̶ ̶D̶r̶a̶y̶t̶o̶n̶ ̶/̶ ̶M̶^r̶ S̶ ̶A̶d̶a̶m̶s̶ ̶/̶ ̶M̶^r̶ ̶G̶ ̶M̶o̶r̶r̶i̶s̶ ̶/̶ ̶M̶^r̶ ̶P̶a̶c̶a̶ ̶/̶ ̶M̶^r̶ ̶J̶a̶y̶.̶_̶_̶". RC (in French), PCC (Item 94), DNA. Copy, PCC (Item 111), DNA. Copy, PCC (Item 114).

TO GEORGE WASHINGTON

Philadelphia, December 8, 1778

Sir

The last Letter which I had the honor of writing to Your Excellency is dated the 6th Instant, in the mean time I have received and presented to Congress your favors of the 4th and 5th, the former is committed to the Board of War.

By direction of Congress I now transmit Copy of a Letter of the 23d Ultimo from the honor:.ble Major General Schuyler.[1] You will be pleased Sir to direct your next Dispatches to the President of Congress, who will not be the subscriber, but in my private Character I shall ever retain that true respect and esteem under which I have so often had the honor of acknowledging myself, w̶i̶t̶h̶

Sir / Your Excellency's Most Obedient & / Most Humble Servant[2]

SOURCE: LB, PCC (Item 13), DNA; addressed "General Washington / by [*blank*]"; dated "8th December".

---

[1] General Schuyler sent intelligence from Saratoga in which he noted "All is quiet in this quarter." The enemy's shipping retired from the station at Crown Point and the troops and "Savages" who had destroyed settlements bordering Lake Champlain returned to Canada. He included an estimate of the enemy's troop strength in Canada and wrote that he had "Intelligence recently received from Canada" that the enemy "are Apprehensive of a visit from us." Philip Schuyler to HL, Nov. 23, 1778, PCC, Item 153, Vol. 3, p. 392ff.

[2] HL noted below text in square brackets "then determined to resign".

HENRY LAURENS: RESIGNATION

Philadelphia, December 9, 1778

Resigned for good & sufficient reasons, which were read in Congress from the Chair, 9ᵗʰ· December 1778.

Henry Laurens.

10ᵗʰ· Offer'd to lodge in Congress the Paper containing the reasons for resignation above alluded to, & also the Books containing Copies of Official Letters written by me as President, some objections by Mʳ· Govʳ· Morris against the first__ [1] & the House came to no determination, both therefore remain for the demand of Congress

Henry Laurens.

SOURCE: AD copied into LB, PCC (Item 13), DNA; dated "10ᵗʰ Decem~ 1778".

HENRY LAURENS: RESIGNATION SPEECH

[*There are several copies of HL's resignation speech, all of which are substantially the same. There are, however, two sets of notes keyed to the text. One set of four notes marked "[a]" through "[d]" appears with a contemporary copy in the hand of Moses Young. A second set of nine notes marked "{a}" through "{i}" appears with a 19th century copy in an unidentified*

---

[1] There is no mention in the *Journal* of HL's offer to give Congress the paper containing his reasons for resigning or Gouverneur Morris's objection. HL's resignation speech is printed in the Worthington C. Ford edition of the *Journals of the Continental Congress,* from a copy printed in the *Pennsylvania Magazine of History and Biography.* Morris, writing to New York governor George Clinton on December 10, announced that John Jay had replaced HL as president and noted his belief that "The Public will I am confident experience many good consequences from the Exchange." New Jersey delegate John Fell recorded the December 10 vote in Congress in which eight states voted for Jay and four for HL, with Virginia not represented. *JCC,* XII, 1202-1206; *PMHB,* XIII (1889), 232-236; *Delegate Letters* (Smith), XI, 324, 328.

hand. Both sets of notes are printed after the speech and are keyed to the appropriate spot in the text by superscript bracketed letters for the first set and superscript braced letters for the second.]

Philadelphia, December 9, 1778

[Gentle]men[1]

Ever [jeal]ous for the dignity of Congress, and prompted by a sense of Duty, I had the honor on Monday of laying before the House, informations which I had received from Citizens of respectable Characters, that a certain Letter, signed S. Deane and address'd to the Citizens of America at large, published in the Pennsylvania Packet of Saturday the 5th. Instant, which I presumed every Member had read, had created anxieties in the minds of the good People of this City, and excited tumults amongst them__ that having received such information, I had carefully perused the Letter, and found it to contain Articles highly derogatory to the honor and interests of these United States.

That I could not be suspected of having prejudices, or of being engaged in any intrigue or Cabal against Mr. Deane, since, I could declare upon my honor, that no Gentleman on the floor knew so much of my sentiments respecting Mr. Deane's Public Character, as I had communicated to that Gentleman himself__ {a} that seeing Mr. Deane had made his Appeal to the People, and had intimated a design of giving them a course of Letters, it was evident, he did not mean to depart from America so suddenly as he had lately declared to this House.

That from these considerations, I held it dishonorable to Congress to hear him the following evening, and thereupon I humbly moved the House "to appoint a Committee of three to consider and report specially upon the contents of the Letter above mentioned__ that in the mean time Mr. Deane be informed that Congress will give him further notice when they desire to hear him in the House."

This motion was seconded by many voices__ an amendment was offered by an Honorable Gentleman__ "That the Printed Letter

---

[1] Bracketed material here and below supplied from 19th century copy.

be read," which being put to question, passed in the negative by a majority of one State.[a] {b}

I then renew'd my motion, founded upon common fame and my own certain knowledge of the facts__ this was over ruled by calling for the Order of the day,{c} for which a single voice, you know Gentlemen is sufficient, and from that time the motion has remained neglected.

I feel upon this occasion, not for any disappointment to myself, but for the honor and dignity of this House, the great Representative of an infant Empire, upon whose conduct the Eyes of Europe are fixed.

I have, from the moment in which my motion was quashed,[b] {d} seriously, and almost constantly reflected on the above recited circumstances, and have again attentively considered Mr. Deane's Address to the People.

I see no cause to regret my conduct on Monday, and I am confirmed in my opinion, that the Address contains groundless and unwarrantable insinuations and intimations respecting the conduct of this House.

Mr. Deane had never offered to this House a Narrative in writing [of his] proceedings in France, in his character of Commercial and Political Agent, nor ha[th he,] even to this day, produced proper Accounts and Vouchers of his expenditure of Pub[lic Mo]ney.

He was notified on the 3d Instant by your P[resident] that Congress [had] resolved to take into consideration, as on that evening, "the [st]ate of their foreign Affairs[; and that] such branches as he had been particularly concerned in, would in due course become subjects of their deliberation without any avoidable or unnecessary delay"[2]

In a Letter of the 4th "he thanked Congress for that intimation."

In the same Letter he informed them "that he had prepared to leave this City, and had made his arrangements accordingly, which it would not be in his power to dispense with for any time," and yet on the 5th he published an Address "to the free and virtuous

---

[2] In this copy only, the quotation marks in the text and the words "without any avoidable or unnecessary delay" were added by HL.

Citizens of America," in which he complains "that the Ears of their Representatives had been shut against him," and tacitly promises them a course of Letters.

He informs the Public that he had been sacrificed for the agrandizement of others.

He charges one of your Commissioners[e] with such improper conduct in his public character, as amounts, in my Ideas, to high Crimes.

He avers that the same Commissioner "had been suspected by their best friends abroad, and those in important Characters and stations," although he had given Congress no such information in writing, which he ought to have done, even long before he commenced his Voyage from France.

He insinuates that the same Commissioner had been improperly forced upon him.

He sets up a charge against another of your Commissioners[f] for a species of peculation and other malversation of conduct, which if true, it was his duty long ago to have exhibited to Congress.

He arraigns the Justice and the Wisdom of Congress.

He charges and questions the conduct of an honorable Member of this House,[g] out of the House, and holds him up to the Public in a criminal light, which ought not to have been done before he had lodged a complaint in Congress, and had failed of their attention. His publication is a sacrifice of the Peace and good Order of these States to Personal resentments, and so far as it regards Congress, it is groundless and unwarrantable; wherefore, be the remainder false or true, it is, in my humble opinion, a pernicious and unprovoked Libel, affrontive to the Majesty of the People.

I am neither a Volunteer advocate for the private characters stricturized in M^r· Deane's Paper, nor an Enemy to M^r· Deane.__ In a word, I view the performance in question as an Act, unbecoming the character of a Public Servant__ altogether unnecessary, and tending to excite fears and jealousies in the minds of those free and virtuous Citizens of America to whom Mʳ· Deane has[3] addressed himself, and also to draw the conduct of Congress into suspicion and contempt__ and I still hold my opinion, that it was the duty of this House to take the Address into consideration before they admitted the Author to a further hearing.

Nevertheless Congress were pleased to adhere to a Resolve passed on Saturday subsequently to the open appearance of that unnecessary and insulting Publication, for hearing [him in] writing, contrary to a Resolution of the fifteenth day of August last, which was obtain[ed] at that time after much debate, by the reasonings and votes of Gentlemen who had inte[rested] themselves [strong]ly in his favor, and from motives assigned which cannot be effaced [from] the remembrance of those Gentlemen who were then present__ [h] and time is Now given to [Mr. Deane] for preparing a detail of his transactions, which, if I understand any thing of Public Business, ought to have [been c]ompleted and ready for presentation before he landed on the American Shore.

I feel my own honor, and much more forcibly the honor of the Public deeply wounded by Mʳ· Deanes' address*[4] and I am persuaded that it will hold out such encouragement [to] our Enemies to continue their persecution, as will, in its consequences, be more detrimental to [our] Cause than the loss of a Battle.__ Mʳ· Deane has not contented himself with the [sc]ope of Dunlap's Newspaper, he has caused his Address to be printed in A thousand Hand [B]ills__ these will afford a sufficient number for penetrating the remotest part of our Union, and [e]nough for the service of our Enemies.*

I know that what I am about to do will give a transient pleasure to our Enemies, [kn]owledge derived from a circumstance which induced me to continue in this Chair after the 31ˢᵗ [day of] October last,[c] more strongly induced me than that unanimous request of this House which I [w]as then honored with. There are Gentlemen upon this floor who are well acquainted with [th]e

---

[3] HL interlined "has" above "had".
[4] The asterisks inserted in this paragraph refer to the following note at the bottom of the page: "The words from * to the end of that Paragraph * were intended, but omitted thro' accident in ~~his~~ the Address to Congress delivered from the Chair."

circumstance alluded to__[i] but Gentlemen, their satisfaction will indeed be transitory, for [I] here again solemnly declare, <u>and they will soon learn it</u>, that I am determined to continue a faithful and diligent labourer in the Cause of my Country, and at the hazard of Life, fortune, and domestic happiness, to contribute, by every means in my power to the perfect establishment of our Independence.

I shall have less cause to regret the carrying my intended purpose into effect, foreseeing that you may immediately fill with advantage the vacancy which will presently happen.

I shall hold myself particularly answerable to my constituents for my present conduct, and in general to all my fellow Citizens, throughout these States, when properly questioned.

Finally, Gentlemen, from the considerations abovementioned, as I cannot consistently with my own honor, nor with utility to my Country, considering the manner in which Business is transacted here,[d] remain any longer in this Chair, I now resign it.

H L.

[Notes on the Speech]

[a]Five States, Ay, for reading the printed Letter; six, No; some of the latter as the President has been informed were influenced by an opinion that it would be waste of time to read what could give them no information and these intended to vote for a Committee__ the question for a Committee was over ruled by management in spinning out time to one o'clock, when a certain Order of the day to be taken up at that hour, and which cannot be postponed but by unanimous ~~illegible~~ consent, was peremptorily called for.

[b]By the device abovementioned

[c]The President had frequently premonished Congress of his intention to resign the Chair on the 31st of October when he should have served in it one whole year agreeable to the Articles of Contederation; therefore on that day being Saturday he reminded the House of his several former intimations, and humbly intreated them to make choice of some other Member to fill the Chair on the following Monday.

The House discovered a general disinclination to the measure, and after some ~~disinclination~~ ↑deliberation↓[5] determined against a decisive opinion until Monday__ On the intervening Sunday Morning the first of November, a Newspaper, printed in the Garrison of New York was put into his hands, and he was pressed to read a Letter published in that Paper by some Person who professed much personal regard for him, founded upon an old acquaintance & friendship, and expressing the Writer's astonishment that such a Man as he described the President to be should sit at the head of that Banditti (or some term of the same import) the American Congress.

This circumstance embarrassed the President, he had been extremely desirous of quitting the Chair but now became averse to gratifying the Enemy, who seemed to have thrown the flattering Letter abovementioned in his way as a temptation, he therefore waited in silence till Monday for the final opinion of Congress.

On Monday he repeated his request that the House would proceed to the choice of a new President; after some conversation and debate the House were pleased to signify by the voice of a respectable Member their perfect satisfaction with his whole conduct, and that it was their unanimous request he would continue to sit as President for some time longer, which the President then chearfully complied with, and he confesses that he felt some degree of exultation in the thought of having it in his power by an event so honorable to himself to demonstrate to his quondam friend in the Garrison, that he was not to be captivated by flattery.

[d]Alluding particularly to the manner in which the motion had been quashed, as well as to manners in general which were well understood. (by the Members then present)[6]

[a]Mr Deane had in private at his special request related to the President the whole, as he then said of his transactions in his twofold character of Commercial Agent and Commissioner to the Court of France. When he had finished his conversation of two hours, the President replied, "According to your relation, Sir, and

---

[5] Interlineation by HL.
[6] Words in parentheses added by HL.

which I will believe, because you have related the whole upon your honor, every thing stands fair on your part, but from my Youth I have in such cases as these been governed by the maxim, <u>hear the other Party</u>, therefore you will excuse me for delaying a final opinion: Another thing Mr Deane, <u>I must say</u>, for I flatter no Man, I think <u>you ought to have brought your Accounts</u>. You could never hope for a better opportunity." N:B. Mr Deane came to Philadelphia in time of profound peace between England and France, in a Convoy of thirteen Ships of the Line__ but had left his Accounts behind him in France, as he informed Congress, "in a safe place." About £250,000 Sterling had passed through his hands, or under his direction.

[b]This amendment was artfully offered in order to bring on debate and spin out, time, and the mover accomplished his end__ it passed in the negative, because every Member had already read the Letter.

[c]This measure had been preconcerted by the Mover of the Amendment above mentioned, who was in the party of Mr Deane.

[d]In effect quashed by the artful manevre which had parried and postponed the motion

[e]Arthur Lee

[f]William Lee

[g]Richard Henry Lee

[h]It had been moved on the 15 August that Mr Deane should render an account of his Mission in writing__ this was opposed by <u>his Party</u>, who urged that a verbal Narrative would be sufficient, and more likely to discover truth than a formal and studied written Account.__ Now in December, the same party urged, merely for the purpose of foisting in (as afterwards appeared) much groundless slander and obloquy upon the Messieurs Lee and leave the same upon record.

[i]The Presidents one years service had expired on the 31st. October when he gave notice of his determination to resign the Chair on Mondy the 2d. November__ and had requested Congress to think in the mean time of a proper person to succeed him. On the intervening Sunday, one of Rivington's New York Gazettes was shown to him, containing a Letter written by somebody, who (after much illiberal abuse upon the Members of Congress in general) speaks in the most favorable and flattering terms of the President

and expresses great regret that a Gentleman with whom he had formerly the honor of boasting an acquaintance and friendship, should be sitting at the head of such a Banditti.

This circumstance embarassed the President__ if said he, I adhere to my Saturdays resolution and retire from the Chair on Monday, the Writer of this scurrilous Letter will boast of having gained his point__ if I retract, I shall act contrary to my now inclination, contrary to the intended rule laid down in our unfinished Articles of Confederation, and moreover I may be charged with vanity or versatility, or both, I will said he to two confidential friends, let the business take its chance.

When Monday the 2ᵈ November arrived, he repeated his motion for choosing a President the Members in general strenuously opposed the motion__ at length they held a consultation in a circle, and deputed Mr Samuel Adams to address the President, and to express their full and entire satisfaction with his past conduct, and the unanimous request of Congress that he would continue in the Chair__ this circumstance afforded an honorable relief to the President, and induced him for the present to submit to the will of Congress__

SOURCE: Copy, HL Papers, ScHi; titled "The Resignation of Henry Laurens President of Congress"; dated "In Congress on Wednesday the 9ᵗʰ December 1778"; docketed "resignation of the President of / Congress, as delivered from the Chair / the 9ᵗʰ December 1778.__". The notes keyed to this document are marked [a] through [d] and docketed by HL "Notes to reasons for / resignation / 9ᵗʰ. Decem 1778.". Copy (19th century), HL Papers, ScHi. The notes keyed to this document are marked {a} through {i}. Copy, MH.

APPENDIX

CATALOG OF DOCUMENTS

The listing below represents a comprehensive list of all known Laurens documents for the period covered by this volume. Documents printed in this volume have been placed in italic type; those omitted, in roman type. The documents are arranged in chronological order with those bearing the same date listed in the following order: (1) letters written by HL, alphabetized by recipient; (2) circular letters; (3) letters written to HL, alphabetized by sender; and (4) other documents. Circular letters are identified by an asterisk. Abbreviations used to identify the sources of the documents are as follows:

Archives Nationales for Archives Nationale, Paris, France.

Archives, For. Min. for Archives du ministère des affaires étrangères, Paris, France.

Carnegie for catalog of Carnegie Book Shop.

Clinton Papers for *The Public Papers of George Clinton, First Governor of New York, 1777-1795, 1801-1804,* ed. Hugh Hastings (10 volumes: New York, 1899-1914).

CSmH for Henry E. Huntington Library and Art Gallery, San Marino, California.

CtHi for Connecticut Historical Society, Hartford, Connecticut.

CtLHi for Litchfield Historical Society, Litchfield, Connecticut.

CtY for Yale University, New Haven, Connecticut.

Deane Papers for *Papers in Relation to the Case of Silas Deane* (Philadelphia, 1855).

DeHi for Delaware Historical Society, Wilmington, Delaware.

DLC for Library of Congress.

DNA for National Archives and Records Administration.

DNDAR for National Society of the Daughters of the American Revolution, Washington, D.C.

Dodd for catalog of Dodd, Mead & Co.

Italy for Biblioteca Nazionale Centrale, Florence, Italy.

GHi for Georgia Historical Society, Savannah, Georgia.

Giametti for V. Giametti, "Le Chevalier de Cambray Digny: An Unsung Hero of the American Revolution."

Goodspeed for catalog of Goodspeed's Book Shop, Inc., Boston, Massachusetts

IHi for Illinois State Historical Society, Springfield, Illinois.

IMunS for Saint Mary of the Lake Seminary, Mundelein, Illinois.

JCC for U.S. Continental Congress. *Journals of the Continental Congress, 1774-178,* ed. Worthington C. Ford, et al. (34 volumes: Washington, D.C., 1904-1905).

Kendall for the Henry W. Kendall Collection of Laurens Papers, Kendall Whaling Museum, Sharon, Massachusetts.

Marcus for catalog of Samuel Marcus, Stationer, Boston.

M-Ar for Massachusetts Secretary of State, Archives Division, Boston, Massachusetts.

MB for Boston Public Library, Boston, Massachusetts.

MdAA for Hall of Records Commission, Annapolis, Maryland.

MdHi for Maryland Historical Society, Baltimore, Maryland.

MeHi for Maine Historical Society, Portland, Maine.

MH for Harvard University Library, Cambridge, Massachusetts.

MHi for Massachusetts Historical Society, Boston, Massachusetts.

MiU-C for The William L. Clements Library, University of Michigan, Ann Arbor, Michigan.

Moore for Frank Moore, ed., *Materials for History printed from Original Manuscripts. with notes and illustrations. Correspondence of Henry Laurens* (New York, 1861).

MWA for American Antiquarian Society, Worcester, Massachusetts.

N for New York State Library, Albany, New York.

Nc-Ar for North Carolina State Department of Archives and History, Raleigh, North Carolina.

NcD for Duke University, Durham, North Carolina.

NHi for the New-York Historical Society, New York, New York.

NHi *Collections* for *Collections* of New-York Historical Society: *The Deane Papers*. Vols. III-V, 1888-1890.

Nh-Ar for New Hampshire State Department of Administration and Control, Division of Archives and Records Management, Concord, New Hampshire.

NhHi for New Hampshire Historical Society, Concord, New Hampshire.

NhD for Dartmouth College, Hanover, New Hampshire.

NjMoHP for National Park Service, Morristown National Historical Park, Morristown, New Jersey.

NjP for Princeton University, Princeton, New Jersey.

NN for The New York Public Library, New York, New York.

NNC for Columbia University Library, New York, New York.

NNPM for Pierpont Morgan Library, New York, New York.

Pa. Archives for *Pennsylvania Archives. Selected and Arranged from Original Documents in the Office of the Secretary of the Commonwealth* (119 vols.: Philadelphia and Harrisburg, 1852-1935).

Pa. Packet for *The Pennsylvania Packet, or the General Advertiser.*

PBMCA for Archives of the Moravian Church, Bethlehem, Pennsylvania.

PCC for Papers of the Continental and Confederation Congresses and the Constitutional Convention, Record Group 360, DNA, Washington, D.C.

PHi for The Historical Society of Pennsylvania, Philadelphia, Pennsylvania.

PPAmP for American Philosophical Society, Philadelphia, Pennsylvania.

Private for private collections.

PRO for Public Record Office, London, England.

PWacD for David Library of the American Revolution, Washington Crossing, Pennsylvania, on deposit at the American Philosophical Society.

R-Ar for Rhode Island Archives, Providence, Rhode Island.

RHi for Rhode Island Historical Society, Providence, Rhode Island.

RNHi for Newport Historical Society, Newport, Rhode Island.

Rosenbach for The Philip H. and A.S.W. Rosenbach Foundation, Philadelphia, Pennsylvania.

RPB for Brown University, Providence, Rhode Island.

Ryden for George Herbert Ryden, ed., *Letters from Caesar Rodney, 1756-1784* (Philadelphia, 1933).

S.C. Gen. Gaz. for *South Carolina & American General Gazette.*

ScHi for South Carolina Historical Society, Charleston, South Carolina.

SCL (ScU) for South Caroliniana Library, University of South Carolina, Columbia, South Carolina.

SHC (NcU) for Southern Historical Collection, University of North Carolina, Chapel Hill, North Carolina.

Vassar for Vassar College, Poughkeepsie, New York.

Vi for Virginia State Library, Richmond, Virginia.

ViU for University of Virginia, Charlottesville, Virginia.

Title	*1778*	*Source*
To George Washington	July 7	DLC; ScHi; MH
From John Laurens	July 7	Kendall
From George Washington	July 7	PCC
To Israel Putnam	July 8	PCC
To George Washington	July 8	PCC
From George Clinton	July 8	PCC
From Count d'Estaing	July 8	Kendall; PCC
From William Heath	July 8	PCC
From Patrick Henry	July 8	PCC
To Richard Caswell	July 9	PCC
To William Heath	July 9	MHi; PCC
To Patrick Henry	July 9	PCC
To Thomas Johnson	July 9	MdAA; PCC
From Benedict Arnold	July 9	PCC
From William Heath	July 9	PCC
From Jeremiah Powell	July 9	PCC
To Count d'Estaing	July 10	PCC
To Henry Fisher	July 10	PCC
To Horatio Gates	July 10	NHi; PCC
To John Houstoun	July 10	PCC

To Thomas Johnson	July 10	MdAA
To the Marquis de Lafayette	July 10	ScHi
To Rawlins Lowndes	July 10	PCC
To Caesar Rodney	July 10	NNC
To George Washington	July 10	DLC; PCC
To Richard Wescott	July 10	PCC
From Silas Deane	July 10	PCC
From Silas Deane	July 10	*Deane Papers*
From Horatio Gates	July 10	PCC
From Patrick Henry	July 10	PCC
Circular to Several States	July 10	PCC
To George Washington	July 11	DLC; PCC
From Carlisle Commission	July 11	DLC; PRO; Kendall
From William Cross	July 11	PCC
From Silas Deane	July 11	NHi *Collections*
From Count d'Estaing	July 11	PCC
From Ebenezer Hazard	July 11	DLC; PCC; MiU-C
From Pennsylvania Council	July 11	NHi
From Jeremiah Wadsworth	July 11	CtHi
From George Washington	July 11	Private; DLC; ScHi
To William Greene	July 12	R-Ar
To William Heath	July 12	MHi; ScHi
To Jeremiah Powell	July 12	M-Ar
To Meshech Weare	July 12	Nh-Ar
To George Clinton	July 12	*Clinton Papers*
From George Washington	July 12	PCC; DLC
From Richard Wescott	July 12	PCC
Circular to Several States	July 12	PCC
To Patrick Henry	July 13	PCC
From Ephraim Blaine	July 13	PCC
From John Laurens	July 13	Kendall
From Conrad-Alexandre Gérard	July 14	PCC
From Conrad-Alexandre Gérard	July 14	PCC
From Conrad-Alexandre Gérard	July 14	PCC
From the Marquis de Lafayette	July 14	ScHi
From George Washington	July 14	PCC; DLC; MHi
To John Lewis Gervais	July 15	ScHi
To Rawlins Lowndes	July 15	ScHi
From Théveneau de Francy	July 15	ScHi
From Board of War	July 16	PCC
From John Lewis Gervais	July 16	Private
From Patrick Henry	July 16	PCC
From William Maxwell	July 16	PCC
From Jacob Read	July 16	PHi

To William Livingston	July 17	PCC
To George Washington	July 17	PCC; DLC
From William Livingston	July 17	PCC
From William Smith	July 17	PCC
From Cornelius Sweers	July 17	PCC
To John Houstoun	July 18	ScHi
To the Marquis de Lafayette	July 18	ScHi
To William Livingston	July 18	ScHi
To John Rutledge	July 18	ScHi
To George Washington	July 18	ScHi; DLC
To John Wells, Jr.	July 18	ScHi
From Theodorick Bland	July 18	PCC
From John Laurens	July 18	PCC
From John Laurens	July 18	Kendall
From John Laurens	July 18	Kendall
From Philip Schuyler	July 19	PCC
From Charles Berge	July 20	PCC
From Commissioners at Paris	July 20	PCC; MHi
From William Heath	July 20	PCC
From David Mason	July 20	PCC
From William Moultrie	July 20	PCC; ScHi
From Samuel A. Otis	July 20	Kendall; ScHi
From Jeremiah Powell	July 20	PCC
To John Nutt	July 21	ScHi
From Baron de Kalb	July 21	NN; ScHi
To Denis Cottineau	July 22	ScHi
From John Armstrong	July 22	PCC
From Horatio Gates	July 22	PCC
From John Laurens	July 22	Kendall
From William Livingston	July 22	ScHi
From Jeremiah Powell	July 22	PCC
From Frederick Tracy	July 22	PCC; CtHi
From George Washington	July 22	ScU-SCL; DLC
From George Washington	July 22	PCC; DLC
To Richard Caswell	July 23	ScHi; Nc-Ar; MH
From Commissioners at Paris	July 23	PCC; ScHi
From the Marquis de Lafayette	July 23	ScHi
From William Livingston	July 23	ScHi
From John Wereat	July 23	PCC
To John Burnet	July 24	ScHi
To Patrick Henry	July 24	PCC
To William Smith	July 24	PCC
To Jonathan Trumbull, Sr.	July 24	PCC
From George Washington	July 24	DLC; ScHi
From Richard Caswell	July 25	Nc-Ar
From Ralph Izard	July 25	PCC; ScHi

From William Livingston	July 25	ScHi
From Jonathan Trumbull, Jr.	July 25	PCC; CtHi
From Meshech Weare	July 25	PCC; MHi
To Théveneau de Francy	July 26	ScHi
To Patrick Henry	July 26	PCC
To John Laurens	July 26	ScHi
From George Washington	July 26	PCC; DLC
To William Gardner	July 27	PCC; ScHi
From John Adams	July 27	MHi
From Chevalier de Cambray	July 27	Kendall
From Nathanael Greene	July 27	PCC; CSmH
From William Moultrie	July 27	PCC
To Théveneau de Francy	July 28	ScHi
To William Smith	July 28	ScHi
From Silas Deane	July 28	PCC
From George Washington	July 28	PCC; DLC
From Commissioners at Paris	July 29	PCC; MHi
From John Lewis Gervais	July 29	Private
From John Lewis Gervais	July 29	Private
From Rawlins Lowndes	July 29	Kendall; ScHi
From Pennsylvania Council	July 29	*Pa. Archives*
From John Wells, Jr.	July 29	Kendall
From James Willing	July 29	ScHi
To Caleb Gibbes	July 30	PCC
To William Heath	July 30	MHi; PCC
To William Palfrey	July 30	PCC
To Jonathan Trumbull, Jr.	July 30	NjMoHP
To George Washington	July 30	PCC
To Alexander Wright	July 30	ScHi
To Richard Marven and Samuel Shaw	July 31	PCC
To George Washington	July 31	ScHi
From Caesar Rodney	July 31	Ryden
From Charles Scott, et al.	Aug.	PCC
From Marquis de Brétigney	Aug. 1	PCC
From Matthew Clarkson	Aug. 1	PCC
From William Malcom	Aug. 1	PCC
From John Sullivan	Aug. 1	PCC
From British Prisoners of War	Aug. 2	PCC
From Cornelius Sweers	Aug. 2	PCC
To Théveneau de Francy	Aug. 3	PCC
From Benedict Arnold	Aug. 3	PCC
From John Campbell	Aug. 3	PCC
From William Livingston	Aug. 3	ScHi
From J. Rocquette, P.A. Elsevier, *& P.Th. Rocquette*	Aug. 3	PHi
From John Rutledge	Aug. 3	DNDAR

From Cornelius Sweers	Aug. 3	PCC
From Jonathan Trumbull, Jr.	Aug. 3	CtHi
From George Washington	Aug. 3	PCC; ScHi; DLC; CtHi
To Rawlins Lowndes	Aug. 4	PCC
From Board of War	Aug. 4	PCC
From John Laurens	Aug. 4	Kendall; ScHi
To Benedict Arnold	Aug. 5	PCC
To Rawlins Lowndes	Aug. 5	ScHi
From Benedict Arnold	Aug. 5	PCC
From John Baynton	Aug. 5	PCC
From Chevalier de Cambray	Aug. 5	Kendall
From Benjamin Flower	Aug. 5	PCC
From Robert H. Harrison	Aug. 5	PCC
From Robert Howe	Aug. 5	ScHi
From William Smith	Aug. 5	Kendall
From Samuel Gollen	Aug. 6	PCC
From John Sullivan	Aug. 6	Moore
From Cornelius Sweers	Aug. 6	PCC
Reply to Conrad-Alexandre Gérard	Aug. 6	PCC
To Benedict Arnold	Aug. 7	PCC
To John Lewis Gervais	Aug. 7	ScHi
To John Wells, Jr.	Aug. 7	ScHi
To Jacob Christopher Zahn	Aug. 7	ScHi
Remonstrance from Carlisle Commission	Aug. 7	PCC; PHi
From Adam Ferguson	Aug. 7	PCC
From Benjamin Flower	Aug. 7	PCC
From Théveneau de Francy	Aug. 7	ScHi
From John Nixon	Aug. 7	PCC
From George Washington	Aug. 7	PCC
From George Washington	Aug. 7	PCC
To John Beatty	Aug. 8	PCC
To Eastern Navy Board	Aug. 8	PCC
To William Greene	Aug. 8	R-Ar; PCC
To William Heath	Aug. 8	MHi; PCC
To Jonathan Trumbull, Sr.	Aug. 8	PCC
To Meshech Weare	Aug. 8	MHi; PCC
From Benedict Arnold	Aug. 8	PCC
From William Maxwell	Aug. 8	PCC
From Timothy Pickering	Aug. 8	PCC
From Timothy Pickering and Richard Peters	Aug. 8	PCC; MHi
From Benjamin Randolph	Aug. 8	PCC
To William Malcom	Aug. 9	PCC
From James Clinton	Aug. 9	PCC
From George Washington	Aug. 9	PCC; DLC
To John Nelson	Aug. 10	PCC

To Baron von Steuben	Aug. 10	NHi; ScHi
From Thomas Mifflin	Aug. 10	PCC
From Louis de La Radière	Aug. 10	PCC
From John Sullivan	Aug. 10	PCC; ScHi; MWA
To Rawlins Lowndes	Aug. 11	ScHi
From John Bailey	Aug. 11	PCC
From William Heath	Aug. 11	PCC
From Thomas Mifflin	Aug. 11	PCC
From Thomas Nelson	Aug. 11	*Pa. Packet*
From John Paterson	Aug. 11	PCC
From Jonathan Trumbull, Sr.	Aug. 11	PCC
From George Washington	Aug. 11	PCC
From Marquis de Brétigney	Aug. 12	PCC
From William Palfrey	Aug. 12	PCC
From Marquis de La Rouerie	Aug. 12	Dodd
Commission: Return Jonathan Meigs	Aug. 12	DLC
To Eastern Navy Board	Aug. 13	PCC
To William Greene	Aug. 13	R-Ar; PCC
To John Laurens	Aug. 13	ScHi
To George Washington	Aug. 13	PCC
From Caleb Gibbes	Aug. 13	PCC
From Chevalier de La Neuville	Aug. 13	PCC
From George Washington	Aug. 13	PCC; DLC
From John Adams	Aug. 14	MHi; ScHi
From Board of War	Aug. 14	PCC
From Théveneau de Francy	Aug. 14	ScHi
From Jeremiah Powell	Aug. 14	PCC
From John Sullivan	Aug. 14	PCC
From George Weedon	Aug. 14	PCC; RPB
To Thomas Mifflin	Aug. 15	PCC
From Benedict Arnold	Aug. 15	PCC
From Board of War	Aug. 15	PCC
From Peter Colt	Aug. 15	PCC
From Thomas Mifflin	Aug. 15	PCC
From Mrs. Wilson	Aug. 15	PCC
To Isaac Foster	Aug. 16	PCC
To William Palfrey	Aug. 16	PCC
To William Shippen	Aug. 16	PCC
To John Sullivan	Aug. 16	NhHi; ScHi; MHi; MH
To Unknown	Aug. 16	*SC Gen. Gaz.*
To George Washington	Aug. 16	PCC
To Meshech Weare	Aug. 16	MHi; PCC
From Baron de Knobelauch	Aug. 16	PCC
From Rawlins Lowndes	Aug. 16	Kendall; ScHi
From Peter Timothy	Aug. 16	PHi

From George Washington	Aug. 16	PCC; ScHi
From George Washington	Aug. 16	PCC
From John Wells, Jr.	Aug. 16	Kendall
Motion re Silas Deane	Aug. 16	PHi
To George Bryan	Aug. 17	Marcus; PCC
To William Livingston	Aug. 17	PCC
From Maria Barrell	Aug. 17	PCC
From John Lewis Gervais	Aug. 17	Private
From John B. Girardeau	Aug. 17	PCC
From Baron de Kalb	Aug. 17	PCC
From Thomas Mifflin	Aug. 17	PCC
From Joseph Nourse	Aug. 17	PCC
From Charles Willson Peale	Aug. 17	PHi
From Frances Pugh	Aug. 17	PHi
From Fanny Raddon	Aug. 17	PCC
From Fanny Raddon	Aug. 17	PCC
From John Sullivan	Aug. 17	N
From Cornelius Sweers	Aug. 17	PCC
From Peter Timothy	Aug. 17	Moore
From Matthew Visscher	Aug. 17	PCC
Committee Report	Aug. 17	PCC
From Baron d'Arendt	Aug. 18	PCC
From John Bigelow	Aug. 18	PCC
From Marquis de Brétigney	Aug. 18	ScHi
From John Lewis Gervais	Aug. 18	Private
From Robert Howe	Aug. 18	PCC
From Baron de Kalb	Aug. 18	PCC
From John Christian Senf	Aug. 18	DLC
To Hannah Sweers	Aug. 19	ScHi
From Benedict Arnold	Aug. 19	PCC
From John Campbell	Aug. 19	PCC
From Mordecai Sheftall	Aug. 19	PCC
From John Sullivan	Aug. 19	PCC; ScHi
From George Washington	Aug. 19	PCC; DLC
To John Bailey	Aug. 20	PCC
To James Clinton	Aug. 20	PCC
To John Nixon	Aug. 20	PCC
To George Washington	Aug. 20	PCC
To George Washington	Aug. 20	PCC
From George Bryan	Aug. 20	ViU
From John Houstoun	Aug. 20	PCC
From John McKinly	Aug. 20	PCC
From Josiah Stoddard	Aug. 20	PCC
From George Washington	Aug. 20	NNPM; DLC; ScHi
To William Livingston	Aug. 21	ScHi

From John Adams	Aug. 21	ScHi; MHi
From William Livingston	Aug. 21	ScHi
From Hannah Sweers	Aug. 21	PCC
From George Washington	Aug. 21	PCC; ScHi; DLC
From George Washington	Aug. 21	PCC
To John Lewis Gervais	Aug. 22	ScHi
To James Pyne	Aug. 22	ScHi
From John Laurens	Aug. 22	Kendall; ScHi
From William Livingston	Aug. 22	PCC
From Anthony Marmajou	Aug. 22	PCC
From Pennsylvania Council	Aug. 22	PCC
From Thomas Proctor	Aug. 22	PCC
From Benjamin Randolph	Aug. 22	PCC
From Caesar Rodney	Aug. 22	DeHi
From Garret Stediford	Aug. 22	PCC
To John Beatty	Aug. 23	ScHi
To Adam Boyd	Aug. 23	PCC
To James Graham	Aug. 23	ScHi
To John Hurt	Aug. 23	PCC
To Baron de Kalb	Aug. 23	PCC
To Noirmont de La Neuville	Aug. 23	PCC
To John Laurens	Aug. 23	ScHi
To Lachlan McIntosh	Aug. 23	ScHi
To George Washington	Aug. 23	PCC
From John Sullivan	Aug. 23	PHi
From John Temple	Aug. 23	PCC
From John Wells, Jr.	Aug. 23	Kendall
From Lachlan McIntosh	Aug. 24	Kendall
From Caesar Rodney	Aug. 24	Ryden
From Cornelius Sweers	Aug. 24	PCC
From Cornelius Sweers	Aug. 24	PCC
From Jeremiah Wadsworth	Aug. 24	PCC; CtHi
From George Washington	Aug. 24	PCC
Receipt	Aug. 24	DLC
To William Smith	Aug. 25	ScHi
From Chevalier Du Plessis	Aug. 25	PHi
From George Walton	Aug. 25	PCC
From George Washington	Aug. 25	DLC; ScHi
From George Washington	Aug. 25	PCC; DLC
To William Maxwell	Aug. 26	ScHi
From Board of War	Aug. 26	PCC
From Carlisle Commission	Aug. 26	PCC; PRO
From Count d'Estaing	Aug. 26	DLC; PCC
From Adam Ferguson	Aug. 26	PCC
From Robert Howe	Aug. 26	PCC
From the Marquis de Lafayette	Aug. 26	ScHi

To John Houstoun	Aug. 27	ScHi; PRO
From John Adams	Aug. 27	PCC
From Louis Duportail	Aug. 27	PCC
From Joseph Reed and John Banister	Aug. 27	PCC
From Jonathan Trumbull, Sr.	Aug. 27	PCC
To Peter Colt	Aug. 28	PCC
To William Heath	Aug. 28	MHi; PCC
To James Knox	Aug. 28	PCC
To John Paterson	Aug. 28	PCC
To John Sullivan	Aug. 28	PCC; RHi
To John Sullivan	Aug. 28	DLC; PCC
To George Washington	Aug. 28	PCC
To George Washington	Aug. 28	PCC
To George Washington	Aug. 28	ScHi
From Board of War	Aug. 28	PCC
From William Greene	Aug. 28	PCC
From the Marquis de Lafayette	Aug. 28	PCC
From John Wells, Jr.	Aug. 28	Kendall
From John & Alexander Wilcocks	Aug. 28	*Pa. Archives*
To John Laurens	Aug. 29	ScHi
To George Washington	Aug. 29	ScHi
From Board of War	Aug. 29	PCC
From Board of War	Aug. 29	PCC
From Baron von Steuben	Aug. 29	Kendall; ScHi
From Baron von Steuben	Aug. 29	PCC
Receipt	Aug. 29	DLC
To Joseph Reed	Aug. 30	PCC
To Charles Stewart	Aug. 30	PCC
To George Washington	Aug. 30	PCC
From Baron d'Arendt	Aug. 30	PCC
From William Heath	Aug. 30	Kendall; ScHi
To John Beatty	Aug. 31	PCC
To George Bryan	Aug. 31	PCC
To Joseph Reed and John Bannister	Aug. 31	PCC
To George Washington	Aug. 31	PCC
From Conrad-Alexandre Gérard	Aug. 31	ScHi
From Rawlins Lowndes	Aug. 31	PCC; Kendall; ScHi
From John Sullivan	Aug. 31	PCC; ScHi
From Jeremiah Wadsworth	Aug. 31	PCC; CtHi
From George Washington	Aug. 31	PCC; ScHi; DLC
Commission: William Gibbon	Aug. 31	DNA
From Robert Wooldridge	Sept.	PCC
To Conrad-Alexandre Gérard	Sept. 1	ScHi
To William Livingston	Sept. 1	ScHi

From George Clinton	Sept. 1	PCC
From Conrad-Alexandre Gérard	Sept. 1	ScHi
From John Laurens	Sept. 1	*SC Gen. Gaz.*
From Baron von Steuben	Sept. 1	NNPM; ScHi
From Jeremiah Wadsworth	Sept. 1	PCC; CtHi
From George Washington	Sept. 1	PCC; DLC; ScHi
From William Heath	Sept. 2	PCC
From John Sullivan	Sept. 2	PCC
From Jeremiah Powell	Sept. 3	PCC
From George Walton	Sept. 3	Kendall; ScHi
To John Beatty	Sept. 4	PCC
From John Berkenhout	Sept. 4	ScHi
From Charles Lee	Sept. 4	PCC
From Joseph Nourse	Sept. 4	PCC
From John Stevens	Sept. 4	DLC
From Cornelius Sweers	Sept. 4	PCC
From George Washington	Sept. 4	CSmH; DLC; ScHi
From George Washington	Sept. 4	PCC; DLC
From George Washington	Sept. 4	PCC; DLC; ScHi
To Auditors of Accounts	Sept. 5	PCC
To John Berkenhout	Sept. 5	PCC
To George Bryan	Sept. 5	PCC
To Richard Caswell	Sept. 5	PCC
To Committee of Arrangement	Sept. 5	PCC
To William Greene	Sept. 5	R-Ar; PCC
To William Heath	Sept. 5	MHi; PCC
To Patrick Henry	Sept. 5	PCC; Vi
To Thomas Johnson	Sept. 5	MdAA; PCC
To William Livingston	Sept. 5	PCC
To William Maxwell	Sept. 5	ScHi
To William Palfrey	Sept. 5	PCC
To Jeremiah Powell	Sept. 5	M-Ar; PCC
To Caesar Rodney	Sept. 5	NjMoHP; PCC
To Jonathan Trumbull, Sr.	Sept. 5	PCC
To Jonathan Trumbull, Sr.	Sept. 5	ScHi
To George Washington	Sept. 5	PCC
To Meshech Weare	Sept. 5	PCC
From Samuel Elbert	Sept. 5	PCC
From William Heath	Sept. 5	PCC
From Robert Howe	Sept. 5	ScHi
From Robert Howe	Sept. 5	PCC; ScHi
From William Malcom	Sept. 5	ScHi; Kendall
From William Read	Sept. 5	ScHi
From Baron von Steuben	Sept. 5	PCC; NHi

Receipt	Sept. 5	ScHi
To Eastern Navy Board	Sept. 6	PCC
To John Lewis Gervais	Sept. 6	ScHi
To John Houstoun	Sept. 6	PCC
To Rawlins Lowndes	Sept. 6	ScHi
To William Maxwell	Sept. 6	PCC
To Charles Cotesworth Pinckney	Sept. 6	ScHi
To John Rutledge	Sept. 6	ScHi
From Conrad-Alexandre Gérard	Sept. 6	ScHi
From Baron von Steuben	Sept. 6	Kendall; NHi; ScHi
From Jeremiah Wadsworth	Sept. 6	PCC; CtHi; MdHi
From John Wells, Jr.	Sept. 6	Kendall
To Charles Lee	Sept. 7	PCC
From John Adams	Sept. 7	PCC; MHi
From Benedict Arnold	Sept. 7	NN
From Thomas Chambers, et al.	Sept. 7	PCC
From Committee of Arrangement	Sept. 7	PCC
From Nathaniel Falconer	Sept. 7	PCC
From Rawlins Lowndes	Sept. 7	Kendall; ScHi
From George Washington	Sept. 7	PCC; DLC
From Auditors of Accounts	Sept. 8	PCC
From George Cottnam	Sept. 8	PCC
From Silas Deane	Sept. 8	PCC
From James Johnston	Sept. 8	PCC
From Philip Schuyler	Sept. 8	PCC
From Anthony Wayne	Sept. 8	PCC; PHi
To Silas Deane	Sept. 9	PCC
From Joseph Clay	Sept. 9	GHi
From Joseph Clay	Sept. 9	GHi
From George Clinton	Sept. 9	PCC
From John Lewis Gervais	Sept. 9	Private
From Romand de Lisle	Sept. 9	PCC
Receipt	Sept. 9	NjMoHP
To Count d'Estaing	Sept. 10	Archives Nationales; PCC; ScHi
To Count d'Estaing	Sept. 10	Archives Nationales
To John Lewis Gervais	Sept. 10	ScHi
To Rawlins Lowndes	Sept. 10	ScHi
To George Washington	Sept. 10	PCC
From John Adams	Sept. 11	PCC; MHi
From John Beatty	Sept. 11	PCC
From Silas Deane	Sept. 11	PCC

From William Livingston	Sept. 11	PCC
From John McKinly	Sept. 11	PCC
To John Cadwalader	Sept. 12	PCC; PHi
To Nathaniel Falconer	Sept. 12	PCC
To Thomas Johnson	Sept. 12	MdAA; PCC
To William Smith	Sept. 12	ScHi
To George Washington	Sept. 12	PCC
From William Heath	Sept. 12	PCC
From Ralph Izard	Sept. 12	PCC; ScHi
From George Washington	Sept. 12	Rosenbach; ScHi; DLC; MH
From George Washington	Sept. 12	PCC
From George Washington	Sept. 12	PCC
To John Beatty	Sept. 13	ScHi
To George Clinton	Sept. 13	NHi; PCC
To Nathanael Greene	Sept. 13	PCC
To William Greene	Sept. 13	R-Ar; PCC
To William Heath	Sept. 13	MHi; PCC
To the Marquis de Lafayette	Sept. 13	PCC; MH
To John Laurens	Sept. 13	ScHi
To William Maxwell	Sept. 13	ScHi
To Jeremiah Powell	Sept. 13	PCC
To Baron von Steuben	Sept. 13	NHi; ScHi
To John Sullivan	Sept. 13	PCC
To Jonathan Trumbull, Sr.	Sept. 13	PCC
To Jeremiah Wadsworth	Sept. 13	PCC
To Meshech Weare	Sept. 13	MHi; PCC
From Baron d'Arendt	Sept. 13	PCC
From Richard Caswell	Sept. 14	PCC; Nc-Ar
From Richard Caswell	Sept. 14	Nc-Ar
From James Laurens	Sept. 14	ScHi
To John Lewis Gervais	Sept. 15	ScHi
To Rawlins Lowndes	Sept. 15	ScHi
To William Read	Sept. 15	ScHi
From Baron d'Arendt	Sept. 15	PCC
From John Beatty	Sept. 15	Dodd
From Board of War	Sept. 15	PCC
From John Laurens	Sept. 15	Kendall
From William Smith	Sept. 15	Kendall
From John Stoddart	Sept. 15	DLC
From Mary Verner	Sept. 15	PCC
To William Henry Drayton	Sept. 16	NN
To George Washington	Sept. 16	PCC
From Richard Caswell	Sept. 16	PCC; Nc-Ar
From William Henry Drayton	Sept. 16	NN

From Eastern Navy Board	Sept. 16	PCC
From Joseph Nourse	Sept. 16	PCC
To John Laurens	Sept. 17	ScHi
To Baron von Steuben	Sept. 17	NHi; ScHi
From Commissioners at Paris	Sept. 17	PCC
From William Hoskins	Sept. 17	PCC
From William Livingston	Sept. 17	ScHi
From Maryland Council	Sept. 17	PCC
From Alexander McNutt	Sept. 17	PCC
From John Morgan	Sept. 17	PCC; ScHi
From Casimir Pulaski	Sept. 17	PCC
To George Bryan	Sept. 18	ScHi
From John Connelly	Sept. 18	PCC
From Alexander Gillon	Sept. 18	ScHi
From John Sullivan	Sept. 18	PCC
From Jonathan Trumbull, Jr.	Sept. 18	PCC; CtHi
From Meshech Weare	Sept. 18	PCC
To Richard Beresford	Sept. 19	ScHi
To John Laurens	Sept. 19	ScHi
From Board of War	Sept. 19	PCC
From John Cadwalader	Sept. 19	PCC; PHi
From Sir Henry Clinton	Sept. 19	PRO
From Michael de Kowatz	Sept. 19	PCC
From John Laurens	Sept. 19	NN
From Arthur Lee	Sept. 19	ScHi
From James Mease	Sept. 19	PCC
To Ebenezer Hancock	Sept. 20	PCC
To George Washington	Sept. 20	PCC
From John Adams	Sept. 20	MHi
From John Lewis Gervais	Sept. 21	Private
From William Heath	Sept. 21	PHi
From William Lee	Sept. 21	ScHi
To Auditors of Accounts	Sept. 22	PCC
To John Clark and James Johnston	Sept. 22	PCC
To William Palfrey	Sept. 22	PCC
From Richard Caswell	Sept. 22	Nc-Ar
From Richard Caswell	Sept. 22	PCC
From Richard Caswell	Sept. 22	Nc-Ar
From Commissioners at Paris	Sept. 22	PCC
From Silas Deane	Sept. 22	PCC
From Field Officers	Sept. 22	PCC
From Robert Howe	Sept. 22	PCC
From Robert Howe	Sept. 22	ScHi
From Robert Howe	Sept. 22	PCC; CSmH; ScHi
From Rawlins Lowndes	Sept. 22	Kendall; ScHi
To John Browne	Sept. 23	Goodspeed

To John Lewis Gervais	Sept. 23	ScHi
To Rawlins Lowndes	Sept. 23	ScHi
To George Washington	Sept. 23	ScHi
From the Marquis de Lafayette	Sept. 23	PCC; MH
From John Sullivan	Sept. 23	PCC
From George Washington	Sept. 23	PCC; DLC
From Jonathan Brewer	Sept. 24	PCC
From Chevalier de Cambray	Sept. 24	Kendall
From Silas Deane	Sept. 24	PCC
From Seth Harding	Sept. 24	PCC
From John Laurens	Sept. 24	Kendall
From William Livingston	Sept. 24	PCC; ScHi
From Resolve Smith	Sept. 24	PCC
From John Wharton	Sept. 24	PCC
S.C. Delegates to Robert Williams	Sept. 24	DLC
From Peter Colt	Sept. 25	PCC
From John Connolly	Sept. 25	PCC
From Lachlan McIntosh	Sept. 25	Kendall
From John Sullivan	Sept. 25	PCC
From Meshech Weare	Sept. 25	PCC; MHi
From John & Alexander Wilcocks	Sept. 25	*Pa. Archives*
To Richard Caswell	Sept. 26	CtY; PCC; Nc-Ar; MH
To Patrick Henry	Sept. 26	PCC
To John Houstoun	Sept. 26	PCC
To Rawlins Lowndes	Sept. 26	PCC
To Rawlins Lowndes	Sept. 26	ScHi
To Jonathan Trumbull, Sr.	Sept. 26	PCC
From George Morgan	Sept. 26	PCC
From James Searle	Sept. 26	PCC
To George Clinton	Sept. 27	PCC
To George Washington	Sept. 27	PCC
From John Adams	Sept. 28	MHi
From William Livingston	Sept. 28	PCC; ScHi
From Francis Wade	Sept. 28	PCC
From Owen Biddle	Sept. 29	PCC
From John Clark, Jr.	Sept. 29	PCC
From John Laurens	Sept. 29	ScHi
From Jean-Baptiste Ternant	Sept. 29	PCC
From Jeremiah Wadsworth	Sept. 29	PCC; CtHi
From George Washington	Sept. 29	PCC; DLC
From Board of War	Sept. 30	PCC
From William Heath	Sept. 30	PCC
From Baron von Steuben	Sept. 31	Kendall; ScHi
From Christopher Hele	Oct.	PCC
From Chevalier de La Neuville	Oct.	PCC

From Marquis de La Rouerie	Oct.	PWacD
From John Stevens	Oct.	PCC
To William Livingston	Oct. 1	PCC
To William Livingston	Oct. 1	ScHi
To Caesar Rodney	Oct. 1	PCC
From John Houstoun	Oct. 1	Kendall; ScHi
From Rawlins Lowndes	Oct. 1	Kendall; ScHi
To William Heath	Oct. 2	MHi
To Baron von Steuben	Oct. 2	NHi; PCC
To John Sullivan	Oct. 2	PCC
To George Washington	Oct. 2	PCC
From John Adams	Oct. 2	PCC; MHi
From John Beatty	Oct. 3	PCC
From Board of War	Oct. 3	PCC
From Samuel Gilbert and Lemuel Holmes	Oct. 3	PCC
From George Washington	Oct. 3	PPAmP; ScHi; DLC
From George Washington	Oct. 3	PCC
To the Pennsylvania Packet	Oct. 3	*Pa. Packet*
To Richard Caswell	Oct. 4	Nc-Ar; PCC
To Patrick Henry	Oct. 4	PCC
To John Houstoun	Oct. 4	PCC
To Thomas Johnson	Oct. 4	MdAA; PCC
To Rawlins Lowndes	Oct. 5	PCC
From Board of War	Oct. 5	PCC
From Jonathan Trumbull, Sr.	Oct. 5	CtHi; ScHi
Commission: James De Bronville	Oct. 5	PCC; PHi
To Robert Howe	Oct. 6	PCC
To William Livingston	Oct. 6	PCC
To Rawlins Lowndes	Oct. 6	ScHi
From James Deane	Oct. 6	PCC
From Philip Schuyler	Oct. 6	PCC
From Jonathan Trumbull, Jr.	Oct. 6	PCC
From Jonathan Trumbull, Sr.	Oct. 6	PCC
From George Washington	Oct. 6	PCC
To George Bryan*	Oct. 7	NhHi; PCC
To Richard Caswell*	Oct. 7	PCC; Nc-Ar
To George Clinton*	Oct. 7	PCC
To Silas Deane	Oct. 7	PCC
To William Greene*	Oct. 7	PCC
To Patrick Henry*	Oct. 7	Vi; PCC
To Thomas Johnson	Oct. 7	PCC
To William Livingston	Oct. 7	PCC
To Jeremiah Powell	Oct. 7	PCC
To Caesar Rodney	Oct. 7	PCC
To Jonathan Trumbull, Sr.	Oct. 7	PCC

To Meshech Weare	Oct. 7	MHi; PCC
From Silas Deane	Oct. 7	PCC
From John Laurens	Oct. 7	Kendall
From William Malcom	Oct. 7	Kendall; ScHi
From George Morgan	Oct. 7	PCC
To Jonathan Trumbull, Sr.	Oct. 8	DLC
From John Connolly	Oct. 8	PCC
From Thomas Hartley	Oct. 8	PCC
From Timothy Pickering	Oct. 8	PCC; MHi
To John Beatty	Oct. 9	PCC
To George Washington	Oct. 9	PCC
From Carl F. Fuhrer and Carl W. Kleinschmidt	Oct. 9	PCC
From Robert Howe	Oct. 9	ScHi
From William Livingston	Oct. 9	ScHi
From William Livingston	Oct. 9	ScHi
From Robert Pringle	Oct. 9	NHi
From William Read	Oct. 9	ScHi
From Jean-Baptiste Ternant	Oct. 9	NNC
To Nathanael Greene	Oct. 10	PCC
To William Heath	Oct. 10	MHi; PCC
To George Washington	Oct. 10	DLC
From John Norman	Oct. 10	PCC
From Pennsylvania Council	Oct. 10	PCC
To Peter Colt	Oct. 12	PCC
To Baron von Steuben	Oct. 12	PHi
To Jonathan Trumbull, Jr.	Oct. 12	PCC
From John Connolly	Oct. 12	NHi
From Silas Deane	Oct. 12	PCC
From Silas Deane	Oct. 12	PCC
From Silas Deane	Oct. 12	PCC
From Silas Deane	Oct. 12	PCC
From Robert Howe	Oct. 12	PCC
From George Morgan	Oct. 12	PCC
From Casimir Pulaski	Oct. 12	PHi
To George Bryan*	Oct. 13	PCC
To Richard Caswell*	Oct. 13	Nc-Ar; PCC
To George Clinton*	Oct. 13	PCC
To Commanding Officer in the Southern Department	Oct. 13	PCC
To William Greene*	Oct. 13	PCC
To William Heath	Oct. 13	MHi; PCC
To Patrick Henry*	Oct. 13	Vi; PCC
To John Houstoun*	Oct. 13	PCC
To Thomas Johnson *	Oct. 13	MdAA; PCC
To William Livingston*	Oct. 13	PCC
To Rawlins Lowndes*	Oct. 13	PCC

To Jeremiah Powell	Oct. 13	NhD; PCC
To Caesar Rodney	Oct. 13	Private; PCC
To Jonathan Trumbull, Sr.	Oct. 13	PCC
To George Washington	Oct. 13	PCC
To Meshech Weare	Oct. 13	Vassar
From Horatio Gates	Oct. 13	PCC; NHi
From Richard Gridley	Oct. 13	PCC
From William Heath	Oct. 13	PCC
From the Marquis de Lafayette	Oct. 13	PCC
From John Laurens	Oct. 13	Kendall
From Rawlins Lowndes	Oct. 13	Kendall; ScHi
From Charles Cotesworth Pinckney	Oct. 13	Kendall; ScHi
From Charles Stewart	Oct. 13	PCC; MH
From Lord Stirling	Oct. 13	PCC; NHi
From Peter Timothy	Oct. 13	DLC
From Jeremiah Wadsworth	Oct. 13	CtHi
From Thomas Conway	Oct. 14	PCC
From Chevalier de La Neuville	Oct. 14	PCC
From John Laurens	Oct. 14	Kendall
From Baron von Steuben	Oct. 14	Kendall; ScHi
From George Washington	Oct. 14	PCC; DLC
From John Wells, Jr.	Oct. 14	Kendall
From Gosuinus Erkelens	Oct. 15	PCC
From Jeremiah Wadsworth	Oct. 15	CtHi
Address to Congress	Oct. 15	PCC
To George Bryan	Oct. 16	PCC
To Richard Caswell	Oct. 16	Nc-Ar
To Joseph Clay	Oct. 16	PCC
To George Clinton	Oct. 16	N; PCC
To Nathanael Greene	Oct. 16	PCC
To William Greene	Oct. 16	R-Ar; PCC
To Patrick Henry	Oct. 16	Vi
To Thomas Johnson	Oct. 16	MdAA
To William Livingston	Oct. 16	PCC
To James Mease	Oct. 16	PCC
To Jeremiah Powell	Oct. 16	PCC
To Caesar Rodney	Oct. 16	CtLHi
To Jonathan Trumbull, Sr.	Oct. 16	PCC
To Jeremiah Wadsworth	Oct. 16	PCC
To George Washington	Oct. 16	PCC
To Meshech Weare	Oct. 16	PCC
From the Marquis de Lafayette	Oct. 16	PCC
From Charles Lee	Oct. 16	PCC
From Casimir Pulaski	Oct. 16	PCC
From Jonathan Trumbull, Sr.	Oct. 16	PCC
Continental Congress: Resolution	Oct. 16	NN; Vi; Private

To Philip Schuyler	Oct. 17	PCC
To Lord Stirling	Oct. 17	ScHi
From Lord Stirling	Oct. 17	NjP; ScHi
From Lord Stirling	Oct. 17	PCC
To Chevalier de Cambray	Oct. 18	Italy
To Richard Caswell	Oct. 18	MeHi; PCC; Nc-Ar
To Patrick Henry	Oct. 18	PCC
To John Houstoun	Oct. 18	PCC
To Rawlins Lowndes	Oct. 18	PCC
To Casimir Pulaski	Oct. 18	PCC
To Joseph Reed	Oct. 18	PCC
To Lord Stirling	Oct. 18	MeHi; PCC
From Edward Hand	Oct. 18	PCC
From Rawlins Lowndes	Oct. 18	Kendall; ScHi
From Lachlan McIntosh	Oct. 18	Kendall
From Caesar Rodney	Oct. 18	PCC; DeHi
From George Washington	Oct. 18	PCC
To Benjamin Lincoln	Oct. 19	PCC
From John Beatty	Oct. 19	PCC
From Casimir Pulaski	Oct. 19	PCC
From Gérard de St. Elme	Oct. 19	PCC
To James Deane	Oct. 20	PCC
To Count d'Estaing	Oct. 20	Archives Nationale
To James Gray	Oct. 20	PCC
To Charles Stewart	Oct. 20	MH; PCC
From Board of War	Oct. 20	PCC
From Lord Stirling	Oct. 20	PCC
From Josiah Stoddard	Oct. 20	PCC
From Jean-Baptiste Ternant	Oct. 20	NN
From Jeremiah Wadsworth	Oct. 20	PCC; CtHi
Board of War: Report	Oct. 20	PCC
To Louis XVI	Oct. 21	PCC; ScHi; PPAmP; PHi
To Louis XVI	Oct. 21	Archives For. Min.; PCC; NHi
From William Heath	Oct. 21	MHi
From Elisha Hinman	Oct. 21	PCC
From Ralph Izard	Oct. 21	DLC
From Casimir Pulaski	Oct. 21	PCC
From Lord Stirling	Oct. 21	PCC; NHi
From Louis De Vrigny	Oct. 21	PCC
From George Washington	Oct. 21	NcD; DLC
To John Beatty	Oct. 22	PCC
To William Heath	Oct. 22	MHi; PCC

To George Washington	Oct. 22	PCC
From Benedict Arnold	Oct. 22	PCC
From Benedict Arnold	Oct. 22	PCC
From Marquis De Brétigney	Oct. 22	PCC
From Dominique L'Eglise	Oct. 22	PCC
From William Livingston	Oct. 22	PCC
From John Stark	Oct. 22	PCC
From George Washington	Oct. 22	DLC
To Peter Colt	Oct. 23	PCC
To Horatio Gates	Oct. 23	NHi; PCC
To John Lewis Gervais	Oct. 23	PCC
To Lord Stirling	Oct. 23	NHi; PCC
To George Washington	Oct. 23	PCC
From Thomas Chittenden	Oct. 23	PCC
From John Laurens	Oct. 23	ScHi
From William Livingston	Oct. 23	MB; ScHi
From Joseph March	Oct. 23	PCC; MH
To William Blount	Oct. 24	PCC
To Chevalier de Cambray	Oct. 24	PCC
To Benjamin Harrison	Oct. 24	PCC
To Patrick Henry	Oct. 24	PCC
To the Marquis de Lafayette	Oct. 24	PCC; ScHi; MH
To Rawlins Lowndes	Oct. 24	ScHi
From Casimir Pulaski	Oct. 24	PCC
From George Washington	Oct. 24	PCC; ScHi; DLC
To Lord Stirling	Oct. 25	Private; PCC
To George Washington	Oct. 25	PCC
From Lord Stirling	Oct. 25	Kendall; ScHi
From Board of War	Oct. 26	PCC
From Adam Ferguson	Oct. 26	*Pa. Packet; Pa.*
Evening Post		
From George Galphin	Oct. 26	ScHi
From the Marquis de Lafayette	Oct. 26	PCC
From the Marquis de Lafayette	Oct. 26	PCC
From the Marquis de Lafayette	Oct. 26	PCC
From the Marquis de Lafayette	Oct. 26	ScHi
From Casimir Pulaski	Oct. 26	PCC
From John Sullivan	Oct. 26	PCC
From George Washington	Oct. 26	PCC; DLC
To Chevalier de Cambray	Oct. 27	Giamatti
To Don Diego Joseph Navarro	Oct. 27	PWacD; PCC
From Peter Colt	Oct. 27	PCC
From Gérard de St. Elme	Oct. 27	PCC
From Thomas Johnson	Oct. 27	PCC
From the Marquis de Lafayette	Oct. 27	PCC
From Casimir Pulaski	Oct. 27	PCC

From Caesar Rodney	Oct. 27	PCC
From Meshech Weare	Oct. 27	PCC; MHi
Certificate: John Tousard	Oct. 27	PHi
To Edward Brice	Oct. 28	PCC
To Chevalier de Failly	Oct. 28	PCC
To Presley Neville	Oct. 28	PCC
To Casimir Pulaski	Oct. 28	PCC
From David Franks	Oct. 28	PCC
To Horatio Gates	Oct. 29	NHi; PCC
To Jeremiah Powell	Oct. 29	PCC
To Josiah Stoddard	Oct. 29	PCC
To Louis de Tousard	Oct. 29	PHi; PCC
From William Heath	Oct. 29	PCC
From William Heath	Oct. 29	PCC
From John McKinly	Oct. 29	PCC
From Jean-Baptiste Ternant	Oct. 29	ScU (SCL)
From George Washington	Oct. 29	DLC
To the Marquis de Lafayette	Oct. 30	PCC
To William Palfrey	Oct. 30	PCC
To George Washington	Oct. 30	PCC
From John Beatty	Oct. 30	DLC
From Marquis de Brétigney	Oct. 30	PCC
From Peter Colt	Oct. 30	PCC
From Horatio Gates	Oct. 30	PCC; NHi
From William Greene	Oct. 30	PCC
From William Killen	Oct. 30	ScHi
From Charles Lee	Oct. 30	PCC
From Phineas Peirce	Oct. 30	PCC
From Philip Schuyler	Oct. 30	PCC
From Jonathan Trumbull, Sr.	Oct. 30	PCC
From Board of War	Oct. 31	PCC
From John Sullivan	Oct. 31	PCC
From George Washington	Oct. 31	PCC; DLC
From Chevalier de Crenis	Nov.	PCC
From Isaac Melcher	Nov.	PCC
To Robert H. Harrison	Nov. 1	PCC
To William Killen	Nov. 1	PCC
To John McKinly	Nov. 1	PCC
To Caesar Rodney	Nov. 1	PHi; PCC
To George Washington	Nov. 1	PCC
From Silas Deane	Nov. 1	PCC
From Lord Stirling	Nov. 1	PCC
From William Heath	Nov. 2	PCC
From Philip Schuyler	Nov. 2	PCC
From John Sullivan	Nov. 2	PCC

Continental Congress: Resolution	Nov. 2	ScHi
To Casimir Pulaski	Nov. 3	PCC
From the Marquis de Brétigney	Nov. 3	PCC
From Peter Craig	Nov. 3	PCC
From Jeremiah Powell	Nov. 3	PCC
From Casimir Pulaski	Nov. 3	PCC
From Lord Stirling	Nov. 3	Kendall; ScHi
From Dominique L'Eglise	Nov. 4	PCC
From Carl F. Fuhrer and Carl W. Kleinschmidt	Nov. 4	PCC
From Caesar Rodney	Nov. 4	PCC; DeHi
To Chevalier Du Plessis	Nov. 5	PCC
To Jean de Gimat	Nov. 5	PCC
To the Marquis de Lafayette	Nov. 5	PCC
To Lord Stirling	Nov. 5	PCC
From Jean de Gimat	Nov. 5	PCC
From William Read	Nov. 5	ScHi
From Peter Scull	Nov. 5	PCC
From Lord Stirling	Nov. 5	PCC
To Gosuinus Erkelens	Nov. 6	PCC
To George Washington	Nov. 6	PCC
From George Clinton	Nov. 6	PCC
From John Laurens	Nov. 6	PCC; ScHi
From William Palfrey	Nov. 6	PCC
From George Washington	Nov. 6	PCC; DLC
From Meshech Weare	Nov. 6	PCC; MHi
To John Beatty	Nov. 7	PCC
To Caesar Rodney	Nov. 7	DeHi; PCC
To Lord Stirling	Nov. 7	PCC
From Commissioners at Paris	Nov. 7	PCC; MHi; ScHi
From David Franks	Nov. 7	PCC
From James Laurens	Nov. 7	ScHi
To William Malcom	Nov. 8	PCC
To Jonathan Trumbull, Sr.	Nov. 8	PCC
From Caesar Rodney	Nov. 8	PCC; DeHi
To George Bryan	Nov. 9	PCC
From Thomas Conway	Nov. 9	PCC
From Conrad-Alexandre Gérard	Nov. 9	PCC
From Patrick Henry	Nov. 9	PCC
From Baron de Kalb	Nov. 9	PCC
From Benjamin Lincoln	Nov. 9	PCC; MHi
From William Livingston	Nov. 9	NN; ScHi
From William Livingston	Nov. 9	ScHi
To John Avery	Nov. 10	PCC
To John Beatty	Nov. 10	PCC
To William Heath	Nov. 10	MHi; PCC

To Philip Schuyler	Nov. 10	PCC
To Jonathan Trumbull, Sr.	Nov. 10	CtHi; ScHi; DLC
From Robert H. Harrison	Nov. 10	PCC
From George Galphin	Nov. 11	ScHi
From Christopher Hele	Nov. 11	PCC
From Officers of the 2nd Light Dragoon Regiment	Nov. 11	PCC
From Lord Stirling	Nov. 11	Kendall; ScHi
From George Washington	Nov. 11	PCC; DLC
To Eastern Navy Board	Nov. 12	PCC
To Nathanael Greene	Nov. 12	PCC
To John Sullivan	Nov. 12	IMunS; PCC
To Jeremiah Wadsworth	Nov. 12	PCC
From Chevalier Du Plessis	Nov. 12	DLC
From George Washington	Nov. 12	PCC; DLC
From Casimir Pulaski	Nov. 13	PCC
From Caesar Rodney	Nov. 13	PCC; DeHi
From Lord Stirling	Nov. 13	Kendall; ScHi
From George Washington	Nov. 13	PCC; DLC
To Richard Caswell	Nov. 14	SHC (NcU); Nc-Ar; PCC
To Nathanael Greene	Nov. 14	PCC
To Patrick Henry	Nov. 14	PCC
To Thomas Johnson	Nov. 14	MdAA; PCC
S.C. Delegates to Rawlins Lowndes	Nov. 14	ScHi
To George Washington	Nov. 14	PCC
From Benedict Arnold	Nov. 14	PCC
From Thomas Hartley	Nov. 14	PCC
From William Livingston	Nov. 14	ScHi
From George Washington	Nov. 14	DLC; ScHi
From George Washington	Nov. 14	PCC
To Charles Stewart	Nov. 15	PCC
To Lord Stirling	Nov. 15	PCC
To George Washington	Nov. 15	PCC
From the Marquis De Brétigney	Nov. 15	PCC
From James Gambier	Nov. 15	PCC
From Lord Stirling	Nov. 15	NN
To George Bryan	Nov. 16	PCC
To Richard Caswell	Nov. 16	Nc-Ar; PCC
To George Clinton	Nov. 16	PCC
To William Greene	Nov. 16	R-Ar; PCC
To Patrick Henry	Nov. 16	PCC
To John Houstoun	Nov. 16	PCC
To Robert Howe	Nov. 16	PCC
To Thomas Johnson	Nov. 16	PCC
To Benjamin Lincoln	Nov. 16	PCC
To William Livingston	Nov. 16	PCC

To Rawlins Lowndes	Nov. 16	PCC
To Jeremiah Powell	Nov. 16	PCC
To Caesar Rodney	Nov. 16	IHi; PCC
To Jonathan Trumbull, Sr.	Nov. 16	PCC; DLC
To Meshech Weare	Nov. 16	MHi; PCC
From Alexander Gillon	Nov. 16	ScHi
From Jonathan Trumbull, Sr.	Nov. 16	PCC; NN
From George Washington	Nov. 16	PCC; DLC
From George Washington	Nov. 16	PCC; DLC
From Benjamin Whitcomb	Nov. 16	PCC
Circular to Governors	Nov. 16	PCC
Receipt	Nov. 16	ScU (SCL)
To Silas Talbot	Nov. 17	PCC; MHi
From Charles F. Bedaulx	Nov. 17	PCC
From Lord Stirling	Nov. 17	NN
From Benjamin Whitcomb	Nov. 17	PCC
Thanksgiving Proclamation	Nov. 17	PHi; NN
To Lord Stirling	Nov. 18	NNC
To George Washington	Nov. 18	PCC
From Charles F. Bedaulx	Nov. 18	PCC
From George Washington	Nov. 18	PCC; DLC
From Silas Deane	Nov. 19	PCC
From Rawleigh Downman and George Hancock	Nov. 19	PCC
From William Heath	Nov. 19	PCC
From Thomas McKean	Nov. 19	ScHi
From Lord Stirling	Nov. 19	ScHi
From George Washington	Nov. 19	DLC
From Meshech Weare	Nov. 19	PCC
To George Washington	Nov. 20	PCC
To George Washington	Nov. 20	DLC
From Conrad-Alexandre Gérard	Nov. 20	PCC
From Thomas Hartley	Nov. 20	PCC
From L.S.	Nov. 20	ScHi
From Henry B. Livingston	Nov. 20	PCC; NHi
From William Livingston	Nov. 20	ScHi
From George Washington	Nov. 20	PCC; DLC
To Stephen Drayton	Nov. 21	PCC
To William Heath	Nov. 21	MHi
To Francis Huger	Nov. 21	PCC
To Edmund Hyrne	Nov. 21	PCC
To Lord Stirling	Nov. 21	PHi
From Lord Stirling	Nov. 21	ScHi
From George Washington	Nov. 21	PCC; DLC
From Chevalier de La Neuville	Nov. 22	PCC
From Casimir Pulaski	Nov. 22	PCC

From Caesar Rodney	Nov. 22	PCC; DeHi
To John Ettwein	Nov. 23	PBMCA
To Arthur Middleton	Nov. 23	ScHi
From Patrick Henry	Nov. 23	PCC
From Samuel Huntington	Nov. 23	NN
From William Livingston	Nov. 23	PCC
From Casimir Pulaski	Nov. 23	PCC
From Philip Schuyler	Nov. 23	PCC
From Lord Stirling	Nov. 23	ScHi
From Jean-Baptiste Ternant	Nov. 23	DLC
From William Thompson	Nov. 23	PCC
From George Washington	Nov. 23	PCC; DLC
From George Washington	Nov. 23	PCC; DLC
To Benjamin Lincoln	Nov. 24	NN; PCC
To Lord Stirling	Nov. 24	Dodd
From Christopher Hele	Nov. 24	PCC
From Robert Howe	Nov. 24	PCC
From Board of War	Nov. 25	PCC
From John Ettwein	Nov. 25	ScHi
From John Houstoun	Nov. 25	Kendall; ScHi
From William Livingston	Nov. 25	Lyon
From Casimir Pulaski	Nov. 25	PCC
To Lord Stirling	Nov. 26	DLC
To George Washington	Nov. 26	PCC
From Baron von Steuben	Nov. 26	PCC
From George Washington	Nov. 26	PCC; DLC
To George Washington	Nov. 27	PCC
From Thomas Galbraith	Nov. 27	PCC
From the Marquis de Lafayette	Nov. 27	PCC
From the Marquis de Lafayette	Nov. 27	PCC
From the Marquis de Lafayette	Nov. 27	PCC
From George Washington	Nov. 27	PCC; DLC
Commission: David Henley	Nov. 27	PCC
To James Gambier	Nov. 28	PCC
To Lord Stirling	Nov. 28	IMunS
To George Washington	Nov. 28	PCC
From Théveneau de Francy	Nov. 28	PCC
From Patrick Henry	Nov. 28	PCC
From Jonathan F. Morris	Nov. 28	PCC
From Baron von Steuben	Nov. 28	Kendall
From Lord Stirling	Nov. 28	Kendall; ScHi
From Lord Stirling	Nov. 28	Kendall; ScHi
To Lord Stirling	Nov. 29	NNPM
To Lord Stirling	Nov. 29	PCC
From Jacob Dirik	Nov. 29	PCC
From Louis de Fleury	Nov. 29	PCC

From the Marquis de Lafayette	Nov. 29	ScHi
From the Marquis de Lafayette	Nov. 29	PCC
From William Livingston	Nov. 29	PCC
From George Morgan	Nov. 29	PCC
From Lord Stirling	Nov. 29	Kendall; ScHi
From James M. Varnum	Nov. 29	PCC
From Silas Deane	Nov. 30	PCC
From William Henry Drayton	Nov. 30	ScHi
From Horatio Gates	Nov. 30	NHi
From Horatio Gates	Nov. 30	PCC; NHi
From Baron de Thuillières	Nov. 30	PCC
From Jonathan Trumbull, Jr.	Nov. 30	CtHi
To Caron de Beaumarchais	Dec.	DNA
From John Connolly	Dec.	PCC
From Massachusetts Board of War	Dec.	PCC
From Marquis de La Rouerie	Dec.	PCC
Notes for Speech to Congress	Dec.	DLC
To Lord Stirling	Dec. 1	Carnegie
From Gosuinus Erkelens	Dec. 1	PCC
From Lord Stirling	Dec. 1	Kendall; ScHi
From Lord Stirling	Dec. 1	PCC; ScHi
To Richard Caswell	Dec. 2	PCC
To George Clinton	Dec. 2	PCC
To Nathanael Greene	Dec. 2	PCC
To William Greene	Dec. 2	R-Ar; PCC
To Patrick Henry	Dec. 2	PCC
To John Houstoun	Dec. 2	PCC
To Thomas Johnson	Dec. 2	MdAA; PCC
To Benjamin Lincoln	Dec. 2	PCC
To William Livingston	Dec. 2	PCC
To Rawlins Lowndes	Dec. 2	PCC
To William Palfrey	Dec. 2	PCC
To Jeremiah Powell	Dec. 2	PCC
To Joseph Reed	Dec. 2	PCC
To Caesar Rodney	Dec. 2	PCC
To Philip Schuyler	Dec. 2	PCC
To Elisha Sheldon	Dec. 2	PCC
To John Sullivan	Dec. 2	PCC
To Jonathan Trumbull, Sr.	Dec. 2	NjMoHP; PCC
To George Washington	Dec. 2	PCC
To Meshech Weare	Dec. 2	Nh-Ar; PCC
From Louis Duportail	Dec. 2	PCC
From Conrad-Alexandre Gérard	Dec. 2	PCC
To Silas Deane	Dec. 3	PCC
To Horatio Gates	Dec. 3	PCC
To William Heath	Dec. 3	PCC; MHi

From John Adams	Dec. 3	PCC
From Augustin Des Epiniers	Dec. 3	PCC
From Horatio Gates	Dec. 3	PCC
From Horatio Gates	Dec. 3	NHi
From John Lewis Gervais	Dec. 3	Private
From William Livingston	Dec. 3	PCC; Private
From Rawlins Lowndes	Dec. 3	Kendall; ScHi
From Casimir Pulaski	Dec. 3	PCC
To Philip Schuyler	Dec. 4	PCC
From Silas Deane	Dec. 4	PCC
From Conrad-Alexandre Gérard	Dec. 4	PCC
From Casimir Pulaski	Dec. 4	PCC
From Lord Stirling	Dec. 4	PCC
From George Washington	Dec. 4	PCC; DLC
Notes on Conversation with Gérard	Dec. 4	ScHi
To Silas Deane	Dec. 5	CtHi
To Augustin Des Epiniers	Dec. 5	PCC
To Lord Stirling	Dec. 5	NN
To George Washington	Dec. 5	PCC
From John H. Carter	Dec. 5	PCC
From John Connolly	Dec. 5	PCC
From Robert H. Harrison	Dec. 5	PCC; DLC
From William Heath	Dec. 5	Kendall; ScHi
From Joseph Reed	Dec. 5	*Pa. Archives*
To Chevalier de La Neuville	Dec. 6	PCC
To the Marquis de Lafayette	Dec. 6	Archives For. Min.
To Lord Stirling	Dec. 6	NHi
To George Washington	Dec. 6	PCC
From John Adams	Dec. 6	PCC; MHi
From Conrad-Alexandre Gérard	Dec. 6	PCC
To Rawlins Lowndes	Dec. 7	ScHi
To Lord Stirling	Dec. 7	NNC
From John Adams	Dec. 7	MHi
From Conrad-Alexandre Gérard	Dec. 7	PCC
From Frederick Verner	Dec. 7	PCC
From George Washington	Dec. 7	PCC; DLC
Motions re Silas Deane	Dec. 7	ScHi
Notes on Court-martial of William Thompson	Dec. 7	ScHi
To Jeremiah Powell	Dec. 8	PCC; M-Ar
To William Thomson	Dec. 8	PCC
To George Washington	Dec. 8	PCC
From John Adams	Dec. 8	PCC; MHi
From Board of War	Dec. 8	PCC
Resignation	Dec. 9	ScHi; MH
Resignation Speech	Dec. 9	PCC

INDEX

Names of vessels and captains in the text, source notes, and footnotes are indexed. After the name of each vessel, the type of vessel and the name of the captain, when known, have been added as information. After the name of each ship captain, the name of his vessel has been added as information. Proper nouns in addresses in the source notes have been indexed. An *sn* following a page number indicates that the entry appears only in the source note of that particular page. Wives are indexed under their husbands' surnames with maiden names given in parentheses, as Gervais, Mary (Sinclair). When there are several spellings of the same name, the editors have indexed the accepted spelling of the name of a well-known personage; for others they have used the spelling which to them seemed most correct. Variants are placed in parentheses. Names of people mentioned in earlier volumes are followed by a volume and page reference in parentheses which indicates the first appearance of that name in this series. Unprinted items listed in the "Catalog of Documents" are indexed and appear under the name of the correspondent in the subentry "letters not printed." The material in the front matter has not been indexed.

Duportail, Louis le Bègue de Presle
(XII, 39): letters not printed, 592,
608; on America's obligation to
France, 104; and defense of the
Delaware River, 153; inspects
fortifications, 441; memorial of,
255
Durst, Mr. (messenger) (XII, 434sn),
67sn, 130sn, 136sn, 137sn, 138sn
Dutch (lang.), 419
Dutch Reformed Church, 420n, 446,
447n
Dutch War of Independence, 418n

Eagle, HMS, 15, 209, 217, 358n, 362;
reported driven on shore, 267
Eagle, packet (Nichols), 264, 265
Eastern Navy Board: letters not
printed, 588, 589, 594, 596, 605
East Florida: British evacuation of,
90n; British possession of, poses
threat to Ga., 535; coast of,
ravaged by privateers, 190; Creek
Indians to assist, 186; as destina-
tion for British regiments, 437n;
Gervais calls for conquest of, 552;
Indians sent to aid British troops,
243n; invasion of Ga. from, 534,
552; patriots in, 189; subjugation
of, sought, 500; as threat to Ga.,
93, 281. See also Amelia Narrows;
Cape Canaveral; Fort Tonyn;
Governor; Lieutenant Governor;
Mosquito Inlet; New Smyrna; St.
Augustine; St. Johns River; St
Marks; St. Marys River
East Florida Campaign, 541;
Brétigney's plan for, 196n, 237,
276, 465n; called for by Congress,
486, 487n; galleys requested for,
488, 527, 540; HL doubts success
of, 516; HL favors, 237; naval
command of, 531n
East Florida Expedition: casualties,
93–94; concluded, 87, 131;

consequences of failure for Ga.,
192; cost of, 263; cost of, to be
borne by Congress, 88, 93;
disputed command of, 88, 94,
385n; health of troops undermined by diet, 87; HL on, 80. 157,
236–237; Houstoun on, 188–192;
and Indian affairs, 169; John
Wells, Jr. on, 93–94, 176; McIntosh
inquires about, 427; object of, 87;
provisions from HL's plantations
for, 86n; reasons for failure, 189,
192, 262, 360; Robert Howe
defends role in, 395n; S.C.
Assembly reviews, 292; service in,
283; Spanish observers on, 196;
mentioned, 42, 86, 174, 187, 248,
295, 375. See also Houstoun, John;
Howe, Robert; Williamson,
Andrew
East Florida Rangers, 187n; claim to
have commissions, 290; invade
Ga., 530n, 552; raid Ga., 289–290,
375; taken prisoner, 333; threaten
Ga. and S.C. frontier, 333
Easton Beach, R.I., 249
Easton Pond, R.I., 249
Ebenezer, Ga., 87n
Eden, William (VIII, 15n), 22, 139
Edinburgh University, 266n, 397
Education, 134n, 215; European,
476n; in England, 314n, 321n; in
Switzerland, 314n; legal, 321n;
medical, 41, 266n. See also College
of New Jersey; College of
Philadelphia; Edinburgh
University; Eton College;
Lincoln's Inn; Medical school;
Middle Temple; Military schools;
Philadelphia Academy; Schools;
Utrecht, University of
Egg Harbor, N.J., 297, 363, 437
Eglise, Dominique L': letters not
printed, 602, 604
Elbert, Samuel: letters from, 268–269

allowance for, 29n; election of, 572n; HL continues as, 464, 542; and House procedures, 221; resignation of, 464n, 571; term of, 464, 577, 579; and Vt. issue, 4n; mentioned, 354

President, S.C., 279, 312n; powers of, 247

Pressmen, 178

Preston, HMS, 15, 423, 462

Preville, Chevalier de, 256

Prevost, Augustine (VIII, 375n), 535n

Prevost, James Mark (IV, 468): and captured HL letter, 238n; exchange with Col. White, 553; invades Ga., 530n, 535; as Lt. Gov. of Ga., 535n

Price, Charles, Jr., 314n; arrives in S.C. from N.Y., 314n, 407, 414; ordered to leave S.C., 409; returns to Ga., 415, 426

Price, Joseph (*Active*) (XI, 315n), 274, 276

Prices: charged by Loyalists, 49; inflated by war, 8, 9, 38, 41, 79, 182, 281, 330n, 485n; in Philadelphia, 79; lower at Charleston when coast is clear, 179; lowered by embargo, 124n; of carriages, 131, 217; of cloth, 38, 181, 291; of corn, 332; of East Indies goods, 281; of European goods, 281; of firewood, 181, 551; of flour, 466n; of forage, 485n; of horses, 8; of indigo, 108, 179, 183, 291, 550; of provisions, 482; of rice, 39, 40, 108, 124n, 179, 272, 332, 335, 551; of shoes, 182; of slaves, 180, 181, 292n; of tobacco, 108; of uniforms, 509; of vessels in S.C., 281; of wagons, 49; of West Indies goods, 281; of wine, 79, 281; raised by embargo, 383n; raised by unrestricted purchases of agents, 55n; regulation of, 2, 518; speculators drive up, 368, 466n;

state regulation of, 518

Prince of Orange, British privateer, 471n

Princess Royal, HMS, 287n, 316n, 356

Princeton, N.J., 75, 206sn, 265, 306sn, 324, 397, 437, 481sn; general hospital at, 314n, 315sn

Pringle, John Julius (X, 3), 74n, 418n

Pringle, Robert (1702–1776) (I, 6n), 397

Pringle, Robert (1755–1811) (XI, 15): letters from, 397

Printers, 137, 178, 180, 548. *See also* Books; Crouch, Charles; Crouch, Mary; Dunlap, John; Gaines, Hugh; Newspapers; Rivington, James; Timothy, Peter; Wells, John, Jr.

Printing offices, 97n

Prisoner exchanges, 147, 207n, 263n, 274, 377n; between S.C. and E.Fla., 90, 174, 344; Congress and, 156, 456n, 461, 537; and Convention Army, 512, 537n; Lafayette seeks resolve on, 543n; negotiations for, 148, 156n, 327n, 433, 547; rules governing, 90, 158, 175, 481. *See also* Cartels; Commissioners for prisoner exchanges; Convention Army; Paroles

Prisoners of war, 293; Convention Army as, 149; E.Fla. Rangers as, 290; Loyalists as, 90, 263n, 264; Senf as, 172; soldiers as, 256; taken by privateer, released, 416n

Prisoners of war, American: at Havana, 503; on British ships, 66, 175; escape, 7n, 89n, 274, 353; held at St. Augustine, 377n; held in N.Y., 205, 274; officers, need pay, 348; provisions for, 480; seek aid from Commissioners at Paris, 472, 475; taken at fall of Charleston, 314n; treatment of, 66, 127n, 158; wife seeks HL's assistance, 306